RESOURCES. TRAINING. SUPPORT.

Look inside for access to new assessment tools and multimedia resources!

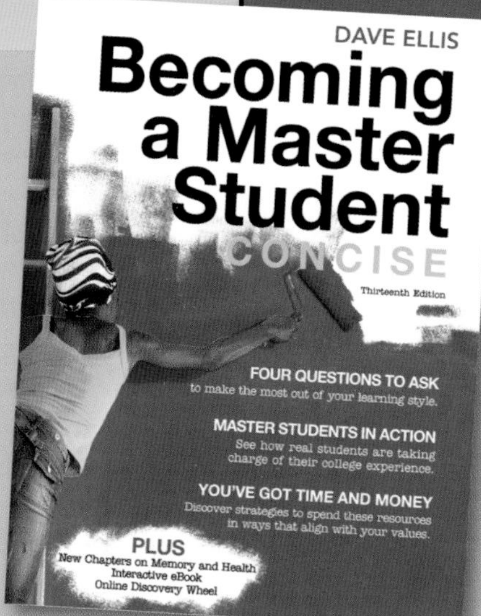

A message from *Becoming a Master Student* author Dave Ellis…

Becoming a Master Student is a book I wrote to help your students be more successful in school and in life. The book presents lots of strategies, hints, tools, and techniques for students to pick from. It's a smorgasbord of suggestions so that students can pick what will work for them to be more successful by their definition of success.

When I first created *Becoming a Master Student*, I wanted a book that was more like a magazine with bite-sized articles divided into even smaller sections that could be read independently. Also, like in a magazine I wanted many of the pages to be an advertisement—not for a product, but for an idea about student success. The articles would advertise to students to read actively, to take notes frequently, to practice self-responsibility, to handle conflict, to manage distress, and much more.

The book is now in the thirteenth edition, and each time we revise it, it's because students and teachers let us know what works and what doesn't. As the population of students changes, and as the ideas about education change and develop, we add new elements to each chapter. The book evolves by our listening to you and to students.

For me one of the greatest joys of writing this book and of teaching this course is in my own development. As teachers, what works best is when we practice what we teach. And each time I practice the skills of *Becoming a Master Student*, I grow professionally and personally.

It really is a joy to put into practice stress management techniques and then live a more calm and relaxed life. It's a joy to practice what we teach about health and then experience the benefits of vibrant health. What I hear from teachers all the time is that when they implement these ideas, their lives change. I know that I have learned way more than students about becoming a master student—because when we teach it, we really learn it. That is the challenge and the joy of this book—not only developing the master students out there, but also developing the master student in you.

Dave

Hear more from author Dave Ellis, explore the philosophy behind ***Becoming a Master Student***, and discover the full range of teaching and learning resources available with this edition at www.cengage.com/community/bams.

Faculty Support and Training

TeamUP Faculty Programs

Our **TeamUP** program provides a range of services to help you implement new ideas and learning tools into your courses. Choose the level of support that works best for you, including:

- **Consultants** who understand your challenges and create a customized solution to meet your unique needs.
- **Trainers** who work with you and your students to fully utilize the power of your technology solutions.
- **Experts** in education who offer opportunities to explore new educational tools and ideas through peer-to-peer and professional insight.

To connect with your **TeamUP** Faculty Programs Consultant, call 1-800-528-8323 or visit www.cengage.com/teamup.

Free eSeminars to Reinvigorate Your Teaching

Convenient, cutting-edge, and practical, the **Wadsworth College Success eSeminar Series** offers opportunities for professional development right at your desk. Our experts present relevant topics ranging from learning styles and active learning strategies to motivation and raising expectations. Take advantage of this no-cost faculty development opportunity. Visit **www.cengage.com/tlc/collegesuccess** to access updated eSeminar schedules and archival presentations.

Custom Solutions: Your Course, Your Way

Let Cengage Learning Custom Solutions help create the perfect learning solution for your course. Add key information about your campus and resources, a campus photo, planner pages, or other content from our College Success programs into your student's copy of *Becoming a Master Student*, Concise, 13e. Visit **custom.cengage.com** for more information.

Annotated Instructor's Edition

Becoming a MASTER STUDENT CONCISE

Thirteenth Edition

Doug Toft
Contributing Editor

Dean Mancina
Golden West College, CA
Faculty Advisor

AUSTRALIA • BRAZIL • JAPAN • KOREA • MEXICO • SPAIN • UNITED KINGDOM • UNITED STATES

ANNOTATED INSTRUCTOR'S EDITION

Becoming a Master Student Concise
Ellis

Senior Sponsoring Editor: Shani Fisher
Development Editor: Daisuke Yasutake
Editorial Assistant: Cat Salerno
Media Editor: Amy Gibbons
Senior Marketing Manager: Kirsten Stoller
Marketing Coordinator: Ryan Ahern
Marketing Communications Manager: Stacey Purviance
Content Project Manager: Jessica Rasile
Senior Art Director: Pam Galbreath
Print Buyer: Julio Esperas
Rights Acquisition Specialist, Images: Jennifer Meyer Dare
Senior Rights Acquisition Specialist, Text: Katie Huha
Text Designer: Susan Gilday
Cover Designer: Yvo Riezebos
Cover Image: Ted Humble-Smith/RF/Getty
Project Management/Composition: MPS Content Services

Library of Congress Control Number: 2010927093

Student Edition:

ISBN-13: 978-0-495-91281-1

ISBN-10: 0-495-91281-6

Annotated Instructor's Edition:

ISBN-13: 978-0-495-91284-2

ISBN-10: 0-495-91284-0

Wadsworth
20 Channel Center Street
Boston, MA 02210
USA

Cengage Learning is a leading provider of customized learning solutions with office locations around the globe, including Singapore, the United Kingdom, Australia, Mexico, Brazil and Japan. Locate your local office at **international.cengage.com/region**

Cengage Learning products are represented in Canada by Nelson Education, Ltd.

For your course and learning solutions, visit **www.cengage.com**.

Purchase any of our products at your local college store or at our preferred online store **www.cengagebrain.com**.

Printed in the United States of America
1 2 3 4 5 6 7 14 13 12 11 10

Contents

Chapter annotations

Please note: Chapter annotations can be found on an insert that appears before the beginning of each of the main text chapters, starting with the introduction.

Using the Annotated Instructor's Edition

Get familiar with the Annotated Instructor's Edition

The Annotated Instructor's Edition of *Becoming a Master Student Concise,* Thirteenth Edition, will help guide you as you use this textbook. Whether you are a first-time user of *Becoming a Master Student* or a long-time fan, there is something here for you. In this Annotated Edition, strategies to aid your teaching are available at the front of the main text, and content-specific ideas appear prior to each chapter. All of these pages have a separate numbering system (AIE Chapter 1, AIE Chapter 2, and so on) so that the textbook pages are numbered the same as the student edition of the text. This allows you to stay on the same page as your students when assigning readings and exercises.

Do a textbook reconnaissance

Flip through the pages of this textbook right now to get the big picture of the thirteenth edition. Look for fresh ideas you can use to support your course objectives. Explore new features, such as the new Skills Snapshot activity at the end of each chapter and the revised Put It to Work case study articles that help students see how the skills learned in each chapter can be applied in the workplace. Note how the annotated instructor information is organized and stands out visually from the student content for your handy reference.

Get to know your TeamUP Faculty Programs consultant

For more than 20 years, TeamUP College Survival has provided consultation and training for the design and implementation of student success and first-year courses. All members of the team of consultants have extensive experience in teaching and administering the first-year course and in facilitating training sessions and conferences. Get to know your consultant today by calling 1-800-856-5727. Or visit the team online at **www.cengage.com/teamup.** Be sure to ask a consultant how you can attend a conference or workshop—for free!

Listen to your peers

Throughout the Annotated Instructor's Edition, you will find tips from the Faculty Advisor for *Becoming a Master Student Concise,* Thirteenth Edition, Dean Mancina of Golden West Community College, and Momika Fileva of Davenport University. Also look for suggestions from the Advisory Board and TeamUP consultants. As you dig into the following chapters, think about what you would say if you could add your voice to theirs. Send an e-mail to csweb.CollegeSurvival@cengage.com to share your comments.

Use the transition guide to find your way

If you have used previous editions of *Becoming a Master Student Concise,* you may need some help finding your favorite articles and exercises. The transition guide on the Instructor Companion Site will help you navigate the changes made to the thirteenth edition. A brief version of this guide is available on page AIE-16.

Make this book your own

The length of student success courses varies, so there may be more content here than you can share during your course. If some sections of the book don't apply to your course at all, skip them. Later, see whether you can help your students gain value from these sections anyway. When you are committed to getting the most out of this book, your students will take note. Use the extra space in the annotated instructor pages to write ideas for lesson plans, activities, quiz questions, guest speakers, and homework assignments. Change the exercises in the book to fit your needs. Create a new technique by combining several others. Create a technique out of thin air! End your course by suggesting that students explore any unread sections of the book as one of the "ways to continue . . ." their journey of student success. See Chapter 10 for more about this.

Model the concepts

Action makes this book work. You are your students' best role model. Completing the exercises along with your students will enable you to stay involved and speak from experience when you discuss each chapter in class. The exercises and readings will help you write, touch, feel, move, see, search, ponder, speak, listen, recall, choose, commit, and create. In this way you join your students on their road to success.

Integrate learning styles into your teaching with the Master Student Map

On the opening page of each chapter, the Master Student Map (**M**etacognitive **A**pplication **P**rocess) guides students toward maximum learning by asking the four basic questions—*Why? What? How?* and *What if?*—that correlate to the Learning Style Inventory as explained in Chapter 1. By becoming aware of their preferred learning style and by using the Master Student Map, students will be better able to understand and practice new styles. Read more about the Master Student Map and how it works on page AIE-19. For additional reinforcement, use the Master Student Map in class as a structure for reviewing the previous chapter and previewing the upcoming one.

Note the style and design elements of each chapter

A toolbar at the top of each page signals when the chapter is coming to an end, with its Put It to Work feature, Quiz, Skills Snapshot, and Master Student Profile. Flip to the back of one of the chapters now. *Becoming a Master Student Concise* provides the building blocks with which a creative and active mind can succeed.

Use the materials before each chapter to help you create lesson plans

There are four instructor pages before each chapter. These sections provide content-related ideas for guest speakers, lectures, activities, homework assignments, and previews/reviews to help bring the classroom alive for your students. The organization of these pages is based on the seven-part lesson plan structure described on page AIE-10. Flip to one of the chapters and review the instructor pages now.

Link to the Web

Throughout this book, students are reminded to visit the College Success CourseMate available at cengagebrain.com. There they'll find articles, videos, online exercises, and links to other useful Web sites. Part of the support for you when using this textbook is a password-protected instructor resource Web site that contains dozens of lesson plan and lecture ideas, activities, handouts, test questions, and more. These tools were submitted by faculty around the country who wanted to share effective strategies they have used in their classrooms. Register now (It's free, of course!) so that you can explore additional resources to use with your students.

Power Processes

The Power Processes at the end of each chapter are a long-standing popular feature of *Becoming a Master Student Concise.* These articles describe approaches to student success that are more philosophical in nature than most of the tools in the text. Review the pre-chapter instructor resources in the book or on the Instructor Companion site for strategies to help your students make full value of these special tools.

Help students take this book to work

Although the focus of this textbook is success in college, students can apply nearly all of the techniques in this book to any career. Students with less experience in the workplace, however, may not see how these tools apply at work. The Put It to Work articles at the end of each chapter use case studies to suggest key strategies that will help students make a seamless transition from success in school to success on the job. Skim one of them now.

Master Student Profiles

Becoming a Master Student Concise has always concluded each chapter with a brief article about a real person who encompasses qualities of a master student. In each new edition of the textbook, several of the stories are replaced with new ones. Read the article "The Master Student" on page 30 and then check out the table of contents now to discover the 10 people on the special roster of Master Students for the thirteenth edition!

chapter
Put It to Work
Quiz
Skills Snapshot

Master Student PROFILE

Al Gore . . . is optimistic

One hundred and nineteen years ago, a wealthy inventor read his own obituary, mistakenly published years before his death. Wrongly believing the inventor had just died, a newspaper printed a harsh judgment of his life's work, unfairly labeling him "The Merchant of Death" because of his invention—dynamite. Shaken by this condemnation, the inventor made a fateful choice to serve the cause of peace.

Seven years later, Alfred Nobel created this prize and the others that bear his name.

Seven years ago tomorrow, I read my own political obituary in a judgment that seemed to me harsh and mistaken—if not premature. But that unwelcome verdict also brought a precious if painful gift: an opportunity to search for fresh new ways to serve my purpose.

Unexpectedly, that quest has brought me here. Even though I fear my words cannot match this moment, I pray what I am feeling in my heart will be communicated clearly enough that those who hear me will say, "We must act." . . .

In the last few months, it has been harder and harder to misinterpret the signs that our world is spinning out of kilter. Major cities in North and South America, Asia and Australia are nearly out of water due to massive droughts and melting glaciers. Desperate farmers are losing their livelihoods. Peoples in the frozen Arctic and on low-lying Pacific islands are planning evacuations of places they have long called home. Unprecedented wildfires have forced a half million people from their homes in one country and caused a national emergency that almost brought down the government in another. Climate refugees have migrated into areas already inhabited by people with different cultures, religions, and traditions, increasing the potential for conflict. Stronger storms in the Pacific and Atlantic have threatened whole cities. Millions have been displaced by massive flooding in South Asia, Mexico, and 18 countries in Africa. As temperature extremes have increased, tens of thousands have lost their lives. We are recklessly burning and clearing our forests and driving more and more species into extinction.

There is an African proverb that says, "If you want to go quickly, go alone. If you want to go far, go together." We need to go far, quickly. . . .

Fifteen years ago, I made that case at the "Earth Summit" in Rio de Janeiro. Ten years ago, I presented it in Kyoto. This week, I will urge the delegates in Bali to adopt a bold mandate for a treaty that establishes a universal global cap on emissions and uses the market in emissions trading to efficiently allocate resources to the most effective opportunities for speedy reductions.

This treaty should be ratified and brought into effect everywhere in the world by the beginning of 2010—two years sooner than presently contemplated. The pace of our response must be accelerated to match the accelerating pace of the crisis itself. . . .

Make no mistake, the next generation will ask us one of two questions. Either they will ask: "What were you thinking; why didn't you act?"

Or they will ask instead: "How did you find the moral courage to rise and successfully resolve a crisis that so many said was impossible to solve?"

Al Gore, "Nobel Lecture," December 10, 2007. Copyright © 2007 The Nobel Foundation, Stockholm, 2007. Reproduced by permission.

© Joseph Sohm/Visions of America/Corbis

(1948–) Former vice president of the United States. Gore refocused his career on climate change, won a Nobel Peace Prize, and—in his film *An Inconvenient Truth*—invented a new type of documentary.

Learn more about Al Gore and other master students at the Master Student Hall of Fame.

BECOMING A MASTER STUDENT 97

Master Teachers in Action

Instructors share their experiences with using *Becoming a Master Student Concise!*

Overall

My retired husband was scanning the text on a plane one day while we were traveling and marveled at the content and scope of the issues covered. After his review, he then said to me, "Can I get a copy?" A former student liked the text so much that she planned to share it with her high school daughter and her daughter's friends because she thought it would help them improve their academic performance.

—JOYCE NORWOOD, SANTA ANA COLLEGE
Photo courtesy of Joyce Norwood

I have used BAMS since its first edition—then because it was the one selected by the course leader and one of the few available. After my first BAMS workshop, I began to better understand the philosophy behind the text—a philosophy that I believe in and practice. But, more importantly, it is student and instructor friendly—filled with ideas and opportunities to practice what we teach (or should I say preach).

—FRANK BAKER, GOLDEN WEST COLLEGE
Photo courtesy of Frank Baker

Features

Discovery Wheel

The Discovery Wheel is brilliant because it allows the students to quickly identify where they may be weak and directs them to the chapter that can assist them.

—CHRIS DOUSE, INDIANA UNIVERSITY-PURDUE UNIVERSITY FORT WAYNE
Photo courtesy of Chris Douse

I really like the Discovery Wheel. I think it's so important for students to get a handle on where they are when they begin the semester, *and* where they are when they finish. I'm surprised how much growth there is! Sometimes it's not shown in "increased" scores on the Discovery Wheel; sometimes the scores go down . . . that's a good thing. It shows that they are really examining their skills and abilities.

—TERRY CARLES, VALENCIA COMMUNITY COLLEGE
Photo courtesy of Terry Carles

Power Process

One of the assignments in my class is a group presentation on a Power Process. Early in the term, students pick a Power Process to work on. Small groups are formed with students interested in the same one. At midterm time, presentations are given. It is one of the highlights of the term.

—JOE RINE, MINNEAPOLIS COMMUNITY & TECHNICAL COLLEGE
Photo courtesy of Joe Rine

The Power Processes are my favorite feature in BAMS. They can be applied to all life situations. They're great for "teachable moments" during the semester as well. I've heard students tell their classmates to "Be Here Now" when they were engaged in side conversations or to apply "I Create It All" when they made excuses for not completing a homework assignment.

—DEBBIE WARFIELD, SEMINOLE COMMUNITY COLLEGE
Photo courtesy of Debbie Warfield

The Power Processes are my favorite feature. They are applicable and very timely. They give students an opportunity to consciously explore problem situations. Sometimes we have a problem, and until we bring it consciousness, it persists. By presenting typical scenarios, my students are able to relate and begin to think outside the box.

—DAWN SHAFFER, CENTRAL PIEDMONT COMMUNITY COLLEGE
Photo courtesy of Dawn Shaffer

Journal Entries and Critical Thinking Exercises

The Journal Entries information and exercises provide a format that invites students to become active participants in the learning process, resulting in the acquisition of skills leading to behavior changes important to personal and academic success.

—LD LOVETT, TRUCKEE MEADOWS COMMUNITY COLLEGE
Photo courtesy of LD Lovett

Using the Annotated Instructor's Edition

Inevitably I end up having a class where what I've been doing just isn't working or, I'm just looking to try something different. I always find exciting ideas to take into class by reviewing these pages.

—TERRY CARLES, VALENCIA COMMUNITY COLLEGE
Photo courtesy of Terry Carles

As a new faculty member (former administrator) I was struggling with the concept of developing an engaging class. I am the product of traditional, lecture style classes, as my bachelor's degree is in finance. I knew that I wanted/needed to engage the students, I just didn't know how, as I had never personally experienced an engaging class! The article, "Creating an Engaging Classroom," was an excellent starting point for me. The course model gave me a great guideline to start with and to try to follow. It also helped to keep me on task as the semester went along and I found myself lecturing too much, as that is what I experienced as a student.

—LEIGH SMITH, LAMAR INSTITUTE OF TECHNOLOGY
Photo courtesy of Leigh Smith

Content

Money

I find that many of our students have no experience with budgeting. They get money from their parents when they overspend, or work extra hours when they get in serious debt. Many will not buy textbooks because money is tight. This is a big, big problem on our large urban campus. Students get into debt and then work 30 or more hours per week to pay it down or for general living expenses. Because of this extra workload, their grades suffer and they lose financial aid and the cycle starts all over again... I like that the exercise found in Chapter 2 makes students realize where (and on what) they're spending money each month. They often complain that they have no money for books or school-related expenses, not realizing that they've spent money on designer clothing and accessories, electronic gadgets, eating out, trips, and so on.

—LETITIA THOMAS, UNIVERSITY AT BUFFALO
Photo courtesy of Letitia Thomas

Classroom Civility

I cover classroom civility in my classes. I have found that we can't assume that students know what is expected of them in terms of what are appropriate college classroom behaviors. For many, they are the first in their family to attend college. There is a misconception among students that because they pay for classes, any behavior is acceptable in the classroom. (The customer is always right!) Many of the students are also under a great deal of stress right now due to the state of the economy. This also influences their behaviors. During the first week of class, we have a discussion on classroom civility, and I have them sign the student agreement.

—DEBBIE WARFIELD, SEMINOLE COMMUNITY COLLEGE
Photo courtesy of Debbie Warfield

MESSAGE FROM Faculty Advisor

Dean Mancina

. . . is a Master Student

Teaching student success classes has given me the humbling honor of facilitating the transformation of students' lives. It makes the hours of prep work and grading worthwhile when a student tells me that this is the best class she's taken in college, or that it has changed her life.

In 1985, I attended a workshop presented by Dave Ellis, hoping to learn new ways to help the students at my community college succeed. By the end of that workshop, I felt that Dave had the answer I was looking for. I returned to Southern California, and with the help of Dave and TeamUP Faculty Programs, I developed a course for Golden West College that has become one of my institution's most popular classes.

Many students come to my college and to my class with low self-expectations. They aren't sure if they are "college material." Some think they might be too old or not smart enough. Some wonder if they have the motivation to do the work or the means to attend college. Most students leave my class with renewed enthusiasm about themselves and their dream of completing an educational program. Many of them get involved in student government and receive scholarships and awards. Two of my former students who became college educators have developed similar courses on their campuses for the students they now teach.

By modeling this book's concepts both in and outside the classroom, I've enjoyed the added side benefit of being happier in my personal life. By modeling this book's concepts both in and outside the classroom, I've enjoyed the added side benefit of being happier in my personal life. I've changed my habits, attitudes, and approaches to problem solving. I've gained confidence as a teacher and member of my campus community. By creating and implementing a course that has been popular and successful, I've earned respect from my colleagues. Over the last 20 years, I've had the wonderful opportunity to help other college and university faculty design and update their courses. And for the last 10 years, I've helped shape the updated editions of this book so that it continues to be current and relevant.

By learning more about learning style theory as presented in Chapter 1, I have become a better teacher. Like many instructors, I prefer to teach the way that I prefer to learn. I just wasn't aware that I was teaching this way and that there are equally effective ways of perceiving and processing information that work better for many of my students. Using the Learning Style Inventory and exercises in my classroom not only has helped my students develop understanding, tolerance, and the skills to adjust to different teaching styles, but it has also helped me understand and reach out to students who prefer to learn differently than I do.

I see myself as a facilitator in the classroom. This book is so well written by Dave Ellis that I just need to follow it, support it, and provide an environment in my classroom that is safe and inviting so that students are encouraged to reach for their dreams.

My suggestions throughout this Annotated Instructor's Edition, and those of Mominka Fileva, are just that—suggestions. As you find your own voice in this material, you will develop your own way of teaching it to your students. Please change, adapt, alter, and re-create my ideas so they work for you and your students. I'd love to hear what you come up with. Write to me at csweb.College Survival@cengage.com.

Teaching a student success course for the first time may seem intimidating. Most of us teach classes in our primary field of expertise, so teaching a course outside our knowledge base can be challenging on many levels. Here are a few suggestions to help you get started.

Finding the master instructor in you

Model the behavior you want to see in your students

If you want your students to be organized, be organized in your class. If you want your students to show up on time, always be punctual yourself.

The textbook is for you, too

You can apply the strategies in this textbook to your professional and personal life. Use the same student success tools to sharpen your memory, manage your time, and improve relationships with colleagues, friends, and loved ones. Use the table of contents and the index to look for strategies to help you start, stop, or change habits in your life.

In a teacher-training workshop, a dedicated instructor once asked, "How can I model and teach promptness if I'm always late to class?" This was an opportunity for personal and professional growth! For us, as for our students, however, change is a choice we choose to make.

Be inquisitive

There are many resources for you to use in the process of developing lesson plans for your student success course. In addition to this Annotated Instructor's Edition, with its suggestions here and on the pages preceding each chapter, explore these additional resources to help you create and improve lesson plans and organize all aspects of your course:

- **Instructor Companion Site**—provides specific tools to use while teaching your course, including video clips, PowerPoint slides, sample syllabi, chapter-by-chapter lecture outlines, teaching tips, exercises, quizzes, Web links, suggestions for service-learning activities, and more. You can edit most of the downloadable files to tailor them for your course.
- **DVDs/videos**—perfect for supplementing your lecture, videos can be used as "guest speakers" in your course. For a complete listing of available videos, and for information about new Power Process videos, flip to the "Master instructor resources" article on page AIE-XX.
- **TeamUP consultants**—available by toll-free phone (1-800-856-5727) and e-mail (serviceandtraining@cengage.com), a consultant can assist you with planning, class activities, research, and implementing a course on your campus. Ask about a customized on-campus training session or how you can attend a TeamUP conference for free.
- **Faculty members on your campus**—invite a respected colleague to lunch to find out how he solves grading, attendance, logistic, and classroom management issues.

Take it one step at a time

Creating the perfect course isn't likely to happen overnight. This textbook explains tools and techniques so clearly that you don't need to try to cover all of them in class. Start by identifying one or two topics in each chapter that you have personally found valuable. Look for activities or lecture ideas at the Instructor Companion Site or in this Annotated Instructor's Edition, and build your lesson plans around the topics that you want to emphasize. Use videos and guest speakers from your campus to augment your class meetings. Reinforce concepts by conducting review sessions and giving weekly quizzes. For additional lesson planning strategies, see the article "Creating engaging classes" on page AIE-XX. *

Creating engaging classes
Using the seven-part course model in your classroom

USING THE FOLLOWING lesson planning model as a framework can provide more opportunities to engage students as active participants and partners in their learning process. The objective is to use varying modes of instruction to facilitate a course that accesses and maximizes each student's method of learning. Try using this seven-part course model as a weekly guideline when developing your lesson plans:

Lectures	**20 percent**
Exercises	**20 percent**
Sharing	**20 percent**
Guest speakers	**20 percent**
Evaluation **Preview/review** **Assignments**	**20 percent**

It will not always be possible to include all parts each week and that's OK. Ideally, over the entire term, the recommendation is to spend 20 percent of class time for lectures; 20 percent for exercises; 20 percent for conversations and sharing; 20 percent for guest speakers; and the remaining 20 percent for previewing/reviewing, quizzes and evaluations, and giving assignments. A complete overview of this course model is available on the Instructor Companion Site. The revised Annotated Instructor's Edition models this structure for every chapter. Flip to the four pages before one of the chapter to see this model put into action.

From Dean Mancina:

Using this seven-part course model can be challenging at first and may seem like more work than lecturing. Although the initial investment to create or redesign your lesson plans may be significant, I discovered that as a result of using this method to design my lesson plans, during class I get to have fun along with my students. Students tell me they enjoy the variety and that the class goes by much faster than many of their other classes.

Here is a sample lesson plan for my 170-minute, once-a-week student success course. If your course meets twice a week, you could do half of these things at each of the two weekly meetings.

CHAPTER 3: Memory

Collect homework (:03)
Preview the class agenda (:07)
Tutorial learning center—guest speakers (:15)
Review Chapter 3 (:30)
Lecture—mnemonic devices (:20)
Activity—loci system (:20)
Sharing successful memory experiences in groups (:20)
Activity—"Love Your Problems" (:30)
Quiz on Chapter 3 (:20)
Assignment—read/do pages XX–XX (Chapter 4) (:05)

Collect homework

I collect homework at the beginning of the class to encourage students to arrive on time. If they are late, they don't get any points for their homework. The collected homework is a randomly selected Journal Entry or other writing assignment from within the text. Additional suggestions regarding collecting and grading homework assignments are available on the Instructor Companion Site.

Preview

I project a PowerPoint slide with the day's agenda before class. I encourage students to copy the agenda into their notes. The agenda can be used as a framework for note taking and helps explain to students the organization of the work we will do in class..

Guest Speaker

Each week I invite guest speakers from support programs to make brief presentations on their services. This helps students learn what kinds of assistance are available at our college. If a guest speaker isn't available for a certain topic, consider showing one of the many videos that accompany this book in class.

Review

I randomly assign students to groups of four to conduct a review of the material they have read prior to coming to class. I provide poster paper and colored pens, and show them how to make a mind map. The students write their first names at the top of each poster and tape the posters to the walls using removable tape. Staying in their groups, they walk around to view the other mind maps, confirming what they have created and noticing what other groups included that they did not. Because they will be taking a quiz at the end of class, students stay motivated and focused for this activity.

Lecture

Lecturing on only one or two topics of the text encourages students to learn from the textbook and frees up class time for the many other activities planned for each class meeting. It's challenging to decide what topics to choose for my lecture. When I first started teaching, I selected topics I was most familiar with and for which felt I could add to beyond what the text said. As I became more confident about the content of the book, I began to focus on topics that students had difficulty fully understanding.

Activity

Though activities take time, they are often more effective than other methods for teaching skills that students retain. Additionally, groups promote more active involvement from students while they learn. The Instructor Companion Site has many activities provided by advisors, consultants, and instructors. Skim them, pick a few that fit your teaching style and time constraints, and try them with your class.

Sharing

Most of the time my students are in groups during class. Over the course of the semester, they get to know each other, and most form a few close friendships. Studies have shown that making friends on campus significantly reduces the likelihood that students will drop out of college. Participating in a sharing period allows students to talk candidly with their peers about their concerns, questions, and frustrations, both at college and at home. I give them a topic for discussion and sometimes, depending on the topic, will ask for group sharing at the end of this segment.

Evaluation

Each week I give a short quiz to my students at the end of the class. Doing so ensures that they read the textbook material, remain focused during class, and stay until the end of the session because they lose points if they miss the quiz.

Assignments

Each week I assign specific pages as a reading assignment, even if I want students to read the entire chapter. I call it "read/do" and list the specific page numbers because I require students to complete all Journal Entries, Discovery/Intention Statements, and Critical Thinking Exercises within the assigned pages.

This seven-part course model is a proven strategy for organizing, planning, and revitalizing lesson plans. Whether you're a novice or a veteran teacher of student success courses, I encourage you to try it. *

Setting up your syllabus

BOTH THE STUDENTS and the purpose and focus of the course will be different at each school. *Becoming a Master Student Concise* is designed to give students and instructors a variety of topics and ideas. By using this Annotated Instructor's Edition and the Instructor Companion Site, you can select material that is most appropriate both for your students and for your course purpose. Specific resources for "Writing your course purpose" and "Creating a course philosophy" are available on the Instructor Companion Site.

There are dozens of approaches to creating your student success course's syllabus. It may be as brief as one page, providing only the most essential information for students, or it may be several pages long, with detailed assignments, due dates, and other information about the course. Here are some ideas to consider:

Choose what to include. In addition to the course name, class time and room, instructor name, office hours, and instructor contact information, here are some common elements that may be included in your syllabus:

- Required textbook information
- Optional textbook information
- Other materials you will require students to have
- Class support Web site URL
- Assignments, with or without instructions and due dates
- Important dates, for midterm, final, and the like
- Official course outline
- Agendas for each class meeting
- Learning outcomes
- Grading method
- Additional recommended readings and/or resources
- Class rules

If you're creating a syllabus for your course for the first time, a more general syllabus may be a better choice. As you progress through the course material, you may discover that some topics take more or less time than you anticipated. A general syllabus makes it easier for you to change due dates for assignments without confusing your students.

Organize and sequence the course topics. The official course outline of record and the total student contact hours for your course will provide you with parameters for organizing the material you will cover during the term. Based on the length of your course, decide how much time you will spend on each topic/chapter. Consider the order in which you will present the topics. Although the text chapters are organized in a logical sequence, once you complete the Introduction and First Steps chapters, each chapter has independent content, so you can teach the chapters in whatever order you prefer. Some teachers let the students prioritize the chapters by voting on each of the chapter topic names.

Identify key dates. After you have organized and sequenced the course topics/chapters, identify key dates for you and your students. Decide when the midterm will be given, when major projects will be due, and which guest speakers you want to invite and when during the term you want them to come.

Choose a grading method. Decide how you will weight quizzes, tests, homework, and other assignments. How many quizzes will you give? Will students be allowed to drop their lowest quiz score? Will there be an option for extra credit? You can protect yourself from student accusations of favoritism by developing an objective system for grading that is applied consistently to each student.

Choose class rules. Class rules include written clarification of the boundaries you set for behavior in the classroom, instructions on the way assignments should be presented for grading, and parameters for how your students should interact with each other. Here is a partial list of topics you may wish to address in your written rules:

- Attendance
- Assignments turned in with no name
- Late assignments
- Word-processed (versus handwritten) assignments
- Side conversations
- Cell phone and laptop computer use in class
- Academic honesty
- Formatting requirements for electronically transmitted assignments (.pdf, .doc, etc.)
- Logging-in frequency for online courses

Evaluate and refine. Each semester, make notes about what works and what doesn't work in your syllabus so that you can modify it for the next term. Consider asking your students at the end of the term to provide feedback as to how the syllabus could have been more helpful to them. *

College 100 - Becoming A Successful Student
Syllabus

Professor:	Dean Mancina
Email:	dmancina@aol.com
Office:	Library 109
Hours:	By appointment Tuesdays, and via email
Phone:	714.892.7711 x 51216
Classroom:	Library 223 • Tuesdays 2:45-5:55 pm
Textbook:	Becoming A Master Student Concise, 13th Edition

The grading system in this course is points-based. Here is a list of graded activities in the course and the maximum points possible.

REGULAR POINTS:	**Maximum**
Text Exercises and other HW (14 @15 pts. each)	+210
Quizzes (12 @ 15 pts. each)	+180
Choose Your Grade	+15
Discovery Wheel #1	+15
Eureka Majors/Career Exploration	+15
Time Monitor	+30
Library Assignments (3 @15 pts each)	+45
Interview w/Campus Personnel	+30
Report on Campus Event	+30
Meeting with Course Instructor	+40
Oral Presentation	+100
Research Project	+100
Review Test #1	+50
Review Test #2	+50
Final Exam	+90
Total Points	**+1000**

MINUS POINTS:	
1. missed class meeting, each	-30
2. missed appointment with /instructor *	-15
3. missed oral presentation *	-15
4. each final exam question skipped	-15

* Cancellations on #2 & 3 require 48 hours' notice to avoid minus points.

BONUS POINTS:	**Maximum**
1. Typing any assignment, each	+2
2. Others, to be assigned, each	+15
3. Individual/Group tutoring hour *(Maximum tutoring pts. = 90)*	+10
4. Assessment Portfolio Builder Exercise	+35

Maximum Total Bonus Per Student = 150

Grading Scale

900+ points =	A	
800-899 =	B	685+ = CR
700-799 =	C	684- = NC *
600-699 =	D	
500-599 =	F	
below 500->	Subject to Withdrawal	

*It is your responsibility to sign up for CR/NC by the GWC Admissions Office deadline.

See also my Course Policies and Classroom Rules handout.

TeamUP College Survival: Committed to STUDENT SUCCESS

CENGAGE'S TEAMUP FACULTY PROGRAMS GROUP is dedicated to providing educators with proven instructional strategies and tools that lead to student success. For the past 24 years, our team of consultants has provided guidance and training for the design and implementation of student success and first-year courses.

The Faculty Program consulting team is available to assist with any stage of student success program development, including::

- Developing student retention strategies
- Implementing student success courses
- Training faculty members
- Helping faculty engage students as active learners
- Transforming the learning environment
- Hosting conferences and workshops

Our team

Our team of consultants has extensive experience in teaching and administering the first-year course and in facilitating training at national education conferences throughout the year. We provide full-time support to help educators establish and maintain effective student success programs.

Web site

Visit our Web site at **www.cengage.com/teamup** for additional resources and more information about TeamUp Facult Programs:

- Get the latest industry information.
- Get updates on the latest technology available through Cengage Learning texts.
- Get connected to our support services.

Conferences/workshops

College Survival conferences and workshops offer highly interactive and informative sessions designed to equip you with ideas and activities that you can apply immediately in your classroom. All educators involved in enhancing instruction and improving students' motivation and performance are encouraged to attend.

About our national conferences. Our two- to three-day conferences provide informative, interactive sessions on a wide range of topics, such as adult learners, learning styles, student retention, motivation, technology, and much more. Presenters include nationally known authors, student success instructors, and College Survival consultants who offer invaluable instructional strategies based on their experience teaching the first-year course. This forum for learning and sharing with colleagues will furnish you with activities and ideas to implement immediately in your course.

About our on-campus workshops. Led by Team UP consultants, our on-campus workshops are customized to the needs of instructors on a particular campus. These workshops will equip you with ideas and activities to enliven the teaching and learning experience. The cost of a workshop is $1,500 a day plus expenses, or free for schools ordering a minimum of $30,000 a year in College Success texts. Ask your Cengage Learning Representative to help you set up a training at your institution.

Who should attend? If you are an educator, new or experienced, who is dedicated to promoting student success in career schools, community colleges, or four-year colleges and universities, these events are for you! Those who will benefit from these workshops include:

- Academic and student affairs administrators
- Student success and freshman seminar coordinators
- Faculty members (full-time and adjunct instructors)
- Retention/enrollment management directors
- Counselors and orientation directors

How can your Cengage Learning Consultant help? Your Cengage Learning TeamUP Consultant can help you with ideas for introducing a topic, creating community in the classroom, designing your syllabus, and figuring out what to do in class tomorrow. All you have to do is contact them. Check the TeamUP Web site to find your consultant: **www.cengage.com/teamup** *

Could your students use an extra $1,000?

CENGAGE STUDENT SUCCESS is proud to present three students each year with a $1,000 scholarship for tuition reimbursement. Each instructor at postsecondary schools in the United States and Canada that offer a student success course is welcome to nominate one student for the scholarship. To be considered, students must write an essay that answers the question "How do you define success?"

Here's one way to get your students to participate. Host a schoolwide competition for students enrolled in a first-year student success or study skills course. Consider having students participate by including the competition in your syllabus as a goal-setting or writing assignment. In your local contest, ask all of your students to write an essay on the topic "How do you define success?" The essay should not exceed 750 words.

Materials to advertise the scholarship competition are available on the Instructor Companion Site. Download flyers for posting on bulletin boards around campus or for posting to online bulletin boards on your course Web site or in your course management system.

Students can send in their individual essays by filling out an entry form (available on the College Success CourseMate) to Cengage Learning. Multiple students from the same school may enter their essays. Entries are due each year on December 15. The winners are announced the following spring on the CourseMate. Invite your students to read the winning essays of previous entrants, also available on the CourseMate. *

Gaining support

Student success courses and first-year seminar programs help students learn to be more effective in school, thereby improving their academic performance and increasing their level of commitment.

Gaining approval and support from administrators is important to the success of your course and requires preparation and communication. This backing is necessary to sustain the course long enough to establish both its effectiveness and its value. These suggestions can help you establish that base of support:

Write a statement of purpose for your course. One possibility is "The purpose of our student success course is to improve students' academic performance and increase their level of commitment to our college."

Refer to your statement of purpose often. When negotiating any aspect of your course, be sure to avoid compromises that would sabotage its purpose from either the institution's or the students' perspective. For example, it would be a mistake to settle for too few course contact hours.

Seek grassroots support. The more people who have a vested interest in your proposal, the more likely it is to be accepted. Ask for assistance from the top of the administrative hierarchy. Draw a political road map encompassing crucial factors for gaining support and identifying key individuals. Include those who have behind-the-scenes influence. Enlist the support of colleagues who trust you. Spend time with key individuals who may not support your concept but are key curriculum decision makers.

Become a retention expert on your campus. Familiarize yourself with all the data, research, and institutional studies related to student performance and retention at your school. Explore options your institution might use to improve student performance and reduce attrition.

More suggestions for gaining support are available at the Instructor Web site: www.cengage.com/success/bams13e.

A guide for instructors who have used previous editions of this book

THE FOUNDATIONS AND THEMES for student success in *Becoming a Master Student Concise* have been used by millions of students. Since the first edition, students and instructors have helped shape this book by providing strategies, insights, and suggestions. As a result of its continuous evaluation and refinement, students are inspired and motivated by this book to adopt, develop, and commit to using the skills needed for success in college and throughout life. These ideas are now a part of the thirteenth edition.

Every word in every article has been evaluated for its helpfulness to students. Statistics have been updated, recent research has been included, and articles have been shortened or lengthened as necessary to maximize clarity of concepts and strategies. Here are some of the major changes you will see in this edition. Please note that a detailed summary of all changes, including moved, deleted, and added articles, is located on the Instructor Companion Site to help you update your lesson plans.

Key textbook feature changes:

- Completely revised Put it to Work articles now feature case studies that will make it even easier for students to relate the themes and concepts to the workplace.
- The Power Process articles are more succinct and have been reduced to one page.
- A new chapter-end exercise "Skills Snapshot" helps students summarize what they learned in each chapter and connects back to their original responses in the Discovery Wheel. This new feature replaces the "Learning styles application exercise," which can now be found online.
- The Master Students in Action feature in the chapter openers helps students connect to real students who have taken this course. Real students share their strategies for success or challenges that they have faced.

Key changes to specific chapters

Introduction: Making Transitions

- **New** article "Classroom civility—what's in it for you," on page 12, introduces the simple student behaviors that create a sense of safety, mutual respect, and community in any place where people gather—including a classroom, tutoring center, library, or instructor's office.
- **New** Journal Entry "Plan for transition," on page 10, helps students figure out a plan to meet new people on campus to help ease the transition into higher education.
- **New** article "Connect to resources," on page 15, provides students with various groups, clubs, and support services that will allow them to answer any questions they may have about their school.

Chapter 1: First Steps

- **New** Critical Thinking Exercise "Develop your multiple intelligences," on pages 31–33, asks students to interact with the expanded chart of the various intelligences discussed in the article "Claim your multiple intelligences," on page 31.

Key revisions to the Learning Styles Inventory include

- Clearer directions on how to take the LSI.
- A **new** Journal Entry that prepares students for taking the Inventory.
- A **new** reflection activity, "Take a snapshot of your learning styles," on page LSI-2, that asks students to reflect on what they've learned. This activity is intended to be completed after students read all of the material about learning styles (including Multiple Intelligences and VAK).
- The "Learning styles across the curriculum" chart, on page LSI-8, connects learning styles to specific strategies that students can use for their other courses.
- **New** material for students to connect their learning style to their courses, future career, and major.
- **New** article "The value of higher education," on page 41, shows students the numerous benefits to continuing their education beyond high school.
- **New** Critical Thinking Exercise "Reprogram your attitude," on page 42, walks students through the process of using affirmations and visualizations to change their attitude.
- **New** Master Student Profile: Lalita Booth, on page 47.

Chapter 2: Time and Money

(Combined Chapters 2 and 9 from previous edition)

- **Revised** article "You've got the time—and the money," on page 49, shows students how they are the ones in control of managing their schedule and budget.
- **New** Mastering Technology feature: "Use Web-based tools to save time," on page 58.
- **New** article "Gearing up: Using a long-term planner," on pages 59–60, helps students understand the value of long-term planning and various tips to become effective at it.
- **New** article "Get the most of out now," on pages 61–62, provides suggestions for being productive and avoiding procrastinating.
- **Revised** Critical Thinking Exercise "The Money Monitor/Money Plan," pages 63–67, simplifies the directions for creating and maintaining a budget.
- **New** Master Student Profile: Al Gore, on page 75.

Chapter 3: Memory

- **New** article "Take your memory out of your closet," on page 77, introduces students to the concept of memory by tying it to the image of a closet.
- **New** article "The memory jungle," on page 78, explains the different types of memory by comparing memory to a jungle.
- **New** article "Memory techniques," on pages 79–83, provides students with various strategies to improve and develop a memory system that fits their learning style.
- **New** Critical Thinking Exercise "Remembering your car keys—or anything else," on page 84, allows students to practice a specific memory technique.
- **New** sidebar "Keep your brain fit for life," on page 84, discusses habits that will help students keep their brain in tip-top shape.
- **New** article "Mnemonic devices," on pages 85–86, details the specifics of this memory technique.
- **New** Critical Thinking Exercise "Get creative," on page 86, asks students to come up with their own mnemonic devices.
- **New** Mastering Technology feature: "Use your computer to enhance memory," on page 87.
- **New** sidebar "Notable failures," on page xx, describes numerous examples of people who had to fail first before becoming successful.
- **New** Critical Thinking Exercise "Move from problems to solutions," on page 89, helps students move from dwelling on problems to coming up with solutions.
- **New** Master Student Profile: Pablo Alvarado, on page 93.

Chapter 4: Reading

(Chapter 3 in previous edition)

- **New** sidebar, "Muscle Reading for ebooks," on page 95, links strategies for print books to online mediums.
- **New** article "Get to the bones of your book with concept maps," on page 100, shows students how this technique can help them find the major ideas in a text.
- **New** Critical Thinking Exercise "Relax," on page 101, describes a way to combat eyestrain and release tension while reading.
- **New** Mastering Technology feature "Find what you want on the Internet," on page 104, will help students take their Internet searches to the next level.
- **New** sidebar "Muscle Reading in Brief," on page 108, gives an abbreviated approach to using this technique when a student is short on time.
- **New** Master Student Profile: Chief Wilma Mankiller, on page 113.

Chapter 5: Notes

(Chapter 4 in previous edition)

- **New** sidebar article "Meeting with your instructor," on page 123, gives strategies to get the most out of talking with your instructor outside of class.
- **New** Mastering Technology feature "Your mind, online," on page 128, lists computer applications that can give students a variety of ways to store text and images, organize them, search them, and even share them with others when appropriate.
- **New** Master Student Profile: Harvey Milk, on page 133.

Chapter 6: Tests

(Chapter 5 in previous edition)

- **New** section in the article "Cooperative learning: Studying in groups," on pages 137–138, about the importance of understanding the learning styles of study group members.
- **New** Mastering Technology feature "Collaboration 2.0," on page 138, lists Web-based applications that allow students to create virtual study groups and collaborate online.
- **New** article "The test isn't over until . . . ," on page 142, explains the benefits of looking over tests after they have been graded.

- **New** Critical Thinking Exercise "Things I like to do," on page 144, shows students how to relieve stress by replacing unpleasant thoughts with pleasant images.
- **New** Journal Entry "Notice your excuses and let them go," on page 145, asks students to come up with their reasons for not studying and find ways to eliminate their excuses.
- **New** Critical Thinking Exercise "Use learning styles for math success" on page 147.
- **New** article "Eight reasons to celebrate mistakes," on page 148, shows students that taking a different attitude towards failure can lead to future success.
- **New** Master Student Profile: Bert and John Jacobs, on page 153.

Chapter 7: Thinking

(Chapter 6 in previous edition)

- **New** Mastering Technology article "Rethinking email," on page 166, lists ways to use critical thinking to manage your inbox.
- **New** Critical Thinking Exercise "Explore emotional reactions," on page 168, helps students understand how to stay effective thinkers when confronted with topics that trigger strong emotional reactions.
- **New** Journal Entry "Reflect on choosing a major," on page 168.
- **New** Master Student Profile: Twyla Tharp, on page 173.

Chapter 8: Communicating

(Chapter 7 in previous edition)

- **New** article "Communicating in a diverse world," on page 175, provides an overview of the importance of learning to communicate with people from various backgrounds.
- **New** article "Developing emotional intelligence," on page 179, helps students recognize feelings and respond to them in a skillful way.
- **New** article "Thriving with diversity," on page 182–183, shows students how to learn from the diverse community available on campus.
- **New** Mastering Technology feature "Master students—Get networked," on page 184, shows ways to use the Internet to get connected to others.
- **New** sidebar "Making the grade in group presentations" on page 188, gives strategies for creating memorable presentations.

Chapter 9: Health

- **New** chapter opener article "Wake up to health," on page 195, links healthy behavior to success in college.
- **New** article "Choose your fuel," on page 196, focuses on the importance of eating healthy.
- **New** sidebar "Prevent and treat eating disorders," on page 196, provides information on the dangers of unhealthy eating habits.
- **New** article "Choose to exercise," on page 197, provides students with reasons to stay active.
- **New** article "Choose freedom from distress," on pages 198–199, gives students strategies to help manage stress and other mental health issues.
- **New** sidebar "Choose to rest," on page 200, endorses the need for proper amounts of sleep.
- **New** article "Choose to stay safe," on pages 201–202, outlines various precautions that students should take when they get on campus.
- **New** sidebar "Observe thyself," on page 202, lists certain changes to a student's body that may be the first sign of needing medical treatment.
- **New** Critical Thinking Exercise "Addiction: How do I know," on page 203, provides students with a series of questions to help them figure out if they should seek help with a potential addiction.
- **New** Mastering Technology sidebar article "Setting limits on screen time" on page 204, helps students manage their time online.
- **New** article "Alcohol and other drugs: THE TRUTH," on page 205–206, explains the idea of drug dependence and provides suggestions for seeking help.
- **New** sidebar "Succeed in quitting smoking," on page 206, outlines various strategies to give up the habit.
- **New** Master Student Profile: Randy Pausch, on page 211.

Chapter 10: What's New

- **New** Mastering Technology sidebar article "Continue your education at Internet University," on page 214, offers online resources that can be applied for lifelong learning.
- **New** Critical Thinking Exercise "Recognize your skills," on page 220, helps students figure out and organize their skills to create a detailed list.
- **New** article "Join a diverse workplace," on page 225, offers strategies for students entering the workforce.
- **New** Exercise "This book shouts, 'Use me!'" on page 230, explains to students how the text can be a valuable tool as they continue their college career.
- **New** Master Student Profile: Lisa Ling, on page 235. *

Master Student Map

ONE OF THE MOST USEFUL FEATURES in *Becoming a Master Student Concise* is the Master Student Map (**M**etacognitive **A**pplication **P**rocess) located on the opening page of each chapter. The Master Student Map is a reasoning model based on the Learning Style Inventory. Even the most inexperienced students can quickly begin to apply this simple, systematic process to monitor their thinking and learning. What makes this model so effective is that by utilizing the strengths of each learning style, students can implement the monitoring aspect of metacognition as soon as they achieve awareness.

Each category of the Master Student Map begins with a basic question designed to engage student interest and lead to the important ideas presented in the chapter. A closer look at the design and formatting of each question in the Master Student Map will reveal the logic behind this innovative approach to introducing chapter topics.

why this chapter matters . . .

The role of this question is to encourage personal interest and a need to know in the learner. Initiating the Master Student Map with this type of question leads Mode 1 learners toward a deeper metacognitive understanding of their thinking, allowing them to call on principles within their prior knowledge that help structure the ideas in the chapter.

what is included . . .

This question is followed by a list of specific, thought-provoking article titles from the chapter. This helps Mode 2 learners probe and analyze the factual and conceptual ideas presented in the chapter and become more aware of what will be expected of them..

how you can use this chapter . . .

Mode 3 students will experience the impact of acclaimed features of *Becoming a Master Student Concise*, such as the Discovery and Intention Journal Entry system, Power Processes, and Master Student Profiles, which uplift and inspire students to make personal commitments and set goals to accomplish. By consciously choosing their attitude about a chapter topic before they begin to study, students gain confidence in their own ability to initiate action and synthesize solutions to pressing problems. In this stage, have students go through the list of articles and mark the ones they predict they will know something about. The articles they do not mark indicate topics they are least familiar with. Being aware of knowledge gaps will give students a better idea of what they need to study for tests

as you read, ask yourself what if . . .

Taking advantage of the action-oriented strength of Mode 4 learners, *What if?* questions lead to more lateral thinking and thus better-quality decisions. Specific skills do not necessarily transfer from one mental schema to another. Asking provocative *What if?* questions triggers the students' imagination to transfer skills and create new schema for developing skills in their other classes. Students are intrigued by inquiry rather than pat answers. *What if?* questions stimulate discussion

Using the Master Student Map

Begin to use the Master Student Map now by reviewing the Instructor Companion Site through the framework of the Master Student Map.

Why the Instructor Companion Site matters. Being prepared and organized for teaching your course will help you to teach first-year students the importance of becoming master students.

What is included. The Instructor Companion Site includes information on how to write your course outline, establish course objectives or student learning outcomes, determine instructional choices, integrate technology, use educational PowerPoint slides that illustrate key articles in the textbook, explore lectures and exercises for each chapter in the book, access DVD segments on the Power Processes to show your students during class, assess assignments and exercises, identify evaluation criteria, and create and maintain a supportive classroom atmosphere for your students.

How you can use this Companion Site. Ask yourself how you could adapt information, ideas, and exercises here to fit the needs of the students at your campus taking your course.

As you read, ask yourself: What if I could use the materials in this course and apply it to the other disciplines I teach?

and further the transfer of skills in situations outside the classroom as well.

Based on the latest theories of brain-active learning, the Master Student Map feature helps students activate relevant memories with regard to the subject matter in the chapter. Because all learning depends on prior knowledge, beginning each chapter with this reasoning model helps students in several ways. First, distractions can be reduced or eliminated because the model allows students to study the most interesting or important topics first. Next, it helps increase the speed of students' learning by organizing the ideas in the beginning pages. Finally, it links all of the ideas in the entire textbook to the learning style of each student in a simple but powerful way.

Another important benefit of the Master Student Map is that it provides the instructor with a clear outline of what is going to be investigated in each chapter and a framework for guiding the discussion. In a pilot study using this model, instructors at Utah Valley State College found these questions to be very helpful as teaching tools primarily because the questions gave them a place to begin instruction and a final destination.

The four basic questions not only help instructors better understand what the students need to know but also serve as a catalyst for both pre- and post-assessment in the students' minds. Instructors who were more adept at viewing the curriculum in a holistic fashion were able to use this feature of overarching guiding questions to help them convey to students the big picture of the chapter in an efficient and meaningful way. Those instructors who were more linear in their thinking leaned toward the *What?* category of guiding questions and allowed their students to discover how the other questions fit in during the course of the discussion. This flexibility instilled confidence in the instructors to teach the magazine format of *Becoming a Master Student Concise* in their own preferred style and enabled them to be more comfortable with the teaching process. Consequently, students reported high satisfaction with both the course instructor and the material. *

Using the Instructor Companion Site

As you review the Instructor Companion Site, ask yourself

what if . . .

I need help teaching a certain skill or concept to my students?

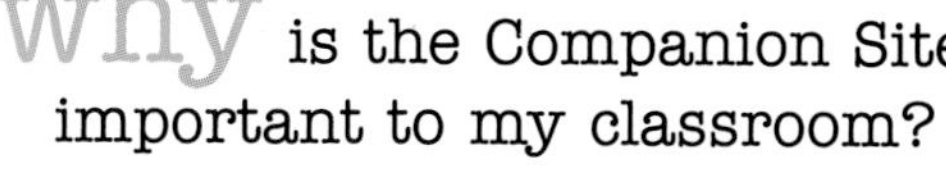

why is the Companion Site important to my classroom?

- Resources to support your instruction have been collected from educators whose previous experiences in the classroom have been met with success.
- Access to instructional materials, provided in electronic format, allows you to easily customize and then print, e-mail, or post materials to a class Web site or course-management system.

how can I use this resource?

- Evaluate resources chapter by chapter while planning your course to determine in-class activities and exercises you will use throughout the semester.
- View PowerPoint slides that are downloadable and customizable to fit your needs.
- Review sample syllabi instructors have generously shared for your inspiration.
- Read the guide and handouts created to accompany the Power-Up! Video/ DVD series.
- Review lecture ideas you may adapt and adopt to clarify key concepts in the textbook.
- Invite guest speakers to your course at the start of the term.
- Practice using technology resources.

what is included?

- Pre- and post-test retention study materials
- Teaching tips
- Lecture ideas
- Warm-up exercises
- Guest speaker ideas
- Relationship building exercises
- Applying skills activities
- Closure exercises
- Prompts for conversation and sharing exercises
- Technology integration suggestions
- Chapter tests
- Answer keys
- Final exam suggestions
- PowerPoint slide shows
- Video clips
- Bibliography
- Information on TeamUp College Survival consulting services
- Resources for gaining support for your first-year experience course
- Information on supplementary resources

Master instructor resources

THE AIE RESOURCE PAGES in this Annotated Instructor's Edition of *Becoming a Master Student Concise* highlight many chapter-specific resource materials that are available to you through Cengage Learning. Take advantage of these valuable tools to assist you in your course. Remember to call your TeamUp consultant if you have any questions about acquiring materials or integrating them into your course, or if you have a suggestion you would like to see implemented in the future.

Instructor Companion Site. This new one-stop resource provides all of the support materials users of previous editions of *Becoming a Master Student Concise* have found in the paper Course Manual and the ClassPrep CD-ROM, plus new content. Material on the Companion Site includes icebreakers, lecture ideas, classroom activities, handouts, PowerPoint slides to integrate into classroom presentations, and additional ideas submitted by instructors who have shared tools they have developed for use with college students.

Powerlecture CD. This Powerlecture CD-ROM contains the *Becoming a Master Student Concise* test bank in the ExamView test-generating software, enhanced instructor PowerPoints, and a PDF of the Course Manual.

College Success CourseMate. College Success CourseMate is easily accessible for students and instructors alike via cengagebrain.com. The site includes new activities and resources for students, including the Discovery Wheel interactive exercise, Skillbuilders, Concept Maps, and a Master Student Hall of Fame featuring Master Student Profiles and biographical information about past and present master students.

WebTutor. The WebTutor offers a number of instructor resources to complement the main text including discussion questions and gradebook content. For students, Power Process media, Video Skillbuilders, and additional resources will enhance their understanding of the text's main points.

Multimedia eBook. The Multimedia eBook allows users to experience the textbook in a whole new way by instantly connecting students to resources including videos and Web site activities that will bring the content in the text to life.

Power-Up! Power Process DVD. Show your students how to put the *power* into Power Processes with *Power-Up!* a new DVD that contains 8- to 9-minute segments on each of the Power Processes in *Becoming a Master Student Concise.* These video segments will enhance your lecture by bringing to life the concepts and metaphors in the text while speaking to the auditory and visual learners in your class. This closed-captioned Power Process DVD is free to adopters. These videos are also found on the Student CourseMate.

Additional videos. A 30-minute video, *The Interviewing Process: Strategies for Making the Right Impression,* takes students through the interviewing process from start to finish, providing them with strategies for successful interviews. The video covers preparation for the interview with instruction on what to wear, questions and answers to think about, and research on the company. Real-life interviewing scenarios on the video provide students with examples of the actual interview process. Also covered is what to do after the interview, including evaluating how it went, seeing what you can learn, and following up.

A financial management video, *Money and Finances,* discusses strategies to help students gain control of their finances and overcome the money problems they may currently be experiencing. Students will hear advice from financial advisor Ann Egan on income and expenses, examine the general principles of budgeting and cash flow, and hear a discussion on financial aid. Through real-world money challenges, including the pitfalls of credit card spending, presented by real students, this video will teach your students to develop the skills of good money management.

The new Master Students and Teachers in Action video provides you with an inside look at how *Becoming A Master Student Concise* is used by professors, including information on their favorite parts, and how specific articles and activities from the text prepares students for achieving success.

Each of the above videos is accompanied by a program overview to guide instructors through its contents, as well as suggestions for classroom activities. These additional aids can be found at the Instructor Companion Site.

PowerPoint slides. PowerPoint slides for selected topics in *Becoming a Master Student Concise* can be downloaded from the Instructor Companion site. These slides can be edited to fit your teaching style and preferences.

CL Assessment and Portfolio Builder. The CL Assessment and Portfolio Builder tool is available for packaging, with *Becoming a Master Student Concise*, as a passkey to a password-protected Web page. This is a personal assessment tool to help students learn more about themselves and prepare for success in college and career. Students will build their portfolios by responding to questions in the modules *Personal, Interpersonal, Career,* and *Community,* and by reflecting on their skills, attitudes, values, and behaviors. The *Accomplishments Report* summarizes the results of students' responses in a format that is perfect for creating a résumé or preparing for interviews. More information about this resource begins on page AIE-27.

3×5 cards. Provided at no charge to instructors who purchase *Becoming a Master Student Concise*, 3×5 cards facilitate classroom participation. The text suggests a variety of uses for 3×5 cards. Instructors and students often report becoming obsessed with them. They find them lurking in closets, hiding under their beds, stuck on their mirrors, pinned to bulletin boards, tucked into pockets, slipped into their notes, marking their places in books, resting next to their telephones, even replacing their address and recipe books. Some instructors ask students to carry 3×5 cards with them for a few days and jot down how they use their time. By doing so, students can monitor what they are doing and the amount of time they spend doing it.

Another way to use 3×5 cards is for attendance. Have students write their names and a question on a 3×5 card. Then have students bring their cards to class each day to hand in as their admission tickets to class. Their questions can then be used to stimulate classroom discussions.

Two-part exercise sheets. Two-part exercise sheets (up to five per book ordered) provide a way to encourage students to participate in class. The final step in any classroom exercise can be for students to write Journal Entries on two-part sheets. If you collect the original, letting students keep a copy for their own use, you can read some of the student discoveries and insights anonymously to the rest of the class. Students are interested in what their peers think. Collecting two-part sheets can also be a convenient way to take attendance. *

Selling this class to students on Day 1

IF YOUR STUDENT SUCCESS course is required, you are likely to have a number of student resisters in your class. In colleges and universities where taking such a course is an option, some students enroll because they think it looks like an "easy A" in the catalog. In either case, you, as the course instructor, can positively influence students on the first day of class so that they'll be more likely to stay and discover for themselves the value of this course. Here are seven suggestions to help build interest and commitment on Day 1:

1. Student testimonial letters. At the end of each semester, ask students to write a letter of advice to a future student in your course. Encourage them to include the information they would have liked to have known on the first day of class. Consider making this assignment part of the final or another assignment for which credit is granted. Distribute copies of these letters to your students during the first class meeting. Because these letters consist of opinions and not always facts, it may be useful to have the students exchange letters or share key information in the letters in groups or with the class as a whole. Students believe the content in these letters from unknown peers, and many will be inspired by what they read. Faculty Advisor Dean Mancina puts these letters in envelopes before handing them out—the sealed envelopes add to the impact!

2. Student guest speakers. This idea can be used as an alternative or in conjunction with the testimonial letters above. At the end of the semester, invite students to return as guest speakers on the first day of your class the following semester. Get their e-mail addresses and/or phone numbers so that you can send them a reminder a week or two before the next term begins. Having two or three students tell their peers how valuable the course is raises the commitment level of students who are still "shopping" for classes during the first week of the term.

3. Show your enthusiasm. If you've taught this course before, you know the profound impact it can have on your students. Share that in a dramatic and enthusiastic way. Let your students know how much impact this course can have on their lives. Share some stories of the success your prior students have achieved, but don't mention names, to protect your students' privacy.

4. Ask, "What do you want?" During the first class, ask students to write down three skills that would be so beneficial that if they could learn them, staying in this course would be "worth it." Brainstorm several such skills first to prompt their thinking. Use two-part paper. Have the students pass one copy forward. Read their responses aloud, anonymously, and announce whether each skill is part of the content of this course. This activity helps personalize the course and demonstrates that the content includes material that students want to learn. It also helps to clarify what this class is *not* about, as it's doubtful your course will cover everything the students want.

5. Talk about the text. *Becoming a Master Student* is one of the most used college textbooks on any subject in North America. This is a proven product that works. Hold the book up and turn to key pages such as the Discovery Wheel. Tell the students this is a book they will not want to trash or sell at the end of the semester, but will keep as a reference tool for the rest of their college years . . . and beyond!

6. Group discussion and anonymous questions. Divide students into groups of four and ask them to brainstorm questions about this course that they don't know the answers to. Have the students submit their questions anonymously on 3×5 cards. Read the questions aloud and answer them. Addressing concerns students may not wish to state openly can help quell anxiety and fears that could result in students dropping the course.

7. Tell the truth. Be honest about both the "good news" and the "bad news." "This course is *not* an easy A! But it's also about more than you thought it was when you enrolled." On the first day, Faculty Advisor Dean Mancina shares this thought with his students: "I don't know why you enrolled in this class, but today I get to convince you to commit to it and stay!" *

The Discovery Wheel

The Discovery Wheel is an opportunity for students to think about the kind of student they are and the kind of student that they want to become. Its 10 sections correspond to the 10 chapters in the text. This exercise is assigned at the outset of the course to help students assess their current strengths and weaknesses in different areas of student success. Students answer a series of questions and then plot their scores on their Discovery Wheel—a graphic illustration of their skill levels. This exercise is also available for students to complete on the College Success CourseMate.

At the end of Chapter 10 is an identical Discovery Wheel. By repeating the exercise at the completion of the course, students can trace their progress in acquiring skills and techniques that can ensure their success in school and later in life.

The purpose of this exercise is to give students the opportunity to change their behavior. Completing the Discovery Wheel a second time allows students to see what behaviors they have changed on their journey to becoming master students.

Having your students complete the Journal Entry that follows the second Discovery Wheel provides them with another opportunity to state how they intend to change. Encourage them to reconsider tools that they did not think they could use the first time they encountered them in the text.

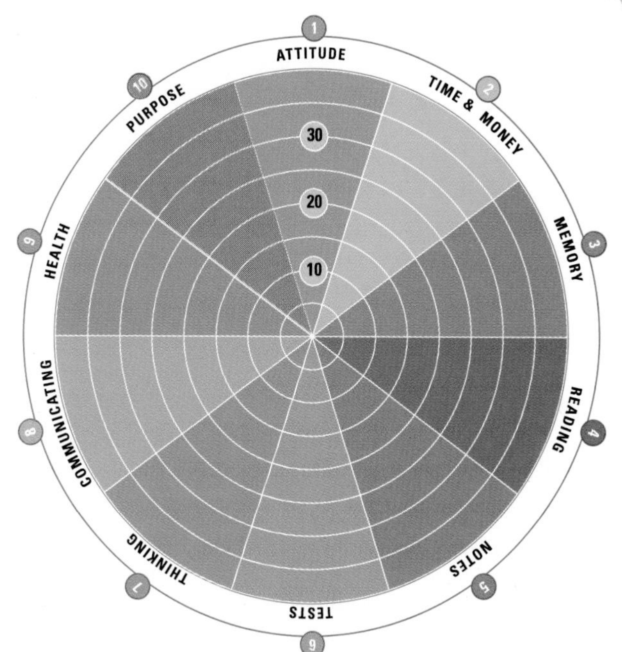

Note: Student scores may be lower on the second Discovery Wheel. That's okay. Lower scores might result from increased self-awareness and honesty, valuable assets in themselves.

Tips for teaching student success online

MANY OF THE STRATEGIES in the Instructor's Edition and on the Instructor Companion site can be adapted for use in your online student success course. For example, the icebreaker activity "Vote with your feet" (page AIE-29) can be used online by having the students read a controversial article. Then at the Discussion Board, each student posts in the Subject Line: Strongly Agree, Agree, Disagree, or Strongly Disagree, with justification for his or her position in the body of the post. Further require that students respond to at least two other student posts in this thread.

One of the most important roles of the online instructor is to ensure a high degree of interactivity and participation by managing the discussion forum. In a classroom, the instructor builds motivation in front of the students by her on-stage demeanor. Online that role is portrayed in the projects, instructions, and guidance the instructor gives, which altogether promote a dynamic, interactive environment for online students. For example, when assigning a text exercise such as the Discovery Wheel, instead of having students turn in the reflective responses to the exercise, have them post a Discovery and/or Intention Statement to the Discussion Board and respond to at least two classmates' posts. If you use the eBook with your online students, assign students to complete the pre-chapter assessment that appears as a link icon at the beginning of each chapter and then post an Intention Statement about the results on the discussion board.

Here are some suggestions to help you manage your online Discussion Board:

- Stagger due dates for postings and replies each week to keep the conversation moving.
- Require discussion participation and make it part of the student's grade in the course.
- Provide post expectations to receive full credit.
- Teach students to create succinct, accurate titles for the subject line of their posts.
- Don't let students use abbreviated writing, teach netiquette.

> "After students read the article "Connect to resources" (page 15), I have my students participate in an online scavenger hunt to discover what support programs are available to them while attending this community college. Many students do not attend classes on campus so I have them search the school Web site and then post on the Discussion Board what they discover. My assignment includes several different questions regarding student resources. Each student must respond to a different question.
>
> **—Connie Marten, Online Instructor, Golden West College**

Consider the following examples of online activities:

1. **Don't fool yourself:** Common mistakes in logic (pages 160–161). After students read the article, instruct them to pick one common mistake in logic and post a personal example to the discussion board. The second part of the assignment includes responding to classmates' posts.

2. **Weekly Journal:** The weekly journal is an avenue for students and the instructor to relate one to one. Solicit feedback from your students. Ask them how they are doing in class. Often an online class may be more difficult or time-consuming than they anticipated. In the journals, students often share frustrations with other classes, work, or not having enough time with family and friends. Direct them to a specific article in the textbook that may help, or quote something from the book in your reply. *

CL Assessment and Portfolio Builder and Career Resource Center

THE CL ASSESSMENT AND PORTFOLIO BUILDER is a personal development tool that engages students in *self-assessment, critical thinking,* and *goal-setting* activities to prepare them for college and the workplace.

Students build a portfolio by responding to questions about their skills, attitudes, values, and behaviors in four key life areas: *Personal, Interpersonal, Career,* and *Community.* The *Accomplishments Report* summarizes the results of their responses and asks students to provide supporting evidence for responses in which they rate themselves as highly proficient. This provides great practice for honing critical thinking skills as well as for creating a résumé or preparing for interviews.

The Accomplishments Report module also provides access to additional resources, such as Cengage Learning's Web-based Career Resource Center, which offers tips, exercises, articles, and ideas to help students succeed on their journey from college to career. *The Bridge from College to Career* lets students practice new skills acquired in college that can be applied as they enter the job market. *Finding the Perfect Job* helps students fine-tune their résumé writing and interviewing skills. And *Skills for Your Future* provides strategies for problem solving and decision making to help students learn to work with others and communicate on the job.

Contact your sales representative or your TeamUp Consultant about shrink-wrapping this tool as a passkey to a protected Web site with *Becoming a Master Student Concise.*

A walk-through of the features

Demo this product via the College Success CourseMate. Visit each of the areas described below and try it yourself.

Each module *(Personal, Interpersonal, Career,* and *Community)* has a series of statements. Students assess their response to each statement by selecting from four choices. Feedback is provided for each response to help guide students in making the most appropriate selection. You can participate in the CL Assessment and Portfolio Builder by selecting the suitable response to each of the statements in the four sections. Those items that you mark as "usually and consistently" will be carried over to the *Accomplishments Report,* the fifth module.

Once the assessment portion has been completed, you are ready to enter evidence into your *Accomplishments Report.* In this section, you will provide supporting evidence for statements that were rated as "usually and consistently" most like your skills, attitudes, values, and behaviors.

The evidence is saved, and a portfolio of accomplishments is generated from these entries. Students can view and update their portfolios throughout the semester, and they can print a hard copy to bring to class or use as a reference during an interview.

After an *Accomplishments Report* is generated, students will see which areas still need documentation. They can explore information and resources for gaining experiences in college using the Career Resource Center. Students can access tips, exercises, articles, and additional Internet links to help them succeed in college and in the workplace. Suggestions for using the CL Assessment and Portfolio Builder to create a résumé and prepare for interviews are also available in the Career Resource Center. *

Icebreakers: Some ideas for first-day-of-class activities

CREATING A SENSE of community in your classroom starts during your first class meeting. Icebreakers can help both you and your students create a comfortable environment that supports self-discovery and honest reflection—two processes that will help your students achieve success. Here are several possible first-day icebreakers to get you started. Refer to the Instructor Companion Site for more activities related to specific chapters that can be used at any time throughout your course.

Becoming a Master Student Concise has many unique messages in the beginning of the text. These messages are helpful for instructors to remember and highlight when starting the course.

"This book is worthless."

Have you ever seen a book start with this statement? All books are worthless unless read, so this book is useless unless students strive to adapt and adopt methods to attain personal and academic success. Students often complain about the cost of their textbooks. Yet the cost is even higher when they pay for a text but do not actively read it and implement its strategies to promote their success. Ask your students what specific steps they will take to ensure they get the most out of their investment in this textbook. Point out the following exercises as specific tasks to help them get started on this journey: "Textbook Reconnaissance," "The Discovery Wheel," and "Learning Style Inventory."

What is a Master Student?

Student success courses are offered at colleges and universities nationwide. Students often exhibit less resistance to taking this course when they realize that their school is not the only one requiring it. The qualities of a successful student are also the qualities of successful employees. This course can help students define the characteristics that promote excellence in their studies and relationships and in preparation for the world of work. Have your students review the article "The Master Student" in Chapter 1. Divide them into groups of four and ask them to list the qualities of people they admire (family members, celebrities, or friends). When each group has named 10 characteristics, create a combined list of 20 for the entire class. Ask students to rank in order the qualities that might contribute to success in school, work, and life.

Ask your students to consider these qualities of success and then write an essay entitled "How do I define success?" Submit the best essay to the Cengage Learning Student Success scholarship competition (see complete details on page AIE-15).

Master Students in Action quotes

Each edition of *Becoming a Master Student Concise* has been revised by considering the valuable insights and ideas of students and educators. Instructors over the years have used the Master Students in Action feature as part of the final examination for their course. Let your students know right from the outset that you will ask them to complete the Master Students in Action form on the College Success CourseMate or e-mail the forms to csweb.CollegeSurvival@cengage.com. Here they can share information about any article or exercise that they have found to be especially valuable to their growth during the course—and why. Ask them to suggest ways in which *Becoming a Master Student Concise* could be valuable to next year's first-year students.

"What do you want?"

Research indicates that more than 60 percent of first-year college and university students are not yet sure of their career choice, even if they have declared a major. A student might choose a major because of parental pressure or the institution's policy rather than because of a passionate commitment to that field of study or career. This lack of clarity about her destination could negatively affect a student's level of dedication and involvement. She might experience a lack of desire or frustration when she encounters difficulties because she does not sense that current distresses might result in long-term benefits.

When they are asked "What do you want?" students can begin to find answers to what they hope to accomplish in the course, in the term, and in the academic year. Consider having your students share their answers in class, in small groups.

Create a college survival kit

Divide students into groups and ask them to brainstorm what this kit would have in it. Ask each group to report out to the class four items that have not been shared by another group.

Scavenger hunt

Create a scavenger hunt list about the services at the college. This encourages students to meet their peers, become familiar with the campus layout, and learn which services are available. The winner of the scavenger hunt might be rewarded by being taken to lunch by the college president.

Student success alumni

Invite former students to speak about their experiences taking the student success course and to describe specific successes they've had in college subsequent to completing this course.

Class as a worksite

Tell the class that you are the supervisor and they are the employees. Ask them the implications for being late, absent, attentive, and productive. Create a list of expected behaviors in the "workplace."

Naming names

Have each student introduce himself with a unique name that describes him. These aliases could be used throughout the term.

Choose your final grade

Many students wonder on the first day about the grade they'll get at the end of the term. Provide a list of each assignment, quiz, and test in the course and the maximum points possible. Ask students to set a goal score for each item. Then tell them to total their scores and see their final (goal) grade. This activity generates good first-day questions about course assignments throughout the term. It also demonstrates course goal setting.

Excuses brainstorm

Faculty Advisor Dean Mancina asks his students to commit to attend every class meeting. He asks students to brainstorm a list of reasons why a student might miss class. As reasons are suggested, he asks students to categorize them as "good," "poor", or "questionable." Students typically disagree about categorizing them, and most excuses end up in the "questionable" category. This activity helps students see how having to decide what exactly is a "good" excuse puts the faculty in an awkward position. It also sets the stage for Dean explaining his absence policy.

Group syllabus questions

Divide students into groups and ask each group to come up with three questions about the syllabus. Respond to the entire class about each of the groups' questions. Students are generally more attentive to responses to their inquiries than to your "lecture" about the syllabus.

Voting with your feet

Eldon McMurray from Utah Valley State College makes four signs—Agree, Disagree, Strongly Agree, and Strongly Disagree—and posts them on the walls of the classroom. At the beginning of the activity, he has the students push the chairs aside and form a group in the middle. Next he reads a controversial statement like, "Being energy independent is more important than global warming."

Then he asks the students to vote with their feet. They simply move to stand by the sign that reflects how they feel about the issue at argument. He picks two or three students and has them defend their "stand." He also teaches them what it means to make a stand. He shows a video clip from the Tiananmen Square uprising in China. *

Encourage students to participate

Your student success course will benefit from class participation that motivates students to contribute and share. As you create a sense of community in your classroom, use these suggestions for increasing overall participation.

Facilitate students getting to know each other. Having students do projects in groups with nonthreatening group assignments (such as "Plan participation activities") helps them to get to know each other. It's less intimidating to participate around people you've met than with strangers. Randomly assign students to different groups for a brief activity each week.

Plan participation activities. Divide your students into small groups (three to four students is ideal) to review articles from the textbook or assignments that may have been completed outside class. Provide some guidelines and post them (on a whiteboard, PowerPoint slide, etc.) so that all students can see them. Suggest the number of minutes that students should talk about each question you have assigned. For example, you may ask your students to do the following: "Identify the time-management strategy that was most interesting to you and describe how you plan to use it in the upcoming week (2 minutes per person)."

After your students have discussed this with their group, bring the discussion back to the classroom as a whole. Create a tally to show which strategy was the most popular. Consider discussing why some of the less popular strategies are beneficial, and challenge your students to try the one they selected and then one of the less popular strategies. As the instructor, also commit to planning to practice these new strategies and collectively report back on results during the next class period. Sharing enthusiasm with students is a master instructor quality that will help to increase positive feedback and results in your course.

Call on students rather than waiting for them to volunteer. Allow all of your students to think about questions that you are asking, permitting time for reflection and contemplation. Suggest that your students who frequently get called on first write down their answers while everyone in the class has time to think. Break the ice by selecting one of your eager students. Then select students who have not had a chance to share. Remind students that participating in class is a great way to connect with the instructor and that a student success class is a perfect classroom for practicing their public speaking skills. Challenge your students to participate in their other courses as much as they participate in this class—it's engaging!

Acknowledging uncomfortableness. Trying new techniques, changing habits, and practicing new behaviors can be uncomfortable at first. Nevertheless, these activities make up much of what a student success course is about. When describing the benefits of the course, it is wise to be honest about the challenges that students face while expressing confidence in their ability to succeed. Ask students to write their names with their nondominant hands, to introduce themselves to one another by shaking their left hands, or to cross their arms in reverse of the way they normally do. Everyone can relate when they all feel the awkwardness of these movements. But with practice, these movements will begin to feel natural. So will participating in class.

Reinforce speaking up. Surprise a student who speaks up with "bonus points" or a coupon for a beverage in the school food service. Dean Mancina's student success course has a required "materials fee" of about $3 per student. This small account funds the purchase of inexpensive educational supplies that are given to students through the term.

Teaching learning styles in your classroom

BECOMING A MASTER STUDENT CONCISE includes three approaches to learning styles: the Learning Style Inventory, multiple intelligences, and the VAK (**v**isual, **a**uditory, and **k**inesthetic) system. That's a lot of information to absorb. It is important to recognize that each approach presents a valid option and is not the final word on learning styles. Encourage your students to look for ideas from any of these methods that they can put to immediate use. When they write Intention Statements, have your students keep these questions in mind: How can I use this idea to *be* more successful in school? What will I *do* differently as a result of reading about learning styles? If I develop new learning styles, what skill will I *have* that I don't have now?

The Learning Style Inventory (LSI). People are fascinated by why they do what they do—and students are no exception. Taking the Learning Style Inventory (LSI) in Chapter 1 gives students a chance to increase their self-awareness as learners. The LSI helps students make sense of what they're experiencing in college.

Developed by Dr. David Kolb at Case Western Reserve University in Cleveland, Ohio, the LSI measures a learner's preferences for *perceiving* information (taking it in) and *processing* information (making sense of what she takes in). When these preferences are plotted on two continuums, four unique modes of learning are formed. Students find that although every individual is capable of employing all four modes, each person has a preferred way of learning.

The Master Student Map on the first page of each chapter highlights these four modes to help students become more effective learners through an understanding of their own learning style preferences. More important, the Master Student Map can help increase students' effectiveness by encouraging them to use those modes that they have previously underutilized.

Detailed information about administering and helping your students interpret the Learning Style Inventory appears on the next page. Support materials are also available at the Instructor Companion Site.

Multiple intelligences. Howard Gardner of Harvard University believes that no single measure of intelligence can tell us how smart we are. Instead, Gardner identifies many types of intelligence, described in *Becoming a Master Student Concise* on pages 31–33. By applying Gardner's concepts, students can explore additional methods for achieving success in school, work, and relationships. *Becoming a Master Student Concise* is designed to help students develop these different intelligences. Charts accompany the definitions of Gardner's multiple intelligences in the text, highlighting the characteristics of each intelligence, the learning strategies that are preferred by people with this type of intelligence, and the careers that might interest them. Have your students apply this information to their core courses. For example, a student with musical/rhythmic intelligence could write songs using lyrics based on class notes and could experiment with various kinds of background music while studying.

When students begin to acknowledge and trust all of their intelligences, they can understand and appreciate themselves more.

The VAK system. The VAK system is a simple and powerful technique that focuses on perception through three sense channels: seeing, or *visual* learning; hearing, or *auditory* learning; and movement, or *kinesthetic* learning. Invite your students to discover their VAK preferences by taking the informal inventory included in the text.

Strategies in the text highlight ways students can build on their current learning preferences and develop new options by utilizing their other sense channels. It is important that you teach students to take in information efficiently through their preferred learning style, but it is equally important that you teach them to study and learn information efficiently through a variety of other learning styles. As their instructor, you can set an example by using a mix of strategies to teach them ways to learn the largest amount of material in the least amount of time.

Additional ideas for implementing variety in your teaching strategies can be found at the Instructor Companion Site. *

Applying the learning styles for critical thinking

Have students use the following scale to rate their confidence in their ability to utilize the four questions *Why? What? How?* and *What if?* to effectively accomplish the tasks listed:.

0 Never confident
1 Rarely confident
2 Occasionally confident
3 Sometimes confident
4 Often confident
5 Almost always confident

___ 1. You are a learner, and your biology professor only shows you *how* to do an experiment. Rate your confidence in your ability to answer any questions (*Why? What?* and/or *What if?*) you still have.

___ 2. After your professor repeats the instructions for an assignment, they are still not clear to you. How confident are you that you can gain the clarity you need to successfully complete the assignment by asking yourself the four questions?

___ 3. As you plan your schedule for the next semester, you find there are a number of English classes to choose from. How confident are you in your ability to discover which class would be best for you to take?

___ 4. You are preparing for a test, but you have little, if any, prior background knowledge about the subject.

___ 5. You have a problem, and you are trying to understand all the factors that have contributed to the problem so that you can solve it.

___ 6. You are reviewing your class notes for a test, and you do not remember why a certain entry was so important for you to remember.

___ 7. You need to choose your career and declare a major, but you are not sure what steps to take first.

___ 8. Your car breaks down, and you are the one responsible for fixing it.

___ 9. You are planning a party, and you have been elected to be in charge of buying the food and arranging for the entertainment.

___10. You are sending out Christmas cards, and you discover that you have more friends and family on your list than you have cards to send.

Administering and interpreting the Learning Style Inventory

THE LEARNING STYLE INVENTORY (LSI) is an important tool to help your students discover their preferred mode of learning. Some instructors have found their students feel overwhelmed when they are left on their own to take the LSI, score it, and interpret the results. Consider the following suggestions.

Begin by introducing the LSI to your students. The article "Learning styles: Discovering how you learn" will help you set the stage. Page 36 highlights the step-by-step directions for completing the LSI, which begins on page LSI-1. Review the directions with your students. If you are assigning the LSI as homework, consider walking students through the scoring process in class first. Or ask them to hold off scoring the inventory until they're in class with you. Guide them in using the interpretive material: Help your students connect it with their own experience. Doing so will pay big dividends. Not only will your students begin to understand why they make the choices they do, but they'll be better partners in the learning process.

Be sure to review the cycle of learning with your students. The examples will be easily identifiable to your students and will encourage them to put the information they have discovered about themselves into practice right away. Begin your discussion by asking students about their preferred way to learn historical information or new technology. Once you have your students in the proper mindset to think about their learning style, they will be better prepared to read the Master Student Map at the beginning of each chapter and will understand the value of completing the Learning Styles Application on the CourseMate.

Beginning on page 37, the article "Using your learning style profile to succeed" will have your students participating in a Mode 4 activity. In the Put it to Work feature at the end of Chapter 1, your students will be invited to think specifically about learning styles and their application in the workplace.

Students can use their understanding of learning styles to make choices that support their academic progress. Ask them to apply *What? Why? How?* and *What if?* questions to the LSI:

- "***Why*** should I involve myself in this learning situation?"

  Self-awareness control is the ability to consciously monitor and intentionally control thinking and establish purposeful reasons for action. Asking the question *Why?* helps students regulate their thinking by establishing purposeful reasons for their actions.

- "***What*** will I need to do to understand the concept?"

  Critical analysis is the ability to identify key ideas, gather necessary information, and recognize the importance of essential ideas. Asking *What?* questions helps students recognize the knowledge level of essential ideas by their order of importance.

- "***How*** is this learning meaningful to me?"

  Reasoned synthesis is the ability to combine essential ideas to create meaningful applications of knowledge. Asking *How?* questions helps students utilize essential ideas and create meaningful applications of their knowledge

- "***What if*** I apply this strategy to my other courses or to my life?"

  Creative transfer application is the ability to adapt applications for different concepts and choose the most effective strategies for specific situations. Asking *What if?* questions helps students imagine alternative applications and choose the most effective strategy for the situation.

Integrating knowledge of learning styles into the curriculum can help instructors design a course that promotes success for all students. As you choose your teaching methods to address various preferences at different points in the course, you meet different students' needs. Students in your classes typically represent all four modes of learning, so some students will sometimes find a good fit with what you are doing, while at other times they'll need to stretch beyond their preferences. Acknowledging different learning styles allows instructors to shift their energy from lecturing to facilitating. Rather than just focusing on the transfer of knowledge, you can use feedback about your students' learning to inform your teaching. Students come to realize that their interactions shape what happens in the classroom, and they become active participants in constructing their learning experience. Working together, instructors and students create an environment that promotes success.

More suggestions for creating lesson plans that support all four modes of learning are available at the Instructor Companion Site. In addition, video clips from the *Learning Style Inventory* video—an overview of the LSI and its application—are available at the Instructor Companion Site. *

Using learning styles to improve learning and problem-solving skills

Students can improve their ability to learn and solve problems in three ways:

1. Develop learning and work relationships with people whose learning strengths and weaknesses are different from theirs.
2. Improve the fit between their learning style strengths and the kinds of learning and problem-solving experiences they face.
3. Practice and develop learning skills in their areas of weakness.

First strategy: Develop supportive relationships. This is the easiest way to improve learning skills. It is important for students to recognize their own learning style strengths and build on them. At the same time, it is important to understand and value other people's different learning styles. Also, students should not assume that they have to solve problems alone. Learning power is increased by working with others. Although students might be drawn to people who have similar learning skills, they'll learn more and experience the learning cycle more fully with friends and coworkers who have different learning skills.

How? If someone has an abstract learning style, such as Mode 3, he can learn to communicate ideas more effectively by associating with those who are more concrete and people oriented, such as learners who prefer Mode 1. A person with a more reflective style can benefit from observing the risk taking and experimentation of people who are more active, such as learners who prefer Mode 4.

Second strategy: Improve the match or fit between students' learning styles and their life situation. This is a more difficult way to achieve better learning performance and life satisfaction.

How? There are a number of ways to do this. For some people, this might mean a change of career to a field where they feel more comfortable with the values and skills required of them. Most people, however, can improve the match between their learning style and their tasks by reorganizing their priorities and activities. They can concentrate on those tasks and activities that lie in their areas of learning strength and rely on other people's help in areas of learning weakness.

Third strategy: Become a flexible learner. Students can do this by strengthening the learning skills in which they are weak. This strategy is the most challenging but also the most rewarding. By becoming flexible, students will be able to cope with problems of all kinds, and they will be more adaptable in changing situations. Because this strategy is more difficult, it requires more time and tolerance for mistakes and failures.

How? First, students should develop a long-term plan. Look for improvements and payoffs over months and years, rather than right now. Next, look for safe opportunities to practice new skills. Students should find situations that can test new skills and will not punish them for failure. Lastly, students should reward themselves! Becoming a flexible learner is hard work.

Embracing diversity

RESEARCH INDICATES THAT although successful students benefit from having a relationship with a caring and competent adult, they are most likely to excel if they receive positive support from a peer group. The information below will help you foster that sense of belonging and assist students of all backgrounds in sharing with each other their discoveries and insights about higher education.

Research also shows that when students interact with diverse student groups, they experience many benefits including these:

- Improved cultural understanding and tolerance
- Decreased cultural prejudice and discrimination
- Stronger connection to the campus community
- Preparation for challenges of global society
- Development of creativity and critical thinking skills

These benefits can be realized only if students extend themselves beyond both real and imagined barriers.

Anthony Antonio, a professor at Stanford University, claims, "The most influential experiences with diversity likely involve the development of interracial [and cross-cultural] friendships."* Learning tolerance and respect for the diversity that makes each student unique will be one of the most important skills students learn in college. By willingly stretching themselves to increase their sensitivity and feel empathy toward others, they will develop personal attributes that will benefit them throughout their lives.

Instructors and students are currently using *Becoming a Master Student Concise* in the United States, Canada, and many other countries. In all probability, a variety of cultural and life experiences will be represented by the students in your class. They will have come from many places and have had varied experiences.

Additional activities on the Instructor Companion Site offer ways to encourage communication among students of different races, ethnicity, ages, countries of origin, and levels of familiarity with the American language and American customs.

The video *Embracing Diversity* highlights a group of students representing diverse cultures, ages, races, and religious and ethnic backgrounds. They share their personal experiences and illustrate by example effective means of communicating across cultures. Attitudes, stereotypes, and biases are examined.

One of the major goals of diversity awareness is to understand how each person fits into the lives and worlds of others. For some of your students, college may be their first experience with someone different from themselves. As you prepare for your course, keep in mind that some kinds of diversity can be less obvious, though just as profound, as others. To the student from rural America, a classmate from New York or Chicago might seem nearly as strange as one from Finland or Zimbabwe, and vice versa.

International students will have additional adjustment issues beyond those of the other students in your class. They are far from home in an unfamiliar culture. Keep in mind that some statements, activities, or attitudes that seem perfectly natural in our society may seem curious or even offensive to students from other countries. Familiarize yourself with cultural differences and issues that could baffle or frustrate these students and work to overcome them before they become obstacles to learning.

Finding common ground can be an important learning experience in the classroom. Routinely pairing students from different backgrounds and circumstances when assigning group projects and activities can provide students with the opportunity to encounter ideas, attitudes, and experiences different from their own. Throughout the semester, schedule a variety of activities involving students in individual, partner, small-group, and whole-class settings that exercise and accentuate the similarities among your students, and also celebrate the wealth of their differences.

School strategies

Promote participation. Involving students in school activities challenges them and stimulates their interest. Promote the benefits of participating by placing ads in school newsletters and posting notes on bulletin boards. Design and display posters. Ask other teachers to announce school activities in their classrooms. Brainstorm ways to get more students involved. Don't overlook asking students for their ideas!

Provide tutors. Encourage students to take advantage of tutors. Maintaining or improving one's performance level and gaining confidence in academic ability help ensure student success.

*Antonio, A.L. (2004). When does race matter in college friendships? Exploring men's diverse and homogeneous friendship groups. *The Review of Higher Education.* 27(4), 553-575.

Structure opportunities for friendships. Having friends is widely accepted as a critical component of making a healthy adjustment to college life and achieving academic success. Friendships can be expanded beyond immediate peer groups to include faculty members, administrative staff, counselors, role models, peers from home environments, community members, or graduate students. Organize icebreakers and get-acquainted exercises during orientation and at other school events. Encourage the use of name tags at these events. Sponsor social activities that include faculty and staff as well as students. Encourage broad participation in all social, academic, cultural, and extracurricular events.

Examine policies and procedures. Review policies and procedures, looking for any subtle (or blatant) messages of racism or other forms of discrimination. If there is no clear disciplinary procedure for infractions of any policy, implement one.

Promote resources. New students who are unfamiliar with the resources at your school cannot use them. Asking the administrators and staff who are responsible for these resources to describe their services during student orientation is only the beginning of what's possible.

Ask administrators and directors of service programs to speak in your class. Suggest that clubs and organizations offering services to diverse students sponsor programs to familiarize students with the resources at your school. Write articles about resources for the school newsletter. An open house at which refreshments are served will encourage students to get to know the facilities and the services that are available. Ask students who have benefited from the resources to give testimonials. Create contests and games that require students to visit various offices, facilities, and services personnel.

Promote the resources at your school so that they attract and serve students. Have tutors and counselors introduce themselves and make short presentations in class. Ask the student advisory board for help.

Make school inviting. Students who feel comfortable are more likely to experience success in school. Do the residence halls offer quiet places to study? Are exercise facilities available at convenient times? Are the needs for student transportation and day care facilities met? Are computers and software programs up to date? How long do students have to wait for assistance in the financial-aid and other student services offices? What is the quality of the food service? How can registration procedures be made more efficient? Do instructors post office hours and keep them? What do admissions representatives say would attract more students?

Hire from different backgrounds. Whenever possible, hiring both men and women from a variety of backgrounds will provide role models for students. Whether they are faculty, staff, or administrators, they should be knowledgeable about diversity issues and committed to being involved with students on campus.

Evaluate faculty. Conduct regular student and peer evaluations of all instructors. Include the criteria of being sensitive to the needs of students and being responsive to the learning styles of all students.

Encourage leadership. Students from diverse backgrounds who are in leadership positions help promote acceptance and inclusion of all students in all areas of school life. Sponsor leadership training programs. Encourage students with leadership potential to consider running for student offices.

Sponsor panel discussions. Invite students from a variety of populations to participate in panel discussions on a wide range of topics. Each panel member can introduce herself (including a description of what it's like to be a member of her particular population on your campus, if appropriate) and then state his point of view about the topic. The discussion can then be opened for questions and answers.

Conduct workshops. Invite faculty and staff to attend workshops on the diverse backgrounds, circumstances, and cultures of students at your institution.

Classroom strategies

Help ensure success. You can individualize your instruction and structure your course so that students experience success. Total success in school is achieved by taking a series of small, successful steps. Set high but realistic expectations. If your course is too easy, students will lose interest. If it is too difficult, students may become discouraged. By continually evaluating students, monitoring their progress, and getting feedback from them, you can plan your classes in ways that help ensure student success.

Provide opportunities to talk. Invite students to speak about their perspectives. Suggest that students talk to others to share their concerns, celebrations, compliments, and complaints. Use small-group discussions and exercises. If you teach online or have a supplemental Web site for your class, use the Discussion Board for this purpose. Promote the idea of visiting with counselors and forming peer support groups. The suggestions for conversations and sharing at the Instructor Companion site include many ideas for stimulating discussions.

Acknowledge and appreciate cultural differences. We can learn from each other and from exploring values that are different from our own. When we exchange ideas, we can expand our perceptions and examine our values. Use conversations, publications, and special events to recognize and celebrate diversity.

Communicate the advantages of being bicultural. Learning new ways of speaking and behaving does not mean denying or letting go of our traditional languages or customs. Adding alternatives does not eliminate anything. Expanding our options increases our ability to operate effectively in a variety of situations and improves our chances of success.

Discuss how the school environment is similar to, and different from, students' home environments. Then discuss ways to make effective transitions back and forth from one to the other. Explore how the expectations of one environment can be assets or liabilities in another. Recognize that a strength in one culture might be a disadvantage in another. Tennis rackets are great on a tennis court, but they don't work very well in a golf game. How can a student adapt so that he is successful in both environments?

Recognize different beliefs regarding time, competitiveness, and respect for authority. In some cultures, punctuality is a plus. In others, time is not measured in hours, minutes, and seconds; instead, it is measured by the movement of the sun, the changing of the seasons, and an intuitive sense of community readiness. In some cultures, competitiveness is a common incentive toward achievement. In others, it is considered antisocial and insulting. Eye contact during conversations is considered respectful in some cultures and disrespectful in others.

You can acknowledge a wide range of beliefs and, at the same time, communicate the expectations of your institution. An advantage to being bicultural is the ability to adopt behaviors that promote success in a specific environment.

Encourage exposure to different backgrounds. Encourage students to break out of old patterns and habits by associating with people from different backgrounds as well as with those whose backgrounds are similar to their own. They could choose new lab partners, form groups with people they don't know for in-class exercises, sit in new areas in the student union, or attend events that are likely to draw crowds different from those with whom they are comfortable. Invite your class to brainstorm ways to gain exposure to people with different backgrounds.

Survey student needs. Evaluate frequently. When you become aware that a student is struggling in a certain area, make an appointment with that student to formulate an action plan.

Individualize feedback. Students appreciate getting specific feedback about their individual performance. Students may initially share cultural concerns or issues in their writing rather than speaking up in class or even individually to you. Write sensitive, relevant comments on papers you return. Send messages and comments to students through the school e-mail. Thank a student who has actively participated as he leaves the classroom.

Set clear expectations. Communicate expectations clearly. State them several times in several different ways. Use examples to illustrate both what is acceptable and what isn't. Invite students to ask questions in class or to contact you during your office hours or via e-mail if they have any questions or concerns.

Be a mediator. As an instructor of a student success course, you can facilitate communication between students and administrators. Pass students' complaints and compliments on to the people who are most directly involved. Ask for responses from those people and report back to the students. Follow up on all communications until the matter is resolved.

Include other cultural experiences. Use speakers, textbooks, classroom materials, activities, and media presentations that incorporate diverse cultural experiences. Ask students, colleagues, administrators, and community members for recommendations.

Use a critical thinking approach. Ask students to decide what they think about relevant issues and why they think it. Then ask them to seek other views and gather evidence to support the various viewpoints. Discuss which view or views are the most reasonable. When discussing issues, you can apply the strategies outlined in the articles on critical thinking in the text to recognize any errors in thinking.

Encourage proaction. When students face uncomfortable, unfamiliar, and difficult situations, they sometimes choose avoidance. They may feel powerless or resentful and choose to withdraw rather than risk embarrassment. Help students consider the long-term costs of giving up. Help them see the benefits of a positive, healthy, and proactive approach. Suggest a variety of alternatives for dealing with the problems they face. Rather than giving up, students can garner support and find or create forums to discuss and resolve their issues.

Allow personal expression. Invite students to translate material into their own words. Ask them how certain techniques, or variations of those techniques, might be applied in their own culture. For example, a gay, lesbian, or transgender student may want to "come out" to the class while sharing in groups or with the whole class. Be ready to provide leadership and support in the event that another student's lack of sensitivity and understanding threatens to create an oppressive rather than supportive environment in your class.

Acknowledge student expertise. Ask students to communicate course content from their unique cultural perspective. Experiencing a concept from a different cultural perspective reinforces it. Give an assignment requiring students to combine a student success strategy with some cultural event, personality, tradition, or value. For example, they could create original music and lyrics or describe the role that a particular success strategy may have played in how a cultural hero changed history.

Use guest speakers. Invite guest speakers to your class who represent successful role models. Ask them to share struggles they have experienced and successes they have achieved. Be sure to include time for a question-and answer period.

Personal strategies

Avoid generalizations. All generalizations are suspect—even this one. Avoid tendencies to lump together all people of one race or culture. Consider speaking up when you hear generalizations being made.

Examine your own prejudices. If you have painful memories that contribute to your prejudices, judgments, and generalizations, examine them. Tell the truth about the costs and benefits of holding on to them. Look at how your history encouraged you to be prejudiced in certain ways. Talk about your prejudices and formulate a plan to heal and grow.

Examine your assumptions about students. Where do you think your students go during their vacations? How would you expect them to spend extra money? What type of music do they enjoy? Who are their heroes? Which holidays do they celebrate? Consider how often your assumptions direct your teaching and your conversations with students. How would your teaching and your conversations be different if you assumed nothing about your students?

Find a translator. Taking a First Step by admitting that you are unfamiliar or uncomfortable with students from other cultures helps bridge the gap. Ask around to find someone who can act as a translator. In this sense, a translator is someone from the students' ethnic or cultural background who has successfully adapted to the mainstream environment. Ask students if they are willing to have this person present when you discuss various issues.

Increase your sensitivity to society's exclusions and inclusions. When you become aware of what to look for, you can see many examples of how one cultural or ethnic group excludes or includes others. Watch advertising and television shows. Listen to speeches. Examine the policies and notice the membership demographics of schools, business organizations, neighborhoods, religious institutions, athletic clubs, and social groups. Look for subtle or hidden messages of exclusion and inclusion as well as blatant, formal structures.

Reach out to students. Be sure students know your office hours. Send written invitations to each student in your class to come visit you during those hours. Talk in class about what students might gain if they schedule an appointment to see you or if they just drop in. Write your reactions to what students have written on papers before you return them. Maintain accurate records about attendance and call students when they miss a class. Use whatever appropriate methods you can think of to let individual students know that you are personally interested in their success. Be a person with whom students can form a supportive, interpersonal relationship.

Give specific feedback. Feedback promotes student success. Be especially sensitive to the unspoken expectations of the environment at your school and in your community. When feedback is given with a sincere desire to promote success, it is likely to be appreciated. *

Critical thinking: It's all over this book

THINKING SKILLS ARE necessary from the first day of the semester, and tools throughout the text are designed to prepare students for the more in-depth coverage provided in Chapter 7: "Thinking."

A first-year experience course can help students develop higher-level thinking and learning skills through self-awareness, self-regulation, and self-instruction. *Becoming a Master Student Concise* offers many opportunities for critical thinking through the introduction of self-awareness tools; strategies for successful studying; and opportunities for connection with other students, faculty, and campus resources.

Self-discovery is encouraged in Chapter 1 through the Discovery Wheel, the Learning Style Inventory, and other learning styles models. The self-awareness that students gain through using these tools provides them with a foundation for honestly assessing their experiences for the rest of their lives. By completing the Discovery Wheel again at the end of the text, students can evaluate the work they have accomplished over the semester.

Time management is a crucial skill for students to develop. The exercises in Chapter 2 help students take a First Step in learning how to manage their time and set short-, medium-, and long-term goals.

As students develop effective thinking and study skills, mastering memory, reading, note taking, and test taking, encourage them to begin to transfer these concepts to their core courses. The application of these skills requires a higher level of thinking and promotes their overall success in college.

Once students reach the "Thinking" chapter, they have experienced the rigors of higher education and are ready to engage in *thorough thinking*. Master students use thorough thinking to select a major, choose courses for the second semester, and plan for their future. They have also actively employed decision-making skills and are ready to transition to the next step of solving problems more creatively and confidently. They exhibit a certain attitude toward success that is highlighted in the way they ask questions, make decisions, and solve problems.

The development of more advanced thinking skills helps students transition to later chapters. There they broaden their scope to consider the impact of decisions and experiences in higher education on such areas as diversity, communication, money, health, their careers, and life beyond.

Throughout the text, students are encouraged to participate actively in developing and implementing concepts. The ideas in the text are not a list of instructions; they are tools that students can try and then decide what works best for them.

The Master Student Map on the first page of each chapter encourages students to ask questions related to the four modes of learning identified in the Learning Style Inventory in Chapter 1. These questions promote curiosity and invite students to explore and investigate new materials.

Discovery and Intention Journal Entries, which appear throughout the text, promote a form of decision making that requires students to make declarations that lead to focused action.

Critical Thinking Exercises promote the application of strategies and allow students to practice problem solving. Students develop thinking techniques and chart their own course.

Put it to Work articles provide students with the chance to begin making connections to their future and to think critically about the application of the skills they learn in college to the workplace. Endorse this type of thinking by asking students to create their own scenarios that apply the skills they are learning in this course to the careers they are considering.

The tools provided in *Becoming a Master Student Concise* are a foundation for this success, and as the instructor, you have the ability to foster the attitudes of a critical thinker in your classroom. Ask your students *how* they will apply these skills. Advertise how these strategies work by suggesting that students ask *What if* questions: "*What if* I apply these test-taking strategies to prepare for exams in my biology course? And *what if* I do not?" *

Classroom Management Strategies

STUDENTS CAN ACHIEVE maximum success in an environment that fosters creativity, critical thinking, focus, and commitment. Developing your classroom management skills can help you create that environment. There are as many approaches to effective classroom management as there are instructors. To be effective, a strategy has to fit your style. For example, if you like a structured, linear environment, set up your class to fit that style. Brainstorm a list of answers to the following question: What is the optimum teaching environment for you and your students? The answers to this question may provide you with guidance in formulating strategies that will provide an environment conducive to learning. Consider asking tenured colleagues what works and what doesn't work for them. They know the culture of the students attending your institution.

After you decide what you want, make sure that you clearly communicate to your students how you conduct your class. Have a conversation with your students about this topic during the first week of class. Follow up with key aspects about your class in writing to enhance clarity. This information might be part of your syllabus or a separate handout.

Finally, implement consistently. Public institutions must be able to defend that students are not being discriminated against. No instructor wants to be accused of treating students with favoritism at any institution, public or private.

Class rules to consider

- *Respect—for peers, for the instructor, and for guest speakers.* What are the minimum standards you want to set?
- *Side conversations.* Some side conversations in class are related to the class topic being discussed, but others may be unrelated to the topic. Seating students in groups promotes more active learning but may also facilitate more side conversations. Side conversations may distract you from your lecture. Further, when two students engage in a side conversation, not only do they miss what's actually happening in class, but the students around them may be distracted as well.
- *Absences.* What is your policy regarding missed class meetings? How will students get the assignments, handouts, information, and class experiences they missed? Flexibility here is helpful for students, but if you're teaching many courses or are a part-time instructor, providing copies of all of your previous handouts and class summaries and taking the time to go over missed classes with students may not be realistic.
- *Arriving late to class.* Some instructors and students are distracted when students arrive late to class. How can late-arriving students minimize the disruption they cause? Will you still accept their homework?
- *Cell phones/laptops/other technologies.* Many students have come to believe that they need to stay in touch with their family and friends even during class. If you don't want students constantly stepping out of the classroom to answer their phones, checking their e-mail, surfing the Web, or texting instead of being engaged in what's happening in class, you'll need to set parameters for the use of such devices.
- *Turning in assignments late.* Will you accept assignments after they are due? If so, what are the limits to that policy, if any?
- *Makeups for missed quizzes and tests.* Can your students arrange to make up a quiz or test they miss?
- *Cheating.* What is your policy regarding cheating?
- *Progressive discipline.* How will you handle violations of your class rules?

Some instructors provide a written list of class rules and review them during class. Other instructors create such a list with the students at the beginning of the course. Such documents can even take the form of a class contract that the instructor and students must sign. *See the example of Dean Mancina's class rules on the next page.*

As for discipline, first find out your college's policies and procedures regarding student discipline for cheating and disruptive classroom behavior. Your dean or another administrator may be responsible for student discipline and can give you guidance and direction that is consistent with the institution's policies. Decide ahead of time what your progressive discipline plan will be if a student violates or refuses to follow your rules. Your behavior in that situation will set an example and inform other students of the consequences of not following your rules. Depending on the specific infraction, you might start by approaching the student individually and reminding her of the rule she has broken. If she repeats the violation, you might call her out in front of the class, remind her that you have already talked to her about this, and say that the next time you will tell her to leave the class. Then follow through with her removal if she violates the rule a third time. *

Dean Mancina's Course Policies & Class Rules

1. The H1N1 flu virus is very contagious. If you're ill, stay home, or go to the GWC Health Center or to your private doctor. You'll lose some points, but just do bonus assignments to make up the points, and check the class website for assignments and handouts. Email me for a summary of the topics discussed in class that you missed.

2. Attendance at each class meeting and completing the Choose Your Grade assignment are required. Be in class on time. **No late assignments are accepted for point credit.**

3. Assignments, quizzes, etc turned in without your name on the front page get zero points.

4. Side Conversations are not permitted.

5. Turn cell phones to Off or Silent and keep them out of sight during class unless I authorize you to use them in class (e.g., to use the calculator).

6. Laptop computers may be used in class, but must focus at all times on College 100 content.

7. Read and follow the GWC Academic Honesty Policy as it is enforced in my class.

8. **Your grade will be based solely on the total points achieved on the activities you complete.** You must keep track of your own grade by using the Grade Monitor handout.

9. You must purchase a 3-ring binder for your text, handouts, notes, and other materials.

10. My course requires online access. Do not use an email address shared with others. Email attachments must be sent in WORD or PDF format. No other formats will be accepted. NOTE: The Blackboard Vista email system is not 100% reliable. To ensure that your emails reach me in a timely manner, I recommend you email me directly at dmancina@aol.com.

11. After 4 weeks, if your total points drop below 50% possible, you may be withdrawn from the course.

12. If you drop this course at any time during the semester, it is your responsibility to officially process the withdrawal paperwork.

13. My class and website are hate-free zones. **Inappropriate, disrespectful, or disruptive behavior will not be tolerated.**

14. Achievement of Student Learning Outcomes is based on the premise that you attend all class meetings, participate actively, and complete all outside of class activities. Generally, students should expect to spend an average of 2 hours outside of class for every hour spent in class in most transferable college courses, including this one.

15. Students with disabilities who believe they may need accommodations should contact the Accessibility Center for Education (ACE) as soon as possible in order to ensure that if ACE finds them qualified, such accommodations are made in a timely and confidential fashion. 714.895.8721 or 714.895.8350 TDD.

Helping your students become master students

The new **chapter opener design** includes a Master Student Map to help students preview chapter concepts and chart their course to success. By using this map, located at the start of each chapter, your students can begin to address each of the four modes of learning described in Chapter 1.

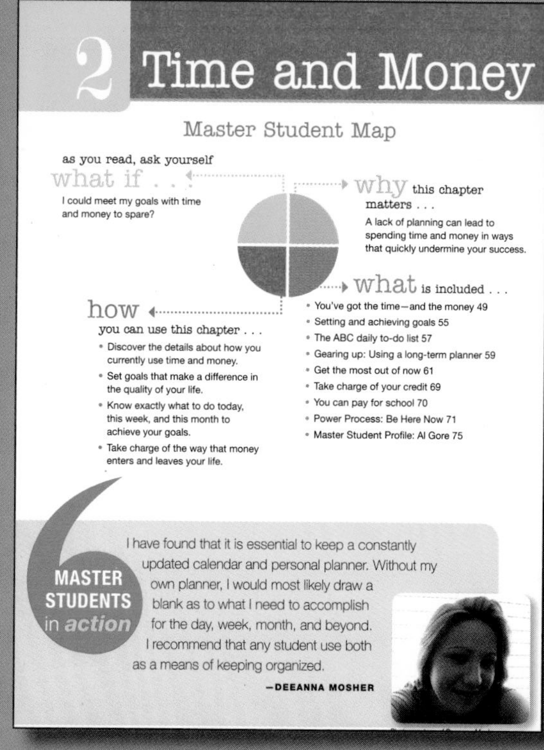

2 Time and Money

Master Student Map

as you read, ask yourself

what if . . .

I could meet my goals with time and money to spare?

why this chapter matters . . .

A lack of planning can lead to spending time and money in ways that quickly undermine your success.

how you can use this chapter . . .

- Discover the details about how you currently use time and money.
- Set goals that make a difference in the quality of your life.
- Know exactly what to do today, this week, and this month to achieve your goals.
- Take charge of the way that money enters and leaves your life.

what is included . . .

- You've got the time—and the money 49
- Setting and achieving goals 55
- The ABC daily to-do list 57
- Gearing up: Using a long-term planner 59
- Get the most out of now 61
- Take charge of your credit 69
- You can pay for school 70
- Power Process: Be Here Now 71
- Master Student Profile: Al Gore 75

MASTER STUDENTS in action

I have found that it is essential to keep a constantly updated calendar and personal planner. Without my own planner, I would most likely draw a blank as to what I need to accomplish for the day, week, month, and beyond. I recommend that any student use both as a means of keeping organized.

—DEEANNA MOSHER

New to the chapter opener is the **Master Students in Action** feature**.** Students can read and relate to real stories of success and struggles in college from their peers.

journal entry 2

Intention Statement

Plan for transition

As a way to ease your transition to higher education, consider setting a goal to meet at least one new person each week for the next month. For example, you could introduce yourself to someone in each of your classes. You could also see your teachers during office hours and meet with your academic advisor.

List your ideas for meeting new people by completing the following sentence.

I intend to . . .

The **Discovery Wheel** has 10 spokes that represents the 10 themes (and chapters) in the book. The self-awareness that students gain through using this tool provides them with a foundation for honestly assessing their experiences for the rest of their lives. By completing the Discovery Wheel again at the end of the text, students can evaluate the work they have accomplished.

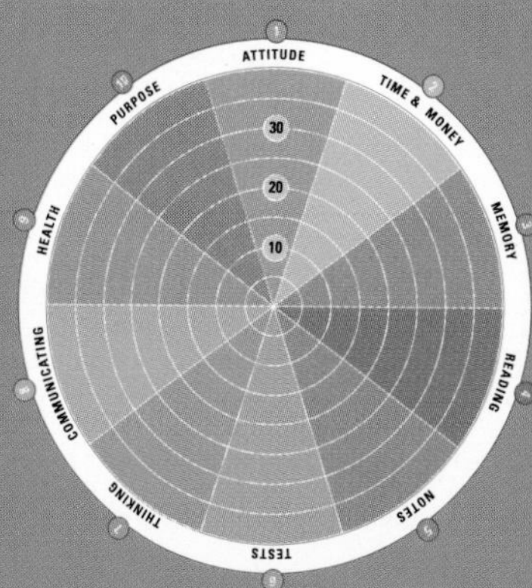

The **Journal Entries** help students interact with the chapter content, declare their goals, and commit to taking action.

The Learning Style Inventory (LSI). People are fascinated by why they do what they do—and students are no exception. Students can take the Kolb Learning Style Inventory (LSI) in Chapter 1 to increase their self-awareness as learners. The LSI, which is printed on carbon-less paper for easy scoring, helps students make sense of what they're experiencing in college. Key updates to the LSI for this edition include

- Clearer directions on how to take the LSI.
- A new Journal Entry that prepares students for taking the Inventory.
- A new reflection activity, "Take a snapshot of your learning styles," that asks students to reflect on what they've learned. This activity is intended to be completed after students read all of the material about learning styles (including multiple intelligences and VAK).
- A learning styles across the curriculum chart that connects learning styles to specific strategies that students can use for their other courses.
- New material to help students connect their learning style to their courses, future career, and major.

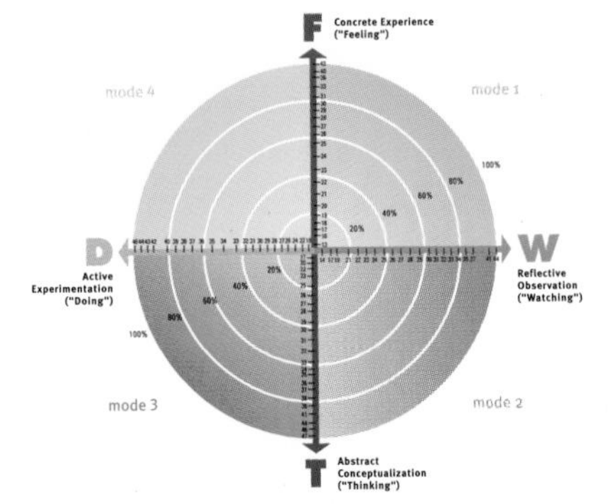

Learning Style Graph

3 Remove the sheet of paper that follows this page. Then transfer your totals from Step 1 on page LSI-3 to the lines on the Learning Style Graph below. On the brown (F) line, find the number that corresponds to your "**Brown** F" total from page LSI-3. Then write an X on this number. Do the same for your "**Teal** W," "**Purple** T," and "**Orange** D" totals. The graph on this page is yours to keep and to refer to and the graph on page LSI-7 is for you to turn into your professor if he or she requires it.

4 Now, pressing firmly, draw four straight lines to connect the four X's, and shade in the area to form a kite. (For an example, see the illustration to the right.) This is your learning style profile. Each X that you placed on these lines indicates your preference for a different aspect of learning.

Concrete experience ("feeling"). The number where you put your X on this line indicates your preference for learning things that have personal meaning and have connections to experiences in your life. The higher your score on this line, the more you like to learn things that you feel are important and relevant to yourself.

Reflective observation ("watching"). Your number on this line indicates how important it is for you to reflect on the things you are learning. If your score is high on this line, you probably find it important to watch others as they learn about an assignment and then report on it to the class. You probably like to plan things out and take the time to make sure that you fully understand a topic.

Abstract conceptualization ("thinking"). Your number on this line indicates your preference for learning ideas, facts, and figures. If your score is high on this line, you probably like to absorb many concepts and gather lots of information on a new topic.

Active experimentation ("doing"). Your number on this line indicates your preference for applying ideas, using trial and error, and practicing what you learn. If your score is high on this line, you probably enjoy hands-on activities that allow you to test out ideas to see what works.

LSI-5

Muscle Reading for ebooks

Find navigation tools. To flip electronic pages, look for *previous* and *next* buttons or arrows on the right and left borders of each page. Many ebooks also offer a "go to page" feature that allows you to key in a specific page number.

For a bigger picture of the text, look for a table of contents that lists chapter headings and subheadings. Click on any of these headings to see whether you can expand the text for that part of the book. Note that charts, illustrations, photos, tables, diagrams and other visuals might be listed separately in the table of contents.

Search. Look for a search box that allows you to enter key words and find all the places in the text where those words are mentioned.

Look for links to related information. Many ebook readers will supply a definition of any word in the text. All you need to do is highlight a word and click on it. Also find out whether your ebook reader will connect you to Web sites related to the topic of your ebook.

Mark it up. Look for ways to electronically underline or highlight text. In addition, see whether you can annotate the book by keying in your own notes tied to specific pages. You might be able to tag each note with a key word and then sort your notes into categories based on these words.

Print. See whether you can connect your ebook device to a printer. You might find it easier to study difficult passages on paper. Note that some ebook publishers impose a limit on how much text you can print.

Monitor battery life. Recharge the battery for your ebook device or laptop computer so that it has enough power to last throughout your work or school day. Seeing your screen go dark when you're in the middle of a paragraph could be a one-way ticket to confusion.

Consult the print version. Sometimes it's hard to beat a good old-fashioned book—especially for dense tables, complex illustrations, and large, color-coded charts. These features might not translate well to a small screen. Go to the library or bookstore to see whether you can find those pages in a printed copy of your ebook.

Sidebars highlight key information and concepts.

mastering technology

FIND WHAT YOU WANT ON THE INTERNET

At one level, searching the Internet is simple. Just go online to a site such as Ask.com, Google, or Yahoo! Look for the search box, and enter a key word or two to describe what you want to find. Then hit the enter key.

You might find exactly what you're looking for in this way. If you don't, then take your Internet searches to the next level:

Use specific key words. Entering *firefox* or *safari* will give you more focused results than entering *web browser*. *Reading strategies* or *note-taking strategies* will get more specific results than *study strategies*. Whenever possible, use proper names. Enter *Beatles* or *Radiohead* rather than *British rock bands*. If you're looking for nearby restaurants, enter *restaurant* and your zip code rather than the name of your city.

Start with fewer key words rather than more. Instead of *ways to develop your career plan*, just enter *career plan*. The extra words might lead to irrelevant results or narrow your search too much.

If you're looking for certain words in a certain order, use quotation marks. *"Audacity of hope"* will return a list of pages with that exact phrase.

Search within a site. If you're looking only for articles about college tuition from the *New York Times*, then add *new york times* or *nytimes.com* to the search box.

When you're not sure of a key word, add a wild-card character. In most search engines, that character is the asterisk (*). If you're looking for the title of a film directed by Clint Eastwood and just can't remember the name, enter *clint eastwood directed **.

Look for more search options. The previous suggestions can keep you from drowning in a sea of useless search results. Many search engines also offer advanced search features and explain how to use them. Look for the word *advanced* or *more* on the site's homepage, and click on the link.

Discover more search strategies.

104 **Chapter Four**

The **Mastering Technology** feature connects chapter content and themes to technology, providing concrete tips on how to effectively use technology to succeed.

Critical Thinking Exercises reinforce concepts learned in each chapter through problem solving, creative thinking, and decision making.

18 critical thinking exercise

Use learning styles for math success

Review the articles about learning styles in Chapter 1: "First Steps." Look for strategies that could promote your success in math. Modify any of the suggested strategies so that they work for you, or invent new techniques of your own. If you're a visual learner, for example, you might color code your notes by writing key terms and formulas in red ink. If you like to learn by speaking and listening, consider reading key passages in your textbooks out loud. And if you're a kinesthetic learner, use "manipulatives"—such as magnetic boards with letters and numbers—when you study math. Whatever you choose, commit to using at least one new strategy. In the space below, describe what you will do.

Power Process

DETACH

This Power Process helps you release the powerful, natural student within you. It is especially useful whenever negative emotions are getting in your way.

Attachments are addictions. When we are attached to something, we think we cannot live without it, just as a drug addict feels he cannot live without drugs. We believe that our well-being depends on maintaining our attachments.

We can be attached to just about anything: beliefs, emotions, people, roles, objects. The list is endless.

One person, for example, might be so attached to his car that he takes an accident as a personal attack. Pity the poor unfortunate who backs into this person's car. He might as well back into the owner himself.

Another person might be attached to her job. Her identity and sense of well-being depend on it. She could become suicidally depressed if she ever got fired.

When we are attached and things don't go our way, we can feel angry, sad, afraid, or confused.

Suppose you are attached to getting an A on your physics test. You feel as though your success in life depends on getting that A. As the clock ticks away, you work harder on the test, getting more stuck. That voice in your head gets louder: "I must get an A. I MUST get an A. I MUST GET AN A!"

Now is a time to detach. Practice observer consciousness. See whether you can just *observe* what's going on, letting go of all your judgments. When you just observe, you reach a quiet state above and beyond your usual thoughts. This is a place where you can be aware of being aware. From this tranquil spot, you can see yourself objectively, as if you were someone else.

Pay attention to your thoughts and physical sensations. If you feel stuck, just notice that. If your palms are sweaty and your stomach is one big knot, just admit it.

Also get a broader perspective. Imagine how much this moment will matter 1 hour, 1 day, 1 week, or 1 year from now.

In addition, practice breathing. Calm your mind and body with relaxation techniques.

Practice detaching before the big test. The key is to let go of automatic emotional reactions when you don't get what you want.

Caution: Giving up an *attachment* to being an A student does not mean giving up *being* an A student. Giving up an attachment to a job doesn't mean giving up the job. When you detach, you get to keep your values and goals. However, you know that you will be OK even if you fail to achieve a goal. You are more than your goals. You are more than your thoughts and feelings. These things come and go. Meanwhile, the part of you that can *just observe* is always there and always safe, no matter what happens.

Behind your attachments is a master student. Release that mastery. Detach.

Learn more about this Power Process online.

© 2010 Katsuo Yamagishi/SPORT/Jupiterimages Corporation

BECOMING A MASTER STUDENT CONCISE 149

Each chapter, including the Introduction, has a **Power Process**, a unique motivational article that empowers success through the application of strategies that relate to a wide variety of circumstances, issues, and problems. Revised for the 13th edition, the Power Process message is now more succinct.

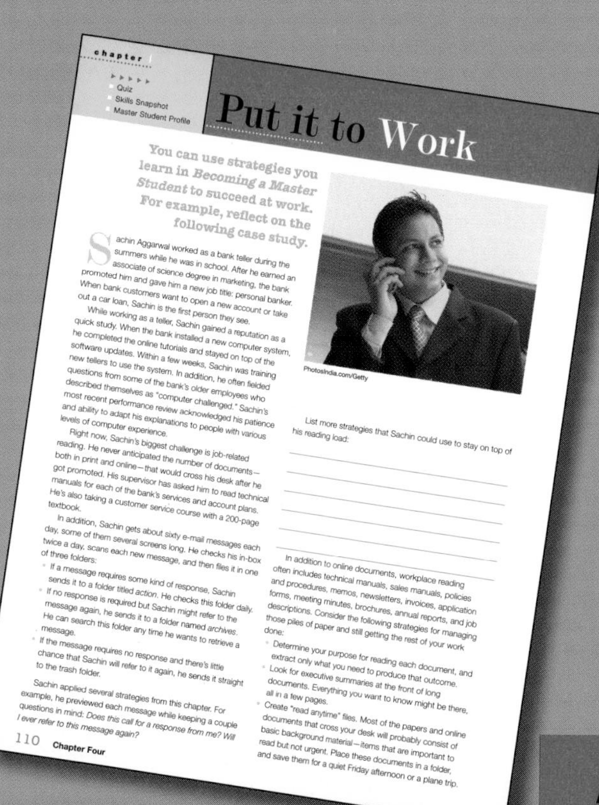

chapter

- Quiz
- Skills Snapshot
- Master Student Profile

Put it to Work

You can use strategies you learn in *Becoming a Master Student* to succeed at work. For example, reflect on the following case study.

Sachin Aggarwal worked as a bank teller during the summers while he was in school. After he earned an associate of science degree in marketing, the bank promoted him and gave him a new job title: personal banker. When bank customers want to open a new account or take out a car loan, Sachin is the first person they see.

While working as a teller, Sachin gained a reputation as a quick study. When the bank installed a new computer system, he completed the online tutorials and stayed on top of the software updates. Within a few weeks, Sachin was training new tellers to use the system. In addition, he often fielded questions from some of the bank's older employees who described themselves as "computer challenged." Sachin's most recent performance review acknowledged his patience and ability to adapt his explanations to people with various levels of computer experience.

Right now, Sachin's biggest challenge is job-related reading. He never anticipated the number of documents—both in print and online—that would cross his desk after he got promoted. His supervisor has asked him to read technical manuals for each of the bank's services and account plans. He's also taking a customer service course with a 200-page textbook.

In addition, Sachin gets about sixty e-mail messages each day, some of them several screens long. He checks his in-box twice a day, scans each new message, and then files it in one of three folders:

- If a message requires some kind of response, Sachin sends it to a folder titled *action*. He checks this folder daily.
- If no response is required but Sachin might refer to the message again, he sends it to a folder named *archives*. He can search this folder any time he wants to retrieve a message.
- If the message requires no response and there's little chance that Sachin will refer to it again, he sends it straight to the trash folder.

Sachin applied several strategies from this chapter. For example, he previewed each message while keeping a couple questions in mind: *Does this call for a response from me? Will I ever refer to this message again?*

PhotosIndia.com/Getty

List more strategies that Sachin could use to stay on top of his reading load:

In addition to online documents, workplace reading often includes technical manuals, sales manuals, policies and procedures, memos, newsletters, invoices, application forms, meeting minutes, brochures, annual reports, and job descriptions. Consider the following strategies for managing those piles of paper and still getting the rest of your work done:

- Determine your purpose for reading each document, and extract only what you need to produce that outcome.
- Look for executive summaries at the front of long documents. Everything you want to know might be there, all in a few pages.
- Create "read anytime" files. Most of the papers and online documents that cross your desk will probably consist of basic background material—items that are important to read but not urgent. Place these documents in a folder, and save them for a quiet Friday afternoon or a plane trip.

110 Chapter Four

Put it to Work reinforces the transferability of skills by encouraging students to think critically about applying what they learn to the workplace. Completely revised for the 13th edition, the articles now feature case studies that help students relate the chapter's themes and concepts to the workplace.

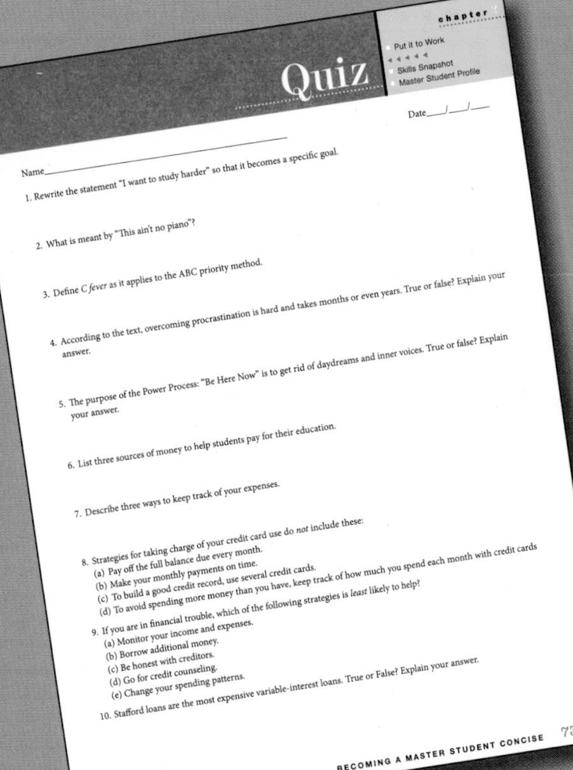

Quiz

chapter

Put it to Work
Skills Snapshot
Master Student Profile

Name________________________ Date___/___/___

1. Rewrite the statement "I want to study harder" so that it becomes a specific goal.

2. What is meant by "This ain't no piano"?

3. Define *C fever* as it applies to the ABC priority method.

4. According to the text, overcoming procrastination is hard and takes months or even years. True or false? Explain your answer.

5. The purpose of the Power Process: "Be Here Now" is to get rid of daydreams and inner voices. True or false? Explain your answer.

6. List three sources of money to help students pay for their education.

7. Describe three ways to keep track of your expenses.

8. Strategies for taking charge of your credit card use do *not* include these:
   (a) Pay off the full balance due every month.
   (b) Make your monthly payments on time.
   (c) To build a good credit record, use several credit cards.
   (d) To avoid spending more money than you have, keep track of how much you spend each month with credit cards

9. If you are in financial trouble, which of the following strategies is *least* likely to help?
   (a) Monitor your income and expenses.
   (b) Borrow additional money.
   (c) Be honest with creditors.
   (d) Go for credit counseling.
   (e) Change your spending patterns.

10. Stafford loans are the most expensive variable-interest loans. True or False? Explain your answer.

BECOMING A MASTER STUDENT CONCISE 73

The updated end-of-chapter **Quiz** allows students to assess their comprehension of the materials covered in each chapter.

New to the 13th edition, the **Skills Snapshot** exercise helps students summarize what they have learned in each chapter and connects back to their original responses in the Discovery Wheel.

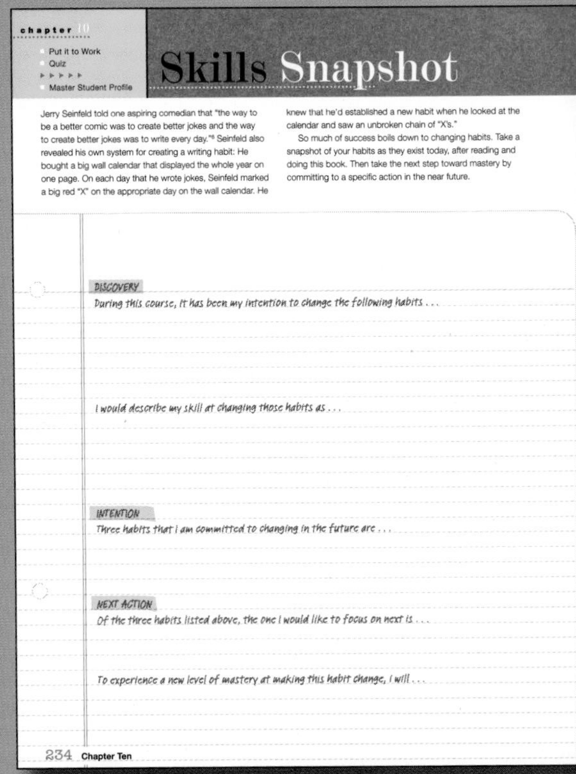

chapter 10

Put it to Work
Quiz
Master Student Profile

Skills Snapshot

Jerry Seinfeld told one aspiring comedian that "the way to be a better comic was to create better jokes and the way to create better jokes was to write every day."[6] Seinfeld also revealed his own system for creating a writing habit: He bought a big wall calendar that displayed the whole year on one page. On each day that he wrote jokes, Seinfeld marked a big red "X" on the appropriate day on the wall calendar. He knew that he'd established a new habit when he looked at the calendar and saw an unbroken chain of "X's."

So much of success boils down to changing habits. Take a snapshot of your habits as they exist today, after reading and doing this book. Then take the next step toward mastery by committing to a specific action in the near future.

DISCOVERY

During this course, it has been my intention to change the following habits . . .

I would describe my skill at changing those habits as . . .

INTENTION

Three habits that I am committed to changing in the future are . . .

NEXT ACTION

Of the three habits listed above, the one I would like to focus on next is . . .

To experience a new level of mastery at making this habit change, I will . . .

234 Chapter Ten

chapter 1

Put it to Work
Quiz
Skills Snapshot

Master Student PROFILE

Lalita Booth is Willing to Work

Sitting in front of a classroom of UCF LEAD Scholars, Lalita Booth looks like any other junior. The brown-eyed, freckle-faced student blends in with her peers in the University of Central Florida (UCF) leadership development program in every way.

That is, until she opens her mouth.

"You're looking at the face of a child abuse survivor, a perpetual runaway, a high-school dropout," she says, as idle chitchat turns to complete silence. "I was a teenage mother, a homeless parent, and a former welfare recipient."

Lalita's parents divorced when she was young; by age 12 she was a runaway pro—asking for permission to go somewhere and then simply not returning for a few days or a few weeks. . . . She became proficient in "couch surfing" at friends' homes. When there was no couch to crash on, the teen would take her nightly refuge behind the closest dumpster and rest in the park during the day.

Furthering her quest to be a grownup, at 17 she married her long-time buddy and fellow high-school dropout, Quinn. Three months later, she found out she was pregnant with her son, Kieren. What normally would be a joyful time was instead a stressful one while the new couple struggled in a prison of deep poverty. The miserable situation began to take its toll, and after just two and a half years of marriage, Quinn was ready to call it quits.

With her new boyfriend, Carl, and her most precious cargo, Kieren, in tow, Booth fled to Boulder, Colorado. Kieren lived with his paternal grandparents for 7 months while Lalita and Carl attempted to get back on their feet.

Being in Colorado proved to be fruitful for the 21-year-old Lalita. It started with an interesting job opportunity as an enrolled agent—an expert in U.S. taxation who can represent taxpayers before the Internal Revenue Service. Lalita could acquire the license without further schooling. Better yet, it would boost her income to $32,000. She buckled down and read all 4,000 pages of the study guide, and, thanks to her nearly photographic memory, she aced the test.

But, once again, she was in the wrong place at the wrong time. Carl's brother in Orlando was very ill, and he needed to move to Florida.

The only way to ensure her independence was to do something that frightened her to the very core—go back to school. . . .

. . . And soon after, she enrolled at Seminole Community College.

. . . In May 2005, Lalita was selected to attend the Salzburg Global Seminar, where she brainstormed ways to solve global problems with a group of international students. The thought-provoking trip led to her mission: to help others escape the choke hold of poverty.

Back in the states, Booth's world became even more dream-like when she won the Jack Kent Cooke Foundation Scholarship. . . .

Lalita Booth strongly believes, and for good reason, that "things that are worth achieving are absolutely unreasonable." She advises, "Set unreasonable goals, and chase them unreasonably."

Adapted from Sarah Sekula, "Escape Artist," *Pegasus*, July/August 2008, *UCF Alumni Life*, 20–26.

Jacque Brund/UCF News and Information

Once homeless, and now a student at the University of Central Florida and accepted to Harvard Business School.

Find more biographical information about Lalita Booth at the Master Student Hall of Fame.

BECOMING A MASTER STUDENT CONCISE 47

Each **Master Student Profile** highlights a person who embodies the qualities of a master student. This edition features new profiles: Lalita Booth (Chapter 1), Al Gore (Chapter 2), Pablo Alvardo (Chapter 3), Chief Wilma Mankiller (Chapter 4), Harvey Milk (Chapter 5), Bert and John Jacobs (Chapter 6), Twyla Tharp (Chapter 7), Randy Pausch (Chapter 9), and Lisa Ling (Chapter 10).

Interactive learning opportunities for your students

Cengage Learning's **College Success CourseMate** brings course concepts to life with interactive learning, study, and exam preparation tools that support the printed textbook. Watch student comprehension soar as your class works with the printed textbook and the textbook-specific website. College Success CourseMate goes beyond the book to deliver what you need!

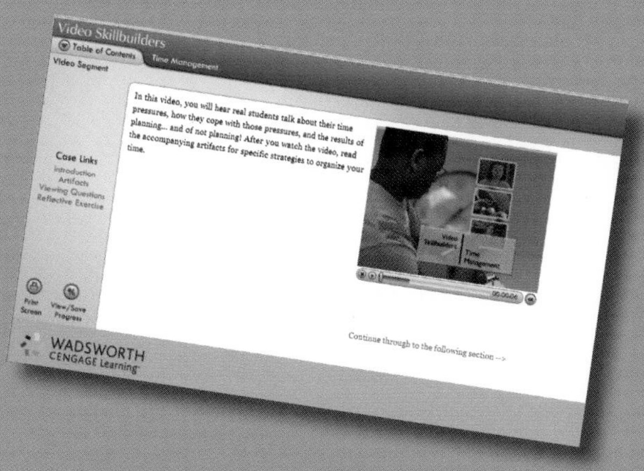

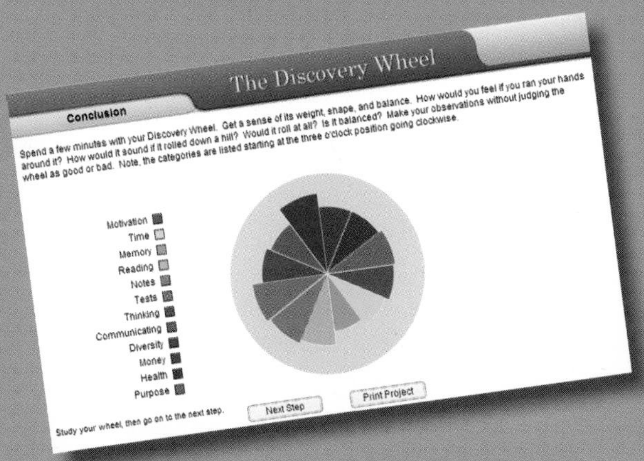

College Success CourseMate includes:

- an interactive eBook
- interactive teaching and learning tools including:
  - Quizzes
  - Flashcards
  - Videos
  - Online Discovery Wheel
  - Video Skillbuilders
  - and more
- Engagement Tracker, a first-of-its-kind tool that monitors student engagement in the course

Learn more at cengage.com/coursemate.

If you want your students to receive access to College Success CourseMate, you must request that the Printed Access Card be bundled with their text. Contact your sales rep for details at www.cengage.com/findrep2.html.

How much of a difference does your college success course make in your students' academic success?

The College Success Factors Index (CSFI) 2.0 (developed by Edmond Hallberg and Kaylene Hallberg, and Loren Sauer) is an online survey that students complete to assess their patterns of behavior and attitudes in 10 key areas that have been proven by research to affect student outcomes for success in higher education.

The CSFI is a perfect assessment tool for demonstrating the difference your College Success course makes in your students' academic success.

- As a pre-course assessment, the CSFI helps incoming students determine their strengths and areas in which they need improvement, allowing you to tailor your course topics to meet their needs.
- An Early Alert indicator flags students who are the most at-risk of falling behind. This information enables instructors to intervene at the beginning of the semester to increase their students' likelihood of success—and improve retention rates.
- Text-specific remediation guides students to appropriate pages in their book for added support.
- Increased reporting functionality provides instructors with access to more information and data about their students.
- As a post-test assessment, it measures student progress and validates your College Success program.

Visit www.cengage.com/success/csfi2 for a product tour and more information.

TeamUP Faculty Programs
College Success Staff Development
Get Trained. Get Connected. Get Support.

The TeamUP Faculty Programs consulting team provides training in developing college success programs, revising existing programs, and integrating our products into your teaching. Whether we work with you online, on the phone, or on campus, we strive to deliver high-quality services through our Faculty Programs, Training, and Media Integration.

For more than a decade, our TeamUP consultants have led the way in providing college success course expertise through on-campus consulting, training, and national workshops and conferences.

Look to TeamUP for

- One- and two-day regional or on-campus training sessions presenting effective pedagogical strategies that can be applied to all disciplines and have proved effective in a variety of college success course curricula.
- Assistance from our TeamUP consultants, each of whom has extensive experience in teaching the first-year course.
- Regional and nationwide conferences that provide two to three days of informative, interactive sessions covering a range of topics presented by authors, student success instructors, and TeamUP consultants.
- Ideas and best practices on how to customize all elements of our technology.
- eSeminars facilitated by experts in the field that allow for professional development from the convenience of your desk.

To connect with your TeamUP Faculty Programs Consultant, call **800–856–5727** or visit **www.cengage.com/teamup**.

Becoming a MASTER STUDENT Concise

Thirteenth Edition

Doug Toft
Contributing Editor

Dean Mancina
Golden West College, CA
Faculty Advisor

WADSWORTH
CENGAGE Learning™

AUSTRALIA • BRAZIL • JAPAN • KOREA • MEXICO • SPAIN • UNITED KINGDOM • UNITED STATES

Becoming a Master Student Concise
Thirteenth Edition
Ellis

Senior Sponsoring Editor: Shani Fisher

Development Editor: Daisuke Yasutake

Editorial Assistant: Cat Salerno

Media Editor: Amy Gibbons

Senior Marketing Manager: Kirsten Stoller

Marketing Coordinator: Ryan Ahern

Marketing Communications Manager: Stacey Purviance

Content Project Manager: Jessica Rasile

Senior Art Director: Pam Galbreath

Print Buyer: Julio Esperas

Rights Acquisition Specialist, Images: Jennifer Meyer Dare

Rights Acquisition Specialist, Text: Katie Huha

Text Designer: Susan Gilday

Cover Designer: Yvo Riezebos

Cover Image: Ted Humble-Smith/RF/Getty

Project Management/Composition: MPS Content Services, A Macmillan Company

Library of Congress Control Number: 2010927093

Student Edition:

ISBN-13: 978-0-495-91281-1

ISBN-10: 0-495-91281-6

Annotated Instructor's Edition:

ISBN-13: 978-0-495-91284-2

ISBN-10: 0-495-91284-0

Wadsworth
20 Channel Center Street
Boston, MA 02210
USA

Cengage Learning is a leading provider of customized learning solutions with office locations around the globe, including Singapore, the United Kingdom, Australia, Mexico, Brazil and Japan. Locate your local office at **international.cengage.com/region**

Cengage Learning products are represented in Canada by Nelson Education, Ltd.

For your course and learning solutions, visit **www.cengage.com.**

Purchase any of our products at your local college store or at our preferred online store **www.cengagebrain.com.**

Printed in the United States of America
1 2 3 4 5 6 7 14 13 12 11 10

Advisory Board

Andrea Anderson
College of Lake County, IL

Beverly Brucks
Illinois Central College

Myra L. Cox
Harold Washington College, IL

Elinor DeWire
Olympic College, WA

Margaret Garroway
Howard Community College, MD

Dawn Gauvreau
Central Carolina Technical College, SC

Eric D. Gullufsen
James A. Rhodes State College, OH

SusAnn Key
Midwestern State University, TX

Kim Kraft
Olympic College, WA

Sunita Kumari
St. Petersburg College, FL

Pamela Moss
Midwestern State University, TX

Berta Parrish
Cuesta College, CA

Kelly Paulin
Columbus State Community College, OH

Patricia Rowe
Columbus State Community College, OH

Randi Russert
Harry S. Truman College, IL

Leigh Smith
Lamar Institute of Technology, TX

Karen Joy Tuinstra
Mesa State College, CO

Brandy Whitlock
Anne Arundel Community College, MD

Past Advisory Board Members

Frank Ardaiolo
Winthrop University, SC

Phyllis Arias
Long Beach City College, CA

Alice Benham
Bowling Green Technical College, KY

Don Becker
Delaware State University

Anita N. Blowers
University of North Carolina at Charlotte

Paula Bradberry
Arkansas State University

Ruthmary Braden
Bellevue Community College, WA

Mary Carstens
Wayne State, MI

Maria Chovan
Golden West College, CA

Irene Cohn
Fullerton College, CA

Jennifer Combs
Fullerton College, CA

Kelly Cox
University of Nevada, Las Vegas

Janet Cutshall
Sussex County Community College, NJ

Ann Deiman
Brown College, MN

Gigi Derballa
Asheville-Buncombe Technical Community College, NC

Linda Dunham
Central Piedmont Community College, NC

Raymond Dunn, Sr.
Broward Community College, FL

Anne Daly Elmer
Cumberland Community College, NH

Charles R. Frederick
Indiana University, Bloomington

Sheryl Hartman
Miami Dade College, FL

Tracy Koski
Columbus State Community College, OH

Christine Landrum
Mineral Area College, MO

Tim Littell
Rhodes State College, OH

Carole Mackewich
Clark College, WA

Kelly Mansfield
Kaplan College, IN

Brenda Marina
University of Akron, OH

Kathleen McGough
Broward Community College, Central Campus, Davie, FL

Cheryl A. McNear
Polytechnic University, NY

Advisory Board

Student Advisory Board

Brief Table of Contents

Andrew Taylor/Shutterstock

Ferenc Szelepcsenyi/ Shutterstock

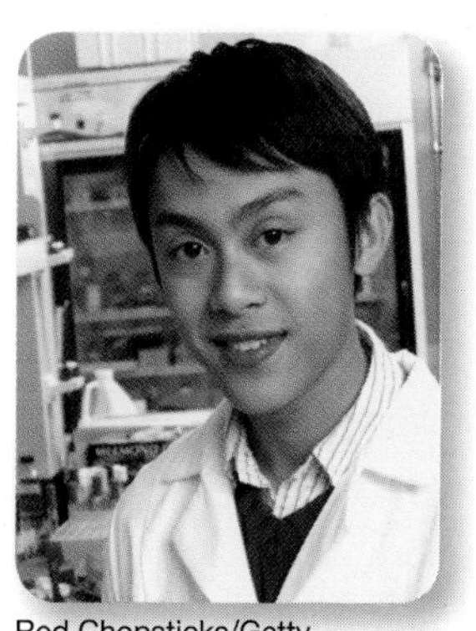
Red Chopsticks/Getty

© Thinkstock/Alamy

Table of Contents

Edmond Van Hoorick/Digital Vision/Getty Images

Making Transitions xii

1 First Steps 20

what if
why
what
how

2 Time and Money 48

Asia Images Group/Getty

3 Memory 76

Angelo Cavalli/Digital Vision/RF/Getty Images

4 Reading 94

© Digital Vision/Picture Quest

5 Notes 114

© iStockphoto.com/anna karwowska

6 Tests 134

Yuri Arcurs/Shutterstock

7 Thinking 154

Rich Reed/National Geographic/Getty

8 Communicating 174

© Masterfile Royalty Free

9 Health 194

ZenShui/Alix Minde/Getty

10 What's Next? 212

Terry Vine/Blend Images/RF/Getty

Making Transitions

Instructor Tools & Tips

> Change and growth take place when a person has risked himself and dares to become involved with experimenting with his own life.
>
> **—Herbert Otto**
>
> The human ability to learn and remember is virtually limitless.
>
> **—Sheila Ostrander and Lynn Schroeder**

Each chapter in the Annotated Instructor Edition is preceded by pages with suggestions for instructors. These suggestions are organized using the 7-part course model on page AIE-10. You can quickly find ideas to use in your classroom for preview, guest speakers, lectures, class activities, sharing, homework, and evaluation.

Preview

The introductory chapter, "Making Transitions," is an important gateway to *Becoming a Master Student* because it sets the stage for entering the culture of higher education and connecting to new surroundings. It also explains how students should write the important Discovery and Intention Journal Entries throughout the book. Encourage your students to read "Making Transitions" the first week of class.

Guest Speaker

Two or three students from your class in the previous term can make great guest speakers for the first week of class. Students respond well to hearing from their peers. You might provide some guidance about the types of experiences the speakers should share. Ask them to briefly discuss why they enrolled in this course and the three most useful tools they learned in the class. Then invite students to ask the guests questions about the course. Consider taping the presentation in case no former students are available to speak.

Here is a guest speaker's comment on how she conducts her first week of class:

> During the first class, I ask my students to preview the text, paying particular attention to the table of contents. I then give students my course syllabus, which lists a suggested schedule of topics for the semester. The students' first assignment is to look at the table of contents and rearrange the schedule of topics in a way that fits their needs. (Another way to do this is to use students' completed Discovery Wheels—see Chapter 1.) During the second class meeting, we list the topics on a flip chart and vote on the order of the chapters. Then we rearrange the syllabus according to the preferences of the students. This method helps me design the course to meet students' immediate needs. Because the course is mandatory, some of the students have negative feelings when they come to class. Allowing them input on the order of the topics sparks interest and gives them ownership of the course.
>
> **—Dr. Jennifer Hurd, TeamUP Consultant**

Lecture

Master Student Map. Teach students how to use the Master Student Map right from the start of *Becoming a Master Student*. If you have ever had trouble convincing your students to read the Introduction, this simply formatted framework will help them grasp the value of this book right away. Use the Master Student Map (**M**etacognitive **A**pplication **P**rocess) as a jumping-off point for sparking classroom discussion. Then teach your students how they can use this model to preview chapter content in this textbook. Take it a step further and show your students how creating a similar schema for textbooks in other courses can help activate background knowledge and provide a "hook" to get them ready for the material within the chapter. Start now by asking your students the following questions. Consider writing them on your whiteboard, posting them to your discussion board in an online course, or creating a PowerPoint presentation with them.

Why? Why is it important to read the Introduction?

What? What kind of information does an Introduction provide for the reader? What information does the Introduction to *Becoming a Master Student* provide?

How? Rate your level of effectiveness with the information presented in the Introduction now. (How much do you already know about the topics presented? How will this book help you become a better student?) Ask yourself, "How can I get more value from my textbook by reading the Introduction?"

What if? What if you skipped the Introduction? Ask yourself, "What if I could use this Introduction right now to become a better student?"

Discovery and Intention Statements (pages 5–6). The Discovery and Intention Journal Entry system allows students to begin the reflective critical thinking process they will need to grasp the concepts and develop the skills studied in this student success course and to transfer those skills to their other classes. This simple yet powerful system is one of the foundations of the textbook. As students read the book, they are often asked to write Discovery Statements about what they are learning and Intention Statements about what they plan to do, based on the new information they are assimilating.

In addition to assigning the many Discovery and Intention Statements in the book, ask students to write statements in class after activities such as guest speakers, videos, or lectures. Here is a basic formula for writing Discovery Statements: "When I [what you experienced], I discovered that [specifically what you became aware of]." Here is a formula for Intention Statements: "I intend to [specifically what action you plan to take] by [time frame or date]. My reward will be [the tangible reward you'll give yourself if you complete your intended goal]."

Organize for success. The inside front cover of *Becoming a Master Student* has a tool for master students: a place to organize key information to have at their fingertips throughout their college experience. Have your students fill in their information while they wait for you to begin class, or leave a few minutes at the end of your first meeting.

Illustrate how students can immediately apply this new strategy to their other courses. Although not every textbook has a place to record information on the inside cover, students can use the inside front and back covers as quick references—for personal information, key facts such as formulas or Web site addresses, and any other information they will need to refer to frequently.

Encourage your students to identify a student in each class who seems responsible and dependable. Have them exchange e-mail addresses and phone numbers and record them. Suggest to students that if they know they won't be in class, they should contact this student ahead of time to ask him or her to pick up extra copies of handouts and request to copy this person's notes.

Take this opportunity to invite your students to visit you during office hours. Provide your e-mail address, phone number, and office location.

Exercises/Activities

1. **Critical thinking Exercise 2: Commitment (page 4).** After students have read the Introduction and completed this exercise, at the following class meeting ask them to open their books to this exercise so that they can review what they wrote. This simple exercise, which takes less than 5 minutes to complete, helps students confirm their commitment to this course and, indirectly, to their entire college experience. To reinforce this exercise and remind students of it throughout the semester, have them write their level of commitment in large letters on a sheet of paper and then sign their name at the bottom. Have them put this paper at the very front of their three-ring binder for this course so that every time they open their binder, they'll be reminded of their commitment to this textbook—and to their student success.

2. **Making the transition to higher education (pages 9–11).** Have your students choose partners and review the list of expectations in this article. Ask them to predict the two transition areas in the list from the article that would cause students the most trouble and to discuss why. Then they should discuss some possible solutions for students who might be facing these problems. To help students con-

nect to the article on a personal level, ask them which of the items listed in the article present a challenge for them.

3. **Ways to change a habit (page 17).** Challenge your students in class to brainstorm a list of habits they would like to start, stop, or change. Then ask them to pick a habit that they would like to commit to change successfully within the next 16 weeks. Using the two-part note paper from TeamUP, have them write down their habit and separate the paper. Tell the students to put one part in a self-addressed envelope and to keep the copy for themselves as a reference and reminder of their habit change plan. Collect the self-addressed envelopes and mail them to the students in four months (after the course is over) as an incentive for them to keep working on their habit change.

4. **Power Process: Discover What You Want (page 19).** Ask your students to begin using the mode 1 suggestion presented by the Master Student Map to think critically about the new Power Process in the Introduction. Explain the purpose of each Power Process to your students: The Power Process will change the way they think, or change their consciousness, because it is their consciousness that determines their behavior.

Ask students to form groups to consider and discuss the following: (1) *Why* this Power Process might matter to them (or to their children, family, coworkers, and the like), (2) *What* this Power Process means with regard to the transition to college, (3) *How* they will make this transition work for them, and (4) *What* they risk by not making this transition now.

5. **First day activity** On the first day of class, ask your students, "What do you want?" Give them 10 minutes to write a list of ten skills they might learn in this class that would be useful for them in college and in their lives. Challenge them to think about things that are worth working hard for. Then have the students form groups of four to share what they wrote. Have them complete this list on two-part paper so that they can keep their list and you can have a copy. This will help you get to know your students right away.

Conversation/Sharing

1. **This book is worthless—if you just read it (pages 1–2).** This article helps you "sell" this course to resistant students, whether your course is required or not. Consider going over the seven pitches presented in this article on the first day of class, even though the students haven't read the article yet.

2. If you share with your class an experience that you had as a student in college, your students may feel that you are more of a partner with them in their educational explorations. Students particularly enjoy hearing stories of the mistakes you might have made! Here's a success story Faculty Advisor Dean Mancina shares with his students when discussing the value of connecting to campus resources:

> "When I applied for my first teaching position coordinating a Tutoring Program at Golden West College, I didn't know that 167 others had also applied! A few months after I was selected for the position, I asked my Dean why I had been selected over so many other applicants, many of whom might have had more experience. He shared with me that I was the only finalist who was able to answer the interview question about organizing, planning, publicizing, and evaluating college programs. I had spoken about my experiences working in student activities when I was a student in college. I had fun meeting other students and working with student government, but it wasn't until that point that I became aware of the other potential benefits of connecting to campus resources. Little did I know that I'd still be at Golden West College 34 years later!
>
> **—Faculty Advisor Dean Mancina,**
> **Golden West College**

Homework

Even though many students won't have purchased the textbook on the first day of class, hold up your copy of the book and show them Critical Thinking Exercise 1: Textbook reconnaissance (page 2). When you assign textbook reading each week, tell students that they must read the articles *and* do all of the Critical Thinking Exercises and Discovery/Intention Journal Entries within the assigned pages. The thinking/writing assignments in the book help students personalize what they are reading.

Evaluation

Frequent quizzes ensure that students focus attention during class and keep up with the text reading assignments. Quizzes also provide students with opportunities for written reflection regarding new discoveries and intentions. In addition, evaluations help you identify topics and concepts that students have not yet mastered. Questions may be based on the textbook reading assignment, guest speakers, class activities, and/or the lecture. Possible answers are provided for the end-of-chapter quizzes in this Annotated Instructor's Edition.

On your request, Cengage Learning will provide packages of three-part NCR quiz paper to facilitate quick quizzes in class. First, make up your quiz question(s). These may be multiple-choice, true or false, short answer, or essay questions. Students answer the quiz question(s) on the white (top) sheet, simultaneously making two copies on the yellow and pink paper. When the quiz time is up, direct students to tear off the white copy and pass it forward. They can no longer change their answers because you have the original white sheet. Then direct them to look up the correct answers in their books and grade their own quizzes. Finally, have them pass the yellow copy forward for your review and to record their scores. Students keep the pink copy.

Additional Digital Resources

INTRO

Course Manual

The online *Course Manual* serves as an invaluable reference for those developing and teaching a College Success course with *Becoming a Master Student Concise*. The *Course Manual* provides advice on general teaching issues such as preparing for classes, classroom management, grading, and communicating with students of various backgrounds, as well as specific strategies on getting the most out of various features in *Becoming a Master Student Concise* and book-specific Web sites. Do a *Course Manual* reconnaissance to find ideas that you can use in your course right now.

Instructor Companion Site

The updated Instructor Companion Site provides resources to help you plan and customize your course. Content specific to the Introduction includes:

- Lecture Ideas
  - Selling the Course
  - What Are the Skills of Successful Students?
- In-Class Exercises
  - Advisor Role Play Exercise
  - Icebreaker with Commitment
  - Student Agreement Contract
- Writing Assignments
  - Working with Academic Advisors
- In-Text Quiz Answers
- PowerPoint Slides

The Instructor Companion Site also contains the following book-specific content:

- ExamView Test Bank
- Online Course Manual
- Sample Syllabi
- Detailed Transition Guide

College Success CourseMate

To help your students gain a better understanding of the topics discussed in *Becoming a Master Student Concise*, encourage them to visit the Colleg Success CourseMate at CengageBrain.com that provides the following resources specific to the Introduction:

- Connect to Text content expands on specific topics marked with an icon within the Introduction.
- Practice Tests allow students to see how well they understand the themes of *Becoming a Master Student Concise.*
- Interactive Concept Maps promote critical thinking by highlighting related ideas to show relationships among concepts.
- Learning Styles Application
- Discussion Topics
- Reflection Questions
- Experiment with chapter strategies.
- Remembering Cultural Differences presents readers with brief articles that touch on aspects of diversity in our rapidly changing world. For the Introduction, the following article will prompt your students to look at contemporary issues in a new way:
  - What and How Cultures Teach
- Power Process Media contains video, PowerPoints, and audio files to take what your students have learned from the Power Processes in their book to the next level. For the Introduction, students will find additional media on:
  - Discover what you want

Along with the chapter-specific content, a General Resources folder is available that contains Toolboxes geared toward specific student types (Community College, Adult Learner, Student Athlete), the Plagiarism Prevention Zone, and the Career Resource Center.

INTRODUCTION

Making Transitions

Master Student Map

as you read, ask yourself

what if . . .

I could use the ideas in this Introduction to master *any* transition in my life?

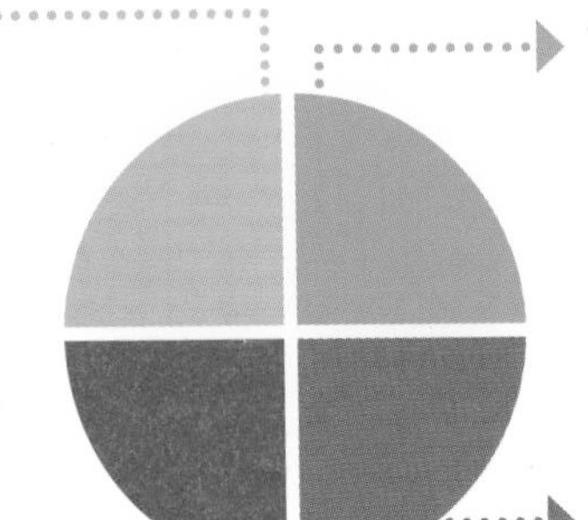

why the Introduction matters . . .

You can ease your transition to higher education and set up a lifelong pattern of success by following the strategies described here.

how you can use this Introduction . . .

- Discover a way to interact with books that multiplies their value.
- Use a journal to translate personal discoveries into powerful new behaviors.
- Connect with people and organizations that support your success.

what is included . . .

MASTER STUDENTS in *action*

Use all of the resources on campus. Get to know your instructors and professors, attend every class, accept all new challenges, get a support group, have outside hobbies and passions, believe in yourself.

—TIMOTHY ALLEN

Photo courtesy of Timothy Allen/ American River College

This book is worthless—if you just read it

THE FIRST EDITION of this book began with the sentence *This book is worthless*. Many students thought beginning this way was a trick to get their attention. It wasn't. Others thought it was reverse psychology. It wasn't that either. Still others thought it meant that the book was worthless if they didn't read it. It meant more than that.

This book is worthless even if you read it—*if reading it is all you do*. What was true of that first edition is true of this one as well. Until you take action and use the ideas in it, *Becoming a Master Student* really is worthless.

The purpose of this book is to help you make a successful transition to higher education by setting up a pattern of success that will last the rest of your life. You probably won't take action and use the ideas in this book until you are convinced that you have something to gain. That's the reason for providing this Introduction—to persuade you to use this book actively.

Before you stiffen up and resist this sales pitch, remember that you have already bought the book. Now you can get something for your money by committing yourself to take action—in other words, by committing yourself to becoming a master student. Here's what's in it for you.

Pitch #1: You can save money now and make more money later. Start with money. Your college education is one of the most expensive things you will ever buy. You might find yourself paying $30 to $100 an hour to sit in class. (See Critical Thinking Exercise 10: "Education by the hour" on page 70 to come up with a specific figure that applies to your own education.)

As a master student, you control the value you get out of your education, and that value can be considerable. The joy of learning aside, college graduates make more money during their lifetimes—and experience less unemployment—than do their non-degreed peers.[1] It pays to be a master student.

Pitch #2: You can rediscover the natural learner in you. Joy is important too. As you become a master student, you will learn to gain knowledge in the most effective way possible—by discovering the joyful, natural learner within you.

Children are great natural students. They quickly master complex skills, such as language, and they have fun doing it. For young children, learning is a high-energy process involving experimentation and discovery—and sometimes broken dishes.

Then comes school. For some students, drill and drudgery replace discovery and dish breaking. Learning can become a drag. You can use this book to reverse that process and rediscover what you knew as a child—that laughter and learning go hand in hand.

Sometimes—and especially in college—learning does take effort. As you become a master student, you will learn many ways to get the most out of that effort.

Pitch #3: You can choose from hundreds of techniques. *Becoming a Master Student* is packed with hundreds of practical, nuts-and-bolts techniques. The best part is, you can begin using them immediately. For example, by doing the textbook reconnaissance suggested on page 2, you might find three powerful learning techniques during a single 15-minute exercise. Even if you doze in lectures, drift off during tests, or dawdle on term papers, you'll find ideas in this book that you can use to become a more effective student.

Not all of these ideas will work for you. That's why there are so many of them in *Becoming a Master Student*. You can experiment with the techniques. As you discover what works, you will develop a unique style of learning to use for the rest of your life.

Pitch #4: You get the best suggestions from thousands of students. The concepts and techniques in this book are here not just because educators and psychologists say they work. They are here because students from all kinds of backgrounds have tried them and agree that they work. These are students who dreaded giving speeches, couldn't read their own notes, and fell behind in their course work. Then they figured out ways to solve those problems. Now you can use their ideas.

Pitch #5: You can learn about yourself. The process of self-discovery is an important theme in *Becoming a Master Student*. Throughout the book, you'll see Discovery Statements and Intention Statements. Use these Journal Entries to write about everything from today's to-do list to your longest-term goals. The big picture is important. Studying for an organic chemistry quiz is a lot easier with a clean desk and a clear idea of the course's importance to you.

Pitch #6: You can use a proven product. Previous editions of this book have proved successful for hundreds of thousands of students. Student feedback has been positive. In particular, students with successful histories have praised the techniques in this book.

Pitch #7: You can learn the secret of student success. If this sales pitch still hasn't persuaded you to use this book actively, maybe it's time to reveal the secret of student success. (Provide your own drum roll here.) The secret is . . . there are no secrets. Give up formulas, keep experimenting, and find strategies that actually help you meet your goals.

The strategies that successful students use are well-known. You have hundreds of them at your fingertips right now in this book. Use them. Modify them. Invent new ones. You're the authority on what works for you.

What makes any technique work is commitment and action. Without them, the pages of *Becoming a Master Student* are just 2 pounds of expensive mulch. Add your participation to the mulch, and these pages become priceless. *

This book is worth $1,000

Cengage Learning is proud to present three students each year with a $1,000 scholarship for tuition reimbursement. Any post-secondary school in the United States and Canada can nominate one student for the scholarship. To be considered, the student must write an essay that answers the question, "How do you define success?"

For more details, visit the College Success CourseMate.

1 critical thinking exercise
Textbook reconnaissance

Start becoming a master student this moment by doing a 15-minute "textbook reconnaissance." A textbook reconnaissance shows you where a course is going. It gives you the big picture. That's useful because brains work best when going from the general to the specific. Getting the big picture before you start makes it easier to recall and understand details later on.

First, read this book's Table of Contents. Do it in 3 minutes or less. Next, look at every page in the book. Move quickly. Scan headlines. Look at pictures. Notice forms, charts, and diagrams.

Your textbook reconnaissance will work even better if you look for ideas to use. When you find one, write the page number and a short description of the idea below. If you run out of room, just continue your list on a separate sheet of paper.

You also can use sticky notes to flag the pages that look useful. You could even use notes of different colors to signal priority, such as green for ideas to use right away and yellow for suggestions to apply later.

The idea behind this technique is simple: It's easier to learn when you're excited, and it's easier to get excited about a course if you know it's going to be useful, interesting, or fun.

Remember, look at every page quickly. And here's another useful tip: Do it now.

Page number	Description

Complete this exercise online.

Get the most out of this book

1. Get used to a new look and tone. This book looks different from traditional textbooks. *Becoming a Master Student* presents major ideas in magazine-style articles. You will discover lots of lists, blurbs, one-liners, pictures, charts, graphs, illustrations, and even a joke or two.

2. Rip 'em out. The pages of *Becoming a Master Student* are perforated because some of the information here is too important to leave in the book and there are some pages your instructor might want to see. For example, Journal Entry 3 asks you to list some important things you want to get out of your education. To keep yourself focused on these goals, you could rip that page out and post it on your bathroom mirror or some other place where you'll see it several times a day.

You can reinsert the pages later by sticking them into the spine of the book. A piece of tape will hold them in place.

3. Skip around. You can use this book in several different ways. Read it straight through. Or pick it up, turn to any page, and find an idea you can use. Look for ideas you can use right now. For example, if you are about to choose a major or are considering changing schools, skip directly to the articles on these topics on pages 164 and 223, respectively.

You might find that this book presents similar ideas in several places. This repetition is intentional. Repetition reinforces key points. Also, a technique that works in one area of your life might work in others as well. Look especially to the Power Processes near the end of each chapter for ideas that you can apply in many ways.

4. If it works, use it. If it doesn't, lose it. If there are sections of this book that don't apply to you at all, skip them—unless, of course, they are assigned. In that case, see whether you can gain value from those sections anyway. When you are committed to getting value from this book, even an idea that seems irrelevant or ineffective at first can turn out to be a powerful tool.

5. Put yourself into the book. As you read about techniques in this book, create your own scenarios and cast yourself in the title role. For example, when reading through Critical Thinking Exercise 1: "Textbook reconnaissance," picture yourself using this technique on your world history textbook.

6. Listen to your peers. On the first page of each chapter you will find Master Students in Action. These short features contain quotations from students who used this text. As you dig into the following chapters, think about what you would say if you could add your voice to theirs.

7. Own this book. Right now, put your name, address, and related information on the inside cover of this book. Don't stop there, though. Determine what you want to get out of school, and create a record of how you intend to get it by reading the Power Processes and completing the Journal Entries in this Introduction. Every time your pen touches a page, you move closer to mastery.

8. Do the exercises. Action makes this book work. To get the most out of this book, do most of the exercises. (It's never too late to go back and do the ones you skipped.) Exercises invite you to write, touch, feel, move, see, search, ponder, speak, listen, recall, choose, commit, and create. You might even sing and dance. Learning often works best when it involves action.

9. Practice critical thinking. The exercises that appear throughout the book encourage contemplation and problem solving. Use these exercises to explore new ways of thinking about chapter topics. Note that other elements of this text, including Chapter 7: "Thinking," and Journal Entries, also promote critical thinking.

10. Learn about learning styles. Check out the Learning Styles Inventory in Chapter 1. This material can help you discover your preferred learning styles and allow you to explore new styles. Then, throughout the rest of that chapter, you'll find suggestions for applying your knowledge of learning styles. Remember that the various modes of learning can be accessed by asking four basic questions: *Why? What? How?* and *What if?*

11. Navigate through learning experiences with the Master Student Map. You can orient yourself for maximum learning every time you open this book by asking those same four questions. That's the idea behind the Master Student Map included on the first page of each chapter, which includes sample answers to those questions. Use the four-part structure of this map to cycle through several learning styles and effectively learn anything.

12. Link to the Web. Throughout this book, you'll notice reminders to visit the College Success CourseMate at CengageBrain.com. When you see these notices, go to the CourseMate for articles, online exercises, and links to other useful Web sites.

13. Read the sidebars. Look for sidebars—short bursts of words and pictures placed between longer articles—throughout this book. These short pieces might offer insights that transform your experience of higher education.

Even though this book is loaded with special features, you'll find some core elements. For example, the two pages that open each chapter include a lead article and an introductory Journal Entry. And at the end of each chapter, you'll find a Power Process, Put It to Work article, chapter quiz, Skills Snapshot, and Master Student Profile —all noted in a toolbar at the top of the page.

14. Practice using technology. Read and use the Mastering Technology features as you make your way through the book. These short boxes help you apply the techniques in the book to get the most out of online learning.

15. Take this book to work. With a little tweaking, in some cases, you can apply nearly all of the techniques in this book to your career. For more details, see the Put It to Work articles near the end of each chapter. Use these articles to make a skillful transition from success in school to success on the job.

Note: As a strategy for avoiding sexist language, this book alternates the use of feminine and masculine pronouns. *

2 critical thinking exercise
Commitment

This book is worthless unless you actively participate in its activities and exercises. One powerful way to begin taking action is to make a commitment. Conversely, if you don't make a commitment, then sustained action is unlikely. The result is a worthless book. Therefore, in the interest of saving your valuable time and energy, this exercise gives you a chance to declare your level of involvement up front. From the options below, choose the sentence that best reflects your commitment to using this book. Write the number in the space provided at the end of the list.

1. "Well, I'm reading this book right now, aren't I?"
2. "I will skim the book and read the interesting parts."
3. "I will read the book, think about it, and do the exercises that look interesting."
4. "I will read the book, do some exercises, and complete some of the Journal Entries."
5. "I will read the book, do some exercises and Journal Entries, and use some of the techniques."
6. "I will read the book, do most of the exercises and Journal Entries, and use some of the techniques."
7. "I will study this book, do most of the exercises and Journal Entries, and use some of the techniques."
8. "I will study this book, do most of the exercises and Journal Entries, and experiment with many of the techniques in order to discover what works best for me."
9. "I promise myself that I will create value from this course by studying this book, doing all the exercises and Journal Entries, and experimenting with most of the techniques."
10. "I will use this book as if the quality of my education depends on it—doing all the exercises and Journal Entries, experimenting with most of the techniques, inventing techniques of my own, and planning to reread this book in the future."

Enter your commitment level and today's date here:
Commitment level _______ Date _______

If you selected commitment level 1 or 2, you might consider passing this book on to a friend. If your commitment level is 9 or 10, you are on your way to success in school. If your level is somewhere in-between, experiment with the techniques and learning strategies you will find in this book. If you find that they work, consider returning to this exercise and raising your level of commitment.

Complete this exercise online.

The Discovery and Intention Journal Entry system

One way to become a better student is to grit your teeth and try harder. There is a better way: The Discovery and Intention Journal Entry system. This system can increase your effectiveness by showing you ways to focus your energy.

USING THE DISCOVERY and Intention Journal Entry system is a little like flying an airplane. Airplanes are seldom exactly on course. Human and automatic pilots are always checking an airplane's positions and making corrections. The resulting flight path looks like a zigzag. The plane is almost always flying in the wrong direction, but because of constant observation and course correction, it arrives at the right destination.

As a student, you can use a similar approach. Journal Entries throughout this book are labeled as Discovery Statements, Intention Statements, or Discovery/Intention Statements. Each Journal Entry contains a short set of suggestions to direct your writing.

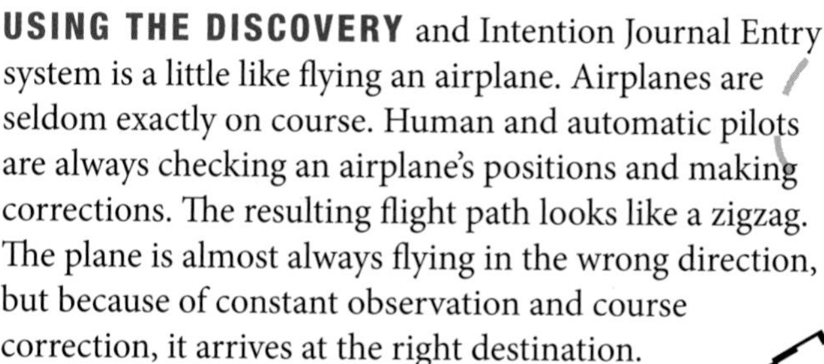

Through Discovery Statements, you gain awareness of "where you are." These statements are a record of what you are learning about yourself as a student—both your strengths and your weaknesses. Discovery Statements can also be declarations of your goals, descriptions of your attitudes, statements of your feelings, transcripts of your thoughts, and chronicles of your behavior.

Sometimes Discovery Statements chronicle an "aha!" moment—a flash of insight that results when a new idea connects with your prior experiences, preferred styles of learning, or both. Perhaps a solution to a long-standing problem suddenly occurs to you. Or a life-changing insight wells up from the deepest recesses of your mind. Don't let such moments disappear. Capture them in Discovery Statements.

Intention Statements can be used to alter your course. These statements are about your commitment to take action based on increased awareness. An intention arises out of your choice to direct your energy toward a specific task and to aim at a particular goal. The processes of discovery and intention reinforce each other.

Even simple changes in behavior can produce results. If you feel like procrastinating, then tackle just one small, specific task related to your intention. Find something you can complete in 5 minutes or less, and do it *now*. For example, access just one Web site related to the topic of your next assigned paper. Spend just 3 minutes previewing a reading assignment. Taking "baby steps" like these can move you into action with grace and ease.

That's the system in a nutshell. Discovery leads to awareness. Intention leads to commitment. The result is focused action, which creates new outcomes in your life.

The purpose of this system is not to get you pumped up and excited to go out there and try harder. In fact, Discovery and Intention Statements are intended to help you work smarter rather than harder.

The process of discovery, intention, and action creates a dynamic and efficient cycle. First, you write Discovery Statements about where you are now and where you want to be. Next, you write Intention Statements about the specific steps you will take to achieve your goals. Finally, you follow up with action—the sooner, the better.

Then you start the cycle again. Write Discovery Statements about whether or how you act on your Intention Statements—and what you learn in the process. Follow up with more Intention Statements about what you will do differently in the future. Then move into action and describe what happens next.

Sometimes a Discovery or Intention Statement will be long and detailed. Usually, it will be short—maybe just a line or two. With practice, the cycle will become automatic.

This process never ends. Each time you repeat the cycle, you get new results. It's all about getting what you want and becoming more effective in everything you do. This is the path of mastery—a path that you can travel for the rest of your life.

By the way, don't panic when you fail to complete an intended task. Straying off course is normal. Simply make the necessary corrections. Consider the first word in the title of this book—*becoming*. This word implies that mastery is not an end state or final goal. Rather, mastery is a process that never ends.

Miraculous progress might not come immediately. Do not be concerned. Stay with the cycle. Give it time. Use Discovery Statements to get a clear view of your world. Then use Intention Statements to direct your actions. Whenever you notice progress, record it.

The following statement might strike you as improbable, but it is true: It can take the same amount of energy to get what you *don't* want in school as it takes to get what you *do* want. Sometimes getting what you don't want takes even *more* effort. An airplane burns the same amount of fuel flying away from its destination as it does flying toward it. It pays to stay on course.

You can use the Discovery and Intention Journal Entry system to stay on your own course and get what you want. Start with the Journal Entries included in the text. Then go beyond them. Write Discovery and Intention Statements of your own at any time, for any purpose. Create new strategies whenever you need them, based on your current situation. Once you get the hang of it, you might discover you can fly. *

Hello Author
I Agree

Rewrite this book

Some books should be preserved in pristine condition. This book is not one of them.

Something happens when you interact with a book by writing in it. *Becoming a Master Student* is about learning, and learning results when you are active. When you make notes in the margin, you can hear yourself talking with the author. When you doodle and underline, you see the author's ideas taking shape. You can even argue with the author and come up with your own theories and explanations. In all of these ways, you become a coauthor of this book. Rewrite it to make it yours.

While you're at it, you can create symbols or codes that will help you when reviewing the text later on. You might insert a "Q" where you have questions or put exclamation points next to important ideas. You could also circle words to look up in a dictionary.

Remember, if any idea in this book doesn't work for you, you can rewrite it. Change an exercise to fit your needs. Create a new technique by combining several others. Create a technique out of thin air!

Find something you agree or disagree with on this page, and write a short note in the margin about it. Or draw a diagram. Better yet, do both. Let creativity be your guide. Have fun.

Begin rewriting now.

Discovery and Intention Statement guidelines

Discovery Statements

1 Record the specifics about your thoughts, feelings, and behavior. Thoughts include inner voices. We talk to ourselves constantly in our heads. When internal chatter gets in your way, write down what you are telling yourself. If this seems difficult at first, just start writing. The act of writing can trigger a flood of thoughts.

Thoughts also include mental pictures. These images are especially powerful. Picturing yourself flunking a test is like a rehearsal to do just that. One way to take away the power of negative images in your mind is to describe them in detail.

Also notice how you feel when you function well. Use Discovery Statements to pinpoint exactly where and when you learn most effectively.

In addition, observe your actions and record them accurately. If you spent 90 minutes chatting online with a favorite cousin instead of reading your anatomy text, write about it and include the details, such as when you did it, where you did it, and how it felt. Record your observations quickly, as soon as you make them.

2 Use discomfort as a signal. When you approach a daunting task, such as a difficult math problem, notice your physical sensations—a churning stomach, perhaps, or shallow breathing or yawning. Feeling uncomfortable, bored, or tired might be a signal that you're about to do valuable work. Stick with it. Tell yourself you can handle the discomfort just a little bit longer. You will be rewarded.

You can experience those rewards right now. Just think of the problem that poses the biggest potential barrier to your success in school. Choose a problem that you face today. (***Hint:*** It might be the thing that's distracting you from reading this article.) If you have a lot of emotion tied up in this problem, that's even better. Write a Discovery Statement about it.

3 Suspend judgment. When you are discovering yourself, be gentle. Suspend self-judgment. If you continually judge your behaviors as "bad" or "stupid" or "galactically imbecilic," sooner or later your mind will revolt. Rather than put up with the abuse, it will quit making discoveries. For your own benefit, be kind to yourself.

4 Tell the truth. Suspending judgment helps you tell the truth about yourself. The saying "The truth will set you free" endures for a reason. The closer you get to the truth, the more powerful your Discovery Statements will be. And if you notice that you are avoiding the truth, don't blame yourself. Just tell the truth about it.

Intention Statements

1 Make intentions positive. The purpose of writing Intention Statements is to focus on what you want rather than what you don't want. Instead of writing "I will not fall asleep while studying chemistry," write, "I intend to stay awake when studying chemistry." Also avoid the word *try*. Trying is not doing. When we hedge our bets with *try*, we can always tell ourselves, "Well, I *tried* to stay awake." We end up fooling ourselves into thinking we succeeded.

2 Make intentions observable. Experiment with an idea from teacher and trainer Robert Mager, who suggests that goals be defined through behaviors that can be observed and measured.[2] Rather than writing "I intend to work harder on my history assignments," write, "I intend to review my class notes, and I intend to make summary sheets of my reading." Then, when you review your progress, you can determine more precisely whether you have accomplished what you intended.

3 Make intentions small and achievable. Give yourself opportunities to succeed by setting goals you can meet. Break large goals into small, specific tasks that can be accomplished quickly. Small and simple changes in behavior—when practiced consistently over time—can have large and lasting effects. If you want to get an A in biology, ask yourself, "What can I do today?" You might choose to study biology for an extra hour. Make that your intention.

When setting your goals, anticipate self-sabotage. Be aware of what you might do, consciously or unconsciously, to undermine your best intentions. If you intend to study differential equations at 9 p.m., notice what you're doing when you sit down to watch a 2-hour movie that starts at 8 p.m.

Also, be careful with intentions that depend on other people. If you write that you intend for your study group to complete an assignment by Monday, then your success depends on the other students in the group.

4 Set timelines that include rewards. Timelines can focus your attention. For example, if you are assigned to write a paper, break the assignment into small tasks and set a precise due date for each one. You might write, "I intend to select a topic for my paper by 9 a.m. Wednesday."

Timelines are especially useful when your intention is to experiment with a technique suggested in this book. The sooner you act on a new idea, the better. Consider practicing a new behavior within 4 hours after you first learn about it.

Remember that you create timelines to help yourself, not to feel guilty. And, you can always change a timeline.

When you meet your goal on time, reward yourself. Rewards that are an integral part of a goal are powerful. For example, your reward for earning a degree might be the career you've always dreamed of. External rewards, such as a movie or an afternoon in the park, are also valuable. These rewards work best when you're willing to withhold them. If you plan to take a nap on Sunday afternoon whether or not you've finished your English chemistry assignment, then the nap is not an effective reward.

Another way to reward yourself is to sit quietly after you have finished your task and savor the feeling. One reason why success breeds success is that it feels good. *

journal entry 1

Discovery Statement

Recalling Excellence

Welcome to the first Journal Entry in this book. You'll find Journal Entries in every chapter, all with a similar design that allows space for you to write.

In the space below, write a description of mastery—a time in your life when you did something well. This experience does not need to be related to school. Describe the details of the situation, including the place, time, and people involved. Also describe the physical sensations and emotions you associate with the event.

I discovered that . . .

You share one thing in common with other students at your career school, college, or university: Entering higher education represents a major change in your life. You've joined a new culture with its own set of rules, both spoken and unspoken.

Making the transition to higher education

WHETHER YOU'VE JUST graduated from high school or have been out of the classroom for decades, you'll discover many differences between secondary and post-secondary education. The sooner you understand such differences, the sooner you can deal with them. Some examples of what you might face include the following:

- *New academic standards.* Once you enter higher education, you'll probably find yourself working harder in school than ever before. Instructors will often present more material at a faster pace. There probably will be fewer tests in higher education than in high school, and the grading might be tougher. Compared to high school, you'll have more to read, more to write, more problems to solve, and more to remember.
- *A new level of independence.* College instructors typically give less guidance about how or when to study. You may not get reminders about when assignments are due or when quizzes and tests will take place. You probably won't get study sheets the night before a test. And anything that's said in class or included in assigned readings might appear on an exam. Overall, you might receive less consistent feedback about how well you are doing in each of your courses. Don't let this tempt you into putting off work until the last minute. You will still be held accountable for all course work. And anything that's said in class or included in assigned readings might appear on an exam.
- *Differences in teaching styles.* Instructors at colleges, universities, and career schools are often steeped in their subject matter. Many did not take courses on how to teach and might not be as interesting as some of your high school teachers. In addition, some professors might seem more focused on research than on teaching.
- *A larger playing field.* The institution you've just joined might seem immense, impersonal, and even frightening. The sheer size of the campus, the variety of courses offered, the large number of departments—all of these opportunities can add up to a confusing array of options.
- *More students and more diversity.* The school you're attending right now might enroll hundreds or thousands more students than your high school. And the range of diversity among these students might surprise you.

In summary, you are now responsible for structuring your time and creating new relationships. Perhaps more than ever before, you'll find that your life is your own creation. You are free to set different goals, explore alternative ways of thinking, change habits, and expand your circle of friends. All this can add up to a new identity—a new way of being in the world.

At first, this world of choices might seem overwhelming or even frightening. You might feel that you're just going through the motions of being a student or playing a role that you've never rehearsed.

That feeling is understandable. Use it to your advantage. Consider that you are assuming a new role in life—that of being a student in higher education. And just as actors enter the minds of the characters that they portray, you can take on the character of a master student.

When you're willing to take responsibility for the quality of your education, you can create the future of your dreams. Keep the following strategies in mind.

Decrease the unknowns. Before classes begin, get a map of the school property and walk through your first day's schedule, perhaps with a classmate or friend. Visit your instructors in their offices and introduce yourself. Anything you can do to get familiar with the new routine will help.

Admit your feelings—whatever they are. School can be an intimidating experience for new students. Anyone can feel anxious, isolated, homesick, or worried. People of diverse cultures, adult learners, commuters, and people with disabilities may feel excluded.

Those emotions are common among new students, and there's nothing wrong with them. Simply admitting the truth about how you feel—to yourself and to someone else—can help you cope. And you can almost always do something constructive in the present moment, no matter how you feel.

If your feelings about this transition make it hard for you to carry out the activities of daily life—going to class, working, studying, and relating to people—then get professional help. Start with a counselor at the student health service on your campus. The mere act of seeking help can make a difference.

Allow time for transition. You don't have to master the transition to higher education right away. Give it some time. Also, plan your academic schedule with your needs in mind. Balance time-intensive courses with others that don't make as many demands.

Find resources. A supercharger increases the air supply to an internal combustion engine. The resulting difference in power can be dramatic. You can make just as powerful a difference in your education if you supercharge it by using all of the resources available to students. In this case, your "air supply" includes people, campus clubs and organizations, and school and community services.

Of all resources, people are the most important. You can isolate yourself, study hard, and get a good education. However, doing this is not the most powerful use of your tuition money. When you establish relationships with teachers, staff members, fellow students, and employers, you can get a *great* education. Build a network of people who will personally support your success in school.

Accessing resources is especially important if you are the first person in your family to enter higher education. As a first-generation student, you are having experiences that people in your family may not understand. Talk to your relatives about your activities at school. If they ask how they can help you,

journal entry 2

Intention Statement

Plan for transition

As a way to ease your transition to higher education, consider setting a goal to meet at least one new person each week for the next month. For example, you could introduce yourself to someone in each of your classes. You could also see your teachers during office hours and meet with your academic advisor.

List your ideas for meeting new people by completing the following sentence.

I intend to . . .

give specific answers. Also, ask your instructors about programs for first-generation students on your campus.

Meet with your academic advisor. One person in particular—your academic advisor—can help you access resources and make the transition to higher education. Meet with this person regularly. Advisors generally know about course requirements, options for declaring majors, and the resources available at your school. Peer advisors might also be available.

When you work with an advisor, remember that you're a paying customer and have a right to be satisfied with the service you get. Don't be afraid to change advisors when that seems appropriate.

Learn the language of higher education. Terms such as *grade point average (GPA), prerequisite, accreditation, matriculation, tenure,* and *syllabus* might be new to you. Ease your transition to higher education by checking your school catalog or school Web site for definitions of these words and others that you don't understand. Also ask your academic advisor for clarification.

Show up for class. In higher education, teachers generally don't take attendance. Yet you'll find that attending class is essential to your success. The amount that you pay in tuition and fees makes a powerful argument for going to classes regularly and getting your money's worth. In large part, the material that you're tested on comes from events that take place in class.

Showing up for class occurs on two levels. The most visible level is being physically present in the classroom. Even more important, though, is showing up mentally. This kind of attendance includes taking detailed notes, asking questions, and contributing to class discussions.

Research on college freshmen indicates a link between regular class attendance and academic success.[3] Succeeding in school can help you get almost anything you want, including the career, income, and relationships you desire. Attending class is an investment in yourself.

Manage out-of-class time. For students in higher education, time management takes on a new meaning. What you do *outside* class matters as much as—or even more than—what you do in class. Instructors give you the raw materials for understanding a subject while a class meets. You then take those materials, combine them, and *teach yourself* outside of class.

To allow for this process, schedule 2 hours of study time for each hour that you spend in class. Also, get a calendar that covers the entire academic year. With the syllabus for each of your courses in hand, note key events for the entire term—dates for tests, papers, and other projects. Getting a big picture of your course load makes it easier to get assignments done on time and to avoid all-night study sessions.

Experiment with new ways to study. You can cope with increased workloads and higher academic expectations by putting all of your study habits on the table and evaluating them. Don't assume that the learning strategies you used in the past—in high school or the workplace—will automatically transfer to your new role in higher education. Keep the habits that serve you, drop those that hold you back, and adopt new ones to promote your success. On every page of this book, you'll find helpful suggestions.

Take the initiative in meeting new people. Introduce yourself to classmates and instructors. You can do this just before or after class. Realize that most of the people in this new world of higher education are waiting to be welcomed. You can help them and help yourself at the same time.

Perhaps you imagined that higher education would be a hotbed of social activity—and now find yourself feeling lonely and disconnected. Your feelings are common. Remember that plugging into the social networks at any school takes time. It's worth the effort. Connecting to school socially as well as academically promotes your success and your enjoyment.

Become a self-regulated learner. Reflect on your transition to higher education. Think about what's working well, what you'd like to change, and ways to make those changes. Psychologists use the term *self-regulation* to describe this kind of thinking.[4] Self-regulated learners set goals, monitor their progress toward those goals, and change their behavior based on the results they get.

Becoming a Master Student promotes self-regulation through the ongoing cycle of discovery, intention, and action. Write Discovery Statements to monitor your behavior and evaluate the results you're currently creating in any area of your life. Write about your level of commitment to school, your satisfaction with your classes and grades, your social life, and your family's support for your education.

Based on your discoveries, write Intention Statements about your goals for this term, this year, next year, and the rest of your college career. Describe exactly what you will do to create new results in each of these time frames. Then follow through with action. In this way, you take charge of your transition to higher education, starting now. *

Find more strategies for mastering the art of transition online.

The topic of this article might seem like a lesson in common sense, yet some students lack civility. They forget the simple behaviors that create a sense of safety, mutual respect, and community in any place—including a classroom, tutoring center, library, or instructor's office.

Classroom civility—what's in it for you

CONSIDER AN EXAMPLE: A student arrives 15 minutes late to a lecture and lets the door slam behind her. She pulls a fast-food burger out of a paper bag (hear the sound of that crackling paper). Then her cell phone rings at full volume—and she answers it. Behaviors like these send a message to everyone in the room: "I'm ignoring you."

Without civility, you lose. Even a small problem with classroom civility can create a barrier for everyone. Learning gets interrupted. Trust breaks down. Your tuition dollars go down the drain.

You might invest hundreds of hours and thousands of dollars in getting a degree. You deserve to enter classrooms that are free of discipline problems and bullies.

Many schools have formal policies about classroom civility. Find out what policies apply to you. The consequences for violating them can be serious and may include dismissal or legal action.

With civility, you win. When you treat instructors with respect, you're more likely to be treated that way in return. A respectful relationship with an instructor could turn into a favorable reference letter, a mentorship, a job referral, or a friendship that lasts for years after you graduate. Politeness pays.

Classroom civility does not mean that you have to be passive or insincere. You can present your opinions with passion and even disagree with an instructor. And you can do so in a way that leaves everyone enriched rather than threatened.

The basics of classroom civility are summarized in the following suggestions. They reflect common sense, and they make an uncommon difference.

Attend classes regularly. Show up for classes on time. If you know that you're going to miss a class or be late, then let your instructor know. Take the initiative to ask your instructor or another student about what you missed.

If you arrive late, do not disrupt class. Close the door quietly and take a seat. When you know that you will have to leave class early, tell your instructor before class begins, and sit near an exit. If you leave class to use the restroom or handle an emergency, do so quietly.

During class, participate fully. Take notes and join in discussions. Turn off your cell phone or any other electronic device that you don't need for class. Remember that sleeping, texting, or doing work for another class is a waste of your time and money.

Instructors often give assignments or make a key point at the end of a class period. Be there when it happens. Wait until class has been dismissed before you pack up your notebooks and other materials.

Communicate respect. When you speak in class, begin by addressing your instructor as *Ms., Mrs., Mr., Professor,* or whatever the teacher prefers.

Discussions gain value when everyone gets a chance to speak. Show respect for others by not monopolizing class discussions. Refrain from side conversations and profanity. When presenting viewpoints that conflict with those of classmates or your instructor, combine the passion for your opinion with respect for the opinions of others.

Respect gets communicated in the smallest details. Maintain good hygiene. Avoid making distracting noises, and cover your mouth if you yawn or cough. Also avoid wearing inappropriate, revealing clothing. Even if you meet your future spouse in class, refrain from public displays of affection.

If you disagree with a class requirement or grade you received, then talk to your instructor about it after class. Your ideas will get more attention if they are presented in a private setting and in a respectful manner.

See civility as a contribution. Every class you enter has the potential to become a community of people who talk openly, listen fully, share laughter, and arrive at life-changing insights. Anything you do to make that vision a reality makes a positive difference. *

Succeeding in higher education—at any age

If you're returning to school after a long break from the classroom, there's no reason to feel out of place. Returning adults and other nontraditional students make up the majority of the student body in many schools.

David Buffington/Blend Images/Getty

BEING AN ADULT learner puts you on a strong footing. With a rich store of life experiences, you can ask meaningful questions and make connections between course work and daily life. Any skills that you've developed to work on teams, manage projects, meet deadlines, and solve problems will be assets in the classroom. Many instructors will especially enjoy working with you.

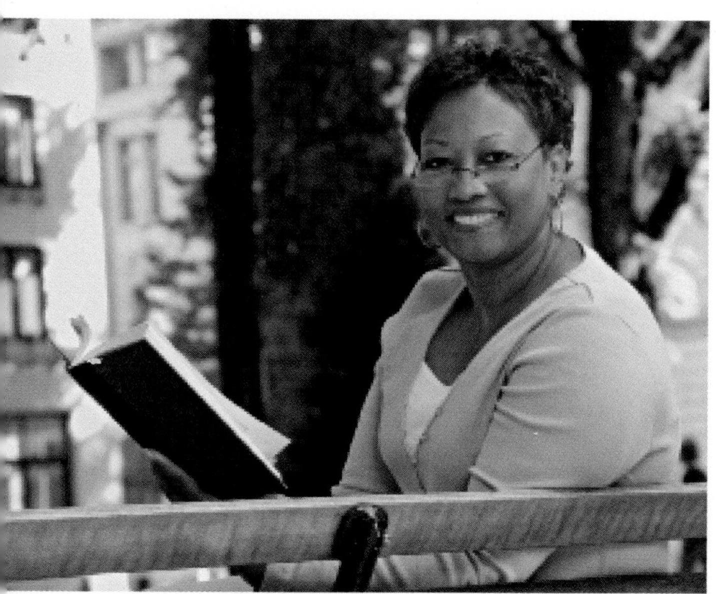
David Buffington/Blend Images/Getty

Following are some suggestions for adult learners who want to ease their transition to higher education. If you're a younger student, commuting student, or community college student, look for useful ideas here as well.

Acknowledge your concerns. Adult learners might express any of the following fears:

- *I'll be the oldest person in all my classes.*
- *I've been out of the classroom too long.*
- *I'm concerned about my math, reading, and writing skills.*
- *I'm worried about making tuition payments.*
- *How will I ever make the time to study, on top of everything else I'm doing?*

Those concerns are understandable. Now consider some facts:

- College classrooms are more diverse than ever before. According to the U.S. Census Bureau, 37 percent of students in the nation's colleges are age 25 and older. The majority of these older students attend school part-time.[5]
- Adult learners can take advantage of evening classes, weekend classes, summer classes, distance learning, and online courses. Also look for classes in off-campus locations, closer to where you work or live.
- Colleges offer financial aid for students of all ages, including scholarships, grants, and low-interest loans.
- You can meet other students and make new friends by taking part in orientation programs. Look for programs that are targeted to adult learners.

- You are now enrolled in a course that can help boost your skills at math, reading, writing, note taking, time management, and other key areas.

Ease into it. If you're new to higher education, consider easing into it. You can choose to attend school part-time before making a full-time commitment. If you've taken college-level classes in the past, find out whether any of those credits will transfer into your current program.

Plan ahead. By planning a week or month at a time, you get a bigger picture of your multiple roles as a student, an employee, and a family member. With that awareness, you can make conscious adjustments in the number of hours you devote to each domain of activity in your life. For example:

- If your responsibilities at work or home will be heavy in the near future, then register for fewer classes next term.
- Choose recreational activities carefully, focusing on those that relax and recharge you the most.
- Don't load your schedule with classes that require unusually heavy amounts of reading or writing.

For related suggestions, see Chapter 2: "Time and Money."

Delegate tasks. If you have children, delegate some of the household chores to them. Or start a meal co-op in your neighborhood. Cook dinner for yourself and someone else one night each week. In return, ask that person to furnish you with a meal on another night. A similar strategy can apply to child care and other household tasks.

Get to know other returning students. Introduce yourself to other adult learners. Being in the same classroom gives you an immediate bond. You can exchange work, home, or cell phone numbers and build a network of mutual support. Some students adopt a buddy system, pairing up with another student in each class to complete assignments and prepare for tests.

Find common ground with traditional students. Traditional and nontraditional students have many things in common. They seek to gain knowledge and skills for their chosen careers. They desire financial stability and personal fulfillment. And, like their older peers, many younger students are concerned about whether they have the skills to succeed in higher education.

Consider pooling resources with younger students. Share notes, edit one another's papers, and form study groups. Look for ways to build on one another's strengths. If you need help using a computer for assignments, you might ask a younger student. In group projects and case studies, you can expand the discussion by sharing insights from your experiences.

Enlist your employer's support. Let your employer in on your educational plans. Point out how the skills you gain in the classroom will help you meet work objectives. Offer informal seminars at work to share what you're learning in school. You might find that your company reimburses its employees for some tuition costs or even grants time off to attend classes.

Get extra mileage out of your current tasks. Look for ways to relate your schoolwork to your job. For example, when you're assigned a research paper, choose a topic that relates to your current job tasks. Some schools even offer academic credit for work and life experience.

Review your subjects before you start classes. Say that you're registered for trigonometry and you haven't taken a math class since high school. Consider brushing up on the subject before classes begin. Also, talk with future instructors about ways to prepare for their classes.

"Publish" your schedule. After you plan your study and class sessions for the week, write up your schedule and post it in a place where others who live with you will see it. If you use an online calendar, print out copies to put in your school binder and on your refrigerator door, bathroom mirror, or kitchen cupboard.

Enroll family and friends in your success. School can cut into your social life. Prepare friends and family members by discussing this issue ahead of time. See Chapter 8: "Communicating" for ways to prevent and resolve conflict.

You can also involve your spouse, partner, children, or close friends in your schooling. Offer to give them a tour of the campus, introduce them to your instructors and classmates, and encourage them to attend social events at school with you.

Take this process a step further and ask the key people in your life for help. Share your reason for getting a degree, and talk about what your whole family has to gain from this change. Ask them to think of ways that they can support your success in school and to commit to those actions. Make your own education a joint mission that benefits everyone. *

Find more strategies for adult learners online.

Connect to resources

NAME A CHALLENGE that you're facing right now, such as finding money to pay for classes, resolving conflicts with a teacher, lining up a job after graduation. Chances are that a school or community resource can help.

Resources are often free—and unused. Following are some examples of resources that might be available to you. Check your school and city Web sites for more options.

Academic advisors can help you select courses, choose a major, plan your career, and adjust in general to the culture of higher education.

Arts organizations connect you to local museums, concert venues, clubs, and stadiums.

Athletic centers often open weight rooms, swimming pools, indoor tracks, basketball courts, and racquetball and tennis courts to all students.

Child care is sometimes made available to students at a reasonable cost through the early childhood education department on campus or at community agencies.

Churches, synagogues, mosques, and temples have members who are happy to welcome fellow worshippers who are away from home.

Computer labs on campus are places where students can go to work on projects and access the Internet. Computer access is often available off-campus as well. Check public libraries for this service. Some students get permission to use computers at their workplace after hours.

Consumer credit counseling can help even if you've really blown your budget. And it's usually free. Do your research, and choose a reputable and not-for-profit consumer credit counselor.

Counseling centers in the community can assist you with a problem when you can't get help at school. Look for career-planning services, rehabilitation offices, outreach programs for veterans, and mental health clinics.

Extracurricular activities are yours to explore. Consider student government, fraternities, sororities, service clubs, religious groups, sports clubs, and political groups. Use these activities to develop new skills, explore possible careers, build contacts for jobs, and build a lifelong habit of volunteering. Make conscious choices about how to divide your time between schoolwork and extracurricular activities. Think carefully about how many hours each week or month you can devote to them. For ideas, see Chapter 2: "Time and Money."

The ***financial aid office*** assists students with loans, scholarships, work-study, and grants.

Governments (city, county, state, and federal) often have programs for students. Check the government listings in your local telephone directory and city Web site.

Hotlines offer a way to get emergency care, personal counseling, and other kinds of help via a phone call. Do an Internet search on *phone hotlines* in your area that assist with the specific kind of help you're looking for. Check your school catalog for more resources.

Job placement offices can help you find part-time employment while you are in school and a full-time job after you graduate.

Legal aid services provide free or inexpensive assistance to low-income people.

Libraries are a treasure chest on campus and in any community. They employ people who are happy to help you locate information.

Newspapers published on campus and in the local community list events and services that are free or inexpensive.

Your ***school catalog*** lists course descriptions, tuition fees, requirements for graduation, and information on everything from the school's history to its grading practices.

School security agencies can tell you what's safe and what's not. They can also provide information about parking, bicycle regulations, and traffic rules.

Special needs and disability services assist college students who have learning disabilities or other specific needs.

Student health clinics often provide free or inexpensive counseling and other medical treatment.

Support groups exist for people with almost any problem, from drug addiction to cancer. You can find people with problems who meet every week to share suggestions, information, and concerns about problems they share.

Tutoring is usually free and is available through academic departments or counseling centers. *

Link to the world of work

STARTING NOW, read this book with a mental filter in place. Ask yourself, "How can I use this idea to meet my career goals? How can I apply this technique to my current job or the next job I see for myself?" The answers can help you thrive in any job, whether you work full-time or part-time.

To stimulate your thinking, look for the Put It to Work articles near the end of each chapter. In addition, invent techniques of your own based on what you read, and test them at work. There's no limit to the possibilities.

For example, use the Discovery and Intention Journal Entry system while you're in the work force. Write Discovery Statements to note your current job skills, as well as areas for improvement. Also use Discovery Statements to describe what you want from your career.

Follow up with Intention Statements that detail specifically what you want to be doing 1 year, 5 years, and 10 years or more from today. Write additional Intention Statements about specific actions you can take to meet those career goals.

As you read, look for more ideas to apply at work. For example, the techniques presented in ***Setting and achieving goals*** (page 55) can help you plan and complete projects on time. Supplement these ideas with suggestions from ***The ABC daily to-do list*** (page 57) and ***Get the most out of now*** (page 61). You might choose to tackle difficult tasks first thing in the day, or at any other time when your energy peaks.

Memory techniques (page 79) will come in handy as you learn the policies and procedures for a new job.

Use the ***Muscle Reading techniques*** in Chapter 4 (page 95) to keep up with journals and books in your field.

The article ***Record*** (page 118) explains different formats for taking notes. Use these tools to document what happens at work-related meetings.

Adapt the ideas mentioned in ***Cooperative learning: Studying in groups*** (page 137) to cooperate more effectively with members of a project team.

Choose freedom from distress (page 198) is full of strategies that can help you manage any situation. Use them when you're under deadline pressure or dealing with a difficult customer.

Use the thinking skills presented in ***Gaining skill at decision making*** (page 162) when it comes time to choose a career, weigh job offers, or make work-related decisions.

Those are just a few suggestions. On every page of this book, you'll find ways to expand your job skills and enhance your personal development. *

You don't need this course—but you might want it

Some students don't believe they need a student success course. They might be right. These students may tell you that many schools don't even offer such a class. That's true.

Consider the benefits of taking this course anyway.

Start with a single question: *What's one new thing that I could do on a regular basis to make a significant, positive difference in my life?* This question might be the most important thing you ask yourself this term. The answer does not have to involve a huge behavior change. Over weeks and months, even a small shift in the way you take notes, read a textbook, or interact with instructors can make a major difference in how well you do in school.

After you ask that question, look for hundreds of possible answers in this book. Your student course will reveal even more.

A student success course gives you strategies for creating the life of your dreams. It's possible that you might arrive at these strategies on your own, given enough time. But why wait? Approach this book and your course as if the quality of your education depends on them. Then watch the benefits start to unfold.

Ways to change a habit

CONSIDER A NEW way to think about the word *habit*. Imagine for a moment that many of our most troublesome problems and even our most basic traits are just habits.

The expanding waistline that your friend is blaming on her spouse's cooking—maybe that's just a habit called overeating.

The fit of rage that a student blames on a teacher—maybe that's just the student's habit of closing the door to new ideas.

Procrastination, stress, and money shortages might just be names that we give to collections of habits—scores of simple, small, repeated behaviors that combine to create a huge result.

When you discover a behavior that undermines your goals or creates a circumstance that you don't want, consider a new attitude: That behavior is just a habit. And it can be changed.

Thinking about ourselves as creatures of habit actually gives us power. Then we are not faced with the monumental task of changing our very nature. Rather, we can take on the doable job of changing our habits. Even a change in behavior that seems insignificant at first can have effects that ripple throughout your life.

Tell the truth

Telling the truth about any habit—from chewing our fingernails to cheating on tests—frees us. When we admit what's really going on in our lives, our defenses come down. We become open to accepting help from others. The support we need to change a habit has an opportunity to show up and make an impact.

Choose and commit to a new behavior

Make a commitment to practice the new habit. Tell key people in your life about your decision to change. Set up a plan for when and how. Answer key questions: When will I apply the new habit? Exactly how will I think, speak, or act differently?

For example, consider the student who always snacks when he studies. This is especially easy, given the place he chooses to study: the kitchen. He can choose to change this habit by studying at a desk in his bedroom instead of at the kitchen table.

Get feedback and support

Getting feedback and support is a crucial step in adopting a new behavior. It is also a point at which many plans for change break down. It's easy to practice your new behavior with great enthusiasm for a few days. After the initial rush of excitement, though, things can get a little tougher. You begin to find excuses for slipping back into old habits: "One more cigarette won't hurt." "I can get back to my diet tomorrow." "It's been a tough day; I deserve this beer."

One way to get feedback is to bring other people into the picture. Ask others to remind you that you are changing your habit if they see you backsliding.

Starting new habits might call for focused, long-lasting support from close friends or family members. Getting support from them can be as simple as a quick phone call: "Hi. Have you started that outline for your research paper yet?" Or it can be as formal as a support group that meets once a week to review everyone's goals and action plans.

Another source of feedback is yourself. Create charts to track your behavior, or write about your progress in your journal. Figure out a way to monitor your progress.

Practice, practice, practice—without self-judgment

Act on your intention over and over again. If you fail or forget, let go of any self-judgment. Just keep practicing the new habit. Allow whatever time it takes to make a change. *

Find more strategies for changing a habit at the College Success CourseMate.

journal entry 

Discovery Statement

Choosing your purpose

Success is a choice—your choice. To get what you want, it helps to know what you want. That is the purpose of this two-part Journal Entry.

You can begin choosing success by completing this Journal Entry right now. If you choose to do it later, then choose a date, time, and place, and block out the time on your calendar.

Date: ______________________________

Time: ______________________________

Place: ______________________________

Part 1

Select a time and place when you know you will not be disturbed for at least 20 minutes. (The library is a good place to do this exercise.) Relax for 2 or 3 minutes, clearing your mind. Next, complete the following sentences. Write in the space below and use additional paper as needed.

When you run out of ideas, stick with it just a bit longer. Be willing to experience a little discomfort. Keep writing. What you discover might be well worth the extra effort.

What I want from my education is . . .

____

____

____

When I complete my education, I want to be able to . . .

____

____

____

I also want . . .

____

____

____

____

____

____

____

____

Part 2

After completing Part 1, take a short break. Reward yourself by doing something that you enjoy. Then come back to this Journal Entry.

Now, review the list you just created of things that you want from your education. See whether you can summarize them in the form of a one-sentence purpose statement. Start this sentence with, "My purpose for being in school is. . . ."

Allow yourself to write many drafts of this purpose statement, and review it periodically as you continue your education. With each draft, see whether you can capture the essence of what you want from higher education and from your life. State this in a vivid way—in a short sentence that you can easily memorize, one that sparks your enthusiasm and makes you want to get up in the morning.

You might find it difficult to express your purpose statement in one sentence. If so, write a paragraph or more. Then look for the sentence that seems most charged with energy for you.

Following are some sample purpose statements:

- My purpose for being in school is to gain skills that I can use to contribute to others.
- My purpose for being in school is to live an abundant life that is filled with happiness, health, love, and wealth.
- My purpose for being in school is to enjoy myself by making lasting friendships and following the lead of my interests.

Write at least one draft of your purpose statement below:

____

____

____

____

____

____

____

____

____

____

Discover What You Want

Imagine a person who walks up to a counter at the airport to buy a plane ticket for his next vacation. "Just give me a ticket," he says to the reservation agent. "Anywhere will do."

The agent stares back at him in disbelief. "I'm sorry, sir," she replies. "I'll need some more details. Just minor things—such as the name of your destination city and your arrival and departure dates."

"Oh, I'm not fussy," says the would-be vacationer. "I just want to get away. You choose for me."

Compare this traveler to another one who walks up to the counter and says, "I'd like a ticket to Ixtapa, Mexico, departing on Saturday, March 23, and returning Sunday, April 7. Please give me a window seat, first class, with vegetarian meals."

Now, ask yourself which traveler is more likely to end up with an enjoyable vacation.

The same principle applies in any area of life. Knowing where we want to go increases the probability that we will arrive at our destination. Discovering what we want makes it more likely that we'll get it. Once our goals are defined precisely, our brains reorient our thinking and behavior to align with those goals—and we're well on the way there.

The example about the traveler with no destination seems far-fetched. Before you dismiss it, though, do an informal experiment: Ask three other students what they want to get out of their education. Be prepared for hemming and hawing, vague generalities, and maybe even a helping of pie in the sky à la mode.

These responses are amazing, considering the stakes involved. Our hypothetical vacationer is about to invest a couple weeks of his time and hundreds of dollars, all with no destination in mind. Students routinely invest years of their lives and thousands of dollars with an equally hazy idea of their destination in life.

Now suppose that you ask someone what she wants from her education and you get this answer: "I plan to get a degree in journalism with double minors in earth science and Portuguese so that I can work as a reporter covering the environment in Brazil." Chances are you've found a master student. The details of a person's vision offer a clue to mastery.

Discovering what you want greatly enhances your odds of succeeding in higher education. Many students quit school simply because they are unsure about what they want from it. With well-defined goals in mind, you can look for connections between what you want and what you study. The more connections you discover, the more likely you'll stay in school—and the more likely you'll get what you want in every area of life.[6]

Learn more about this Power Process online.

Edmond Van Hoorick/Digital Vision/Getty Images

1 First Steps

Instructor Tools & Tips

> "You either change things or you don't. Excuses rob you of power and induce apathy.
>
> —**Agnes Whistling Elk**
>
> In oneself lies the whole world, and if you know how to look and learn, then the door is there and the key is in your hand. Nobody on earth can give you either that key or the door to open, except yourself.
>
> —**J. Krishnamurti**

Preview

Many students taking a student success course start out the semester with a high level of enthusiasm and energy. That's good because there's a lot of meaty and important foundation material in the Introduction and in Chapters 1 and 2. If students learn the important concepts presented in these chapters, they are well on the way to achieving their educational goals. Remind your students that this chapter is about First Steps—and this includes exercises in self-discovery, making transitions, and motivation. Use the Master Student Map on the chapter opener page to inspire your students, stimulate class discussion, and preview the chapter topics.

Guest Speaker

Consider inviting the elected President of the Student Government to speak to your students as a follow-up to the article "The Value of Higher Education" (page 41). Prompt the President to discuss why he became involved in student activities and what he's gotten out of the experience.

If a speaker isn't available, consider using the Master Student Profile articles as guest speakers. Each chapter of this text includes a profile of a person who embodies several qualities of a master student. Invite your students to look for timeless qualities in the people they read about. Growing up with difficult situations, Lalita Booth observed the world around her and chose a different type of life for herself. She discovered that going back to school was the key to the life she wanted to create. Use this story to start a conversation about the external challenges students face while pursuing a post-secondary education.

Lecture

Learning Style Inventory (pages LSI-1–LSI-8). Being aware of learning styles is an important strategy for success because it helps students understand differences in the ways people perceive and process new information. Your students will learn about their own preferred style of learning and how this tool can help them observe and ascertain the preferred teaching styles of their professors.

The Learning Style Inventory (LSI) is a unifying theme woven throughout *Becoming a Master Student.* Activities are crafted to engage students not only in the strengths of their own learning preferences but in the strengths of other styles as well. The Master Student Map at the beginning of each chapter can help students internalize the strategies taught in each chapter. Study skills do not transfer from a student success class to other courses accidentally. It takes a talented and prepared instructor to help students build other schema and develop the confidence that is necessary to transfer new strategies to different learning settings. Teaching this might seem intimidating for first-time instructors. Remember, when you teach with *Becoming a Master Student,* you are not alone. Your support materials include a talented team of TeamUP consultants. Call (1-800-856-5727) or visit **www.cengage.com/teamup** today!

Additional resources to help guide you in administering the LSI and applying the Master Student Map and Learning Styles Application are on the Instructor Companion site. A video for instructors is also available online.

Claim your multiple intelligences (page 31). Howard Gardner's theory of several types of intelligence complements this chapter's discussion of different learning styles: both recognize that there are alternative ways for people to learn and assimilate knowledge. This article provides students with concepts for exploring additional methods to achieve success in school, work, and relationships. A chart on pages 32–33 presents an overview of the characteristics of each type of intelligence, suggests possible learning strategies for each, and links the different types with possible careers. Have your students further explore these career choices as they consider different majors or areas of focused study.

Exercises/Activities

1. Learning by seeing, hearing, and moving: The VAK system (pages 39–40). Learning by seeing (visual learning), hearing (auditory learning), and moving (kinesthetic learning) allows students to perceive information through their senses. Engage your students by asking them to take the informal inventory and to continue to take First Steps of self-discovery. Have your students submit Discovery Statements to highlight the new strategies they have discovered and Intention Statements to describe the new options for learning that they intend to implement.

2. The Master Student (page 30). After students read this article outside of class, reinforce the concept of mastery with the following team-building activity in class. Randomly assign students to groups of four and ask each group to select five of the most important master student qualities. The group members must agree on the five qualities they pick and be able to justify their decision to choose them. Have each group report to the whole class on their choices.

3. Attitudes, affirmations, and visualizations (page 42). Self-awareness is the key to self-regulation and eventually self-mastery. This article encourages students to begin positive self-talk early in the course. Affirmations are employed to help students sustain a positive self-image and develop attitudes that lead to success. To help students grasp the power of visualization, try the classroom exercise "Creating their place." Begin this exercise by providing students with names for this place such as power place, caring place, peaceful place, or happy place. Students select the name that feels best to them. This allows all students, introverts and extroverts, to be positive about their choice. Instruct students to close their eyes and create this place in their mind. Follow a script (which is available on the Instructor Companion site) to help them discover the effectiveness of guided visualization. Once they have created this "mind place" in class two or three times, it can help reduce stress and test anxiety, and it can serve as a strategic memory tool.

4. Power Process: Ideas Are Tools (page 43). Each Power Process can be illustrated by a simple yet meaningful object lesson. For example, to illustrate this Power Process, bring a drinking straw, a spoon, a hammer, and a piece of chalk or whiteboard marker to class. Ask for volunteers to help write an assignment on the board. Hand out the various "ideas/tools" for them to use to write on the board. In seconds, all of the students will realize the power of this process. Although each of these ideas is an excellent tool for the job it was designed to do, only the student with the right tool is successful at the current task.

Conversation/Sharing

The article on Motivation (pages 28–29) provides students with tools that enable them to take responsibility for their own motivation in college. Motivation is often high at the beginning of the semester but may drop as the term progresses. Have students form groups of four and share which of the tools each student intends to use to keep motivation high for the entire term. Ask each group to provide a summary of their group's findings to the whole class.

Homework

The Discovery Wheel (pages 23–26) is an opportunity for students to take a First Step in telling the truth about the kind of student they are and the kind of student they want to become. This is not a test but an opportunity for change. Students complete the Discovery Wheel in Chapter 1 and then again in Chapter 10. This enables them to measure their progress. Results from the Discovery Wheel exercises can be used in your course in a variety of ways. Consider the following suggestions:

- Ask students to list their intentions or commitments for improving particular skills during the term. At the end of the term, they can assess their progress in those areas by using the Discovery Wheel in Chapter 10.
- As an alternative to the textbook version of the Discovery Wheel, have your students fill out the online interactive Discovery Wheel found on the College

Success Coursemate. Note that this online version does not include number ratings, so the results will be formatted differently from the results of the Discovery Wheel in the text.

- Create an assignment requiring students to contact people on campus or in the community who can assist them in enhancing particular skills. For example, the reading center can provide specific strategies for improving comprehension, word attack skills, and concentration.
- Allow the Discovery Wheel exercises to help shape course content. You can use the results to plan future lessons or to determine what students want to learn or accomplish during the course as a result of their self-assessments.
- Ask students to form small groups and coach each other. Coaching could include how to capitalize on and share talents and how to strengthen areas for growth. If you choose to do this activity, let students know your reasons for forming small groups. For many, self-assessment is personal, and sharing the results might seem risky. Ask students to coach themselves. They can imagine that the self-assessment is for someone special whose success in school and life is important to them. Ask students to take their best suggestions and implement them.
- Create a resource network. Take the titles of the sections of the Discovery Wheel (Attitude, Time and Money, Memory, and so on) and list each title on a piece of paper. Ask students to sign their names to a particular piece of paper if they are willing to assist others in enhancing their skills in this area. Then distribute the lists to the class or post them on your course Web site.

Evaluation

Quiz ideas for Chapter 1:

- Ask students about the role of truth in the mastery of student success.
- Ask students about discoveries from completing the Discovery Wheel.
- Ask students about their preferred Learning Style and the characteristics of students who like to learn using this style.
- Ask students about the challenges in college for someone with their Learning Style.
- Ask students to name and give examples of two multiple intelligences.
- Ask students to describe key points in the article "The value of higher education."
- Ask students to explain three of the master student qualities they desire to possess.

Here is another quiz idea from an Advisory Board Member:

> "To save class time for instruction and discussion, I tell my students that I am going to select only one 10-point question for the quiz. It will be one of the questions in the book quiz. I present the question and ask students to respond using the three-part quiz forms (available through your sales rep). When they are through answering the question, I remind students to write their name on the quiz before tearing off the white sheet and handing it in. Then they compare answers with the person next to them to seek insights from each other. If they did not have the answer, I tell them that if they return the pink sheet with the answers to all ten questions, I will give them 7 out of 10 points.
>
> **—Eldon McMurray, Utah Valley State College**

Additional Digital Resources

CHAPTER 1

Course Manual

The online *Course Manual* serves as an invaluable reference for those developing and teaching a College Success course with *Becoming a Master Student Concise*. The *Course Manual* provides advice on general teaching issues such as preparing for classes, classroom management, grading, and communicating with students of various backgrounds, as well as specific strategies on getting the most out of various features in *Becoming a Master Student Concise* such as the Discovery Wheel, Learning Styles Inventory, and book-specific Web sites. Do a *Course Manual* reconnaissance to find ideas that you can use in your course right now.

Instructor Companion Site

The updated Instructor Companion Site provides resources to help you plan and customize your course. Content specific to Chapter 1 includes:

- Lecture Ideas
  - Corkscrews are Tools
  - Connecting VAK Self-Awareness, Brain Science, and Learning Styles in Your Mind
- In-Class Exercises
  - Co-creating a Syllabus
  - The Importance of Intention
  - Master Student Qualities
- Writing Assignments
  - Application Portfolio for Becoming a Master Student
- In-Text Quiz Answers
- PowerPoint Slides

The Instructor Companion Site also contains the following book-specific content:

- ExamView Test Bank
- Online Course Manual
- Sample Syllabi
- Detailed Transition Guide

College Success CourseMate

To help your students gain a better understanding of the topics discussed in *Becoming a Master Student Concise*, encourage them to visit the College Success CourseMate at CengageBrain.com, which provides the following resources specific to Chapter 1:

- Online version of the Discovery Whee
- Connect to Text content expands on specific topics marked with an icon within Chapter 1.
- Practice Tests allow students to see how well they understand the themes of *Becoming a Master Student Concise.*
- Interactive Concept Maps promote critical thinking by highlighting related ideas to show relationships among concepts.
- Learning Styles Application
- Discussion Topics
- Reflection Questions
- Assessment Questions
- Experiment with chapter strategies
- Video Skillbuilders bring to life techniques that will help students to excel in college and beyond. The following videos should give your students more information regarding topics covered in Chapter 1:
  - Motivation and Goal Setting: Staying Motivated and Making a Contribution
  - Learning Styles: The VAK
  - Learning Styles: The Kolb Learning Style Inventory
  - Motivation and Goal Setting: Staying Motivated as an Adult Learner
- Remembering Cultural Differences presents readers with brief articles that touch on aspects of diversity in our rapidly changing world. For Chapter 1, the following article will prompt your students to look at contemporary issues in a new way:
  - Culture in the Classroom
- Master Student Profiles provide additional information on the people covered in this book feature. For Chapter 1, students will find expanded coverage and links about:
  - Lalita Booth
- Power Process Media contains video, PowerPoints, and audio files to take what your students have learned from the Power Processes in their book to the next level. For Chapter 1, students will find additional media on:
  - Ideas Are Tools

Along with the chapter-specific content, a General Resources folder is available that contains Toolboxes geared toward specific student types (Community College, Adult Learner, Student Athlete), the Plagiarism Prevention Zone, and the Career Resource Center.

1 First Steps

Master Student Map

as you read, ask yourself

what if . . .

I could create new outcomes in my life by accepting the way I am right now?

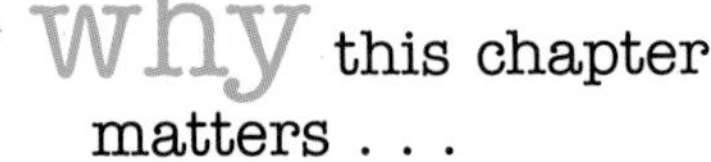

why this chapter matters . . .

Success starts with telling the truth about what *is* working—and what *isn't*—in our lives right now.

how you can use this chapter . . .

- Experience the power of telling the truth about your current skills.
- Discover your preferred learning styles and develop new ones.
- Choose attitudes that promote your success.

what is included . . .

MASTER STUDENTS in *action*

At the beginning of the term, I would have said that I learned best by doing (hands-on). But now that I have grown and expanded the boundaries of my mind's learning capabilities, I learn best with a mixture of all three (watching, listening, and doing). This is because I have come to realize that all three types of learning are connected through a balance, leading one to discover the "perfect" method of learning. —**DEONDRÉ LUCAS**

Photo courtesy of Deondré Lucas

First Step:
Truth is a key to mastery

THE FIRST STEP technique is simple: Tell the truth about who you are and what you want. End of discussion. Now proceed to Chapter 2.

Well, it's not *quite* that simple.

The First Step is one of the most valuable tools in this book. It magnifies the power of all the other techniques. It is key to becoming a master student.

Urging you to tell the truth sounds like moralizing, but there is nothing moralizing about a first step. It is a practical, down-to-earth way to change behavior. No technique in this book has been field-tested more often or more successfully—or under tougher circumstances.

The principle of telling the truth is applied universally by people who want to turn their lives around. For members of Alcoholics Anonymous, the First Step is acknowledging that they are powerless over alcohol. For people who join Weight Watchers, the First Step is admitting how much they weigh.

It's not easy to tell the truth about our weaknesses. And for some of us, it's even harder to recognize our strengths. Maybe we don't want to brag. Maybe we're attached to a poor self-image. Yet using the First Step technique in *Becoming a Master Student* means telling the truth about our positive qualities too.

It might help to remember that weaknesses are often strengths taken to an extreme. The student who carefully revises her writing can make significant improvements in a term paper. If she revises too much and hands in the paper late, though, her grade might suffer. Any success strategy carried too far can backfire.

Whether written or verbal, the ways that we express our First Steps are more powerful when they are specific. For example, if you want to improve your note-taking skills, you might write, "I am an awful note taker." It would be more effective to write, "I can't read 80 percent of the notes I took in Introduction to Psychology last week, and I have no idea what was important in that class." Be just as specific about what you plan to achieve. You might declare, "I want to take legible notes that help me predict what questions will be on the final exam."

Completing the exercises in this chapter can help you tap resources you never knew you had. They're all First Steps. It's just that simple. The truth has power. *

journal entry

Discovery/Intention Statement

Take a 10-minute First Step

Take 5 minutes to skim the Discovery Wheel exercise starting on page 23. Find one statement that describes a skill you already possess—a personal strength that will promote your success in school. Write that statement here:

____

____

____

____

____

The Discovery Wheel might also prompt some thoughts about skills you want to acquire. Describe one of those skills by completing the following sentence.

I discovered that . . .

____

____

____

____

____

Now, take another 5 minutes skim the appropriate chapter in this book for at least three articles that could help you develop this skill. For example, if you want to take more effective notes, turn to Chapter 5. List the names of your chosen articles here.

I intend to read . . .

____

____

____

____

____

3 critical thinking exercise
Taking the First Step

The purpose of this exercise is to give you an extended chance to discover and acknowledge your own strengths, as well as areas for improvement. For many students, this exercise is the most difficult one in the book. To make the exercise worthwhile, do it with courage.

Some people suggest that looking at areas for improvement means focusing on personal weaknesses. They view it as a negative approach that runs counter to positive thinking. Well, perhaps. Positive thinking is a great technique. So is telling the truth, especially when we see the whole picture—the negative aspects as well as the positive ones.

If you admit that you can't add or subtract and that's the truth, then you have taken a strong, positive First Step toward learning basic math. On the other hand, if you say that you are a terrible math student and that's not the truth, then you are programming yourself to accept unnecessary failure.

The point is to tell the truth. This exercise is similar to the Discovery Statements that appear in every chapter. The difference is that, in this case, for reasons of confidentiality, you won't write down your discoveries in the book.

Be brave. If you approach this exercise with courage, you are likely to disclose some things about yourself that you wouldn't want others to read. You might even write down some truths that could get you into trouble. Do this exercise on separate sheets of paper; then hide or destroy them. Protect your privacy.

To make this exercise work, follow these suggestions.

Be specific. It is not effective to write, "I can improve my communication skills." Of course you can. Instead, write down precisely what you can *do* to improve your communication skills—for example, "I can spend more time really listening while the other person is talking, instead of thinking about what I'm going to say next."

Look beyond the classroom. What goes on outside school often has the greatest impact on your ability to be an effective student. Consider your strengths and weaknesses that you may think have nothing to do with school.

Be courageous. This exercise is a waste of time if it is done half-heartedly. Be willing to take risks. You might open a door that reveals a part of yourself that you didn't want to admit was there. The power of this technique is that once you know what is there, you can do something about it.

Part 1

Time yourself, and for 10 minutes write as fast as you can, completing each of the following sentences at least 10 times with anything that comes to mind. If you get stuck, don't stop. Just write something—even if it seems crazy.

I never succeed when I . . .

I'm not very good at . . .

Something I'd like to change about myself is . . .

Part 2

When you have completed the first part of the exercise, review what you have written, crossing off things that don't make any sense. The sentences that remain suggest possible goals for becoming a master student.

Part 3

Here's the tough part. Time yourself, and for 10 minutes write as fast as you can, completing the following sentences with anything that comes to mind. As in Part 1, complete each sentence at least 10 times. Just keep writing, even if it sounds silly.

I always succeed when I . . .

I am very good at . . .

Something I like about myself is . . .

Part 4

Review what you have written, and circle the things that you can fully celebrate. This list is a good thing to keep for those times when you question your own value and worth.

Complete this exercise online.

4

critical thinking exercise

The Discovery Wheel

The Discovery Wheel is another opportunity to tell the truth about the kind of student you are and the kind of student you want to become.

This is not a test. There are no trick questions, and the answers will have meaning only for you.

Here are two suggestions to make this exercise more effective. First, think of it as the beginning of an opportunity to change. There is another Discovery Wheel at the end of this book. You will have a chance to measure your progress there, so be honest about where you are now. Second, lighten up. A little laughter can make self-evaluations a lot more effective.

Here's how the Discovery Wheel works. By the end of this exercise, you will have filled in a circle similar to the one on this page. The Discovery Wheel circle is a picture of how you see yourself as a student. The closer the shading comes to the outer edge of the circle, the higher the evaluation of a specific skill. In the example to the right, the student has rated her reading skills low and her note-taking skills high.

The terms *high* and *low* are not meant to reflect judgment. The Discovery Wheel is not a permanent picture of who you are. It is a picture of how you view your strengths and weaknesses as a student today. To begin this exercise, read the following statements and award yourself points for each one, using the point system described below. Then add up your point total for each section, and shade the Discovery Wheel on page 26 to the appropriate level.

5 points: This statement is always or almost always true of me.

4 points: This statement is often true of me.

3 points: This statement is true of me about half the time.

2 points: This statement is seldom true of me.

1 point: This statement is never or almost never true of me.

Complete this exercise online.

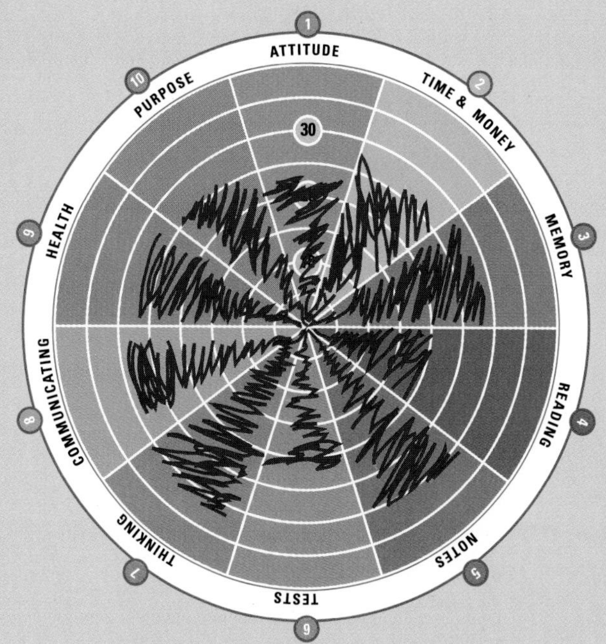

1. _____ I enjoy learning.

2. _____ I understand and apply the concept of multiple intelligences.

3. _____ I connect my courses to my purpose for being in school.

4. _____ I make a habit of assessing my personal strengths and areas for improvement.

5. _____ I am satisfied with how I am progressing toward achieving my goals.

6. _____ I use my knowledge of learning styles to support my success in school.

7. _____ I am willing to consider any idea that can help me succeed in school—even if I initially disagree with that idea.

8. _____ I regularly remind myself of the benefits I intend to get from my education.

_____ **Total score (1) Attitude**

1. _____ I set long-term goals and periodically review them.

2. _____ I set short-term goals to support my long-term goals.

3. _____ I write a plan for each day and each week.

4. _____ I assign priorities to what I choose to do each day.

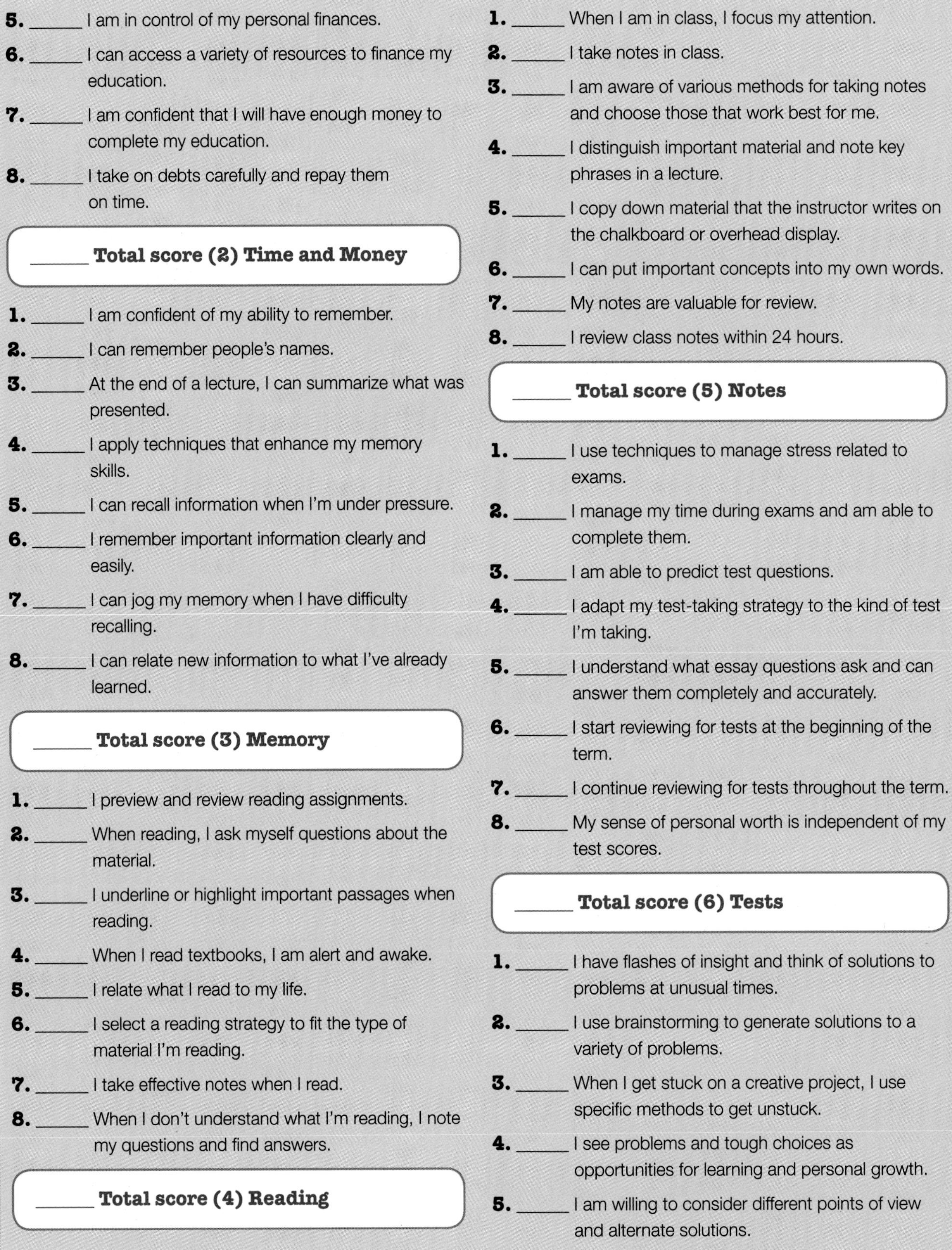

5. ______ I am in control of my personal finances.

6. ______ I can access a variety of resources to finance my education.

7. ______ I am confident that I will have enough money to complete my education.

8. ______ I take on debts carefully and repay them on time.

______ Total score (2) Time and Money

1. ______ I am confident of my ability to remember.

2. ______ I can remember people's names.

3. ______ At the end of a lecture, I can summarize what was presented.

4. ______ I apply techniques that enhance my memory skills.

5. ______ I can recall information when I'm under pressure.

6. ______ I remember important information clearly and easily.

7. ______ I can jog my memory when I have difficulty recalling.

8. ______ I can relate new information to what I've already learned.

______ Total score (3) Memory

1. ______ I preview and review reading assignments.

2. ______ When reading, I ask myself questions about the material.

3. ______ I underline or highlight important passages when reading.

4. ______ When I read textbooks, I am alert and awake.

5. ______ I relate what I read to my life.

6. ______ I select a reading strategy to fit the type of material I'm reading.

7. ______ I take effective notes when I read.

8. ______ When I don't understand what I'm reading, I note my questions and find answers.

______ Total score (4) Reading

1. ______ When I am in class, I focus my attention.

2. ______ I take notes in class.

3. ______ I am aware of various methods for taking notes and choose those that work best for me.

4. ______ I distinguish important material and note key phrases in a lecture.

5. ______ I copy down material that the instructor writes on the chalkboard or overhead display.

6. ______ I can put important concepts into my own words.

7. ______ My notes are valuable for review.

8. ______ I review class notes within 24 hours.

______ Total score (5) Notes

1. ______ I use techniques to manage stress related to exams.

2. ______ I manage my time during exams and am able to complete them.

3. ______ I am able to predict test questions.

4. ______ I adapt my test-taking strategy to the kind of test I'm taking.

5. ______ I understand what essay questions ask and can answer them completely and accurately.

6. ______ I start reviewing for tests at the beginning of the term.

7. ______ I continue reviewing for tests throughout the term.

8. ______ My sense of personal worth is independent of my test scores.

______ Total score (6) Tests

1. ______ I have flashes of insight and think of solutions to problems at unusual times.

2. ______ I use brainstorming to generate solutions to a variety of problems.

3. ______ When I get stuck on a creative project, I use specific methods to get unstuck.

4. ______ I see problems and tough choices as opportunities for learning and personal growth.

5. ______ I am willing to consider different points of view and alternate solutions.

6. ______ I can detect common errors in logic.

7. ______ I construct viewpoints by drawing on information and ideas from many sources.

8. ______ As I share my viewpoints with others, I am open to their feedback.

______ **Total score (7) Thinking**

1. ______ I am candid with others about who I am, what I feel, and what I want.

2. ______ Other people tell me that I am a good listener.

3. ______ I can communicate my upset feelings and anger without blaming others.

4. ______ I can make friends and create valuable relationships in a new setting.

5. ______ I am open to being with people I don't especially like in order to learn from them.

6. ______ I can effectively plan, research, and complete a large writing assignment.

7. ______ I approach conflict with other people as a problem to solve, not a contest to win.

8. ______ I speak confidently in class and make effective presentations.

______ **Total score (8) Communicating**

1. ______ I have enough energy to study and work—and still enjoy other areas of my life.

2. ______ If the situation calls for it, I have enough reserve energy to put in a long day.

3. ______ The way I eat supports my long-term health.

4. ______ The way I eat is independent of my feelings of self-worth.

5. ______ I exercise regularly to maintain a healthful weight.

6. ______ My emotional health supports my ability to learn.

7. ______ I notice changes in my physical condition and respond effectively.

8. ______ I am in control of any alcohol or other drugs I put into my body.

______ **Total score (9) Health**

1. ______ I see learning as a lifelong process.

2. ______ I relate school to what I plan to do for the rest of my life.

3. ______ I learn by making a contribution to the lives of other people.

4. ______ I have a written career plan and update it regularly.

5. ______ I am gaining skills to succeed in a diverse workplace.

6. ______ I take responsibility for the quality of my education—and my life.

7. ______ I live by a set of values that translates into daily actions.

8. ______ I am willing to accept challenges even when I'm not sure how to meet them.

______ **Total score (10) Purpose**

Filling in your Discovery Wheel

Using the total score from each category, shade in each section of the Discovery Wheel. Use different colors, if you want. For example, you could use green to denote areas you want to work on. When you have finished, complete the Journal Entry on the next page.

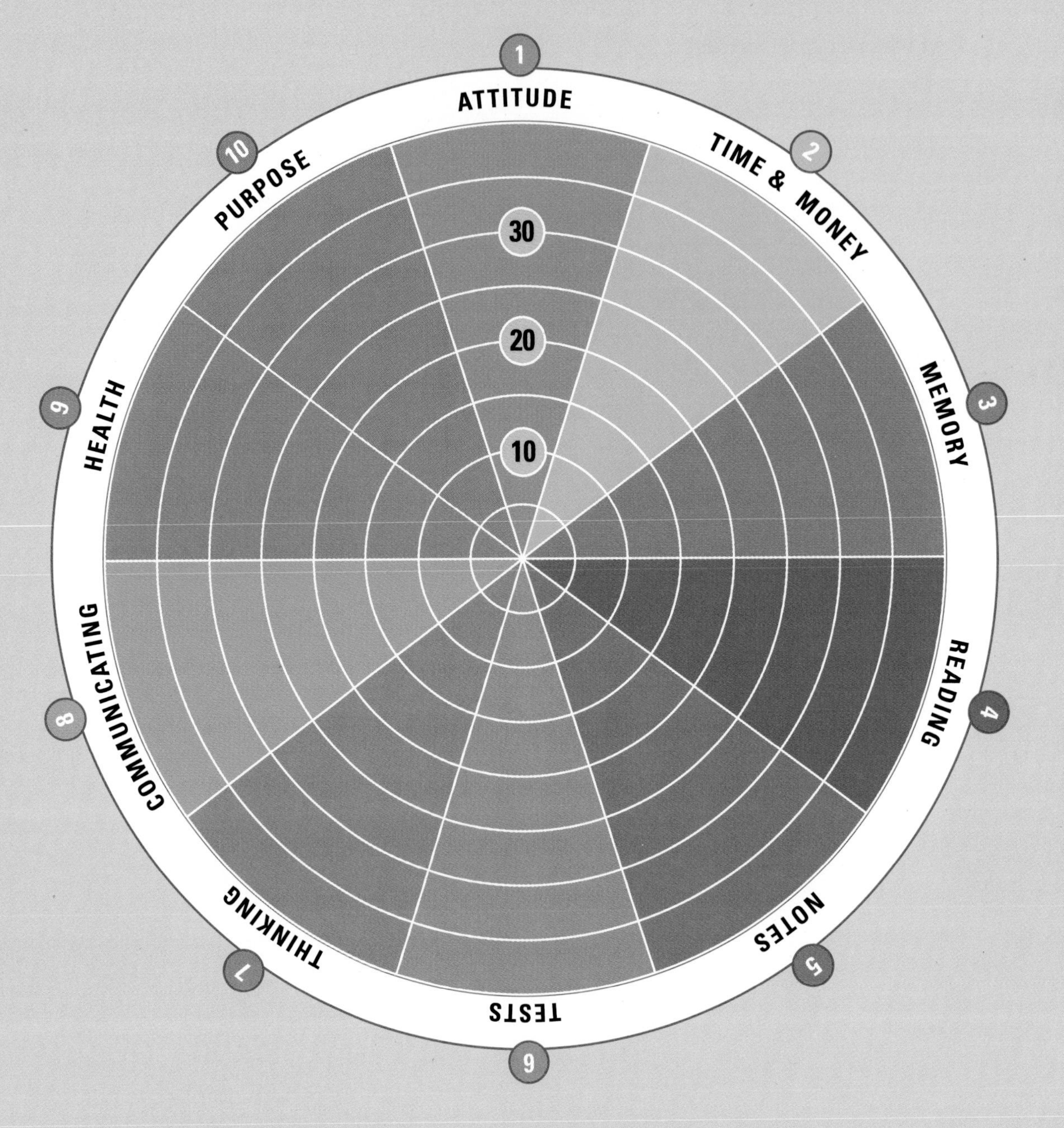

journal entry 5

Discovery/Intention Statement

Roll your Discovery Wheel

Now that you have completed your Discovery Wheel, it's time to get a sense of its weight, shape, and balance. Can you imagine running your hands around it? If you could lift it, would it feel light or heavy? How would it sound if it rolled down a hill? Would it roll very far? Would it wobble? Make your observations without judging the wheel as good or bad. Simply be with the picture you have created.

After you have spent a few minutes studying your Discovery Wheel, complete the following sentences in the spaces below them. Don't worry about what to write. Just put down whatever comes to mind. Remember, this is not a test.

This wheel is an accurate picture of my ability as a student because . . .

____

____

My self-evaluation surprises me because . . .

____

____

The two areas in which I am strongest are . . .

____

____

The areas in which I want to improve are . . .

____

____

I want to concentrate on improving these areas because . . .

____

____

Now, select one of your discoveries, and describe how you intend to benefit from it. Complete the statement below.

To gain some practical value from this discovery, I will . . .

____

____

mastering technology

SUPPLEMENT YOUR TEXT WITH COMPUTER RESOURCES

Today, your purchase of a textbook often gives you access to a suite of related resources, including companion Web sites that are regularly updated and other digital media. One way to get your money's worth from a text is to fully use these resources, even if they are not assigned.

- To begin, check out the College Success CourseMate for this concise edition of *Becoming a Master Student*. There you'll discover ways to take your involvement with this book to a deeper level. For example, access the Web site to do an online version of the Discovery Wheel exercise. Then look for videos, additional exercises, articles, PowerPoint slides, practice tests, and forms.
- Look for Web sites created by your instructors for other courses. Ask them for the URLs. Check your course syllabus for more details. When your course does have a Web site, explore its features in detail.
- Using keywords related to your course, search the Internet for related sites. Look for content that expands on topics presented in class.
- Find out whether your instructors offer "virtual office hours"—times when they are willing to answer questions via e-mail or instant messaging.
- Search for online homework help in specific subjects. Many schools and public libraries post such sites.
- Visit your school's Web site. Look for lists of campus organizations, extracurricular activities, and student services.

Image copyright olly, 2010. Used under license from Shutterstock.com

Motivation—"I'm just not in the mood"

IN LARGE PART, this chapter is about your motivation to succeed in school. There are at least two ways to think about motivation. One way is to use the terms *self-discipline*, *willpower*, and *motivation* to describe something missing in ourselves. We use these words to explain another person's success—or our own shortcomings: "If I were more motivated, I'd get more involved in school." "Of course she got an A. She has self-discipline." "If I had more willpower, I'd lose weight." It seems that certain people are born with lots of motivation, while others miss out on it.

A second approach to thinking about motivation is to stop assuming that it is mysterious, determined at birth, or hard to come by. Perhaps there's nothing missing in you. What we call motivation could be something that you already possess: the ability to do a task even when you don't feel like it. This is a habit that you can develop with practice. The following suggestions offer ways to do that.

Promise it. Motivation can come simply from being clear about your goals and acting on them. Say that you want to start a study group. You can commit yourself to inviting people and setting a time and place to meet. Promise your classmates that you'll do this, and ask them to hold you accountable. Self-discipline, willpower, motivation—none of these mysterious characteristics needs to get in your way. Just make a promise and keep your word.

Befriend your discomfort. Sometimes keeping your word means doing a task you'd rather put off. The mere thought of doing laundry, reading a chapter in a statistics book, or proofreading a term paper can lead to discomfort. In the face of such discomfort, you can procrastinate. Or you can use this barrier as a means to getting the job done.

Begin by investigating the discomfort. Notice the thoughts running through your head, and speak them out loud: "I'd rather walk on a bed of coals than do this." "This is the last thing I want to do right now."

Also observe what's happening with your body. For example, are you breathing faster or slower than usual? Is your breathing shallow or deep? Are your shoulders tight? Do you feel any tension in your stomach?

Once you're in contact with your mind and body, stay with the discomfort for a few minutes longer. Don't judge it as good or bad. Accepting the thoughts and body sensations robs them of power. They might still be there, but in time they can stop being a barrier for you.

Discomfort can be a gift—an opportunity to do valuable work on yourself. On the other side of discomfort lies mastery.

Change your mind—and your body. You can also get past discomfort by planting new thoughts in your mind or changing your physical stance. For example, instead of slumping in a chair, sit up straight or stand up. You can also get physically active by taking a short walk. Notice what happens to your discomfort.

Work with your thoughts. Replace "I can't stand this" with "I'll feel great when this is done" or "Doing this will help me get something I want."

Sweeten the task. Sometimes you can be held back by just one aspect of a task. You can stop procrastinating merely by changing that aspect. If distaste for your physical environment keeps you from studying, you can change that environment. Reading about social psychology might seem like a yawner when you're alone in a dark corner of the house. Moving to a cheery, well-lit library can sweeten the task.

Talk about how bad it is. One way to get past negative attitudes is to take them to an extreme. When faced with an unpleasant task, launch into a no-holds-barred gripe session. Pull out all the stops: "There's no way I can start my income taxes now. This is terrible beyond words—an absolute disaster. This is a catastrophe of global proportions!" Griping taken this far can restore perspective. It shows how self-talk can turn inconveniences into crises.

Turn up the pressure. Sometimes motivation is a luxury. Pretend that the due date for your project has been moved up one day, one week, or one month. Raising the stress level slightly can spur you into action. Then the issue of motivation seems beside the point, and meeting the due date moves to the forefront.

Turn down the pressure. The mere thought of starting a huge task can induce anxiety. To get past this feeling, turn down the pressure by taking "baby steps." Divide a large project into small tasks. In 30 minutes or less, you could preview a book, create a rough outline for a paper, or solve two or three math problems. Careful planning can help you discover many such steps to make a big job doable.

Ask for support. Other people can become your allies in overcoming procrastination. For example, form a support group and declare what you intend to accomplish before each meeting. Then ask members to hold you accountable. If you want to begin exercising regularly, ask another person to walk with you three times weekly. People in support groups ranging from Alcoholics Anonymous to Weight Watchers know the power of this strategy.

Adopt a model. One strategy for succeeding at any task is to hang around the masters. Find someone you consider successful, and spend time with her. Observe this person and use her as a model for your own behavior. You can "try on" this person's actions and attitudes. Look for tools that feel right for you. This person can become a mentor to you.

Compare the payoffs to the costs. All behaviors have payoffs and costs. Even unwanted behaviors such as cramming for exams or neglecting exercise have payoffs. Cramming might give you more time that's free of commitments. Neglecting exercise can give you more time to sleep.

One way to let go of such unwanted behaviors is first to celebrate them—even embrace them. We can openly acknowledge the payoffs.

Celebration can be especially powerful when you follow it up with the next step—determining the costs. For example, skipping a reading assignment can give you time to go to the movies. However, you might be unprepared for class and have twice as much to read the following week.

Maybe there is another way to get the payoff (going to the movies) without paying the cost (skipping the reading assignment). With some thoughtful weekly planning, you might choose to give up a few hours of television and end up with enough time to read the assignment *and* go to the movies.

Comparing the costs and benefits of any behavior can fuel our motivation. We can choose new behaviors because they align with what we want most.

Do it later. At times, it's effective to save a task for later. For example, writing a résumé can wait until you've taken the time to analyze your job skills and map out your career goals. Putting it off does not show a lack of motivation—it shows planning.

When you choose to do a task later, turn this decision into a promise. Estimate how long the task will take, and schedule a specific date and time for it on your calendar.

Heed the message. Sometimes lack of motivation carries a message that's worth heeding. For example, consider the student who majors in accounting but seizes every chance to be with children. His chronic reluctance to read accounting textbooks might not be a problem. Instead, it might reveal his desire to major in elementary education. His original career choice might have come from the belief that "real men don't teach kindergarten." In such cases, an apparent lack of motivation signals a deeper wisdom trying to get through. *

In 1482, Leonardo da Vinci wrote a letter to a wealthy baron, applying for work. Here is an excerpt from the letter: "I can contrive various and endless means of offense and defense. . . . I have all sorts of extremely light and strong bridges adapted to be most easily carried. . . . I have methods for destroying every turret or fortress. . . . I will make covered chariots, safe and unassailable. . . . In case of need I will make big guns, mortars, and light ordnance of fine and useful forms out of the common type." And then he added, almost as an afterthought, "In times of peace I believe I can give perfect satisfaction and to the equal of any other in architecture . . . can carry out sculpture . . . and also I can do in painting whatever may be done."

The *Mona Lisa*, for example.

The Master Student

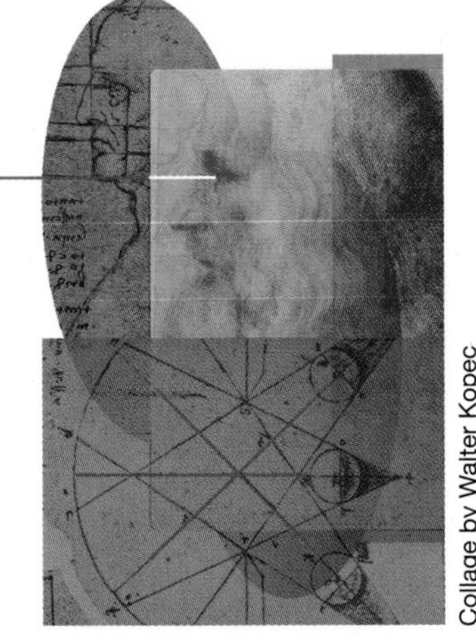

Collage by Walter Kopec

THIS BOOK is about something that cannot be taught. It's about becoming a master student.

Mastery means attaining a level of skill that goes beyond technique. For a master, methods and procedures are automatic responses to the needs of the task. Work is effortless; struggle evaporates. The master carpenter is so familiar with her tools that they are part of her. Because these masters don't have to think about the details of the process, they bring more of themselves to their work.

Mastery can lead to flashy results—an incredible painting, for example, or a gem of a short story. Often the result of mastery is a sense of profound satisfaction, well-being, and timelessness. Work seems self-propelled. The master is in control by being out of control. He lets go and allows the creative process to take over. That's why after a spectacular performance by an athlete or performer, observers often say, "He played full out and made it look like he wasn't even trying."

Likewise, the master student is one who plays full out but makes learning look easy. She works hard without seeming to make any effort. She's relaxed *and* alert, disciplined *and* spontaneous, focused *and* fun-loving.

You might say that those statements don't make sense. Mastery, in fact, doesn't make sense. It cannot be captured with words. It defies analysis. Mastery cannot be taught. It can only be learned and experienced.

Look around and you'll begin to see the endless diversity of master students. These people are old and young, male and female. They exist in every period of history. And they come from every culture, race, and ethnic group.

Also remember to look to yourself. No one can teach us to be master students; we already are master students. We are natural learners by design. As students, we can rediscover that every day.

In each chapter of this text there is an example of a person who embodies one or more qualities of a master student. As you read these Master Student Profiles, ask questions based on the modes of learning explained in this chapter: Why is this person considered a master student? What attitudes or behaviors helped to create her mastery? How can I develop those qualities? What if I could use his example to create positive new results in my own life?

Also reflect on other master students you've read about or know personally. The master student is not a vague or remote ideal. Rather, master students move freely among us.

In fact, there's one living inside your skin. *

Claim your multiple intelligences

Center: © Tanya Constantine/Getty, *clockwise from bottom left:* © Vladimir Godnik/Getty, © Scott T. Baxter/Getty, © George Doyle/Getty, © Meg Takamura, © Stockbyte/Getty, © Gregor Schuster/Getty, © Tim Laman/Getty, © Doug Menuez/Getty, collage by Walter Kopec

PEOPLE OFTEN THINK that being smart means the same thing as having a high IQ, and that having a high IQ automatically leads to success. However, psychologists are finding that IQ scores do not always foretell which students will do well in academic settings—or after they graduate.[1]

Howard Gardner of Harvard University believes that no single measure of intelligence can tell us how smart we are. Instead, Gardner defines intelligence in a flexible way as "the ability to solve problems, or to create products, that are valued within one or more cultural settings." He also identifies several types of intelligence.[2]

People using **verbal/linguistic intelligence** are adept at language skills and learn best by speaking, writing, reading, and listening. They are likely to enjoy activities such as telling stories and doing crossword puzzles.

People who use **mathematical/logical intelligence** are good with numbers, logic, problem solving, patterns, relationships, and categories. They are generally precise and methodical, and are likely to enjoy science.

When people learn by creating images and by placing objects in a space, they display **visual/spatial intelligence.** They think in pictures and understand best by seeing the subject. They enjoy charts, graphs, maps, mazes, tables, illustrations, art, models, puzzles, and costumes.

People using **bodily/kinesthetic intelligence** prefer physical activity. They enjoy activities such as building things, woodworking, dancing, skiing, sewing, and crafts. They generally are coordinated and athletic, and they would rather participate in games than just watch.

Students using **musical/rhythmic intelligence** enjoy expression through songs, rhythms, and musical instruments. They are responsive to various kinds of sounds, remember melodies easily; and might enjoy drumming, humming, and whistling.

People using **intrapersonal intelligence** are exceptionally aware of their own feelings and values. They are generally reserved, self-motivated, and intuitive.

Outgoing people show evidence of **interpersonal intelligence.** They do well with cooperative learning and are sensitive to the feelings, intentions, and motivations of others. They often make good leaders.

People using **naturalist intelligence** love the outdoors and recognize details in plants, animals, rocks, clouds, and other natural formations. These people excel in observing fine distinctions among similar items.

Each of us has all of these intelligences to some degree. And each of us can learn to enhance them. Experiment with learning in ways that draw on a variety of intelligences—including those that might be less familiar. When we acknowledge all of our intelligences, we can constantly explore new ways of being smart. *

5 critical thinking exercise
Develop your multiple intelligences

Gardner's theory of multiple intelligences complements the discussion of different learning styles found later in this chapter. The main point is that there are many ways to gain knowledge and acquire new behaviors. You can use Gardner's concepts to explore a range of options for achieving success in school, work, and relationships.

The chart on the next pages summarizes the content of "Claim your multiple intelligences" and suggests ways to apply the main ideas. Instead of merely glancing through this chart, get active. Place a check mark next to any of the "Possible characteristics" that describe you. Also check off the "Possible learning strategies" that you intend to use. Finally, underline or highlight any of the "Possible careers" that spark your interest.

Remember that the chart is *not* an exhaustive list or a formal inventory. Take what you find merely as points of departure. You can invent strategies of your own to cultivate different intelligences.

Type of intelligence	Possible characteristics	Possible learning strategies	Possible careers
Verbal/linguistic	❑ You enjoy writing letters, stories, and papers. ❑ You prefer to write directions rather than draw maps. ❑ You take excellent notes from textbooks and lectures. ❑ You enjoy reading, telling stories, and listening to them.	❑ Highlight, underline, and write notes in your textbooks. ❑ Recite new ideas in your own words. ❑ Rewrite and edit your class notes. ❑ Talk to other people often about what you're studying.	Librarian, lawyer, editor, journalist, English teacher, radio or television announcer
Mathematical/logical	❑ You enjoy solving puzzles. ❑ You prefer math or science class over English class. ❑ You want to know how and why things work. ❑ You make careful, step-by-step plans.	❑ Analyze tasks so you can order them in a sequence of steps. ❑ Group concepts into categories, and look for underlying patterns. ❑ Convert text into tables, charts, and graphs. ❑ Look for ways to quantify ideas—to express them in numerical terms.	Accountant, auditor, tax preparer, mathematician, computer programmer, actuary, economist, math or science teacher
Visual/spatial	❑ You draw pictures to give an example or clarify an explanation. ❑ You understand maps and illustrations more readily than text. ❑ You assemble things from illustrated instructions. ❑ You especially enjoy books that have a lot of illustrations.	❑ When taking notes, create concept maps, mind maps, and other visuals (see Chapter 5: Notes). ❑ Code your notes by using different colors to highlight main topics, major points, and key details. ❑ When your attention wanders, focus it by sketching or drawing. ❑ Before you try a new task, visualize yourself doing it well.	Architect, commercial artist, fine artist, graphic designer, photographer, interior decorator, engineer, cartographer
Bodily/kinesthetic	❑ You enjoy physical exercise. ❑ You tend not to sit still for long periods of time. ❑ You enjoy working with your hands. ❑ You use a lot of gestures when talking.	❑ Be active in ways that support concentration; for example, pace as you recite, read while standing up, and create flash cards. ❑ Carry materials with you, and practice studying in several different locations. ❑ Create hands-on activities related to key concepts; for example, create a game based on course content. ❑ Notice the sensations involved with learning something well.	Physical education teacher, athlete, athletic coach, physical therapist, chiropractor, massage therapist, yoga teacher, dancer, choreographer, actor

Type of intelligence	Possible characteristics	Possible learning strategies	Possible careers
Musical/rhythmic	❑ You often sing in the car or shower. ❑ You easily tap your foot to the beat of a song. ❑ You play a musical instrument. ❑ You feel most engaged and productive when music is playing.	❑ During a study break, play music or dance to restore energy. ❑ Put on background music that enhances your concentration while studying. ❑ Relate key concepts to songs you know. ❑ Write your own songs based on course content.	Professional musician, music teacher, music therapist, choral director, musical instrument sales representative, musical instrument maker, piano tuner
Intrapersonal	❑ You enjoy writing in a journal and being alone with your thoughts. ❑ You think a lot about what you want in the future. ❑ You prefer to work on individual projects over group projects. ❑ You take time to think things through before talking or taking action.	❑ Connect course content to your personal values and goals. ❑ Study a topic alone before attending a study group. ❑ Connect readings and lectures to a strong feeling or significant past experience. ❑ Keep a journal that relates your course work to events in your daily life.	Minister, priest, rabbi, professor of philosophy or religion, counseling psychologist, creator of a home-based or small business
Interpersonal	❑ You enjoy group work over working alone. ❑ You have plenty of friends and regularly spend time with them. ❑ You prefer talking and listening over reading or writing. ❑ You thrive in positions of leadership.	❑ Form and conduct study groups early in the term. ❑ Create flash cards, and use them to quiz study partners. ❑ Volunteer to give a speech or lead group presentations on course topics. ❑ Teach the topic you're studying to someone else.	Manager, school administrator, salesperson, teacher, counseling psychologist, arbitrator, police officer, nurse, travel agent, public relations specialist, creator of a midsize to large business
Naturalist	❑ As a child, you enjoyed collecting insects, leaves, or other natural objects. ❑ You enjoy being outdoors. ❑ You find that important insights occur during times you spend in nature. ❑ You read books and magazines on nature-related topics.	❑ During study breaks, take walks outside. ❑ Post pictures of outdoor scenes where you study, and play recordings of outdoor sounds while you read. ❑ Invite classmates to discuss course work while taking a hike or going on a camping trip. ❑ Focus on careers that hold the potential for working outdoors.	Environmental activist, park ranger, recreation supervisor, historian, museum curator, biologist, criminologist, mechanic, woodworker, construction worker, construction contractor or estimator

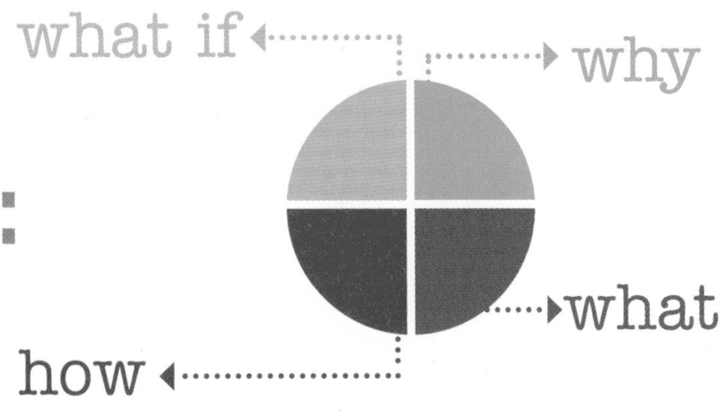

Learning styles: Discovering how you learn

RIGHT NOW, you are investing substantial amounts of time, money, and energy in your education. What you get in return for this investment depends on how well you understand the process of learning and use it to your advantage.

If you don't understand the learning process, you might feel bored or confused in class. You might have no idea how to respond after getting a low grade. Over time, frustration can mount to the point where you question the value of being in school.

Some students answer that question by dropping out of school. These students lose a chance to create the life they want, and society loses the contributions of educated workers.

You can prevent that outcome. Gain strategies for going beyond boredom and confusion. Discover new options for achieving goals, solving problems, listening more fully, speaking more persuasively, and resolving conflicts between people. Start by understanding the different ways that people create meaning from their experience and change their behavior. In other words, learn about *how* we learn.

We learn by perceiving and processing

When we learn well, says psychologist David Kolb, two things happen.[3] First, we *perceive*—that is, we notice events and "take in" new experiences. Second, we *process*, or "deal with," experiences in a way that helps us make sense of them.

Some people especially enjoy perceiving through *concrete experience*. They like to absorb information through their five senses. They learn by getting directly involved in new experiences. When solving problems, they rely on intuition as much as intellect. These people typically function well in unstructured classes that allow them to take initiative.

Other people favor perceiving by *abstract conceptualization*. They take in information best when they can think about it as a subject separate from themselves. They analyze, intellectualize, and create theories. Often these people take a scientific approach to problem solving and excel in traditional classrooms.

People also process experiences differently. Some people favor processing information by *reflective observation*. They prefer to stand back, watch what is going on, and think about it. They consider several points of view as they attempt to make sense of things and generate many ideas about how something happens. They value patience, good judgment, and a thorough approach to learning.

Other people like to process experience by *active experimentation*. They prefer to jump in and start doing things immediately. These people do not mind taking risks as they attempt to make sense of things; this helps them learn. They are results-oriented and look for practical ways to apply what they have learned.

Perceiving and processing—an example

Suppose that you get a new cell phone. It has more features than any phone you've used before. You have many options for learning how to use it. For example, you could do any of the following:

- Just get your hands on the phone right away, press some buttons, and see if you can dial a number or send a text message.
- Read the instruction manual and view help screens on the phone before you try to make a call.
- Recall experiences you've had with phones in the past and what you've learned by watching other people use their cell phones.
- Ask a friend who owns the same type of phone to coach you as you experiment with making calls and sending messages.

These actions illustrate the different ways of perceiving and processing:

- Getting your hands on the phone right away and seeing if you can make it work is an example of learning through concrete experience.

- Reading the manual and help screens before you use the phone is an example of learning through abstract conceptualization.
- Recalling what you've experienced in the past is an example of learning through reflective observation.
- Asking a friend to coach you through a "hands-on" activity with the phone is an example of learning through active experimentation.

Four modes of learning and four questions

Your learning style is the unique way that in which you blend the possible ways of perceiving and processing experience. Learning styles can be described in many ways. To keep things simple, just think in terms of four *modes* of learning.

Mode 1 learners are concrete and reflective. They seek a purpose for new information and a personal connection with the content. They want to know that a course matters, and how it challenges or fits in with what they already know. These learners embrace new ideas that relate directly to their current interests and career plans. In summary, Mode 1 learners ask, *Why* learn this?

Mode 2 learners are abstract and reflective. They crave information. When learning something, they want to know the main facts, ideas, and procedures. They seek a theory to explain events and are interested in what experts have to say. Often these learners like ideas that are presented in a logical, organized way. They break a subject down into its key elements or steps and master each one in a systematic way. Mode 2 learners ask, *What* is the content?

Mode 3 learners are abstract and active. They hunger for an opportunity to try out what they're studying. They want to take theories and test them by putting them into practice. These learners thrive when they have well-defined tasks, guided practice, and frequent feedback. Mode 3 learners ask, *How* does this work?

Mode 4 learners are concrete and active. They get excited about going beyond classroom assignments. They apply what they're learning in various situations and use theories to solve real problems. Mode 4 learners ask, *What if* I tried this in a different setting?

The four modes—an example

Becoming a Master Student is specifically designed to move you through all four modes of learning.

At the beginning of each chapter, you complete a Journal Entry designed to connect the chapter content to your current life experience. The aim is to help you see the chapter's possible benefits and discover a purpose for reading further. You answer the Mode 1 question—*Why* learn this?

Next, you read articles that are filled with ideas and suggestions for succeeding in school and the workplace. All these readings provide answers to the Mode 2 question—*What* is the content?

You also use exercises to practice new skills with and get feedback from your instructor and other students. These exercises are answers to the Mode 3 question—*How* does this work?

Finally, at the end of each chapter, a "Put It to Work" article and " Take a Skills Snapshot" exercise helps you apply the chapter content to different situations and choose your next step toward mastery. You discover answers to the Mode 4 question—*What if* I tried this in a different setting?

Also notice the Master Student Map at the beginning of each chapter. It presents the chapter content as answers to these above four questions. For example, the Master Student Map for this chapter (page 20) suggests *why* this chapter matters: "Success starts with telling the truth about what *is* working—and what *isn't*—in our lives right now." There's a list of *what* topics are included and suggestions for *how* you can use this chapter. Finally, you're encouraged to ask, "*What if* I could create new outcomes in my life by accepting the way I am right now?"

Becoming a flexible learner

Kolb believes that effective learners are flexible. They can learn using all four modes. They consistently ask *Why? What? How?* and *What if?*—and use a full range of activities to find the answers.

Becoming a flexible learner promotes your success in school and in the workplace. By developing all four modes of learning, you can excel in many types of courses. You can learn from instructors with many different styles of teaching. You can expand your options for declaring a major and choosing a career. You can experiment with a variety of strategies and create new options for learning *anything*.

Above all, you can recover your natural gift for learning. Rediscover a world where the boundaries between learning and fun, between work and play, all disappear. While immersing yourself in new experiences, blend the sophistication of an adult with the wonder of a child. This is one path that you can travel on for the rest of your life.

The following elements of this chapter are designed to help you take the next steps toward becoming a flexible learner:

- To discover how you currently prefer to learn, take the Learning Style Inventory that follows.

- Read the article "Using your learning style profile to succeed" to learn ways to expand on your preferences.
- For additional perspectives on learning styles, see the articles "Claim your multiple intelligences" and "Learning by seeing, hearing, and moving—The VAK system." *

Directions for completing the Learning Style Inventory

To help you become more aware of learning styles, Kolb developed the Learning Style Inventory (LSI). This inventory is included on the next several pages. Responding to the items in the LSI can help you discover a lot about ways you learn.

The LSI is not a test. There are no right or wrong answers. Your goal is simply to develop a profile of your current learning style. So, take the LSI quickly. You might find it useful to recall a recent time when you learned something new at school, at home, or at work. However, do not agonize over your responses.

Note that the LSI consists of twelve sentences, each with four different endings. You will read each sentence, and then write a "4" next to the ending that best describes the way you currently learn. Then you will continue ranking the other endings with a "3," "2," or "1," representing the ending that least describes you. You must rank each ending. *Do not leave any endings blank.* Use each number only once for each question.

Following are more specific directions:

1. Read the instructions at the top of page LSI-1. When you understand example A, you are ready to begin.
2. Before you write on page LSI-1, remove the sheet of paper following page LSI-2.
3. While writing on page LSI-1, press firmly so that your answers will show up on page LSI-3.
4. After you complete the twelve items on page LSI-1, go to page LSI-3. *

Find more information and examples related to learning styles online.

journal entry

Discovery Statement

Prepare for the Learning Styles Inventory

As a warm-up for the LSI and articles that follow, spend a minute or two thinking about times in the past when you felt successful at learning. Underline or highlight any of the following statements that describe those situations:

I was in a highly structured setting, with a lot of directions about what to do and feedback on how well I did at each step.

I was free to learn at my own pace and in my own way.

I learned as part of a small group.

I learned mainly by working alone in a quiet place.

I learned in a place where there was a lot of activity going on.

I learned by forming pictures in my mind.

I learned by *doing* something—moving around, touching something, or trying out a process for myself.

I learned by talking to myself or explaining ideas to other people.

I got the "big picture" before I tried to understand the details.

I listened to a lecture and then thought about it after class.

I read a book or article and then thought about it afterward.

I used a variety of media—such as a videos, films, audio recordings, or computers—to assist my learning.

I went beyond taking notes and wrote in a personal journal.

I was considering where to attend school and knew I had to actually set foot on each campus before choosing.

I was shopping for a car and paid more attention to how I felt about test driving each one than to the sticker prices or mileage estimates.

I was thinking about going to a movie and carefully read the reviews before choosing one.

Reviewing the above list, do you see any patterns in the way you prefer to learn? If you do see any patterns, briefly describe them here.

____

____

____

Learning Style Inventory

Complete items 1–12 below. Use the following example as a guide:

A. When I learn: __2__ I am happy. __3__ I am fast. __4__ I am logical. __1__ I am careful.

Remember: **4** = Most like you **3** = Second most like you **2** = Third most like you **1** = Least like you

Before completing the items, remove the sheet of paper following this page. While writing, press firmly.

1. When I learn:	_____ I like to deal with my feelings.	_____ I like to think about ideas.	_____ I like to be doing things.	_____ I like to watch and listen.
2. I learn best when:	_____ I listen and watch carefully.	_____ I rely on logical thinking.	_____ I trust my hunches and feelings.	_____ I work hard to get things done.
3. When I am learning:	_____ I tend to reason things out.	_____ I am responsible about things.	_____ I am quiet and reserved.	_____ I have strong feelings and reactions.
4. I learn by:	_____ feeling.	_____ doing.	_____ watching.	_____ thinking.
5. When I learn:	_____ I am open to new experiences.	_____ I look at all sides of issues.	_____ I like to analyze things, breaking them down into their parts.	_____ I like to try things out.
6. When I am learning:	_____ I am an observing person.	_____ I am an active person.	_____ I am an intuitive person	_____ I am a logical person.
7. I learn best from:	_____ observation.	_____ personal relationships.	_____ rational theories.	_____ a chance to try out and practice.
8. When I learn:	_____ I like to see results from my work.	_____ I like ideas and theories.	_____ I take my time before acting.	_____ I feel personally involved in things.
9. I learn best when:	_____ I rely on my observations.	_____ I rely on my feelings.	_____ I can try things out for myself.	_____ I rely on my ideas.
10. When I am learning:	_____ I am a reserved person.	_____ I am an accepting person.	_____ I am a responsible person.	_____ I am a rational person.
11. When I learn:	_____ I get involved.	_____ I like to observe.	_____ I evaluate things.	_____ I like to be active.
12. I learn best when:	_____ I analyze ideas.	_____ I am receptive and open-minded.	_____ I am careful.	_____ I am practical.

Take a snapshot of your learning styles

This page is intended to be completed as a culminating exercise. Before you work on this exercise, complete the Learning Styles Inventory and read the following articles:

Claim your multiple intelligences, page 31

Learning styles: Discovering how you learn, page 34

Using your learning style profile to succeed, page 37

Learning by seeing, hearing, and moving—the VAK system, page 39

Any inventory of your learning styles is just a snapshot that gives a picture of who you are today. Your answers are not right or wrong. Your score does not dictate who you can become in the future. The key questions are simply "How do I currently learn?" and "How can I become a more successful learner?"

Take a few minutes right now to complete the following sentences describing your latest insights into the way you learn. When you finish, plan to follow up on those insights.

If someone asked me, "What do you mean by learning styles, and can you give me an example?" I'd say . . .

I would describe my current learning style(s) as . . .

If someone asked me to define intelligence, I'd say . . .

When learning well, I tend to use the following senses . . .

I apply my knowledge of learning styles by using certain strategies, such as . . .

When I study or work with people whose learning styles differ from mine, I will respond by . . .

To explore new learning styles, I will . . .

Remove this sheet before completing the Learning Style Inventory.

This page is inserted to ensure that the other writing you do in this book doesn't show through on page LSI-3.

Remove this sheet before completing the Learning Style Inventory.

This page is inserted to ensure that the other writing you do in this book doesn't show through on page LSI-3.

Scoring your Inventory

Now that you have taken the Learning Style Inventory, it's time to fill out the Learning Style Graph (page LSI-5) and interpret your results. To do this, please follow the next five steps.

1 First, add up all of the numbers you gave to the items marked with brown **F** letters. Then write down that total to the right in the blank next to "**Brown** F." Next, add up all of the numbers for "**Teal** W," "**Purple** T," and "**Orange** D," and also write down those totals in the blanks to the right.

2 Add the four totals to arrive at a GRAND TOTAL, and write down that figure in the blank to the right. (Note: The grand total should equal 120. If you have a different amount, go back and re-add the colored letters; it was probably just an addition error.) Now remove this page and continue with Step 3 on page LSI-5.

scorecard

Brown F	total ______
Teal W	total ______
Purple T	total ______
Orange D	total ______
GRAND TOTAL	______

F	T	D	W
W	T	F	D
T	D	W	F
F	D	W	T
F	W	T	D
W	D	F	T
W	F	T	D
D	T	W	F
W	F	D	T
W	F	D	T
F	W	T	D
T	F	W	D

Remove this page after you have
completed Steps 1 and 2 on page LSI-3.
Then continue with Step 3 on page LSI-5.

Learning Style Graph

3 Remove the sheet of paper that follows this page. Then transfer your totals from Step 1 on page LSI-3 to the lines on the Learning Style Graph below. On the brown (F) line, find the number that corresponds to your "**Brown** F" total from page LSI-3. Then write an X on this number. Do the same for your "**Teal** W," "**Purple** T," and "**Orange** D" totals. The graph on this page is yours to keep and to refer to and the graph on page LSI-7 is for you to turn into your professor if he or she requires it.

4 Now, pressing firmly, draw four straight lines to connect the four X's, and shade in the area to form a kite. (For an example, see the illustration to the right.) This is your learning style profile. Each X that you placed on these lines indicates your preference for a different aspect of learning.

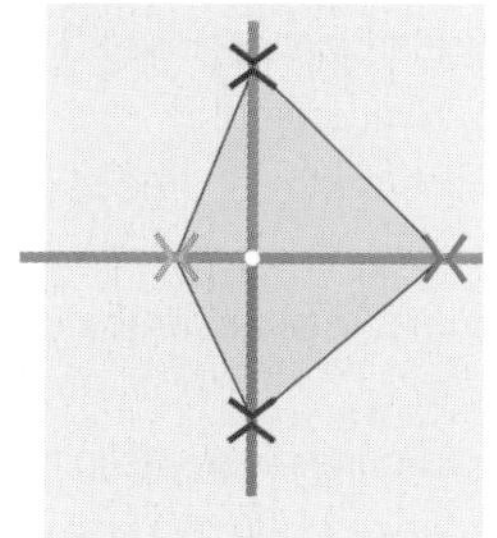

Concrete experience ("feeling"). The number where you put your X on this line indicates your preference for learning things that have personal meaning and have connections to experiences in your life. The higher your score on this line, the more you like to learn things that you feel are important and relevant to yourself.

Reflective observation ("watching"). Your number on this line indicates how important it is for you to reflect on the things you are learning. If your score is high on this line, you probably find it important to watch others as they learn about an assignment and then report on it to the class. You probably like to plan things out and take the time to make sure that you fully understand a topic.

Abstract conceptualization ("thinking"). Your number on this line indicates your preference for learning ideas, facts, and figures. If your score is high on this line, you probably like to absorb many concepts and gather lots of information on a new topic.

Active experimentation ("doing"). Your number on this line indicates your preference for applying ideas, using trial and error, and practicing what you learn. If your score is high on this line, you probably enjoy hands-on activities that allow you to test out ideas to see what works.

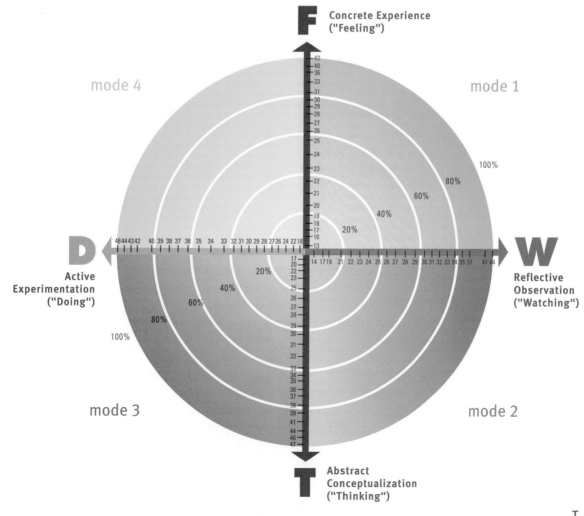

F
Concrete Experience
("Feeling")

mode 4

mode 1

D
Active
Experimentation
("Doing")

W
Reflective
Observation
("Watching")

20% 40% 60% 80% 100%

mode 3

mode 2

T
Abstract
Conceptualization
("Thinking")

Learning styles across the curriculum

You can get another perspective on learning styles by thinking about ways to succeed in the various subjects that you study. For example, a math course will draw on different ways of perceiving and processing information than a course in African-American literature or modern dance. When you feel stuck in a particular subject, see if you can get unstuck by applying a strategy based on your knowledge of learning styles. The following chart offers some examples. Start with them, and create more on your own.

Subject Area	Possible Strategies for Mastery
Humanities: English, literature, public speaking, history, religion, philosophy, fine arts	• Deepen your reading skills by previewing and reviewing each assignment (see Chapter 5: "Reading"). • Keep a dictionary handy and create an updated list of new words and their definitions. • Experiment with several different formats for taking notes (see Chapter 6: "Notes"). • Keep a personal journal to practice writing and make connections between the authors and ideas that you're studying. • Take part in class discussions and welcome chances to speak in front of groups.
Math and natural sciences: algebra, geometry, calculus, chemistry, biology, physics	• Before registering for a course, make sure that you are adequately prepared through prior course work. • In your notes, highlight basic principles—definitions, assumptions, axioms. • Learn concepts in the sequence presented by your instructor. • If you feel confused, ask a question immediately. • Attend all classes, practice solving problems every day, and check your work carefully. • Translate word problems into images or symbols; translate images and symbols into words. • Balance abstract ideas with concrete experiences, including laboratory sessions and study groups. • Take math courses back to back so you can apply what you learn in one level of a math course immediately to the next level.
Social sciences: sociology, psychology, economics, political science, anthropology, geography	• Pay special attention to theories—key terms and statements that are used to explain relationships between observations and predict events. • Expect complex and contradictory theories, and ask your instructor about ways to resolve disagreements among experts in the field. • Ask your instructor to explain the scientific method and how it is used to arrive at theories in each social science. • Ask about the current state of evidence for each theory. • Ask for examples of a theory and look for them in your daily life.
Foreign languages: learning to speak, read, and write any language that is new to you	• Pay special attention to the "rules"—principles of grammar, noun forms, and verb tense. For each principle, list correct and incorrect examples. • Spend some time reading, writing, or speaking the language every day. • Welcome the opportunity to practice speaking in class, where you can get immediate feedback. • Start or join a study group in each of your language classes. • Spend time with people who are already skilled in speaking the language. • Travel to a country where the language is widely spoken. • Similar to math courses, take your language courses back to back to ensure fluency.

Remove this sheet before completing the Learning Style Graph

This page is inserted to ensure that the other writing you do in this book doesn't show through on page LSI-7.

Remove this sheet before completing the Learning Style Graph

This page is inserted to ensure that the other writing you do in this book doesn't show through on page LSI-7.

Returning to the big picture about learning styles

This chapter introduces many ideas about how people learn—four modes, multiple intelligences, and the VAK system. That's a lot of information! And these are just a few of the available theories. You may have heard about inventories other than the Learning Style Inventory, such as the Myers-Briggs Type Indicator® (MBTI®) Instrument.* Do an Internet search on *learning styles,* and you'll find many more.

To prevent confusion, remember that there is one big idea behind these theories about learning styles. They all promote *metacognition* (pronounced "metta-cog-NI-shun"). *Meta* means "beyond" or "above." *Cognition* refers to everything that goes on inside your brain—perceiving, thinking, and feeling. So, metacognition refers to your ability to view your attitudes and behaviors from beyond—that is, understand more fully the way you learn. From that perspective, you can choose to think and act in new ways. *Metacognition is one of the main benefits of higher education.*

In addition, theories about learning styles share the following insights:

- People differ in important ways.
- We can see differences as strengths—not deficits.
- Relationships improve when we take differences into account.
- Learning is continuous—it is a *process,* as well as a series of outcomes.
- We *create* knowledge rather than simply absorbing it.
- We have our own preferences for learning.
- We can often succeed by matching our activities with our preferences.
- Our preferences can expand as we experiment with new learning strategies.
- The deepest learning takes place when we embrace a variety of styles and strategies.

Remember that teachers in your life will come and go. Some will be more skilled than others. None of them will be perfect. With a working knowledge of learning styles, you can view any course as one step along a path to learning what you want, using the ways that *you* choose to learn. Along this path toward mastery, you become your own best teacher.

*MBTI and Myer-Briggs Type Indicator are registered trademarks of Consulting Psychologists Press, Inc.

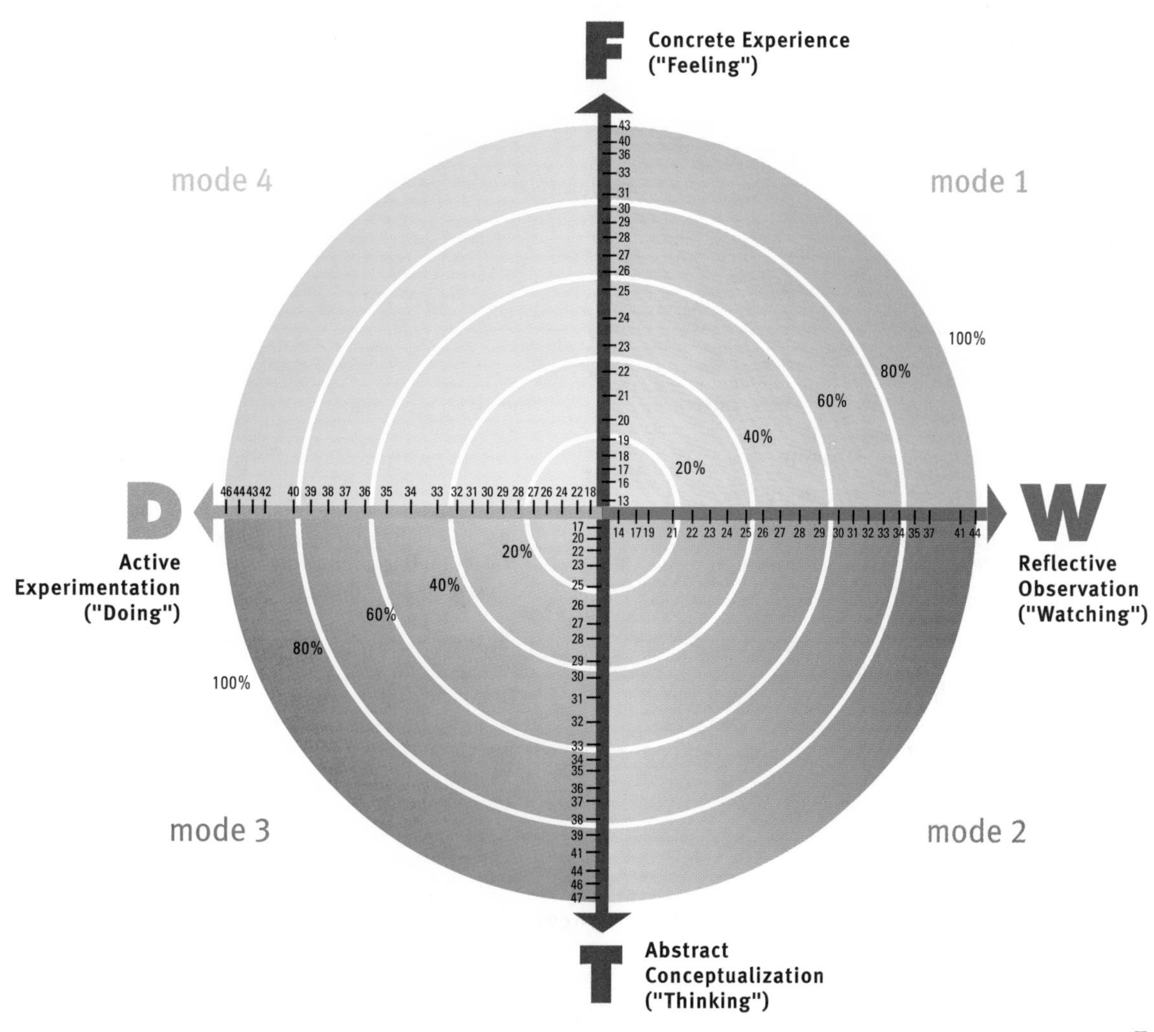

Balancing your preferences

The chart below identifies some of the natural talents as well as challenges for people who have a strong preference for any one mode of learning. For example, if most of your kite is in Mode 2 of the Learning Style Graph, then look at the lower right-hand corner of the following chart to see if this is an accurate description of yourself.

After reviewing the description of your preferred learning mode, read all of the sections for the other modes that start with the words "People with other preferred modes." These sections explain what actions you can take to become a more balanced learner.

Concrete Experience

Active Experimentation

Reflective Observation

Abstract Conceptualization

mode 4

Strengths:
- Getting things done
- Leadership
- Risk taking

Too much of this mode can lead to:
- Trivial improvements
- Meaningless activity

Too little of this mode can lead to:
- Work not completed on time
- Impractical plans
- Lack of motivation to achieve goals

People with other preferred modes can develop Mode 4 by:
- Making a commitment to objectives
- Seeking new opportunities
- Influencing and leading others
- Being personally involved
- Dealing with people

mode 1

Strengths:
- Imaginative ability
- Understanding people
- Recognizing problems
- Brainstorming

Too much of this mode can lead to:
- Feeling paralyzed by alternatives
- Inability to make decisions

Too little of this mode can lead to:
- Lack of ideas
- Not recognizing problems and opportunities

People with other preferred modes can develop Mode 1 by:
- Being aware of other people's feelings
- Being sensitive to values
- Listening with an open mind
- Gathering information
- Imagining the implications of ambiguous situations

mode 3

Strengths:
- Problem solving
- Decision making
- Deductive reasoning
- Defining problems

Too much of this mode can lead to:
- Solving the wrong problem
- Hasty decision making

Too little of this mode can lead to:
- Lack of focus
- Reluctance to consider alternatives
- Scattered thoughts

People with other preferred modes can develop Mode 3 by:
- Creating new ways of thinking and doing
- Experimenting with fresh ideas
- Choosing the best solution
- Setting goals
- Making decisions

mode 2

Strengths:
- Planning
- Creating models
- Defining problems
- Developing theories

Too much of this mode can lead to:
- Vague ideals ("castles in the air")
- Lack of practical application

Too little of this mode can lead to:
- Inability to learn from mistakes
- No sound basis for work
- No systematic approach

People with other preferred modes can develop Mode 2 by:
- Organizing information
- Building conceptual models
- Testing theories and ideas
- Designing experiments
- Analyzing quantitative data

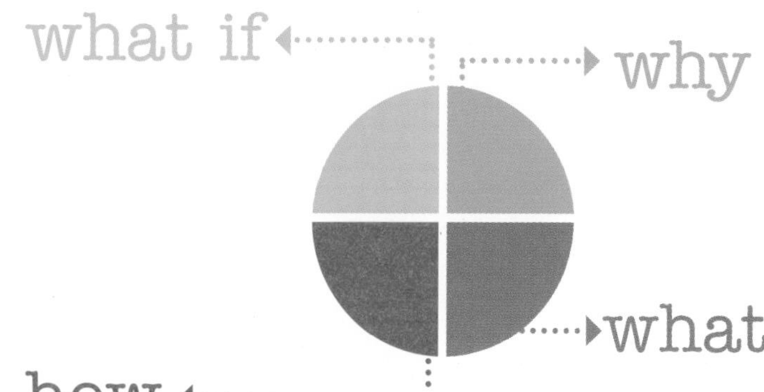

Using your learning style profile to succeed

Develop all four modes of learning

Each mode of learning highlighted in the Learning Styles Inventory represents a unique blend of concrete experience, reflective observation, abstract conceptualization, and active experimentation. You can explore new learning styles simply by adopting new habits related to each of these activities. Consider the following suggestions as places to start. Also remember that any insight derived from exploring learning styles will make a difference in your life only when it leads to changes in your behavior.

To gain concrete experiences:

- Attend a live demonstration or performance related to your course content.
- Engage your emotions by reading a novel or seeing a video related to your course.
- Interview an expert in the subject you're learning or a master practitioner of a skill you want to gain.
- Conduct role-plays, exercises, or games based on your courses.
- Conduct an informational interview with someone in your chosen career, or "shadow" that person for a day on the job.
- Look for a part-time job, internship, or volunteer experience that complements what you do in class.
- Deepen your understanding of another culture and extend your foreign language skills by studying abroad.

To become more reflective:

- Keep a personal journal, and write about connections among your courses.
- Form a study group to discuss and debate topics related to your courses.
- Set up a Web site, computer bulletin board, e-mail listserv, or online chat room related to your major.
- Create analogies to make sense of concepts; for instance, see whether you can find similarities between career planning and putting together a puzzle.
- Visit your course instructor during office hours to ask questions.
- Take time during social events with friends and relatives to briefly explain what your courses are about.

To develop abstract thinking:

- Take notes on your reading in outline form; consider using word-processing software with an outlining feature.
- Supplement assigned texts with other books, magazine and newspaper articles, and related Web sites.
- Attend lectures given by your current instructors and others who teach the same subjects.
- Take ideas presented in text or lectures and translate them into visual form—tables, charts, diagrams, and maps (see Chapter 5: "Notes").
- Create visuals and use computer software to recreate them with more complex graphics and animation.

To become more active:

- Conduct laboratory experiments or field observations.
- Go to settings where theories are being applied or tested; for example, volunteer at a local business or observe a lab school classroom.
- Make predictions based on theories you learn, and then see if events in your daily life confirm your predictions.
- Try out a new behavior described in a lecture or reading, and observe its consequences in your life.

Use the modes to explore your major

If you enjoy learning in Mode 1, you probably value creativity and human relationships. When choosing a major, consider the arts, English, psychology, or political science.

If Mode 2 is your preference, then you enjoy gathering information and building theories. A major related to math or science might be ideal for you.

If Mode 3 is your favorite, then you like to diagnose problems, arrive at solutions, and use technology. A major related to health care, engineering, or economics could be a logical choice for you.

And if your preference is Mode 4, you probably enjoy taking the initiative, implementing decisions, teaching, managing projects, and moving quickly from planning into action. Consider a major in business or education.

As you prepare to declare a major, remain flexible. Use a your knowledge of learning styles to open up possibilities rather than restrict them.

Use the modes of learning to explore your career

Knowing about learning styles becomes especially useful when planning your career.

People who excel at Mode 1 are often skilled at "tuning in" to the feelings of clients and coworkers. These people can listen with an open mind, tolerate confusion, be sensitive to people's feelings, open up to problems that are difficult to define, and create a variety of solutions. If you like Mode 1, you may be drawn to a career in counseling, social services, the ministry, or another field that centers on human relationships. You might also enjoy a career in the performing arts.

People who prefer Mode 2 like to do research and work with ideas. They are skilled at gathering data, interpreting information, and summarizing—activities that help them arrive at the "big picture." They may excel at careers that center on science, math, technical communications, or planning. Mode 2 learners may also work as college teachers, lawyers, technical writers, or journalists.

People who like Mode 3 are drawn to solving problems, making decisions, and checking on progress toward goals. Careers in medicine, engineering, information technology, or another applied science are often ideal for them.

People who enjoy Mode 4 like to influence and lead others. These people are often described as "doers" and "risk takers." They like to take action and complete projects. Mode 4 learners often excel at managing, negotiating, selling, training, and teaching. They might also work for a government agency.

Keep in mind that there is no strict match between certain learning styles and certain careers. Learning is essential to success in all careers.

Accept change—and occasional discomfort

Seek out chances to develop new modes of learning. If your instructor asks you to form a group to complete an assignment, avoid joining a group where everyone shares your learning style. Work on project teams with people who learn differently than you. Get together with people who both complement and challenge you.

Also look for situations where you can safely practice new skills. If you enjoy reading, for example, look for ways to express what you learn by speaking, such as leading a study group on a textbook chapter.

Discomfort is a natural part of the learning process. Allow yourself to notice any struggle with a task or lack of interest in completing it. Remember that such feelings are temporary and might ease as you continue to balance your learning preferences. By choosing to move through discomfort, you consciously expand your ability to learn in new ways. *

Use the modes to learn from *any* instructor

Students who experience difficulty in school might say, "My teacher doesn't get me." Or, "The tests are too hard for me." Or, "In class, we never have time for questions." Or, "The instructor doesn't teach to my learning style."

Such statements can prevent you from taking responsibility for your education. To stay in charge of your learning, consider adopting attitudes such as the following:

I will look for the potential value in learning this information.

I can learn something useful in any situation, even if I don't like it at first.

I will experiment with this suggestion to see if it works.

No matter who's teaching this course, I am responsible for what I learn.

I will master this subject by using several modes of learning.

Remember that you can take action on such statements even if you don't fully agree with them yet. One way to change your attitudes is to adopt new behaviors, see how they work, and watch for new results in your life.

Even when teachers don't promote all four modes of learning, you can take charge of the way you learn. In the process, you consciously direct your growth and create new options.

Learning by seeing, hearing, and moving: The VAK system

YOU CAN APPROACH the topic of learning styles with a simple and powerful system—one that focuses on just three ways of perceiving through your senses:

- Seeing, or *visual learning*
- Hearing, or *auditory learning*
- Movement, or *kinesthetic learning*

To recall this system, remember the letters *VAK*, which stand for **v**isual, **a**uditory, and **k**inesthetic. The theory is that each of us prefers to learn through one of these sense channels. In addition, we can enrich our learning with activities that draw on the other channels.

To reflect on your VAK preferences, answer the following questions. Each question has three possible answers. Circle the answer that best describes how you would respond in the stated situation. This is not a formal inventory—just a way to prompt some self-discovery.

When you have problems spelling a word, you prefer to

1. Look it up in the dictionary.
2. Say the word out loud several times before you write it down.
3. Write out the word with several different spellings and then choose one.

You enjoy courses the most when you get to

1. View slides, overhead displays, videos, and readings with plenty of charts, tables, and illustrations.
2. Ask questions, engage in small-group discussions, and listen to guest speakers.
3. Take field trips, participate in lab sessions, or apply the course content while working as a volunteer or intern.

When giving someone directions on how to drive to a destination, you prefer to

1. Pull out a piece of paper and sketch a map.
2. Give verbal instructions.
3. Say, "I'm driving to a place near there, so just follow me."

When planning an extended vacation to a new destination, you prefer to

1. Read colorful, illustrated brochures or articles about that place.
2. Talk directly to someone who's been there.
3. Spend a day or two at that destination on a work-related trip before taking a vacation there.

You've made a commitment to learn to play the guitar. The first thing you do is

1. Go to a library or music store and find an instruction book with plenty of diagrams and chord charts.
2. Pull out your favorite CDs, listen closely to the guitar solos, and see whether you can sing along with them.
3. Buy or borrow a guitar, pluck the strings, and ask someone to show you how to play a few chords.

You've saved up enough money to lease a car. When choosing from among several new models, the most important factor in your decision is

1. The car's appearance.
2. The information you get by talking to people who own the cars you're considering.
3. The overall impression you get by taking each car on a test drive.

You've just bought a new computer system. When setting up the system, the first thing you do is

1. Skim through the printed instructions that come with the equipment.
2. Call up someone with a similar system and ask her for directions.
3. Assemble the components as best as you can, see if everything works, and consult the instructions only as a last resort.

You get a scholarship to study abroad next semester, which starts in just 3 months. You will travel to a country where French is the most widely spoken language. To learn as much French as you can before you depart, you

1. Buy a video-based language course that's recorded on a DVD.
2. Set up tutoring sessions with a friend who's fluent in French.
3. Sign up for a short immersion course in an environment in which you speak only French, starting with the first class.

Now take a few minutes to reflect on the meaning of your responses. All of the answers numbered "1" are examples of visual learning. The "2s" refer to auditory learning, and the "3s" illustrate kinesthetic learning. Finding a consistent pattern in your answers indicates that you prefer learning through one sense channel to using the others. Or you might find that your preferences are fairly balanced.

In any case, increase your options for success by learning through *all* your sense channels. For example, you can enhance visual learning by leaving room in your class notes to add your own charts, diagrams, tables, and other visuals later. You can also key your handwritten notes into a computer file and use software that allows you to add colorful fonts and illustrations.

To enhance auditory learning, reinforce your memory of key ideas by talking about them. When studying, stop often to summarize key points and add examples in your own words. After doing this several times, dictate your summaries into a voice recorder and transfer the files to an iPod or similar device. Listen to these files while walking to class or standing in line at the store.

For kinesthetic learning, you've got plenty of options as well. Look for ways to translate course content into three-dimensional models that you can build. While studying biology, for example, create a model of a human cell using different colors of clay. Whenever possible, supplement lectures with lab sessions, demonstrations, field trips, and other opportunities for hands-on activity. Also recite key concepts from your courses while you walk or exercise.

These are just a few examples. In your path to mastery of learning styles, you can create many more of your own. *

Reminder: Go back to page LSI-2 to complete the "Take a Snapshot of Your Learning Styles" exercise.

The value of higher education

When you're waist-deep in reading assignments, writing papers, and studying for tests, you might well ask yourself, "Is all this effort going to pay off someday?" That's a fair question. And it addresses a core issue—the value of getting an education beyond high school.

BE REASSURED. The potential benefits of higher education are enormous.

Gain a broad vision

It's been said that a large corporation is a collection of departments connected only by a plumbing system. As workers in different fields become more specialized, they run the risk of forgetting how to talk to one another.

Higher education can change that. One benefit of studying the liberal arts is the chance to gain a broad vision. People with a liberal arts background are aware of the various kinds of problems tackled in psychology and theology, philosophy and physics, literature and mathematics. They understand how people in all of these fields arrive at conclusions and how these fields relate.

Master the liberal arts

According to one traditional model, education means mastering two essential tasks: the use of language and the use of numbers. We master the use of language through the basic processes of communication: reading, writing, speaking, and listening. And courses in mathematics and science help us understand the world in quantitative terms. The abilities to communicate and calculate are essential to almost every profession. Excellence at these skills has long been considered an essential characteristic of an educated person.

The word *liberal* comes from the Latin verb *libero*, which means "to free." Liberal arts are those that promote critical thinking. Studying them can free us from irrational ideas, half-truths, racism, and prejudice. The liberal arts grant us freedom to explore alternatives and create a system of personal values. These benefits are priceless —the very basis of personal fulfillment and political freedom.

Discover values beyond working

We do not spend all of our waking hours at our jobs. That fact leaves us with a choice that affects the quality of our lives: how to spend leisure time. By cultivating our interest in the arts and community affairs, the liberal arts provide us with many options for activities outside work. Our studies add a dimension to life that goes beyond having a job and paying the bills.

Discover new interests

Taking a broad range of courses has the potential to change your direction in life. A student previously committed to a career in science might try out a drawing class and eventually switch to a degree in studio arts. Or a person who swears that she has no aptitude for technical subjects might change her major to computer science after taking an introductory computer course.

Raise your standards

Most of the writing in newspapers and magazines becomes dated quickly. In contrast, many of the books you read in higher education have passed the hardest test of all—time. Such works have created value for people for decades, sometimes for centuries. These creations are inexhaustible. We can return to them time after time and gain new insights. These are the works we can justifiably call great. Hanging out with them transforms us. Getting to know them exercises our minds, just as running exercises our bodies.

By studying the greatest works in many fields, we raise our standards. We learn ways to distinguish what is superficial and fleeting from what is lasting and profound.

Learn skills that apply across careers

Jobs that involve responsibility, prestige, and higher incomes depend on self-management skills. These skills include knowing ways to manage time, resolve conflicts, set goals, learn new skills, and relate to people of diverse cultures. Higher education is a place to learn and practice such skills.

Most of us will have multiple careers in our lifetimes. In this environment of constant change, making a living means learning skills that apply across careers. *

Attitudes and affirmations, and visualizations

I'M A GREAT STUDENT!

"I HAVE A bad attitude." Some of us say this as if we were talking about having the flu. An attitude can be as strong as the flu, but it isn't something we have to accept. You can change your attitudes through regular practice with affirmations and visualizations.

An affirmation is a statement describing what you want. The most effective affirmations are personal, positive, and written in the present tense. To use affirmations, first determine what you want. Then describe yourself as if you already have it. To get what you want from your education, you could write, "I, Malika Jones, am a master student. I take full responsibility for my education. I learn with joy, and I use my experiences in each course to create the life that I want."

Effective affirmations include detail. Use brand names, people's names, and your own name. Involve all of your senses—sight, sound, smell, taste, touch. Take a positive approach. Instead of saying, "I am not fat," say, "I am slender."

Once you have written an affirmation, repeat it. Practice saying it out loud several times a day. Do this at a regular time, such as just before you go to sleep or just after you wake up.

You can combine affirmations with visualization—the technique of seeing yourself being successful. Choose what you want to improve. Then describe in writing what it would look like, sound like, and feel like to have that improvement in your life. If you are learning to play the piano, write down briefly what you would see, hear, and feel if you were playing skillfully. If you want to improve your relationships with your children, write down what you would see, hear, and feel if you were communicating with them successfully. Once you have a clear image, practice it in your imagination. Then wait for the results to unfold in your life. *

6 critical thinking exercise
Reprogram your attitude

Step 1

Pick something in your life that you would like to change. It can be related to anything—relationships, work, money, or personal skills. Below, write a brief description of what you choose to change.

Step 2

Add more details about the change you described in Step 1. Write down how you would like the change to come about. Be outlandish. Imagine that you are about to ask your fairy godmother for a wish that you know she will grant. Be detailed.

Step 3

Here comes the fairy godmother. Use affirmations and visualizations to start yourself on the path to creating exactly what you wrote about in Step 2. Below, write at least 2 affirmations that describe your dream wish. Also, briefly outline a visualization that you can use to picture your wish. Be specific, detailed, and positive.

Complete this exercise online.

Ideas Are Tools

There are many ideas in this book. When you first encounter them, don't believe any of them. Instead, think of the ideas as tools.

For example, you use a hammer for a purpose—to drive a nail. You don't try to figure out whether the hammer is "right." You just use it. If it works, you use it again. If it doesn't work, you get a different hammer.

People have plenty of room in their lives for different kinds of hammers, but they tend to limit their openness to different kinds of ideas. A new idea, at some level, is a threat to their very being—unlike a new hammer, which is simply a new hammer.

Most of us have a built-in desire to be right. Our ideas, we often think, represent ourselves.

Some ideas are worth dying for. But please note: This book does not contain any of those ideas. The ideas on these pages are strictly "hammers."

Imagine someone defending a hammer. Picture this person holding up a hammer and declaring, "I hold this hammer to be self-evident. Give me this hammer or give me death. Those other hammers are flawed. There are only two kinds of people in this world: people who believe in this hammer and people who don't."

That ridiculous picture makes a point. This book is not a manifesto. It's a toolbox, and tools are meant to be used.

If you read about a tool in this book that doesn't sound "right" or one that sounds a little goofy, remember that the ideas here are for using, not necessarily for believing. Suspend your judgment. Test the idea for yourself. If it works, use it. If it doesn't, lose it.

Any tool—whether it's a hammer, a computer program, or a study technique—is designed to do a specific job. A master mechanic carries a variety of tools because no single tool works for all jobs. If you throw a tool away because it doesn't work in one situation, you won't be able to pull it out later when it's just what you want. So if an idea doesn't work for you and you are satisfied that you gave it a fair chance, don't throw it away. File it away instead. The idea might come in handy soon.

And remember, this book is not about figuring out the "right" way. Even the "ideas-are-tools" approach is not "right."

It's a hammer . . . (or maybe a saw).

Learn more about this Power Process online.

Edmond Van Hoorick/Digital Vision/Getty Images

Put it to Work

You can use strategies you learn in *Becoming a Master Student* to succeed at work. Get started by reflecting on the following case study.

Shortly after graduating with an associate in arts (A.A.) degree in business administration, Sylvia Lopez joined a market research firm as a staff accountant. After a week, she wanted to quit. She didn't think she would ever learn to deal with her coworkers. Their personalities just seemed too different.

For example, there was a project manager, Ed Washington. He spent hours a day on the phone calling prospective customers who had responded to the corporate Web site. Because Ed's office door was always open and he had a loud voice, people inevitably overheard his calls. It seemed to Sylvia that Ed spent a lot of time socializing with clients—asking about their hobbies and family lives. Even though Ed was regarded as a skilled salesperson, Sylvia wondered when he actually got any work done.

Sylvia also felt uncomfortable with Linda Martinez, the firm's accounting analyst and her direct supervisor. Linda kept her office door closed most of the time. In contrast to Ed, Linda hardly ever stopped to chat informally. Instead of taking lunch breaks, she typically packed a bag lunch and ate it while checking e-mail or updating the company databases. Linda had a reputation as a top-notch employee. Yet the only time people saw her was at scheduled staff meetings. Linda led those meetings and distributed a detailed agenda in advance. Although Ed was on a first-name basis with everyone in the office, Linda made it clear that she wished to be addressed as "Ms. Martinez."

After thinking for several days about how to survive in the same office with such different coworkers, Sylvia chose to simply accept those differences. In her journal, she reflected on her experiences with Ed and Linda, noting her observations and listing specific ways to improve her working relationships with both of them.

Sylvia made it her intention to stop by Ed's office several times each week, always allowing some time for "small talk" before asking a work-related question.

She also sent an e-mail to Linda with this request: "I value working with you, and I'd like to make sure my performance is up to par. Is there any way I can get regular feedback from you about how I'm doing?"

Sylvia applied several strategies from this chapter. For example, she

- Observed her coworkers and looked for clues to their styles.
- Accepted the differences in her coworkers and looked for ways to build on each person's strengths.
- Used her journal as a tool for reflective observation.
- Used other modes of learning by planning new responses to Ed and Linda—and taking action on her plans.

List more strategies that would be useful to Sylvia in this situation.

____

____

____

____

Once you've discovered differences in people's styles, look for ways to accommodate them. As you collaborate on projects with coworkers, for example, encourage them to answer the four learning style questions:

Ask *Why?* to define the purpose and desired outcomes of a project. Help participants answer these questions: What's in this for our organization? What's in this for me?

Ask *What?* to set goals, assign major tasks, and set due dates for each task.

Ask *How?* as you complete your tasks. In project meetings, discuss what's working well, and brainstorm ways to improve performance.

Ask *What if?* to discuss what the team is learning from the project and ways to apply that learning to the larger organization.

Quiz

Name____ Date____/____/____

1. Define the term *mastery* as it is used in this chapter.
   Mastery implies a level of skill that goes beyond technique; it is something that cannot be taught. Often the result of mastery is a sense of profound satisfaction, well-being, and timelessness. Likewise, the master student is one who plays full out and makes learning look easy. She works hard without seeming to make any effort. She's relaxed *and* alert, disciplined *and* spontaneous, focused *and* fun-loving. (Answers will vary.) (*The Master Student*, p. 30)
2. The First Step technique refers only to telling the truth about your weaknesses. True or false? Explain your answer.
   False. The First Step is all about telling the truth about your areas for improvement: This involves telling the truth about what *is* working as well as what isn't, who you are, and what you want. (Answers will vary.)
   (*First Step: Truth is a key to mastery*, p. 21)
3. The four modes of learning are associated with certain questions. Give the appropriate question for each mode.
   • Mode 1: Why? • Mode 2: What? • Mode 3: How? • Mode 4: What if?
   (*Learning styles: Discovering how you learn*, pp. 34–36)
4. Briefly explain two possible benefits of getting an education beyond high school.
   Describe two of the following benefits: • Gain a broad vision • Master the liberal arts • Discover values beyond working • Discover new interests • Learn skills that apply across careers (*The value of higher education*, p. 41)
5. *Becoming a Master Student* is specifically designed to help you develop one or two modes of learning. True or false? Explain your answer.
   False. After helping you identify your preferred learning mode, the text explains what actions you can take to become a more balanced learner and how to develop all four modes of learning. (*Using your learning style profile to succeed*, pp. 37–38)
6. List three types of intelligence defined by Howard Gardner. Then describe one learning strategy related to each type of intelligence that you listed.
   List three of the following:
   - Verbal/linguistic: Practice learning by reciting new ideas in your own words.
   - Mathematical/logical: Practice learning by looking for ways to quantify ideas.
   - Visual/spatial: Find pictures and graphs in a book and practice analyzing them without reading the accompanying text.
   - Musical/rhythmic: Try studying with different kinds of music in the background and analyze which, if any, seem to aid in your learning.
   - Interpersonal: Form a study group with classmates to discuss homework, text, and class discussions.

   (*Claim your multiple intelligences*, p. 31)
7. According to the Power Process: "Ideas Are Tools," the key to success at using any suggestion in this book is *believing* in it. True or false? Explain your answer.
   False. The ideas in this text are for using, not for believing. Each idea can be used as a tool to help students become master students. Not every idea will fit—the challenge is to discover why an idea is right or not right for you and to ask yourself the questions that will expand your toolbox with more ideas. (Answers will vary). (*Power Process: Ideas Are Tools*, p. 43)
8. According to this chapter, theories about learning styles share several insights, including these:
   (a) We *create* knowledge rather than simply absorbing it.
   (b) We have our own preferences for learning.
   (c) We can often succeed by matching our activities with our preferences.
   (d) Our preferences can expand as we experiment with new learning strategies.
   (e) All of the above.
   (e) All of the above. (*Learning styles: Discovering how you learn*, pp. 34–36)
9. This chapter presents two viewpoints on the nature of motivation. Briefly explain the difference between them.
   One view presents motivation as a quality or trait that some people are born with. The other view is that motivation is a habit that we can develop with practice. In the first view, we are powerless to change our motivation. In the second view, we can improve our ability to motivate ourselves to accomplish our goals. (*Motivation—"I'm just not in the mood,"* pp. 28–29)
10. Write an example of an effective affirmation and an example of an ineffective affirmation.
    Effective affirmations are personal, positive, and written in the present tense. They include details like brand names, people's names, and your own name.
    Effective: I, Mary Jones, am a confident student who is responsible for her own education.
    Ineffective: I want to be a confident student who is responsible for her own education. (Answers will vary.)
    (*Attitudes, affirmations, and visualizations*, p. 42)

Skills Snapshot

The Discovery Wheel in this chapter includes a section labeled *Attitude*. For the next 10 to 15 minutes, go beyond your initial responses to that exercise. Take a snapshot of your skills as they exist today, after reading and doing this chapter.

Begin by reflecting on some recent experiences. Then take another step toward mastery by choosing to follow up on your reflections with a specific action.

SELF-AWARENESS

Three things I do well as a student are . . .

Three ways that I'd like to improve as a student are . . .

STYLES

If asked to describe my learning style in one sentence, I would say that I am . . .

To become a more flexible learner, I could . . .

FLEXIBILITY

When I disagree with what someone else says, my first response is usually to . . .

In these situations, I could be more effective by . . .

NEXT ACTION

I'll know that I've adopted new attitudes to support my success when I'm able to say . . .

To reach that level of mastery, the most important thing I can do next is to . . .

Master Student PROFILE

Lalita Booth
is Willing to Work

Jacque Brund/UCF News and Information

Sitting in front of a classroom of UCF LEAD Scholars, Lalita Booth looks like any other junior. The brown-eyed, freckle-faced student blends in with her peers in the University of Central Florida (UCF) leadership development program in every way.

That is, until she opens her mouth.

"You're looking at the face of a child abuse survivor, a perpetual runaway, a high-school dropout," she says, as idle chitchat turns to complete silence.

"I was a teenage mother, a homeless parent, and a former welfare recipient."

Lalita's parents divorced when she was young; by age 12 she was a runaway pro—asking for permission to go somewhere and then simply not returning for a few days or a few weeks.

. . . She became proficient in "couch surfing" at friends' homes. When there was no couch to crash on, the teen would take her nightly refuge behind the closest dumpster and rest in the park during the day.

Furthering her quest to be a grownup, at 17 she married her long-time buddy and fellow high-school dropout, Quinn. Three months later, she found out she was pregnant with her son, Kieren. What normally would be a joyful time was instead a stressful one while the new couple struggled in a prison of deep poverty. The miserable situation began to take its toll, and after just two and a half years of marriage, Quinn was ready to call it quits.

With her new boyfriend, Carl, and her most precious cargo, Kieren, in tow, Booth fled to Boulder, Colorado. Kieren lived with his paternal grandparents for 7 months while Lalita and Carl attempted to get back on their feet.

Being in Colorado proved to be fruitful for the 21-year-old Lalita. It started with an interesting job opportunity as an enrolled agent—an expert in U.S. taxation who can represent taxpayers before the Internal Revenue Service. Lalita could acquire the license without further schooling. Better yet, it would boost her income to $32,000. She buckled down and read all 4,000 pages of the study guide, and, thanks to her nearly photographic memory, she aced the test.

But, once again, she was in the wrong place at the wrong time. Carl's brother in Orlando was very ill, and he needed to move to Florida.

The only way to ensure her independence was to do something that frightened her to the very core—go back to school. . . .

. . . And soon after, she enrolled at Seminole Community College.

. . . In May 2005, Lalita was selected to attend the Salzburg Global Seminar, where she brainstormed ways to solve global problems with a group of international students. The thought-provoking trip led to her mission: to help others escape the choke hold of poverty.

Back in the states, Booth's world became even more dream-like when she won the Jack Kent Cooke Foundation Scholarship. . . .

Lalita Booth strongly believes, and for good reason, that "things that are worth achieving are absolutely unreasonable." She advises, "Set unreasonable goals, and chase them unreasonably."

Adapted from Sarah Sekula, "Escape Artist," *Pegasus*, July/August 2008, *UCF Alumni Life*, 20–26.

Once homeless, and now a student at the University of Central Florida and accepted to Harvard Business School.

Find more biographical information about Lalita Booth at the Master Student Hall of Fame.

2 Time and Money

Instructor Tools & Tips

> Even if you are on the right track, you'll get run over if you just sit there.
>
> **—Will Rogers**
>
> While we might vigorously maintain that we know that "money can't buy happiness" and "the best things in life are free," honesty requires that we look deeper. Our behavior tells a different story.
>
> **—Joe Dominguez and Vicki Robin**
>
> An hour of effective, precise, hard, disciplined and integrated thinking can be worth a month of hard work.
>
> **—David Kekich**

Preview

Chapter 2 addresses one of the great challenges for students—managing their time and money. Whether they are traditional students attending college right out of high school or returning students attending college for the first time after an absence from formal education, your students each have only 168 hours per week to allocate to their many priorities. Time is an equal opportunity resource. As you help your students choose how to allocate their 168 hours per week, set goals, and overcome procrastination, remind them that planning increases their options. The same idea applies to money. Money is the most common reason students give for withdrawing from college. With tuition increases on the rise, the need for first-year college students to develop a mature financial literacy is crucial to their college survival. New articles will help students explore ways to manage money during tough times and relate their learning style to how they spend their money. Planning in regards to time and money offers them the freedom to act in response to their intentions rather than to their moods. And planning vastly increases the odds of getting what they want.

Guest Speaker

Consider inviting experts from your college or from off-campus who work in fields that emphasize planning, goal setting, or organization. A representative from the Counseling Department may provide some planning tips and also share information about advisement, scheduling, and personal counseling services. The Financial Aid Director from your campus can talk to students about financial aid opportunities, deadlines, and forms they need to fill out.

Here are two guest speakers for you:

> I think the Time Monitor exercise is one of the most valuable in the book. Until students track their time, most have no idea how they use/waste their time. Because time management is so very important, have students do the same exercise of tracking their time toward the end of the semester. Comparing the two should reflect changes. There should be a direct correlation between their time management and the success they are having in school, work, and life.
>
> **—Jo Ella Fields, Oklahoma State University**
>
> Discussing money in class can raise student privacy concerns. My student success course is about students taking an honest look at themselves, learning new ways of being a student, and creating plans to achieve their created goals. And while a more personal discussion about money might be more powerful, I tend toward generalizations and let the students internalize these concepts and apply them privately to their individual financial circumstances.
>
> **—Dean Mancina**

Lecture

Here is a lecture idea from Faculty Advisor Eldon McMurray that relates to planning and money management: There are three ways college students can avoid the absolute financial disasters awaiting them—avoiding late fees, keeping a current account register, and protecting oneself from identity theft.

Avoiding late fees. Prioritizing spending with a simple budget can help students avoid paying late fees. Discuss the importance of paying credit card bills on time. Point out that after just one late payment, some credit card companies boost interest rates beyond 31 percent and charge late fees of $25 in most cases. And some credit card companies raise rates if you miss a deadline on another card, even if you have a spotless record with them.

Suggest that students pay scheduled bills automatically if possible. Setting up a separate account so that their set bills will be paid automatically from their bank account saves students the hassle of writing monthly checks and worrying about mail delays; it also protects them from costly missed deadlines.

Keeping a current account register. Maintaining an up-to-date account register can be the difference between graduating and dropping out. Barry Oats, a former collegiate football player, suggests a trick he learned from legendary football coach Lavell Edwards that can help any student: Simply play your money like a weekly football game.

First, make a financial "game plan" for the week by predicting your income and expenses. On Thursday night, do a "half-time check" to make sure your income tops your expenses. Finally, on Sunday afternoon reconcile your accounts by matching your receipts with your game plan. If you have cash left over after accounting for all your spending, you win!

Protecting oneself from identity theft. Here are some ideas to share with students to help them avoid identity theft: Purchase a simple paper shredder and destroy all ATM receipts as soon as the transactions appear on your monthly bank statement. *Never* give your credit or debit card or your PIN (personal identification number) to anyone. Always ask whether you can swipe your own card in department stores. Watch your card from the moment it leaves your hand until the clerk returns it to you/ Make sure that the clerk is not copying or imaging your card.

Exercises/Activities

1. **Why? What? How? and What if?** Tap into all the different learning styles of your students by asking these questions in class (write them on the board or post them to your online course discussion board):

Why? Why does this book cover planning and money?

What? What is planning? Read through the list of articles in this chapter and pick three that look interesting. What about these three articles interests you?

How? How would you rate your level of success with the ideas covered in this chapter? (How much do you already know about prioritizing your time, setting goals, or spending and managing your money?)

What if? What if you start to apply these strategies to your life right now? And what if you don't?

2. **The ABC daily to-do list (page 57).** Some students have had prior experience with to-do lists. Their testimonials in class can help convince students who have not yet tried to-do lists to experiment with them. The ABC priority aspect is usually a new concept for all students. Learning this technique helps them make better decisions about *what* to do and *when* to do it. Practicing this skill in groups during class helps students get started with to-do lists.

3. **The 7-day antiprocrastination plan (page 62).** Many students report that procrastination is their number one obstacle to success in school, work, and their personal lives. After they have read the antiprocrastination article and sidebar, divide them into groups of four and ask them to list situations in which they often procrastinate. Then discuss as a group which of the antiprocrastination strategies might be most appropriate for each situation. Making this an active-learning exercise puts the strategies in motion. Have the students create summary charts on poster paper and then present a brief report to the rest of the class.

4. **Get the most out of now (pages 61–62).** After students have read this article, divide them into groups of four and ask them to discuss which of the tools they have had success with in the past. Then ask them to discuss five tools that they are interested in trying and to make a verbal commitment to each of their group members. At the beginning of the next class, ask students to report back to their groups to discuss which strategies worked and which did not.

5. **Take charge of your credit (page 69).** At the beginning of the semester, tell students to keep all credit card offers they receive in the mail. Have them bring the offers to class on a specific day. Divide the class into groups and ask them to analyze the offers in terms of the promotional interest rate, regular interest rate, credit limits, annual fees,

and penalties for late payments. Then ask the students whether any of the offers in their group provides a better deal than the rate, limit, fees, and penalties on the credit card(s) they currently use. Most students won't know these facts about their current credit card(s). This is a good lead-in to an assignment to investigate their credit cards.

6. **Power Process: Be Here Now (page 71).** This Power Process teaches the skill of focusing attention—a skill essential for taking effective notes in class, maximizing comprehension when reading textbooks, and memorizing content. After students read the article and you review it with them in class, have them stand up and find a partner for this brief "hand mirror" exercise. Facing their partner, students put their hands up, palms facing toward their partner, without touching. In this position, students appear as a mirror image of their partner. Without speaking, for 1 minute, one student is in charge of moving her hands slowly in different directions—up, down, left, right, forward, backward. Her partner focuses his attention and mirrors the movement of her hands with his hands, even when they do not move symmetrically. After 1 minute, they reverse roles for another minute. Afterward, discuss the paradox that it feels both easy and difficult to focus attention for just 60 seconds.

Conversation/Sharing

The Master Student Profile about Al Gore describes ways to approach and solve problems. In groups of four, ask students to select either a world or a local problem toward which they would like to contribute their time and energy. Then brainstorm creative solutions to the problem. As a whole class, share ideas and discuss master student qualities that students can develop while attending college. Additional information, including links to outside resources, related to Al Gore and other master students is available on the College Success Coursemate, in the Master Student Hall of Fame.

Homework

The Time Monitor/Time Plan Process (pages 50–54). Assign the monitoring step of this exercise the week before you get to this chapter, because the exercise asks students to monitor their activities first so that they will have a detailed picture of how they spend their time. When students complete this exercise *before* they read the chapter, they are motivated to learn strategies to make the most of their 168 hours per week. It is not easy to keep track of oneself for 24 hours a day for a week, so talk about the importance of this exercise ahead of time. To show students that you know how challenging this exercise is, share with them that you did it yourself.

The Money Monitor/Money Plan (pages 63–67). This activity is similar to the Time Monitor/Time Plan. The first step in managing their money is to see objectively how much money they have and how they spend it. If they think back to the invaluable knowledge they obtained from the Time Monitor/Time Plan, they will be willing to spend the time to complete this admittedly lengthy task for the awareness it will provide them.

Gearing up: Using a long-term planner (pages 59–60). The words *planning* and *time management* strike terror into many students' hearts. Yet this is the number one skill research tells us that students need. Tell students that they cannot control time, but they *can* control the way they respond to it. They cannot control the past, but they *can* have an impact on their future by planning the semester. The master monthly calendar is an opportunity for you to help your students plan an entire semester. Using the blank monthly calendar in the textbook (with additional forms at the back of the text or available on the College Success Coursemate), have students create their master plan based on the course syllabi from all of their classes. Have them transfer dates for tests and papers and ask them to plug in interim deadlines, such as "Write draft." Some students have success when, during this exercise, they also create a timeline for each of the bigger projects. An example is available on the Instructor Companion site.

Evaluation

Quiz ideas for Chapter 2:

- Write a Discovery Statement regarding time monitoring/planning.
- Write an Intention Statement regarding goal setting.
- Name antiprocrastination tools.
- Describe strategies for getting the most out of now.
- Write a Discovery Statement regarding the Power Process: "Be Here Now."

In addition, ask students to describe ways of making more money while in college. Ask students to write specific Intention Statements about protecting their money online. Ask students how they intend to spend less money. Ask them to discuss one or more money management strategies that are especially useful during tough economic times. Ask students how they can take charge of their credit cards.

Additional Digital Resources

CHAPTER 2

Course Manual

The online *Course Manual* serves as an invaluable reference for those developing and teaching a College Success course with *Becoming a Master Student Concise*. The *Course Manual* provides advice on general teaching issues such as preparing for classes, classroom management, grading, communicating with students of various backgrounds as well as specific strategies on getting the most out of various features in *Becoming a Master Student Concise* and book-specific Web sites. Do a *Course Manual* reconnaissance to find ideas that you can use in your course right now.

Instructor Companion Site

The updated Instructor Companion Site provides resources to help you plan and customize your course. Content specific to Chapter 2 includes:

- Lecture Ideas
  - Committing to Coming to Class
  - Planning Sets You Free
  - Structured Time and Freedom
  - Money Makes the World Go Around
- In-Class Exercises
  - 3×5 Goal Setting
  - How Do I Manage My Time?
  - Education by the Hour
  - The Long-Term Budget
- Writing Assignments
  - Goal-Setting Paper
- In-Text Quiz Answers
- PowerPoint Slides

The Instructor Companion Site also contains the following book-specific content:

- ExamView Test Bank
- Online Course Manual
- Sample Syllabi
- Detailed Transition Guide

College Success CourseMate

To help your students gain a better understanding of the topics discussed in *Becoming a Master Student Concise*, encourage them to visit the College Success CourseMate at CengageBrain.com that provides the following resources specific to Chapter 2:

- Connect to Text content expands on specific topics marked with an icon within the Introduction.
- Practice Tests allow students to see how well they understand the themes of *Becoming a Master Student Concise*.
- Interactive Concept Maps promote critical thinking by highlighting related ideas to show relationships among concepts.
- Learning Styles Application
- Discussion Topics
- Reflection Questions
- Assessment Questions
- Experiment with chapter strategies
- Video Skillbuilders bring to life techniques that will help students to excel in college and beyond. The following videos should give your students more information regarding topics covered in Chapter 2:
  - Time Management
  - Managing Your Finances
- Remembering Cultural Differences presents readers with brief articles that touch on aspects diversity in our rapidly changing world. For Chapter 2, the following article will prompt your students to look at contemporary issues in a new way:
  - The Concept of Time
- Master Student Profiles provide additional information on the people covered in this book feature. For Chapter 2, students will find expanded coverage and links about:
  - Al Gore
- Power Process Media contains video, PowerPoints, and audio files to take what your students have learned from the Power Processes in their book to the next level. For Chapter 2, students will find additional media on:
  - Be Here Now

Along with the chapter-specific content, a General Resources folder is available that contains Toolboxes geared toward specific student types (Community College, Adult Learner, Student Athlete), the Plagiarism Prevention Zone, and the Career Resource Center.

2 Time and Money

Master Student Map

as you read, ask yourself

what if . . . ?

I could meet my goals with time and money to spare?

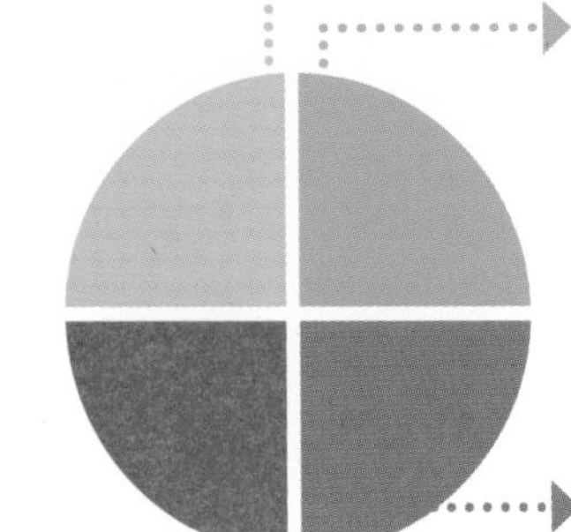

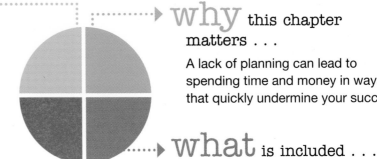

why this chapter matters . . .

A lack of planning can lead to spending time and money in ways that quickly undermine your success.

how you can use this chapter . . .

- Discover the details about how you currently use time and money.
- Set goals that make a difference in the quality of your life.
- Know exactly what to do today, this week, and this month to achieve your goals.
- Take charge of the way that money enters and leaves your life.

what is included . . .

MASTER STUDENTS in *action*

I have found that it is essential to keep a constantly updated calendar and personal planner. Without my own planner, I would most likely draw a blank as to what I need to accomplish for the day, week, month, and beyond. I recommend that any student use both as a means of keeping organized.

—DEEANNA MOSHER

Photo courtesy of Deeanna Mosher

You've got the time— and the money

THE WORDS *time management* may call forth images of restriction and control. You might visualize a prune-faced Scrooge hunched over your shoulder, stopwatch in hand, telling you what to do every minute. The whole situation is bad news.

Here's the good news: You do have enough time for the things you want to do. All it takes is thinking about the possibilities and making conscious choices.

Time is an equal opportunity resource. All of us, regardless of gender, race, creed, or national origin, have exactly the same number of hours in a week. No matter how famous we are, no matter how rich or poor, we get 168 hours to spend each week—no more, no less.

Approach time as if you are in control. Sometimes it seems that your friends control your time, your boss controls your time, your teachers or your parents or your kids or somebody else controls your time. Maybe that is not true, though. When you say you don't have enough time, you might really be saying that you are not spending the time you *do* have in the way that you want.

The same idea applies to money. When you say you don't have enough money, the real issue might be that you are not spending the money you *do* have in the way that you want.

Most money problems result from spending more than is available. It's that simple, even though we often do everything we can to make the problem much more complicated. The solution also is simple: Don't spend more than you have. If you are spending more than you have, then increase your income, decrease your spending, or do both.

Again, you are in control of what you spend. This idea has never won a Nobel Prize in Economics, but you won't go broke applying it.

Everything written about time and money management boils down to two ideas. One involves knowing exactly *what* you want. The other involves knowing *how* to get what you want. State your wants as written goals. Then choose actions that will help you meet those goals.

Strategies for managing time and money are not complicated. In fact, they're not even new. These strategies are all based on the cycle of discovery, intention, and action that you're already practicing in this book. Throw in the ability to add and subtract, and you have everything you need to manage your time and your money.

You can spend these valuable resources in ways that align with your values. That's the purpose of this chapter. *

journal entry 7

Discovery/Intention Statement

Create value from this chapter

Think back to a time during the past year when you rushed to finish a project at the last minute or when you did not have enough money to achieve a goal that was important to you. List at least one thing you might have done to create either outcome.

I discovered that I . . .

____

____

____

____

____

Now take a few minutes to skim this chapter. Look for ways to produce new outcomes with your time or money. List five techniques that you intend to use, along with their associated page numbers.

Strategy	**Page number**

7

critical thinking exercise

The Time Monitor/ Time Plan Process

The purpose of this exercise is to transform time into a knowable and predictable resource. Complete this exercise over a 2-week period.

- During the first week, you *monitor* your activities to get detailed information about how you actually spend your time.
- After you analyze your first week in Journal Entry 8, you *plan* the second week.
- During the second week, you *monitor* your activity again and compare it with your plan.
- Based on everything you've learned, you *plan* again.

For this exercise, monitor your time in 15-minute intervals, 24 hours a day, for 7 days. Record how much time you spend sleeping, eating, studying, attending lectures, traveling to and from class, working, watching television, listening to music, taking care of the kids, running errands—everything.

If this sounds crazy, hang on for a minute. This exercise is not about keeping track of the rest of your life in 15-minute intervals. It is an opportunity to become conscious of how you spend your time—your life. Use the Time Monitor/Time Plan process only for as long as it helps you do that.

When you know exactly how you spend your time, you can make choices with open eyes. You can spend more time on the things that are most important to you and less time on the unimportant. Monitoring your time puts you in control of your life.

Here's an eye-opener for many students. If you think you already have a good idea of how you manage time, predict how many hours you will spend in a week on each category of activity listed in the form on page 52. (Four categories are already provided; you can add more at any time.) Make your predictions before your first week of monitoring. Write them in the margin to the left of each category. After monitoring your time for 1 week, see how accurate your predictions were.

The following charts are used for monitoring and planning, and include instructions for using them. Some students choose other materials, such as 3x5 cards, calendars, campus planners, or time management software. You might even develop your own way to monitor your time.

1. **Get to know the Time Monitor/Time Plan.** Look at the sample Time Monitor/Time Plan on page 51. Note that each day has two columns—one labeled "Monitor" and the other labeled "Plan." During the first week, you will use only the "Monitor" column, just like this student did.

   On Monday, the student in this example got up at 6:45 a.m., showered, and got dressed. He finished this activity and began breakfast at 7:15. He put this new activity in at the time he began and drew a line just above it. He ate from 7:15 to 7:45. It took him 15 minutes to walk to class (7:45 to 8:00), and he attended classes from 8:00 to 11:00.

   When you begin an activity, write it down next to the time you begin. Round off to the nearest 15 minutes. If, for example, you begin eating at 8:06, enter your starting time as 8:00. Over time, it will probably even out. In any case, you will be close enough to realize the benefits of this exercise.

   Keep your Time Monitor/Time Plan with you every minute you are awake for 1 week. Take a few moments every 2 or 3 hours to record what you've done. Or enter a note each time you change activities.

2. **Remember to use your Time Monitor/Time Plan.** It might be easy to forget to fill out your Time Monitor/Time Plan. One way to remember is to create a visual reminder for yourself. You can use this technique for any activity you want to remember.

   Relax for a moment, close your eyes, and imagine that you see your Time Monitor/Time Plan. Imagine that it has arms and legs and is as big as a person. Picture the form sitting at your desk at home, in your car, in one of your classrooms, or in your favorite chair. Visualize it sitting wherever you're likely to sit. When you sit down, the Time Monitor/Time Plan will get squashed unless you pick it up and use it.

   You can make this image more effective by adding sound effects. The Time Monitor/Time Plan might scream, "Get off me!" Or, because time can be related to money, you might associate the Time Monitor/Time Plan with the sound of an old-fashioned cash register. Imagine that every time you sit down, a cash register rings to remind you it's there.

Do this exercise online.

MONDAY 9 / 12	Monitor	Plan
	Get up	
	Shower	
7:00		7:00
7:15	Breakfast	
7:30		
7:45	Walk to class	
8:00	Econ 1	8:00
8:15		
8:30		
8:45		
9:00		9:00
9:15		
9:30		
9:45		
10:00	Bio 1	10:00
10:15		
10:30		
10:45		
11:00		11:00
11:15	Study	
11:30		
11:45		
12:00		12:00
12:15	Lunch	
12:30		
12:45		
1:00		1:00
1:15	Eng. Lit	
1:30		
1:45		
2:00		2:00
2:15	Coffeehouse	
2:30		
2:45		
3:00		3:00
3:15		
3:30		
3:45		
4:00		4:00
4:15	Study	
4:30		
4:45		
5:00		5:00
5:15	Dinner	
5:30		
5:45		
6:00		6:00
6:15		
6:30	Babysit	
6:45		
7:00		7:00

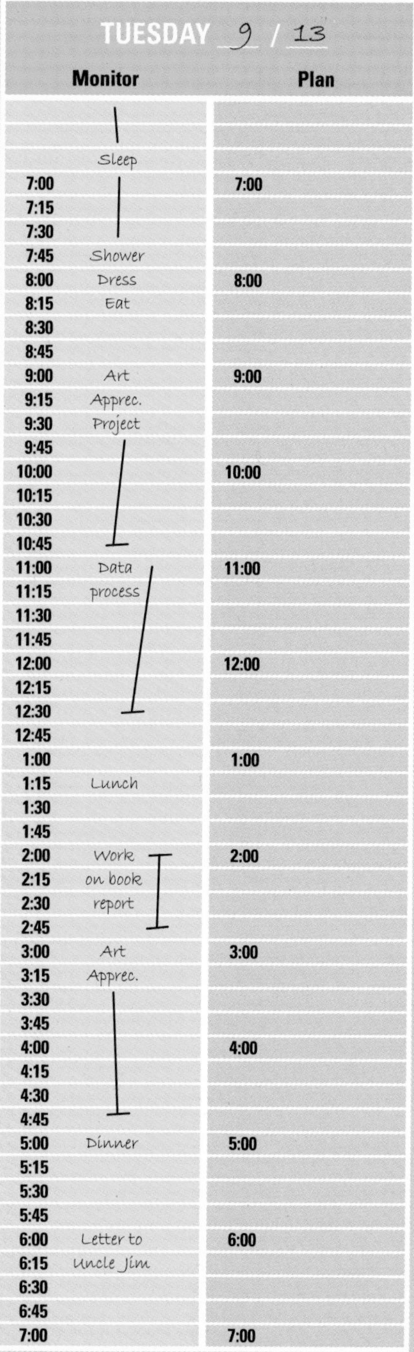

TUESDAY 9 / 13	Monitor	Plan
	Sleep	
7:00		7:00
7:15		
7:30		
7:45	Shower	
8:00	Dress	8:00
8:15	Eat	
8:30		
8:45		
9:00	Art	9:00
9:15	Apprec.	
9:30	Project	
9:45		
10:00		10:00
10:15		
10:30		
10:45		
11:00	Data	11:00
11:15	process	
11:30		
11:45		
12:00		12:00
12:15		
12:30		
12:45		
1:00		1:00
1:15	Lunch	
1:30		
1:45		
2:00	Work	2:00
2:15	on book	
2:30	report	
2:45		
3:00	Art	3:00
3:15	Apprec.	
3:30		
3:45		
4:00		4:00
4:15		
4:30		
4:45		
5:00	Dinner	5:00
5:15		
5:30		
5:45		
6:00	Letter to	6:00
6:15	Uncle Jim	
6:30		
6:45		
7:00		7:00

3. **Evaluate the Time Monitor/Time Plan.** After you've monitored your time for 1 week, group your activities together by categories. The form on page 52 lists the categories "sleep," "class," "study," and "meals." Think of other categories you could add. "Grooming" might include showering, putting on makeup, brushing teeth, and getting dressed. "Travel" could include walking, driving, taking the bus, and riding your bike. Other categories might be "exercise," "entertainment," "work," "television," "domestic," and "children."

Write in the categories that work for you, and then do the following:

- Guess how many hours you *think* you spent on each category of activity. List these hours in the "Estimated" column.

- List the *actual* number of hours you spent on each activity, adding up the figures from your daily time monitoring. List these hours in the "Monitored" column. Make sure that the grand total of all categories is 168 hours.
- Now take a minute, and let these numbers sink in. Compare the totals in the "Estimated" and "Monitored" columns.

Notice your reactions. You might be surprised. You might feel disappointed or even angry about where your time goes.

Use those feelings as motivation to plan your time differently. Go to the "Planned" column, and choose how much time you *want* to spend on various categories during the coming week. As you do this, allow yourself to have fun. Approach planning in the spirit of adventure. Think of yourself as an artist who's creating a new life.

In several months, you might want to take another detailed look at how you spend your life. Fill in the "Monitor" and "Plan" columns on pages 53-54 simultaneously. Use a continuous cycle of monitoring and planning to get the full benefits of this exercise for the rest of your life. Let time management become more than a technique. Transform it into a habit—a constant awareness of how you spend your lifetime.

WEEK OF ___ / ___ / ___ /			
Category	**Estimated**	**Monitored**	**Planned**
Sleep			
Class			
Study			
Meals			

MONDAY ___ / ___ / ___ /

Monitor	Plan
7:00	7:00
7:15	
7:30	
7:45	
8:00	8:00
8:15	
8:30	
8:45	
9:00	9:00
9:15	
9:30	
9:45	
10:00	10:00
10:15	
10:30	
10:45	
11:00	11:00
11:15	
11:30	
11:45	
12:00	12:00
12:15	
12:30	
12:45	
1:00	1:00
1:15	
1:30	
1:45	
2:00	2:00
2:15	
2:30	
2:45	
3:00	3:00
3:15	
3:30	
3:45	
4:00	4:00
4:15	
4:30	
4:45	
5:00	5:00
5:15	
5:30	
5:45	
6:00	6:00
6:15	
6:30	
6:45	
7:00	7:00
7:15	
7:30	
7:45	
8:00	8:00
8:15	
8:30	
8:45	
9:00	9:00
9:15	
9:30	
9:45	
10:00	10:00
10:15	
10:30	
10:45	
11:00	11:00
11:15	
11:30	
11:45	
12:00	12:00

TUESDAY ___ / ___ / ___ /

Monitor	Plan
7:00	7:00
7:15	
7:30	
7:45	
8:00	8:00
8:15	
8:30	
8:45	
9:00	9:00
9:15	
9:30	
9:45	
10:00	10:00
10:15	
10:30	
10:45	
11:00	11:00
11:15	
11:30	
11:45	
12:00	12:00
12:15	
12:30	
12:45	
1:00	1:00
1:15	
1:30	
1:45	
2:00	2:00
2:15	
2:30	
2:45	
3:00	3:00
3:15	
3:30	
3:45	
4:00	4:00
4:15	
4:30	
4:45	
5:00	5:00
5:15	
5:30	
5:45	
6:00	6:00
6:15	
6:30	
6:45	
7:00	7:00
7:15	
7:30	
7:45	
8:00	8:00
8:15	
8:30	
8:45	
9:00	9:00
9:15	
9:30	
9:45	
10:00	10:00
10:15	
10:30	
10:45	
11:00	11:00
11:15	
11:30	
11:45	
12:00	12:00

WEDNESDAY ___ / ___ / ___ /

Monitor	Plan
7:00	7:00
7:15	
7:30	
7:45	
8:00	8:00
8:15	
8:30	
8:45	
9:00	9:00
9:15	
9:30	
9:45	
10:00	10:00
10:15	
10:30	
10:45	
11:00	11:00
11:15	
11:30	
11:45	
12:00	12:00
12:15	
12:30	
12:45	
1:00	1:00
1:15	
1:30	
1:45	
2:00	2:00
2:15	
2:30	
2:45	
3:00	3:00
3:15	
3:30	
3:45	
4:00	4:00
4:15	
4:30	
4:45	
5:00	5:00
5:15	
5:30	
5:45	
6:00	6:00
6:15	
6:30	
6:45	
7:00	7:00
7:15	
7:30	
7:45	
8:00	8:00
8:15	
8:30	
8:45	
9:00	9:00
9:15	
9:30	
9:45	
10:00	10:00
10:15	
10:30	
10:45	
11:00	11:00
11:15	
11:30	
11:45	
12:00	12:00

THURSDAY ___ / ___ / ___ /

Monitor	Plan
7:00	7:00
7:15	
7:30	
7:45	
8:00	8:00
8:15	
8:30	
8:45	
9:00	9:00
9:15	
9:30	
9:45	
10:00	10:00
10:15	
10:30	
10:45	
11:00	11:00
11:15	
11:30	
11:45	
12:00	12:00
12:15	
12:30	
12:45	
1:00	1:00
1:15	
1:30	
1:45	
2:00	2:00
2:15	
2:30	
2:45	
3:00	3:00
3:15	
3:30	
3:45	
4:00	4:00
4:15	
4:30	
4:45	
5:00	5:00
5:15	
5:30	
5:45	
6:00	6:00
6:15	
6:30	
6:45	
7:00	7:00
7:15	
7:30	
7:45	
8:00	8:00
8:15	
8:30	
8:45	
9:00	9:00
9:15	
9:30	
9:45	
10:00	10:00
10:15	
10:30	
10:45	
11:00	11:00
11:15	
11:30	
11:45	
12:00	12:00

FRIDAY ___ / ___ / ___ /

Monitor	Plan
7:00	7:00
7:15	
7:30	
7:45	
8:00	8:00
8:15	
8:30	
8:45	
9:00	9:00
9:15	
9:30	
9:45	
10:00	10:00
10:15	
10:30	
10:45	
11:00	11:00
11:15	
11:30	
11:45	
12:00	12:00
12:15	
12:30	
12:45	
1:00	1:00
1:15	
1:30	
1:45	
2:00	2:00
2:15	
2:30	
2:45	
3:00	3:00
3:15	
3:30	
3:45	
4:00	4:00
4:15	
4:30	
4:45	
5:00	5:00
5:15	
5:30	
5:45	
6:00	6:00
6:15	
6:30	
6:45	
7:00	7:00
7:15	
7:30	
7:45	
8:00	8:00
8:15	
8:30	
8:45	
9:00	9:00
9:15	
9:30	
9:45	
10:00	10:00
10:15	
10:30	
10:45	
11:00	11:00
11:15	
11:30	
11:45	
12:00	12:00

SATURDAY ___ / ___ / ___ /

Monitor	Plan

SUNDAY ___ / ___ / ___ /

Monitor	Plan

Many of us have vague, idealized notions of what we want out of life. These notions float among the clouds in our heads. They are wonderful, fuzzy, safe thoughts such as "I want to have more free time," "I want to be financially secure," or "I want to be happy."

Setting and achieving goals

THE GOALS ABOVE are great possibilites. But when we state our goals in such general ways, we can become confused about ways to actually achieve them. If you really want to meet a goal, then translate it into specific, concrete behaviors. Find out what that goal looks like. Listen to what it sounds like. Pick it up and feel how heavy that goal is. Inspect the switches, valves, joints, cogs, and fastenings of the goal. Make your goal as real as a chain saw.

In writing, state each goal as an observable action or measurable result. Think in detail about how things will be different once your goal is achieved. List the changes in what you'd see, feel, touch, taste, hear, be, do, or have.

Suppose that one of your goals is to become a better student by studying harder. You're headed in a powerful direction; now translate that goal into a concrete action, such as "I will study 2 hours for every hour I'm in class." Likewise, turn "Get a good education" into "Graduate with a BS degree in engineering by 2015." Specific goals make clear what actions are needed or what results are expected.

To get a comprehensive vision of your future, divide goals into several *time frames*. Long-term goals are major targets in your life that can take 5 or more years to achieve. Mid-term goals are outcomes that you want to produce in 1 to 5 years. And short-term goals are specific things to achieve in a year or less.

Also write goals in several *categories*—education, career, finances, health, family life, social life, spiritual life, and anything else that occurs to you. Writing down exactly what you want to experience in all these areas can help you create the life of your dreams. *

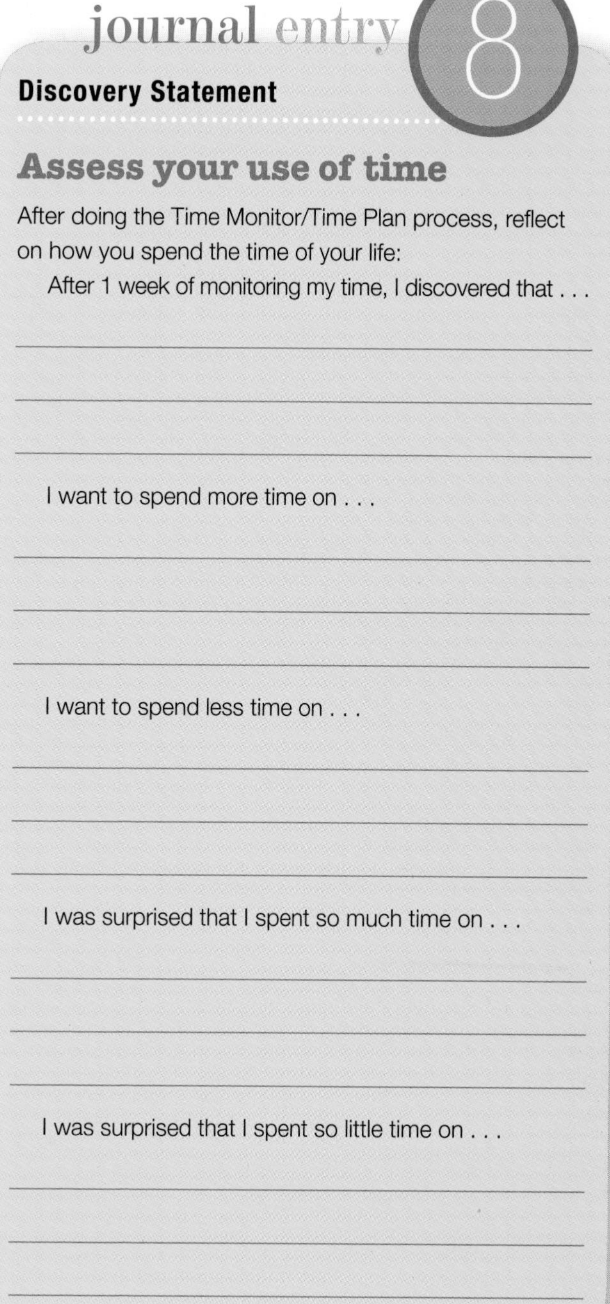

journal entry 8

Discovery Statement

Assess your use of time

After doing the Time Monitor/Time Plan process, reflect on how you spend the time of your life:

After 1 week of monitoring my time, I discovered that . . .

I want to spend more time on . . .

I want to spend less time on . . .

I was surprised that I spent so much time on . . .

I was surprised that I spent so little time on . . .

8 critical thinking exercise
Get real with your goals

One way to make goals effective is to examine them up close. That's what this exercise is about. Using a process of brainstorming and evaluation, you can break a long-term goal into smaller segments until you have taken it completely apart. When you analyze a goal to this level of detail, you're well on the way to meeting it.

For this exercise, you will use a pen, extra paper, and a watch with a second hand. (A digital watch with a built-in stopwatch feature is even better.) Timing is an important part of the brainstorming process, so follow the stated time limits. This entire exercise takes about an hour.

Part 1: Long-term goals

Brainstorm. Begin with an 8-minute brainstorm. Use a separate sheet of paper for this part of the exercise. For 8 minutes, write down everything you think you want in your life. Write as fast as you can, and write whatever comes into your head. Leave no thought out. Don't worry about accuracy. The object of a brainstorm is to generate as many ideas as possible.

Evaluate. After you have finished brainstorming, spend the next 6 minutes looking over your list. Analyze what you wrote. Read the list out loud. If something is missing, add it. Look for common themes or relationships among your goals. Then select three long-term goals that are important to you—goals that will take 5 or more years to achieve. Write these goals in the space below.

Before you continue, take a minute to reflect on the process you've used so far. What criteria did you use to select your top three goals?

Part 2: Mid-term goals

Brainstorm. Read out loud the three long-term goals you listed above. Choose one of them. Then brainstorm a list of goals you might achieve in the next 1 to 5 years that would allow you to accomplish that one long-term goal. These are mid-term goals. Spend 8 minutes on this brainstorm. Go for quantity.

Evaluate. Analyze your brainstorm of mid-term goals. Then select three that are most important to meeting the long-term goal you picked. Allow yourself 6 minutes for this part of the exercise. Write your selections in the space below.

Again, pause for reflection before going on to the next part of this exercise. Why do you see these three goals as more important than the other mid-term goals you generated? On a separate sheet of paper, write about your reasons for selecting these three goals.

Part 3: Short-term goals

Brainstorm. Review your list of mid-term goals, and select one. In another 8-minute brainstorm, generate a list of short-term goals—those you can attain in a year or less that will lead to accomplishing that mid-term goal. Write down everything that comes to mind. Do not evaluate or judge these ideas yet. For now, the more ideas you write down, the better.

Evaluate. Analyze your list of short-term goals. The most effective brainstorms are conducted by suspending judgment, so you might find some bizarre ideas on your list. That's fine. Now is the time to cross them out. Next, evaluate your remaining short-term goals, and select three that you are willing and able to accomplish. Allow yourself 6 minutes for this part of the exercise. Then write your selections in the space below.

The more you practice, the more effective you can be at choosing goals that have meaning for you. You can repeat this exercise, focusing on the other long-term goals you listed or creating new ones.

Complete this exercise online.

One of the most effective ways to stay on track and actually get things done is to use a daily to-do list. Although the Time Monitor/Time Plan gives you a general picture of the week, your daily to-do list itemizes specific tasks you want to complete within the next 24 hours.

Step 1: Brainstorm tasks
Step 2: Estimate time
Step 3: Rate each task by priority
Step 4: Cross off tasks
Step 5: Evaluate

The ABC daily to-do list

ONE ADVANTAGE of keeping a daily to-do list is that you don't have to remember what to do next. It's on the list.

Step 1 Brainstorm tasks

To get started, list all of the tasks you want to get done tomorrow. Each task will become an item on a to-do list. Just list everything you want to accomplish on a sheet of paper or planning calendar, or in a special notebook. You can also use 3x5 cards, writing one task on each card. Cards work well because you can slip them into your pocket or rearrange them, and you never have to copy to-do items from one list to another.

Step 2 Estimate time

For each task you wrote down in Step 1, estimate how long it will take you to complete it. This can be tricky. If you allow too little time, you end up feeling rushed. If you allow too much time, you become less productive. If you are unsure, overestimate rather than underestimate how long you will take for each task. Next, add up the time needed to complete all your to-do items. Also add up the number of unscheduled hours in your day. Then compare the two totals. If you have more hours of to-do items than unscheduled hours, that's a potential problem. To solve it, proceed to Step 3.

Step 3 Rate each task by priority

To prevent overscheduling, decide which to-do items are the most important, given the time you have available. One suggestion for making this decision comes from the book *How to Get Control of Your Time and Your Life*, by Alan Lakein: Simply label each item A, B, or C.[1] The A's are urgent—things that must be done immediately. The B's on your list are important, but not urgent. Finally, the C's are often small, easy tasks that can be done at any time. Once you've labeled the items on your to-do list, schedule time for all of the A's. The B's and C's can be done randomly during unscheduled parts of your day.

Step 4 Cross off tasks

Keep your to-do list with you at all times. Cross off activities when you finish them, and add new ones when you think of them. If you're using 3x5 cards, you can toss away or recycle the cards with completed items. Crossing off tasks and releasing cards can be fun.

When using the ABC priority method, you might experience C fever. Symptoms include the uncontrollable urge to drop that A task and begin crossing C's off your to-do list. When your history paper is due tomorrow, you might feel compelled to vacuum the rug, call your third cousin in Tulsa, and make a trip to the store for shoelaces. If you notice symptoms of C fever, ask yourself, "Does this item *really* need to be done now?" Then calmly return to the A's.

Step 5 Evaluate

At the end of the day, look for A priorities you didn't complete. Look for items that repeatedly turn up as B's or C's on your list and never seem to get done. Consider changing them to A's or dropping them altogether. Similarly, you might consider changing an A that didn't get done to a B or C priority. Then start on tomorrow's to-do list.

In any case, make starting your own to-do list an A priority. *

Find more strategies for daily planning online.

mastering technology

USE WEB-BASED TOOLS TO SAVE TIME

Time management tools generally fall into three major categories, no matter which system or set of techniques you use:

- **Lists** of goals and planned actions for meeting those goals (to-do items).
- **Calendars** for scheduling appointments and keeping track of due dates.
- **Contact managers**—sometimes called *personal relationship managers*—for keeping track of other people's addresses, phone numbers, e-mail addresses, and other contact information, along with notes from meetings with colleagues, clients, customers, or coworkers.

Today you can choose from dozens of free online applications that fill these functions. Online applications can save you time because they're accessible from *any* computer, in any location—as long as it's connected to the Web. Cell phone applications are also available to help you organize your time. If you use online or cell phone applications, you don't have to keep track of information scrawled on pieces of paper or transfer files from computer to computer. All the data you've entered from any computer are at your fingertips, at any time.

Many Web-based applications are aimed directly at students. A few of the options are described below. To find more, do an Internet search using the key words *web*, *tools*, and *students*.

Purpose	Application	Uses
Calendar	Google Calendar (www.google.com/calendar)	Keep track of scheduled events and share them with other people; coordinate your data with other Google online applications.
Calendar	30 Boxes (30boxes.com)	Keep track of scheduled events, and share them with other people.
Goal setting	43Things (www.43things.com)	List goals, and track your progress toward them as part of an online community.
Goal setting	myGoals.com (www.mygoals.com)	List goals, get automatic action reminders, and choose from a library of "GoalPlans" based on expert-recommended content.
Lists	Gubb (www.gubb.net)	Create and edit lists (including to-do lists), check off completed items, assign due dates to items, and send lists via e-mail or text messaging.
Lists	Remember the Milk (www.rememberthemilk.com)	Create and manage tasks online and offline, and send yourself reminders.
Multipurpose	Google Docs (docs.google.com)	Create and share documents, spreadsheets, presentations, and forms.
Multipurpose	Zoho (www.zoho.com)	Create and share documents, spreadsheets, presentations, and forms; create a wiki (a Web site that anyone can edit); send and receive e-mail; manage to-do lists; create a calendar; chat online; and clip content (audio, video, text, and images) from the Web.
Multipurpose	Yahoo (www.yahoo.com)	Send and receive e-mail, manage contact information, take notes, and create a calendar.
Multipurpose	OpenOffice (www.openoffice.org)	Create documents, spreadsheets, presentations, graphics, and databases.

Find an updated list of Web-based applications online.

Gearing up: Using a long-term planner

Planning a day, a week, or a month ahead is a powerful practice. Using a long-term planner—one that displays an entire quarter, semester, or year at a glance—can yield even more benefits.

WITH A LONG-TERM planner, you can eliminate a lot of unpleasant surprises. Long-term planning allows you to avoid scheduling conflicts—the kind that obligate you to be in two places at the same time 1 month from now. You can also anticipate busy periods, such as finals week, and start preparing for them. Say good-bye to all-night cram sessions; say hello to serenity.

Find a long-term planner, or make your own. Photocopy the long-term planner that appears on the following page, or look for other options. Many office supply stores carry academic planners in paper form that cover an entire school year. Computer software for time management offers the same features. You can also be creative and make your own long-term planner. A big roll of newsprint pinned to a bulletin board or taped to a wall will do nicely.

Enter scheduled dates that extend into the future. Use your long-term planner to list commitments that extend beyond the current month. Enter test dates, lab sessions, days that classes will be canceled, and other events that will take place over this term and next term.

Create a master assignment list. Find the syllabus for each course you're currently taking. Then, in your long-term planner, enter the due dates for all of the assignments in all of your courses. This step can be a powerful reality check.

The purpose of this technique is to not to make you feel overwhelmed with all the things you have to do. Rather, its aim is to help you take a First Step toward recognizing the demands on your time. Armed with the truth about how you use your time, you can make more accurate plans.

Include nonacademic events. In addition to tracking academic commitments, you can use your long-term planner to mark significant events in your life outside school. Include birthdays, doctors' appointments, concert dates, credit card payment due dates, and car maintenance schedules.

Use your long-term planner to divide and conquer. Big assignments such as term papers or major presentations pose a special risk. When you have 3 months to do a project, you might say to yourself, "That looks like a lot of work, but I've got plenty of time. No problem." But 2 months, 3 weeks, and 6 days from now, it could suddenly be a problem.

For some people, academic life is a series of last-minute crises punctuated by periods of exhaustion. You can avoid that fate. The trick is to set due dates *before* the final due date.

When planning to write a term paper, for instance, enter the final due date in your long-term planner. Then set individual due dates for each milestone in the writing process—creating an outline, completing your research, finishing a first draft, editing the draft, and preparing the final copy. By meeting these interim due dates, you make steady progress on the assignment throughout the term. That sure beats trying to crank out all those pages at the last minute. *

Find printable copies of this long-term planner online.

Week of	Monday	Tuesday	Wednesday	Thursday	Friday	Saturday	Sunday
9 / 5							
9 / 12		English quiz					
9 / 19			English paper due		Speech #1		
9 / 26	Chemistry test					Skiing at the lake	
10 / 3		English quiz			Speech #2		
10 / 10				Geography project due			
10 / 17				--- No classes ---			

Name ______________________________

LONG-TERM PLANNER ___ / ___ / ___ to ___ / ___ / ___

Week of	Monday	Tuesday	Wednesday	Thursday	Friday	Saturday	Sunday
___ / ___							
___ / ___							
___ / ___							
___ / ___							
___ / ___							
___ / ___							
___ / ___							
___ / ___							
___ / ___							
___ / ___							
___ / ___							
___ / ___							
___ / ___							
___ / ___							
___ / ___							
___ / ___							
___ / ___							
___ / ___							
___ / ___							
___ / ___							
___ / ___							
___ / ___							
___ / ___							
___ / ___							
___ / ___							
___ / ___							
___ / ___							
___ / ___							
___ / ___							
___ / ___							

Get the most out of now

© Image copyright Ferenc Szelepcsenyi, 2009. Used under license from Shutterstock.com

Study difficult (or boring) subjects first. If your chemistry problems put you to sleep, get to them first, while you are fresh. We tend to give top priority to what we enjoy studying, yet the courses that we find most difficult often require the most creative energy. Save your favorite subjects for later. If you find yourself avoiding a particular subject, get up an hour earlier to study it before breakfast. With that chore out of the way, the rest of the day can be a breeze.

Be aware of your best time of day. Many people learn best in daylight hours. If this is true for you, schedule study time for your most difficult subjects before nightfall.

Use waiting time. Five minutes waiting for a subway, 20 minutes waiting for the dentist, 10 minutes in between classes—waiting time adds up fast. Have short study tasks ready to do during these periods. For example, you can carry 3x5 cards with facts, formulas, or definitions and pull them out anywhere.

Study 2 hours for every hour you're in class. Students in higher education are regularly advised to allow 2 hours of study time for every hour spent in class. If you are taking 15 credit hours, then plan to spend 30 hours a week studying. The benefits of following this advice will be apparent at exam time.

This guideline is just that—a guideline, not an absolute rule. Use the Time Monitor/Time Plan exercise in this chapter to discover what works for you.

Also avoid marathon study sessions. When possible, study in shorter sessions. Three 3-hour sessions are usually more productive than one 9-hour session. If you must study in a large block of time, work on several subjects, and avoid studying similar topics one after the other.

Learn to say no. Saying no is a time-saver and a valuable life skill for everyone. Some people feel it is rude to refuse a request. But you can say no effectively and courteously. Others want you to succeed as a student. When you tell them that you can't do what they ask because you are busy educating yourself, most people will understand.

Manage interruptions. Notice how others misuse your time. Be aware of repeat offenders. Ask yourself whether there are certain friends or relatives who consistently interrupt your study time. If avoiding the interrupter is impractical, send a clear message: "What you're saying is important. Can we schedule a time to talk about it when I can give you my full attention?"

Ask: "What is one task I can accomplish toward achieving my goal?" This technique is helpful when you face a big, imposing job. Pick out one small task related to that job, preferably one you can complete in about 5 minutes. Then do it. The satisfaction of getting one thing done can spur you on to get one more thing done. Meanwhile, the job gets smaller.

Ask: "Is this a piano?" Carpenters who construct rough frames for buildings have a saying they use when they bend a nail or accidentally hack a chunk out of a two-by-four: "Well, this ain't no piano." It means that perfection is not necessary. Ask yourself if what you are doing needs to be perfect. Perhaps you don't have to apply the same standards of grammar to lecture notes that you would apply to a term paper. If you can complete a job 95 percent perfectly in 2 hours and 100 percent perfectly in 4 hours, ask yourself whether the additional 5 percent improvement is worth doubling the amount of time you spend.

Ask: "Am I making time for things that are important but not urgent?" If we spend most of our time putting out fires, we can feel drained and frustrated. According to Stephen R. Covey, this chain of events occurs when we forget to take time for things that are not urgent but are truly important.[2] Examples of truly important activities include exercising regularly, reading, praying or meditating, spending quality time alone or with family members and friends, traveling, and cooking nutritious meals. Each of these activities can contribute directly to a long-term goal or life mission. Yet when schedules get tight, we often forgo these things, waiting for that elusive day when we'll "finally have more time." That day won't come until we choose to make time for what's truly important.

Ask: "Could I find the time if I really wanted to?" The way people speak often rules out the option of finding more time. An alternative is to speak about time with more possibility.

The next time you're tempted to say, "I just don't have time," pause for a minute. Question the truth of this statement. Could you find 4 more hours this week for studying? Suppose that someone offered to pay you $10,000 to find those 4 hours. Suppose too that you will get paid only if you don't lose sleep, call in sick for work, or sacrifice anything important to you. Could you find the time if vast sums of money were involved?

Remember that when it comes to school, vast sums of money *are* involved.

Ask: "Am I willing to promise it?" This time-management idea might be the most powerful of all: If you want to find time for a task, promise yourself—and others—that you'll get it done.

To make this technique work, do more than say that you'll try or that you'll give it your best shot. Take an oath, as you would in court. Give it your word.

At times you might go too far. Some promises may be truly beyond you, and you might break them. However, a broken promise is not the end of the world.

Promises can work magic. When your word is on the line, it's possible to discover reserves of time and energy you didn't know existed. *

Discover even more ways to get the most out of now.

The 7-day anti-procrastination plan

Overcoming procrastination does not have to be a process that takes month or years. Experiment with ending this habit over the next 7 days.

MONDAY Make it Meaningful. What is important about the task you've been putting off? List all the benefits of completing that task. To remember this strategy, keep in mind that it starts with the letter ***M,*** as in the word ***Monday.***

TUESDAY Take it Apart. Break big jobs into a series of small ones you can do in 15 minutes or less. This strategy starts with the letter ***T,*** so mentally tie it to ***Tuesday.***

WEDNESDAY Write an Intention Statement. If you can't get started on a term paper, you might write, "I intend to write a list of at least 10 possible topics by 9 p.m. I will reward myself with an hour of guilt-free recreational reading." In your memory, file the first word in this strategy—***write***—with ***Wednesday.***

THURSDAY Tell Everyone. Publicly announce your intention to get a task done. Tell your spouse, roommate, friends, parents, or children. Include anyone who will ask whether you've completed the assignment or who will suggest ways to get it done. Associate ***tell*** with ***Thursday.***

FRIDAY Find a Reward. Remember to reward yourself only if you complete the task. Then notice how it feels. ***Friday*** is a fine day to ***find*** a reward.

SATURDAY Settle it Now. Do it now. Link ***settle*** with ***Saturday.***

SUNDAY Say No. If you realize that you really don't intend to do something, quit telling yourself that you will. That's procrastinating. Just say no. Then you're not procrastinating. ***Sunday*** is a great day to finally let go and just ***say*** no.

9

critical thinking exercise
The Money Monitor/Money Plan

Many of us find it easy to lose track of money. It likes to escape when no one is looking. And usually, no one *is* looking. That's why the simple act of noticing the details about money can be so useful—even if this is the only idea from this chapter that you ever apply.

Use this exercise as a chance to discover how money flows into and out of your life. The goal is to record all the money you receive and spend over the course of 1 month. This sounds like a big task, but it's simpler than you might think. Besides, there's a big payoff for this action. With increased awareness of income and expenses, you can make choices about money that will change your life. Here's how to begin.

1. Tear out the Money Monitor/Money Plan form on page 66.
Make photocopies of this form to use each month. The form helps you do two things. One is to get a big picture of the money that flows in and out of your life. The other is to plan specific and immediate changes in how you earn and spend money.

2. Keep track of your income and expenses.
Use your creativity to figure out how you want to carry out this step. The goal is to create a record of exactly how much you earn and spend each month. Use any method that works for you. Be sure to keep it simple. Following are some options:

Carry 3x5 cards in your pocket, purse, backpack, or briefcase. Every time you buy something or get paid, record a few details on a card. List the date. Add a description of what you bought or what you got paid. Note whether the item is a source of income (money coming in) or an expense (money going out). Be sure to use a separate card for each item. This makes it easier to sort your cards into categories at the end of the month and fill out your Money Monitor/Money Plan.

Save all receipts and file them. Although this method does not require you to carry any 3x5 cards, it does require that you faithfully hang on to every receipt and record of payment. Every time you buy something, ask for a receipt. Then stick it in your wallet, purse, or pocket. When you get home, make notes about the purchase on the receipt. Then file the receipts in a folder labeled with the current month and year (for example, *1/12 to 2/12*). Every time you get a paycheck during that month, save the stub and add it to the folder. If you do not get a receipt or record of payment, whip out a 3x5 card and create one of your own. Detailed receipts will help you later on when you file taxes, categorize expenses (such as food and entertainment), and check your purchases against credit card statements.

Use personal finance software. Learn to use Quicken or a similar product that allows you to record income and expenses on your computer and to sort them into categories.

Use online banking services. If you have a checking account that offers online services, take advantage of the records that the bank is already keeping for you. Every time you write a check, use a debit card, or make a deposit, the transaction will show up online. You can use a computer to log in to your account and view these transactions at any time. If you're unclear about how to use online banking, go to your bank and ask for help.

Experiment with several of the above options. Settle into one that feels most comfortable to you. Or create a method of your own. Anything will work, as long as you end each month with an *exact and accurate* record of your income and expenses.

3. On the last day of the month, fill out your Money Monitor/Money Plan.
Pull out a blank Money Monitor/Money Plan. Label it with the current month and year. Fill out this form using the records of your income and expenses for the month.

Notice that the far left column of the Money Monitor/Money Plan includes categories of income and expenses. (You can use the blank rows for categories of income and expenses that are not already included.) Write your total for each category in the middle column.

For example, if you spent $300 at the grocery store this month, write that amount in the middle column next to "Groceries." If you work a part-time job and received two paychecks for the month, write the total in the middle column next to "Employment." See the sample Money Monitor/Money Plan on the next page for more examples.

Remember to split expenses when necessary. For example, you might write one check each month to pay the balance due on your credit card. The purchases listed on your credit card bill might fall into several categories. Total up your expenses in each category, and list them separately.

Suppose that you used your credit card to buy music online, purchase a sweater, pay for three restaurant meals, and buy two tanks of gas for your car. Write the online music expense next to "Entertainment." Write the amount you paid for the sweater next to "Clothes." Write the total you spent at the restaurants next to "Eating Out." Finally, write the total for your gas stops next to "Gas."

Now look at the column on the far right of the Money Monitor/Money Plan. This column is where the magic happens. Review each category of income and expense. If you plan to reduce your spending in a certain category during the next month, write a minus sign (–) in the far right column. If you plan a spending increase in any category next month, write a plus sign (+) in the far right column. If you think that a category of income or expense will remain the same next month, leave the column blank.

Look again at the sample Money Monitor/Money Plan. This student plans to reduce her spending for clothes, eating out, and entertainment (which for her includes movies and DVD rentals). She plans to increase the total she spends on groceries. She figures that even so, she'll save money by cooking more food at home and eating out less.

Notice one more thing about the Money Monitor/Money Plan: It does not require you to create a budget. Budgets—like diets—often fail. Many people cringe at the mere mention of the word *budget*. To them it is associated with scarcity, drudgery, and guilt. The idea of creating a budget conjures up images of a penny-pinching Ebenezer Scrooge shaking a bony, wrinkled finger at them and screaming, "You spent too much, you loser!"

That's not the idea behind the Money Monitor/Money Plan. In fact, there is no budget worksheet for you to complete each month. And no one is pointing a finger at you. Instead of budgeting, you simply write a plus sign or a minus sign next to each expense or income category that you *freely choose* to increase or decrease next month.

If you're short on money, one possible solution is to increase your income. This approach is reasonable. It also has a potential problem: When their income increases, many people continue to spend more than they make. To avoid this problem, manage your expenses no matter how much money you make. For starters:

- *Reduce the big-ticket items*. Choices about where to live, for example, can save you thousands of dollars. Sometimes a place a little farther from campus, or a smaller house or apartment, will be much less expensive.
- *Reduce the small-ticket items*. Reducing or eliminating the money you spend on low-cost purchases can make a big difference over time. For example, $3 spent at the coffee shop every day adds up to $1,095 over a year. That kind of spending can give anyone the jitters.
- *Reduce the cost of eating*. Instead of hitting a restaurant, head to the grocery store. Fresh fruits, fresh vegetables, and whole grains are not only better for you than processed food—they also cost less. Create a list of your five favorite home-cooked meals, and learn how to prepare them. Keep the ingredients for these meals always on hand. To reduce your grocery bills, buy these ingredients in bulk.
- *Reduce your phone bill*. If you use a cell phone, pull out a copy of your latest bill. Review how many minutes you used last month. Perhaps you could get by with a less expensive phone, fewer minutes, fewer text messages, and a cheaper plan.
- *Reduce your entertainment expenses—and still have fun*. When you spend money on entertainment, ask yourself what the benefits will be and whether you could get the same benefits for less money. You can read magazines for free at the library, for example. Most libraries also loan CDs and DVDs for free.
- *To manage your spending, consider the "envelope system."* After reviewing your monthly income and expenses, for example, put a certain amount of cash each week in an envelope labeled "Entertainment/Eating Out." When the envelope is empty, stop spending money on these items for the rest of the week. If you use online banking, see whether you can create separate accounts for various spending categories. Then deposit a fixed amount of money into each of those accounts. This is an electronic version of the envelope system.

After you've filled out your first Money Monitor/Money Plan, take a moment to congratulate yourself. You have actively collected and analyzed the data needed to take charge of your financial life. No matter how the numbers add up, you are now in conscious control of your money. Repeat this exercise every month. It will keep you on a steady path to financial freedom.

Do this exercise online.

Sample Money Monitor/Money Plan
Month________ Year_____

Income	This Month	Next Month
Employment	500	
Grants	100	
Interest from Savings		
Loans	300	
Scholarships	100	
Total Income	1000	

Expenses	This Month	Next Month
Books and Supplies		
Car Maintenance		
Car Payment		
Clothes		–
Deposits into Savings Account		
Eating Out	50	–
Entertainment	50	–
Gas	100	
Groceries	300	+
Insurance (Car, Life, Health, Home)		
Laundry	20	
Phone	55	
Rent/Mortgage Payment	400	
Tuition and Fees		
Utilities	50	
Total Expenses	1025	–

Money Monitor/Money Plan
Month________ Year_____

Income	This Month	Next Month
Employment		
Grants		
Interest from Savings		
Loans		
Scholarships		
Total Income		

Expenses	This Month	Next Month
Books and Supplies		
Car Maintenance		
Car Payment		
Clothes		
Deposits into Savings Account		
Eating Out		
Entertainment		
Gas		
Groceries		
Insurance (Car, Life, Health, Home)		
Laundry		
Phone		
Rent/Mortgage Payment		
Tuition and Fees		
Utilities		
Total Expenses		

Money Monitor/Money Plan
Month________ Year_____

Income	This Month	Next Month
Employment		
Grants		
Interest from Savings		
Loans		
Scholarships		
Total Income		

Expenses	This Month	Next Month
Books and Supplies		
Car Maintenance		
Car Payment		
Clothes		
Deposits into Savings Account		
Eating Out		
Entertainment		
Gas		
Groceries		
Insurance (Car, Life, Health, Home)		
Laundry		
Phone		
Rent/Mortgage Payment		
Tuition and Fees		
Utilities		
Total Expenses		

journal entry 9

Discovery/Intention Statement

Reflect on your Money Monitor/Money Plan

Now that you've experimented with the Money Monitor/ Money Plan process, reflect on what you're learning. To start creating a new future with money, complete the following statements.

After monitoring my income and expenses for 1 month, I was surprised to discover that . . .

When it comes to money, I am skilled at . . .

When it comes to money, I am *not* so skilled at . . .

I could increase my income by . . .

I could spend less money on . . .

After thinking about the most powerful step I can take right now to improve my finances, I intend to . . .

Take charge of your credit

A GOOD CREDIT rating will serve you for a lifetime. With this asset, you'll be able to borrow money any time you need it. A poor credit rating, however, can keep you from getting a car or a house in the future. You might also have to pay higher insurance rates, and you could even be turned down for a job.

To take charge of your credit, borrow money only when truly necessary. If you do borrow, then make all of your payments, and make them on time. This is especially important for managing credit cards and student loans.

Use credit cards with caution

An unpaid credit card balance is a sure sign that you are spending more money than you have. To avoid this outcome, keep track of how much you spend with credit cards each month. Pay off the card balance each month, on time, and avoid finance or late charges.

If you do accumulate a large credit card balance, go to your bank and ask about ways to get a loan with a lower interest rate. Use this loan to pay off your credit cards. Then promise yourself never to accumulate credit card debt again.

To simplify your financial life and take charge of your credit, consider using only one card. Choose one with no annual fee and the lowest interest rate.

As of February 22, 2010, credit card companies must comply with new regulations designed to protect consumers. In most cases, for example, a company cannot raise interest rates within the first year of a new account. And if you are under age 21, you will need to show that you can make credit card payments, or get a cosigner. For more information, go online to www.federalreserve.gov and search for *new credit card rules*.

Manage student loans

A college degree is one of the best investments you can make. But you don't have to go broke to get that education. Make this investment with the lowest debt possible.

The surest way to manage debt is to avoid it altogether. If you do take out loans, borrow only the amount that you cannot get from other sources—scholarships, grants, employment, gifts from relatives, and personal savings.

Also set a target date for graduation, and stick to it. The fewer years you go to school, the lower your debt.

If you transfer to another school, consider costs carefully. In addition to choosing schools on the basis of reputation, consider tuition, fees, housing, and financial aid packages.

When borrowing money for school, shop carefully. Go to the financial aid office and ask whether you can get a Stafford loan. These are fixed-rate, low-interest loans from the federal government.

If your parents are helping to pay for your education, they can apply for a PLUS loan. There is no income limit, and parents can borrow up to the total cost of their children's education.

Some lenders will forgive part of a student loan if you agree to take a certain job for a few years, such as teaching in a public school in a low-income neighborhood or working as a nurse in a rural community. This arrangement is called an *income-based repayment plan*. Ask someone in the financial aid office if it is an option for you.

If you take out student loans, find out exactly when the first payment is due on each of them. Don't assume that you can wait to start repayment until you find a job. Any bill payments that you miss will hammer your credit score.

Also ask your financial aid office about whether you can consolidate your loans. This means that you lump them all together and owe just one payment every month. Loan consolidation makes it easier to stay on top of your payments and protect your credit score. *

Find more strategies online for credit mastery.

If you're in trouble

Financial problems are common. Solve them in ways that protect you for the future.

Get specific data. Complete Exercise 9: "The Money Monitor/Money Plan" included earlier in this chapter.

Be honest with creditors. Determine the amount that you are sure you can repay each month, and ask the creditor if that would work for your case.

Go for credit counseling. Most cities have agencies with professional advisors who can help straighten out your financial problems.

Change your spending patterns. If you have a history of overspending (or underearning), change *is* possible. This chapter is full of suggestions.

You can pay for school

Education is one of the few things you can buy that will last a lifetime. It won't rust, corrode, break down, or wear out. It can't be stolen, burned, repossessed, or destroyed. Once you have a degree, no one can take it away. That makes your education a safer investment than real estate, gold, oil, diamonds, or stocks.

There are many ways to pay for school. The kind of help you get depends on your financial need. In general, financial need equals the cost of your schooling minus what you can reasonably be expected to pay.

Financial aid includes money you don't pay back (grants and scholarships), money you do pay back (loans), and work-study programs. Most students who get financial aid receive a package that includes several examples of each type.

To find out more, visit your school's financial aid office on a regular basis. Also go online. Start with Student Aid on the Web at studentaid.ed.gov.

Once you've lined up financial aid, keep it flowing. Find out the requirements for renewing loans, grants, and scholarships. Remember that many financial aid packages depend on your making "satisfactory academic progress." Also, programs change constantly. Money may be limited, and application deadlines are critical.

Scholarships, grants, and loans backed by the federal government are key sources of money for students. State governments often provide grants and scholarships as well. So do credit unions, service organizations such as Kiwanis International, and local chambers of commerce. Sometimes relatives will provide financial help. For more information on loans, refer back to the article "Take Charge of Your Credit."

Determine how much money you need to finish your degree and where you will get it. Having a plan for paying for your entire education makes it easier to finish your degree. *

Go online to learn about more ways to pay for school.

Education by the hour

As a tool for becoming more aware of time *and* money, determine exactly what it costs you to go to school. Fill in the blanks below using totals for a semester, quarter, or whatever term system your school uses.

Note: Include only the costs that relate directly to going to school. For example, under "Transportation," list only the amount that you pay for gas to drive back and forth to school—not the total amount you spend on gas for a semester.

Tuition	$______
Books	$______
Fees	$______
Transportation	$______
Clothing	$______
Food	$______
Housing	$______
Entertainment	$______
Other expenses (such as insurance, medical costs, and child care)	$______
Subtotal	$______
Salary you could earn per term if you weren't in school	$______
Total (A) (Subtotal + Salary)	$______

Now figure out how many classes you attend in one term. This is the number of your scheduled class periods per week multiplied by the number of weeks in your school term. Put that figure below:

Total (B) ______

Divide the **Total (B)** into the **Total (A),** and put that amount here:

$______

This is what it costs you to go to one class one time.

On a separate sheet of paper, describe your responses to discovering this figure. Also list anything you will do differently as a result of knowing the hourly cost of your education.

Do this exercise online.

2 TIME AND MONEY

Be Here Now

Being right here, right now is such a simple idea. It seems obvious. Where else can you be but where you are? When else can you be there but when you are there?

The answer is that you can be somewhere else at any time—in your head. It's common for our thoughts to distract us from where we've chosen to be. When we let this happen, we lose the benefits of focusing our attention on what's important to us in the present moment.

To "be here now" means to do what you're doing when you're doing it. It means to be where you are when you're there. Students consistently report that focusing attention on the here and now is one of the most powerful tools in this book.

We all have a voice in our head that hardly ever shuts up. If you don't believe it, conduct this experiment: Close your eyes for 10 seconds, and pay attention to what is going on in your head. Please do this right now.

Notice something? Perhaps a voice in your head was saying, "Forget it. I'm in a hurry." Another might have said, "I wonder when 10 seconds is up?" Another could have been saying, "What little voice? I don't hear any little voice."

That's the voice.

This voice can take you anywhere at any time—especially when you are studying. When the voice takes you away, you might appear to be studying, but your brain is at the beach.

All of us have experienced this voice, as well as the absence of it. When our inner voices are silent, time no longer seems to exist. We forget worries, aches, pains, reasons, excuses, and justifications. We fully experience the here and now. Life is magic.

Do not expect to be rid of the voice entirely. That is neither possible nor desirable. Your inner voice serves a purpose. It enables you to analyze, predict, classify, and understand events out there in the "real" world. The trick is to consciously choose when to be with your inner voice and when to let it go.

Instead of trying to force a stray thought out of your head—a futile enterprise—simply notice it. Accept it. Tell yourself, "There's that thought again." Then gently return your attention to the task at hand. That thought, or another, will come back. Your mind will drift. Simply notice again where your thoughts take you, and gently bring yourself back to the here and now.

The idea behind this Power Process is simple. When you plan for the future, plan for the future. When you listen to a lecture, listen to a lecture. When you read this book, read this book. And when you choose to daydream, daydream. Do what you're doing when you're doing it.

Be where you are when you're there. Be here now . . . and now . . . and now.

Learn more about this Power Process online.

Put it to Work

You can use strategies in *Becoming a Master Student* to succeed at work. Get started by reflecting on the following case study.

Steve Carlson is a technical writer. He works for DCS, a company that makes products for multimedia teleconferencing—both hardware and software. He joined DCS a year ago, after graduating with a BA in technical communications.

Steve works in a department that creates sales brochures, user manuals, and Web sites that relate to DCS products. His manager is Louise Chao.

One Friday afternoon, Louise knocks on the door of Steve's office. She wants Steve to do a rush project—a new product brochure to be researched, written, designed, and printed in 2 weeks. Louise is on the way to another meeting and only has 5 minutes to talk.

After Louise describes the project, Steve checks a large paper calendar hanging on a wall in his office. This calendar shows the status of Steve's active projects. On this calendar are due dates for researching, outlining, and writing about a dozen documents. Each due date is color coded—red for urgent projects, green for other active projects, and gray for planned projects that are not yet active. Steve uses the wall calendar to plan his work and visually represent his project load.

"I need at least 3 full days to research and write the brochure you're talking about," Steve says. "In addition, meetings with our designer and revisions would take up another 2 days. So, I'd want to free up at least 1 week of my time to get this brochure done."

Steve points to the projects shown in red on his wall calendar. It's clear that his schedule is full of urgent projects.

"Louise, I know this brochure is important to you," he says. "Can we schedule a time to meet about this? We could choose a project to delay for a week so that I could meet your request."

Steve applied several strategies from this chapter to plan projects and stay within budget:

- Estimate time.
- Rate each task by priority.
- Create a master monthly calendar.
- Set clear starting and stopping times.
- Use a long-term planner to divide and conquer.

Asia Images Group/Getty

List more strategies that would be useful to Steve in this situation.

____

____

____

____

____

Consider the following ideas if you feel overwhelmed at work:

- Use the Time Monitor/Time Plan process to analyze the way you currently use your time at work.
- Look for low-value activities to delegate or eliminate.
- Before committing to a project, brainstorm a list of project-related tasks, and estimate the amount of time each task requires.
- Note your peak periods of energy during the workday, and schedule your most challenging tasks for those times.
- Schedule fixed blocks of time during the week when you will not be available for meetings; use this time to tackle your to-do list.
- Set aside 1 hour each week to review the status of long-term projects.
- When delegating tasks to members of a project team, set a clear due date for each task.
- Keep a list of things that coworkers have promised to send you or tasks that they've agreed to complete.

Find more strategies for managing time at work.

Quiz

Name____ Date____/____/____

1. Rewrite the statement "I want to study harder" so that it becomes a specific goal.
   I will study one more hour each night, Monday through Friday, for the next 30 days. After that, I will reflect on and evaluate the impact it has had on my performance in college. (Answers will vary.) (*Setting and achieving goals*, p. 55)
2. What is meant by "This ain't no piano"?
   If a nail is bent or a chunk is accidentally hacked out of a two-by-four during the rough framing of a building, a carpenter might say, "This ain't no piano." It means perfection is not necessary. Consider whether what you are doing needs to be perfect: Is it a piano or not? (*Get the most out of now,* pp. 61–62)
3. Define *C fever* as it applies to the ABC priority method.
   The C items on your to-do list do not require immediate attention. C fever is the uncontrollable urge to drop that A task and begin crossing C's off of the list. A and B tasks are often more difficult and time-consuming. (*The ABC daily to-do list*, p. 57)
4. According to the text, overcoming procrastination is hard and takes months or even years. True or false? Explain your answer.
   False. Most of the strategies are easy and can be done immediately. The challenge is to replace the procrastination habits with nonprocrastination habits. (*The 7-day antiprocrastination plan*, p. 62)
5. The purpose of the Power Process: "Be Here Now" is to get rid of daydreams and inner voices. True or false? Explain your answer.
   It is neither possible nor desirable to get rid of daydreams and inner voices. The trick is to consciously choose when to be with your inner voice and when to let it go.
   Instead of trying to force a stray thought out of your head, simply notice and accept it. Then gently return your attention to the task at hand. (Answers will vary) (*Power Process: Be Here Now*, p. 71)
6. List three sources of money to help students pay for their education.
   List three of the following sources: grants, scholarships, student loans, and work-study programs, all of which may be included in financial aid packages; financial help may also be available from relatives. (*You can pay for school,* p. 70)
7. Describe three ways to keep track of your expenses.
   Describe three of the following methods:
   - Carry 3×5 cards in your pocket, purse, backpack, or briefcase. Every time you buy something record a few details on a card. List the date. Add a description of what you bought.
   - Save all receipts and file them. Every time you buy something, get a receipt, make notes about the purchase on the receipt, and then file the receipts in a folder labeled with the current month and year.
   - Use personal finance software. Learn to use Quicken or a similar product that allows you to record income and expenses on your computer and to sort them into categories.
   - Use online banking services. If you have a checking account that offers online services, take advantage of the records that the bank is already keeping for you. (*The Money Monitor/Money Plan*, pp. 63–67)
8. Which of the folloiwng is *not* a good strategy for taking charge of your credit card:
   (a) Pay off the full balance due every month.
   (b) Make your monthly payments on time.
   (c) To build a good credit record, use several credit cards.
   (d) To avoid spending more money than you have, keep track of how much you spend each month with credit cards.
   (c) To build a good credit record, use several credit cards. (*Take charge of your credit*, p. 69)
9. If you are in financial trouble, which of the following strategies is *least* likely to help?
   (a) Monitor your income and expenses.
   (b) Borrow additional money.
   (c) Be honest with creditors.
   (d) Go for credit counseling.
   (e) Change your spending patterns.
   (b) Borrow additional money. (*If you're in trouble*, p. 69)
10. Stafford loans are the most expensive variable-interest loans. True or false? Explain your answer.
    False. Stafford loans are fixed-rate, low-interest loans from the federal government.
    (*Take charge of your credit*, p. 69)

Skills Snapshot

The Discovery Wheel in Chapter 1, Critical Thinking Exercise 4, includes a section labeled "Time and Money." For the next 10 to 15 minutes, go beyond your initial responses to that exercise. Take a snapshot of your skills as they exist today, after reading and doing this chapter.

Begin by reflecting on some recent experiences. Then take the next step in your mastery of time by choosing the strategy you'd like to experiment with next.

GOALS

I would describe my ability to set specific goals as . . .

The most important goal for me to achieve during this school year is . . .

PLANNING

When setting priorities for what to do each day, the first thing I consider is . . .

I keep track of my daily to-do items by . . .

MANAGING INCOME AND EXPENSES

Right now my main sources of income are . . .

One big monthly expense that I could reduce right away is . . .

NEXT ACTION

I'll know that I've reached a new level of mastery with time and money when . . .

To reach that level of mastery, the most important thing I can do next is to . . .

Master Student PROFILE

Al Gore ... is optimistic

© Joseph Sohm/Visions of America/Corbis

(1948–) Former vice president of the United States, Gore refocused his career on climate change, won a Nobel Peace Prize, and—in his film *An Inconvenient Truth*—invented a new type of documentary.

One hundred and nineteen years ago, a wealthy inventor read his own obituary, mistakenly published years before his death. Wrongly believing the inventor had just died, a newspaper printed a harsh judgment of his life's work, unfairly labeling him "The Merchant of Death" because of his invention—dynamite. Shaken by this condemnation, the inventor made a fateful choice to serve the cause of peace.

Seven years later, Alfred Nobel created this prize and the others that bear his name.

Seven years ago tomorrow, I read my own political obituary in a judgment that seemed to me harsh and mistaken—if not premature. But that unwelcome verdict also brought a precious if painful gift: an opportunity to search for fresh new ways to serve my purpose.

Unexpectedly, that quest has brought me here. Even though I fear my words cannot match this moment, I pray what I am feeling in my heart will be communicated clearly enough that those who hear me will say, "We must act." . . .

In the last few months, it has been harder and harder to misinterpret the signs that our world is spinning out of kilter. Major cities in North and South America, Asia and Australia are nearly out of water due to massive droughts and melting glaciers. Desperate farmers are losing their livelihoods. Peoples in the frozen Arctic and on low-lying Pacific islands are planning evacuations of places they have long called home. Unprecedented wildfires have forced a half million people from their homes in one country and caused a national emergency that almost brought down the government in another. Climate refugees have migrated into areas already inhabited by people with different cultures, religions, and traditions, increasing the potential for conflict. Stronger storms in the Pacific and Atlantic have threatened whole cities. Millions have been displaced by massive flooding in South Asia, Mexico, and 18 countries in Africa. As temperature extremes have increased, tens of thousands have lost their lives. We are recklessly burning and clearing our forests and driving more and more species into extinction.

There is an African proverb that says, "If you want to go quickly, go alone. If you want to go far, go together." We need to go far, quickly. . . .

Fifteen years ago, I made that case at the "Earth Summit" in Rio de Janeiro. Ten years ago, I presented it in Kyoto. This week, I will urge the delegates in Bali to adopt a bold mandate for a treaty that establishes a universal global cap on emissions and uses the market in emissions trading to efficiently allocate resources to the most effective opportunities for speedy reductions.

This treaty should be ratified and brought into effect everywhere in the world by the beginning of 2010—two years sooner than presently contemplated. The pace of our response must be accelerated to match the accelerating pace of the crisis itself. . . .

Make no mistake, the next generation will ask us one of two questions. Either they will ask: "What were you thinking; why didn't you act?"

Or they will ask instead: "How did you find the moral courage to rise and successfully resolve a crisis that so many said was impossible to solve?"

Al Gore, "Nobel Lecture," December 10, 2007.

Learn more about Al Gore and other master students at the Master Student Hall of Fame.

3 Memory

Instructor Tools & Tips

> The art of true memory is the art of attention.
>
> **—Samuel Johnson**

> Memory is the mother of imagination, reason and skill . . . . This is the companion, this is the tutor, the poet, the library with which you travel.
>
> **—Mark Van Doren**

Preview

A primary objective of student success courses is to foster the fundamental skill of memorizing key information. Simplified memory is a biological brain change. In one of the most remarkable discoveries about memory and the human brain, neuroscientists at Washington University in St. Louis, using functional MRI technology, pointed to literal changes in the brain's activity as different learning processes took place. Educational psychologists recently discovered that all long-term memories are set by emotional markers.[1] New learning is accomplished when, within the brain's cognitive neural structure, the student's existing emotional markers match or connect the new information to be learned within the existing brain structure. Understanding the principles of brain-active learning presented in this chapter will help students learn more in less time. It is frustrating when we can't remember something we're certain that we know, especially in a high-stakes situation, such as during a test or at a job interview.

This chapter opens with new information about the brain—how it changes physically by growing more connections between neurons. Understanding that the limbic processor is the gateway to learning and to remembering what they learn can help students become more confident that their brains really are "college material." How your students feel about what they are learning has become more important than ever. Help your students improve their memory by learning to "wire" those neural networks into place.

Guest Speaker

Here is a guest speaker for you:

> I have always loved the Memory techniques . . . . In my classes I stress the importance of making all techniques your own. Needless to say, the custom-made memory system is right on target! Throughout the list of techniques, I especially like that each technique has a clear-cut example for the student. It also gives each student choices.
>
> **—Advisory Board Member Maria Parnell, Brevard Community College, Florida**

Consider inviting a Psychology or Anatomy colleague as your guest speaker to talk to your students about how the brain works. Your current or former students can also be used as guest speakers. Faculty Advisor Eldon McMurray from Utah State College invites student leaders (upper-class students who help teach this course) to present the Master Student Profiles. Most students are more receptive to hearing about these profiles from their peers. For this chapter, I ask my student leaders to talk about *Why* Pablo Alvarado is an example of a master student; *What* qualities Alvarado has that they would like to emulate; *How* they could obtain and practice these qualities; and *What if,* like Pablo Alvarado, they fought for what they believed in.

Lecture

Consider lecturing about some of the Memory techniques you used when you were a student. Explain how students can use these techniques to maximize their effectiveness in college classes.

Another approach is to invite students to ask you for additional information about tools that can enhance memory. Here's how Eldon McMurray explained Q-Cards, flash cards that have questions on both sides, to a student. This explanation could be expanded as a lecture for all students about this useful tool.

> I had a frustrated student tell me that, although she had studied and studied, she had failed her exam in biology. We reviewed her study methods: She had created flash cards by putting a question on one side and the answer on the other. Her review questions did not align well with the instructor's test questions, so she was unable to retrieve answers from her memory during the exam. Q-Cards have a question on both sides. Here's the trick: The question on each side of the card contains the answer to the question on the other side. This portable studying device helps students break information into manageable pieces and forces them to use a higher level of thinking. You can promote even further connection with materials by asking students to draw pictures to help them remember concepts. Reviewing these materials consistently before an exam will aid students' recall.
>
> **—Eldon McMurray**

For additional lecture ideas, visit the Chapter 3 Lecture Ideas on the Instructor Companion site.

Exercises/Activities

1. **The memory jungle (page 78).** Students enjoy the book's analogy of the memory as a jungle. For the visual learner, it is helpful to use the interactive version on the College Success CourseMate to illustrate the concept in a step-by-step manner. You can project it onto a screen in class as a means for review, or you can have students visit the site outside class.

2. **Put it to Work (page 90).** This exercise can be used as an opportunity for building relationships. Start students off in groups of four. Have them use tools described in the article on memory techniques (pages 79–83) to help remember the names of the people in each small group. Then the groups combine to make groups of 8, then 16, then 32, and so on, until everyone in the class can say the first name of every classmate. Then talk about how it feels when someone remembers your name.

3. **Mnemonic devices (pages 85–86).** Get your students involved in creating mnemonic devices in class and they will discover how easy it is to apply these devices outside class. Have your students memorize the Bill of Rights using the peg system that is explained on page 86. To enhance recall, use Q-Cards. To reinforce neural connections, draw pictures.

4. **The loci system (pages 85–86).** Humor can be an effective memory motivator. Demonstrate in class how making up a funny story can help with memorizing word lists. Start by asking for a show of hands from students who think they can memorize 12 words in 12 minutes. Some students will raise their hands. Then ask how many students think they can remember the words in order—that is, if asked for word number 7, number 3, or number 5, can they recall that word after 12 minutes? Usually, only one or two students will raise their hands. Then have the students create a list of 12 nouns. For example, they might create the following list, which you write on the board for reference:

1. Alligator	7. Hamburger
2. Clown	8. Hot air balloon
3. Kitten	9. Television
4. Hummer (car)	10. Criminal
5. Shopping mall	11. Pillow
6. Shoes	12. Monkey

Now, make a note of the time on the clock, and the goal completion time 12 minutes later. As a class, make up a funny story using the numbers and words. If you don't want to make up a story on the spot, use the list above so that you can have the following story ready to go:

Once upon a time, 1 alligator came across 2 clowns with 3 kittens. The alligator was initially surprised when they gave him one of the kittens, but was shocked when he watched 4 of them get into a Hummer and drive off! At 5 p.m. that afternoon, the alligator went to the local shopping mall because he wanted to buy 6 new shoes. After all that shopping, he was very hungry so he ate 7 hamburgers. On his way home, he saw 8 hot air balloons on the horizon. He returned home, and at 9 p.m. that evening he turned on his television to watch his favorite reality show about 10 criminals.

In this particular episode, they were fighting over 11 pillows. When 12 monkeys were released into their cell, chaos broke out!

The students usually find the story foolishly humorous, which helps them remember it. Repeat the story again, reminding them to focus completely on the story you're telling ("Be here now"). Repeat it a third time, and ask them to join you and talk through the story in unison. The next step is to erase or cover up the words on the board and recite the story again in unison. Next, go up and down the rows telling the story, but have each student in turn give the word that goes with that number. If a student can't recall the word, ask him to say the story aloud from the beginning. By the time the student gets to the word, he usually can recall it. This usually takes a total of about 9 to 10 minutes. Next, say a number, and ask students to raise their hands if they know the word that goes with that number. Select one student to confirm the word. Continue until it is clear that everyone knows all the words and the numbers associated with them.

In conclusion, point out that if students can memorize 12 random words in 12 minutes, in order, then they can also memorize important terms for tests fairly quickly if they focus their attention and create a system for memorization. This chapter contains many memorization tools. Most students initially think they can't memorize 12 words in order in 12 minutes, so this exercise boosts confidence in their memory too.

5. **Power Process: Love Your Problems (and Experience Your Barriers) (page 89).** One of many problem-solving tools in *Becoming a Master Student*, this Power Process helps students explore an alternative to avoiding problems that they encounter in college. By embracing a problem, they can diffuse its energy and find a solution. To illustrate this process with an in-class activity, bring a word puzzle or mind game to class. Students who hate these types of puzzles get frustrated. Competitive students become anxious because each wants to be the first to solve it. Allow time for your students to try to solve the problem by loving it. Tell them to relax; enjoy the process; notice their frustration level, competitiveness, and anxiety; and just love the problem. Many students are able to solve the puzzle, individually or in groups. The Instructor Companion site has a sample puzzle that you can hand out to your students as part of this exercise.

Conversation/Sharing

Divide students into small groups to discuss the topic of memorization in college. Students should share their frustration with memorization as well as a successful experience they've had remembering something important.

You can facilitate a conversation using the Master Student Map.

After your students begin to read about memory and learn to activate the connections between neurons, you will have empowered them to connect memory to their Learning Styles.

Why? Why do master students need to have confidence in their ability to remember what they study?

What? What is memory? Read through the list of articles in this chapter and pick three that look interesting. What about these three articles interests you?

How? How can knowing more about how your memory works improve your memory skills? How will this help you in college and in life?

What if? What if you start to apply these memory techniques to your other classes? And what if you don't?

Homework

Remembering your car keys—or anything else (page 84). This exercise helps students practice Learning Styles Mode 3, "How can I use this?" Students are asked to apply the strategies they are learning to a specific, personal memorization situation. An alternative to this assignment would be to ask students to bring in a memorization task from one of their current classes for discussion and analysis in class in groups.

Get creative (page 86). Students enjoy this creative opportunity to invent their own mnemonic device.

Move from problems to solutions (page 88). Here students discover that they can solve their own problems and that such solutions are usually the most effective.

Evaluation

Ask students to describe four memory techniques from the chapter that work for them and to explain how they have used them. Ask students to describe the memory technique "Remember something else." Ask students to explain three ways to keep their brain fit for life. Ask students to explain what "love your problems" means. Ask students why Pablo Alvarado is considered a master student.

Additional Digital Resources

Course Manual

The online *Course Manual* serves as an invaluable reference for those developing and teaching a College Success course with *Becoming a Master Student Concise*. The *Course Manual* provides advice on general teaching issues such as preparing for classes, classroom management, grading, and communicating with students of various backgrounds, as well as specific strategies on getting the most out of various features in *Becoming a Master Student Concise* and book-specific Web sites. Do a *Course Manual* reconnaissance to find ideas that you can use in your course right now.

Instructor Companion Site

The updated Instructor Companion Site provides resources to help you plan and customize your course. Content specific to Chapter 3 includes:

- Lecture Ideas
  - Four Ways to Forget
- In-Class Exercises
  - Your Memory Is Better Than You May Think!
  - The Memory Story
  - Mental Stretch Breaks
- In-Text Quiz Answers
- PowerPoint Slides

The Instructor Companion Site also contains the following book-specific content:

- ExamView Test Bank
- Online Course Manual
- Sample Syllabi
- Detailed Transition Guide

College Success CourseMate

To help your students gain a better understanding of the topics discussed in *Becoming a Master Student Concise*, encourage them to visit the College Success CourseMate at CengageBrain.com that provides the following resources specific to Chapter 3:

- Connect to Text content expands on specific topics marked with an icon within the Introduction.
- Practice Tests allow students to see how well they understand the themes of *Becoming a Master Student Concise.*
- Interactive Concept Maps promote critical thinking by highlighting related ideas to show relationships between concepts.
- Learning Styles Application
- Discussion Topics
- Reflection Questions
- Assessment Questions
- Experiment with chapter strategies
- Video Skillbuilders bring to life techniques that will help students to excel in college and beyond. The following videos should give your students more information regarding topics covered in Chapter 3:
  - Memory Strategies
- Remembering Cultural Differences presents readers with brief articles that touch on aspects of diversity in our rapidly changing world. For Chapter 3, the following article will prompt your students to look at contemporary issues in a new way:
  - The Value of Oral Tradition
- Master Student Profiles provide additional information on the people covered in this book feature. For Chapter 3, students will find expanded coverage and links about:
  - Pablo Alvarado
- Power Process Media contains video, PowerPoints, and audio files to take what your students have learned from the Power Processes in their book to the next level. For Chapter 3, students will find additional media on:
  - Love Your Problems

Along with the chapter-specific content, a General Resources folder is available that contains Toolboxes geared toward specific student types (Community College, Adult Learner, Student Athlete), the Plagiarism Prevention Zone, and the Career Resource Center.

3 Memory

Master Student Map

as you read, ask yourself

what if . . .

I could use my memory to its full potential?

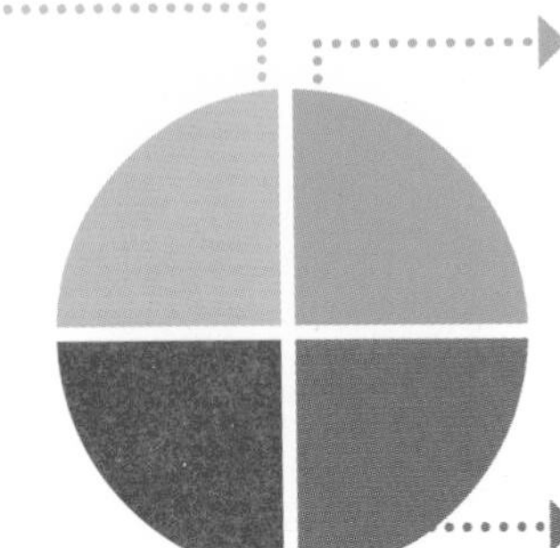

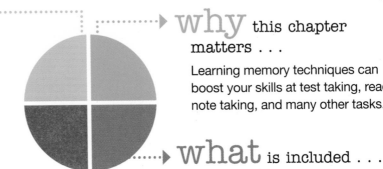

why this chapter matters . . .

Learning memory techniques can boost your skills at test taking, reading, note taking, and many other tasks.

what is included . . .

how you can use this chapter . . .

- Focus your attention.
- Make conscious choices about what to remember.
- Recall facts and ideas with more ease.

MASTER STUDENTS in *action*

Before I read the "Memory" chapter, I had trouble remembering what I studied when taking a test or quiz. Visualization is by far the most useful technique I have come across in this book. While I'm taking the test, I visualize the book or paper that I studied from. It also helps with names. I visualize something funny to go along with someone's name. **—TAUNI ALDINGER**

Photo courtesy of Tauni Aldinger

Take your memory out of the closet

ONCE UPON A time, people talked about human memory as if it were a closet. You stored individual memories there as you would old shirts and stray socks. Remembering something was a matter of rummaging through all that stuff. If you were lucky, you found what you wanted.

This view of memory creates some problems. For one thing, closets can get crowded. Things too easily disappear. Even with the biggest closet, you eventually run out of space. If you want to pack some new memories in there—well, too bad. There's no room.

Brain researchers shattered this image to bits. Memory is not a closet. It's not a place or a thing. Instead, memory is a *process*.

On a conscious level, memories appear as distinct and unconnected mental events: words, sensations, images. They can include details from the distant past—the smell of cookies baking in your grandmother's kitchen or the feel of sunlight warming your face through the window of your first-grade classroom.

On a biological level, each of those memories involves millions of nerve cells, or neurons, firing chemical messages to one another. If you could observe these exchanges in real time, you'd see regions of cells all over the brain glowing with electrical charges at speeds that would put a computer to shame.

When a series of cells connects several times in a similar pattern, the result is a memory. Psychologist Donald Hebb uses the following aphorism to describe this principle: "Neurons which fire together, wire together."[1] It means that memories are not really stored. Instead, remembering is a process in which you *encode* information as links between active neurons that fire together. You also *decode*, or reactivate, neurons that wired together in the past.

Memory is the probability that certain patterns of brain activity will occur again in the future. In effect, you recreate a memory each time you recall it.

Whenever you learn something new, your brain changes physically by growing more connections between neurons. The more you learn, the greater the number of connections. For all practical purposes, there's no limit to how many memories your brain can encode.

There's a lot you can do to wire those neural networks into place. That's where the memory techniques described in this chapter come into play. Step out of your crowded mental closet into a world of infinite possibilities. *

journal entry 10

Discovery/Intention Statement

Create value from this chapter

Write a sentence or two describing the way you feel when you want to remember something but have trouble doing so. Think of a specific incident in which you experienced this problem, such as a time when you tried to remember someone's name or a fact you needed during a test.

I discovered that I . . .

Now spend 5 minutes skimming this chapter, and up to five memory strategies you intend to use. List the strategies below, and note the page numbers where they are explained.

Strategy	Page number

3

MEMORY

The memory jungle

> **Think of your memory as a vast, overgrown jungle. Also imagine that every thought, mental picture, or perception you ever had is represented by an animal in this jungle.**

3

MEMORY

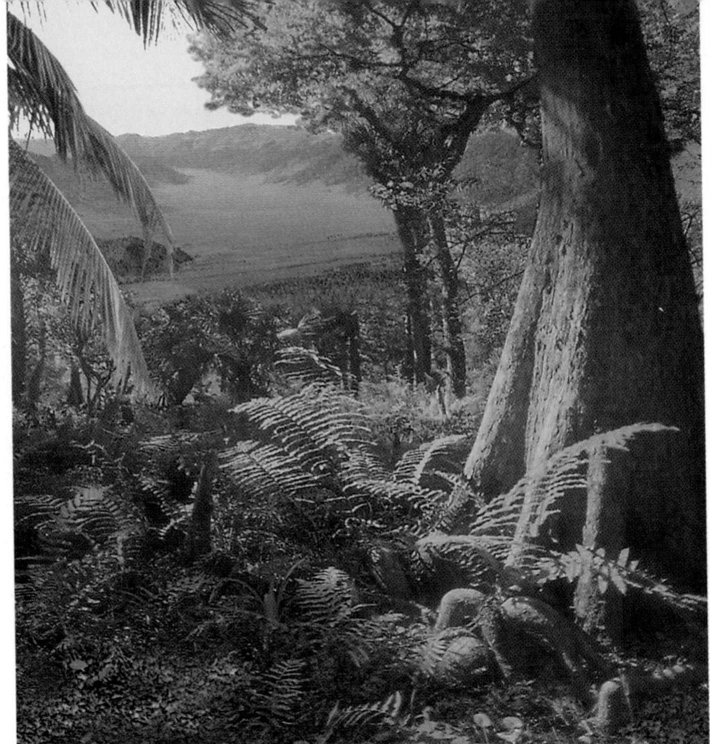

© Photodisc

EVERY SINGLE IDEA or event you've ever perceived by any of your five senses is a thought animal. Some of the thought animals, such as the color of your seventh-grade teacher's favorite sweater, are well hidden. Other thoughts, such as your cell phone number or the position of the reverse gear in your car, are easier to find.

The memory jungle has two rules: Each thought animal must pass through the meadow at the entrance to the jungle. And once an animal enters the jungle, it never leaves.

The meadow represents short-term memory. You use this kind of memory when you look up a telephone number and hold it in your memory long enough to make a call. Short-term memory appears to have a limited capacity (the meadow is small) and disappears fast (animals pass through the meadow quickly).

The jungle itself represents long-term memory. This kind of memory allows you to recall information from day to day, week to week, and year to year. Remember that thought animals never leave the long-term memory jungle. Then use the following visualizations to recall useful concepts about memory.

Visualization #1: A well-worn path

Imagine what happens as a thought—in this case, we'll call it an elephant—charges across short-term memory and into the jungle. The elephant leaves a trail of broken twigs and hoof prints that you can follow. The more often the elephant retraces the path, the clearer the path becomes. Likewise, the more often you recall information, and the more often you encode the same information, the easier it is to find.

Visualization #2: A herd of thoughts

Now, create a mental picture of many animals gathering at a clearing—like thoughts gathering at a central location in memory. It is easier to retrieve thoughts that are grouped together, just as it is easier to find a herd of animals than it is to find a single elephant.

In a similar way, pieces of information are easier to recall if you can associate them with similar information. For example, you can more readily remember a particular player's batting average if you can associate it with other baseball statistics.

Visualization #3: Turning your back

Imagine releasing the elephant into the jungle, turning your back, and counting to 10. When you turn around, the elephant is gone.

This is exactly what happens to most of the information you receive. Forgetting means that thought animals have wandered off. A solution is to review quickly. Do not take your eyes off the thought animal as it crosses the short-term memory meadow. Look at it again (review it) soon after it enters the long-term memory jungle. Wear a path in your memory immediately. *

Go online for more information on the memory jungle.

Memory techniques

Experiment with the following techniques to develop a flexible, custom-made memory system that fits your style of learning.

Be selective. As you dig into your textbooks and notes, make choices about what is most important to learn. Imagine that you are going to create a test on the material, and consider the questions you would ask. When reading, look for chapter previews, summaries, and review questions. Pay attention to anything printed in bold type. Also notice visual elements—tables, charts, graphs, and illustrations. They are all clues pointing to what's important. During lectures, notice what the instructor emphasizes. Anything that's presented visually—on the board, in overheads, or with slides—is probably key.

Make it meaningful. You remember things better if they have meaning for you. One way to create meaning is to learn from the general to the specific. Before you begin your next reading assignment, skim the passage to locate the main idea. If you're ever lost, step back and look at the big picture. The details then might make more sense.

You can organize any list of items—even random items—in a meaningful way to make them easier to remember. In his book *Information Anxiety*, Richard Saul Wurman proposes five principles for organizing any body of ideas, facts, or objects:[2]

Principle	Example
Organize by **time**	Events in history or in a novel flow in chronological order.
Organize by **location**	Addresses for a large company's regional offices are grouped by state and city.
Organize by **category**	Nonfiction library materials are organized by subject categories.
Organize by **continuum**	Products rated in most consumer guides or online stores are grouped from highest in price to lowest in price, or highest in quality to lowest in quality.
Organize by **alphabet**	Entries in a book index are listed in ABC order.

Learn actively. Action is a great memory enhancer. Test this theory by studying your assignments with the same energy that you bring to the dance floor or the basketball court.

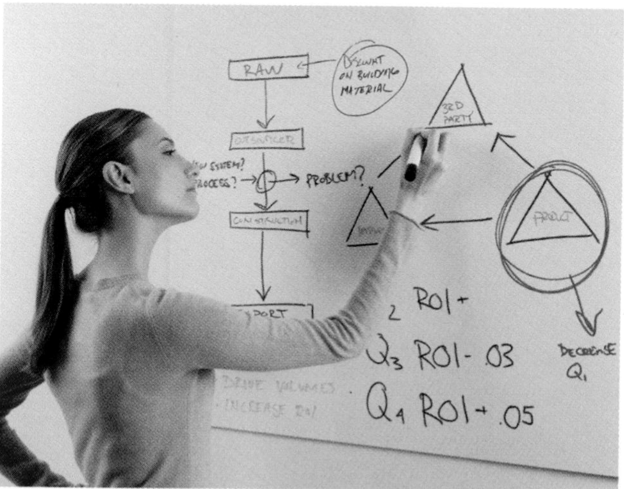

Influx Productions /Lifesize/Getty Images

You can use simple, direct methods to infuse your learning with action. When you sit at your desk, sit up straight. Sit on the edge of your chair, as if you were about to spring out of it and sprint across the room.

Also, experiment with standing up when you study. It's harder to fall asleep in this position. Some people insist that their brains work better when they stand. Pace back and forth and gesture as you recite material out loud. Use your hands. Get your body moving.

Don't forget to move your mouth. During a lecture, ask questions. With your textbooks, read key passages out loud. Use a louder voice for the main points.

Relax. When you're relaxed, you absorb new information quickly and recall it with greater ease and accuracy. Students who can't recall information under the stress of a final exam can often recite the same facts later when they are relaxed. Relaxing might seem to contradict the idea of active learning, but it doesn't. Relaxation is a state of alertness, free of tension, during which your mind can play with new information, roll it around, create associations with it, and apply many of the other memory techniques. See Critical Thinking Exercise 14: "Relax" in Chapter 4 for some tips on how to relax.

Create pictures. Draw diagrams. Make cartoons. Use these images to connect facts and illustrate

Example 1

20 MEMORY TECHNIQUES	
Point	Details
1. Be selective	Choose what not to remember. Look for clues to important material.
2. Make it meaningful	Organize by time, location, category, continuum, or alphabet.
3. Create associations	Link new facts with facts you already know.
4. Learn actively	Sit straight. Stand while studying. Recite while walking.
5. Relax	Release tension. Remain alert.

Example 2

STIMULATE THE ECONOMY WITH TAX CUTS?	
Opinion	Support
Yes	Savings from tax cuts allow businesses to invest money in new equipment. Tax cuts encourage businesses to expand and hire new employees.
No	Years of tax cuts under the Bush administration failed to prevent the mortgage credit crisis. Tax cuts create budget deficits.
Maybe	Tax cuts might work in some economic conditions.
	Budget deficits might be only temporary.

relationships. You can "see" and recall associations within and among abstract concepts more easily when you visualize both the concepts and the associations. The key is to use your imagination. Creating pictures reinforces visual and kinesthetic learning styles.

For example, Boyle's law states that at a constant temperature, the volume of a confined ideal gas varies inversely with its pressure. Simply put, cutting the volume in half doubles the pressure. To remember this concept, you might picture someone "doubled over" using a bicycle pump. As she increases the pressure in the pump by decreasing the volume in the pump cylinder, she seems to be getting angrier. By the time she has doubled the pressure (and halved the volume), she is boiling ("Boyle-ing") mad.

You can also create pictures as you study by using *graphic organizers*. These preformatted charts prompt you to visualize relationships among facts and ideas.

One example is a *topic-point-details* chart. At the top of this chart, write the main topic of a lecture or reading assignment. In the left column, list the main points you want to remember. In the right column, list key details related to each point. See Example 1 for the beginning of a chart based on this article.

You could use a similar chart to prompt critical thinking about an issue. Express that issue as a question, and write it at the top. In the left column, note the opinion about the issue. In the right column, list notable facts, expert opinions, reasons, and examples that support each opinion. Example 2 is about tax cuts as a strategy for stimulating the economy.

Sometimes you'll want to remember the main actions in a story or historical event. Create a timeline by drawing a straight line. Place points in order on that line to represent key events. Place earlier events toward the left end of the line and later events toward the right. Example 3 shows a timeline of events relating to the start of the U.S. war with Iraq.

When you want to compare or contrast two things, play with a Venn diagram. Represent each thing as

Example 3

3/19/03	3/30/03	4/9/03	5/1/03	5/29/03
U.S. invades Iraq	Rumsfeld announces location of WMD	Soldiers topple statue of Saddam	Bush declares mission accomplished	Bush: We found WMD

a circle. Draw the circles so that they overlap. In the overlapping area, list characteristics that the two things share. In the outer parts of each circle, list the unique characteristics of each thing. Example 4 below compares the two types of journal entries included in this book—Discovery Statements and Intention Statements.

The graphic organizers described here are just a few of the many kinds available. Search online for more examples. Have fun and invent graphic organizers of your own.

Recite and repeat. When you repeat something out loud, you anchor the information in two different senses. First, you get the physical sensation in your throat, tongue, and lips when voicing the concept. Second, you hear it. The combined result is synergistic, just as it is when you create pictures. That is, the effect of using two different senses is greater than the sum of their individual effects.

The "out loud" part is important. Reciting silently in your head can be useful—in the library, for example—but it is not as effective as making noise. Your mind can trick itself into thinking it knows something when it doesn't. Your ears are harder to fool.

Repetition is important, too. Repetition is a common memory device because it works. Repetition blazes a trail through the pathways of your brain, making the information easier to find. Repeat a concept out loud until you know it; then say it five more times.

Recitation works best when you recite concepts in your own words. For example, if you want to remember that the acceleration of a falling body due to gravity at sea level equals 32 feet per second per second, you might say, "Gravity makes an object accelerate 32 feet per second faster for each second that it's in the air at sea level." Putting a concept into your own words forces you to think about it.

Have some fun with this technique. Recite by writing a song about what you're learning. Sing it in the shower. Use any style you want (Country, jazz, rock, or rap—when you sing out loud, learning's a snap!)

Or imitate someone. Imagine your textbook being read by Will Ferrell, Madonna, or Clint Eastwood ("Go ahead, punk. Make my density equal mass over volume.")

Write it down. The technique of writing things down is obvious, yet easy to forget. Writing a note to yourself helps you remember an idea, even if you never look at the note again.

You can extend this technique by writing down an idea not just once, but many times. Let go of the old image of being forced to write "I will not throw paper wads" a hundred times on the chalkboard after school. When you choose to remember something, repetitive writing is a powerful tool.

Writing engages a different kind of memory than speaking. Writing prompts us to be more logical, coherent, and complete. Written reviews reveal gaps in knowledge that oral reviews miss, just as oral reviews reveal gaps that written reviews miss.

Engage your emotions. One powerful way to enhance your memory is to make friends with your amygdala. This area of your brain lights up with extra neural activity each time you feel a strong emotion. When a topic excites love, laughter, or fear, the amygdala sends a flurry of chemical messages that say, in effect: *This information is important and useful. Don't forget it.*

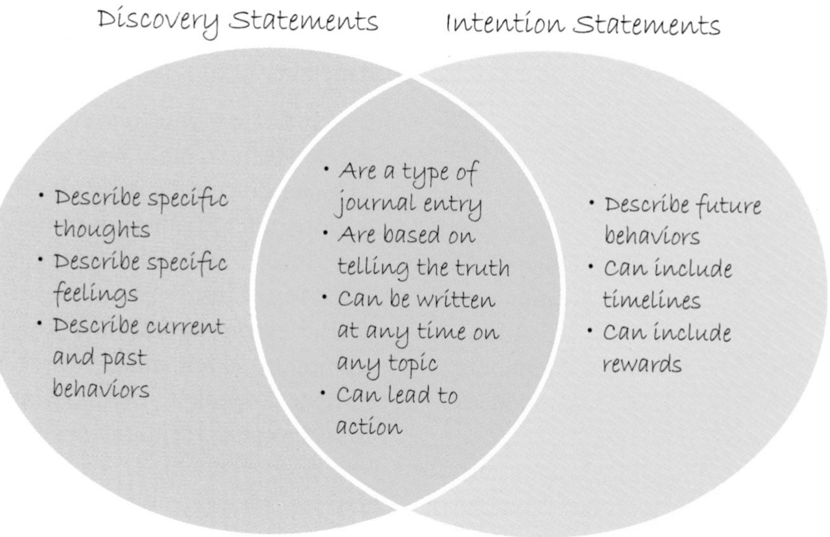

You're more likely to remember course material when you relate it to a goal—whether academic, personal, or career—that you feel strongly about. This is one

Example 4
Discovery Statements
Intention Statements
• Describe specific thoughts
• Describe specific feelings
• Describe current and past behaviors
• Are a type of journal entry
• Are based on telling the truth
• Can be written at any time on any topic
• Can lead to action
• Describe future behaviors
• Can include timelines
• Can include rewards

reason why it pays to be specific about what you want. The more goals you have and the more clearly they are defined, the more channels you create for incoming information.

You can use this strategy even when a subject seems boring at first. If you're not naturally interested in a topic, then *create* interest. Find a study partner in the class—if possible, someone you know and like—or form a study group. Also consider getting to know the instructor personally. When a course creates a bridge to human relationships, you engage the content in a more emotional way.

3 MEMORY

Overlearn. One way to fight mental fuzziness is to learn more than you need to know about a subject simply to pass a test. You can pick a subject apart, examine it, add to it, and go over it until it becomes second nature.

This technique is especially effective for problem solving. Do the assigned problems, and then do more problems. Find another textbook, and work similar problems. Then make up your own problems and solve them. When you pretest yourself in this way, the potential rewards are speed, accuracy, and greater confidence at exam time.

Distribute learning. As an alternative to marathon study sessions, experiment with several shorter sessions spaced out over time. You might find that you can get far more done in three 2-hour sessions than in one 6-hour session.

Distributing your learning is a brain-friendly activity. You cannot absorb new information and ideas during all of your waking hours. If you overload your brain, it will find a way to shut down for a rest—whether you plan for it or not. By taking periodic breaks while studying, you allow information to sink in. During these breaks, your brain is taking the time to rewire itself by growing new connections between cells.

The idea of allowing time for consolidation does have an exception. When you are so engrossed in a textbook that you cannot put it down, when you are consumed by an idea for a term paper and cannot think of anything else—keep going. The master student within you has taken over. Enjoy the ride.

Elaborate. According to Harvard psychologist Daniel Schacter, all courses in memory improvement are based on a single technique—elaboration. *Elaboration* means consciously encoding new information. Repetition is one basic way to elaborate. However, current brain research indicates that other types of elaboration are more effective for long-term memory.[3]

One way to elaborate is to ask yourself questions about incoming information: "Does this remind me of something or someone I already know?" "Is this similar to a technique that I already use?" and "Where and when can I use this information?"

When you first learned to recognize Italy on a world map, your teacher probably pointed out that the country is shaped like a boot. This is a simple form of elaboration.

The same idea applies to more complex material. When you meet someone new, for example, ask yourself, "Does she remind me of someone else?" Or when reading this book, preview the material using the Master Student Map that opens each chapter.

Remember something else. When you are stuck and can't remember something that you're sure you know, remember something else that is related to it.

If you can't remember your great-aunt's name, remember your great-uncle's name. During an economics exam, if you can't remember anything about the aggregate demand curve, recall what you do know about the aggregate supply curve. If you cannot recall specific facts, remember the example that the instructor used during her lecture. Any piece of information is encoded in the same area of the brain as a similar piece of information. You can unblock your recall by stimulating that area of your memory.

A brainstorm is a good memory jog. If you are stumped when taking a test, start writing down lots of answers to related questions, and—pop!—the answer you need could appear.

Notice when you do remember. Everyone has a different memory style. Some people are best at recalling information they've read. Others have an easier time remembering what they've heard, seen, or done.

To develop your memory, notice when you recall information easily, and ask yourself what memory techniques you're using naturally. Also notice when you find it difficult to recall information. Be a reporter. Get the facts, and then adjust your learning techniques. And remember to congratulate yourself when you remember.

Use it before you lose it. Even information encoded in long-term memory becomes difficult to recall when we don't use it regularly. The pathways to the information become faint from disuse. For example, you can probably remember your current phone number. What was your phone number 10 years ago?

This example points to a powerful memory technique. To remember something, access it a lot. Read it, write it, speak it, listen to it, apply it—find some way to make contact with the material regularly. Each time you do so, you widen the neural pathway to the material and make it easier to recall the next time.

Another way to make contact with the material is to teach it. Teaching demands mastery. When you explain the function of the pancreas to a fellow student, you discover quickly whether you really understand it yourself.

Study groups are especially effective because they put you on stage. The friendly pressure of knowing that you'll teach the group helps focus your attention.

Intend to remember. To instantly enhance your memory, form the simple intention to *learn it now* rather than later. The intention to remember can be more powerful than any single memory technique. The simple act of focusing your attention at key moments can do wonders for your memory.

Test this idea for yourself. The next time you're introduced to someone, direct 100 percent of your attention to hearing that person's name. Do this consistently, and see what happens to your ability to remember names. *

Find more memory strategies online.

3

MEMORY

Set a trap for your memory

Say that you're walking to class and suddenly remember that your accounting assignment is due tomorrow. Switch your watch to the opposite wrist. Now you're "trapped." Every time you glance at your wrist and remember that you have switched your watch, it becomes a reminder that you were supposed to remember something else. (You can do the same with a ring.)

If you empty your pockets every night, put an unusual item in your pocket in the morning to remind yourself to do something before you go to bed. For example, to remember to call your younger sister on her birthday, pick an object that reminds you of her—a photograph, perhaps—and put it in your pocket. When you empty your pocket that evening and find the photo, you're more likely to make the call.

Everyday rituals that you seldom neglect, such as feeding a pet, listening to the weather report, and unlacing your shoes, provide opportunities for setting traps. For example, tie a triple knot in your shoelace as a reminder to set the alarm for your early morning study group meeting. You can even use imaginary traps. To remember to write a check for the phone bill, picture your phone hanging on the front door. In your mind, create the feeling of reaching for the doorknob and grabbing the phone instead. When you get home and reach to open the front door, the image is apt to return to you.

Link two activities together, and make the association unusual.

11 critical thinking exercise

Remembering your car keys—or anything else

Pick something you frequently forget or misplace. Some people chronically lose their car keys or forget to write down appointments on their calendar. Others let anniversaries and birthdays slip by.

Pick an item or a task you're prone to forget. Then design a strategy for remembering it. Use any of the techniques from this chapter, research others, or make up your own from scratch. Describe your technique and the results in the space provided.

In this exercise, as in most of the exercises in this book, a failure is also a success. Don't be concerned with whether your technique will work. Design it, and then find out whether it works. If it doesn't work for you this time, use another method.

Keep your brain fit for life

Memories are encoded as physical changes in the brain. Your brain is an organ that needs regular care and exercise. Higher education gives you plenty of chances to exercise that organ. Don't let those benefits fade after you leave school. Starting now, adopt habits to keep your brain lean and fit for life. Consider these research-based suggestions from the Alzheimer's Association.[4]

Stay mentally active. If you sit at a desk most of the workday, take a class. If you seldom travel, start reading maps of new locations and plan a cross-country trip. Seek out museums, theaters, concerts, and other cultural events. Even after you graduate, consider learning another language or taking up a musical instrument. Learning gives your brain a workout, much like sit-ups condition your abs.

Stay socially active. Having a network of supportive friends can reduce stress levels. In turn, stress management helps to maintain connections between brain cells. Stay socially active by working, volunteering, and joining clubs.

Stay physically active. Physical activity promotes blood flow to the brain. It also reduces the risk of diabetes, cardiovascular disease, and other diseases that can impair brain function.

Adopt a brain-healthy diet. A diet rich in dark-skinned fruits and vegetables boosts your supply of antioxidants—natural chemicals that nourish your brain. Examples of these foods are raisins, blueberries, blackberries, strawberries, raspberries, kale, spinach, brussels sprouts, alfalfa sprouts, and broccoli. Avoid foods that are high in saturated fat and cholesterol, which may increase the risk of Alzheimer's disease.

Drink alcohol moderately, if at all. A common definition of moderate consumption for people of legal drinking age is a limit of one drink per day for women and two drinks per day for men. Heavier drinking can affect memory. In fact, long-term alcoholics tend to develop conditions that impair memory. One such condition is Korsakoff's syndrome, a disorder that causes people to forget incidents immediately after they happen.

Protect your heart. In general, what's good for your heart is good for your brain. Protect both organs by eating well, exercising regularly, managing your weight, staying tobacco-free, and getting plenty of sleep. These habits reduce your risk of heart attack, stroke, and other cardiovascular conditions that interfere with blood flow to the brain.

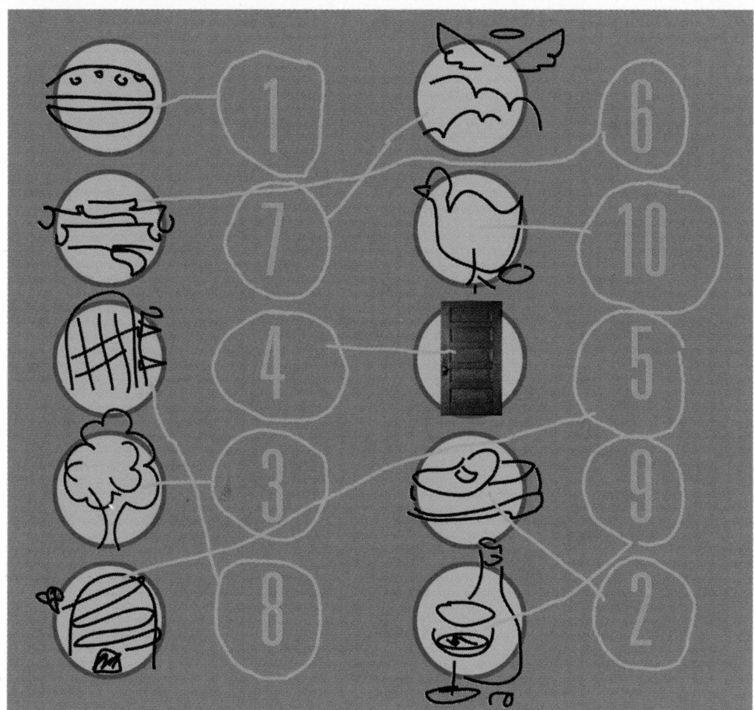

The peg system is a mneumonic device based on matching words that rhyme, such as *one* and *bun*.

Door: © Photospin; *illustration:* Walter Kopec

Mnemonic devices

It's pronounced "ne-MON-ik." The word refers to tricks that can increase your ability to recall everything from grocery lists to speeches.

3

MEMORY

SOME ENTERTAINERS USE mnemonic devices to perform "impossible" feats of memory, such as recalling the names of everyone in a large audience after hearing them just once. Using mnemonic devices, speakers can go for hours without looking at their notes. The possibilities for students are endless.

There is a catch, though. Mnemonic devices have three serious limitations:

- They don't always help you understand or digest material. Mnemonics rely only on rote memorization.
- The mnemonic device itself is sometimes complicated to learn and time-consuming to develop.
- Mnemonic devices can be forgotten.

In spite of their limitations, mnemonic devices can be powerful. These devices fall into five general categories: new words, creative sentences, rhymes and songs, the loci system, and the peg system.

Make up new words. Acronyms are words created from the initial letters of a series of words. Examples include NASA (**N**ational **A**eronautics and **S**pace **A**dministration) and laser (**l**ight **a**mplification by **s**timulated **e**mission of **r**adiation).

You can make up your own acronyms to recall a series of facts. A common mnemonic acronym is Roy G. Biv, which has helped millions of students remember the colors of the visible spectrum (**r**ed, **o**range, **y**ellow, **g**reen, **b**lue, **i**ndigo, and **v**iolet). IPMAT helps biology students remember the stages of cell division (**i**nterphase, **p**rophase, **m**etaphase, **a**naphase, and **t**elophase).

Use creative sentences. Acrostics are sentences that help you remember a series of letters that stand for something. For example, the first letters of the words in the sentence *Every good boy does fine* (E, G, B, D, and F) are the music notes associated with the lines of the treble clef staff.

Create rhymes and songs. Madison Avenue advertising executives spend billions of dollars a year on advertisements designed to burn their messages into your memory. The song "It's the Real Thing" was used to market Coca-Cola, despite the soda's artificial ingredients.

Rhymes have been used for centuries to teach basic facts. "*I* before *e*, except after *c*" has helped many a student on spelling tests.

Use the loci system. The word *loci* is the plural of *locus*, a synonym for *place* or *location*. Use the loci system to create visual associations with familiar locations. Unusual associations are the easiest to remember.

The loci system is an old one. Ancient Greek orators used it to remember long speeches, and politicians use it today. For example, if a politician's position were that road taxes must be raised to pay for school equipment, his loci visualizations before a speech might have looked like the following.

First, as he walks in the door of his house, he imagines a large *porpoise* jumping through a hoop. This reminds him to begin by telling the audience the *purpose* of his speech.

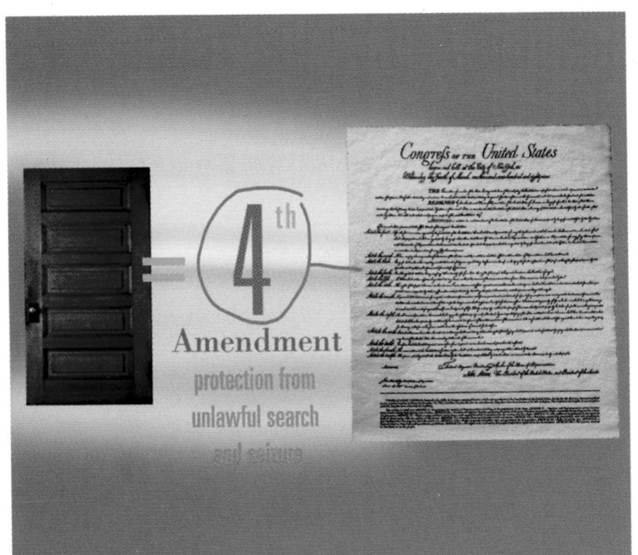

© Photospin

Next, he visualizes his living room floor covered with paving stones, forming a road leading into the kitchen. In the kitchen, he pictures dozens of schoolchildren sitting on the floor because they have no desks.

Now it's the day of the big speech. The politician is nervous. He's perspiring so much that his clothes sticks to his body. He stands up to give his speech, and his mind goes blank. Then he starts thinking to himself:

> I can remember the rooms in my house. Let's see, I'm walking in the front door and—wow!—I see a porpoise. That reminds me to talk about the purpose of my speech. And then there's that road leading to the kitchen. Say, what are all those kids doing there on the floor? Oh, yeah, now I remember—they have no desks! We need to raise taxes on roads to pay for their desks and the other stuff they need in classrooms.

Use the peg system. The peg system is a technique that employs key words that are paired with numbers. Each word forms a "peg" on which you can "hang" mental associations. To use this system effectively, learn the following peg words and their associated numbers well:

bun goes with 1
shoe goes with 2
tree goes with 3
door goes with 4
hive goes with 5
sticks goes with 6
heaven goes with 7
gate goes with 8
wine goes with 9
hen goes with 10

You can use the peg system to remember the Bill of Rights (the first ten amendments to the U.S. Constitution). For example, amendment number *four* is about protection from unlawful search and seizure. Imagine people knocking at your *door* who are demanding to search your home. This amendment means that you do not have to open your door unless those people have a proper search warrant. *

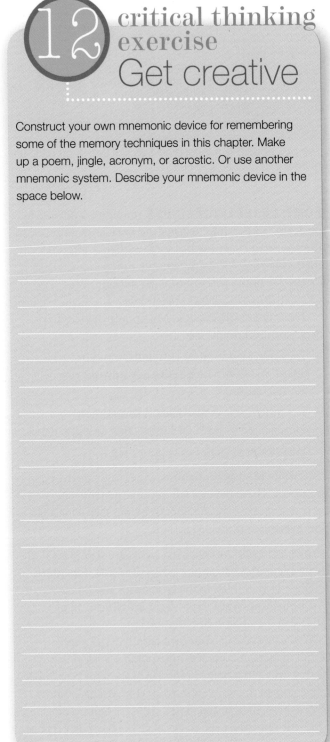

12 critical thinking exercise
Get creative

Construct your own mnemonic device for remembering some of the memory techniques in this chapter. Make up a poem, jingle, acronym, or acrostic. Or use another mnemonic system. Describe your mnemonic device in the space below.

mastering technology

USE YOUR COMPUTER TO ENHANCE MEMORY

The outlining feature of a word-processing program offers a powerful way to apply some of the memory techniques in this chapter. Use this feature to create summaries of textbook chapters and lecture notes:

- Divide a book chapter or set of handwritten notes into sections.
- Open up a new document in your word-processing program, and list the main points from each section.
- Shift to the outline view of your document, and turn each point into a level-one heading.
- Enter key facts and other details as normal text under the appropriate heading.
- When reviewing for a test, shift your document into outline view so that only the headings are displayed. Scan them as you would scan the headlines in a newspaper.
- In the outline view, see whether you can recall the details you included. Then open up the normal text underneath each headline to check the accuracy of your memory.

Outlining your notes allows you to organize information in a meaningful way. And stating key points in your own words helps you learn actively.

You can also use PowerPoint or other presentation software to create flash cards. Add illustrations, color, and other visual effects—a simple and fun way to draw on your visual intelligence.

A related option is to go online. Do an Internet search with the words *flash*, *card*, and *online*. You'll find a list of sites that allow you to select from a library of printable flash cards—or create and print your own cards.

Notable failures

As you experiment with memory techniques, you may try a few that fail at crucial moments—such as during a test. Just remember that many people before you have failed miserably before succeeding brilliantly. Consider a few examples.

In his first professional race, cyclist **Lance Armstrong** finished last.

The first time **Jerry Seinfeld** walked onstage at a comedy club as a professional comic, he looked out at the audience and froze.

When **Lucille Ball** began studying to be an actress in 1927, she was told by the head instructor of the John Murray Anderson Drama School, "Try any other profession."

In high school, actor and comic **Robin Williams** was voted "Least Likely to Succeed."

Walt Disney was fired by a newspaper editor because he "lacked imagination and had no good ideas."

R. H. Macy failed seven times before his store in New York City caught on.

Emily Dickinson had only seven poems published in her lifetime.

Decca Records turned down a recording contract with the **Beatles** with an unprophetic evaluation: "We don't like their sound. Groups of guitars are on their way out."

In 1954, Jimmy Denny, manager of the Grand Ole Opry, fired **Elvis Presley** after one performance.

Babe Ruth is famous for his past home run record, but for decades he also held the record for strikeouts. **Mark McGwire** broke that record.

After **Carl Lewis** won the gold medal for the long jump in the 1996 Olympic Games, he was asked to what he attributed his longevity, having competed for almost 20 years. He said, "Remembering that you have both wins and losses along the way. I don't take either one too seriously."

"I've missed more than 9,000 shots in my career," **Michael Jordan** said. "I've lost almost 300 games. Twenty-six times I've been trusted to take the game winning shot . . . and missed. I've failed over and over and over again in my life. That is why I succeed."

Adapted from "But They Did Not Give Up," www.des.emory.edu/mfp/OnFailingG.html (accessed January 27, 2010).

Find more notable failures online.

13 critical thinking exercise
Move from problems to solutions

Many students find it easy to complain about school and to dwell on problems. This exercise gives you an opportunity to change that habit and respond creatively to any problem you're currently experiencing—whether it be with memorizing or some other aspect of school or life.

The key is to dwell more on solutions than on problems. Do that by inventing as many solutions as possible for any given problem. See whether you can turn a problem into a *project* (a plan of action) or a *promise* to change some aspect of your life. Shifting the emphasis of your conversation from problems to solutions can raise your sense of possibility and unleash the master learner within you.

In the space below, describe at least three problems that could interfere with your success as a student. The problems can be related to courses, teachers, personal relationships, finances, or anything else that might get in the way of your success.

My problem is that . . .

My problem is that . . .

My problem is that . . .

Next, brainstorm at least five possible solutions to each of those problems. Ten solutions would be even better. (You can continue brainstorming on a separate piece of paper or on a computer.) You might find it hard to come up with that many ideas. That's OK. Stick with it. Stay in the inquiry, give yourself time, and ask other people for ideas.

I can solve my problem by . . .

I can solve my problem by . . .

I can solve my problem by . . .

Love Your Problems (And Experience Your Barriers)

We all have problems and barriers that block our progress or prevent us from moving into new areas. Often, the way we respond to our problems places limitations on what we can be, do, and have.

Problems often work like barriers. When we bump up against one of our problems, we usually turn away and start walking along a different path. All of a sudden—bump!—we've struck another barrier. And we turn away again.

As we continue to bump into problems and turn away from them, our lives stay inside the same old boundaries. Inside these boundaries, we are unlikely to have new adventures. We are unlikely to keep learning.

If we respond to problems by loving them instead of resisting them, we can expand the boundaries in which we live our lives.

The word *love* might sound like an overstatement. In this Power Process, the word means to unconditionally accept the fact that your problems exist. The more we deny or resist a problem, the stronger it seems to become. When we accept the fact that we have a problem, we can find effective ways to deal with it.

Suppose one of your barriers is being afraid of speaking in front of a group. You could get up in front of the group and pretend that you're not afraid. Or you could tell yourself, "I'm not going to be scared," and then try to keep your knees from knocking. Generally, these strategies don't work.

A more effective approach is to love your fear. Go to the front of the room, look out into the audience, and say to yourself, "I am scared. I notice that my knees are shaking and my mouth feels dry, and I'm having a rush of thoughts about what might happen if I say the wrong thing. Yup, I'm scared, and I'm not going to fight it. I'm going to give this speech anyway."

The beauty of this Power Process is that you continue to take action—giving your speech, for example—no matter what you feel. You walk right up to the barrier and then *through* it. You might even find that if you totally accept and experience a barrier, such as fear, it shrinks or disappears. Even if that does not happen right away, you still open up to new experiences and gain new chances to learn.

Loving a problem does not need to stop us from solving it. In fact, fully accepting and admitting a problem usually helps us take effective action—which can free us of the problem once and for all.

Learn more about this Power Process online.

Put it to Work

You can use strategies in *Becoming a Master Student* to succeed at work. Get started by reflecting on the following case study.

Paula Chang is a nurse at a large urban hospital. Paula just joined the staff in the cardiology department, which includes 40 nurses, doctors, and other health care workers. She was hired 2 months after graduating with a nursing degree from a nearby university.

Among Paula's goals for her new career was to learn the names of her colleagues by the end of the first week on the job. She succeeded.

One afternoon, the department head, Dr. Frank Rangel, invited Paula into his office for an informal chat. Frank had heard several colleagues talking about Paula's ability to remember names. He wanted to congratulate her—and learn a thing or two about memory techniques from his youngest team member.

"You're the first person on my staff who's ever managed to learn so many names so quickly," said Frank. "What's your secret?"

"No secrets, honest," Paula replied. "It's all about attitude, I guess. I simply made it a priority to remember names. I remember a teacher I had in college who had anywhere from 50 to 100 students in his lecture classes. On the first day of class, he went around the room and asked each of us for our name. It took a lot of time, but then he called us by name for the rest of the semester. I remember feeling so touched by that. I promised I would do the same thing when I started my first job."

Frank smiled and said, "That's impressive. Memorizing so many names so quickly is a neat trick. But I'm just wondering: Does it really make a difference?"

"Yes, I think so," Paula said. "For one thing, I feel more confident right away about my surroundings. I feel more comfortable asking questions when I remember names."

Paula also shared an idea with Frank for future new employees. As a visual learner, she learns better by seeing photos of people and associating pictures with names. So Paula volunteered to take pictures of her colleagues to help everyone learn names.

Paula applied several strategies from this chapter:

- Create pictures.
- Engage your emotions.
- Intend to remember.

© Image copyright Stephen Coburn, 2009. Used under license from Shutterstock.com

List more memory strategies that Paula could use:

____

____

____

____

____

____

Also consider the following suggestions when you want sharpen your memory for names in the workplace. See whether you can adapt these techniques to remembering any kind of detailed, factual information.

- Think of someone you already know who has the same first name as a new coworker. Visualize these two people standing side by side. Look for strong differences or similarities between them.
- Use rhymes or alliteration (the repetition of sounds). If Tim is slim or Sandra wears a scarf, you've got a natural "hook" for remembering their names.
- Use a new person's name every chance you get. In a meeting, for example, refer to "Jim's idea" or "Susan's question."
- Make small talk with people when you first meet them. Associate one key fact—such as a person's hometown or favorite hobby—with an image of the person's face.

Name________________________________ Date____/____/____

1. In the article about the memory jungle, the meadow
   (a) Is a place that every animal (thought or perception) must pass through.
   (b) Represents short-term memory.
   (c) Represents the idea that one type of memory has a limited capacity.
   (d) All of the above.
   (d) All of the above. (*The memory jungle,* p. 78)
2. Define the word *elaborate* as a memory technique and give one example of this strategy.
   Elaboration means consciously encoding new information. Repetition is one basic way to elaborate. Other types of elaboration that are more effective for long-term memory include asking yourself questions about incoming information: "Does this remind me of something or someone I already know?" "Is this similar to a technique that I already use?" and "Where and when can I use this information?" For example, when you meet someone new, ask yourself, "Does he or she remind me of someone else?" (*Memory techniques*, pp. 79–83)
3. Explain three ways to organize a list of items.
   Explain three of the following ways to organize any list of items—even random items—in a meaningful way to make them easier to remember:
   - Organize by **time**—for example, in chronological order.
   - Organize by **location**—for example, by state and city.
   - Organize by **category**—for example, by subject categories.
   - Organize by **continuum**—for example, from highest in quality to lowest in quality.
   - Organize by **alphabet**—for example, ABC order. (*Memory techniques*, pp. 79–83)
4. Define *acronym*, and give an example of one.
   An acronym is a word created from the first letters in a series of words. Examples include **NASA** (**N**ational **A**eronautics and **S**pace **A**dministration), **radar** (**ra**dio **d**etecting **a**nd **r**anging), **scuba** (**s**elf-**c**ontained **u**nderwater **b**reathing **a**pparatus), and **laser** (**l**ight **a**mplification by **s**timulated **e**mission of **r**adiation). (*Mnemonic devices,* pp. 85–86)
5. Memorization on a deep level can take place if you
   (a) Repeat the idea.
   (b) Repeat the idea.
   (c) Repeat the idea.
   (d) All of the above.
   (d) All of the above. (*Memory techniques*, pp. 79–83)
6. Mnemonic devices are the most efficient ways to memorize. True or false? Explain your answer.
   True. These memory tricks can help you learn information quickly. Therefore, they are efficient. However, they may not be effective for long-term memorization or for understanding. (*Mnemonic devices,* pp. 85–86)
7. Briefly describe at least three memory techniques other than mnemonics.
   Briefly describe any three of the following techniques:
   - Be selective.
   - Make it meaningful.
   - Learn actively.
   - Relax.
   - Create pictures.
   - Recite and repeat.
   - Write it down
   - Engage your emotions.
   - Overlearn.
   - Distribute learning.
   - Elaborate.
   - Remember something else.
   - Notice when you do remember.
   - Use it before you lose it.
   - Intend to remember. (*Memory techniques*, pp. 79–83)
8. Give two examples of staying active as you learn.
   Give two of the following examples:
   - Sit up straight.
   - Sit on the edge of your chair.
   - Stand up when you study.
   - Pace back and forth and gesture as you recite material out loud.
   - Ask questions during a lecture.
   - Read key passages out loud.
   - Use a louder voice for the main points. (*Memory techniques*, pp. 79–83)
9. Briefly define the word *love* as it is used in the Power Process: "Love Your Problems (and Experience Your Barriers)."
   Embrace your problems, instead of resisting or avoiding them. (*Power Process: Love Your Problems [and Experience Your Barriers],* p. 89)
10. According to the text, one memory technique is to make friends with your amygdala. Briefly explain the meaning of this sentence.
    The amygdala is the area of your brain that activates when you feel a strong emotion. When a topic excites love, laughter, or fear, the amygdala tells the brain that the incoming information is important and should be remembered. So, you should be as aware of it as possible. (Answers will vary.) (*Memory techniques,* pp. 86–89)

Skills Snapshot

The Discovery Wheel in Chapter 1 includes a section labeled *Memory*. For the next 10 to 15 minutes, go beyond your initial responses to that exercise. Take a snapshot of your skills as they exist today, after reading and doing this chapter.

Begin by reflecting on some recent experiences. Then take the next step toward memory mastery by committing to a specific action in the near future.

Recalling key facts more quickly and accurately could help me be more effective in the following situations . . .

Memory techniques that I already use include . . .

I'll know that I've reached a new level of mastery with remembering ideas and information when . . .

To reach that level of mastery, the most important thing I can do next is to . . .

Master Student PROFILE

Pablo Alvarado

Pablo Alvarado, National Day Laborer Organizing Network (NDLON) - Los Angeles, CA: 2004 Award Recipients," Institute for Sustainable Communities, Leadership for a Changing World, Institute for Sustainable Communities, 2009, http://www.leadershipfor change.org/awardees/ awardee.php3?ID=201.

(1954–) Executive director of the National Day Laborer Organizing Network, who uses soccer, music, and coalition building to foster humane conditions for day laborers.

As an immigrant worker from El Salvador, Pablo Alvarado has a special connection to the Latin American immigrants who have traveled far from their homes in search of work to support their families. These are the people who wait on street corners, in parking lots, or in parks, hoping for temporary employment—which is usually hard physical labor. Their average monthly earnings range from $350 to $1,000. They suffer discrimination, unsafe working conditions, and underpayment or nonpayment for their work, and many live in fear of deportation. Also, in many parts of the country, new civic ordinances prevent day laborers from soliciting work in public places, which makes finding work even more difficult. In addition, day laborers are frequent targets of violence and law enforcement hostility.

In El Salvador, Alvarado's family members were farmers who grew beans, corn, and coffee for their own use. Every day, his father hauled water from a nearby town to sell in their village. At harvest time, young Alvarado worked 10 hours a day at nearby coffee plantations to have money to buy his clothes and school supplies. Although Alvarado's mother never went to school and his father only attended as far as the third grade, his parents insisted that he and his siblings get an education.

In the midst of civil war, when he was 12 years old, Alvarado became a teaching assistant for a literacy class that served his neighbors, and he witnessed the power of education to bring social improvement and better living conditions. "On my way to and from school, I would walk over bodies, which were left on the side of the road. When I was in eighth grade, several teachers were killed and others fled because they were accused of being guerrilla sympathizers," Alvarado recalls.

At 16, Alvarado used his communications skills to serve as a lay preacher. His teachings contained elements of Liberation Theology, applying the Gospels to current socioeconomic and political struggles. He earned high-school teaching credentials in 1989 from Universidad de El Salvador, but "just as many immigrants have done, I fled my country because of political and economic reasons."

Working as an undocumented immigrant in the United States, Alvarado toiled as a gardener, factory assembly line worker, driver, and painter, and he experienced the pain of isolation and discrimination. While working at a studio-equipment factory, he witnessed hostility between Salvadorans and Mexicans. "Drawing on my childhood experiences, I engaged other coworkers and organized a soccer team that greatly improved relations among workers." That was the beginning of Alvarado's leadership in the United States. "The soccer experience is now part of the national movement, as day laborers in Los Angeles and Washington, D.C., have created their own soccer leagues," he says.

Some of his organizing techniques are unusual, but effective. Besides soccer teams, his organization also sponsors chess teams, marathon races, and popular theater. "On the street corners, workers start by relating to each other as competition (for jobs)," Alvarado explains. "When brought together on a soccer field, their dynamic changes to camaraderie, which then extends back to organizing on the street corners."

"Pablo Alvarado, National Day Laborer Organizing Network (NDLON)—Los Angeles, CA: 2004 Award Recipients," Institute for Sustainable Communities, Leadership for a Changing World, 2009, http://www.leadershipforchange.org/awardees/awardee.php3?ID=201.

Find more biographical information about Pablo Alvarado at the Master Student Hall of Fame.

4 Reading

Instructor Tools & Tips

Reading furnishes our mind only with materials of knowledge; it is thinking that makes what we read ours.

—John Locke

There would seem to be almost no limit to what people can and will misunderstand when they are not doing their utmost to get at a writer's meaning.

—Ezra Pound

Preview

Chapter 4 is the first chapter in the text's academic development section, which also includes Chapters 5 and 6. This section of the book employs a time-sensitive critical thinking approach to organize academic learning by considering strategies to employ before, during, and after learning. All three chapters (Chapter 4: "Reading," Chapter 5: "Notes," and Chapter 6: "Tests") follow this approach, which makes Chapter 2: "Time and Money" even more relevant to student success.

Much of this chapter might appear to be a review of the skills students should have learned in elementary or high school, but the reality is that many students do not learn the critical reading skills they need to survive and thrive the academic rigors of college. College reading is more than just the ability to read words. College reading requires critical reading, which is a complex thinking process unlike any other "subject" students will study in school. The academic literacy training that students receive in this chapter will prove invaluable throughout their academic careers. Motivation, maturity, and life experiences all lead students to value the skills of reading comprehension and reading speed more than they might have as children. Most importantly, you can help your students accelerate their ability to learn new material by helping them activate any prior knowledge to engage with the reading they must do to succeed. Encourage your students to use the information they have learned about the brain in the memory chapter to enhance their skill at reading.

Also included in this chapter is an updated article about how to use the library.

Guest Speaker

This is a good time to invite a librarian as your guest speaker to talk to students about how they can use the library to research topics for classes. See also the related assignment in the Homework section.

Another option is to invite instructors from a variety of disciplines to talk about reading strategies appropriate to their course content. Ask them to come prepared to answer the following questions for your students:

Why? Why is the reading material in your discipline area unique?

What? What strategies would work best for tackling the reading material in your discipline area? Suggest that your discipline expert bring a sample passage (as a handout) for students so that they can use this new strategy to read it.

How? How can students improve their reading comprehension in your discipline area using these strategies?

What if? What if the students are still having trouble with reading in this discipline? What resources do you suggest (on-campus labs, ancillary textbooks, Web sites, and the like)?

Here's a guest speaker for you:

The article, "Reading with children underfoot," is one of my favorites. I usually have many students in my online college survival course who are parents. Often, somewhere along the way, they will mention the problems they have with studying because of their kids. I immediately suggest that they read this article, and I have received some really positive feedback from the students who have not only read the article but have successfully used some of the techniques. Many of them have written back to me to thank me for alerting them to this article before it became part of an assigned chapter. Their children have also responded positively to the attention they receive while "helping" Mom or Dad to study!

—Diane Beecher,
Lake Superior College, Minnesota

Lecture

Students may ask, "Why use Muscle Reading? I have been reading since first grade!" Muscle Reading is designed as a balanced literacy approach. It incorporates the three aspects of a metacognitive learning system. This means that it presents specific strategies for students to use before, during, and after reading.

Students may also grumble that this approach to reading requires "too much work." Lecture on Muscle Reading by walking them through the nine steps using the next chapter, "Notes." Tell them to *Preview* the chapter by turning the pages, looking at graphs, pictures, article titles, and anything else that stands out for them. Next, on a sheet of paper, have them create an *Outline* by listing the titles of the articles, double-spacing between the article titles. Instruct the students to turn each title into a *Question*. Then have them *Read* the chapter, highlighting/*Underlining* the *Answers* they discover to their outline list of questions. Ask them to *Recite, Review,* and periodically *Review Again* their outline questions and highlighted answers in the book. This lecture and demonstration will help your students see how the nine-step process can be efficiently streamlined while retaining its effectiveness. For more information, review the sidebar article, "Muscle Reading in Brief," on page 108.

Exercises/Activities

1. Three Phases of Muscle Reading (page 96–98). Divide your class into three groups: Before, During, and After. Have each group prepare a 10-minute presentation on the three steps within their given phase. Each group aims for a memorable lesson that provides examples of their strategies. In conclusion, the three groups come up with a sample test question to help determine how the rest of the class understood their presentation.

2. Power Process: Notice Your Pictures and Let Them Go (page 109). Present this Power Process as a problem-solving technique. When students feel frustrated because reality does not match their expectations, "Notice Your Pictures and Let Them Go" helps them let go of those expectations and experience what their reality *does* have to offer. In class, have students individually brainstorm "pictures" that interfere with their success in college. Examples include "I'm not smart enough to get a college degree" or "I'll never graduate—I can't stick with anything for four years." Then ask students to select one picture to "let go." Have them write their picture on a piece of paper and fold it up. Take the entire class outside and have the students tear their papers (negative pictures) into shreds and throw them in the dumpster—literally letting them go! Return to class and have students write briefly about a new, positive picture to replace the negative one they have let go. For some students, this will be a personal exercise, and they may not feel comfortable talking about it with others. Other students may be willing to share with the class their experience of letting their negative picture go.

3. Master Student Profile: Wilma Mankiller (page 113). Divide students into groups and ask each group to come up with ways that they can be leaders on their college campus or in their local community. Have them write their ideas on large sheets of poster paper and tape them to the walls in your classroom. Have students stay in groups and walk around the room to read the other lists.

Conversation/Sharing

Now that your students have practiced using the Master Student Map in previous chapters, see whether they can generate their own questions before you present yours to the class.

Why? Why does *Becoming a Master Student* include a chapter on reading?

What? Read through the list of articles and select three that you believe will enhance your reading skills.

How? How can you be more successful in college with these additional strategies for successful reading?

What if? What if you apply these reading strategies to your coursework for other classes?

Homework

The twenty-first century researcher—using your library (pages 103–104). After students have read this article and heard from a librarian (as a guest speaker), give them an assignment to go to the college library to (1) find a broad, current issue topic for a college research paper and (2) use the online catalog to discover narrow topics within the broad topic. For the first step, you may want to have them use *CQ Researcher,* a reference book most college libraries have, so they learn about a useful book in the library that can help them find current issue topics for future research paper assignments.

Developing critical thinking strategies throughout the semester will help your students master their college-level reading. Use this exercise to help students further develop their skills. This assignment works best as either an extra-credit assignment or as homework.

When reading is tough (page 99). One of the strategies suggested for understanding difficult reading material is to read another publication on the same subject. This is one example of critical thinking skills—explaining and assessing alternative views on an issue.

Apply this strategy now. Ask your students to find and read a newspaper or magazine article that's relevant to one of their current reading assignments from another course. Have your students summarize and compare the viewpoints on the subject presented by both authors. Ask them to list the major questions addressed, along with the answers that are offered, and have them highlight points of disagreement and agreement.

Finally, have your students consider the methods that the authors use to reach their conclusions and the evidence they present. Have students determine whether one author's viewpoint is more reasonable, given all of the suitable evidence. Then ask them to write a paragraph that supports their conclusion.

If you assign this for extra credit or homework, be sure to clarify for your students exactly what materials they should submit. Consider asking them to submit their articles or a bibliography page. If you are trying to encourage students to become familiar with technology, ask them to forward the materials to you in an e-mail attachment or post the materials to your online course management system.

Evaluation

Ask students to explain the nine steps of the Muscle Reading process. Ask students to describe tools to use when reading tough material and to list techniques for reading faster. Ask students to explain in writing to a student who is a single parent how to study with children underfoot.

Additional Digital Resources

Course Manual

The online *Course Manual* serves as an invaluable reference for those developing and teaching a College Success course with *Becoming a Master Student Concise*. The *Course Manual* provides advice on general teaching issues such as preparing for classes, classroom management, grading, and communicating with students of various backgrounds, as well as specific strategies on getting the most out of various features in *Becoming a Master Student Concise* and book-specific Web sites. Do a *Course Manual* reconnaissance to find ideas that you can use in your course right now.

Instructor Companion Site

The updated Instructor Companion Site provides resources to help you plan and customize your course. Content specific to Chapter 4 includes:

- Lecture Ideas
  - Liking the Instructor—or Form versus Content
  - Appropriate Reading Rates
- In-Class Exercises
  - First Impressions
  - Critical Reading as a Process
  - Numbered Notes
- In-Text Quiz Answers
- PowerPoint Slides

The Instructor Companion Site also contains the following book-specific content:

- ExamView Test Bank
- Online Course Manual
- Sample Syllabi
- Detailed Transition Guide

College Success CourseMate

To help your students gain a better understanding of the topics discussed in *Becoming a Master Student Concise*, encourage them to visit the College Success CourseMate at CengageBrain.com that provides the following resources specific to Chapter 4:

- Connect to Text content expands on specific topics marked with an icon within the Introduction.
- Practice Tests allow students to see how well they understand the themes of *Becoming a Master Student Concise*.
- Interactive Concept Maps promote critical thinking by highlighting related ideas to show relationships among concepts.
- Learning Styles Application
- Discussion Topics
- Reflection Questions
- Assessment Questions
- Experiment with chapter strategies
- Remembering Cultural Differences presents readers with brief articles that touch on aspects of diversity in our rapidly changing world. For Chapter 4, the following article will prompt your students to look at contemporary issues in a new way:
  - Where Have All the Readers Gone?
- Master Student Profiles provide additional information on the people covered in this book feature. For Chapter 4, students will find expanded coverage and links about:
  - Chief Wilma Mankiller
- Power Process Media contains video, PowerPoints, and audio files to take what your students have learned from the Power Processes in their book to the next level. For Chapter 4, students will find additional media on:
  - Notice Your Pictures and Let Them Go

Along with the chapter-specific content, a General Resources folder is available that contains Toolboxes geared toward specific student types (Community College, Adult Learner, Student Athlete), the Plagiarism Prevention Zone, and the Career Resource Center.

4 Reading

Master Student Map

as you read, ask yourself

what if . . . ?

I could finish my reading with time to spare and easily recall the key points?

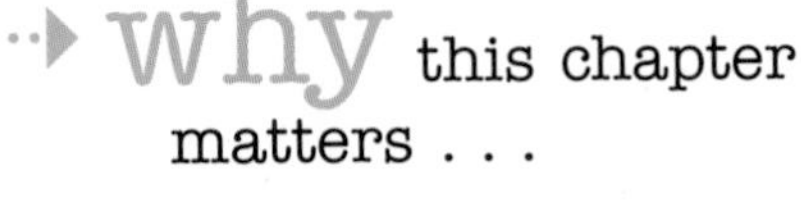

why this chapter matters . . .

Higher education requires extensive reading of complex material.

how you can use this chapter . . .

- Analyze what effective readers do and experiment with new techniques.
- Increase your vocabulary and adjust your reading speed for different types of material.
- Comprehend difficult texts with more ease.

what is included . . .

MASTER STUDENTS in *action*

One night when I was reading, I had so much on my mind I reread the page probably five times. I finally just put the book down and cleared my mind. I put on some of my favorite music, and I took a fantasy trip by thinking about all my upcoming exciting things that I would be doing. It helped me forget all the distracting thoughts that were going through my mind. When I was done, I got back to my reading with no trouble at all. —**LINDSEY GIBLIN**

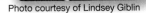

Photo courtesy of Lindsey Giblin

Muscle Reading

PICTURE YOURSELF SITTING at a desk with a book in your hands. Your eyes are open, and it looks as if you're reading. Suddenly your head jerks up. You blink. You realize your eyes have been scanning the page for 10 minutes, and you can't remember a single thing you have read.

Or picture this: You've had a hard day. You were up at 6 a.m. to get the kids ready for school. A coworker called in sick, and you missed your lunch trying to do his job as well as your own. You picked up the kids, then had to shop for dinner. Dinner was late, of course, and the kids were grumpy.

Finally, you get to your books at 8 p.m. You begin a reading assignment on something called "the equity method of accounting for common stock investments." "I am preparing for the future," you tell yourself, as you plod through two paragraphs and begin the third. Suddenly, everything in the room looks different. Your head is resting on your elbow, which is resting on the equity method of accounting. The clock reads 11:00 p.m. Say good-bye to 3 hours.

Sometimes the only difference between a sleeping pill and a textbook is that the textbook doesn't have a warning on the label about operating heavy machinery.

Contrast this scenario with the image of an active reader. This person

- Stays alert, poses questions about what she reads, and searches for the answers.
- Recognizes levels of information within the text, separating the main points and general principles from supporting details.
- Quizzes herself about the material, makes written notes, and lists unanswered questions.
- Instantly spots key terms and takes the time to find the definitions of unfamiliar words.
- Thinks critically about the ideas in the text and looks for ways to apply them.

That sounds like a lot to do. Yet skilled readers routinely accomplish all these things and more—while enjoying reading.

One way to experience this kind of success is to approach reading with a system in mind. An example is Muscle Reading. You can use Muscle Reading to avoid mental mini-vacations and reduce the number of unscheduled naps during study time, even after a hard day.

Muscle Reading is a way to decrease your difficulties and struggles by increasing your energy and skills. Once you learn this system, you might actually spend less time on your reading and get more out of it.

This is not to say that Muscle Reading will make your education a breeze. Muscle Reading might even look like more work at first. Effective textbook reading is an active, energy-consuming, sit-on-the-edge-of-your-seat business. That's why this strategy is called Muscle Reading. *

journal entry 11

Discovery/Intention Statement

Discover what you want from this chapter

Recall a time when you encountered problems with reading, such as words you didn't understand or paragraphs you paused to reread more than once. Sum up the experience and how you felt about it by completing the following statement:

I discovered that I . . .

Now list three to five specific reading skills you want to gain from this chapter.

I intend to . . .

Three phases of Muscle Reading

MUSCLE READING IS a three-phase technique you can use to extract the ideas and information you want.

Phase 1 includes steps to take *before* you read.

Phase 2 includes steps to take *while* you read.

Phase 3 includes steps to take *after* you read.

Each phase has three steps.

PHASE ONE:
Before you read
Step 1: **Preview**
Step 2: **Outline**
Step 3: **Question**

PHASE TWO:
While you read
Step 4: **Read**
Step 5: **Underline**
Step 6: **Answer**

PHASE THREE:
After you read
Step 7: **Recite**
Step 8: **Review**
Step 9: **Review again**

Images: © Masterfile Royalty Free, collage by Walter Kopec

4 READING

To assist your recall of Muscle Reading strategies, memorize three short sentences:

Pry Out Questions.

Root Up Answers.

Recite, Review, and Review again.

These three sentences correspond to the three phases of the Muscle Reading technique. Each sentence is an acrostic. The first letter of each word stands for one of the nine steps listed above. To jog your memory, write the first letters of the Muscle Reading acrostic in a margin or at the top of your notes. Then check off the steps you intend to follow. Alternatively, you can write the Muscle Reading steps on 3x5 cards and use them for bookmarks.

PHASE 1: Before you read

Step 1: Preview

Before you start reading, preview the entire assignment.

If you are starting a new book, look over the table of contents and flip through the text page by page. If you're going to read one chapter, flip through the pages of that chapter. Even if your assignment is merely a few pages in a book, you can benefit from a brief preview of the table of contents.

Keep an eye out for summary statements. Many textbooks have summaries in the introduction or at the end of each chapter. If the assignment is long or complex, read the summary first. Also read chapter headings and subheadings. Like the headlines in a newspaper, these headings are usually printed in large, bold type. Headings are brief summaries in themselves. Inspect drawings, diagrams, charts, tables, graphs, and photographs as well.

When previewing, seek out familiar concepts, facts, or ideas. These items can help increase comprehension by linking new information to previously learned material. Look for ideas that spark your imagination or curiosity.

Keep the preview short. If the entire reading assignment will take less than an hour, your preview might take 5 minutes.

Step 2: Outline

Outlining actively organizes your thoughts about the assignment and can help make complex information easier to understand. If your textbook provides chapter outlines, spend some time studying them. When an outline is not provided, sketch a brief one in the margin of your book or at the beginning of your notes on a separate sheet of paper. Later, as you read and take notes, you can add to your outline.

Headings in the text can serve as major and minor entries in your outline. When you outline, feel free to rewrite headings so that they are more meaningful to you.

The amount of time you spend on the outlining step will vary. For some assignments, a 10-second mental outline is all you might need. For other assignments (fiction and poetry, for example), you can skip this step altogether.

Step 3: Question

Before you begin a careful reading, determine what you want from the assignment. Will you be reading just to get the main points? Key supporting details? Additional details? All of the above? Also imagine what kinds of questions about this material could show up on a test. Then put your questions in writing.

Another useful technique is to turn chapter headings and subheadings into questions. For example, if a heading is "Transference and Suggestion," you can ask yourself, "What are *transference* and *suggestion*? How does *transference* relate to *suggestion*?" Make up a quiz as if you were teaching this subject to your classmates. If there are no headings, look for key sentences and turn them into questions. These sentences usually show up at the beginnings or ends of paragraphs and sections.

Demand your money's worth from your textbook. If you do not understand a concept, write specific questions about it.

PHASE 2: While you read

Step 4: Read

Before you dive into the first paragraph, take a few moments to reflect on what you already know about this subject. This technique prepares your brain to accept the information that follows.

As you read, visualize the material. Form mental pictures of the concepts as they are presented. If you read that a voucher system can help control cash disbursements, picture a voucher handing out dollar bills.

Get a feel for the subject. For example, let's say you are reading about a microorganism—a paramecium—in your biology text. Imagine what it would feel like to run your finger around the long, cigar-shaped body of the organism. Imagine feeling the large fold of its gullet on one side and the tickle of the hairy little cilia as they wiggle in your hand.

Muscle Reading for ebooks

Find navigation tools. To flip electronic pages, look for *previous* and *next* buttons or arrows on the right and left borders of each page. Many ebooks also offer a "go to page" feature that allows you to key in a specific page number.

For a bigger picture of the text, look for a table of contents that lists chapter headings and subheadings. Click on any of these headings to see whether you can expand the text for that part of the book. Note that charts, illustrations, photos, tables, diagrams and other visuals might be listed separately in the table of contents.

Search. Look for a search box that allows you to enter key words and find all the places in the text where those words are mentioned.

Look for links to related information. Many ebook readers will supply a definition of any word in the text. All you need to do is highlight a word and click on it. Also find out whether your ebook reader will connect you to Web sites related to the topic of your ebook.

Mark it up. Look for ways to electronically underline or highlight text. In addition, see whether you can annotate the book by keying in your own notes tied to specific pages. You might be able to tag each note with a key word and then sort your notes into categories based on these words.

Print. See whether you can connect your ebook device to a printer. You might find it easier to study difficult passages on paper. Note that some ebook publishers impose a limit on how much text you can print.

Monitor battery life. Recharge the battery for your ebook device or laptop computer so that it has enough power to last throughout your work or school day. Seeing your screen go dark when you're in the middle of a paragraph could be a one-way ticket to confusion.

Consult the print version. Sometimes it's hard to beat a good old-fashioned book—especially for dense tables, complex illustrations, and large, color-coded charts. These features might not translate well to a small screen. Go to the library or bookstore to see whether you can find those pages in a printed copy of your ebook.

Step 5: Underline

If you own the book, deface it. Have fun writing in it. Underline important concepts or information that you want to review later. Underlining calls out key points and offers a secondary benefit: When you read with a highlighter, pen, or pencil in your hand, you involve your kinesthetic senses of touch and motion. Being physical with your books can help build strong neural pathways in your memory.

Avoid underlining too soon. Underlining after you read each paragraph can work well. At other times, you may want to wait until you complete a chapter or section to make sure you know the key points. Then mark up the text.

Underline sparingly—usually less than 10 percent of the text. If you mark up too much on a page, you defeat the purpose: to flag the most important material for review.

In addition to underlining, you can mark up a text in the following ways:

- Place an asterisk (*) or an exclamation point (!) in the margin next to an especially important sentence or term.
- Circle key terms and words to look up later in a dictionary.
- Write short definitions of key terms in the margin.
- Write a Q in the margin to highlight possible test questions, passages you don't understand, and questions to ask in class.
- Write personal comments in the margin, such as points of agreement or disagreement with the author.
- Write mini-indexes in the margin—that is, the numbers of other pages in the book where the same topic is discussed.
- Number each step in a list or series of related points.

Step 6: Answer

As you read, write answers to your questions from Step 3. Jot down new questions, and note when you don't find the answers you are looking for. Use these notes to ask questions in class, or see your instructor personally.

When you read, create an image of yourself as a person in search of the answers. You are a detective, watching for every clue, sitting erect in your straight-back chair, demanding that your textbook give you what you want—the answers.

PHASE 3: After you read

Step 7: Recite

Talk to yourself about what you've read. Or talk to someone else. When you finish a reading assignment, make a speech about it.

One way to get yourself to recite is to look at each underlined point. Note what you marked; then put the book down and start talking out loud. Explain as much as you can about that particular point.

Step 8: Review

Sound the trumpets! This point is critical: A review within 24 hours moves information from your short-term memory to your long-term memory. Review within 1 day. If you read it on Wednesday, review it on Thursday. During this review, look over your notes and clear up anything you don't understand. Recite some of the main points again.

Step 9: Review again

The final step in Muscle Reading is the weekly or monthly review. This step can be very short—perhaps only 4 or 5 minutes per assignment. Go over your notes. Read the highlighted parts of your text, and recite one or two of the more complicated points.

You can accomplish these short reviews anytime, anywhere, if you are prepared. Conduct a 5-minute review while you are waiting for a bus to arrive, your socks to dry, or the water to boil. You can use 3x5 cards as a handy review tool. Write ideas, formulas, concepts, and facts on cards, and carry them with you. These short review periods can be effortless and fun. *

Find examples of Muscle Reading strategies online.

When reading is tough

> **When you are confused, tell the truth about it. Successful readers monitor their understanding of reading material. They do not see confusion as a mistake or a personal shortcoming. Instead, they take it as a cue to change their reading strategies.**

Read it again. Somehow, students get the idea that reading means opening a book and dutifully slogging through the text—line by line, page by page—moving in a straight line from the first word to the last. Actually, this method can be an ineffective way to read much of the published material you'll encounter in college.

Feel free to shake up your routine. Make several passes through tough reading material. During a preview, just scan the text to look for key words and highlighted material. Next, skim the entire chapter or article again, spending a little more time and taking in more than you did during your preview. Finally, read in more depth, proceeding word by word through some or all of the text.

Difficult material—such as the technical writing in science texts—is often easier the second time around. Isolate difficult passages and read them again, slowly.

If you read an assignment and are completely lost, do not despair. Sleep on it and then return to the assignment the next day.[1]

Look for essential words. If you are stuck on a paragraph, mentally cross out all of the adjectives and adverbs, and then read the sentences without them. Find the important words—usually verbs and nouns.

Hold a mini-review. Pause briefly to summarize—either verbally or in writing—what you've read so far. Stop at the end of a paragraph and recite, in your own words, what you have just read. Jot down some notes, or create a short outline or summary.

Read it out loud. Make noise. Read a passage out loud several times, each time using a different inflection and emphasizing a different part of the sentence. Be creative. Imagine that you are the author talking.

Talk to your instructor. Admit when you are stuck, and make an appointment with your instructor. Most teachers welcome the opportunity to work individually with students. Be specific about your confusion. Point out the paragraph that you found toughest to understand.

Stand up. Changing positions periodically can combat fatigue.

Skip around. Jump to the next section or to the end of a tough article or chapter. You might have lost the big picture. Simply seeing the next step, the next main point, or a summary might be all you need to put the details in context. Retrace the steps in a chain of ideas, and look for examples. Absorb facts and ideas in whatever order works for you—which may be different from the author's presentation.

Find a tutor. Many schools provide free tutoring services. If your school does not, other students who have completed the course can assist you.

Use another text. Find a similar text in the library. Sometimes a concept is easier to understand if it is expressed another way. Children's books—especially children's encyclopedias—can provide useful overviews of baffling subjects.

Pretend you understand, and then explain it. Pretend that the material is clear as a bell and explain it to another person, or even to yourself. Write down your explanation. You might be amazed by what you know.

Stop reading. When none of the above suggestions work, do not despair. Admit your confusion and then take a break. Catch a movie, go for a walk, study another subject, or sleep on it. The concepts you've already absorbed might come together at a subconscious level as you move on to other activities. Allow some time for that process. When you return to the reading material, see it with fresh eyes. *

Get to the bones of your book with concept maps

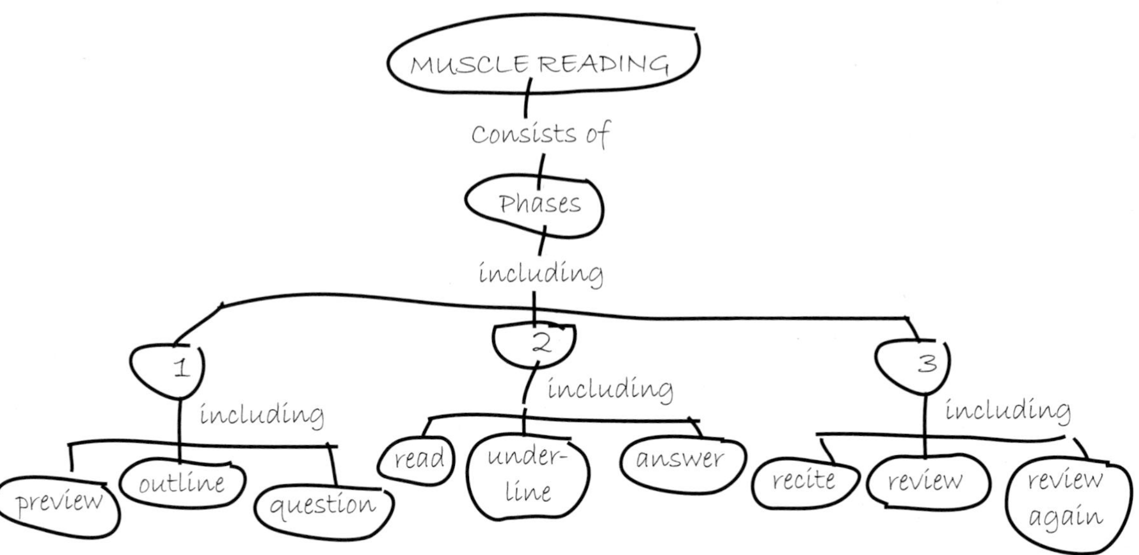

Concept mapping, pioneered by Joseph Novak and D. Bob Gowin, is a tool to make major ideas in a book leap off the page.[2] In creating a concept map, you reduce an author's message to its essence—its bare bones. Concept maps can also be used to display the organization of lectures and discussions.

Concepts and links are the building blocks of knowledge. A *concept* is a name for a group of related things or ideas. *Links* are words or phrases that describe the relationship between concepts. Consider the following paragraph:

> Muscle Reading consists of three phases. Phase 1 includes tasks to complete before reading. Phase 2 tasks take place during reading. Finally, Phase 3 includes tasks to complete after reading.

In this paragraph, examples of concepts are *Muscle Reading, reading, phases, tasks, Phase 1, Phase 2,* and *Phase 3*. Links include *consists of, includes, before, during,* and *after*.

To create a concept map, list concepts and then arrange them in a meaningful order from general to specific. Then fill in the links between concepts, forming meaningful statements.

Concept mapping promotes critical thinking. It alerts you to missing concepts or faulty links between concepts. In addition, concept mapping mirrors the way that your brain learns—that is, by linking new concepts to concepts that you already know.

To create a concept map, use the following steps:

1. **List the key concepts in the text.** Aim to express each concept in three words or less. Most concept words are nouns, including terms and proper names. At this point, you can list the concepts in any order.

2. **Rank the concepts so that they flow from general to specific.** On a large sheet of paper, write the main concept at the top of the page. Place the most specific concepts near the bottom. Arrange the rest of the concepts in appropriate positions throughout the middle of the page. Circle each concept.

3. **Draw lines that connect the concepts.** On these connecting lines, add words that describe the relationship between the concepts. Again, limit yourself to the fewest words needed to make an accurate link—three words or less. Linking words are often verbs, verb phrases, or prepositions.

4. **Finally, review your map.** Look for any concepts that are repeated in several places on the map. You can avoid these repetitions by adding more links between concepts. *

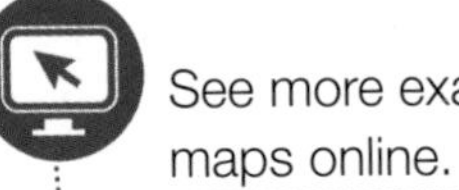

See more examples of concept maps online.

Reading *fast*

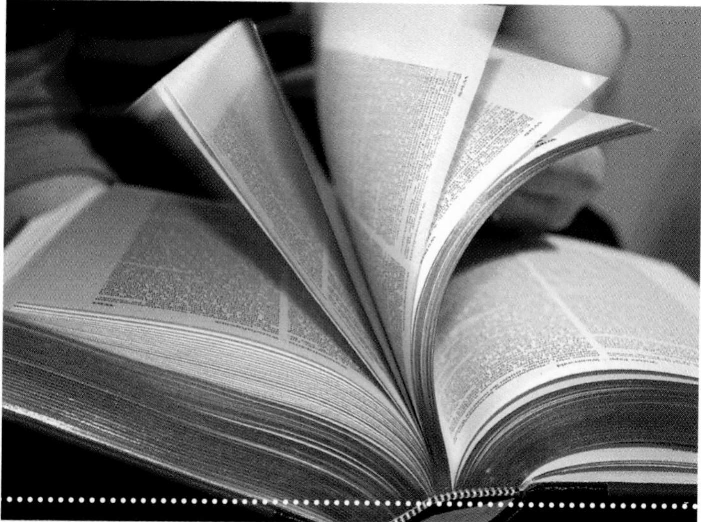

© Chris Pancewicz/Alamy

DO AN EXPERIMENT right now. Read the rest of this article as fast as you can. After you finish, come back and reread the same paragraphs at your usual rate. As you do, note how much you remember from your first sprint through the text. You might be surprised to find out how well you comprehend material even at dramatically increased speeds. Build on that success by experimenting with the following guidelines.

Move your eyes faster. When we read, our eyes leap across the page in short bursts called *saccades* (pronounced "să-käds"). A saccade is also a sharp jerk on the reins of a horse—a violent pull to stop the animal quickly. Our eyes stop like that, too, in pauses called *fixations*.

Although we experience the illusion of continuously scanning each line, our eyes actually take in groups of words, usually about three at a time. For more than 90 percent of reading time, our eyes are at a dead stop in those fixations.

Your eyes can move faster if they take in more words with each burst—for example, six instead of three. To practice taking in more words between fixations, find a newspaper with narrow columns. Then read down one column at a time, and fixate only once per line.

In addition to using the above techniques, simply make a conscious effort to fixate less. You might feel a little uncomfortable at first. That's normal. Just practice often, for short periods of time.

Notice and release ineffective habits. Our eyes make regressions; that is, they back up and reread words. You can reduce regressions by paying attention to them. Use the handy 3x5 card to cover words and lines that you have just read. You can then note how often you stop and move the card back to reread the text. Don't be discouraged if you stop often at first. Being aware of it helps you regress less frequently.

Also notice vocalizing. To read faster, avoid reading out loud and moving your lips. Also avoid subvocalizing—that is, mentally "hearing" the words as you read them. To stop doing this, just be aware of it.

When you first attempt to release these habits, choose simpler reading material. That way, you can pay closer attention to your reading technique. Gradually work your way up to more complex material.

If you're pressed for time, skim. When you're in a hurry, experiment by skimming the assignment instead of reading the whole thing. Read the headings, subheadings, lists, charts, graphs, and summary paragraphs. Summaries are especially important. They are usually found at the beginning or end of a chapter or section.

Stay flexible. Remember that speed isn't everything. Skillful readers vary their reading rate according to their purpose and the nature of the material. An advanced text in analytic geometry usually calls for a different reading rate than the Sunday comics.

With that in mind, remember the first rule of reading fast: Just do it! *

14 critical thinking exercise
Relax

Eyestrain can be the result of continuous stress. Take a break from your reading and use this exercise to release tension.

1. Sit on a chair or lie down, and take a few moments to breathe deeply.
2. Close your eyes, place your palms over them, and visualize a perfect field of black.
3. Continue to be aware of the blackness for 2 or 3 minutes while you breathe deeply.
4. Now remove your hands from your eyes, and open your eyes slowly.
5. Relax for a minute more; then continue reading.

Read with a dictionary in your lap

HAVING A LARGE vocabulary makes reading more enjoyable and increases the range of materials you can explore. In addition, building your vocabulary gives you more options for self-expression when speaking or writing.

Strengthen your vocabulary by taking delight in words. Look up unfamiliar terms. Pay special attention to words that arouse your curiosity.

© Stockbyte/Getty Images

Students regularly use two kinds of paper dictionaries: the desk dictionary and the unabridged dictionary. A desk dictionary is an easy-to-handle abridged dictionary that you can use many times in the course of a day. Keep this book within easy reach (maybe in your lap) so you can look up unfamiliar words while reading. You can find a large, unabridged dictionary in a library or bookstore. It provides more complete information about words and definitions than your desk dictionary, and also includes synonyms, usage notes, and word histories. Or you may prefer using one of several online dictionaries, such as Dictionary.com.

Construct a word stack. When you come across an unfamiliar word, write it down on a 3x5 card. Below the word, copy the sentence in which it was used, along with the page number. You can look up each word immediately, or you can accumulate a stack of these cards and look up the words later. Write the definition of each word on the back of the 3x5 card, adding the *diacritics*—marks that tell you how to pronounce it.

To expand your vocabulary and learn the history behind the words, take your stack of cards to an unabridged dictionary. As you find related words in the dictionary, add them to your stack. These cards become a portable study aid that you can review in your spare moments.

Learn—even when your dictionary is across town. When you are listening to a lecture and hear an unusual word, or when you are reading on the bus and encounter a word you don't know, you can still build your word stack. Pull out a 3x5 card and write down the word and its sentence. Later, you can look up the definition and write it on the back of the card.

Divide words into parts. Another suggestion for building your vocabulary is to divide an unfamiliar word into syllables and look for familiar parts. This strategy works well if you make it a point to learn common prefixes (beginning syllables) and suffixes (ending syllables). For example, the suffix *-tude* usually refers to a condition or state of being. Knowing this makes it easier to conclude that *habitude* refers to a usual way of doing something and that *similitude* means being similar or having a quality of resemblance.

Infer the meaning of words from their context. You can often deduce the meaning of an unfamiliar word simply by paying attention to its context—the surrounding words, phrases, sentences, paragraphs, or images. Later, you can confirm your deduction by consulting a dictionary.

Practice looking for context clues such as these:

- *Definitions.* A key word might be defined right in the text. Look for phrases such as *defined as* or *in other words.*
- *Examples.* Authors often provide examples to clarify a word meaning. If the word is not explicitly defined, then study the examples. They're often preceded by the phrases *for example, for instance,* or *such as.*
- *Lists.* When a word is listed in a series, pay attention to the other items in the series. They might define the unfamiliar word through association.
- *Comparisons.* You might find a new word surrounded by synonyms—words with a similar meaning. Look for synonyms after words such as *like* and *as.*
- *Contrasts.* A writer might juxtapose a word with its *antonym* (opposite). Look for phrases such as *on the contrary* and *on the other hand.* ✻

The twenty-first-century researcher—using your library

© Masterfile Royalty Free

LIBRARIES HOUSE TREASURES. In addition to housing print and audiovisual publications, libraries give you access to online sources. Remember that much published material is available only in print. The book—a form of information technology that's been with us for centuries—still has something to offer the twenty-first-century researcher.

Ask a librarian. Libraries give you access to a resource that goes even beyond the pages of a book or a Web site. That resource is a real person—a librarian. Librarians are trained explorers who can guide your expedition into the information jungle. They chose this line of work because they enjoy helping people. They also understand that some people feel nervous about finding materials. Asking a librarian for help can save you hours.

Librarians have various specialties. Start with a reference librarian. If the library has the material that you want, this person will find it. If not, he will direct you to another source. This source might be a business, community agency, or government office.

Take a tour. Libraries—from the smallest one in your hometown to the Smithsonian in Washington, D.C.—consist of just three basic elements:

- *Catalogs*—databases that list all of the library's accessible materials.
- *Collections*—materials, such as periodicals (magazines and newspapers), books, pamphlets, audiovisual materials, and materials available from other collections via interlibrary loan.
- *Computer resources*—Internet access; connections to campus-wide computer networks; and databases stored on CD-ROMs, on CDs, on DVDs, or online.

Before you start your next research project, take some time to investigate all three elements of your campus or community library. Start with a library orientation session or tour. Step into each room, and ask what's available there. Also find out whether the library houses any special collections. You might find one related to your major or another special interest.

Search the catalog. Some catalogs include listings for several libraries. To find materials, do a key word search—much like using a search engine on the Internet.

The catalog lists materials by subject, author, and title. Each listing includes a Library of Congress or Dewey decimal system number. These call numbers are used to shelve and locate materials. When you find a book by its call number, look at the materials around it on the shelf. There you will find other sources of information on the same topic.

Some catalogs let you see whether material is on the shelf or checked out. You may even be able to put a hold on materials that are currently in circulation. Ask a librarian whether you can do these things from a computer at your home or workplace.

Inspect the collection. When inspecting a library's collections, look for materials such as the following:

- *Encyclopedias.* Use leading print and online encyclopedias, such as *Encyclopaedia Britannica.* Specialized encyclopedias cover many fields and include, for example, *Encyclopedia of Psychology*, *Encyclopedia of the Biological Sciences*, *Encyclopedia of Asian History*, and *McGraw-Hill Encyclopedia of Science and Technology.*
- *Biographies.* Read accounts of people's lives in works such as *Who's Who*, *Dictionary of American Biography*, and *Biography Index: A Cumulative Index to Biographical Material in Books and Magazines.*
- *Critical works.* Read what scholars have to say about works of art and literature in Oxford Companion volumes (such as *Oxford Companion to Art* and *Oxford Companion to African American Literature*).
- *Statistics and government documents.* Among the many useful sources are *Statistical Abstract of the United States*, *Handbook of Labor Statistics*,

Occupational Outlook Handbook, and U.S. Census Bureau publications.

- *Almanacs, atlases, and gazetteers.* See the *World Almanac and Book of Facts*, the *New York Times Almanac*, and the *CIA World Factbook*.
- *Dictionaries.* Consult the *American Heritage Dictionary of the English Language*, *Oxford English Dictionary*, and other specialized dictionaries such as the *Penguin Dictionary of Literary Terms and Literary Theory* and the *Dictionary of the Social Sciences*.
- *Indexes and databases.* Databases contain publication information, summaries, and sometimes the full text of an article available for downloading or printing from your computer. Your library houses print and CD-ROM databases and subscribes to some online databases. Other resources are accessible through online library catalogs or Web links.
- *Reference works in specific subject areas.* Examples include *The Oxford Companion to Art* and the *Concise Oxford Companion to Classical Literature*.
- *Periodical articles.* Find articles in periodicals (works issued periodically, such as scholarly journals, popular magazines, and newspapers) by using a periodical index. Use electronic indexes for recent works and print indexes for earlier works—especially for works written before 1980.[3]

Access computer resources. Many libraries have access to special databases that are not available on the Internet. A reference librarian can tell you about them. Also ask about ebooks (electronic books). These texts are delivered straight to your computer.

Inspect your finds. Once you find materials about a particular topic, inspect each one. Allow sufficient time for this step. Scan all the materials to find the most useful ones, and read them several times.

With print materials, give special attention to the preface, publication data, table of contents, bibliography, glossary, endnotes, and index. (Nonprint materials, including online documents, often include similar types of information.) Also scan any headings, subheadings, and summaries. If you have time, read a chapter or section.

Then evaluate materials according to the following:

Relevance. Look for materials that deal directly with your research questions. If you're in doubt about the relevance of a particular source, ask yourself, "Will this material help me achieve the purpose of my research? Does it support my thesis?"

Currency. Notice the publication date of your material (usually found in the front matter on the copyright page). If your topic is time sensitive, set some guidelines about how current you want your sources to be.

Credibility. Look for biographical information about the author: education, training, and work experience that qualifies this person to publish on the topic. Also notice any possible sources of bias, such as political affiliations or funding sources, that might color the author's point of view. *

mastering technology

FIND WHAT YOU WANT ON THE INTERNET

At one level, searching the Internet is simple. Just go online to a site such as Ask.com, Google, or Yahoo! Look for the search box, and enter a key word or two to describe what you want to find. Then hit the enter key.

You might find exactly what you're looking for in this way. If you don't, then take your Internet searches to the next level:

Use specific key words. Entering *firefox* or *safari* will give you more focused results than entering *web browser*. *Reading strategies* or *note-taking strategies* will get more specific results than *study strategies*. Whenever possible, use proper names. Enter *Beatles* or *Radiohead* rather than *British rock bands*. If you're looking for nearby restaurants, enter *restaurant* and your zip code rather than the name of your city.

Start with fewer key words rather than more. Instead of *ways to develop your career plan*, just enter *career plan*. The extra words might lead to irrelevant results or narrow your search too much.

If you're looking for certain words in a certain order, use quotation marks. *"Audacity of hope"* will return a list of pages with that exact phrase.

Search within a site. If you're looking only for articles about college tuition from the *New York Times*, then add *new york times* or *nytimes.com* to the search box.

When you're not sure of a key word, add a wild-card character. In most search engines, that character is the asterisk (*). If you're looking for the title of a film directed by Clint Eastwood and just can't remember the name, enter *clint eastwood directed **.

Look for more search options. The previous suggestions can keep you from drowning in a sea of useless search results. Many search engines also offer advanced search features and explain how to use them. Look for the word *advanced* or *more* on the site's homepage, and click on the link.

Discover more search strategies.

English as a Second Language

If you grew up reading and speaking a language other than English and are new to the English language, you might fall under the category of English as a Second Language (ESL) student, or English Language Learner (ELL). Experiment with the following suggestions to learn English with more success.

4

READING

Build confidence

Many ESL/ELL students feel insecure about using English in social settings, including the classroom. Choosing not to speak, however, can delay your mastery of English and isolate you from other students.

As an alternative, make it your intention to speak up in class. List several questions beforehand, and plan to ask them. Also, schedule a time to meet with your instructors during office hours to discuss any material that you find confusing. These strategies can help you build relationships while developing English skills.

In addition, start a conversation with at least one native speaker of English in each of your classes. For openers, ask about their favorite instructors or ideas for future courses to take.

English is a complex language. Whenever you extend your vocabulary and range of expression, the likelihood of making mistakes increases. The person who wants to master English yet seldom makes mistakes is probably being too careful. Do not look upon mistakes as a sign of weakness. Mistakes can be your best teachers—if you are willing to learn from them.

Remember that the terms *English as a Second Language* and *English Language Learner* describe a difference—not a deficiency. The fact that you've entered a new culture and are mastering another language gives you a broader perspective than people who speak only one language. And if you currently speak two or more languages, you've already demonstrated your ability to learn.

Errors	Corrections
Sun is bright.	The sun is bright.
He cheerful.	He is cheerful.
I enjoy to play chess.	I enjoy playing chess.
Good gifts received everyone.	Everyone received good gifts.
I knew what would present the teachers.	I knew what the teachers would present.
I like very much museums.	I like museums very much.
I want that you stay.	I want you to stay.
Is raining.	It is raining.
My mother she lives in Iowa.	My mother lives in Iowa.
I gave the paper to she.	I gave the paper to her.
They felt safety in the car.	They felt safe in the car.
He has three car.	He has three cars.
I have helpfuls family members.	I have helpful family members.
She don't know nothing.	She knows nothing.

Analyze errors in using English

To learn from your errors, make a list of those that are most common for you. Next to the error, write a corrected version. For some examples, see the chart above.

Remember that native speakers of English also use this technique—for instance, by making lists of words they frequently misspell.

Also keep in mind that errors in speaking English often result from basic differences between languages. The sentence "I bought car" does not obey the rules of English grammar. Correct versions are "I bought a car" and "I bought the car." However, an expression like "I bought car" might be acceptable in Chinese and Japanese languages that omit articles such as "a" and "the."

Learn by speaking and listening

You probably started your English studies by using textbooks. Writing and reading in English are important. Both can help you add to your English vocabulary and master grammar. To gain greater fluency and improve your pronunciation, also make it your goal to *hear* and *speak* English.

For example, listen to radio talk shows. Imitate the speaker's pronunciation by repeating phrases and sentences that you hear. During conversations, notice the facial expressions and gestures that accompany certain English words and phrases.

If you speak English with an accent, do not be concerned. Many people speak clear, accented English. Work on your accent only if you can't be easily understood.

Take advantage of opportunities to read and hear English at the same time. For instance, turn on English subtitles when watching a film on DVD. Also, check your library for books on tape or CD. Check out the printed book, and follow along as you listen.

Use computer resources

Some online dictionaries allow you to hear words pronounced. These sites include Answers.com (www.answers.com) and Merriam-Webster Online (www.m-w.com).

Other resources include online book sites with a read-aloud feature. An example is Project Gutenberg (www.gutenberg.org; search on "Audio Books"). Speaks for Itself (www.speaksforitself.com) is a free download that allows you to hear text from Web sites read aloud.

Also, check general Web sites for ESL students. A popular one is Dave's ESL Café (www.eslcafe.com), which will lead you to others.

Gain skills in note taking and testing

When taking notes, remember that you don't have to capture everything that an instructor says. To a large extent, the art of note taking consists of choosing what *not* to record. Listen for key words, main points, and important examples. Remember that instructors will often repeat these things. You'll have more than one chance to pick up on the important material. When you're in doubt, ask for repetition or clarification. For additional suggestions, see Chapter 5: "Notes."

Taking tests is a related challenge. You may find that certain kinds of test questions—such as multiple-choice items—are more common in the United States than in your native country. Chapter 6: "Tests" can help you master these and many other types of tests.

When in doubt, use expressions you understand

Native speakers of English use many informal expressions that are called *slang*. You are more likely to find slang in spoken conversation than in written English.

Native speakers also use *idioms*—colorful expressions with meanings that are not always obvious. Idioms can often be misunderstood. For instance, a "fork in the road" does not refer to an eating utensil discarded on a street. Rather, it is a place where a part of the road branches off.

Learning how to use slang and idioms is part of gaining fluency in English. However, these elements of the language are tricky. If you mispronounce a key word or leave one out, you can create a misunderstanding. In important situations—such as applying for a job, writing an essay, or meeting with a teacher—use only those expressions you fully understand.

Later, during informal conversations with friends, try out new expressions. Ask for feedback on your use of them.

Create a community of English learners

Learning as part of a community can increase your mastery. For example, when completing a writing assignment in English, get together with other people who are learning the language. Read each other's papers and suggest revisions. Plan on revising your paper a number of times based on feedback from your peers.

You might feel awkward about sharing your writing with other people. Accept that feeling—and then remind yourself of everything you have to gain by learning from a group. In addition to learning English more quickly, you can raise your grades and make new friends.

Native speakers of English might be willing to assist your group. Ask your instructors to suggest someone. This person can benefit from the exchange of ideas and the chance to learn about other cultures.

Celebrate your gains

Every time you analyze and correct an error in English, you make a small gain. Celebrate those gains. Taken together over time, they add up to major progress in mastering English as a second language. *

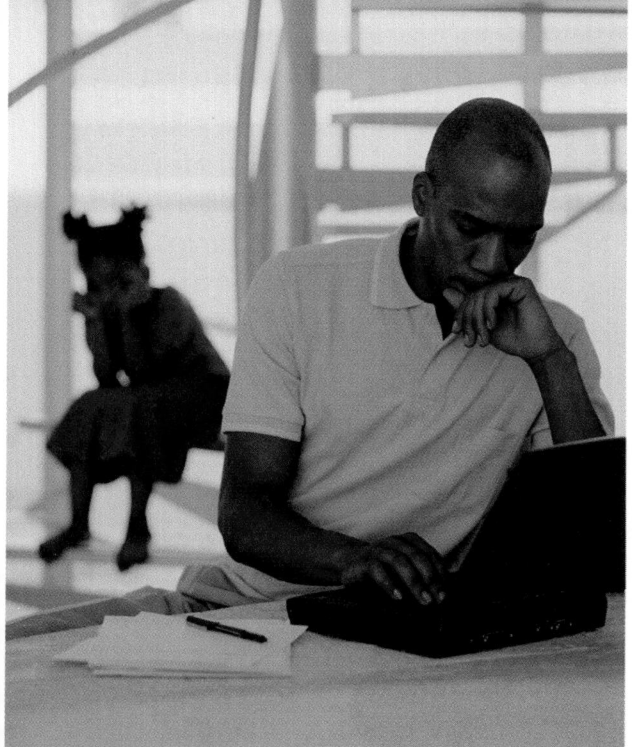

© Digital Vision/Picture Quest/Getty Images

Reading with children underfoot

IT IS POSSIBLE to have effective study time as well as quality time to spend with your children. The following suggestions come mostly from students who are also parents. The specific strategies you use will depend on your schedule and the ages of your children.

Attend to your children first. When you first come home from school, keep your books out of sight. Spend at least 10 minutes with your children before you settle in to study. Give them hugs and ask about their day. Then explain that you have some work to do. Your children might reward you with 30 minutes of quiet time. A short time of full, focused attention from a parent can be more satisfying than longer periods of partial attention.

Of course, this suggestion won't work with infants or toddlers. Schedule sessions of concentrated study for when these children are asleep.

Use "pockets" of time. See whether you can arrange study time at school before you come home. If you arrive at school 15 minutes early and stay 15 minutes late, you can squeeze in an extra half-hour of study time that day. Also look for opportunities to study between classes.

Before you shuttle children to soccer games or dance classes, throw a book in the car. While your children are warming up for the game or changing clothes, steal another 15 minutes to read.

Plan special activities for your child. Find a regular playmate for your child. Some children can pair off with close friends and safely retreat to their rooms for hours of private play. You can check on them occasionally and still get lots of reading done.

Another option is to take your children to a public playground. While they swing, slide, and dig in the sand, you can dig into your textbooks. Lots of physical activity will tire out your children in constructive ways. If they go to bed a little early, that's extra time for you to read.

After you set up appropriate activities for your children, don't attend to them every second, even if you're nearby as they play. Obviously, you want to break up fights, stop unsafe activity, and handle emergencies. Short of such incidents, though, you're free to read.

Create a special space for your child. Set aside one room or area of your home as a play space. Childproof this space. The goal is to create a place where children can roam freely and play with minimal supervision. Consider allowing your child in this area *only* when you study. Your homework time then becomes your child's reward.

If you're cramped for space, just set aside some special toys for your child to play with during your study time. When you're sitting at your desk, your child might enjoy sitting at a small table and doing an "assignment." While she plays with stickers or flips through some children's books, you can review your notes.

Use television responsibly. Another option is to use television as a babysitter—when you can control the programming. Rent a DVD for your child to watch as you study. If you're concerned about the quality of programming your child is watching, select educational programs that keep his mind active and engaged.

See whether your child can use headphones while watching television. That way, the house stays quiet while you study.

Allow for interruptions. It's possible that you'll be interrupted even if you set up special activities for your child in advance. If so, schedule the kind of studying that can be interrupted. For instance, you could write out or review flash cards with key terms and definitions. Save the tasks that require sustained attention for other times.

Plan study breaks with children. Another option is to spend 10 minutes with your children for every 50 minutes that you study. View this time not as an interruption but as a study break.

Alternatively, you can schedule time to be with your children when you've finished studying. Let your children in on the plan: "I'll be finished reading at 7:30. That gives us a whole hour to play before you go to bed."

Many children like visible reminders that "their time" is approaching. An oven timer works well for this purpose. Set it for 15 minutes of quiet time. Follow that with 5 minutes of show-and-tell, storybooks, or another activity with your child. Then set the timer for another 15 minutes of studying, another break, and so on.

Develop a routine. Young children love routines. They often feel more comfortable and secure when they know what to expect. You can use this characteristic to your benefit. One option is to develop a regular time for studying and let your child know this schedule: "I have to do my homework between 4 p.m. and 5 p.m. every day." Then enforce it.

Bargain with children. Reward them for respecting your schedule. In return for quiet time, give your child an extra allowance or a special treat. Children might enjoy gaining "credits" for this purpose. Each time they give you an hour of quiet time for studying, make an entry on a chart, put a star on their bulletin board, or give them a coupon. After they've accumulated a certain number of entries, stars, or coupons, they can cash them in for a big reward—a movie or a trip to the zoo.

Ask other adults for help. This suggestion for studying with children relates to a message repeated throughout the book: Enlist other people to help support your success. Getting help can be as simple as asking your spouse, partner, neighbor, or fellow student to take care of the children while you study. Offer to trade child care with a neighbor: You will take his kids and yours for 2 hours on Thursday night if he'll take them for 2 hours on Saturday morning. Some parents start blockwide babysitting co-ops based on the same idea.

Find community activities and services. Ask whether your school provides a day care service. In some cases, these services are available to students at a reduced cost. Community agencies such as the YMCA might offer similar programs.

You can also find special events that appeal to children. Storytelling hour at the library is one example. While your child is being entertained and supervised, you can stay close by. Use the time in this quiet setting to read a chapter or review class notes.

Make it a game. Reading a chemistry textbook with a 3-year-old in the same room is not as preposterous as it sounds. The secret is to involve your child. For instance, use this time to recite. Make funny faces as you say the properties of the transition elements in the periodic table. Talk in a weird voice as you repeat Faraday's laws. Draw pictures and make up an exciting story about the process of titration.

Read out loud to your children, or use them as an audience for a speech. If you invent rhymes, poems, or songs to help you remember formulas or dates, teach them to your children. Be playful. Kids are attracted to energy and enthusiasm.

Whenever possible, involve family members in tasks related to reading. Older children can help you with research tasks—finding books at the library, looking up news articles, or even helping with typing.

When you can't read everything, just read something. Your objection to reading with children nearby may sound like this one: "I just can't concentrate. There's no way I can get it all done while children are around."

That's OK. Even if you can't absorb an entire chapter while the kids are running past your desk, you can skim the chapter. Or you can just read the introduction and summary. When you can't get it *all* done, just get *something* done.

Caution: If you always read this way, your education might be compromised. Supplement this strategy with others so that you can get all of your reading done. *

Discover more ways to study with children underfoot.

Muscle Reading in Brief

Here's a shorter version of Muscle Reading that you might want to use when you are short on time:

- **Preview and question.** Flip through the pages, looking at anything that catches your eye—headings, subheadings, illustrations, photographs. Turn the title of each article into a question. For example, "Muscle Reading" can become "What is Muscle Reading?" List your questions on a separate sheet of paper, or write each question on a 3x5 card.
- **Read to answer your questions.** Read each article. Then go back over the text and underline or highlight answers to your questions.
- **Recite and review.** When you're done with the chapter, close the book. Recite by reading each question—and answering it—out loud. Review the chapter by looking up the answers to your questions.

Power Process

Notice Your Pictures and Let Them Go

One of the brain's primary jobs is to manufacture images. We use mental pictures to make predictions about the world, and we base much of our behavior on those predictions.

Pictures can sometimes get in our way. Take the student who plans to attend a school he hasn't visited. He chose this school for its strong curriculum and good academic standing, but his brain didn't stop there. In his mind, the campus has historic buildings with ivy-covered walls and tree-lined avenues. The professors, he imagines, will be as articulate as Barack Obama and as entertaining as Conan O'Brien. The cafeteria will be a cozy nook serving everything from delicate quiche to strong coffee. He will gather there with fellow students for hours of stimulating, intellectual conversation. The library will have every book, while the computer lab will boast the newest technology.

The school turns out to be four gray buildings downtown, next to the bus station. The first class he attends is taught by an overweight, balding professor wearing a purple and orange bird-of-paradise tie. The cafeteria is a nondescript hall with machine-dispensed food, and the student's apartment is barely large enough to accommodate his roommate's tuba. This hypothetical student gets depressed. He begins to think about dropping out of school.

The problem with pictures is that they can prevent us from seeing what is really there. That is what happened to the student in this story. His pictures prevented him from noticing that his school is in the heart of a culturally vital city—close to theaters, museums, government offices, clubs, and all kinds of stores. The professor with the weird tie is not only an expert in his field but also a superior teacher. The school cafeteria is skimpy because it can't compete with the variety of inexpensive restaurants in the area.

Our pictures often lead to our being angry or disappointed. We set up expectations of events before they occur. Sometimes we don't even realize that we have these expectations. The next time you discover you are angry, disappointed, or frustrated, look to see which of your pictures aren't being fulfilled.

When you notice that pictures are getting in your way, in the gentlest manner possible, let your pictures go. Let them drift away like wisps of smoke picked up by a gentle wind.

Sometimes when we let go of old pictures, it's helpful to replace them with new, positive pictures. These new images can help you take a fresh perspective. The new pictures might not feel as comfortable and genuine as your old ones, but it's important to let those pictures go. No matter what picture is in your head, you can still be yourself.

Learn more about this Power Process online.

▸▸▸▸▸
- Quiz
- Skills Snapshot
- Master Student Profile

Put it to Work

You can use strategies you learn in *Becoming a Master Student* to succeed at work. For example, reflect on the following case study.

PhotosIndia.com/Getty

Sachin Aggarwal worked as a bank teller during the summers while he was in school. After he earned an associate of science degree in marketing, the bank promoted him and gave him a new job title: personal banker. When bank customers want to open a new account or take out a car loan, Sachin is the first person they see.

While working as a teller, Sachin gained a reputation as a quick study. When the bank installed a new computer system, he completed the online tutorials and stayed on top of the software updates. Within a few weeks, Sachin was training new tellers to use the system. In addition, he often fielded questions from some of the bank's older employees who described themselves as "computer challenged." Sachin's most recent performance review acknowledged his patience and ability to adapt his explanations to people with various levels of computer experience.

Right now, Sachin's biggest challenge is job-related reading. He never anticipated the number of documents—both in print and online—that would cross his desk after he got promoted. His supervisor has asked him to read technical manuals for each of the bank's services and account plans. He's also taking a customer service course with a 200-page textbook.

In addition, Sachin gets about sixty e-mail messages each day, some of them several screens long. He checks his in-box twice a day, scans each new message, and then files it in one of three folders:

- If a message requires some kind of response, Sachin sends it to a folder titled *action*. He checks this folder daily.
- If no response is required but Sachin might refer to the message again, he sends it to a folder named *archives*. He can search this folder any time he wants to retrieve a message.
- If the message requires no response and there's little chance that Sachin will refer to it again, he sends it straight to the trash folder.

Sachin applied several strategies from this chapter. For example, he previewed each message while keeping a couple questions in mind: *Does this call for a response from me? Will I ever refer to this message again?*

List more strategies that Sachin could use to stay on top of his reading load:

____

____

____

____

____

____

In addition to online documents, workplace reading often includes technical manuals, sales manuals, policies and procedures, memos, newsletters, invoices, application forms, meeting minutes, brochures, annual reports, and job descriptions. Consider the following strategies for managing those piles of paper and still getting the rest of your work done:

- Determine your purpose for reading each document, and extract only what you need to produce that outcome.
- Look for executive summaries at the front of long documents. Everything you want to know might be there, all in a few pages.
- Create "read anytime" files. Most of the papers and online documents that cross your desk will probably consist of basic background material—items that are important to read but not urgent. Place these documents in a folder, and save them for a quiet Friday afternoon or a plane trip.

Quiz

Name____ Date____/____/____

1. Name the acrostic that can help you remember the steps of Muscle Reading.
   Pry **O**ut **Q**uestions, **R**oot **U**p **A**nswers, **R**ecite, **R**eview, and **R**eview again. (*Three phases of Muscle Reading,* pp. 96–98)
2. Briefly describe two ways to infer the meaning of a word from its context.
   Briefly describe two of the following ways:
   - *Definitions*. A key word might be defined right in the text.
   - *Examples*. Authors often provide examples to clarify a word meaning.
   - *Lists*. When a word is listed in a series, the other items in the series might define the unfamiliar word through association.
   - *Comparisons*. You might find a new word surrounded by synonyms.
   - *Contrasts*. A writer might juxtapose a word with its *antonym.* (*Read with a dictionary in your lap*, p. 102)
3. Give three examples of what to look for when previewing a reading assignment.
   Describe at least three of the following:
   - Look over the table of contents.
   - Survey the entire assignment by looking at each page.
   - Look for summary statements.
   - Look for familiar concepts, facts, or ideas while previewing.
   - Read all chapter headings and subheadings.
   - Inspect drawings, diagrams, charts, tables, graphs, and photographs.
   - Look for ideas that spark your imagination or curiosity. (*Three phases of Muscle Reading,* pp. 96–98)
4. Choose three headings from this chapter and turn them into questions that can assist your reading.
   - Heading: *Muscle Reading*—Question: What is Muscle Reading?
   - Heading: *Three Phases of Muscle Reading*—Question: How does Muscle Reading work?
   - Heading: *Get to the bones of your book with concept maps*—What are concept maps? (*Three phases of Muscle Reading,* pp. 96–98)
5. In addition to underlining and highlighting, there are other ways to mark up a text. List three possibilities.
   List any three of the following ways:
   - Use asterisks or exclamation points near important sentences.
   - Circle key terms.
   - Write short definitions of key terms in the margin.
   - Mark possible test questions with a *Q* in the margin.
   - Write personal comments in the margin.
   - Write related page number references in the margin.
   - Number steps in a list or series of related points. (*Three phases of Muscle Reading,* pp. 96–98)
6. To get the most benefit from marking a book, underline at least 20 percent of the text. True or false? Explain your answer.
   False. Underlining is generally more effective when only the most important material is flagged. A small portion of underlined text, less than 10 percent, is usually sufficient for review. (*Three phases of Muscle Reading,* pp. 96–98)
7. Explain at least three techniques you can use when reading is tough.
   Explain at least three of the following techniques:
   - Read it again.
   - Look for essential words.
   - Hold a minireview.
   - Read it out loud.
   - Talk to your instructor.
   - Stand up.
   - Skip around.
   - Find a tutor.
   - Use another text.
   - Pretend you understand and then explain it.
   - Stop reading. (*When reading is tough,* p. 99)
8. According to the Power Process in this chapter, what is a potential problem with having mental pictures?
   The problem is that sometimes mental pictures can prevent us from seeing reality. We set up expectations of events before they occur. However, there is sometimes a disconnect between our expectations (pictures) and reality. This is when pictures get in our way. Many times, the disconnect makes us angry, disappointed, and frustrated. When you notice that pictures are getting in your way, in the most gentle manner possible, let your pictures go and replace them with new images that can help you take a fresh perspective on reality. (Answers will vary.)
   (*Power Process: Notice Your Pictures and Let Them Go*, p. 109)
9. Libraries of any size consist of just three basic elements. True or false? Explain your answer.
   True. Libraries of any size consist of just three basic elements:
   - *Catalogs*—databases that list all of the library's accessible materials.
   - *Collections*—periodicals, books, pamphlets, audiovisual materials, and materials available from other collections via inter-library loan.
   - *Computer resources*—Internet access; connections to campus-wide computer networks; and databases stored on CD-ROMs, CDs, DVDs, or online. (*The twenty-first-century researcher—using your library*, pp. 103–104)
10. List at least three techniques for increasing your reading speed.
    Discuss at least three of the following techniques:
    - Experiment with intentionally reading as fast as possible.
    - Move your eyes faster.
    - Notice and release ineffective habits.
    - Avoid vocalizing and subvocalizing.
    - If you're pressed for time, skim.
    - Stay flexible by varying your reading rate according to your purpose and the nature of the material.
    - Practice on easy material. (*Reading fast,* p. 101)

Skills Snapshot

Now that you've learned about Muscle Reading, review the *Reading* section of the Discovery Wheel on page 112. Think about whether that evaluation of your reading skills is still accurate. After studying this chapter, you might want to make some major changes in the way you read. Or perhaps you are a more effective reader than you thought you were.

In either case, take a snapshot of your current reading skills by completing the following sentences.

BEFORE YOU READ

If someone asked me how well I keep up with my assigned reading, I would say that . . .

To get the most out of a long reading assignment, I start by . . .

WHILE YOU READ

To focus my attention while I read, I . . .

When I take notes on my reading, my usual method is to . . .

AFTER YOU READ

When it's important for me to remember what I read, I . . .

When I don't understand something that I've read, I overcome confusion by . . .

NEXT ACTION

I'll know that I've reached a new level of mastery with reading when . . .

To reach that level of mastery, the most important thing I can do next is to . . .

Chief Wilma Mankiller . . . was a leader

Wilma Mankiller came from a large family that spent many years on the family farm in Oklahoma. They were, of course, poor, but not desperately so. "As far back as I can remember there were always books around our house," she recalls in her autobiography, *Mankiller: A Chief and Her People*. "This love of reading came from the traditional Cherokee passion for telling and listening to stories. But it also came from my parents, particularly my father. . . ."

Unfortunately, a poor local economy made the Mankiller family an easy target for the Bureau of Indian Affairs relocation program of the 1950s. . . . In 1959, the family moved to San Francisco, where Wilma's father could get a job and where Wilma began her junior high school years. This was not a happy time for her. She missed the farm and she hated the school where white kids teased her about being Native American and about her name.

Mankiller decided to leave her parents and go to live with her maternal grandmother, Pearl Sitton, on a family ranch inland from San Francisco. The year she spent there restored her confidence, and after returning to the Bay Area, she got increasingly involved with the world of the San Francisco Indian Center. . . .

When a group of Native Americans occupied Alcatraz Island in November 1969, in protest of U.S. Government policies, which had, for hundreds of years, deprived them of their lands, Mankiller participated in her first major political action.

"It changed me forever," she wrote. "It was on Alcatraz . . . where at long last some Native Americans, including me, truly began to regain our balance."

. . . She returned to Oklahoma in the 1970s, where she worked at the Urban Indian Resource Center and volunteered in the community. In 1981, she founded and then became director of the Cherokee Community Development Department, where she orchestrated a community-based renovation of the water system and was instrumental in lifting an entire town, Bell, Oklahoma, out of squalor and despair. In 1983, she ran for Deputy Chief of the Cherokee Nation.

The campaign was not an easy one. There had never been a woman leader of a Native American tribe. She had many ideas to present and debate, but encountered discouraging opposition from men who refused to talk about anything but the fact that she was a woman. Her campaign days were troubled by death threats, and her tires were slashed. She sought the advice of friends for ways to approach the constant insults, finally settling on a philosophy summed up by the epithet, "Don't ever argue with a fool, because someone walking by and observing you can't tell which one is the fool." In the end, Mankiller had her day: She was elected as first woman Deputy Chief, and over time her wise, strong leadership vindicated her supporters and proved her detractors wrong.

In 1985, when Chief Ross Swimmer left for Washington, D.C., Mankiller was obligated to step into his position, becoming the first woman to serve as Principal Chief of the Cherokee Nation.

Susannah Abbey, "Community Hero: Chief Wilma Mankiller," My Hero, November 17, 1006, www.myhero.com/myhero/hero.asp?hero=w_mankiller.

© Peter Turnley/CORBIS

(1945–2010) The first woman to become principal chief of the Cherokee Nation. Chief Wilma Mankiller also was awarded the Presidential Medal of Freedom, the nation's highest civilian honor

Find more biographical information on Wilma Mankiller at the Master Student Hall of Fame online.

5 Notes

Instructor Tools & Tips

> Rather than try to gauge your note-taking skill by quantity, think in this way: Am I simply doing clerk's work or am I assimilating new knowledge and putting down my own thoughts? To put down your own thoughts you must put down your own words. . . . If the note taken shows signs of having passed through a mind, it is a good test of its relevance and adequacy.
>
> **—Jacques Barzun and Henry Graff**

Preview

Linking Chapters 4, 5, and 6 together is very important because students sometimes tend to compartmentalize the skills presented in these chapters. Introducing note taking as a four-part process asks students to understand *Why* it is important to capture the context of *What* they are taking notes on. This chapter will help your students identify *What* note-taking strategies are effective: observing, recording, and reviewing. Each part of the process is essential and interdependent with the others. After your students learn new strategies for taking notes, ask them *How* they will apply these strategies to their other courses. Practice is an important element in adopting or adapting effective note-taking techniques. Encourage your students to test the new methods over time before they evaluate the effectiveness of a particular method. In class discussions, give students time to interpret the effectiveness of their note taking. Remember to suggest that learning styles have a significant impact on note-taking skill. Students can also apply *What if* by connecting Chapters 4, 5, and 6 together into a study-skills section for the course.

Guest Speaker

At this point in the term, students should be aware of how they are doing in their classes. It may be a good time to invite guest speakers from academic support services to talk to your students about how to get additional help they may need. Possibilities include the coordinators of the Writing Center, Tutoring Program, or Academic Success Center.

Here is a colleague from North Carolina discussing another note-taking tool:

> I share an additional tool for note taking with my students: **Use the power of doodling.** If you find that you often have drawn circles around every hole on the paper and have added doodles in every open space in your notes, perhaps you need to use your "doodle power" to your advantage. Doodlers often find that they put more vigor into their artistic efforts than they do into the content of their notes. Consider using this energy to create notes in the style of a comic strip with stick figures (for speed) and balloons for dialogue. As you invest your energy in depicting the information on paper, you will become more involved in the presentation instead of allowing the doodles to distract you.
>
> **—Sam Sink, Wilkes Community College, North Carolina**

Lecture

Eldon McMurray tells his students, "You are your own best instructor." As an in-class discussion, he asks students to tell him about their favorite recording artists or sports figures. He asks questions such as "Where does she live?" and "How old is he?" Then he switches over to asking students about their professors. He almost always gets a blank stare when he asks, "What do you know about your math instructor?" Then he reviews the article "Enroll your instructor in your education" (page 123), challenging his students to brainstorm ideas on how they can learn more about their instructors and how this connectedness will help them in class. Some shy students particularly like the idea of conducting Internet research and reading about their instructors online.

Many new college students have no idea what they should do when they miss a class. They fail to contact either their instructor or their classmates to find out what handouts, information, and assignments they missed. As a follow-up to the article "What to do when you miss a class" (page 117), consider providing a brief lecture on this topic. It's also a good time to review classroom and campus attendance policies with your students.

Consider using the PowerUp DVD segment "I Create It All" as a lecture review of this important Power Process about self-responsibility.

Exercises/Activities

1. Target class exercise. Ask your students to select three of their other courses in which they would like to put their advanced note-taking system into practice. By applying the note-taking concepts to their other courses, they start to realize the power of the ideas presented in *Becoming a Master Student.* To give them a head start and to help them understand how setting the stage can contribute to effective note taking, have them prepare for taking notes in class by outlining the textbook reading that the professor's lecture will cover that day.

2. Getting your money's worth, or "What am I paying for this ticket?" Set up this demonstration by having a student come up at the beginning of the class and pay you $20 for a front-row seat. If there is no front-row seat available, ask a student to move so that the paying student can sit there. Do this very seriously, and the irony of the object lesson will catch everyone's attention.

Ask students where they would expect to sit at a concert if they paid $40 or more to attend. Then ask why tickets are so much more expensive for front-row center seats at a concert, or at the center court of a professional basketball game, or on the 50-yard line of a football game. All they have to do to get the best seat in class is be on time or come a little early.

3. "Be here now" in class. Ask students to designate the upper right-hand corner of their class note page as their "Be here now" corner. When they catch their mind wandering, they can jot down a note and then bring their attention back to the speaker. Practicing this helps them stay focused.

4. Note-taking tools. After students have read about the various note-taking strategies, discuss them in class. Divide the class into groups of four, and assign each group one of the new techniques to practice while you give a short lecture. Provide a safety net for this exercise by telling students that you will give them a detailed handout of the lecture at the end of class. This way, they don't have to worry about missing important information while they are trying out a new note-taking tool. After the lecture, the students discuss—with their group and then as a class—what they discovered about using the new strategy, including their initial perceptions of its strengths and weaknesses. This in-class practice encourages students to try a new note-taking tool in their other courses.

5. Power Process: I Create It All (page 129). This in-class activity helps bring this process alive. After students have read this process and seen the "I Create It All" segment from the PowerUp DVD, ask them to recall a recent situation that went well for them at college, work, or home. Give them a few minutes to summarize the situation in their notes. Then ask them to list six ways that they created that successful situation. After they are done, ask for volunteers to share their success and how they created it. Then repeat the exercise, this time identifying a recent situation that did *not* work out well for them. For some students, this part may be much harder to do. Discuss this in class, with students volunteering to share their stories.

6. Master Student Profile: Harvey Milk (page 133). As a follow-up activity to this article, divide students into groups and ask them to think about challenges that they may face in college or in the workplace. Then brainstorm possible ways to overcome the problems. As a whole class, share ideas and discuss master student qualities that students can develop while attending college.

Conversation/Sharing

Ask students to discuss the characteristics that made Harvey Milk a master student, using the list of words and phrases provided in Chapter 1. Also ask them to identify *What* traits Milk had that they feel they do not personally possess. This can be followed by further sharing on *How* students can gain these qualities.

This chapter provides a good opportunity to facilitate a conversation and sharing about online courses. Some students love them; some hate them. Ask students to share what they have liked and/or disliked about online courses so that those who haven't tried these courses will have more information before it's time to register for the next term.

Homework

Master Student Map (page 114). Students can begin practicing new note-taking techniques immediately after reading this chapter. As your students begin to transfer and apply what they learn in this course to their other courses, more aha! moments will begin to occur.

Why? Why learn about new methods of note taking?

What? What is the Cornell format? What is mind mapping?

How? How can reviewing your notes help you be more successful in school?

What if? What if you observe, record, and review your notes in a new way in all of your classes?

Review: The note-taking process flows (page 122). For many students, 24 hours is too long to wait before reviewing and processing their notes into long-term memory. For difficult classes or upper-division theory-based courses, ask your students to answer the questions using the strengths of each mode in the Master Student Map exercises. Students can summarize their notes during their review by answering these key questions: *Why* is this idea important? *What* are the details I need to know? *How* will I remember and prepare to be tested on this material? *What if* the test is multiple choice? *What if* the test is an essay format?

Critical Thinking Exercise 16: Revisit your goals (page 126). One powerful way to achieve any goal is to periodically assess your progress in meeting it. Critical Thinking Exercise 16 provides your students with an opportunity to reflect on the materials that have been covered to date. Students are asked to reflect on their goals set in Critical Thinking Exercise 8 (page 56) and make adjustments to their plan. While discussing this exercise, suggest that your students look back at their Discovery Wheel and review their progress to date. Students will be given a formal post-course Discovery Wheel in Chapter 10.

Evaluation

Ask students to describe the Cornell note-taking system. Ask students to describe strategies for taking notes when instructors talk fast. Ask students what it takes to become an online learner. Ask students to explain how the Power Process: "I Create It All" can help them be more successful in college.

Additional Digital Resources

Course Manual

The online *Course Manual* serves as an invaluable reference for those developing and teaching a College Success course with *Becoming a Master Student Concise*. The *Course Manual* provides advice on general teaching issues such as preparing for classes, classroom management, grading, and communicating with students of various backgrounds, as well as specific strategies on getting the most out of various features in *Becoming a Master Student Concise* and book-specific Web sites. Do a *Course Manual* reconnaissance to find ideas that you can use in your course right now.

Instructor Companion Site

The updated Instructor Companion Site provides resources to help you plan and customize your course. Content specific to Chapter 5 includes:

- Lecture Ideas
  - Exploring Note-Taking Methods
- In-Class Exercises
  - Adapt Your Note-Taking Style
  - Mind Map Review
  - Recording Your Notes
  - Now, This is Studying
  - What Level Are You on?
- In-Text Quiz Answers
- PowerPoint Slides

The Instructor Companion Site also contains the following book-specific content:

- ExamView Test Bank
- Online Course Manual
- Sample Syllabi
- Detailed Transition Guide

College Success CourseMate

To help your students gain a better understanding of the topics discussed in *Becoming a Master Student Concise*, encourage them to visit College Success CourseMate at CengageBrain.com that provides the following resources specific to Chapter 5:

- Connect to Text content expands on specific topics marked with an icon within the Introduction.
- Practice Tests allow students to see how well they understand the themes of *Becoming a Master Student Concise.*
- Interactive Concept Maps promote critical thinking by highlighting related ideas to show relationships among concepts.
- Learning Styles Application
- Discussion Topics
- Reflection Questions
- Assessment Questions
- Experiment with chapter strategies
- Video Skillbuilders bring to life techniques that will help students to excel in college and beyond. The following videos should give your students more information regarding topics covered in Chapter 5:
  - Taking Notes to Improve Your Grade
  - Textbook Note Taking: Student Methods
- Remembering Cultural Differences presents readers with brief articles that touch on aspects of diversity in our rapidly changing world. For Chapter 5, the following article will prompt your students to look at contemporary issues in a new way:
  - From Hieroglyphics to Handwriting in the Computer Age
- Master Student Profiles provide additional information on the people covered in this book feature. For Chapter 5, students will find expanded coverage and links about:
  - Harvey Milk
- Power Process Media contains video, PowerPoints, and audio files to take what your students have learned from the Power Processes in their book to the next level. For Chapter 5, students will find additional media on:
  - I Create It All

Along with the chapter-specific content, a General Resources folder is available that contains Toolboxes geared toward specific student types (Community College, Adult Learner, Student Athlete), the Plagiarism Prevention Zone, and the Career Resource Center.

5 Notes

Master Student Map

as you read, ask yourself

what if . . .?

I could take notes that remain informative and useful for weeks, months, or even years to come?

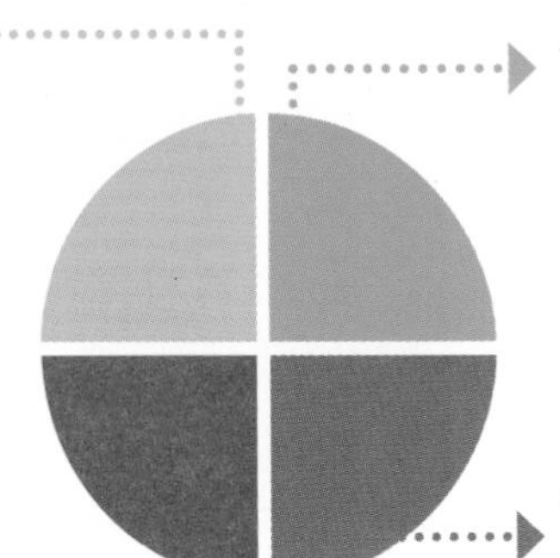

why this chapter matters . . .

Note taking helps you remember information and influences how well you do on tests.

what is included . . .

how you can use this chapter . . .

- Experiment with several formats for note taking.
- Create a note-taking format that works especially well for you.
- Take effective notes in special situations—such as while reading and when instructors talk fast.

MASTER STUDENTS in *action*

Being responsible is what your career depends on: going to class, turning in assignments on time, studying for exams in advance, and, most importantly, knowing when to go out and when to stay home. Becoming a master student means setting and accomplishing goals—not to prove anything to anyone but to yourself.

—MAURICIO RUEDA

Photo courtesy of Mauricio Rueda

The note-taking process flows

ONE WAY TO understand note taking is to realize that taking notes is just one part of the process. Effective note taking consists of three parts: observing, recording, and reviewing. First, you observe an "event"—a statement by an instructor, a lab experiment, a slide show of an artist's works, or a chapter of required reading. Then you record your observations of that event; that is, you "take notes." Finally, you review what you have recorded.

Each part of the note-taking process is essential, and each depends on the others. Your observations determine what you record. What you record determines what you review. And the quality of your review can determine how effective your next observations will be. For example, if you review your notes on the Sino-Japanese War of 1894, the next day's lecture on the Boxer Rebellion of 1900 will make more sense.

Legible and speedy handwriting is also useful in taking notes. Knowledge about outlining is handy too. A nifty pen, a new notebook, and a laptop computer are all great note-taking devices. However, they're all worthless—unless you participate as an energetic observer *in* class and regularly review your notes *after* class. If you take those two steps, you can turn even the most disorganized chicken scratches into a powerful tool.

Sometimes note taking looks like a passive affair, especially in large lecture classes. One person at the front of the room does most of the talking. Everyone else is seated and silent, taking notes. The lecturer seems to be doing all of the work.

Don't be deceived. Observe more closely, and you'll see some students taking notes in a way that radiates energy. They're awake and alert, poised on the edge of their seats. They're writing—a physical activity that expresses mental engagement. These students listen for levels of ideas and information, make choices about what to record, and compile materials to review.

In higher education, you might spend hundreds of hours taking notes. Making them more effective is a direct investment in your success. Think of your notes as a textbook that *you* create—one that's more current and more in tune with your learning preferences than any textbook you could buy. *

journal entry 12

Discovery/Intention Statement

Get what you want from this chapter

Think about the possible benefits of improving your skills at note taking. Recall a recent incident in which you had difficulty taking notes. Perhaps you were listening to an instructor who talked fast, or you got confused and stopped taking notes altogether. Describe the incident in the space below.

Now preview this chapter to find at least three strategies that you can use right away to help you take better notes. Sum up each of those strategies in a few words, and note the page numbers where you can find out more about each suggestion.

Strategy	Page number

Describe a specific situation in which you promise to apply one of the strategies you listed above.

I intend to . . .

OBSERVE
The note-taking process flows

Woman: Getty; *frames:* Shutterstock, collage by Walter Kopec

SHERLOCK HOLMES, a fictional master detective and student of the obvious, could track down a villain by observing the fold of his scarf and the mud on his shoes. In real life, a doctor can save a life by observing a mole—one a patient has always had—that undergoes a rapid change. A student can save hours of study time by observing that she gets twice as much done at a particular time of day. Keen observers see facts and relationships. To sharpen your classroom observation skills, experiment with the following techniques.

Complete outside assignments. Nothing is more discouraging (or boring) than sitting through a lecture about the relationship of Le Chatelier's principle to the study of kinetics if you've never heard of Henri Louis Le Chatelier or kinetics. The more familiar you are with a subject, the more easily you can understand lectures. Instructors usually assume that students complete assignments, and they construct their lectures accordingly.

Bring materials. Make sure you have a pen, pencil, notebook, and any other materials you need. Bring your textbook to class, especially if the lectures relate closely to the text.

Sit front and center. The closer you sit to the lecturer, the harder it is to fall asleep. The closer you sit to the front, the fewer interesting or distracting classmates are situated between you and the instructor. Material on the board is easier to read from up front. Also, you can hear the instructor better, and she can see you when you have a question.

Sitting up front enables you to become a constructive force in the classroom. By returning the positive energy that an engaged teacher gives out, you can reinforce the teacher's enthusiasm and enhance your experience of the class. Sitting close to the front is a way to commit yourself to getting what you want out of school.

Conduct a short preclass review. Arrive early and then put your brain in gear by reviewing your notes from the previous class. Scan your reading assignment. Look at the sections you have underlined or highlighted. Review assigned problems and exercises. Note questions you intend to ask.

Release distractions. You can use writing in a more direct way to clear your mind of distracting thoughts. Pause for a few seconds and write those thoughts down. If you're distracted by thoughts of errands you need to run after class, list them on a 3x5 card that you will stick in your pocket. Once your distractions are out of your mind and safely stored on paper, you can gently return your attention to taking notes.

Be with the instructor. Imagine that you and the instructor are the only ones in the room and that the lecture is a personal conversation between the two of you. Pay attention to the instructor's body language and facial expressions. Look the instructor in the eye. Remember that the power of this suggestion is immediately reduced by digital distractions—Web surfing, e-mail checking, or text messaging.

Postpone debate. When you hear something you disagree with, note your disagreement and let it go for the moment. It is OK to absorb information you don't agree with. Just absorb it with the mental tag "My instructor says . . . , and I don't agree with it."

Let go of judgments about lecture styles. Don't let your attitude about an instructor's lecture style, habits, or appearance get in the way of your education. To decrease the power of your judgments, notice them and let them go. You can even let go of judgments about rambling, unorganized lectures and organize the

What to do when you miss a class

For most courses, you'll benefit by attending every class session. If you miss a class, catch up as quickly as possible. Here are some ways to do that:

Clarify policies on missed classes. On the first day of classes, find out about your instructors' policies on absences. See whether you will be allowed to make up assignments, quizzes, and tests. Also ask about doing extra-credit assignments.

Contact a classmate. Early in the semester, identify a student in each class who seems responsible and dependable. Exchange e-mail addresses and phone numbers. If you know you won't be in class, contact this student ahead of time. When you notice that your classmate is absent, pick up extra copies of handouts, make assignment lists, and offer copies of your notes.

Contact your instructor. If you miss a class, e-mail, phone, or fax your instructor, or put a note in his mailbox. Ask whether he has another section of the same course that you can attend so you won't miss the lecture information. Also ask about getting handouts you might need before the next class meeting.

Consider technology. If there is a Web site for your class, check it for assignments and the availability of handouts you missed. Free online services such as NoteMesh allow students to share notes with one another. These services use wiki software, which allows you to create and edit Web pages using any browser. Before using such tools, however, check with your instructors for their policies on note sharing.

material yourself. While taking notes, separate the key points from the examples and supporting evidence. Note the places where you got confused, and make a list of questions to ask.

Participate in class activities. Ask questions. Volunteer for demonstrations. Join in class discussions.

Relate the class to your goals. If you have trouble staying awake in a particular class, write at the top of your notes how that class relates to a specific goal. Identify the reward or payoff for reaching that goal.

Think critically about what you hear. This suggestion might seem contrary to "postpone debate." It's not. Think critically *after* class, as you review and edit your notes. List questions and write down your agreements and disagreements.

Watch for clues in repetition. When an instructor repeats a phrase or an idea, make a note of it. Repetition is a signal that the instructor thinks the information is important.

Listen for clues in key phrases. Introductory, concluding, and transition remarks include phrases such as *the following three factors, in conclusion, the most important consideration, in addition to*, and *on the other hand*. Phrases like these signal relationships, definitions, new subjects, conclusions, cause and effect, and examples. They reveal the structure of a lecture. You can use these phrases to organize your notes.

Watch the board or PowerPoint presentation for clues. If an instructor takes the time to write something down on the board or show a PowerPoint presentation, consider the material to be important. Copy all diagrams and drawings, equations, names, places, dates, statistics, and definitions.

Watch the instructor's eyes for clues. If an instructor glances at her notes and then makes a point, it is probably a signal that the information is especially important. Anything she reads from her notes is a potential test question.

Highlight the obvious clues. Instructors often hint strongly or tell students point-blank that certain information is likely to appear on an exam. Make stars or other special marks in your notes next to this information. Instructors are not trying to hide what's important.

Notice the instructor's interest level. If the instructor is excited about a topic, it is more likely to appear on an exam. Pay extra attention when she seems more animated than usual. *

Find more strategies for observing online.

RECORD
The note-taking process flows

THE FORMAT AND STRUCTURE of your notes are more important than the speed or elegance of your handwriting. Discover this for yourself with the following techniques.

General techniques for note taking

Use key words. An easy way to sort the extraneous material from the important points is to take notes using key words. Key words or phrases contain the essence of communication. They include

- Concepts, technical terms, names, and numbers.
- Linking words, including words that describe action, relationship, and degree (for example, *most*, *least*, and *faster*).

Key words evoke images and associations with other words and ideas. They trigger your memory. That characteristic makes them powerful review tools. One key word can initiate the recall of a whole cluster of ideas. A few key words can form a chain from which you can reconstruct an entire lecture.

To see how key words work, take yourself to an imaginary classroom. You are now in the middle of an anatomy lecture. Picture what the room looks like, what it feels like, how it smells. You hear the instructor say:

> OK, what happens when we look directly over our heads and see a piano falling out of the sky? How do we take that signal and translate it into the action of getting out of the way? The first thing that happens is that a stimulus is generated in the neurons—receptor neurons—of the eye. Light reflected from the piano reaches our eyes. In other words, we see the piano.
>
> The receptor neurons in the eye transmit that sensory signal—the sight of the piano—to the body's nervous system. That's all they can do—pass on information. So we've got a sensory signal coming into the nervous system. But the neurons that initiate movement in our legs are effector neurons. The information from the sensory neurons must be transmitted to effector neurons or we will get squashed by the piano. There must be some kind of interconnection between receptor and effector neurons. What happens between the two? What is the connection?

Key words you might note in this example include *stimulus, generated, receptor neurons, transmit, sensory signals, nervous system, effector neurons*, and *connection*. You can reduce the instructor's 163 words to these 12 key words. With a few transitional words, your notes might look like this:

Stimulus (piano) generated
in receptor neurons (eye)

Sensory signals transmitted
by nervous system to
effector neurons (legs)

What connects receptor to
effector?

Note the last key word of the lecture above: *connection*. This word is part of the instructor's question and leads to the next point in the lecture. Be on the lookout for questions like this. They can help you organize your notes and are often clues for test questions.

Use pictures and diagrams. Make relationships visual. Copy all diagrams from the board, and invent your own.

Copy material from the board and PowerPoint presentations. Record all formulas, diagrams, and problems that the teacher presents on the board or in a PowerPoint presentation. Copy dates, numbers, names, places, and other facts. If it's presented visually in class, put it in your notes. You can even use your own signal or code to flag that material.

Use a three-ring binder. Three-ring binders have several advantages over other kinds of notebooks. First, pages can be removed and spread out when you review. This way, you can get a complete picture of a lecture. Second, the three-ring-binder format allows you to insert handouts right into your notes. Third, you can insert your own out-of-class notes in the correct order.

Use only one side of a piece of paper. When you use one side of a page, you can review and organize all your notes by spreading them out side by side. Most students find the benefit well worth the cost of the paper. Perhaps you're concerned about the environmental impact of consuming more paper. If so, you can use the blank side of old notes and use recycled paper.

Keep your own thoughts separate. For the most part, avoid making editorial comments in your lecture notes. The danger is that when you return to your notes, you might mistake your own ideas for those of the instructor. If you want to make a comment, clearly label it as your own.

Label, number, and date all notes. Develop the habit of labeling and dating your notes at the beginning of each class. Number the page, too. Sometimes the sequence of material in a lecture is important. Write your name and phone number in each notebook in case you lose it.

Use standard abbreviations. Be consistent with your abbreviations. If you make up your own abbreviations or symbols, write a key explaining them in your notes. The goal is to avoid vague abbreviations. When you use an abbreviation such as *comm.* for *committee*, you run the risk of not being able to remember whether you meant *committee*, *commission*, *common*, or *commit*. One way to abbreviate clearly is to leave out vowels. For example, *talk* becomes *tlk*, *said* becomes *sd*, *American* becomes *Amrcn*.

Leave blank space. Notes tightly crammed into every corner of the page are hard to read and difficult to use for review. Give your eyes a break by leaving plenty of space. Later, when you review, you can use the blank spaces in your notes to clarify points, write questions, and add other material.

Take notes in different colors. You can use colors as highly visible organizers. For example, signal important points with red or use one color of ink for notes about the text and another color for lecture notes.

The Cornell method

A note-taking system that has worked for students around the world is the *Cornell method*, originally developed by Walter Pauk at Cornell University.[1] The cornerstone of this method is what Pauk calls the *cue column*—a wide margin on the left-hand side of the paper. The cue column is the key to the Cornell method's many benefits. Here's how to use it.

Format your paper. On each sheet of your notepaper, draw a vertical line, top to bottom, about 2 inches from the left edge of the paper. This line creates the cue column—the space to the left of the line. You can also find Web sites that allow you to print out pages in this format. Just do an Internet search using the key words *cornell method pdf*.

Take notes, leaving the cue column blank. As you read an assignment or listen to a lecture, take notes on the right-hand side of the paper. Fill up this column with sentences, paragraphs, outlines, charts, or drawings. Do not write in the cue column. You'll use this space later, as you do the next steps.

Condense your notes in the cue column. Think of the notes you took on the right-hand side of the paper as a set of answers. In the cue column, list potential test questions that correspond to your notes. Write one question for each major term or point.

As an alternative to questions, you can list key words from your notes. Yet another option is to pretend that your notes are a series of articles on different topics. In the cue column, write a newspaper-style headline for each "article."

In any case, be brief. If you cram the cue column full of words, you defeat its purpose—to reduce the number of words and length of your notes.

Write a summary. Pauk recommends that you reduce your notes even more by writing a brief summary at the bottom of each page. This step offers you another way to engage actively with the material.

Cue column	Notes
What are the 3 phases of Muscle Reading?	Phase 1: Before you read Phase 2: While you read Phase 3: After you read
What are the steps in phase 1?	1. Preview 2. Outline 3. Question
What are the steps in phase 2?	4. Read 5. Underline 6. Answer
What are the steps in phase 3?	7. Recite 8. Review 9. Review again
What is an acronym for Muscle Reading?	Pry = preview Out = outline Questions = question Root = read Up = underline Answers = answer Recite Review Review again

Summary
Muscle Reading includes 3 phases: before, during, and after reading. Each phase includes 3 steps. Use the acronym to recall all the steps.

5 NOTES

Use the cue column to recite. Cover the right-hand side of your notes with a blank sheet of paper. Leave only the cue column showing. Then look at each item you wrote in the cue column and talk about it. If you wrote questions, answer each question. If you wrote key words, define each word and talk about why it's important. If you wrote headlines in the cue column, explain what each one means and offer supporting details. After reciting, uncover your notes and look for any important points you missed.

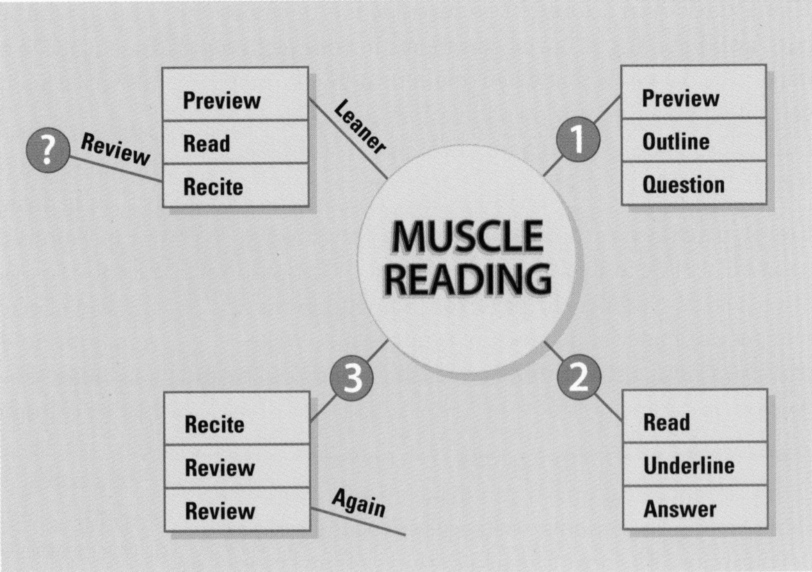

Mind mapping

Mind mapping, a system developed by Tony Buzan,[2] can be used in conjunction with the Cornell method to take notes. In some circumstances, you might want to use mind maps exclusively.

Mind maps quickly, vividly, and accurately show the relationships between ideas. Also, mind mapping helps you think from general to specific. By choosing a main topic, you focus first on the big picture, then zero in on subordinate details. By using only key words, you can condense a large subject into a small area on a mind map. You can review more quickly by looking at the key words on a mind map than by reading notes word for word.

Give yourself plenty of room. To create a mind map, use blank paper that measures at least 11 by 17 inches. If that's not available, turn regular notebook paper on its side so that you can take notes in a horizontal (instead of vertical) format. If you use a computer to take notes in class, consider investing in software that allows you to create digital mind maps that can include graphics, photos, and URL links.

Determine the main concept of the lecture, article, or chapter. As you listen to a lecture or read from your text, figure out the main concept. Write it in the center of the paper and circle it, underline it, or highlight it with color. You can also write the concept in large letters. Record concepts related to the main concept on lines that radiate outward from the center. An alternative is to circle or box in these concepts.

Use key words only. Whenever possible, reduce each concept to a single word per line, circle, or box in your mind map. Although this reduction might seem awkward at first, it prompts you to summarize and to condense ideas to their essence. That results in fewer words for you to write now and fewer to review when it's time to prepare for tests. (Using shorthand symbols and abbreviations can help.) Key words are usually nouns and verbs that communicate the bulk of the speaker's ideas. Choose words that are rich in associations and that can help you recreate the lecture.

Discovery/Intention Statement

Create more value from lectures

Think back on the last few lectures you have attended. How do you currently observe (listen to) lectures? What specific behaviors do you have as you sit and listen? Briefly describe your responses in the space below.

I discovered that I . . .

____

____

____

____

Now write an Intention Statement about any changes you want to make in the way you respond to lectures.

I intend to . . .

____

____

____

____

First-level heading

I. Muscle Reading includes 3 phases.

Second-level heading

A. Phase 1: Before you read

1. Preview

Third-level heading

2. Outline
3. Question

B. Phase 2: While you read

4. Read
5. Underline
6. Answer

C. Phase 3: After you read

7. Recite
8. Review
9. Review again

Distinguish levels with indentations only:

Muscle Reading includes 3 phases

Phase 1: Before you read

Preview

Distinguish levels with bullets and dashes:

MUSCLE READING INCLUDES 3 PHASES

• Phase 1: Before you read

– Preview

Distinguish headings by size:

MUSCLE READING INCLUDES 3 PHASES

Phase 1: Before you read

Preview

Create links. A single mind map doesn't have to include all of the ideas contained in a lecture, book, or article. Instead, you can link mind maps. For example, draw a mind map that sums up the five key points in a chapter. Then make a separate, more detailed mind map for each of those key points. Within each mind map, include references to the other mind maps. This technique helps explain and reinforce the relationships among many ideas. Some students pin several mind maps next to one another on a bulletin board or tape them to a wall. This allows for a dramatic—and effective—look at the big picture.

Outlining

A traditional outline shows the relationships among major points and supporting ideas. Technically, each word, phrase, or sentence that appears in an outline is called a *heading*. Headings are arranged in different levels:

- In the first, or top, level of headings, note the major topics presented in a lecture or reading assignment.
- In the second level of headings, record the key points that relate to each topic in the first-level headings.
- In the third level of headings, record specific facts and details that support or explain each of your second-level headings. Each additional level of subordinate heading supports the ideas in the previous level of heading.

Roman numerals offer just one way to illustrate the difference between levels of headings. See the following examples. *

See more examples of notes in various formats online.

REVIEW
The note-taking process flows

Review within 24 hours. This note-taking technique might save you hours of review time later in the term. If you review your notes soon enough after class, you can move that information from short-term to long-term memory. And you can do it in just a few minutes—often 10 minutes or less.

The sooner you review your notes, the better, especially if the content is difficult. In fact, you can start reviewing *during* class. When your instructor pauses to set up the overhead display or erase the board, scan your notes. Dot the *i*'s, cross the *t*'s, and write out unclear abbreviations.

Another option is to get to your next class as quickly as you can. Then use the 4 or 5 minutes before the lecture begins to review the notes you just took in the previous class. If you do not get to your notes immediately after class, you can still benefit by reviewing them later in the day. A review right before you go to sleep can also be valuable.

Think of the day's unreviewed notes as leaky faucets, constantly dripping and losing precious information until you shut them off with a quick review. Remember, it's possible to forget most of the material within 24 hours—unless you review.

Edit your notes. During your first review, fix words that are illegible. Check to see that your notes are labeled with the date and class and that the pages are numbered. Write out abbreviated words that might be unclear to you later. Make sure you can read everything. If you can't read something or don't understand something you *can* read, mark it. Make a note to ask your instructor or another student about it.

Some students open up a computer file and key in their handwritten notes. Typed notes are easier to read and take up less space. The process of typing them also forces you to organize and review the material.

Fill in key words in the left-hand column. This task is important if you are to get the full benefit of using the Cornell method. Using the key word principles described earlier in this chapter, go through your notes and write key words or phrases in the left-hand column. These key words will speed up the review process later. Then, as you review your notes, cover the right column with a sheet of paper so that you can see only the key words in the left-hand margin. Take each key word in order and recite as much as you can about it. Then uncover your notes and look for any important points you missed.

Conduct short weekly review periods. Once a week, review all of your notes again. These review sessions don't need to take a lot of time. Even a 20-minute weekly review period is valuable. Some students find that a weekend review—say, on Sunday afternoon—helps them stay in continuous touch with the material. Scheduling regular review sessions on your calendar helps develop the habit.

Create summaries. Mind mapping is an excellent way to summarize large sections of your course notes or reading assignments. Create one map that shows all the main topics you want to remember. Then create another map about each main topic. After drawing your maps, look at your original notes, and fill in anything you missed. This system is fun and quick.

Another option is to fit all your review notes on a single sheet of paper. Use any note-taking format that you want—mind map, outline, Cornell method, or a combination of all of them. The beauty of this technique is that it forces you to pick out main ideas and key details. There's not enough room for anything else!

Some instructors might let you use a summary sheet during an exam. But even if you can't use it, you'll benefit from creating one while you study for the test. Summarizing is a powerful way to review. *

Enroll your instructor in your education

FACED WITH AN instructor you don't like, you have two basic choices. One is to label the instructor a "dud" and let it go at that. This choice puts you at the mercy of circumstance. It gives your instructor sole responsibility for the quality of your education and the value of your tuition payments.

There is another option. Don't give away your power. Instead, take responsibility for your education. See whether you can enlist instructors as partners in getting what you want from higher education.

Research the instructor. When deciding what classes to take, look for formal and informal sources of information about instructors. One source is the school catalog. Alumni magazines or newsletters or the school newspaper might run articles on teachers. At some schools, students post informal evaluations of instructors on Web sites. Also talk to students who have taken courses from the instructor you're researching.

Show interest in class. Students give teachers moment-by-moment feedback in class. That feedback comes through posture, eye contact, responses to questions, and participation in class discussions. If you find a class boring, recreate the instructor through a massive display of interest. Ask lots of questions. Sit up straight, make eye contact, and take detailed notes. Your enthusiasm might enliven your instructor. If not, you are still creating a more enjoyable class for yourself.

Release judgments. Separate liking from learning. You can still learn from instructors, even if you don't like them personally. Maybe your instructor reminds you of someone you don't like—your annoying Aunt Edna, a rude store clerk, or the fifth-grade teacher who kept you after school. Your attitudes are in your own head and beyond the instructor's control. Likewise, an instructor's beliefs about politics, religion, or feminism are not related to teaching ability. Being aware of such things can help you let go of negative judgments.

Get to know the instructor. Meet with your instructor during office hours. Teachers who seem boring in class can be fascinating in person. Prepare to notice your pictures and let them go. Students who do well in higher education often get to know at least one instructor outside of class.

Submit professional work. Prepare papers and projects as if you were submitting them to an employer. Imagine that your work will determine whether you get a promotion and pay raise. Instructors often grade hundreds of papers during a term. Your neat, orderly, well-organized paper can stand out and lift a teacher's spirits.

Seek alternatives. You might feel more comfortable with another teacher's style or method of organizing course materials. Consider changing teachers, asking another teacher for help outside class, or attending an additional section taught by a different instructor. You can also learn from other students, courses, tutors, study groups, books, and DVDs. Be a master student, even when you have teachers you don't like. Your education is your own creation. *

Discover more ways to create positive relationships with instructors.

5

NOTES

Meeting with your instructor

Meeting with an instructor outside class can save hours of study time and help your grade. To get the most from these meetings, consider doing the following:

- Come prepared with a list of questions and any materials you'll need. During the meeting, take notes on the instructor's suggestions.
- Show the instructor your class notes to see whether you're capturing essential material.
- Get feedback on outlines that you've created for papers.
- Ask about ways to prepare for upcoming exams.
- Avoid questions that might offend your instructor—for example, "I missed class on Monday. Did we do anything important?"
- When the meeting is over, thank your instructor for making time for you.

Instead of trying to resolve a conflict with an instructor in the few minutes before or after class, schedule a time during office hours. During this meeting, state your concerns in a respectful way. Then focus on finding solutions.

When your instructor talks *fast*

Ask the instructor to slow down. This solution is the most obvious. If asking the instructor to slow down doesn't work, ask her to repeat what you missed.

Take more time to prepare for class. Familiarity with a subject increases your ability to pick up on key points. If an instructor lectures quickly or is difficult to understand, conduct a thorough preview of the material to be covered.

Be willing to make choices. When an instructor talks fast, focus your attention on key points. Instead of trying to write everything down, choose what you think is important. Occasionally, you will make a wrong choice and neglect an important point. Worse things could happen. Stay with the lecture, write down key words, and revise your notes immediately after class.

Exchange photocopies of notes with classmates. Your fellow students might write down something you missed. At the same time, your notes might help them. Exchanging photocopies can fill in the gaps.

Leave large empty spaces in your notes. Leave plenty of room for filling in information you missed. Use a symbol that signals you've missed something, so you can remember to come back to it.

See the instructor after class. Take your class notes with you, and show the instructor what you missed.

Use an audio recorder. Recording a lecture gives you a chance to hear it again whenever you choose. Some audio recording software allows you to vary the speed of the recording. With this feature, you can actually slow down the instructor's speech.

Before class, take notes on your reading assignment. You can take detailed notes on the text before class. Leave plenty of blank space. Take these notes with you to class, and simply add your lecture notes to them.

Go to the lecture again. Many classes are taught in multiple sections. That gives you the chance to hear a lecture at least twice—once in your regular class and again in another section of the class.

Learn shorthand. Some note-taking systems, known as shorthand, are specifically designed for getting ideas down fast. Books and courses are available to help you learn these systems. You can also devise your own shorthand method by inventing one- or two-letter symbols for common words and phrases.

Ask questions—even if you're totally lost. Many instructors allow a question session. This is the time to ask about the points you missed. At times you might feel so lost that you can't even formulate a question. That's OK. One option is to report this fact to the instructor. He can often guide you to a clear question. Another option is to ask a *related* question. Doing this might lead you to the question you really wanted to ask. *

Television note taking

You can use evening news broadcasts to practice listening for key words, writing quickly, focusing your attention, and reviewing. With note taking, as with other skills, the more you practice, the better you become.

The next time you watch the news, use pen and paper to jot down key words and information. If you get behind, relax, leave a space, and return your attention to the broadcast.

During the commercials, review and revise your notes. At the end of the broadcast, spend 5 minutes reviewing all of your notes. Create a mind map of a few news stories; then sum up the news of the day for a friend.

This exercise will help you develop an ear for key words. Because you can't ask questions or request that the speaker slow down, you train yourself to stay totally in the moment.

Don't be discouraged if you miss a lot the first time around. Do this exercise several times, and observe how your mind works.

If you find it too difficult to take notes during a fast-paced television news show, check your local broadcast schedule for a news documentary. Documentaries are often slower paced. Another option is to record a program and then take notes. You can stop the recording at any point to review your notes.

You can also ask a classmate to do this exercise, and then compare notes the next day.

Taking notes while reading

Review notes

Take review notes when you want more detailed notes than writing in the margin of your text allows. You might want to single out a particularly difficult section of a text and make separate notes—or make summaries of overlapping lecture and text material. Because you can't underline or make notes in library books, these sources will require separate notes too.

To take more effective review notes, follow these suggestions: Use a variety of formats. Translate text into Cornell notes, mind maps, or outlines. Combine these formats to create your own. Translate diagrams, charts, and other visual elements into words. Then reverse the process by translating straight text into visual elements.

However, don't let the creation of formats get in your way. Even a simple list of key points and examples can become a powerful review tool.

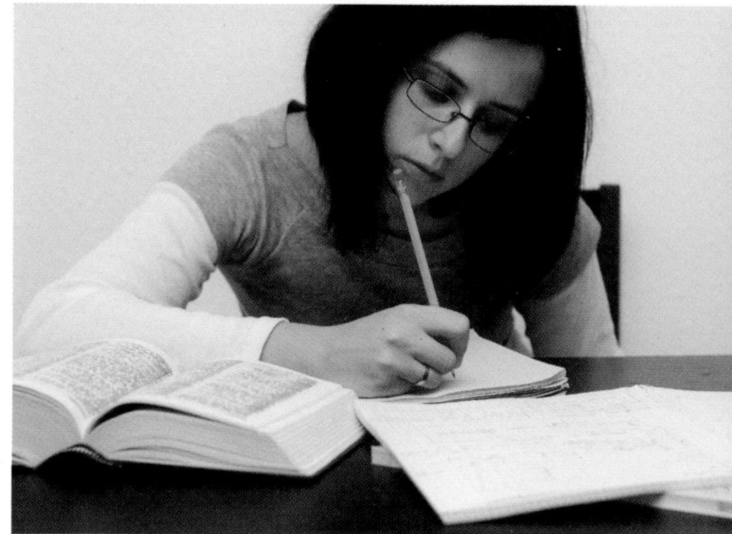

© iStockphoto.com/anna karwowska

Research notes

Take research notes when preparing to write a paper or deliver a speech. One traditional method of research is to take notes on index cards. You write one idea, fact, or quotation per card. The advantage of limiting each card to one item of information is that you can easily arrange cards according to the sequence of your outline—and ongoing changes in your outline.

Taking notes on a computer offers the same flexibility as index cards. In addition, you can take advantage of software features that help you create tables of contents, indexes, graphics, and other elements you might want to use in your project later on.

No matter which method you use, your research notes will fall into two main categories.

The first category includes the actual ideas and facts that you will use to create the content of your paper or presentation. The second category is information about your sources. For example, a source card for a book will show the author, title, date and place of publication, and publisher. You'll need such information later in the writing process as you create a complete list of your sources (bibliography) and a list of sources for specific quotes or paraphrased material (footnotes or endnotes). Keep track of this information as you conduct research.

Ask your instructor about what source information to record. When recording your own ideas, simply note the source as "me."

Be sure to avoid plagiarism. When people take words or images from a source and present them as their own, they are committing plagiarism. Even when plagiarism is accidental, the consequences can be harsh. For essential information on this topic, see "Academic integrity: Avoid plagiarism" on page 186.

If you're taking notes on a computer and using Internet sources, be especially careful to avoid plagiarism. When you copy text or images from a Web site, separate those notes from your own ideas. Use a different font for copied material, or enclose it in quotation marks.

Schedule time to review all the information and ideas that your research has produced. By allowing time for rereading and reflecting on all the notes you've taken, you create the conditions for genuine understanding.

Start by summarizing major points of view on your topic. Note points of agreement and disagreement among your sources.

Then look for connections in your material, including ideas, facts, and examples that occur in several sources. Also look for connections between your research and your life—ideas that you can verify based on personal experience.

Finally, see whether you can find direct answers to the questions that you had when you started researching. These answers could become headings in your paper. *

Find examples of effective research and review notes online.

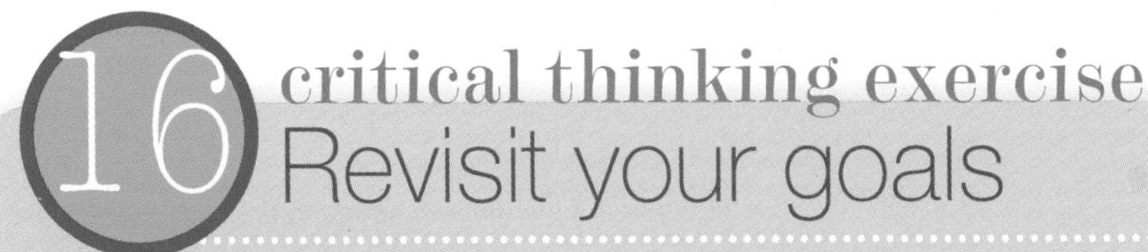

16 critical thinking exercise Revisit your goals

One powerful way to achieve any goal is to periodically assess your progress in meeting it. This step is especially important with long-term goals—those that can take years to achieve.

When you did Critical Thinking Exercise 8: "Get real with your goals" on page 56, you focused on one long-term goal and planned a detailed way to achieve it. This process involved setting mid-term and short-term goals that will lead to achieving your long-term goal. Take a minute to review that exercise and revisit the goals you set. Then complete the following steps.

1. Take your long-term goal from Critical Thinking Exercise 8, and rewrite it in the space below. If you can think of a more precise way to state it, feel free to change the wording.

2. Next, check in with yourself. How do you feel about this goal? Does it still excite your interest and enthusiasm? On a scale of 1 to 10, how committed are you to achieving this goal? Write down your level of commitment in the space below.

3. If your level of commitment is 5 or less, you might want to drop the goal and replace it with a new one. To set a new goal, just turn back to Critical Thinking Exercise 8 and do it again. Release any self-judgment about dropping your original long-term goal. Letting go of one goal creates space in your life to set and achieve a new one.

4. If you're committed to the goal you listed in Step 1 of this exercise, consider whether you're still on track to achieve it. Have you met any of the short-term goals related to this long-term goal? If so, list your completed goals here.

   Before going on to the next step, take a minute to congratulate yourself and celebrate your success.

5. Finally, consider any adjustments you'd like to make to your plan. For example, write additional short-term or mid-term goals that will take you closer to your long-term goal. Or cross out any goals that you no longer deem necessary. Make a copy of your current plan in the space below.

Long-term goal (to achieve within your lifetime):

Supporting mid-term goals (to achieve in 1 to 5 years):

Supporting short-term goals (to achieve within the coming year):

5

NOTES

Becoming an online learner

IF YOU ARE taking an online course or a course that is heavily supported by online materials, note taking could be a new challenge. You can print out anything that appears on a computer screen—online course materials, articles, books, manuscripts, e-mail messages, chat room sessions, and more. A potential problem is that you might skip the note-taking process altogether ("I can just print out everything!") You then miss the chance to internalize a new idea by restating it in your own words—a principal benefit of note taking.

Result: Material passes from computer to printer without ever intersecting with your brain.

To prevent this problem, find ways to engage actively with online materials. Take review notes in Cornell, mind map, concept map, or outline format. Write Discovery and Intention Statements to capture key insights from the materials and to state ways you intend to apply them. Also, talk about what you're learning. Recite key points out loud, and discuss what you read online with other students.

Of course, it's fine to print out online material. If you do, treat your printouts like textbooks, and apply the steps of Muscle Reading explained in Chapter 4. In addition, consider the following ways to create the most value from course content that's delivered online.

Do a trial run with technology. Verify your access to course Web sites, including online tutorials, PowerPoint presentations, readings, quizzes, tests, assignments, bulletin boards, and chat rooms. Ask your instructors for Web site addresses, e-mail addresses, and passwords. Work out any bugs when you start the course and well before that first assignment is due.

If you're planning to use a computer lab on campus, find one that meets course requirements. Remember that on-campus computer labs may not allow you to install all the software needed to access Web sites for your courses or textbooks.

Develop a contingency plan. Murphy's Law of Computer Crashes states that technology tends to break down at the moment of greatest inconvenience. You might not believe this piece of folklore, but it's still wise to prepare for it:

- Find a "technology buddy" in each of your classes—someone who can contact the instructor if you lose Internet access or experience other computer problems.

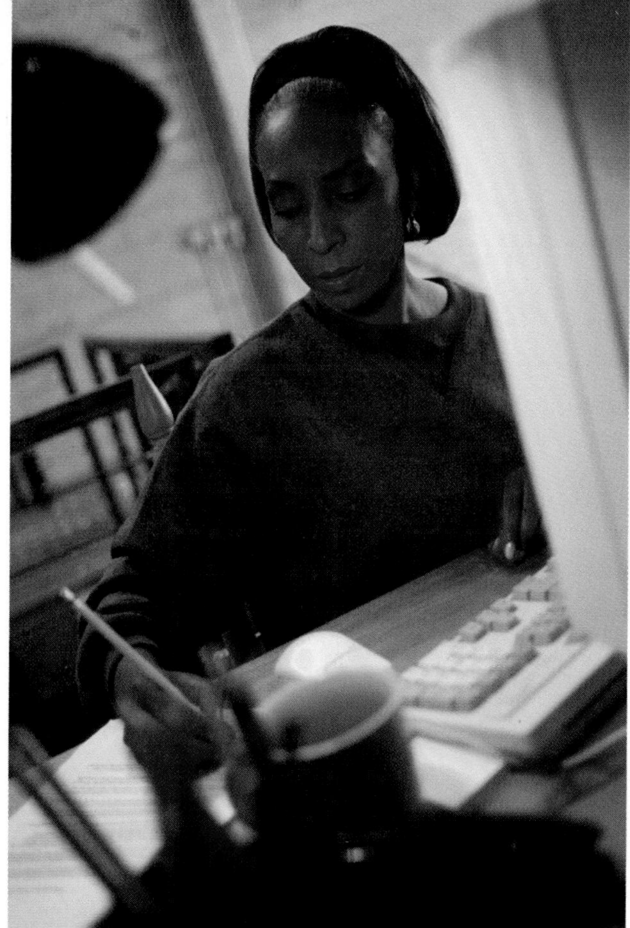

© JUPITERIMAGES/Brand X Pictures/Alamy

- Every day, make backup copies of files created for your courses.
- Keep extra printer supplies—paper and toner or ink cartridges—on hand at all times. Don't run out of necessary supplies on the day a paper is due.

Set up folders and files for easy reference. Create a separate folder for each class on your computer's hard drive. Give each folder a meaningful name, such as *biology-spring-2012*. Place all files related to a course in the appropriate folder. Doing this can save you from one of the main technology-related time wasters: searching for lost files.

Name individual files with care. Avoid changing extensions that identify different types of files, such as .ppt for PowerPoint presentations or .pdf for files in the Adobe Reader portable document format. Changing extensions might lead to problems when you're looking for files later or sharing them with other users.

Take responsibility. If you register for an online course with no class meetings, you might miss the motivating presence of an instructor and classmates. Instead, manufacture your own motivation. Be clear about what you'll gain by doing well in the course. Relate course content to your major and career goals. Don't wait to be contacted by your classmates and instructor. Initiate that contact on your own.

If you feel confused about anything you're learning, ask for help right away. This is especially important when you don't see the instructor face to face in class. Some students simply drop online courses rather than seek help. E-mail or call the instructor before you make that choice. If the instructor is on campus, you might be able to arrange for a meeting during office hours.

Prevent procrastination. Courses that take place mostly or totally online can become invisible in your weekly academic schedule. This tendency reinforces the temptation to put off dealing with these courses until late in the term. You can avoid this fate:

- Early in the term, create a detailed schedule for online courses. In your calendar, list a due date for each assignment. Break big assignments into smaller steps, and schedule a due date for each step.
- Consider scheduling times in your daily or weekly calendar to complete online course work. Give these scheduled sessions the same priority as regular classroom meetings. At these times, check for online announcements relating to assignments, tests, and other course events.
- When you receive an online assignment, e-mail any questions immediately. If you want to meet with an instructor in person, request an appointment several days in advance.
- Download or print out online course materials as soon as they're posted on the class Web site. These materials might not be available later in the term.
- If possible, submit online assignments early. Staying ahead of the game will help you avoid an all-nighter at the computer during finals week.

Focus your attention. Some students are used to visiting Web sites while watching television, listening to loud music, or using instant messaging software. When applied to online learning, these habits can reduce your learning and imperil your grades. To succeed with technology, turn off the television, quit online chat sessions, and turn down the music. Whenever you go online, stay in charge of your attention.

Ask for feedback. To get the most from online learning, request feedback from your instructor via e-mail. When appropriate, also ask for conferences by phone or in person.

Sharing files offers another source of feedback. For example, Microsoft Word has a Track Changes feature that allows other people to insert comments into your documents and make suggested revisions. These edits are highlighted on the screen. Use such tools to get feedback on your writing from instructors and peers.

Note: Be sure to check with your instructors to see how they want students enrolled in their online courses to address and label their e-mails. Many teachers ask their online students to use a standard format for the subject area so they can quickly recognize e-mails from them.

Contact other students. Make personal contact with at least one other student in each of your classes—especially classes that involve lots of online course work. Create study groups to share notes, quiz each other, critique papers, and do other cooperative learning tasks. This kind of support can help you succeed as an online learner. *

mastering technology

YOUR MIND, ONLINE

Imagine how useful—and fun—it would be to download everything you've ever read or thought and then instantly locate what you know about a particular topic. Something like this *is* possible today. Computer applications give you a variety of ways to store text and images, organize them, search them, and even share them with others when appropriate. These applications fall into three categories.

Online notebooks Springpad, Zoho Notebook, and similar online applications allow you to "clip" images and text from various Web pages, categorize all this content, and add your own notes.

Personal information managers Examples of personal information managers include Evernote, Yojimbo, and DEVONThink. These applications share many features with online notebooks. However, some of them allow you to also add "offline" content, such as digital photos of business cards and receipts. You can search through all this content by using tags and key words.

Browser extensions Zotero is a Firefox extension that allows you to store Web pages, PDF files, and notes in rich-text format. This tool makes it easy to cite the sources of text and images and to convert your citations into a bibliography—a great way to avoid plagiarism.

I Create It All

"I create it all" means treating experiences, events, and circumstances in your life *as if* you created them. This is a powerful tool for times of trouble. In a crisis, "I create it all" can lead the way to solutions.

"I create it all" is one of the most unusual and bizarre suggestions in this book. It certainly is not a belief. Use it when it works. Don't when it doesn't.

Keeping that in mind, consider how powerful this Power Process can be. It is really about the difference between two distinct positions in life: being a victim or being responsible.

A victim of circumstances is controlled by outside forces. We've all felt like victims at one time or another. Sometimes we felt helpless.

In contrast, we can take responsibility. Responsibility is "response-ability"—the ability to choose a *response* to any event. You can choose your *response* to any event, even when the event itself is beyond your control.

Many students approach grades from the position of being victims. When the student who sees the world this way gets an F, she reacts something like this: "Another F! Well, of course. That teacher couldn't teach her way out of a wet paper bag. And that textbook—what a bore!"

The problem with this viewpoint is that it's all about making excuses. The student is robbing herself of the power to get any grade other than an F. She's giving all of her power to a bad teacher and a boring textbook.

There is another way, called *taking responsibility*. You can recognize that you choose your grades by choosing your actions. Then you are the source, rather than the result, of the grades you get.

The student who got an F could react like this: "Another F! Oh, shoot! Well, hmmm. . . . What did I do to create it?"

Now, that's power. By asking, "How did I contribute to this outcome?" you are no longer the victim. This student might continue by saying, "Well, let's see. I didn't review my notes after class. That might have done it." Or, "I went out with my friends the night before the test. That probably helped me fulfill some of the requirements for getting an F."

The point is this: When the F is the result of your friends, the book, or the teacher, you probably can't do anything about it. However, if you *chose* the F, you can choose a different grade next time. In this circumstance and many others, you are in charge.

Learn more about this Power Process online.

Put it to Work

Developing the ability to take useful notes during meetings is one way to make yourself valued in the workplace. It might even help you get promoted. With this in mind, look for ways to apply suggestions from this chapter at work.

sozaijiten/Datacraft/Getty

Hanae Niigata is a part-time office manager for a large cardiovascular clinic. Her responsibilities include handling incoming calls, scheduling patient visits, maintaining medical records, and completing other tasks assigned by physicians and nurses.

Hanae's career focus is health care. She has worked as a home health aide and is currently enrolled in school. Her goal is to obtain a degree in nursing and work as a registered nurse.

Hanae has a reputation as a hard worker. Even in a noisy environment with frequent interruptions, she completes tasks that require attention to detail and sustained concentration. She catches errors on medical records that her coworkers tend to miss. In addition, Hanae is often the first person in the office to whom people turn when they have a problem to solve. Even in the most difficult circumstances, she can generate a list of options—including solutions that occur to no one else.

Recently, Hanae attended a 2-hour course on a new telephone system soon to be installed in her office. She was told to take detailed notes so she could teach the system to several receptionists. Hanae was shocked that the old system was being replaced. In her opinion, it was user-friendly.

As the training session began, Hanae diligently attempted to write down almost everything the instructor said. While doing so, she repeatedly found herself distracted by the thought that her manager was replacing a perfectly good phone system with some "sure-to-be-a-nightmare, high-tech garbage."

After completing the course, Hanae sat down with her manager to fill him in on the new system. As she thumbed through her notes, she realized they didn't make much sense to her, even though she had just finished writing them. She couldn't recall much of the course from memory either, leaving her with little information to share with her manager.

Hanae routinely applies strategies from this book to many areas of her work. For example, she applies the Power Process: Be Here Now to help her pay attention amid distractions and catch errors on medical records. In addition, she is a creative thinker and problem solver, using several strategies you will learn in Chapter 7: "Thinking." But when it came to the training session, she didn't apply any of the book's note-taking strategies. List strategies that Hanae could have used to take more effective notes on the training session that she attended:

____

____

____

____

____

When you are at work, consider using the three "A's" when you take notes during a meeting. Record key details about the following:

- *Attendance*. Notice who shows up. Your employer might expect meeting notes to include a list of attendees.
- *Agreements*. The purpose of most meetings is to reach an agreement about something—a policy, project, or plan. Note each agreement. If you're not sure whether an agreement was reached, ask for clarification.
- *Actions*. During meetings, people often commit to take some type of action in the future. Record each proposed follow-up action and who agreed to do it.

Quiz

Name______________________________ Date___/___/___

1. What are the three major steps of effective note taking as explained in this chapter? Summarize each step in one sentence.
   List each of the following and describe in a sentence:
   • Observe: Notice spoken or written words. • Record: Take notes. • Review: Reread notes frequently.
   (Answers will vary.) (*The note-taking process flows,* pp. 116–122)
2. List three ways to edit your notes.
   List three of the following techniques:
   • Fix words that are illegible. • Check whether notes are labeled with the date and class and whether the pages are numbered. • Write out abbreviated words that might be unclear later. • Mark anything you don't understand and make a note to ask your instructor or another student about it. • Type your handwritten notes.
   (*Review: The note-taking process flows*, p. 122)
3. What are some advantages of sitting in the front and center of the classroom?
   Possible advantages to sitting front and center in a lecture include the following:
   • The closer you sit to the lecturer, the harder it is to fall asleep. • The closer you sit to the front, the fewer interesting or distracting classmates between you and instructor there are to watch. • Material on the board is easier to read from the front of the classroom. • The instructor can see you more easily when you have a question. • Sitting up front is a way to commit yourself to getting what you want out of your education. • Sitting up front enables you to become a constructive force in the classroom. • When you sit in front, you are declaring your willingness to take a risk and participate.
   (Answers will vary.) (*Observe: The note-taking process flows,* pp. 116–117)
4. Instructors sometimes give clues that the material they are presenting is important. List three types of clues.
   List at least three of the following:
   • Be alert to repetition. • Listen for introductory, concluding, and transition words and phrases.
   • Watch the board or PowerPoint presentation. • Watch the instructor's eyes. • Highlight the obvious clues.
   • Notice the instructor's interest level. (*Observe: The note-taking process flows,* pp. 116–117)
5. Postponing judgment while taking notes means that you have to agree with everything that the instructor says. True or false? Explain your answer.
   False. When you hear something you disagree with, note your disagreement and let it go for the moment. It is okay to absorb information you don't agree with. Just absorb it with the mental tag that you don't agree and that you will ask about it later. (*Observe: The note-taking process flows,* pp. 116–117)
6. Describe what to include in the cue column when you take notes in the Cornell format.
   In the cue column, list potential test questions that correspond to your notes. You can also list key words from your notes. Another option is to pretend that your notes are a series of articles on different topics. In the cue column, write a newspaper-style headline for each "article." In any case, be brief. If you cram the cue column full of words, you defeat its purpose—to reduce the number of words and length of your notes. (*Record: The note-taking process flows,* pp.118–121)
7. Describe two types of key words. Then write down at least five key words from this chapter.
   Two types of key words include:
   • Concepts, technical terms, names, and numbers. They are usually nouns.
   • Linking words that describe action, relationship, and degree. They are usually verbs.
   Key words in this chapter include Cornell format, mind mapping, research notes, "I create it all," observe, record, review, front and center, preclass review, and postpone debate.
   (Answers will vary.) (*Record: The note-taking process flows,* pp.118–121)
8. Effective students do not combine several different formats for taking notes. True or false? Explain your answer.
   False. To take more effective review notes, use a variety of formats. Combine formats to create your own. However, don't let the creation of formats get in your way. Even a simple list of key points and examples can become a powerful review tool.
   (*Taking notes while reading*, p. 125)
9. Describe at least three strategies for reviewing notes.
   Describe at least three of the following:
   • Review within 24 hours. • Edit your notes. • Fill in key words in the left-hand column.
   • Conduct short weekly review periods. • Create summaries.
   (Answers will vary.) (*Review: The note-taking process flows*, p. 122)
10. Briefly define the word *responsibility* as it is used in the Power Process: "I Create It All."
    As used in this process, responsibility means taking ownership of your actions and responses to things that happen in your life. (Answers will vary.) (*Power Process: I Create It All,* p. 129)

Skills Snapshot

The Discovery Wheel in Chapter 1 includes a section labeled *Notes*. For the next 10 to 15 minutes, go beyond your initial responses to that exercise. Take a snapshot of your skills as they exist today, after reading and doing this chapter.

Begin by reflecting on some of your recent experiences with note taking. These experiences can include classroom notes, as well as notes on your reading assignments. Then take the next step toward mastery by committing to a specific action in the near future.

OBSERVING

If my attention wanders while taking notes, I refocus by . . .

When I strongly disagree with the opinion of a speaker or author, I respond by . . .

RECORDING

The formats I usually use to take notes are . . .

A new note-taking format that I'd like to experiment with is . . .

REVIEWING

If asked to rate the overall quality of the notes that I've taken in the last week, I would say that . . .

In general, I find my notes to be most useful when they . . .

NEXT ACTION

I'll know that I've reached a new level of mastery with note taking when . . .

Master Student PROFILE

Harvey Milk

. . . was courageous

People told Harvey Milk that no openly gay man could win political office. Fortunately, he ignored them.

There was a time when it was impossible for people—straight or gay—even to imagine a Harvey Milk. The funny thing about Milk is that he didn't seem to care that he lived in such a time. After he defied the governing class of San Francisco in 1977 to become a member of its board of supervisors, many people—straight and gay—had to adjust to a new reality he embodied: that a gay person could live an honest life and succeed. That laborious adjustment plods on—now forward, now backward—though with every gay character to emerge on TV and with every presidential speech to a gay group, its eventual outcome favoring equality seems clear.

The few gays who had scratched their way into the city's [San Francisco's] establishment blanched when Milk announced his first run for supervisor in 1973, but Milk had a powerful idea: He would reach downward, not upward, for support. He convinced the growing gay masses of "Sodom by the Sea" that they could have a role in city leadership, and they turned out to form "human billboards" for him along major thoroughfares. In doing so, they outed themselves in a way once unthinkable. It was invigorating.

While his first three tries for office failed, they lent Milk the credibility and positive media focus that probably no openly gay person ever had. Not everyone cheered, of course, and death threats multiplied. Milk spoke often of his ineluctable assassination, even recording a will naming acceptable successors to his seat and containing the famous line: "If a bullet should enter my brain, let that bullet destroy every closet door."

Two bullets actually entered his brain. It was November 27, 1978, in city hall, and Mayor George Moscone was also killed. Fellow supervisor Daniel White, a troubled anti-gay conservative, had left the board, and he became unhinged when Moscone denied his request to return. White admitted the murders within hours. . . .

A jury gave him just 5 years with parole. Defense lawyers had barred anyone remotely pro-gay from the jury and brought a psychologist to testify that junk food had exacerbated White's depression. (The so-called Twinkie defense was later banned.) Milk's words had averted gay riots before, but after the verdict, the city erupted. More than 160 people ended up in the hospital.

Milk's killing probably awakened as many gay people as his election had. His death inspired many associates—most notably Cleve Jones, who later envisioned the greatest work of American folk art, the AIDS quilt. But while assassination offered Milk something then rare for openly gay men—mainstream empathy—it would have been thrilling to see how far he could have gone as a leader. He had sworn off gay bathhouses when he entered public life, and he may have eluded the virus that killed so many of his contemporaries. He could have guided gay America through the confused start of the AIDS horror. Instead, he remains frozen in time, a symbol of what gays can accomplish and the dangers they face in doing so.

John Cloud, "Harvey Milk," *Time*, June 14, 1999, http://205.188.238.181/time/time100/heroes/profile/milk01.html.

(1930–1978) One of America's first openly gay men to win political office, Harvey Milk was assassinated by a former San Francisco city supervisor.

Learn more about Harvey Milk and other master students at the Master Student Hall of Fame.

6 Tests

Instructor Tools & Tips

> Learn from the mistakes of others—you can never live long enough to make them all yourself.
>
> **—John Luther**
>
> Keep in mind that neither success nor failure is ever final.
>
> **—Roger Babson**

Preview

Test taking is a high-priority issue for students. Discussing this topic together in class can help students prepare more successfully before tests while learning to manage anxiety during tests. This chapter reinforces how the strategies in *Becoming a Master Student* can help students reduce stress at school, at work, and at home. An article on math test strategies can help your students achieve higher scores. Encourage your students to do a chapter reconnaissance to discover ways to predict test questions or to glean information from a test after it has been returned.

Guest Speaker

Consider inviting faculty members from different departments to talk to your class about their expectations regarding tests. Ask them to prepare a few suggestions for studying materials in their discipline. Prompt them to provide information on the importance of attending class, reading assigned textbook materials, and completing homework assignments. Have students prepare questions to ask these faculty members during a question-and-answer session.

Another guest speaker idea is to invite the administrator responsible for student discipline. In addition to explaining the office's broader role at the college, prompt the administrator to talk about the college's policies regarding cheating. When students cheat and get caught, they don't talk about it, so students have a misperception that no one is getting caught. The administrator's firsthand discussion of the topic may hit home with students who have considered cheating or have cheated in the past.

Another suggestion for a guest speaker is to invite a counselor or staff member from the Student Health Center to talk about test anxiety and relaxation techniques.

Lecture

What to do when you're stuck. Lecture on what students should do when they are stuck on a test question. Here are some strategies. A copy of this material is available on the Instructor Companion site.

- **Read it again.** Eliminate the simplest sources of confusion, such as misreading the question.
- **Skip the question for now.** This advice is simple—and it works. Tell students to let their subconscious mind work on the answer while they respond to other questions. The trick is to truly let go of the puzzling question—for the moment. Questions that nag at the back of your mind can undermine your concentration and interfere with your recall while you are answering other questions.
- **Look for answers in other test questions.** A term, name, date, or other fact that escapes you might appear in another question on the test itself. Use other questions to stimulate your memory.
- **Treat intuition with care.** In quick-answer questions (multiple choice, true/false), go with your first instinct about which answer is correct. If you think your first answer is wrong because you misread the question, though, do change your answer.
- **Visualize the answer's "location."** Think of the answer to any test question as being recorded someplace in your notes or assigned reading. Close your eyes, take a deep breath, and see whether you can visualize that place—its location on a page in the materials you studied for the test.
- **Rewrite the question.** See whether you can put a confusing question into your own words. Doing so might release the answer.
- **Free-write.** Just start writing anything at all. On scratch paper or in the margins of your test booklet, record any response to the test question that pops into your head. Instead of just sitting there, stumped,

- you're doing something—and that can reduce anxiety. Writing might also trigger a mental association that answers the question.
- **Write an approximate answer.** If you simply cannot think of a direct, accurate answer to the question, give it a shot anyway. Answer the question as well as you can, even if you don't think your answer is fully correct. This technique might help you get partial credit for short-answer questions, essay questions, and problems on math or science tests.

Eight reasons to celebrate mistakes (page 148). From Faculty Advisor Dean Mancina: "Sometimes I flub up a piece of my lecture or an in-class group activity. My students love to see that happen! I made a sign with the eight reasons to celebrate mistakes and had our graphics center blow it up into a poster that I have posted in my classroom. When I make a mistake, rather than trying to cover it up, I walk over to the poster, review the list, and pick one of the reasons to celebrate it, right then and there! The students see me model making a mistake without shame—a real application of the tool. Depending on how many mistakes I make during the semester, some of my students get a frequent review of this strategy!"

Exercises/Activities

1. Cooperative learning: Studying in groups (pages 137–138). This article addresses the topic of working together in group study sessions. Use the Master Student Map to begin the discussion of tests and cooperative learning. Divide your class into four groups, assigning each group one of the learning styles. Next, with their books closed, ask students to write down as many answers to their question *(Why? What? How? What if?)* in relation to test taking as they can in 1 minute. After a minute, have each group pick their best answer and report about it to the class. Then have the students open their textbooks and compare their lists to the Master Student Map.

Why? Why does this chapter appear in *Becoming a Master Student*?

What? What is included in this chapter?

How? How can you use this chapter?

What if? What if you use the techniques in this chapter to be better prepared for tests?

2. What to do *before* the test (page 136). This article is important to students because so many of them cram at the last minute and therefore have never practiced these strategies. Mind maps are powerful visual review tools that can be an effective tool for students who don't know how to study effectively for tests. Have your students get into groups of four, pick a chapter from *Becoming a Master Student,* and create a mind map of the chapter's content on poster paper with colored markers. Tell them to sign their names at the top of the paper. This helps ensure that everyone is actively participating in the group. Hang the completed posters on the wall in the classroom, and then have the students walk around in their groups to review their classmates' work. Having had an opportunity to practice creating mind map summaries in class, they are likely to be more comfortable trying the technique on their own outside class. This activity also allows students to practice the important skill of working in groups.

3. Ways to predict test questions (page 136). Divide students into groups and have them practice predicting test questions for the weekly quizzes that you give in class. Their questions should be based on what they see as the key points you have presented in lectures, activities, and homework, and the key points in the articles in the text. They are often surprised at how easy and effective this tool is!

4. Power Process: Detach (page 149). After you have lectured on how to develop and write good essay exam answers and have emphasized the importance of thinking, planning, and clear writing, divide your students into groups of four and have them answer the following question: "Fully explain the Power Process: 'Detach.' " This activity provides them with an opportunity to practice developing an essay answer in a cooperative learning environment. It's also valuable because some students don't fully understand this process without class discussion. After the groups write their group essay answers, have them pass their papers to another group who then "grade" the essay. Read the highest-scoring answer, and provide your analysis as to the essay's strengths and weaknesses. Here's a modification of this exercise from an instructor:

> One thing that I tell my students about essay tests is to write as if they were writing to someone who knows absolutely nothing about the subject. In that way, they should include all the basic information that they might not otherwise think of. I also use LIBEC, which was in a College Survival newsletter several years ago. LIBEC stands for **l**egible, **i**ntroduction, **b**ody, **e**xample, and **c**onclusion. We talk about these steps and then my students (in groups) write answers to questions I make up from the reading in the chapter. They exchange answers with their group members and check to see whether all the areas were covered. They enjoy working on an essay question with others and then evaluating what others have done.
>
> **—Barbara Fowler, Longview Community College, Missouri**

Conversation/Sharing

As the article "The test isn't over until . . . " (page 142) explains, it is vital for students to find out what questions they missed on a test and to understand why they missed them. Students can use the learning styles questions *(Why? What? How? What if?)* to review their tests. *Why* did I get this question wrong? *What* is the correct answer? *How* should I have studied this material? And they need to understand the consequences: *What if* I do not learn the correct answer for future tests? These four questions are a great foundational structure for this self-analysis. After a quiz or test, divide students into groups and have them share their analyses with each other so that they can all do better on the next evaluation. On a related note, here's a suggestion from an instructor:

> I have always tried to instruct my students to learn something from the tests that they take. This can be an area where the students can gain so much information and yet it is often overlooked. The information in the chart (page 142) is also helpful. This is a great way to say a lot in a small space.
>
> **—Ray Emett, Salt Lake Community College**

Homework

Journal Entry 15 Discovery/Intention Statement (page 145). Ask students to take a look at how they sabotage their opportunities to "create it all" by making excuses. This self-analysis will help them break the excuses habit by writing their discoveries and intentions about excuses.

Journal Entry 16 Discovery Statement (page 145). Having students complete and turn in this journal entry regarding how they feel about tests can be helpful to you in understanding the key problem areas for your students before, during, and after a test. Review students' responses to this exercise and tailor your lectures and activities to address the needs expressed.

Critical Thinking Exercise 18: Use learning styles for math success (page 147). This exercise helps students see how they can use their preferred learning style to create tools to help them succeed in math.

Evaluation

Giving a quiz that includes multiple-choice, true/false, short-answer, and essay questions will give students an opportunity to practice new skills they've learned in this chapter. It will also provide them with feedback about where they have achieved success in building new skills and where more practice is needed. For example, ask the following quiz question about Master Students Bert and John Jacobs: "Briefly describe how Bert and John Jacobs feel about keeping a positive attitude. Then state whether you agree with it or not, and justify your position." Using the three-part quiz forms available from your Cengage sales representative facilitates students' self-evaluation of their quiz performance and provides them with immediate feedback about their test-taking skills.

Additional Digital Resources

Course Manual

The online *Course Manual* serves as an invaluable reference for those developing and teaching a College Success course with *Becoming a Master Student Concise*. The *Course Manual* provides advice on general teaching issues such as preparing for classes, classroom management, grading, and communicating with students of various backgrounds, as well as specific strategies on getting the most out of various features in *Becoming a Master Student Concise* and book-specific Web sites. Do a *Course Manual* reconnaissance to find ideas that you can use in your course right now.

Instructor Companion Site

The updated Instructor Companion Site provides resources to help you plan and customize your course. Content specific to Chapter 6 includes:

- Lecture Ideas
  - Comparing Athletic Competitions to Tests
  - Using Bloom's Taxonomy to Prepare for Tests
  - Test Anxiety and Stress
- In-Class Exercises
  - The Fribbled What?
  - Mid-Term Project
  - The Power of Positive Peer Influence
- In-Text Quiz Answers
- PowerPoint Slides

The Instructor Companion Site also contains the following book-specific content:

- ExamView Test Bank
- Online Course Manual
- Sample Syllabi
- Detailed Transition Guide

College Success CourseMate

To help your students gain a better understanding of the topics discussed in *Becoming a Master Student Concise*, encourage them to visit the text's CourseMate at CengageBrain.com that provides the following resources specific to Chapter 6:

- Connect to Text content expands on specific topics marked with an icon within Chapter 6.
- Practice Tests allow students to see how well they understand the themes of *Becoming a Master Student Concise.*
- Interactive Concept Maps promote critical thinking by highlighting related ideas to show relationships among concepts.
- Video Skillbuilders bring to life techniques that will help students to excel in college and beyond. The following videos should give your students more information regarding topics covered in Chapter 6:
  - Test Taking: Understanding Tests
  - Test Taking: Preparing for Tests
- Learning Styles Application
- Discussion Topics
- Reflection Questions
- Assessment Questions
- Experiment with chapter strategies
- Remembering Cultural Differences presents readers with brief articles that touch on aspects of diversity in our rapidly changing world. For Chapter 6, the following article will prompt your students to look at contemporary issues in a new way:
  - A Historical Look at Exams
- Master Student Profiles provide additional information on the people covered in this book feature. For Chapter 6, students will find expanded coverage and links about:
  - Bert and John Jacobs
- Power Process Media contains video, PowerPoints, and audio files to take what your students have learned from the Power Processes in their book to the next level. For Chapter 6, students will find additional media on:
  - Detach

Along with the chapter-specific content, a General Resources folder is available that contains Toolboxes geared toward specific student types (Community College, Adult Learner, Student Athlete), the Plagiarism Prevention Zone, and the Career Resource Center.

6 Tests

Master Student Map

as you read, ask yourself

what if . . .?

I could let go of anxiety about tests—or anything else?

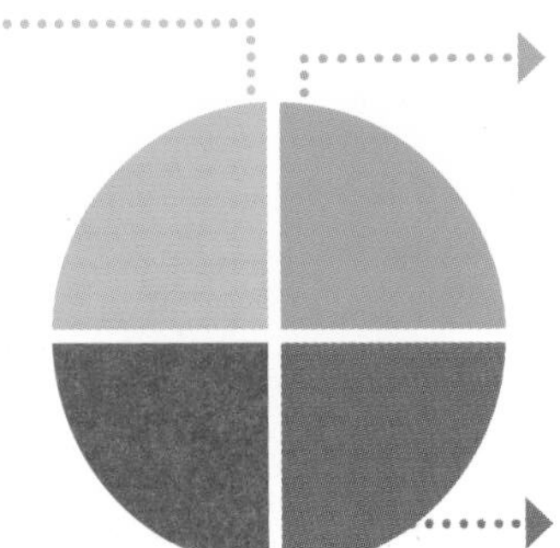

why this chapter matters . . .

Adopting a few simple techniques can make a major difference in how you feel about tests—and how you perform on them.

how you can use this chapter . . .

- Predict test questions and use your study time more effectively.
- Harness the power of cooperative learning by studying with other people.
- Gain strategies for raising your scores on tests.
- Separate your self-image from your test scores.

what is included . . .

MASTER STUDENTS in *action*

When studying for a test, the first thing I usually do is to read over my notes. Sometimes I re-read the chapter just to make sure I comprehend what the chapter is saying. I find it very helpful to go online to the publisher's Web site and do the practice exams. By doing the practice exams, I get a better perspective of what the critical points are in the chapters. I like to go through the chapter outline because sometimes the answers are in the outlines.

—LEA DEAN

Photo courtesy of Lea Dean

Disarm tests

ON THE SURFACE, tests don't look dangerous. Maybe that's why we sometimes treat them as if they were land mines. Suppose a stranger walked up to you on the street and asked, "Does a finite abelian P-group have a basis?" Would you break out in a cold sweat? Would your muscles tense up? Would your breathing become shallow?

Probably not. Even if you had never heard of a finite abelian P-group, you probably would remain coolly detached. However, if you find the same question on a test and you have never heard of a finite abelian P-group, your hands might get clammy.

Grades (A to F) are what we use to give power to tests. However, there are lots of misconceptions about what grades are. Grades are not a measure of intelligence or creativity. They are not an indication of our ability to contribute to society. Grades are simply a measure of how well we do on tests.

Some people think that a test score measures what a student has accomplished in a course. This is false. A test score is a measure of what a student scored on a test. If you are anxious about a test and blank out, the grade cannot measure what you've learned. The reverse is also true: If you are good at taking tests and you are a lucky guesser, the score won't be an accurate reflection of what you know.

Grades are not a measure of self-worth. Yet we tend to give test scores the power to determine how we feel about ourselves. Common thoughts include "If I fail a test, I am a failure" or "If I do badly on a test, I am a bad person." The truth is that if you do badly on a test, you are a person who did badly on a test. That's all.

Carrying around misconceptions about tests and grades can put undue pressure on your performance. It's like balancing on a railroad track. Many people can walk along the rail and stay balanced for long periods. Yet the task seems entirely different if the rail is placed between two buildings, 52 stories up.

It is easier to do well on exams if you don't put too much pressure on yourself. Don't give the test some magical power over your own worth as a human being. Academic tests are not a matter of life and death. Scoring low on important tests—standardized tests, medical school exams, bar exams, CPA exams—usually means only a delay.

Whether the chance of doing poorly is real or exaggerated, worrying about it can become paralyzing. The way to deal with tests is to keep them in perspective. Keep the railroad track on the ground. *

journal entry

Discovery/Intention Statement

Use this chapter to transform your experience of tests

Mentally re-create a time when you had difficulty taking a test. Do anything that helps you reexperience this event. Briefly describe that experience in the space below. For example, you could list some of the questions you had difficulty answering, or explain how you felt after finding out your score on the test.

I discovered that I . . .

Now wipe your mental slate clean, and declare your intention to replace it with a new scenario. Describe how you want your experience of test taking to change. For example, you might write: "I intend to walk into every test I take feeling well rested and thoroughly prepared."

I intend to . . .

Preview this chapter, looking for at least five strategies that can help you accomplish your goal. List those strategies below, and note the page numbers where you can find out more about them.

Strategy	**Page number**

What to do before the test

Do daily reviews. Daily reviews include short preclass and postclass reviews of lecture notes. You should also conduct brief daily reviews with textbooks: Before reading a new assignment, scan your notes and the sections you underlined or highlighted in the previous assignment. In addition, use the time you spend waiting for the bus or doing the laundry to conduct short reviews.

Do weekly reviews. Review each subject at least once a week, allowing about 1 hour per subject. Include reviews of assigned reading and lecture notes. Look over any mind map summaries or flash cards you have created. Also practice working on sample problems.

Do major reviews. Major reviews are usually most helpful when conducted the week before finals or other critical exams. They help you integrate concepts and deepen your understanding of material presented throughout the term. These are longer review periods—2 to 5 hours at a stretch, with sufficient breaks. Remember that the effectiveness of your review begins to drop after an hour or so unless you give yourself a short rest.

Schedule reviews. Schedule specific times in your calendar for reviews. Start reviewing key topics at least 5 days before you'll be tested on them. This allows plenty of time to find the answers to questions and close any gaps in your understanding.

Create study checklists. List reading assignments by chapters or page numbers. List dates of lecture notes. Write down various types of problems you will need to solve. Write down other skills to master. Include major ideas, definitions, theories, formulas, and equations. For math and science tests, choose some problems and do them over again as a way to review for the test. Remember that this study checklist is not a review sheet; it is a to-do list. Checklists contain the briefest possible description of each item to study.

Create flash cards. Flash cards can be used to make portable test questions. On one side of some 3x5 cards, write questions. On the other side, write the answers. It's that simple. Always carry a pack of flash cards with you, and review them whenever you have a minute to spare.

Take a practice test. Write up your own questions, and take this practice test several times before the actual exam. You might type this "test" so that it looks like the real thing. If possible, take your practice test in the same room where you will take the actual test. *

See examples of mind map summary sheets and other review tools online.

6 TESTS

Ways to predict test questions

Ask about the nature of the test. Eliminate as much guesswork as possible. Ask your instructor to describe upcoming tests. Do this early in the term so you can be alert for possible test questions throughout the course.

Put yourself in your instructor's shoes. If you were teaching the course, what kinds of questions would you put on an exam?

Look for possible test questions in your notes and readings. Label a separate section in your notebook "Test Questions." Add several questions to this section after every lecture and assignment.

Look for clues to possible questions during class. During lectures, you can predict test questions by observing what an instructor says and how he says it. Instructors often give clues. They might repeat important points several times, write them on the board, or return to them in later classes.

Save all quizzes, papers, lab sheets, and graded materials of any kind. Quiz questions have a way of reappearing, in slightly altered form, on final exams.

Remember the obvious. Be on the lookout for these words: *This material will be on the test.*

Cooperative learning: Studying in groups

© Image copyright Yuri Arcurs, 2009. Used under license from Shutterstock.com

STUDY GROUPS CAN lift your mood on days when you just don't feel like working. If you skip a solo study session, no one else will know. If you declare your intention to study with others who are depending on you, then your intention gains strength.

Study groups are especially important if going to school has thrown you into a new culture. Joining a study group with people you already know can help ease the transition. To multiply the benefits of working with study groups, seek out people of other backgrounds, cultures, races, and ethnic groups. You can get a whole new perspective on the world, along with some valued new friends. You can also experience what it's like to be part of a diverse team, which is an important asset in today's job market.

Form a study group

Choose a focus for your group. Many students assume that the purpose of a study group is to help its members prepare for a test. That's one valid purpose—but there are others.

Through his research on cooperative learning, psychologist Joe Cuseo identified several kinds of study groups.[1] For instance, members of *test review* groups compare answers and help one another discover sources of errors. *Note-taking* groups focus on comparing and editing notes, often meeting directly after the day's class. Members of *research* groups meet to help one another find, evaluate, and take notes on background materials for papers and presentations. *Reading* groups can be useful for courses in which test questions are based largely on textbooks. Meet with classmates to compare the passages you underlined or highlighted and the notes you made in the margins of your books.

Look for dedicated students. Find people you are comfortable with and who share your academic goals. Look for students who pay attention, participate in class, and actively take notes. Invite them to join your group.

Of course, you can recruit members in other ways. One way is to make an announcement during class. Another option is to post signs asking interested students to contact you. You can also pass around a sign-up sheet before class. These methods can reach many people, but they do take more time to achieve results. In addition, you have less control over who applies to join the group.

Limit groups to four people. Research on cooperative learning indicates that four people is an ideal group size.[2] Larger ones can be unwieldy.

Studying with friends is fine, but if your common interests are pizza and jokes, you might find it hard to focus.

Hold a planning session. Ask two or three people to get together for a snack and talk about group goals, meeting times and locations, and other logistics. You don't have to make an immediate commitment.

As you brainstorm about places to meet, aim for a quiet meeting room with plenty of space to spread out materials.

Do a trial run. Test the group first by planning a one-time session. If that session works, plan another. After a few successful sessions, you can schedule regular meetings.

Conduct your group

Ask your instructor for guidelines on study group activity. Many instructors welcome and encourage study groups. However, they have different ideas about what kinds of collaboration are acceptable. Some activities—such as sharing test items or writing papers from a shared outline—are considered cheating and can have serious consequences. Let your instructor know that you're forming a group, and ask for clear guidelines.

Set an agenda for each meeting. At the beginning of each meeting, reach agreement on what you intend to do. Set a time limit for each agenda item, and determine a quitting time. End each meeting with assignments for all members to complete before the next meeting.

Assign roles. To make the most of your time, ask one member to lead each group meeting. The leader's role is to keep the discussion focused on the agenda and ask for contributions from all members. Assign another person to act as recorder. This person will take notes on the meeting, recording possible test questions, answers, and main points from group discussions. Rotate both of these roles so that every group member takes a turn.

Cycle through learning styles. As you assign roles, think about the learning styles present in your group. Some people excel at raising questions and creating lots of ideas. Others prefer to gather information and think critically. Some like to answer questions and make decisions, while others excel at taking action. Each of these distinct modes of learning are explained in "Learning styles: Discovering how you learn" on page 34-36. To create an effective group, match people with their preferred activities. You should also change roles within the group periodically. This gives group members a chance to explore new learning styles.

Teach each other. Teaching is a great way to learn something. Turn the material you're studying into a list of topics and assign a specific topic to each person, who will then teach it to the group. When you're done presenting your topic, ask for questions or comments. Prompt each other to explain ideas more clearly, find gaps in understanding, consider other points of view, and apply concepts to settings outside the classroom.

Test one another. During your meeting, take a practice test created from questions contributed by group members. When you're finished, compare answers. You can also turn testing into a game by pretending you're on a television game show. Use sample test questions to quiz one another.

Compare notes. Make sure that all the group's members heard the same thing in class and that you all recorded the important information. Ask others to help explain material in your notes that is confusing to you.

Create wall-size mind maps or concept maps to summarize a textbook or series of lectures. Work on large sheets of butcher paper, or tape together pieces of construction paper. When creating a mind map, assign one branch to each member of the study group. Use a different colored pen or marker for each branch of the mind map. (For more information on concept maps and mind maps, see Chapter 5: "Notes.")

Monitor effectiveness. On your meeting agenda, include an occasional discussion about your group's effectiveness. Are you meeting consistently? Is the group helping members succeed in class?

Use this time to address any issues that are affecting the group as a whole. If certain members are routinely unprepared for study sessions, brainstorm ways to get them involved. If one person tends to dominate meetings, reel her in by reminding her that everyone's voice needs to be heard.

To resolve conflict among group members, keep the conversation constructive. Focus on solutions. Move from vague complaints ("You're never prepared") to specific requests ("Will you commit to bringing 10 sample test questions next time?"). Asking a "problem" member to lead the next meeting might make an immediate difference. *

mastering technology

COLLABORATION 2.0

Web-based applications allow you to create virtual study groups and collaborate online. For example, create and revise documents with sites such as Google Docs (www.docs.google.com) and Zoho Writer (www.writer.zoho.com).

Create and share PowerPoint and keynote presentations with tools such as SlideShare (www.slideshare.net).

Use Basecamp (www.basecamphq.com) or 5pm (www.5pmweb.com) to manage projects. You can share files, create a group calendar, assign tasks, chat online, post messages, and track progress toward milestones (key due dates).

Create group mind maps with MindMeister (www.mindmeister.com) and Mindomo (www.mindomo.com).

For more options, do an Internet search with the key words *collaborate online*.

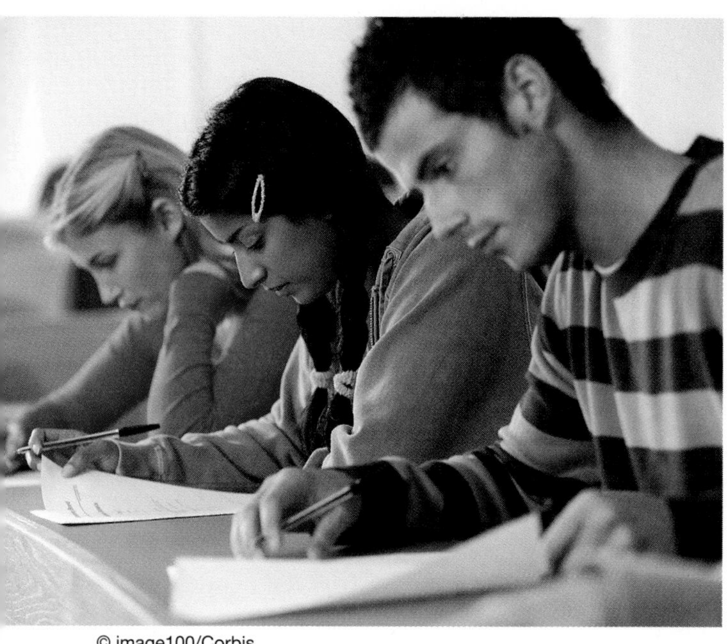

© image100/Corbis

What to do during the test

PREPARE YOURSELF for the test by arriving early. Being early often leaves time to do a relaxation exercise. While you're waiting for the test to begin and talking with classmates, avoid asking the question, "How much did you study for the test?" This question might fuel anxious thoughts that you didn't study enough.

As you begin

Ask the teacher or test administrator whether you can use scratch paper during the test. (If you use a separate sheet of paper without permission, you might appear to be cheating.) If you *do* get permission, use this paper to jot down memory aids, formulas, equations, definitions, facts, or other material you know you'll need and might forget. An alternative is to make quick notes in the margins of the test sheet.

Pay attention to verbal directions given as a test is distributed. Then scan the whole test immediately. Evaluate the importance of each section. Notice how many points each part of the test is worth; then estimate how much time you'll need for each section. Use point value as your guide. For example, don't budget 20 percent of your time for a section that is worth only 10 percent of the points.

Read the directions slowly. Then reread them. It can be agonizing to discover that you lost points on a test merely because you failed to follow the directions. When the directions are confusing, ask to have them clarified.

Now you are ready to begin the test. If necessary, allow yourself a minute or two of "panic" time. Notice any tension you feel, and apply one of the techniques explained in the article "Let go of test anxiety" later in this chapter.

Answer the easiest, shortest questions first. This gives you the experience of success. It also stimulates associations and prepares you for more difficult questions. Pace yourself, and watch the time. If you can't think of an answer, move on. Follow your time plan.

If you are unable to answer a test question, keep an eye out throughout the test for context clues that may remind you of the correct answer. You might spot evidence that helps you to eliminate wrong answers.

Multiple-choice questions

- *Answer each question in your head first.* Do this step before you look at the possible answers. If you come up with an answer that you're confident is right, look for that answer in the list of choices.
- *Read all possible answers before selecting one.* Sometimes two answers will be similar and only one will be correct.
- *Test each possible answer.* Remember that multiple-choice questions consist of two parts: the stem (an incomplete statement or question at the beginning) and a list of possible answers. Each answer, when combined with the stem, makes a complete statement or question-and-answer pair that is either true or false. When you combine the stem with each possible answer, you are turning each multiple-choice question into a small series of true/false questions. Choose the answer that makes a true statement.
- *Eliminate incorrect answers.* Cross off the answers that are clearly not correct. The answer you cannot eliminate is probably the best choice.

True/false questions

- *Read the entire question.* Separate the statement into its grammatical parts—individual clauses and phrases—and then test each part. If any part is false, the entire statement is false.
- *Look for qualifiers.* Qualifiers include words such as *all, most, sometimes,* or *rarely.* Absolute qualifiers such as *always* or *never* generally indicate a false statement.
- *Find the devil in the details.* Double-check each number, fact, and date in a true/false statement. Look for numbers that have been transposed or facts that have been slightly altered. These are signals of a false statement.
- *Watch for negatives.* Look for words such as *not* and *cannot.* Read the sentence without these words and see whether you come up with a true or a false statement. Then reinsert the negative words and see whether the statement makes more sense. Watch especially for sentences with two negative words. As in math operations, two negatives cancel each other out: *We cannot say that Chekhov never succeeded at short story writing* means the same as *Chekhov succeeded at short story writing.*

Computer-graded tests

- Make sure that the answer you mark corresponds to the question you are answering.
- Check the test booklet against the answer sheet whenever you switch sections and whenever you come to the top of a column.
- Watch for stray marks on the answer sheet; they can look like answers.
- If you change an answer, be sure to erase the wrong answer thoroughly, removing all pencil marks completely.

Open-book tests

- Carefully organize your notes, readings, and any other materials you plan to consult when writing answers.
- Write down any formulas you will need on a separate sheet of paper.
- Bookmark the table of contents and index in each of your textbooks. Place stick-on tabs or paper clips on other important pages of books (pages with tables, for instance).
- Create an informal table of contents or index for the notes you took in class.
- Predict which material will be covered on the test, and highlight relevant sections in your readings and notes.

Short-answer/fill-in-the-blank tests

- Concentrate on key words and facts. Be brief.
- Remember that overlearning material can really pay off. When you know a subject backward and forward, you can answer this type of question almost as fast as you can write.

Matching tests

- Begin by reading through each column, starting with the one with fewer items. Check the number of items in each column to see whether they're equal. If they're not, look for an item in one column that you can match with two or more items in the other column.
- Look for any items with similar wording, and make special note of the differences between these items.
- Match words that are similar grammatically. For example, match verbs with verbs and nouns with nouns.
- When matching individual words with phrases, first read a phrase. Then look for the word that logically completes the phrase.
- Cross out items in each column when you are through with them.

Essay questions

Managing your time is crucial in answering essay questions. Note how many questions you have to answer, and monitor your progress during the test period. Writing shorter answers and completing all of the questions on an essay test will probably yield a better score than leaving some questions blank.

Find out what an essay question is asking—precisely. If a question asks you to *compare* the ideas of Sigmund Freud and Karl Marx—no matter how eloquently you *explain* them—you are on a one-way trip to No Credit City.

Before you write, make a quick outline. An outline can help speed up the writing of your detailed answer. You're less likely to leave out important facts. Even if you don't have time to finish your answer, your outline could win you some points. To use test time efficiently, keep your outline brief. Focus on key words to use in your answer.

Introduce your answer by getting to the point. General statements such as "There are many interesting facets to this difficult question" can cause acute irritation to teachers grading dozens of tests.

One way to get to the point is to begin your answer with part of the question. Suppose the question is,

"Discuss how increasing the city police budget might or might not contribute to a decrease in street crime." Your first sentence might be this: "An increase in police expenditures will not have a significant effect on street crime for the following reasons." Your position is clear. You are on your way to an answer.

Next, expand your answer with supporting ideas and facts. Start out with the most solid points. Be brief and avoid filler sentences.

Write legibly. Grading essay questions is in large part a subjective process. Sloppy, difficult-to-read handwriting might actually lower your grade.

Write on one side of the paper only. If you write on both sides of the paper, writing may show through and obscure the words on the other side. If necessary, use the blank side to add points you missed. Leave a generous left-hand margin and plenty of space between your answers. Later on, you can add points that you missed.

Finally, if you have time, review your answers for grammar and spelling errors, clarity, and legibility. *

F is for feedback, not failure

When some students get an F on an assignment, they interpret that letter as a message: "You are a failure." That interpretation is not accurate. Getting an F means only that you failed a test—not that you failed your life.

From now on, imagine that the letter *F* when used as a grade represents another word: *feedback*. An F is an indication that you didn't understand the material well enough or that you could stand to brush up on your test-taking skills. It's a message to do something differently before the next test or assignment.

If you interpret F as *failure*, you don't get to change anything. But if you interpret F as *feedback*, you can change your thinking and behavior in ways that promote your success.

To transform failure into success, harness the power of the Discovery and Intention Journal Entry system. Write Discovery Statements about the possible source of the F. Follow up Intention Statements about what to differently as you prepare for and take your next test. Then complete the cycle by acting on your intention.

6

TESTS

Words to watch for in essay questions

The following words are commonly found in essay test questions. They give you precise directions about what to include in your answer. Get to know these words well. When you see them on a test, underline them. Also look for them in your notes. Locating such key words can help you predict test questions.

Analyze: Break into separate parts and discuss, examine, or interpret each part.

Compare: Examine two or more items. Identify similarities and differences.

Contrast: Show differences. Set in opposition.

Criticize: Make judgments. Evaluate comparative worth. Criticism often involves analysis.

Define: Explain the exact meaning—usually, a meaning specific to the course or subject. Definitions are usually short.

Describe: Give a detailed account. Make a picture with words. List characteristics, qualities, and parts.

Discuss: Consider and debate or argue the pros and cons of an issue. Write about any conflict. Compare and contrast.

Explain: Make an idea clear. Show logically how a concept is developed. Give the reasons for an event.

Prove: Support with facts (especially facts presented in class or in the text).

Relate: Show the connections between ideas or events. Provide a larger context for seeing the big picture.

State: Explain precisely.

Summarize: Give a brief, condensed account. Include conclusions. Avoid unnecessary details.

Trace: Show the order of events or the progress of a subject or event.

Notice how these words differ. For example, *compare* asks you to do something different from *contrast*. Likewise, *criticize* and *explain* call for different responses. If any of these terms are still unclear to you, look them up in an unabridged dictionary.

Review these key words and other helpful vocabulary terms by using the flash cards online.

The test isn't over until . . .

MANY STUDENTS BELIEVE that a test is over as soon as they turn in the answer sheet. Consider another point of view: You're not done with a test until you know the answer to any question that you missed—and *why* you missed it.

Tests in many courses are cumulative—the content on the first test is assumed to be working knowledge for the second test, midterm, or final exam. When you understand the reasons for missed questions and lost points, you learn something. You also increase your odds of achieving better scores later in the course. Here are some ways to maximize the value of any test.

Immediately following the test. After finishing a test, your first thought might be to nap, snack, or celebrate. Restrain those impulses for a short while so that you can reflect on the test.

To begin, sit down in a quiet place. Take a few minutes to write some Discovery Statements related to your experience of taking the test. Describe how you felt about taking the test, how effective your review strategies were, and whether you accurately predicted the questions that appeared on the test.

Follow up with an Intention Statement or two. State what, if anything, you will do differently to prepare for the next test. Be specific.

When the test is returned. A returned test that includes a teacher's comments can be very valuable. First, make sure that the point totals are correct, and check for any grading errors. Next, ask these questions:

- On what material did the teacher base test questions—readings, lectures, discussions, or other class activities?
- What types of questions appeared in the test—objective (such as matching items, true/false questions, or multiple choice), short answer, or essay?
- What types of questions did you miss?
- Can you learn anything from the instructor's comments that will prepare you for the next test?
- What strategies did you use to prepare for this test? What would you do differently for your next test?

Also, see whether you can correct any answers that lost points. Carefully analyze the source of your errors, and find a solution. Consult the chart below for help. *

Source of test error	Possible solutions
Study errors—studying material that was not included on the test, or spending too little time on material that *did* appear on the test	• Ask your teacher about specific topics that will be included on a test. • Practice predicting test questions. • Form a study group with class members to create mock tests.
Careless errors, such as skipping or misreading directions	• Read and follow directions more carefully—especially when tests are divided into several sections with different directions. • Set aside time during the next test to proofread your answers.
Concept errors—mistakes made when you do not understand the underlying principles needed to answer a question or solve a problem	• Look for patterns in the questions you missed. • Make sure that you complete all assigned readings, attend all lectures, and show up for laboratory sessions. • Ask your teacher for help with specific questions.
Application errors—mistakes made when you understand underlying principles but fail to apply them correctly	• Rewrite your answers correctly. • When studying, spend more time solving sample problems. • Predict application questions that will appear in future tests, and practice answering them.
Test mechanics errors—missing more questions in certain parts of the test than others, changing correct answers to incorrect ones at the last minute, leaving items blank, miscopying answers from scratch paper to the answer sheet	• Set time limits for taking each section of a test, and stick to them. • Proofread your test answers carefully. • Look for patterns in the kind of answers you change at the last minute. • Change answers only if you can state a clear and compelling reason to do so.

The high costs of cheating

Cheating on tests can be a tempting strategy. It offers the chance to get a good grade without having to study.

INSTEAD OF STUDYING, we could spend more time watching TV, partying, sleeping, or doing anything that seems like more fun. Another benefit is that we could avoid the risk of doing poorly on a test—which could happen even if we *do* study.

Remember that cheating carries costs. Here are some consequences to consider.

We risk failing the course or getting expelled. The consequences for cheating are serious. Cheating can result in failing the assignment, failing the entire course, getting suspended, or getting expelled from school entirely. Documentation of cheating may also prevent you from being accepted to other schools.

We learn less. Some students argue that cheating is OK in courses that don't matter much. Actually, *all* courses matter. We can create value from any of them. If we look deeply enough, we can discover some idea or acquire some skill to prepare us for future courses or a career after graduation.

We lose time and money. Getting an education costs a lot of money. It also calls for years of sustained effort. Cheating sabotages our purchase. We pay full tuition and invest our energy without getting full value for it.

Fear of getting caught promotes stress. When we're fully aware of our emotions about cheating, we might discover intense stress. Even if we're not stressed, we're likely to feel *some* level of discomfort about getting caught.

Violating our values promotes stress. We might be able to cheat without getting caught. Yet we can still feel an additional layer of stress about violating our own ethical standards. At certain levels, stress can compromise our physical health and overall quality of life.

Cheating on tests can make it easier to violate our integrity again. Human beings become comfortable with behaviors that they repeat. Cheating is no exception.

Think about the first time you drove a car. You might have felt excited—even a little frightened. Now driving is probably second nature, and you don't give it much thought. Repeated experience with driving creates familiarity, which lessens the intense feelings you had during your first time at the wheel.

We can experience the same process with almost any behavior. Cheating once can make it easier to cheat again. And if we become comfortable with compromising our integrity in one area of life, we might find it easier to compromise in other areas.

Cheating lowers our self-concept. Whether or not we are fully aware of it, cheating sends us the message that we are not smart enough or responsible enough to make it on our own. We deny ourselves the celebration and satisfaction of authentic success.

An alternative to cheating is to become a master student. Ways to do this are described on every page of this book. *

Perils of high-tech cheating

Digital technology offers many blessings. It also expands the options for cheating during a test. For example, one student loaded class notes into a Sidekick (a handheld cellular device) and tried to read them. Another student dictated his class notes into files stored on his iPod and tried to listen to them. At one school, students used cell phones to take photos of test questions. They sent the photos to classmates outside the testing room, who responded by text-messaging the answers.[3]

All of these students were caught. Teachers are becoming sophisticated about detecting high-tech cheating. Some schools have cameras in exam rooms. Others use software that monitors the programs running on students' computers during tests. And some schools simply ban all digital devices during tests.

There's no need to learn the hard way—through painful consequences—about the high costs of high-tech cheating. Using the suggestions in this chapter can help you succeed on tests *and* preserve your academic integrity.

Let go of test anxiety

If you freeze during tests and flub questions when you know the answers, you might be dealing with test anxiety. Experiment with these solutions.

Yell "Stop!" When you notice that your mind is consumed with worries and fears—that your thoughts are spinning out of control—mentally yell, "Stop!" If you're in a situation that allows it, yell it out loud. This action can allow you to redirect your thoughts. Once you've broken the cycle of worry or panic, you can use any of the following techniques.

Dispute your thoughts. Certain thoughts tend to increase test anxiety. They often boil down to this statement: *Getting a low grade on a test is a disaster.* Do the math, however: A 4-year degree often involves taking 32–40 courses (8–10 courses per year over 4 years for a full-time student). This means that your final grade on any one course amounts to only 2 or 3 percent of your total grade point average.

Praise yourself. Many of us take the first opportunity to belittle ourselves: "Way to go, dummy! You don't even know the answer to the first question on the test." We wouldn't dream of treating a friend this way, yet we do it to ourselves. An alternative is to give yourself some encouragement: "I am prepared. I can do a great job on this test."

Consider the worst. Rather than trying to put a stop to your worrying, consider the very worst thing that could happen. Take your fear to the limit of absurdity: "Well, if I fail this test, I might fail the course, lose my financial aid, and get kicked out of school. Then I won't be able to get a job, so the bank will repossess my car, and I'll start drinking." Keep going until you see the absurdity of your predictions. After you stop chuckling, you can backtrack to discover a reasonable level of concern.

Breathe. You can calm down the physical sensations within your body by focusing your attention on your breathing. If you notice that you are taking short, shallow breaths, begin to take longer and deeper breaths.

Describe sensations. Describe your feelings of anxiety to yourself in detail. Don't resist them. When you completely admit and accept a physical sensation, it might even disappear.

Exercise aerobically. Performing aerobic exercise is an excellent way to reduce stress overall. Exercise regularly during the days you review for a test. See what effect it has on your ability to focus and relax during the test.

Get help. If you use any of the above techniques for a couple of weeks and they fail to work, then expand your options. Sometimes getting help with a specific situation—such as a lack of money—can relieve a source of stress that affects your success in school. Turn to the appropriate campus resource, such as your doctor, a counselor at your student health center, or the financial aid office. No matter what the source of anxiety, help is always available. *

Things I like to do

One way to relieve stress is to mentally substitute a pleasant image for unpleasant thoughts. Brainstorm a list of things you like to do. Start your list in the space below and continue on a separate piece of paper. Then use these images to calm yourself in stressful situations.

journal entry 

Discovery/Intention Statement

Notice your excuses and let them go

Do a timed, 4-minute brainstorm of all the reasons, rationalizations, justifications, and excuses you have used to avoid studying. Be creative. Start listing your thoughts in the space below and expand on additional paper:

Now write a Discovery Statement about the list you just created.

I discovered that I . . .

Next, review your list, pick the excuse that you use the most, and circle it. In the space below, write an Intention Statement about what you will do to begin eliminating your favorite excuse. Make this Intention Statement one that you can keep, with a timeline and a reward.

I intend to . . .

journal entry 

Discovery Statement

Explore your feelings about tests

Complete the following sentences.

As exam time gets closer, one thing I notice that I do is . . .

When it comes to taking tests, I have trouble . . .

The night before a test, I usually feel . . .

The morning of a test, I usually feel . . .

During a test, I usually feel . . .

After a test, I usually feel . . .

When I learn a test score, I usually feel . . .

Do this Journal Entry online.

Getting ready for math tests

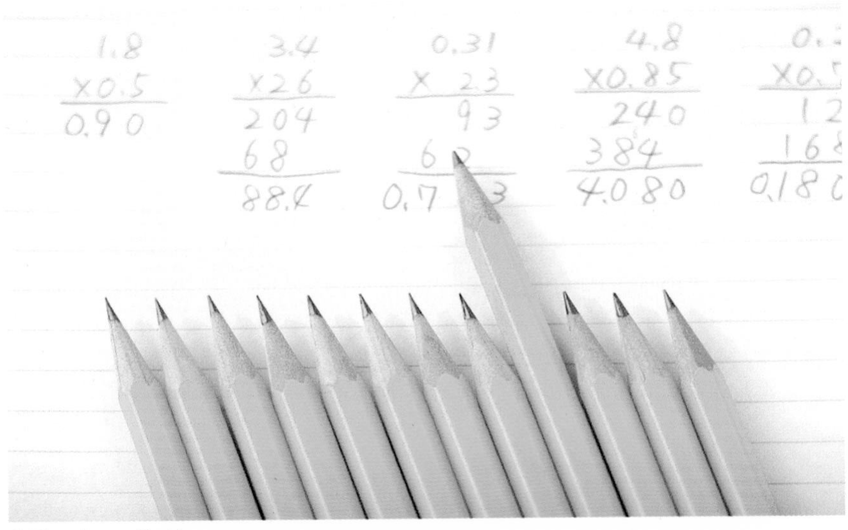

© Bloomimage/Corbis

Connect math to life. Pause occasionally to get an overview of the branch of math that you're studying. What's it all about? What basic problems is it designed to solve? How do people apply this knowledge in daily life? For example, many architects, engineers, and space scientists use calculus daily.

Take a First Step. Math is cumulative. Concepts build upon each other in a certain order. If you struggled with algebra, you may have trouble with trigonometry or calculus.

To ensure that you have an adequate base of knowledge, tell the truth about your current level of knowledge and skill. Before you register for a math course, locate assigned texts for the prerequisite courses. If the material in those books seems new or difficult for you, see the instructor. Ask for suggestions on ways to prepare for the course.

Remember that it's OK to continue your study of math from your current level of ability, whatever that level might be.

Choose teachers with care. Whenever possible, find a math teacher whose approach to math matches your learning style. Talk with several teachers until you find one you enjoy.

Another option is to ask around. Maybe your academic advisor can recommend math teachers. Also ask classmates to name their favorite math teachers—and to explain the reasons for their choices.

In some cases, only one teacher will be offering the math course you need. The suggestions that follow can be used to learn from a teacher regardless of her teaching style.

Take math courses back to back. Approach math in the same way that you learn a foreign language. If you take a year off in between Spanish I and Spanish II, you won't gain much fluency. To master a language, you take courses back to back. It works the same way with math, which is a language in itself.

Form a study group. During the first week of each math course, organize a study group. Ask each member to bring five problems to group meetings, along with solutions. Also exchange contact information so that you can stay in touch via e-mail, phone, and text messaging.

Avoid short courses. Courses that you take during summer school or another shortened term are condensed. You might find yourself doing far more reading and homework each week than you do in longer courses. If you enjoy math, the extra intensity can provide a stimulus to learn. But if math is not your favorite subject, give yourself extra time. Enroll in courses spread out over more calendar days.

Participate fully. Success in math depends on your active involvement. Attend class regularly. Complete homework assignments *when they're due*—not just before the test. If you're confused, get help right away from an instructor, tutor, or study group. Instructors' office hours, free on-campus tutoring, and classmates are just a few of the resources available to you. Also build on class participation by scheduling time for homework. Make daily contact with math.

Prepare for several types of tests. Math tests often involve lists of problems to solve. Ask your instructor about what type of tests to expect. Then prepare for the tests using strategies from this chapter.

Ask questions fearlessly. It's a cliché and it's true: In math, there are no dumb questions. Ask whatever questions will aid your understanding. Keep a running list of them, and bring the list to class.

Make your text your top priority. Math courses are often text driven. Class activities closely follow the book. This means that it is important to complete your reading assignments. Master one concept before going on to the next, and stay current with your reading. Be willing to read slowly and reread sections as needed.

Read actively. To get the most out of your math texts, read with paper and pencil in hand. Work out examples. Copy diagrams, formulas, and equations. Use chapter summaries and introductory outlines to organize your learning. From time to time, stop, close your book, and mentally reconstruct the steps in solving a problem. Before you memorize a formula, understand the basic concepts behind it.

Practice solving problems. When preparing for math tests, work *lots* of problems. Find out whether practice problems or previous tests are on file in the library, in the math department, or with your math teacher. Isolate the types of problems that you find the most difficult. Practice them more often. Be sure to get help with these kinds of problems *before* exhaustion or frustration sets in.

Practice working problems fast. Time yourself. This is a great activity for math study groups.

Practice test taking. Part of preparing for any math test is rehearsal. Instead of passively reading through your text or scanning class notes, do a practice test:

- Print out a set of practice problems, and set a timer for the same length of time as your testing period.
- Whenever possible, work practice problems in the same room where you will take the actual test.
- Use only the kinds of supporting materials—such as scratch paper or lists of formulas—that will be allowed during the test.
- As you work problems, use deep breathing or another technique to enter a more relaxed state.

Ask appropriate questions. During the test, if you don't understand a test item, ask for clarification. The worst that can happen is that an instructor or proctor will politely decline to answer your question.

Write legibly. Put yourself in the instructor's place. Imagine the prospect of grading stacks of illegible answer sheets. Make your answers easy to read. If you show your work, underline key sections and circle your answer.

Do your best. There are no secrets involved in getting ready for math tests. Master some stress management techniques, do your homework, get answers to your questions, and work sample problems. If you've done those things, you're ready for the test and deserve to do well. If you haven't done all those things, just do the best you can.

Remember that your personal best can vary from test to test, and even from day to day. Even if you don't answer all test questions correctly, you can demonstrate what you *do* know right now.

During the test, notice when solutions come easily. Savor the times when you feel relaxed and confident. If you ever feel math anxiety in the future, these are the times to remember.[4] *

18 critical thinking exercise: Use learning styles for math success

Review the articles about learning styles in Chapter 1: "First Steps." Look for strategies that could promote your success in math. Modify any of the suggested strategies so that they work for you, or invent new techniques of your own. If you're a visual learner, for example, you might color code your notes by writing key terms and formulas in red ink. If you like to learn by speaking and listening, consider reading key passages in your textbooks out loud. And if you're a kinesthetic learner, use "manipulatives"—such as magnetic boards with letters and numbers—when you study math. Whatever you choose, commit to using at least one new strategy. In the space below, describe what you will do.

Eight reasons to celebrate mistakes

Most of us are haunted by the fear of failure. We dread the thought of making mistakes or being held responsible for a major breakdown. We shudder at the missteps, fearing they could cost us grades, careers, money, or even relationships. It's possible to take an entirely different attitude toward mistakes. Rather than fearing them, we could actually *celebrate* them.

A creative environment is one in which failure is not fatal. Innovation requires risk taking, despite the chance of failure. And that's just one reason to celebrate mistakes. Following are eight more.

1 Celebration allows us to notice the mistake. Celebrating mistakes gets them out into the open. This activity is the opposite of covering up mistakes or blaming others for them. Hiding mistakes takes a lot of energy. That energy that could be channeled into correcting errors.

2 Mistakes are valuable feedback. There's an old story about the manager of a major corporation who made a mistake that cost his company $100,000. The manager predicted that he would be fired. Instead, his boss said, "Fire you? I can't afford to do that. I just spent $100,000 training you." This story may be fictional, but it makes a point: Mistakes are part of the learning process. In fact, mistakes are often more interesting and more instructive than are successes.

3 Mistakes demonstrate that we're taking risks. People who play it safe make few mistakes. Making mistakes can be evidence that we're stretching to the limit of our abilities—growing, risking, and learning. Fear of making mistakes can paralyze us. Celebrating mistakes helps us move into gear and get things done.

4 Celebrating mistakes reminds us that it's OK to make them. When we celebrate a mistake, we remind ourselves that the person who made the mistake is not bad—just human. This is *not* a recommendation that you purposely set out to make mistakes. Mistakes are not an end in themselves. Rather, their value lies in what we learn from them. When we make a mistake, we can admit it and correct it.

5 Celebrating mistakes includes everyone. Celebrating mistakes reminds us that the exclusive club named the Perfect Performance Society has no members. All of us make mistakes. When we notice them, we can work together. Blaming others or the system prevents the cooperative efforts that can improve our circumstances.

6 Mistakes occur only when we aim at a clear goal. We can express concern about missing a target only if the target is there in the first place. If there's no target or purpose, there's no concern about missing it. Making a mistake affirms something of great value—that we have a plan.

7 Mistakes happen only when we're committed to making things work. Systems work when people are willing to be held accountable. Openly admitting mistakes promotes accountability. Imagine a school where there's no concern about quality and effectiveness. Teachers usually come to class late. Residence halls are never cleaned, and scholarship checks are always late. The administration is in chronic debt, students seldom pay tuition on time, and no one cares. In this school, the word *mistake* would have little meaning. Mistakes become apparent only when people are committed to improvement. Mistakes go hand in hand with a commitment to quality.

8 Celebrating mistakes cuts the problem down to size. On top of the mistake itself, there is often a layer of regret about having *made* the mistake in the first place. When we celebrate mistakes, we release that extra baggage. Then we can get down to the business of correcting the mistake. *

DETACH

This Power Process helps you release the powerful, natural student within you. It is especially useful whenever negative emotions are getting in your way.

Attachments are addictions. When we are attached to something, we think we cannot live without it, just as a drug addict feels he cannot live without drugs. We believe that our well-being depends on maintaining our attachments.

We can be attached to just about anything: beliefs, emotions, people, roles, objects. The list is endless.

One person, for example, might be so attached to his car that he takes an accident as a personal attack. Pity the poor unfortunate who backs into this person's car. He might as well back into the owner himself.

Another person might be attached to her job. Her identity and sense of well-being depend on it. She could become suicidally depressed if she ever got fired.

When we are attached and things don't go our way, we can feel angry, sad, afraid, or confused.

Suppose you are attached to getting an A on your physics test. You feel as though your success in life depends on getting that A. As the clock ticks away, you work harder on the test, getting more stuck. That voice in your head gets louder: "I must get an A. I MUST get an A. I MUST GET AN A!"

Now is a time to detach. Practice observer consciousness. See whether you can just *observe* what's going on, letting go of all your judgments. When you just observe, you reach a quiet state above and beyond your usual thoughts. This is a place where you can be aware of being aware. From this tranquil spot, you can see yourself objectively, as if you were someone else.

Pay attention to your thoughts and physical sensations. If you feel stuck, just notice that. If your palms are sweaty and your stomach is one big knot, just admit it.

Also get a broader perspective. Imagine how much this moment will matter 1 hour, 1 day, 1 week, or 1 year from now.

In addition, practice breathing. Calm your mind and body with relaxation techniques.

Practice detaching before the big test. The key is to let go of automatic emotional reactions when you don't get what you want.

Caution: Giving up an *attachment* to being an A student does not mean giving up *being* an A student. Giving up an attachment to a job doesn't mean giving up the job. When you detach, you get to keep your values and goals. However, you know that you will be OK even if you fail to achieve a goal. You are more than your goals. You are more than your thoughts and feelings. These things come and go. Meanwhile, the part of you that can *just observe* is always there and always safe, no matter what happens.

Behind your attachments is a master student. Release that mastery. Detach.

Learn more about this Power Process online.

Put it to Work

You can use strategies from *Becoming a Master Student* to succeed at work. To discover how your test-taking skills can transfer to your career, reflect on the following case study.

During his senior year of high school, Chang Lee read about the favorable job market for medical assistants. He set a goal to enroll in a local community college, earn his associate of arts (A.A.) degree in medical assisting, work for a few years, and then return to school for a nursing degree.

This career plan was a logical one for Chang. His mother worked as a psychiatric nurse, and he'd always been interested in health care. He figured that his degree would equip him with marketable skills and a way to contribute to society.

Chang's choice was a good one for him. He excelled in his classes. With his career goal in mind, he often asked himself, "How could I use this information to become a better medical assistant?"

During his second year of college, Chang landed an internship with a large medical clinic near campus. The clinic offered him a job after he graduated, and he accepted.

Chang enjoyed the day-to-day tasks of medical assisting. He helped doctors run medical tests and perform physical exams. In addition, he ordered lab work and updated medical records.

After 3 months on the job, Chang was on a first-name basis with many of the clinic's regular patients. No matter how busy the clinic's schedule, Chang made time for people. When they finished describing their symptoms, he frequently asked, "Is there anything else that's on your mind?" Then he listened without interrupting. Chang's ability to put people at ease made him popular with patients, who often asked specifically to see him.

The only part of his job that Chang dreaded was performance reviews, which took place twice during each year of employment. Even though he was respected by coworkers, Chang felt nervous whenever the topic of evaluating work performance came up. "It just reminds me too much of final exams during school," he said. "I like my job, and I try to do it well every day. Having a performance review just raises my anxiety level and doesn't really benefit me."

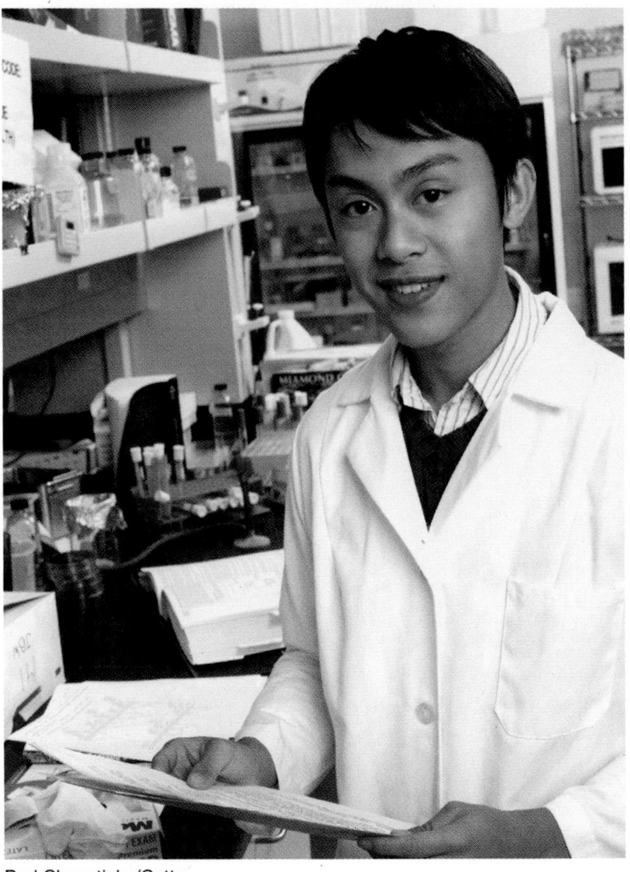

Red Chopsticks/Getty

Chang applied several strategies recommended in this book. For example, he demonstrated a knowledge of learning styles by tying the content of his courses to concrete experience ("How can I *use* this information?").

Describe some strategies that Chang could use to deal with anxiety related to performance reviews:

____

____

____

____

____

Remember that you might face performance reviews, licensing exams, certification exams, and other tests in your career field. Like Chang, you can apply many techniques from this chapter to the workplace. For example, joining study groups while you are in school can help you expand your learning styles and succeed in project teams. Use higher education to develop teamwork skills.

Name____ Date____/____/____

1. **According to the text, test scores measure your accomplishments in a course. True or false? Explain your answer.**
   False. Test scores are a measure of how well we do on tests. (*Disarm tests,* p. 135)
2. **When answering multiple-choice questions, it is better to read all of the possible answers before answering the question in your head. True or false? Explain your answer.**
   False. Answer the question in your head before you look at any of the options. If you come up with an answer you are confident is right, then look for that answer in the list of choices. (*What to do during the test,* pp. 139–141)
3. **Absolute qualifiers such as *always* or *never* generally indicate a false statement. True or false? Explain your answer.**
   True. Qualifiers include words such as *all, most, sometimes,* and *rarely*. Absolute qualifiers are words like *always* and *never*—such extremes generally indicate a false statement. (*What to do during the test,* pp. 139–141)
4. **Briefly explain the difference between a daily review and a major review.**
   Daily reviews include short preclass and postclass reviews of lecture notes and brief text reviews. Major reviews are usually done about a week before an exam and are much longer study periods, such as 2 to 5 hours per session. (*What to do before the test,* p. 136)
5. **Define the term *study checklist*, and give three examples of what to include on such a checklist.**
   Checklists are to-do lists that contain the briefest possible description of each item to study. List at least three of the following examples of what to include
   - Reading assignments listed by page or chapter number.
   - Dates of lecture notes.
   - Types of problems to be solved.
   - Skills to master.
   - Major ideas, definitions, theories, formulas, and equations

   (Answers will vary.) (*What to do before the test,* p. 136)
6. **Describe how using the Power Process: "Detach" differs from giving up.**
   "Giving up" means to stop taking action toward a goal you have. In contrast, detachment involves accepting emotions and understanding the details of those emotions. Once you accept and fully experience your emotions, you can more easily move beyond them. Yet, the more you deny them, the more they persist. When we are detached, we perform better. (*Power Process: Detach,* p. 149)
7. **Study groups can focus on which of the following?**
   (a) Comparing and editing class notes
   (b) Brainstorming ideas for papers and presentations
   (c) Finding and explaining key passages in assigned readings
   (d) Creating and taking practice tests
   (e) All of the above
   (e) All of the above (*Cooperative learning: Studying in groups,* pp. 137–138)
8. **Explain a connection between taking a First Step and succeeding in math courses.**
   Because math is cumulative and concepts build upon each other in a certain order, it is important to ensure that you have an adequate base of knowledge. The first step to success is to tell the truth about your current level of knowledge and skill. Before you register for a math course, locate assigned texts for the prerequisite courses. If the material in those books seems new or difficult for you, see the instructor. Ask for suggestions on ways to prepare for the course. (Answers will vary.) (*Getting ready for math tests*, pp. 146–147)
9. **Describe three techniques for dealing with test anxiety.**
   Describe at least three of the following:
   - Yell "Stop!"
   - Dispute your thoughts.
   - Praise yourself.
   - Consider the worst.
   - Breathe.
   - Describe sensations.
   - Exercise aerobically.
   - Get help. (*Let go of test anxiety,* p. 144)
10. **List a common source of test errors and two ways to prevent such errors.**
    List one of the following sources and possible solutions:
    - Study errors: Practice predicting test questions; form a study group.
    - Careless errors: Read directions more carefully; proofread your answers.
    - Concept errors: Look for patterns in your errors; complete all readings/assignments; ask your teacher for help.
    - Application errors: Rewrite your answers correctly; spend more time on solving sample problems; predict and answer application questions.
    - Test mechanics errors: Set time limits for taking each section of a test; proofread your test answers; look for patterns in your errors; change answers only if you are certain. (*The test isn't over until . . .,* p. 142)

Skills Snapshot

Now that you've had some concrete experience with the strategies presented in this chapter, take a minute to reflect on your responses to the Tests section of the Discovery Wheel on page 23-25. Expand on those responses by completing the following sentences.

PREPARING FOR TESTS

When studying for a test, the first thing I usually do is to . . .

In addition, I . . .

TAKING TESTS

One strategy that helps me with objective tests (true/false and multiple choice) is . . .

One strategy that helps me with short-answer and essay tests is . . .

MANAGING TEST ANXIETY

On the day of a test, my level of confidence is generally . . .

If I feel stressed about a test, I respond by . . .

NEXT ACTION

I'll know that I've reached a new level of mastery with tests when . . .

To reach that level of mastery, the most important thing I can do next is to . . .

Bert and John Jacobs

. . . are positive

© John Rich Photography

Bert Jacobs (1965–) and John Jacobs (1968–), whose jobs are "chief executive optimist" and "chief creative optimist," started their business by selling their T-shirts out of the back of a van.

"Life is good" says the T-shirt, the hoodie, the baseball cap, and the onesie, to which one might reasonably respond in these days of doom and gloom: Really?

When Bert and John Jacobs launched their self-described optimistic apparel company out of a Boston apartment 15 years ago, we were smack in the middle of the go-go '90s, and those three little words—part lifestyle, part mantra, part last-ditch effort by a pair of struggling T-shirt entrepreneurs to make rent money—seemed to mirror the national mood.

Today, not so much. Which, oddly enough, might make this something of a golden moment for the Life is good company.

"It is generally people who face the greatest adversity who embrace this message the most," says Bert Jacobs, whose company Web site features a section of "inspiring letters that fuel us all to keep spreading good vibes." The letters include testimonials from survivors of a grizzly bear attack, a young amputee, and a soldier stationed in Iraq.

Life is good doesn't have a demographic, the brothers like to say, but rather a psychographic: the optimists. And while one might imagine that their numbers are dwindling at roughly the same rate as their retirement accounts, some observers suggest otherwise. . . .

That's not to say Life is good is immune to the downturn, but in this company's case it's all relative. . . .

Until last year the company, whose annual sales top $100 million, had never had a year with less than 30 percent growth. In 2008, it grew only 10 percent, a slowdown that Jacobs notes (in apropos parlance) is "not exactly something you bum out about." Especially since the company hasn't spent a dime on advertising. . . .

Life is good was tested once before, not by the company's customers but its employees. In the days following 9/11, a number of managers approached Bert Jacobs and said that they weren't feeling right about spreading the company's signature tidings. Some had lost friends in the attacks. Maybe life wasn't so good, and maybe this was not the message the American people wanted to hear.

But the company forged ahead, launching its first (wildly successful) nationwide fund-raiser. Jacobs calls it the pivotal moment in the company's history. This led to the formation of the Life is good Kids Foundation, which has since raised millions of dollars for children facing life-threatening challenges.

"Our company has this fantastic positive energy and our brand is capable of bringing people together," he says. "We know there's trauma and violence and hardship. Life is good isn't the land of Willy Wonka. We're not throwing Frisbees all day. We live in the real world. But you can look around you and find good things any time."

For more information on Bert and John Jacobs and Life is good, visit www.lifeisgood.com

Joan Anderson, "A Positive Outlook? Apparel company says bad times make its message more vital," *The Boston Globe*, March 17, 2009, www.boston.com/lifestyle/fashion/articles/2009/03/17/a_positive_outlook/?page=1.

Learn more about Bert and John Jacobs at the Master Student Hall of Fame.

7 Thinking

Instructor Tools & Tips

> I always wanted to be somebody, but I should've been more specific.
>
> **—Lily Tomlin**

> Creativity was in each one of us as a small child. In children it is universal. Among adults it is almost nonexistent. The great question is: What has happened to this enormous and universal human capacity?
>
> **—Tillie Olsen**

Preview

Critical thinking is an essential skill for success in the classroom and in the workplace. Although critical thinking has already been introduced through the Master Student Map, Skills Snapshots, Journal Entries, and Critical Thinking Exercises, Chapter 7 takes a more in-depth look at how students can practice the strategies presented in Chapters 1 through 6, using higher levels of thinking. At this point, your students will probably have taken their first tests in some of their other courses and will have become familiar with the learning strategies presented in the earlier chapters of *Becoming a Master Student*. Now you can help them take the next step toward thinking critically in higher education. The skills they learn in this chapter can be applied immediately to one decision that most of your students must make—choosing a major.

A primary objective of the student success course is to nurture the fundamental skill of critical thinking. From the beginning of this text, your students have been using the Master Student Map as a means of thinking critically. When they ask *Why* they need this chapter, have them complete a chapter reconnaissance of *What* new materials are in this chapter. Together you can discuss *How* these new ideas will help them become better students. Remind your students that, with these techniques, they can open the door of possibility *(What if?)* to solve problems more creatively and make decisions with confidence.

Guest Speaker

Critical thinking is a priority in many workplace scenarios. A police officer, attorney, or law school professor would be a great guest speaker for this chapter. These guests can provide students with a dramatic reality check that will help you reinforce the importance of critical thinking in the real world. Ask your guests to prepare to talk for approximately 10 minutes on the importance of critical thinking in their jobs.

Another guest speaker idea is to invite a colleague from the department that offers critical and/or creative thinking courses, or logic courses. Ask this speaker to talk about classes that students can take to expand on the concepts they learn in this chapter.

Choosing a major is an important decision that troubles many students. Invite the director of your Career Center to speak to your class about the center's services.

Lecture

Use the following excerpt from Vincent Ryan Ruggiero's *Instructor's Resource Manual to Accompany Becoming a Critical Thinker,* Fifth Edition, copyright 2006 (reprinted by permission), to help you prepare lectures for this chapter:

> As a result of the historic neglect of thinking, many people harbor misconceptions about thinking instruction. The following misconceptions are the most damaging:
>
> **That thinking can't be taught.** A related misconception is that thinking can be taught only to "gifted" people. The basis of both misconceptions is the pessimistic view that intelligence is fixed and therefore cannot be increased. Formal research and the experience of innumerable thinking-skills instructors disprove this notion.
>
> **That thinking is taught automatically in certain courses.** Some people reason that English courses teach thinking automatically because they deal with the expression of ideas and because expression is intimately connected to thought. Others make similar claims for science because it deals with scientific method, history because it deals with the record of human thought and

ANNOTATED INSTRUCTOR'S EDITION

action, or psychology because it deals with behavior. Research has long made clear that no course content, by itself, can teach thinking; in other words, thinking skills are developed only when students receive direct instruction in them and have frequent opportunities for guided practice.

That thinking skills are necessarily subject-specific. According to this view, economists use one set of thinking skills, biologists another, and anthropologists yet another; no generic thinking skills exist. Yet close examination of what thinkers do in everyday situations reveals great similarity in their patterns of thought. Moreover, the patterns of error are also remarkably similar. That is why the list of logical fallacies has remained essentially the same since the time of the ancient Greeks. Though different academic disciplines may employ certain patterns of thinking more often and in slightly different ways than others, the fundamental fact is that the human mind created the academic disciplines and is neither defined nor limited by them.

That students learn to think by being exhorted or inspired. Exhortation and inspiration can surely motivate students to learn, but these approaches have little if any teaching force, particularly where skills are involved. No one ever learned to master driving a car or playing the piccolo or dribbling a basketball by hearing a lecture. Similarly, intellectual skills are learned by doing and by receiving guidance and encouragement from knowledgeable people.

Exercises/Activities

1. **Four ways to solve problems (page 162).** Have students practice problem solving and noticing assumptions by completing an in-class case study. Have them do this in groups of four. Individually, they read the short case study in class. Then they discuss it in their group. Facilitate a full-class discussion so that students can hear what other groups came up with. For examples and more information about using case studies in your classroom, go to the Instructor Companion site.

2. Here's a suggestion from TeamUp Consultant Michelle Martin:

> As a warm-up exercise or icebreaker for this chapter, I put my students into groups and give each group an ordinary household object (such as a napkin, candle, coaster, cup). Then I have the groups brainstorm ways to use the objects in a different fashion from the most obviously intended purpose. This helps students embrace different ways of thinking and stretches their minds to see things in new ways.

3. **Becoming a critical thinker (pages 156–157).** Select a current controversial topic and bring in background information from newspapers and magazines about the topic. Divide students into groups and have them work through the issue using the four-step process described in the article "Becoming a critical thinker." Have each group present a 90-second summary report to the class about their position on the issue and their justification for that position.

Conversation/Sharing

Use the think-pair-share discussion pattern to facilitate a dialog about the media's influence on our lives. First, ask students to think critically about the topic and then have them free-write for a minute about their thoughts on the matter and about the learning style questions. They need to feel that they can jot down their own ideas without worrying about what you might expect or want them to say. Then have students work in pairs to share their ideas. Cycle through the learning style questions and then discuss the topic as a class. More detailed information about this exercise is available on the Instructor Companion site.

Homework

Examining different points of view. This is an in-class and homework alternative to the Conversation/Sharing activity above. Have students read a newspaper article about a current controversial issue and then answer the first two learning style questions (*Why?* and *What?*) based on the information in the article. Then have them form groups of four to discuss their ideas. Eventually, someone will say that there is not enough information in the article to explore all of the various views on the topic. This provides you with an opportunity to ask students to continue this project outside the classroom, using campus resources (such as the library and the Internet) to fully answer the second and third (*What?* and *How?*) learning style questions. They should also work on the fourth question *(What if?)* at home. At the next class meeting, have your students discuss their findings and draw conclusions.

Gaining skill at decision making (page 162). Selecting classes is an important decision for students, but too often the hectic process of registering for classes results in a schedule based on convenience rather than critical decision making. Ask students to follow the systematic procedure described in the article "Gaining skill at decision making" to decide which classes to take next semester—before the schedule of classes has been published.

Choosing your major (pages 164–165). After your students have listened to the guest lecture from the Director of the Career Center, have them do a follow-up assignment that involves visiting the Career Center and exploring possible majors. Ask them to write a brief report on what they learned at the center about themselves and about potential careers and/or majors. Have students work through Critical Thinking Exercise 20 and Journal Entry 18 to further explore their thoughts on selecting a major.

Here is a suggestion from an instructor:

> Choosing your major is a major topic in my course. My background is in career counseling. Statistics back up the assumption that students make better grades and are less likely to drop out if they have selected a major and have a good handle on a future career. In my class (and at our school) students are required to complete an exploration paper. They set academic and career goals (even if it's to select a major and career) [and] generate career ideas using a variety of methods (including interest/skills/personality inventories). Students select one career and major to research, complete an informational interview, and finally write a paper reviewing what they have done/researched and any conclusions they have drawn.
>
> **—Terry Carles, Valencia Community College**

Power Process: Find a Bigger Problem (page 169). Some students feel trapped by their personal situation or by learning problems, to the point that their ability to succeed in school is seriously impaired. This article can help students recognize that there are other ways to view their problems. Students can look for ways to get involved in activities that take them outside their own circumstances. Each term, organize a community service project with a local agency as a way to demonstrate that "finding a bigger problem" helps bring their own problems into perspective.

Evaluation

With the skills students have learned about essay test answers in Chapter 6, they are prepared to answer essay questions that require critical thinking. Ask them to justify their answers to open-ended questions about common mistakes in logic, problem solving, or thinking critically about information on the Internet.

Additional Digital Resources

CHAPTER 7

Course Manual

The online *Course Manual* serves as an invaluable reference for those developing and teaching a College Success course with *Becoming a Master Student Concise*. The *Course Manual* provides advice on general teaching issues such as preparing for classes, classroom management, grading, and communicating with students of various backgrounds, as well as specific strategies on getting the most out of various features in *Becoming a Master Student Concise* and book-specific Web sites. Do a *Course Manual* reconnaissance to find ideas that you can use in your course right now.

Instructor Companion Site

The updated Instructor Companion Site provides resources to help you plan and customize your course. Content specific to Chapter 7 includes:

- Lecture Ideas
  - Thriving in the Age of Information
- In-Class Exercises
  - Increasing Awareness
  - Circle Brainstorming
  - Speech Creativity Exercise
  - Who Says So? A Critical Thinking Lesson
- In-Text Quiz Answers
- PowerPoint Slides

The Instructor Companion Site also contains the following book-specific content:

- ExamView Test Bank
- Online Course Manual
- Sample Syllabi
- Detailed Transition Guide

College Success CourseMate

To help your students gain a better understanding of the topics discussed in *Becoming a Master Student Concise*, encourage them to visit the CourseMate at CengageBrain.com that provides the following resources specific to Chapter 7:

- Connect to Text content expands on specific topics marked with an icon within Chapter 7.
- Practice Tests allow students to see how well they understand the themes of *Becoming a Master Student Concise.*
- Interactive Concept Maps promote critical thinking by highlighting related ideas to show relationships among concepts.
- Video Skillbuilders bring to life techniques that will help students to excel in college and beyond. The following videos should give your students more information regarding topics covered in Chapter 7:
  - Critical Thinking: What is Critical Thinking?
  - Critical Thinking in Action: Career Planning
  - Exploring Majors
- Learning Styles Application
- Discussion Topics
- Reflection Questions
- Assessment Questions
- Experiment with chapter strategies
- Remembering Cultural Differences presents readers with brief articles that touch on aspects of diversity in our rapidly changing world. For Chapter 7, the following article will prompt your students to look at contemporary issues in a new way:
  - Perceptions of Engagement
- Master Student Profiles provide additional information on the people covered in this book feature. For Chapter 7, students will find expanded coverage and links about:
  - Twyla Tharp
- Power Process Media contains video, PowerPoints, and audio files to take what your students have learned from the Power Processes in their book to the next level. For Chapter 7, students will find additional media on:
  - Find a Bigger Problem

Along with the chapter-specific content, a General Resources folder is available that contains Toolboxes geared toward specific student types (Community College, Adult Learner, Student Athlete), the Plagiarism Prevention Zone, and the Career Resource Center.

7 Thinking

Master Student Map

as you read, ask yourself

what if . . .

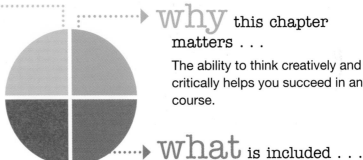

I could solve problems more creatively and make decisions in every area of life with more confidence?

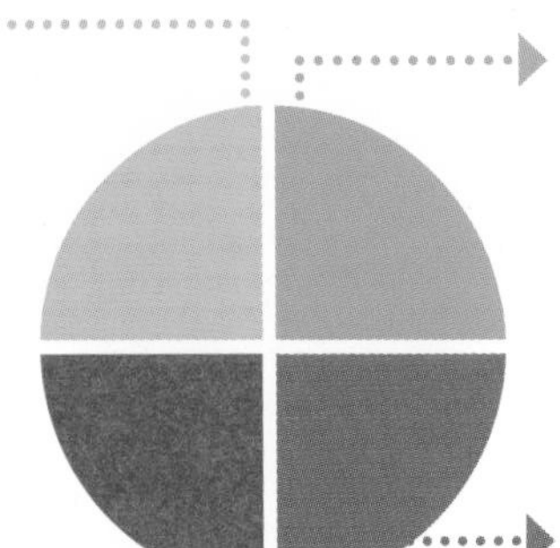

why this chapter matters . . .

The ability to think creatively and critically helps you succeed in any course.

how you can use this chapter . . .

- Read, write, speak, and listen more effectively.
- Learn strategies to succeed at problem solving.
- Apply thinking skills to practical decisions, such as choosing a major.

what is included . . .

MASTER STUDENTS in *action*

I think critical thinking is when you're presented with a problem or a scenario and you don't just go with your gut reaction. You have to look at the problem from many different angles and weigh different options before you decide what is the right answer.

—LAUREN SWIDLER

Photo courtesy of Lea Dean

Critical thinking: A survival skill

SOCIETY DEPENDS ON persuasion. Advertisers want us to spend money on their products. Political candidates want us to "buy" their stands on the issues. Teachers want us to agree that their classes are vital to our success. Parents want us to accept their values. Authors want us to read their books and Web sites. Broadcasters want us to spend our time in front of the radio or television, consuming their programs and not those of the competition. The business of persuasion has an impact on all of us.

It's easy to lose our wits in the crosscurrent of competing ideas—unless we develop skills in critical thinking. When we think critically, we make choices with open eyes.

Novelist Ernest Hemingway once said that all of us could benefit from having a "built-in, automatic crap detector."[1] That inelegant comment points to a basic truth: As critical thinkers, we are constantly on the lookout for thinking that's inaccurate, sloppy, or misleading.

At various times in human history, nonsense has been taken for the truth. For example, people once believed that

- Use of blood-sucking leeches is the recommended treatment for most disease.
- Illness results from an imbalance in the four vital fluids: blood, phlegm, water, and bile.
- Caucasians are inherently more intelligent than people of other races.
- Racial intermarriage will lead to genetically inferior children.
- Racial integration of the armed forces will destroy soldiers' morale.
- Women are incapable of voting intelligently.
- We will never invent anything smaller than a transistor. (That was before the computer chip.)
- Computer technology will usher in the age of the paperless office.

The critical thinkers of history arose to challenge such ideas. These courageous men and women pointed out that—metaphorically speaking—the emperor had no clothes.

Critical thinking is a path to freedom from half-truths and deception. You have the right to question everything that you see, hear, and read. Acquiring this ability is a major goal of a liberal education.

In addition, critical thinking helps us thrive with diversity. Thinking uncovers bias and prejudice. Questioning our assumptions is a First Step to communicating with people of other races, ethnic backgrounds, and cultures.

It's been said that human beings are rational creatures. Yet no one is born a critical or creative thinker. These are learned skills. Use the suggestions in this chapter to claim the thinking powers that are your birthright. The skilled thinker is one aspect of the master student who lives inside you. *

journal entry 

Discovery/Intention Statement

Choose to create value from this chapter

Think back to a time when you felt unable to choose among several different solutions to a problem or several stands on a key issue in your life. In the space below, describe this experience.

I discovered that . . .

____

____

____

Now scan this chapter to find useful suggestions for decision making, problem solving, and critical thinking. Note below at least four techniques that look especially promising to you.

Strategy	**Page number**

Finally, declare your intention to explore these techniques in detail and apply them to a situation coming up during this term.

I intend to use critical thinking strategies to . . .

____

____

____

____

Becoming a critical thinker

Critical thinking is a path to intellectual adventure. Although there are dozens of possible approaches, the process boils down to *asking and answering questions.*

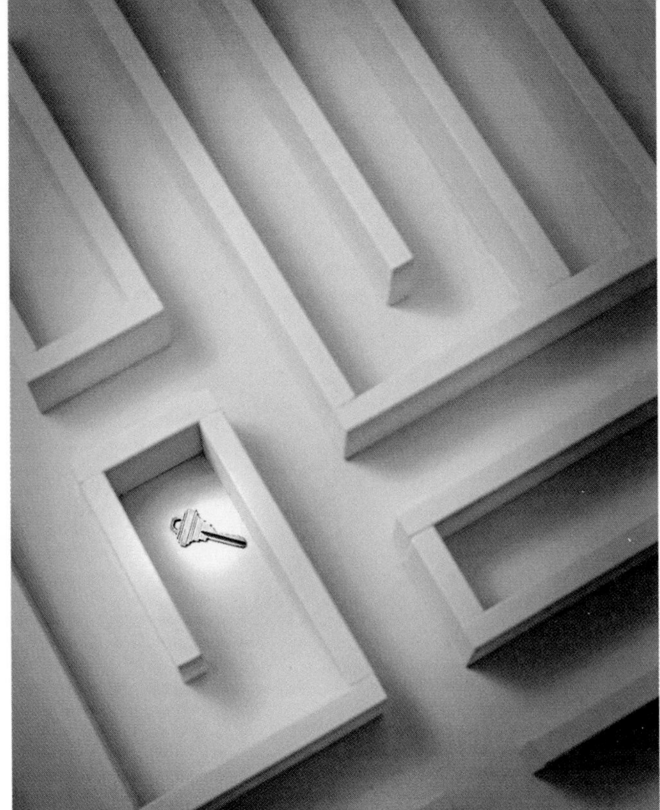
© Steve Cole/Getty

ACCORDING TO "Learning styles: Discovering how you learn" (page 34), there are four modes of learning based on four questions: *Why? What? How?* and *What if?* These questions are also powerful guides to critical thinking. Following are a variety of tools for answering those questions. For more handy implements, see *Becoming a Critical Thinker*, by Vincent Ryan Ruggiero.

1 Why am I considering this issue? Critical thinking and personal passion go together. Begin critical thinking with a question that matters to you. Seek a rationale for your learning. Understand why it is important for you to think about a specific topic. You might want to arrive at a new conclusion, make a prediction, choose a major, choose a mate, or solve a pressing problem. By finding a personal connection with an issue, your interest in acquiring and retaining new information increases.

2 What are various points of view on this issue? Imagine Karl Marx, Cesar Chavez, and Warren Buffet assembled in one room to choose the most desirable economic system. Picture Mahatma Gandhi, Nelson Mandela, and General George Patton lecturing at a United Nations conference on conflict resolution. Visualize Al Gore, Bill Gates, and Ban Ki-moon in a discussion about distributing the world's resources equitably. When seeking out alternative points of view, let such scenarios unfold in your mind.

Dozens of viewpoints exist on every important issue—reducing crime, ending world hunger, preventing war, educating our children, and countless other concerns. In fact, few problems have any single, permanent solution. Each generation produces its own answers to critical questions, based on current conditions. Our search for answers is a conversation that spans centuries. On each question, many voices are waiting to be heard.

You can take advantage of this diversity by seeking out alternative views with an open mind. When talking to another person, be willing to walk away with a new point of view—even if it's the one you brought to the table, but now supported with new evidence.

Examining different points of view is an exercise in analysis, which you can do with the suggestions that follow.

Define terms. Imagine a situation in which two people are arguing about whether an employer should limit health care benefits to members of a family. To one person, the word *family* means a mother, father, and children; to the other person, the word *family* applies to any individuals who live together in a long-term, supportive relationship. Chances are, the debate will go nowhere until these two people realize that they're defining the same word in different ways.

Conflicts of opinion can often be resolved—or at least clarified—when we define our key terms up front. This is especially true with abstract, emotion-laden terms such as *freedom*, *peace*, *progress*, or *justice*. Blood has been shed over the meaning of those words. Define them with care.

Look for assertions. Speakers and writers present their key terms in a larger context called an *assertion*. An assertion is a complete sentence that answers a key question. For example, consider this sentence from the article "The Master Student" in Chapter 1 "Mastery means attaining a level of skill that goes beyond technique." This sentence is an assertion that answers an important question: How do we recognize mastery?

Look for at least three viewpoints. When asking questions, let go of the temptation to settle for just a single answer. Once you have come up with an answer, say to yourself, "Yes, that is one answer. Now what's another?" Using this approach can sustain an inquiry, fuel creativity, and lead to conceptual breakthroughs.

Be prepared: The world is complicated, and critical thinking is a complex business. Some of your answers might contradict others. Resist the temptation to have all of your ideas fit together in a neat, orderly bundle.

Practice tolerance. Taking a position on important issues is natural. When we stop having an opinion on things, we've probably stopped breathing. Problems occur when we become so attached to our current viewpoints that we refuse to consider alternatives.

Many ideas that are widely accepted in Western cultures—for example, civil liberties for people of color and the right of women to vote—once were considered dangerous. Viewpoints that seem outlandish today might become widely accepted a century, a decade, or even a year from now. Remembering this idea can help us practice tolerance for differing beliefs. In doing so, make room for new ideas that might alter our lives.

3 How well is each point of view supported? Uncritical thinkers shield themselves from new information and ideas. As an alternative, you can follow the example of scientists, who constantly search for evidence that contradicts their theories.

To begin, look for logic and evidence. The aim of using logic is to make statements that are clear, consistent, and coherent. As you examine a speaker's or writer's assertions, you might find errors in logic—assertions that contradict each other or assumptions that are unfounded.

Also look at the evidence used to support points of view. Evidence comes in several forms, including facts, expert testimony, and examples. To think critically about evidence, ask questions such as the following:

- Are all or most of the relevant facts presented?
- Are the facts consistent with one another?
- Are facts presented accurately—or in a misleading way?
- Are enough examples included to make a solid case for the viewpoint?
- Do the examples truly support the viewpoint?
- Are the examples typical? That is, could the author or speaker support the assertion with other examples that are similar?
- Is the expert credible—in other words, is the expert truly knowledgeable about the topic?

As you look for answers, remember to understand before criticizing. Polished debaters are good at summing up their opponents' viewpoints—often better than the people who support those viewpoints themselves. Likewise, critical thinkers take the time to understand a statement of opinion before agreeing or disagreeing with it.

In the process, you might discover several "hot spots"—topics that provoke strong opinions and feelings. Some examples are abortion, homosexuality, gun control, and the death penalty. Make a clear intention to accept your feelings about such topics and to continue using critical thinking techniques. One way to cool down is to remember that we can change or even give up our current opinions without giving up ourselves. That's a key message behind the Power Processes: "Ideas Are Tools" and "Detach."

Also be willing to be uncertain. Some of the most profound thinkers have practiced the art of thinking by using a magic sentence: "I'm not sure yet." Those are words that many people do not like to hear. Our society rewards quick answers and quotable sound bites. We're under considerable pressure to utter the truth in 10 seconds or less.

In such a society, it is courageous and unusual to pause, to look, to examine, to be thoughtful, to consider many points of view—and to be unsure. When a society adopts half-truths in a blind rush for certainty, critical thinkers are willing to embrace uncertainty.

4 What if I could combine various points of view or create a new one? The search for truth is like painting a barn door by tossing an open can of paint at it. Few people who throw at the door will miss it entirely. Yet no one can cover the whole door in a single toss.

People who express a viewpoint are seeking the truth. No reasonable person claims to understand the whole truth about anything. Instead, each viewpoint can be seen as one approach among many possible alternatives. If you don't think that any one opinion is complete, then see whether you can combine different perspectives on the issue.

Remember to put those perspectives in writing. Thoughts can move at blinding speed. Writing slows down that process. Gaps in logic that slip by us in thought or speech are often exposed when we commit the same ideas to paper. Writing down our thoughts allows us to compare, contrast, and combine points of view more clearly—and become critical thinkers. *

Find more strategies for becoming a critical thinker.

Ways to create ideas

Conduct a brainstorm

Brainstorming is a technique for creating plans, finding solutions, and discovering new ideas. When you are stuck on a problem, brainstorming can break the logjam. For example, if you run out of money before payday every month, you can brainstorm ways to make your money last longer. You can brainstorm ways to pay for your education. You can brainstorm ways to find a job.

The overall purpose of brainstorming is to generate as many solutions as possible. Sometimes the craziest, most outlandish ideas, while unworkable in themselves, can lead to new ways to solve problems. Use the following steps to try out the brainstorming process:

- *Focus on a single problem or issue.* State your focus as a question. Open-ended questions that start with the words *what, how, who, where,* and *when* often make effective focusing questions.
- *Relax.* Creativity is enhanced by a state of relaxed alertness. If you are tense or anxious, use relaxation techniques such as those described in "Let go of test anxiety" in Chapter 6.
- *Set a quota or goal for the number of solutions you want to generate.* Goals give your subconscious mind something to aim for.
- *Set a time limit.* Use a clock to time your brainstorming session to the minute. Digital sports watches with built-in stopwatches work well. Experiment with various lengths of time. Both short and long brainstorms can be powerful.
- *Allow all answers.* Brainstorming is based on attitudes of permissiveness and patience. Accept every idea. If it pops into your head, put it down on paper. Quantity, not quality, is the goal. Avoid making judgments and evaluations during the brainstorming session. If you get stuck, think of an outlandish idea, and write it down. One crazy idea can unleash a flood of other, more workable solutions.
- *Brainstorm with others.* Group brainstorming is a powerful technique. Group brainstorms take on lives of their own. Assign one member of the group to write down solutions. Feed off the ideas of others, and remember to avoid evaluating or judging anyone's ideas during the brainstorm.

After your brainstorming session, evaluate the results. Toss out any truly nutty ideas, but not before you give them a chance.

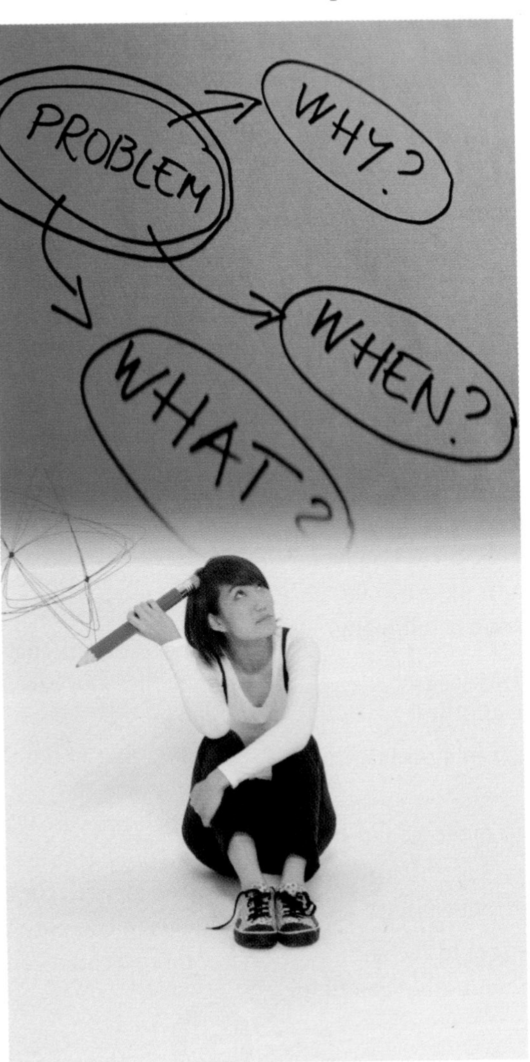

Woman: Floresco Productions/OJO Images/Getty; *words:* Shutterstock; collage by Walter Kopec

Focus and let go

Focusing and letting go are alternating parts of the same process. Intense focus taps the resources of your conscious mind. Letting go gives your subconscious mind time to work. When you focus for intense periods on a question and then take a break, the conscious and subconscious parts of your brain work in harmony.

Remember that periods of inspiration might last only seconds. Be gentle with yourself when you notice that your concentration has lapsed. That might be a time to let go. *Letting go* means not forcing yourself to be creative. Practice focusing for short periods at first, and then give yourself a break. In fact, take a nap when you are tired. Thomas Edison took frequent naps. Then the lightbulb clicked on.

Cultivate creative serendipity

The word *serendipity* was coined by the English author Horace Walpole from the title of an ancient Persian fairy tale, "The Three Princes of Serendip." The princes had a knack for making lucky discoveries. Serendipity is that knack, and it involves more than luck. It is the ability to see something valuable that you weren't looking for.

History is full of people who make serendipitous discoveries. Country doctor Edward Jenner noticed "by accident" that milkmaids seldom got smallpox. The result was his discovery that mild cases of cowpox immunized them. Penicillin was also discovered "by accident." Scottish scientist Alexander Fleming was growing bacteria in a laboratory petri dish. A spore of *Penicillium notatum*, a kind of mold, blew in the window and landed in the dish, killing the bacteria. Fleming isolated the active ingredient, which was eventually used to save thousands of lives.

You can train yourself in the art of serendipity. Keep your eyes open. You might find a solution to an accounting problem in a Saturday morning cartoon. You might discover a topic for your term paper at the corner convenience store. Multiply your contacts with the world. Resolve to meet new people. Join a study or discussion group. Read. Go to plays, concerts, art shows, lectures, and movies. Watch television programs you normally wouldn't watch.

Keep idea files

We all have ideas. People who treat their ideas with care are often labeled "creative." They recognize ideas *and* keep track of them.

One way to keep track of ideas is to write them down on 3x5 cards. Also keep a journal. Record observations about the world around you, conversations with friends, important or offbeat ideas—anything.

To fuel your creativity, read voraciously, including newspapers and magazines. Keep letter-size file folders of important correspondence, magazine and news articles, and other material. You can also create idea files on a computer using word-processing, outlining, or database software.

Collect and play with data

Look from all sides at the data you collect. Switch your attention from one aspect to another. Examine each fact, and avoid getting stuck on one particular part of a problem. Turn a problem upside down by picking a solution first and then working backward. Ask other people to look at the data. Solicit opinions.

Look for the obvious solutions or the obvious "truths" about the problem—then toss them out. Ask yourself, "Well, I know X is true, but if X were *not* true, what would happen?" Or ask the reverse: "If that *were* true, what would follow next?"

Put unrelated facts next to each other and invent a relationship between them, even if it seems absurd at first. Make imaginary pictures with the data. Condense it. Categorize it. Put it in chronological order. Put it in alphabetical order. Put it in random order. Order it from most to least complex. Reverse all of those orders. Look for opposites.

It has been said that there are no new ideas—only new ways to combine old ideas. Creativity is the ability to discover those combinations.

Refine ideas and follow through

Many of us ignore the part of the creative process that involves refining ideas and following through. How many great moneymaking schemes have we had that we never pursued? How many good ideas have we had for short stories that we never wrote? How many times have we said to ourselves, "You know, what they ought to do is attach two handles to one of those things, paint it orange, and sell it to police departments; they'd make a fortune"? And we never realize that we are "they." Genius resides in the follow-through—the application of perspiration to inspiration.

Trust the process

Learn to trust the creative process—even when no answers are in sight. We are often reluctant to look at problems if no immediate solution is at hand. Trust that a solution will show up. Frustration and a feeling of being stuck are often signals that a solution is imminent. *

19
critical thinking exercise
Fix-the-world brainstorm

This exercise works well with four to six people. Pick a major world problem such as hunger, poverty, terrorism, overpopulation, or pollution. Then conduct a 10-minute brainstorm about the steps an individual could take to contribute to solving the problem.

Use the brainstorming techniques explained in the article "Ways to create ideas." Remember not to evaluate or judge the solutions during the process. The purpose of a brainstorm is to generate a flow of ideas and record them all.

After the brainstorming session, discuss the process and the solutions that it generated. Did you feel any energy from the group? Was a long list of ideas generated? Are several of them worth pursuing?

Don't *fool* yourself: Common mistakes in logic

LOGIC IS A BRANCH of philosophy that seeks to distinguish between effective and ineffective reasoning. Students of logic look for valid steps in an *argument*, or a series of statements. The opening statements of the argument are the *premises*, and the final statement is the *conclusion*.

Effective reasoning is not just an idle pastime for unemployed philosophers. Learning to think logically offers many benefits. When you think logically, you take your reading, writing, speaking, and listening skills to a higher level. You can avoid costly mistakes in decision making. You can join discussions and debates with more confidence, cast your election votes with a clear head, and become a better-informed citizen.

Over the last 2,500 years, specialists have listed some classic land mines in the field of logic—common mistakes in thinking that are called *fallacies*. The study of fallacies could fill a yearlong course. Following are some examples to get you started. Knowing about them before you string together a bunch of assertions can help you avoid getting fooled.

Jumping to conclusions. Jumping to conclusions is the only exercise that some lazy thinkers get. This fallacy involves drawing conclusions without sufficient evidence.

Consider the bank officer who hears about a student's failing to pay back an education loan. After that, the officer turns down all loan applications from students. This person has formed a rigid opinion on the basis of hearsay. Jumping to conclusions—also called *hasty generalization*—is at work here.

Following are more examples of this fallacy:

- *When I went to Mexico for spring break, I felt sick the whole time. Mexican food makes people sick.*
- *Google's mission is to "organize the world's information." Their employees must be on a real power trip.*
- *During a recession, more people go to the movies. People just want to sit in the dark and forget about their money problems.*

Rich Reed/National Geographic/Getty

Each item in the above list includes two statements, and the second statement does not necessarily follow from the first. More evidence is needed to make any possible connection.

Attacking the person. This fallacy flourishes at election time. An example is the candidate who claims that her opponent failed to attend church regularly during the campaign. Candidates who indulge in personal attacks about private matters are attempting an intellectual sleight of hand. They want to divert our attention from the truly relevant issues.

Appealing to authority. A professional athlete endorses a brand of breakfast cereal. A famous musician features a soft drink company's product in a rock video. The promotional brochure for an advertising agency lists all of the large companies that have used its services.

In each case, the people involved are trying to win your confidence—and your dollars—by citing authorities. The underlying assumption is usually this: *Famous people and organizations buy our product. Therefore, you should buy it too.* Or, *You should accept this idea merely because someone who's well-known says it's true.*

Appealing to authority is usually a substitute for producing real evidence. It invites sloppy thinking. When our only evidence for a viewpoint is an appeal to authority, it's time to think more thoroughly.

Pointing to a false cause. The fact that one event follows another does not necessarily mean that the two events have a cause-and-effect relationship. All we can actually say is that the events might be correlated. For example, as children's vocabularies improve, they can get more cavities. This does not mean that cavities are the result of an improved vocabulary. Instead, the increase in cavities is due to other factors such as physical maturation and changes in diet or personal care.

Thinking in all-or-nothing terms. Consider these statements: *Doctors are greedy. You can't trust politicians. Students these days are in school just to get high-paying jobs; they lack idealism. Homeless people don't want to work.*

These opinions imply the word *all*. They gloss over individual differences, claiming that all members of a group are exactly alike. They also ignore key facts—for instance, that some doctors volunteer their time at free medical clinics and that many homeless people are children who are too young to work. All-or-nothing thinking is one of the most common errors in logic.

Creating a straw man. The name of this fallacy comes from the scarecrows traditionally placed in gardens to ward off birds. A scarecrow works because it looks like a man. Likewise, a person can attack ideas that *seem* like his opponent's ideas—but are actually absurd. For example, some legislators attacked the Equal Rights Amendment by describing it as a measure to abolish separate bathrooms for men and women. In fact, supporters of this amendment proposed no such thing.

Begging the question. Speakers and writers beg the question when their colorful language glosses over an idea that is unclear or unproven. Consider this statement: *Support the American tradition of individual liberty and oppose mandatory seat belt laws!* Anyone who makes such a statement "begs" (fails to answer) a key question: Are laws that require drivers to use seat belts actually a violation of individual liberty?

Confusing fact and opinion. Facts are statements verified by direct observation or compelling evidence that creates widespread agreement. In recent years, some politicians argued for tax cuts on the grounds that the American economy needed to create more jobs. However, it's not a fact that tax cuts automatically create more jobs. This statement is hard to verify, and there's actually evidence against it.

Appealing to "the people". Consider this statement: *Millions of people use Wikipedia as their main source of factual information. Wikipedia must be the best reference work in the world.* This is a perfect example of the *ad populum* fallacy. (In Latin, that phrase means "to the people.") The essential error is assuming that popularity, quality, and accuracy are the same.

Appealing to "the people" taps into our universal desire to be liked and to associate with a group of people who agree with us. No wonder this fallacy is also called "jumping on the bandwagon." Following are more examples:

- *Internet Explorer is the most widely used Web browser. It must be the best one.*
- *Dan Brown's books, including* The Da Vinci Code, *did not sell as well as the Harry Potter books by J. K. Rowling. I guess we know who's the better writer.*
- *Same-sex marriages must be immoral. Most Americans think so.*

You can refute such statements by offering a single example: Many Americans once believed that slavery was moral and that people of color should not be allowed to vote. That did not make either belief right. *

Practice hunting for fallacies.

Uncovering assumptions

Assumptions are invisible and powerful. And often they are unconscious. People can remain unaware of their most basic and far-reaching assumptions—the very ideas that shape their lives.

Some assumptions block our success. Take the person who says, "I don't worry about saving money for the future. I think life is meant to be enjoyed today—not later." This statement rests on at least two assumptions: *saving money is not enjoyable* and *we can enjoy ourselves only when we're spending money*.

It would be no surprise to find out that this person runs out of money near the end of each month and depends on cash advances from high-interest credit cards. He is shielding himself from some ideas that could erase his debt: Saving money can be a source of satisfaction, and many enjoyable activities cost nothing.

Practice looking for assumptions. Put them in writing. Then see whether you can find any exceptions to the assumptions. This technique will help you become a more critical thinker—and keep from getting fooled.

Gaining skill at decision making

WE MAKE DECISIONS all the time, whether we realize it or not. Even avoiding decisions is a form of decision making. The student who says that she can't decide whether to study for a test might really be saying, "I've decided this course is not important" or "I've decided not to give this course much time." To escape such a fate, decide right now to experiment with the following suggestions.

Recognize decisions. Decisions are specific and lead to focused action. When we decide, we narrow down. We give up actions that are inconsistent with our decision. Deciding to eat fruit for dessert instead of ice cream rules out the next trip to the ice cream store.

Base your decisions on a life plan. The benefit of having long-term goals for our lives is that they provide a basis for many of our daily decisions. Being certain about what we want to accomplish this year and this month makes today's choices more clear.

Use time as an ally. Sometimes we face dilemmas—situations in which any course of action leads to undesirable consequences. In such cases, consider putting a decision on hold. Wait it out. Do nothing until the circumstances change, making one alternative clearly preferable to another.

Use intuition. Some decisions seem to make themselves. A solution pops into our mind, and we gain newfound clarity. Using intuition is not the same as forgetting about the decision or refusing to make it. Intuitive decisions usually arrive after we've gathered the relevant facts and faced a problem for some time.

Think *choices*. Consider that the word *decide* derives from the same roots as *suicide* and *homicide*. In the spirit of those words, a decision forever "kills" all other options. That's kind of heavy. Instead, use the word *choice*, and see whether it frees up your thinking. When you *choose*, you express a preference for one option over others. However, those options remain real possibilities for the future. Choose for today, knowing that as you gain more wisdom and experience, you can choose again. *

Four ways to solve problems

Think of problem solving as a process with four Ps: Define the *problem*, generate *possibilities*, create a *plan*, and *perform* your plan.

1 Define the problem. To define a problem effectively, understand what a problem is—a mismatch between what you want and what you have. Problem solving is all about reducing the gap between these two factors.

2 Generate possibilities. Now put on your creative thinking hat. Open up. Brainstorm as many possible solutions to the problem as you can. At this stage, quantity counts. As you generate possibilities, gather relevant facts. For example, when you're faced with a dilemma about what courses to take next term, get information on class times, locations, and instructors. If you haven't decided which summer job offer to accept, gather information on salary, benefits, and working conditions.

3 Create a plan. After rereading your problem definition and list of possible solutions, choose the solution that seems most workable. Think about specific actions that will reduce the gap between what you have and what you want. Visualize the steps you will take to make this solution a reality, and arrange them in chronological order. To make your plan even more powerful, put it in writing.

4 Perform your plan. This step gets you off your chair and out into the world. Now you actually *do* what you have planned. Ultimately, your skill in solving problems lies in how well you perform your plan. Through the quality of your actions, you become the architect of your own success.

Find more strategies for problem solving.

Define your values; align your actions

One key way to choose what's next in your life is to define your values. Values are the things in life that you want for their own sake. Values guide your choices, including your moment-by-moment choices of what to do and what to have. Your values define who you are and the way that you want to live.

SOME PEOPLE ARE guided by values that they automatically adopt from others or by values that remain largely unconscious. Other people focus on short-term gain and forget about how their behavior violates their values over the long term (a perspective that helped to create the recent economic recession). All these people could be missing the opportunity to live a life that's truly of their own choosing.

Investing time and energy to define your values is a pivotal suggestion in this book. In fact, *Becoming a Master Student* is based on a particular value system that underlies suggestions given throughout the book. This system is based on the importance of these principles:

- Focused attention
- Self-responsibility
- Integrity
- Risk taking
- Contributing

You'll find these values and related ones directly stated in the Power Processes throughout the text. For instance:

"Discover What You Want" is about the value of living a purpose-based life.

"Ideas Are Tools" points to the value of being willing to experiment with new ideas.

"Be Here Now" expresses the value of focused attention.

"Love Your Problems (and Experience Your Barriers)" is about seeing difficulties as opportunities to develop new skills.

"Notice Your Pictures and Let Them Go" is about adopting an attitude of open-mindedness.

"I Create It All" is about taking responsibility for our beliefs and behaviors.

"Detach" reminds us that our core identity and value as a person does not depend on our possessions, our circumstances, or even our accomplishments.

"Find a Bigger Problem" is about offering our lives by contributing to others.

"Employ Your Word" expresses the value of making and keeping agreements.

"Surrender" points to the value of human community and the power of asking for help.

"Be It" is specifically about the power of attitudes—the idea that change proceeds from the inside out as we learn to see ourselves in new ways.

These are key values, and there are more. One is a respect for the power of language, along with the idea that we can reshape our lives by raising the quality of our conversations. Another value is courage—the willingness to set goals and take action to achieve them, which sometimes means taking risks.

In addition, most of the skills you read about in these pages have their source in values. The Time Monitor/Time Plan process, for example, calls for focused attention. Even the simple act of sharing your notes with a student who missed a class is an example of contributing.

Gaining a liberal education is all about adopting and acting on values. As you begin to define your values, consider the people who have gone before you. In creeds, scriptures, philosophies, myths, and sacred stories, the human race has left a vast and varied record of values. Be willing to look everywhere, including sources that are close to home. The creed of your local church or temple might eloquently describe some of your values. So might the mission statement of your school, company, or club. Another way to define your values is to describe the qualities of people you admire.

Also use Intention Statements to translate your values into behavior. Although defining your values is powerful, it doesn't guarantee any results. To achieve your goals, use your values to choose your next action. *

Choosing your major

ONE DECISION that troubles many students in higher education is the choice of an academic major. Here is an opportunity to apply your skills at critical thinking, decision making, and problem solving. The following four suggestions can guide you through this process.

1 Discover options

Follow the fun. Perhaps you look forward to attending one of your classes and even like completing the assignments. This is a clue to your choice of major. See whether you can find similar clues in the subjects and extracurricular activities that you've enjoyed over the years. Look for a major that allows you to continue and expand on these experiences.

Sit down with a stack of 3x5 cards and brainstorm answers to the following questions:

- What do you enjoy doing most with your unscheduled time?
- Imagine that you're at a party and having a fascinating conversation. What is this conversation about?
- What Web sites do you frequently visit or have bookmarked in a Web browser?
- What kind of problems do you enjoy solving—those that involve people? Products? Ideas?
- What interests are revealed by your choices of reading material, television shows, and other entertainment?
- What would an ideal day look like for you? Describe where you'd live, who would be with you, and what you'd do throughout the day. Do any of these visions suggest a possible major?

Questions like these are not frivolous. They can uncover a "fun factor" that energizes you to finish the work of completing a major.

Consider your abilities. In choosing a major, ability counts as much as interest. Einstein enjoyed playing the violin, but his love of music didn't override his choice of a career in science. In addition to considering what you enjoy, think about times and places when you excelled. List the courses that you aced, the work assignments that you mastered, and the hobbies that led to rewards or recognition. Let your choice of a major reflect a discovery of your passions *and* potentials.

Use techniques for self-discovery. Writing is a path to the kind of self-knowledge involved in choosing your major. Start with the exercises and Journal Entries in this book. Review what you've written, looking for statements about your interests and abilities.

Also consider questionnaires and inventories that are designed to match your interests with specific majors. Your academic advisor or someone in your school's career planning office can give you more details. For some fun, take several inventories and meet with an advisor to interpret the results.

Remember that there is no questionnaire, inventory, test, or formula for choosing a major or career. Likewise, there is no expert who can make these choices for you. Inventories can help you gain self-knowledge, and other people can offer valuable perspectives. However, what you *do* with all this input is entirely up to you.

Link to long-term goals. Your choice of a major can fall into place once you determine what you want in life. Before you choose a major, back up to a bigger picture. List your core values, such as contributing to society, achieving financial security and professional recognition, enjoying good health, or making time for fun. Also write down specific goals that you want to accomplish 5 years, 10 years, or even 50 years from today.

Ask other people. Key people in your life might have valuable suggestions about your choice of major. Ask for their ideas, and listen with an open mind. At the same time, distance yourself from any pressure to choose a major or career that fails to interest you. If you make a choice based solely on the expectations of other people, you could end up with a major or even a career you don't enjoy.

Gather information. Check your school's catalog or Web site for a list of available majors. Here is a gold mine of information. Take a quick glance and highlight all the majors that interest you. Then talk to students who have declared them. Also read descriptions of courses required for these majors. Chat with instructors who teach courses in these areas, and ask for copies of their class syllabi. Go the bookstore and browse required texts. Based on all this information, write a list of prospective majors. Discuss them with an academic advisor and someone at your school's career-planning center.

Invent a major. When choosing a major, you might not need to limit yourself to those listed in your school catalog. Many schools now have flexible programs that allow for independent study. Through such programs, you might be able to combine two existing majors or invent an entirely new one of your own.

Think critically about the link between your major and your career. You might be able to pursue a rewarding career by choosing among *several* different majors. Even students planning to apply for law school or medical school have flexibility in their choice of majors. Also remember that many people are employed in jobs with little relationship to their major. And you might choose a career in the future that is unrelated to any currently available major.

2 Make a trial choice

Pretend that you have to choose a major today. Based on the options for a major that you've already discovered, write down the first three ideas that come to mind. Review the list for a few minutes, and then just choose one. Also see Critical Thinking Exercise 20, "Make a Trial Choice of Major."

3 Test your trial choice

When you've made a trial choice of major, take on the role of a scientist. Treat your choice as a hypothesis, and then design a series of experiments to evaluate and test it. For example:

- Schedule office meetings with instructors who teach courses in the major. Ask about required course work and career options in the field.
- Discuss your trial choice with an academic advisor or career counselor.
- Enroll in a course related to your possible major. Remember that introductory courses might not give you a realistic picture of the workloads involved in advanced courses. Also, you might not be able to register for certain courses until you've actually declared a related major.
- Find a volunteer experience, internship, part-time job, or service-learning experience related to the major.
- Interview students who have declared the same major. Ask them in detail about their experiences and suggestions for success.
- Interview someone who works in a field related to the major.
- Think about whether you can complete your major given the amount of time and money that you plan to invest in higher education.
- Consider whether declaring this major would require a transfer to another program or even another school.

4 Choose again

Keep your choice of a major in perspective. There is no single "correct" choice. Your unique set of skills can probably guide you to several different majors. Odds are that you'll change your major at least once—and that you'll change careers several times during your life. Look at choosing a major as the start of a continuing path that involves discovery, choice, and passionate action. *

Find more strategies for choosing a major.

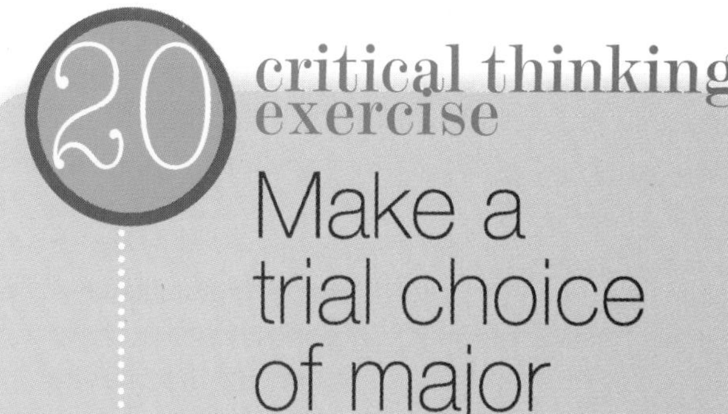

20
critical thinking exercise
Make a trial choice of major

This exercise presents another method for choosing a major. Search your school's course catalog for a list of majors, and cross out all of the majors that you already know are not right for you. You will probably eliminate well over half the list.

Now scan the remaining majors. Next to the ones that definitely interest you, write "yes." Next to majors that you're willing to consider and are still unsure about, write "maybe."

Focus on your "yes" choices. See whether you can narrow them down to three majors. List those here:

Finally, write an asterisk next to the major that interests you most right now. This is your trial choice of major.

Think critically about information on the Internet

SOURCES OF INFORMATION on the Internet range from the reputable (such as the Library of Congress) to the flamboyant (such as the *National Enquirer*). This fact underscores the need for thinking critically about everything you see online. Taking a few simple precautions when you surf the Net can keep you from crashing onto the rocky shore of misinformation.

Look for overall quality. Examine the features of the Web site in general. Notice the effectiveness of the text and visuals as a whole. Also note how well the site is organized and whether you can navigate the site's features with ease.

Next, take a more detailed look at the site's content. Examine several of the site's pages. Look closely for consistency of facts, quality of information, and competency with grammar and spelling. Are the links within the site easy to navigate?

In addition, evaluate the site's links to related Web pages. Look for links to pages of reputable organizations. Click on a few of those links. If they lead you to dead ends, it might indicate that the site you're evaluating is not updated often and may not be a reliable source for current information.

Finally, look for the date that pages were posted. This is another clue to how often the site is updated.

Look at the source. Think about the credibility of the person or organization that posts the Web site. Look for a list of author credentials and publications.

Notice if the site shows any evidence of bias or special interest. Perhaps the site's sponsoring organization wants you to buy a service, a product, or a point of view. This fact might suggest that the information on the site is not objective, and therefore is questionable.

The domain in the uniform resource locator (URL) for a Web site can give you clues about sources of information and possible bias. For example, distinguish among information from a for-profit commercial enterprise (URL ending in .com); a nonprofit organization (.org); a government agency (.gov); and a school, college, or university (.edu).

Note: Wikis (peer-edited sites) such as Wikipedia do not employ editors to screen out errors or scrutinize questionable material before publication. Be careful about using these sites when researching a paper or presentation. Also, be cautious about citing blogs, which often are not reviewed for accuracy.

Look for documentation. When you encounter an assertion on a Web page or some other Internet resource, note the types and quality of the evidence offered. Look for credible examples, quotations from authorities in the field, documented statistics, or summaries of scientific studies. *

mastering technology

RETHINKING E-MAIL

When facing an inbox stuffed with hundreds of messages, some people choose to declare "e-mail bankruptcy." They send out a message to everyone on their contact list: "I'm going to delete all my e-mails. Please resend anything important. Sorry." That's one way to tame the e-mail tiger, and there are other options.

Change the way you use e-mail. Spend a few minutes every day doing e-mail triage. If a message requires some kind of response from you, send it to a folder titled *action*. Check this folder often. If no response is required but you might refer to the message again, send it to a folder named *archives*. Trash all other messages.

In addition, be stingy. Send messages only when absolutely necessary, and keep them short. Reply to messages only when your response adds something essential to the conversation. Unsubscribe from mailing lists, and get the latest news with an online "feed reader" such as Google Reader or Bloglines.

Explore alternatives to e-mail. Use instant messaging, text messaging, and microblogging (for example, using Twitter) to send quick updates. Post more detailed messages via a page on Facebook, LinkedIn, or other social networking site. Consider creating a blog as a way to exchange comments with site visitors.

Use your voice, feet, and face. Instead of sending an e-mail to a neighbor or coworker, pick up the phone. Or get away from the computer screen and make a personal visit. Your face can brighten someone's day more than impersonal lines on a computer screen.

Overcome stereotypes with critical thinking

© 2010 Chad Baker/Ryan McVay / Jupiterimages Corporation

CONSIDER ASSERTIONS such as these: "College students like to drink heavily," "People who speak English as a second language are hard to understand," and "Americans who criticize the president are unpatriotic."

These assertions are examples of stereotyping—generalizing about a group of people based on the behavior of isolated group members. When we stereotype, we gloss over individual differences and assume that every member of a group is the same.

Stereotypes infiltrate every dimension of human individuality. People are stereotyped on the basis of their race, ethnic group, religion, political affiliation, geographic location, birthplace, accent, job, age, gender, sexual orientation, IQ, height, hair color, or hobbies.

In themselves, generalizations are neither good nor bad. In fact, they are essential. Mentally sorting people, events, and objects into groups allows us to make sense of the world. When we consciously or unconsciously make generalizations that rigidly divide the people of the world into "us" versus "them," then we create stereotypes and put on the blinders of prejudice.

You can take several steps to free yourself from stereotypes.

Look for errors in thinking. Some of the most common errors in thinking are the following:

- *Selective perception.* Stereotypes can literally change the way we see the world. If we assume that homeless people are lazy, for instance, we tend to notice only the examples that support our opinion. Stories about homeless people who are too young or too ill to work will probably escape our attention.
- *Self-fulfilling prophecy.* When we interact with people based on stereotypes, we set them up in ways that confirm our thinking. For example, when people of color were denied access to higher education based on stereotypes about their intelligence, they were deprived of opportunities to demonstrate their intellectual gifts.
- *Self-justification.* Stereotypes can allow people to assume the role of victim and to avoid taking responsibility for their own lives. An unemployed white male might believe that affirmative action programs are making it impossible for him to get a job—even as he overlooks his own lack of experience or qualifications.

Create categories in a more flexible way. Stereotyping has been described as a case of "hardening of the categories." Avoid this problem by making your categories broader. Instead of seeing people based on their skin color, you could look at them on the basis of their heredity. (People of all races share most of the same genes.) Or you could make your categories narrower. Instead of talking about "religious extremists," look for subgroups among the people who adopt a certain religion. Distinguish between groups that advocate violence and those that shun it.

Test your generalizations about people through action. You can test your generalizations by actually meeting people of other cultures. It's easy to believe almost anything about certain groups of people as long as we never deal directly with individuals. Inaccurate pictures tend to die when people from different cultures study together, work together, and live together. Consider joining a school or community organization that will put you in contact with people of other cultures. Your rewards will include a more global perspective and an ability to thrive in a multicultural world.

Be willing to see your own stereotypes. The Power Process: "Notice Your Pictures and Let Them Go" can help you see your own stereotypes. One belief about yourself that you can shed is *I have no pictures about people from other cultures.* Even people with the best of intentions can harbor subtle biases. Admitting this possibility allows you to look inward even more deeply for stereotypes.

Every time we notice an inaccurate picture buried in our mind and let it go, we take a personal step toward embracing diversity. *

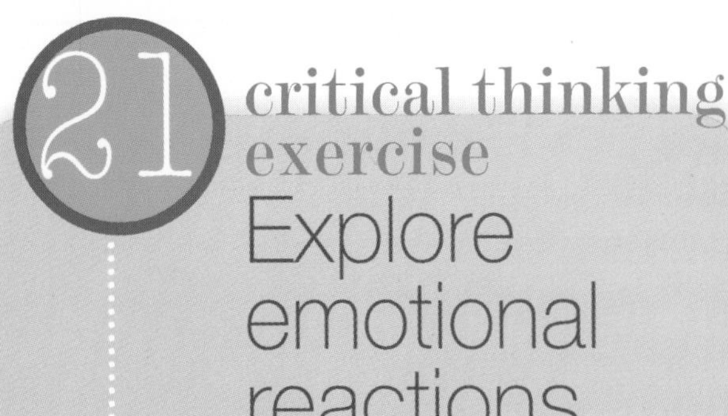

critical thinking exercise 21

Explore emotional reactions

Each of us has certain "hot spots"—issues that trigger strong emotional reactions. These topics may include abortion, gay and lesbian rights, capital punishment, and funding for welfare programs. There are many other examples, varying from person to person.

Examine your own hot spots by writing a word or short phrase summarizing each issue about which you feel very strongly. Also describe what you typically say or do when each issue comes up in conversation. For instance, "When people start talking about how much they admire Sarah Palin, I immediately roll my eyes." Begin your list of hot spots in the space below and continue on separate paper as needed.

After you have completed your list, think about what you can do to become a more effective thinker when you encounter one of these issues. For example, you could breathe deeply and count to 5 before you offer your own point of view. Or, you might preface your opinion with an objective statement such as "There are many valid points of view on this issue. Here's the way I see it, and I'm open to your ideas."

journal entry 18

Discovery/Intention Statement

Reflect on choosing a major

Reflect for a moment on your experience with Critical Thinking Exercise 20: "Make a trial choice of major." If you had already chosen a major, did doing the exercise confirm that choice? Did you uncover any new or surprising possibilities for declaring a major?

I discovered that I . . .

Now consider the major that is your current top choice. Think of publications you plan to read, resources you plan to investigate, and people you intend to meet in order to gather more information about this major.

I intend to . . .

Plan to repeat this Journal Entry several times. You might find yourself researching several majors and changing your mind. That's fine. Just start thinking about your major now.

Find a Bigger Problem

It is impossible to live a life that's free of problems. Besides, problems serve a purpose. They provide opportunities to participate in life. Problems stimulate us and pull us forward.

Seen from this perspective, our goal becomes not to eliminate problems, but to find problems that are worthy of us. Worthy problems are those that inspire critical and creative thinking. They lead us to draw on our talents, define our purpose, and increase our skills. Solving these problems offers the greatest benefits for others and ourselves. Viewed in this way, bigger problems give more meaning to our lives.

Problems expand to fill whatever space is available. Suppose that your only problem for today were to write a follow-up letter to a job interview. You could spend the entire day thinking about what you were going to say, writing the letter, finding a stamp, going to the post office—and then thinking about all of the things you forgot to say.

Now suppose that you got a phone call with an urgent message: A close friend has been admitted to the hospital and wants you to come right away. It's amazing how quickly and easily that letter can get finished when there's a bigger problem on your plate.

True, the smaller problems still need to be solved. The goal is simply to solve them in less time and with less energy.

Bigger problems are easy to find—world hunger, child abuse, environmental pollution, terrorism, human rights violations, drug abuse, street crime, energy shortages, poverty, and wars. These problems and others on the same scale await your attention and involvement.

Tackling a bigger problem does not have to be depressing. In fact, it can be energizing—a reason for getting up in the morning. A huge project can channel your passion and purpose.

When we take on a bigger problem, we play full out. We do justice to our potentials. We love what we do and do what we love. We're awake, alert, and engaged. Playing full out means living our lives as if our lives depended on it.

Perhaps a little voice in your mind is saying, "That's crazy. I can't do anything about global problems." In the spirit of critical thinking, put that idea to the test. Get involved in solving a bigger problem. Then notice how you can, indeed, make a difference. And just as important, notice how smaller problems dwindle—or even vanish.

Learn more about this Power Process online.

Skip Brown/National Geographic/RF/Getty Images

Put it to Work

You can apply thinking skills to practical decisions in the workplace, such as making ethical choices. Start by reflecting on the following case study.

Photo courtesy of Lea Dean

Maria Sanchez graduated with an associate's degree in legal assistance and has been working for two years as a paralegal at a large law firm.

As a paralegal, Maria cannot set legal fees, give legal advice, or present cases in court. Despite these restrictions, she does many of the same things that lawyers do. Maria's current job centers on legal research—finding laws, judicial decisions, legal articles, and other materials that are relevant to her assigned cases.

Recently Maria applied for a new job that opened up in the firm. In addition to legal research, this job involves drafting legal arguments and motions to be filed in court. It would mean a promotion and a raise for Maria.

When Maria applied for the job, she expressed strong interest in it. She believes that her chances are excellent. She also knows that Bill, the other paralegal in the firm, is not interested in the job and will soon announce that he's leaving the firm to pursue another career.

One day, Maria found the first draft of an e-mail that her supervisor had printed out and accidentally placed in a stack of legal documents for Maria to read. The e-mail was a note of congratulations that offered the new paralegal job to Bill. Maria called her parents and told them that she faced an immediate decision: "Do I tell my supervisor that Bill plans to quit? Do I tell Bill about the e-mail? Do I keep quiet, or consider looking for a job in another firm? I'm confused about the ethical thing to do."

As a creative thinker, Maria has already begun brainstorming options. She also sees the importance of choosing her next step and taking action. List some strategies that she could use to make her decision:

____

____

____

____

If you face a decision at work that raises ethical issues, one option is to turn your personal moral standards into a set of practical questions. These questions can guide your thinking about possible actions to take. For example:

- Is this action legal?
- Is this action consistent with the mission, goals, and policies of my organization?
- Is this action consistent with my personal values?
- If I continue taking such actions, will I be happy with the kind of person I will become?
- Will I be able to defend this action tomorrow? Next month? Next year?
- In taking this action, will I set an example that I want other people to follow?
- Am I willing to make this action public—to talk about it openly with coworkers, family members, and friends?

Quiz

Name____ Date____/____/____

1. List the four questions described in this chapter that can assist you in becoming a critical thinker.
   (a) Why am I considering this issue? (b) What are various points of view on this issue?
   (c) How well is each point of view supported? (d) What if I could combine various points of view or create a new one?
   (*Becoming a critical thinker,* pp. 156–157)
2. Briefly describe one strategy for answering each question you listed in your response to Question 1.
   (a) Why? Seek a rationale for your learning, understand why a topic is important, arrive at a new conclusion, make a prediction, solve a problem, find a personal connection.
   (b) What? Define terms, look for assertions, look for at least three viewpoints, practice tolerance.
   (c) How? Look for logic and evidence, consider the source, understand before criticizing, watch for hot spots, be willing to be uncertain.
   (d) What if? Put various perspectives in writing; compare, contrast, and combine points of view; try seeing each viewpoint as one approach among many possible alternatives. (Answers will vary.) (*Becoming a critical thinker*, pp. 156–157)
3. Guidelines for brainstorming do *not* include
   (a) Setting a time limit.
   (b) Setting a quota for the number of ideas to create.
   (c) Focusing on a single problem or issue.
   (d) Stopping the process every five minutes or so to evaluate the quality of the ideas.
   (d) Stopping the process every five minutes or so to evaluate the quality of the ideas. (*Ways to create ideas*, pp. 158–159)
4. List three questions to ask when thinking about an ethical issue.
   Ask three of the following questions: • Is this action legal? • Is this action consistent with the mission, goals, and policies of my organization? • Is this action consistent with my personal values? • If I continue taking such actions, will I be happy with the kind of person I will become? • Will I be able to defend this action tomorrow? Next month? Next year? • In taking this action, will I set an example that I want other people to follow? (Answers will vary.) (*Put it to Work*, p. 170)
5. Briefly describe three strategies for creative thinking.
   Describe three of the following: Conduct a brainstorm, focus and let go, cultivate serendipity, keep idea files, collect and play with data, refine ideas and follow through, trust the process. (Answers will vary.) (*Ways to create ideas,* pp. 158–159)
6. List three ways to test your choice of a major.
   List three of the following: • Ask instructors who teach courses in the major about required course work and career options in the field. • Discuss your trial choice with an academic advisor or career counselor. • Enroll in a course related to your possible major. • Find a volunteer experience, internship, part-time job, or service learning experience related to the major. • Interview students who have declared the same major. • Interview someone who works in a field related to the major. • Think about whether you can complete your major given the amount of time and money that you plan to invest in higher education. • Consider whether declaring this major would require a transfer to another program or even another school. (Answers will vary.) (*Choosing your major*, pp. 164–165)
7. Name one type of logical fallacy and give an example of it.
   Name and give an example of one of the following: • Jumping to conclusions. • Attacking the person. • Appealing to authority. • Pointing to a false cause. • Thinking in all-or-nothing terms. • Creating a straw man. • Begging the question. • Confusing fact and opinion. • Appealing to "the people." (Answers will vary.) (*Don't* fool *yourself: Common mistakes in logic,* pp. 160–161)
8. According to the Power Process in this chapter, the goal of critical thinking is a life that is free from problems. True or false? Explain your answer.
   False. The goal is not to eliminate problems, but to find problems that draw on our talents, move us toward our purpose, and increase our skills. Solving these problems offers the greatest benefits for others and ourselves. Viewed in this way, bigger problems give more meaning to our lives. (Answers will vary.) (*Power Process: Find a Bigger Problem,* p. 169)
9. Name a logical fallacy involved in this statement: "Everyone who's ever visited this school agrees that it's the best in the state."
   Two logical fallacies in this statement are jumping to conclusions and all-or-nothing thinking.
   (*Don't* fool *yourself: Common mistakes in logic,* pp. 160–161)
10. According to the text, the words *choose* and *decide* have the same meaning. True or false? Explain your answer.
    False. Using the word *choose* frees up your thinking as it expresses a preference for one thing over another, rather than eliminating other options completely as happens when you "decide." (*Gaining skill at decision making,* p. 162)

Skills Snapshot

Now that you've experimented with some new strategies for thinking, take a few minutes to revisit your responses to the "Thinking" section of the Discovery Wheel exercise on page 25. Then complete the following sentences.

CREATIVE AND CRITICAL THINKING

When I'm asked to come up with a topic for a paper or speech, the first thing I do is . . .

When I'm asked for my opinion about a political candidate, the first thing I take into account about the candidate is . . .

APPLIED THINKING

In declaring my major, the steps I plan to take include . . .

One of the biggest problems I face right now is . . .

To come up with a solution for this problem, I will . . .

NEXT ACTION

I'll know that I've reached a new level of mastery with critical and creative thinking skills when . . .

To reach that level of mastery, the most important thing I can do next is to . . .

Master Student PROFILE

Twyla Tharp

. . . is creative

Every creative person has to learn to deal with failure, because failure, like death and taxes, is inescapable. If Leonardo and Beethoven and Goethe failed on occasion, what makes you think you'll be the exception?

I don't mean to romanticize failure. . . . Believe me, success is preferable to failure. But there is a therapeutic power to failure. It cleanses. It helps you put aside who you aren't and reminds you of who you are. Failure humbles. . . .

When I tape a three-hour improvisational session with a dancer and find only 30 seconds of useful material in the tape, I am earning straight A's in failure. Do the math: I have rejected 99.7 percent of my work that day. It would be like a writer knocking out a 2,000-word chapter and upon rereading deciding that only three words were worth keeping. Painful, yes, but for me absolutely necessary.

What's so wonderful about wasting that kind of time? It's simple: The more you fail in private, the less you will fail in public. In many ways, the creative act is editing. You're editing out all the lame ideas that won't resonate with the public. It's not pandering. It's exercising your judgment. It's setting the bar a little higher for yourself, and therefore for your audience. . . .

Some of my favorite dancers at New York City Ballet were the ones who fell the most. I always loved watching Mimi Paul; she took big risks onstage and went down often. Her falls reminded you that the dancers were doing superhuman things onstage, and when she fell, I would realize, "Damn, she's human." And hitting the ground seemed to transform Mimi: It was as though the stage absorbed the energy of her fall and injected it back into her with an extra dose of fearlessness. Mimi would bounce back up, ignore the fall, and right before my eyes would become superhuman again. I thought, "Go Mimi!" She became greater because she had fallen. Failure enlarged her dancing.

That should be your model for dealing with failure.

When you fail in public, you are forcing yourself to learn a whole new set of skills, skills that have nothing to do with creating and everything to do with surviving.

Jerome Robbins liked to say that you do your best work after your biggest disasters. For one thing, it's so painful that it almost guarantees that you won't make those mistakes again. Also, you have nothing to lose; you've hit bottom and the only place to go is up. A fiasco compels you to change dramatically. The golfer Bobby Jones said, "I never learned anything from a match I won." He respected defeat and profited from it. . . .

My heroes in *The Odyssey* are the older warriors who have been through many wars. They don't hide their scars, they wear them proudly as a kind of armor. When you fail—when your short film induces yawns or your photographs inspire people to say "That's nice" (ouch!) or your novel is trashed in a journal of opinion that matters to you—the best thing to do is acknowledge your battle scars and gird yourself for the next round. Tell yourself, "This is a deep wound. But it's going to heal and I will remember the wound. When I go back into the fray, it will serve me well."

Reprinted with permission from *The Creative Habit: Learn It and Use It for Life* by Twyla Tharp with Mark Reiter.

© Petre Buzoianu/Corbis

(1941–)
Choreographer who has worked with her own company, the Joffrey Ballet, the Paris Opera Ballet, London's Royal Ballet, and the American Ballet Theatre. She also created dances for the films *Hair*, *Ragtime*, and *Amadeus*.

To learn more about the life and work of Twyla Tharp, visit the Master Student Hall of Fame online.

8 Communicating

Instructor Tools & Tips

> "Listening means trying to see the problem the way the speaker sees it—which means not sympathy, which is feeling for him, but empathy, which is feeling with him.
>
> **—S. I. Hayakawa**
>
> You have two ears and one mouth. Remember to use them in more or less that proportion.
>
> **—Paula Bern**

Preview

Communication is discussed indirectly in many chapters of *Becoming a Master Student*. By taking a closer look at effective communication in this chapter, you can help your students develop the related skills of speaking, listening, and writing, now that they have the necessary foundations to work toward mastery. This chapter also provides an opportunity to discuss conflict resolution, public speaking (including overcoming fear of public speaking), and plagiarism.

Communication abilities are essential workplace skills that can be practiced and mastered in the college setting. Use this Annotated Instructor's Edition and other resources available to you to highlight and discuss key concepts in class and to devise assignments that allow students to practice communication skills outside the classroom. And consider this fact: Developing relationships through effective communication is essential for first-year student success and retention at your college.

Guest Speaker

A librarian or a colleague from the Speech/Communications department makes a timely guest speaker as a lead-in to the articles on plagiarism and speaking in class. Share the related articles with the guest speaker ahead of time so that the speaker can design their presentation to complement the text. Let students know who is coming so that they can prepare questions to ask your guest speaker.

Lecture

Appropriate lecture topics for this chapter include becoming a skilled listener, effective writing, plagiarism, speaking in class, and the Power Process: "Employ Your Word." Consider inviting a guest lecturer for one or more of these topics. You can also use the PowerUP! DVD to lecture for you on the Power Process. For additional lecture ideas, visit the Instructor Companion site.

Exercises/Activities

1. Choosing to speak (page 177). Students who have not taken an interpersonal communications course often do not know how to create "I" statements. Dividing students into groups and having them practice writing and speaking using "I" statements can help them master this skill and enable them to gauge their effectiveness in communicating.

2. Choosing to speak (page 177). This is one of Dave Ellis's favorite class activities. Ask students to pair up with a classmate they have gotten to know during the semester. One student will be the speaker; the other, the listener. The speaker says, "What I like about you is . . ." and finishes the sentence with a quality he likes in that person. He continues to repeat this sentence for 45 seconds, each time stating a different quality. If your students get stuck and cannot think of a quality, encourage them to say, "What I like about you is *everything*" over and over again until they can think of another specific compliment. This keeps the barrage of compliments going. The listener receives the compliments and acknowledges them nonverbally. After 45 seconds, the students switch roles and repeat the exercise. End this activity with a class discussion about how it feels to *give* and to *receive* compliments.

3. Speaking in class (pages 187–188). In this activity, students prepare and present a 5-minute "process" speech describing how to do or make something. This assignment provides them with an opportunity to stand up and speak before the entire class. To lay the groundwork, review the criteria for an effective speech. Faculty Advisor Dean Mancina presents a sample speech to the class to grade using his grading form. Students prepare and practice their speech at home and then sign up to present the speech during class. Students earn credit for essential points made during the introduction, body, and conclusion of their speech. Delivering a speech in a familiar and comfortable environment helps reduce speech anxiety for students, who will likely make future presentations in other courses. For suggestions on grading student speeches, review information provided on the Instructor Companion site.

4. Speaking in class (pages 187–188). Participating in class is another excellent way for students to practice speaking in public. Many students experience communication apprehension when they are called on in class or when they must speak before a group. Ask your students to write a Discovery Statement about their memory of this type of situation. Have them describe their physical sensations, the effectiveness of their presentations, feedback from the audience, and so forth. Ask your students to write an Intention Statement concerning how they intend to participate in class in order to experience talking to a group of people. Ask them to be specific about which class they intend to speak in, how they will set up the opportunity to speak (e.g., having questions ready, sitting in front, or asking to give a presentation), and how they intend to record their observations of the experience.

5. Speaking in class (pages 187–188). Students may be assigned to do many different types of oral reports for their courses, but one form deserves particular attention: the classroom debate. Instructors use this assignment for many reasons, including these:

- It teaches students how to think critically about complex issues.
- It helps students to understand, respect, and adapt to differences of opinion.
- It provides a way of comparing and contrasting different theories and viewpoints.
- It develops students' ability to create prompt, analytical responses to arguments.
- It teaches students how to collect and analyze arguments and evidence.
- It teaches audience members how to listen to and analyze arguments.
- It develops presentation skills and student confidence.[1]

Conversation/Sharing

Your students will definitely be energized to discuss this chapter. It will be especially easy for them to create schema using their prior knowledge of the subject before learning new information. Spend time focusing on the *What if?* in this chapter. Ask students *What if* they use the ideas presented in this chapter to help them succeed in the workplace. Ask your students to consider the importance of communication for the majors they have chosen or to their future career choices.

Homework

Strategies for effective writing (pages 185–186). Are you looking for an assignment that can help your students practice their writing *and* provide them with an opportunity to win a $1,000 scholarship? This is a perfect place to announce the Cengage Learning Scholarship Essay Contest. Host a contest in your classes, select the best essay (that answers the scholarship essay question, posted on the *Becoming a Master Student* CourseMate site), and submit this winning essay to the national contest. Remind your students that they have the formula for writing a successful essay in their hands! Previous winning essays are available at the Student CourseMate site, for reflection.

Strategies for effective writing (pages 185–186). It is essential for you to emphasize to your students that writing is as important in the workplace as it is in the classroom. Stress that learning to write well pays many dividends and that writing effectively can help students express themselves. Writing will help them to organize information and adapt their ideas to different audiences. Finally, point out that good writing is a marketable skill. To verify this, have your students look at help wanted ads in the newspaper or online and determine how many job descriptions call for good writing skills. Have your students look for other transferable skills that they can master in the classroom and utilize in the workplace. Students can write Discovery and Intention Statements after reviewing the help wanted ads. Ask your students to highlight skills other than writing that will be applicable to their intended career choice.

Academic integrity: Avoid plagiarism (page 186). If students understand how to cite sources properly and feel confident about their ability to do so, many are less likely to "cheat," either intentionally or simply because they don't know how to cite. Consider asking students to go to their college library, find a current controversial topic, and use library reference books, such as the *Opposing Viewpoints* series, to choose a position on their controversial topic. Next, have them find three facts in periodicals or books that directly support their position. Finally, ask them to type their three facts and cite them properly using MLA or APA format. Many students don't know how to find topics in the library, locate reference books, and research a topic using the library's online catalog. Ask a librarian to explain how to use the library to your students. The librarian can visit your class as a guest speaker or speak to your students during a class visit to the library.

Power Process: Employ Your Word (page 189). To help illustrate the effectiveness of this Power Process, have students individually think about and then write two promises, one to themselves and one to a significant person in their lives. This exercise helps demonstrate how to use the ideas in the article. Remind students that the promises they are making are, culturally, the highest level of commitment we make to each other.

Master Student Profile: Sampson Davis (page 193). Remind students that the Master Student Profiles can be a source of inspiration. You can also use the Master Student Profiles to discuss the topics covered in the article. Ask your students why they think that Sampson Davis was selected for the communication chapter. You can assign additional reading or research (another opportunity for students to practice their writing) related to this article. Have your students begin with the biographical information and links that are provided on the *Becoming a Master Student* CourseMate site.

Evaluation

Ask students to describe ways to manage conflict. Present an example of a problem between a student and the Admissions/Records Office and ask students to share how they would effectively complain in order to get the situation resolved. Ask students for examples of ways to stay safe during online social networking. Ask students to write Discovery and Intention Statements regarding the Power Process: "Employ Your Word."

Additional Digital Resources

Course Manual

The online *Course Manual* serves as an invaluable reference for those developing and teaching a College Success course with *Becoming a Master Student Concise*. The *Course Manual* provides advice on general teaching issues such as preparing for classes, classroom management, grading, and communicating with students of various backgrounds, as well as specific strategies on getting the most out of various features in *Becoming a Master Student Concise* and book-specific Web sites. Do a *Course Manual* reconnaissance to find ideas that you can use in your course right now.

Instructor Companion Site

The updated Instructor Companion Site provides resources to help you plan and customize your course. Content specific to Chapter 8 includes:

- Lecture Ideas
  - Communication is Straightforward?
- In-Class Exercises
  - Assertiveness Inventory
  - Attendance Brainstorm
  - Turn a Complaint into a Request
  - Making Relationships Work While You're a Student
- In-Text Quiz Answers
- PowerPoint Slides

The Instructor Companion Site also contains the following book-specific content:

- ExamView Test Bank
- Online Course Manual
- Sample Syllabi
- Detailed Transition Guide

College Success CourseMate

To help your students gain a better understanding of the topics discussed in *Becoming a Master Student Concise*, encourage them to visit the text's CourseMate at CengageBrain.com that provides the following resources specific to Chapter 8:

- Connect to Text content expands on specific topics marked with an icon within the Chapter 8.
- Practice Tests allow students to see how well they understand the themes of *Becoming a Master Student Concise.*
- Interactive Concept Maps promote critical thinking by highlighting related ideas to show relationships among concepts.
- Video Skillbuilders bring to life techniques that will help students to excel in college and beyond. The following videos should give your students more information regarding topics covered in Chapter 8:
  - Persuasive Communication: Effective Strategies
  - Persuasive Communication: Communicating in a Group
- Learning Styles Application
- Discussion Topics
- Reflection Questions
- Assessment Questions
- Experiment with chapter strategies
- Remembering Cultural Differences presents readers with brief articles that touch on aspects of diversity in our rapidly changing world. For Chapter 8, the following article will prompt your students to look at contemporary issues in a new way:
  - Ethnicity Issues in Communications
- Master Student Profiles provide additional information on the people covered in this book feature. For Chapter 8, students will find expanded coverage and links about:
  - Sampson Davis
- Power Process Media contains video, PowerPoints, and audio files to take what your students have learned from the Power Processes in their book to the next level. For Chapter 8, students will find additional media on:
  - Employ Your Word

Along with the chapter-specific content, a General Resources folder is available that contains Toolboxes geared toward specific student types (Community College, Adult Learner, Student Athlete), the Plagiarism Prevention Zone, and the Career Resource Center.

8 Communicating

Master Student Map

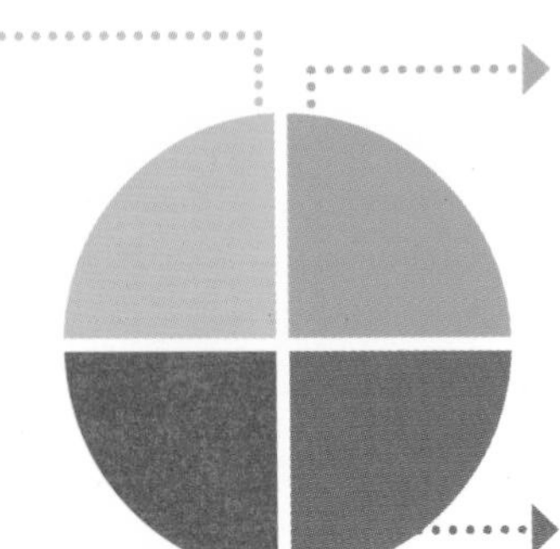

as you read, ask yourself

what if . . .

I could consistently create the kind of relationships that I've always wanted?

why this chapter matters . . .

Your communication abilities—including your skills in listening, speaking, and writing—are as important to your success as your technical skills.

how you can use this chapter . . .

- Listen, speak, and write in ways that promote your success.
- Prevent and resolve conflicts with other people.
- Use your capacity to make and keep agreements as a tool for creating your future.

what is included . . .

MASTER STUDENTS in *action*

Dealing with conflict online is totally different than in person. I find that even if something is "resolved" online, it will probably come up in person anyway, so why not just talk face to face?

—CAT SALERNO

Photo courtesy of Lea Dean

Communicating in a diverse world

ACCORDING TO THE National Association of Colleges and Employers, what interviewers look for most of all in job applicants is skill in communicating—the ability to write and speak clearly and persuasively. Coincidentally, this is also the skill that they find most consistently missing in new graduates.[1]

Communication can be defined as the process of creating shared meaning. When two people agree about the meaning of an event, they stand on common ground. They've communicated.

However, communication is a constant challenge. When people speak or listen, they don't exchange meaning. They exchange only symbols—words, images, gestures—which are open to interpretation. This means that communication is always flawed to some extent. We can never be sure that the message we send is the message that others receive.

Also remember that people differ in more ways than we can measure. The people sitting next to you in class or at work may come from many cultures. Each of them has a unique bundle of life experiences. Each of them creates meaning in a unique way. Adapting to diversity is a challenge that's always present in communication.

In the workplace, you will face diversity. Your coworkers might span three, four, or even five generations. Their race, ethnic group, religion, sexual orientation, and level of physical ability might differ greatly from yours. According to the U.S. Census Bureau, members of minority groups are the fastest growing part of the labor force.[2]

In addition, you will join an international workplace. American companies in the twenty-first century will buy from the world and sell to the world. You might work on project teams with people located in another city, state, or country.

Misunderstandings between people of different cultures can add noise to their interactions. In communication theory, the term *noise* refers to any factor that distorts meaning. Noise can be external (a lawn mower outside a classroom) or internal (fear, anger, false assumptions, or lack of information).

Communication ultimately works best when each of us has plenty of time to receive what others send—and the opportunity to send a complete message when it's our turn. This is challenging. When emotions run high, people can totally forget when it's their turn to receive and when it's their turn to send. Everyone talks and nobody listens.

However, with practice we can overcome many of the difficulties in human communication. That's what this chapter is about. As you enhance your skills at listening, speaking, and writing, you can enter a diverse world with confidence. *

journal entry 19

Discovery/Intention Statement

Commit to create value from this chapter

Think of a time when you experienced an emotionally charged conflict with another person. Were you able to resolve this dispute effectively? If so, list the strategies you used in the following space.

I discovered that I . . .

____

____

____

____

Now scan this chapter for ideas that can help you get your feelings and ideas across more skillfully in similar situations. List at least three ideas here, along with the page numbers where you can read more about them.

Strategy	Page Number

Describe an upcoming situation in which you intend to apply a technique that you listed above.

I intend to . . .

____

____

____

____

Choosing to listen

People love a good listener. Skilled salespeople, managers, coworkers, teachers, parents, and friends are skilled listeners. To become a skilled listener, begin from a clear intention to listen well. Then use the following techniques to become even more effective.

Be quiet. Silence is more than staying quiet while someone is speaking. Let the speaker finish and then wait several seconds before you respond. This gives the speaker time to catch her breath and gather her thoughts. She might want to continue. The short break also gives you time to form your response and helps you avoid listening with your answer running.

Maintain eye contact. Look at the other person while he speaks. This demonstrates your attentiveness and helps keep your mind from wandering. Your eyes also let you observe the speaker's body language and behavior. (Remember too that eye contact is valued more in some cultures than others.)

Send acknowledgments. Words and nonverbal gestures convey to the speaker that you are interested and that you are receiving his message. Examples include "Mmm-hmm," "OK," "Yes," and head nods. These acknowledgments do not imply your agreement. They just indicate that you are listening.

Suspend judgments. Once you're confident that you accurately understand a speaker's point of view, you are free to agree or disagree with it. The key to effective listening is understanding before evaluating.

Choose when to speak. When we listen to another person, we often interrupt with our own stories, opinions, suggestions, and comments. Instead, delay your verbal responses. This does not mean that you remain totally silent while listening. It means waiting for an appropriate moment to respond.

Feed back meaning. Sometimes you can help a speaker clarify her message by paraphrasing it. This does not mean parroting what she says. Instead, briefly summarize. Feed back what you see as the essence of the person's message: "Let me see whether I understood what you said . . . ." or "What I'm hearing you say is . . . ." Often, the other person will say, "No, that's not what I meant. What I said was . . . ." There will be no doubt when you get it right.

Listen for requests. This works especially well with complaints. "This class is a waste of my time" can be heard as "Please tell me what I'll gain if I participate actively in class." "The instructor talks too fast" might be asking "What strategies can I use to take notes when the instructor covers material rapidly?" Hearing complaints as requests gives us more choices. We can choose whether to grant the request or help the speaker translate his complaint into an action plan.

Allow emotion. In the presence of full listening, some people will share things that they feel deeply about. They might shed a few tears, cry, shake, or sob. If you feel uncomfortable when this happens, see whether you can accept the discomfort for a little while longer. Emotional release can bring relief and trigger unexpected insights.

Ask for more. Say, "Is there anything more you want to say about that?" This question sends the speaker a message that you truly value what he has to say.

Be careful with questions and advice. Questions are directive. They can take conversations in a new direction, which may not be where the speaker wants to go. Ask questions only to clarify the speaker's message. Also be cautious about giving advice. Remember that people are different, and do not assume that you know what's best for someone else.

Take care of yourself. If you don't want to listen, be honest: "What you're telling me is important, and I'm pressed for time right now. Can we set aside another time to talk about this?" It's OK not to listen. *

Find more strategies for full listening.

Choosing to speak

You have been talking with people for most of your life, and you usually manage to get your messages across. There are times, though, when you don't. Often, these times are emotionally charged. To become a skilled speaker, begin with a sincere intention to reach common ground with your listener. Then experiment with the suggestions that follow.

Replace "you" messages with "I" messages. Psychologist Thomas Gordon suggests that when communication is emotionally charged, you should limit your statements to descriptions about yourself.[3] Replace "you" messages with "I" messages:

"You are rude" can become "I feel upset."

"You make me mad" could be "I feel angry."

"You must be crazy" can be "I don't understand."

"You don't love me anymore" could become "I'm afraid we're drifting apart."

"I" messages don't judge, blame, criticize, or insult. They don't invite the other person to counterattack with more of the same.

To create an "I" message, stick to the facts. Talk about what you—or anyone else—can see, hear, smell, taste, or touch. Avoid judgments, interpretations, or opinions. Instead of saying, "You're a slob," say, "Last night's lasagna pan was still on the stove this morning." You can also include your feelings: "When I saw that, I felt sad about the state of our household."

Remember that questions are not always questions. We sometimes use questions that aren't questions to sneak our opinions and requests into conversations. "Doesn't it upset you?" means "It upsets me." "Shouldn't we hang the picture over here?" means "I want to hang the picture over here." Communication improves when we just say, "I'm upset" and "Let's hang the picture over here."

Notice barriers to sending messages. It's easy to make excuses for not communicating. If you have fear or some other concern about sending a message, be aware of it. Don't expect the concern to go away. Realize that you can communicate even with your concerns. You can choose to make them part of the message: "I am going to tell you how I feel, and I'm afraid that you will think it's stupid."

Speak candidly. When we brood on negative thoughts and refuse to speak them out loud, we lose perspective. And when we keep joys to ourselves, we diminish our satisfaction. A solution is to share regularly what we think and feel. Psychotherapist Sidney Jourard referred to such openness and honesty as *transparency* and wrote eloquently about how it can heal and deepen relationships.[4]

Sometimes candid speaking can save a life. For example, if you think a friend is addicted to drugs, telling her so in a supportive, nonjudgmental way is a sign of friendship.

This suggestion comes with a couple of caveats. First, there is a big difference between speaking candidly about your problems and griping about them. Gripers usually don't seek solutions. They just want everyone to know how unhappy they are. Instead, talk about problems as a way to start searching for solutions.

Second, avoid bragging. Other people are turned off by constant references to how much money you have, how great your partner is, how numerous your social successes are, or how much status your family enjoys. There is a difference between sharing excitement and being obnoxious.

Speak up! Imagine a community in which people freely and lovingly speak their minds—without fear or defensiveness. That can be your community. Look for opportunities to practice speaking strategies. Join class discussions. Start conversations about topics that excite you. Ask for information and clarification. Ask for feedback on your skills.

Also speak up when you want support. After you have a clear statement of your goals and a plan for achieving them, let family members and friends know. When appropriate, let them know how they can help. You may be surprised at how often people respond to a genuine request for support. *

Find more strategies for speaking your mind.

Discovery/Intention Statement

Discover communication styles

The concept of communication styles can be useful when you want to discover sources of conflict with another person—or when you're in a conversation with someone from a different culture.

Consider the many ways in which people express themselves verbally. These characteristics can reflect an individual's preferred communication style:

- *Extroversion*—talking to others as a way to explore possibilities for taking action.
- *Introversion*—thinking through possibilities alone before talking to others.
- *Dialogue*—engaging in a discussion to hear many points of view before coming to a conclusion or decision.
- *Debate*—arguing for a particular point of view from the outset of a discussion.
- *Openness*—being ready to express personal thoughts and feelings early in a relationship.
- *Reserve*—holding back on self-expression until a deeper friendship develops.
- *A faster pace of conversation*—speaking quickly and forcefully while filling any gaps in conversation.
- *A slower pace of conversation*—speaking slowly and quietly while taking time to formulate thoughts.

These are just a few examples of differences in communication styles. You might be able to think of others.

The point is that people with different communication styles can make negative assumptions about each other. For example, those who prefer fast-paced conversations might assume that people who talk slowly are indecisive. And people who prefer slower-paced conversations might assume that people who talk quickly are pushy and uninterested in anyone else's opinion.

Take this opportunity to think about your preferred communication styles and assumptions. Do they enhance or block your relationships with other people? Think back over the conversations you've had during the past week. Then complete the following sentences, using additional paper as needed.

1. I discovered that I prefer conversations that allow me to . . .

2. I discovered that I usually feel uncomfortable in conversations when other people . . .

3. When people do the things listed in Item 2, I might make certain assumptions, such as . . .

4. As an alternative to making the assumptions listed in Item 3, I intend to . . .

Developing emotional intelligence

Emotional intelligence means recognizing feelings and responding to them in skillful ways. Daniel Goleman, author of *Emotional Intelligence: Why It Can Matter More Than IQ*, concludes that "IQ washes out when it comes to predicting who, among a talented pool of candidates within an intellectually demanding profession, will become the strongest leader." At that point, emotional intelligence starts to become more important.[5]

IF YOU'RE EMOTIONALLY intelligent, you're probably described as someone with good "people skills." That's shorthand for being aware of your feelings, acting in thoughtful ways, showing concern for others, resolving conflict, and making responsible decisions. You can deepen these skills with the following strategies:

Recognize three elements of emotion

Imagine that you suddenly perceive a threat, such as a supervisor who's screaming at you. Your heart starts beating quickly and your stomach tightens (physical sensations). Thoughts race through your head: *This is a disaster. Everyone's watching.* Finally, you take action, which could mean yelling back or fleeing.

Strong emotional reactions consist of these three elements: physical sensations, thoughts, and action. Usually they happen so fast that you can barely distinguish them. Separating them is a first step toward emotional intelligence.

Name your emotions

Naming your emotions is a First Step to going beyond the "fight or flight" reaction. People with emotional intelligence have a rich vocabulary to describe a wide range of emotions. Do an Internet search with the key words *feeling list.* Read through the lists you find for names that you can give to your feelings.

Accept your emotions

Another step toward emotional intelligence is accepting your emotions. This can be challenging if you've been taught that some emotions are "good" while others are "bad." Experiment with another viewpoint: Emotions are complicated. They have many causes that are beyond your control, including what other people do. Because you do not choose your emotional reactions from moment to moment, you cannot be held morally responsible for them. However, you can be held responsible for what you *do* in response to any emotion.

Express your emotions

One possible response to any emotion is expressing it. The key is to speak without blaming others for the way you feel. The basic tool for doing so is using "I" messages, as described on page 177.

Respond rather than react

Move from mindless reactions to mindful actions. See whether you can introduce an intentional gap between sensations and thoughts on the one hand and your next action on the other hand. To do this more often:

- Run a "mood meter." Observe your moods several times a day. On a 3x5 card, note the time of day and your emotional state. Rate your mood on a scale of 1 (relaxed and positive) to 10 (angry, sad, or afraid).
- Write Discovery Statements. In your journal, write about situations in daily life that trigger strong emotions. Describe these events and your usual responses to them.
- Write Intention Statements. After seeing patterns in your emotions, you can consciously choose to behave in new ways. Instead of yelling back at the angry supervisor, for example, make it your intention to remain silent and breathe deeply. Then say, "I'll respond after we've both had a chance to cool down."

Make decisions with emotional intelligence

Emotional intelligence can help you make decisions. When considering a choice, ask yourself, "How am I likely to *feel* if I do this?" You can use "gut feelings" to tell when an action might violate your values or hurt someone.

Think of emotions as energy. Anger, sadness, and fear send currents of sensation through your body. Ask yourself how you can channel that energy into constructive action. *

Learn more ways to develop emotional intelligence.

Managing conflict

Conflict management is one of the most practical skills you'll ever learn. Here are strategies that can help.

Back up to common ground. Begin by listing all of the points on which you are *not* in conflict: "I know that we disagree about how much to spend on a new car, but we do agree that the old one needs to be replaced." Often, such comments put the problem in perspective and pave the way for a solution.

State the problem. Using "I" messages, as explained earlier in this chapter, state the problem. Tell people what you observe, feel, think, want, and intend to do. Allow the other people in a particular conflict to do the same. Each person might have a different perception of the problem. That's fine. Let the conflict come into clear focus. It's hard to fix something unless people agree on what's broken.

Remember that the way you state the problem largely determines the solution. Defining the problem in a new way can open up a world of possibilities. For example, "I need to find a new apartment" is a problem statement that dictates one solution. "We could use some agreements about who cleans our apartment" opens up more options. If you make an agreement with your roommates that works, you might not feel the need to move.

State all points of view. If you want to defuse tension or defensiveness, set aside your opinions for a moment. Take the time to understand the other points of view. Sum up those viewpoints in words that the other parties can accept. When people feel that they've been heard, they're often more willing to listen.

Focus on solutions. After stating the problem, dream up as many solutions as you can. Be outrageous. Don't hold back. Next, evaluate the solutions you brainstormed. Choose one solution that is most acceptable to everyone involved, and implement it.

Focus on the future. Instead of rehashing the past, talk about new possibilities. Think about what you can do to prevent problems in the future. State how you intend to change, and ask others for their contributions to the solution.

Commit to the relationship. The thorniest conflicts usually arise between people who genuinely care for each other. Begin by affirming your commitment to the other person: "I care about you, and I want this relationship to last. So I'm willing to do whatever it takes to resolve this problem." Also ask the other person for a similar commitment.

Allow strong feelings. Being upset is all right. Feeling angry is often appropriate. Crying is OK. Allowing other people to see the strength of our feelings can help resolve the conflict. Often what's on the far side of anger is love. When we express and release resentment, we might discover genuine compassion in its place.

Notice your need to be "right." Some people approach conflict as a situation where only one person wins. That person has the "right" point of view. Everyone else loses. When this happens, step back. See whether you can approach the situation in a neutral way. Define the conflict as a problem to be solved, not as a contest to be won. There might be more than one acceptable solution. Let go of being "right," and aim for being effective at resolving conflict instead.

Sometimes this means apologizing. Conflict sometimes arises from our own errors. Others might move quickly to end the conflict when we acknowledge this fact and ask for forgiveness.

Slow down the communication. In times of great conflict, people often talk all at once. Words fly like speeding bullets, and no one listens. When everyone is talking at once, choose either to listen or to talk—not both at the same time. Just send your message. Or just receive the other person's message. Usually, this technique slows down the pace and allows everyone to become more levelheaded.

Communicate in writing. What can be difficult to say to another person face to face might be effectively communicated in writing. When people in conflict write letters or e-mails to each other, they automatically apply many of the suggestions in this article. Writing is a way to slow down the communication and ensure that only one person at a time is sending a message.

Remember that it is possible for people to misunderstand what you write in a letter or e-mail. To avoid further problems, make clear what you are not saying: "I am saying that I want to be alone for a few days. I am not saying that I want you to stay away forever." Saying what you are not saying is often useful in face-to-face communication as well.

© Masterfile Royalty Free

Get an objective viewpoint. Use a mediator—an objective, unbiased third party. Even an untrained mediator, as long as it's someone who is not a party to the conflict, can do much to decrease tension. Mediators can help everyone get their point of view across. The mediator's role is not to give advice but to keep the discussion on track and moving toward a solution.

Allow for cultural differences. People respond to conflict in different ways, depending on their cultural background. Some stand close, speak loudly, and make direct eye contact. Other people avert their eyes, mute their voices, and increase physical distance. When it seems to you that other people are sidestepping or escalating a conflict, consider whether your reaction is based on cultural bias.

Agree to disagree. Sometimes we do all of the problem solving we can do and the conflict still remains. Recognize that honest disagreement is a fact of life. We can peacefully coexist with other people—and respect them—even though we don't agree on fundamental issues. Conflict can be accepted even when it is not resolved.

See the conflict within you. Sometimes the turmoil we see in the outside world has its source in our own inner world. When we're angry or upset, we can take a minute to look inside. Perhaps we are ready to take offense—waiting to pounce on something the other person said. Perhaps, without realizing it, we did something to create the conflict. Or maybe the other person is simply saying what we don't want to admit is true. When these things happen, we can shine a light on our own thinking. A simple spot-check might help the conflict disappear—right before our eyes. *

Discover more ways to manage conflict.

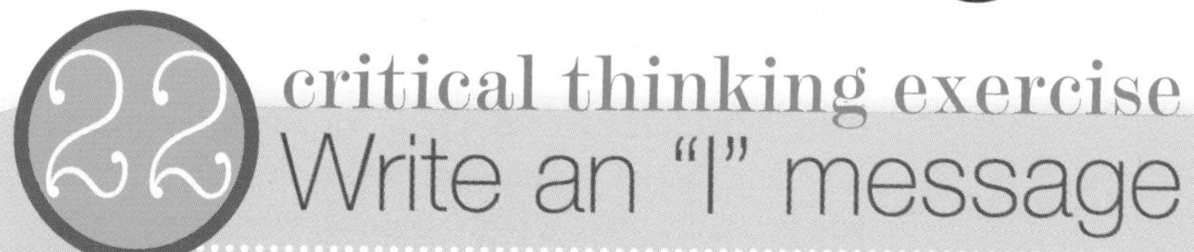

22 critical thinking exercise
Write an "I" message

First, pick something about school that irritates you. Then pretend that you are talking to a person who is associated with this irritation. In the following space, write down what you would say to this person as a "you" message.

Now write the same complaint as an "I" message.

8

COMMUNICATNG

Thriving with diversity

© iStockphoto.com/Andrea Gingerich

Higher education could bring you into the most diverse environment of your life. Your fellow students could come from many different ethnic groups, cultures, and countries.

CONSIDER THE LARGER community involved with your school—faculty members, staff members, alumni, donors, and their families. This community can include anyone from an instructor's newborn infant (age 0) to a retired instructor (age 80). Think of all the possible differences in their family backgrounds, education, job experience, religion, marital status, sexual orientation, and political viewpoints. Few institutions in our society can match the level of diversity found on some campuses.

To get the most from your education, use this environment to your advantage. Through your encounters with many types of people, gain new perspectives and new friends. Acquire skills for communicating effectively in multicultural classrooms and a global economy.

You can start by making friends from many cultures. Do this through internships and extracurricular activities that involve diverse people. Then your cultural competence will unfold in a natural, spontaneous way. Also experiment with the following strategies.

Switch cultural lenses. Diversity skills begin with learning about yourself and understanding the lenses through which you see the world. One way to do this is to intentionally switch lenses—that is, to consciously perceive familiar events in a new way.

For example, think of a situation in your life that involved an emotionally charged conflict among several people. Now mentally put yourself inside the skin of another person in that conflict. Ask, "How would I view this situation if I were that person? Or if I were a person of the opposite gender? Or if I were member of a different racial or ethnic group? Or if I were older or younger?"

Do this consistently and you'll discover that we live in a world of multiple realities. There are many different ways to interpret any event—and just as many ways to respond, given our individual differences.

Look for differences between individualist and collectivist cultures. As you switch lenses, remember some basic differences between cultures. For example, individualist cultures flourish in the United States, Canada, and Western Europe. If your family has deep roots in one of these areas, you were probably raised to value personal fulfillment and personal success. You received recognition or rewards when you stood out from your peers by earning the highest grades in your class, scoring the most points during a basketball season, or demonstrating another form of individual achievement.

In contrast, collectivist cultures value cooperation over competition. Group progress is more important than individual success. Credit for an achievement is widely shared. If you were raised in such a culture, you probably place a high value on your family and were taught to respect your elders. Collectivist cultures dominate Asia, Africa, and Latin America.

In short, individualist cultures emphasize "I," while collectivist cultures emphasize "we." Forgetting about the differences between them can strain a friendship or wreck an international business deal.

If you were raised in an individualist culture, consider the following strategies when communicating with others:

- Remember that someone from a collectivist culture may place a high value on "saving face." This involves more than simply avoiding embarrassment. This person may not want to be singled out from other members of a group even for a positive achievement. If you have a direct request for this person or want to share something that could be taken as a personal criticism, save it for a private conversation.

- Respect titles and last names. Although Americans often like to use first names immediately after meeting someone, in some cultures this practice is acceptable only among family members. Especially in work settings, use last names and job titles during your first meetings. Allow time for informal relationships to develop.
- Put messages in context. For members of collectivist cultures, words convey only part of an intended message. Notice gestures and other nonverbal communication as well.

If you were raised in a collectivist culture, you can creatively "reverse" the items in this list. For instance, remember that direct questions from an American student or coworker are meant not to offend but only to clarify an idea. Don't be surprised if you are called by a nickname, if no one asks about your family, or if you are rewarded for a personal achievement. And in social situations, remember that indirect cues might not get another person's attention. Practice asking clearly and directly for what you want.

Look for common ground. Students in higher education often find that they worry about many of the same things—including tuition bills, the quality of dormitory food, and the shortage of on-campus parking spaces. And our fundamental goals as human beings—such as health, physical safety, and economic security—are desires that cross culture lines.

The key is to honor the differences among people while remembering what we have in common. Diversity is not just about our differences; it's about our similarities. On a biological level, less than 1 percent of the human genome accounts for visible characteristics such as skin color. In terms of our genetic blueprint, we are more than 99 percent the same.[6]

Look for individuals, not group representatives. Sometimes the way we speak glosses over differences among individuals and reinforces stereotypes. For example, a student who is worried about her grade in math may express concern over "all those Asian students who are skewing the class curve." Or a white music major may assume that her African American classmate knows a lot about jazz or hip-hop music. We can avoid such errors by seeing people as individuals—not spokespersons for an entire group.

Be willing to accept feedback. Members of another culture might let you know that some of your words or actions had a meaning other than what you intended. A comment that seems harmless to you may be offensive to them, and they may tell you directly about it.

Avoid responding to such feedback with comments such as "Don't get me wrong," "You're taking this way too seriously," or "You're too sensitive."

Instead, listen without resistance. Open yourself to what others have to say. Remember to distinguish between the intention of your behavior from its actual impact on other people. Then take the feedback you receive and ask how you can use it to communicate more effectively in the future.

If you are new at responding to diversity, then expect to make some mistakes along the way. However, as long as you approach people in a spirit of tolerance, your words and actions can always be changed.

Speak up against discrimination. You might find yourself in the presence of someone who tells a racist joke, makes a homophobic comment, or utters an ethnic slur. When this happens, you have a right to state what you observe, share what you think, and communicate how you feel.

Depending on the circumstance, you might say,

- "That's a stereotype and we don't have to fall for it."
- "Other people are going to take offense at that. Let's tell jokes that don't put people down."
- "I realize that you don't mean to offend anybody, but I feel hurt and angry by what you just said."
- "As members of the majority culture around here, we can easily forget how comments like that affect other people."

Also keep in mind that someone from a specific ethnic or cultural background can also be the source of negative comments about that culture. Speak up against discriminatory comments from any source.

This kind of speaking may be the most difficult communicating you ever do. And if you don't do it, you give the impression that you agree with biased speech.

In response to your candid comments, many people will apologize and express their willingness to change. Even if they don't, you can still know that you practiced integrity by aligning your words with your values. *

Staying smart in cyberspace—safe social networking

WEB SITES SUCH AS MySpace and Facebook create value for their users. Activity in these online communities can also have unexpected consequences. You might find examples of "cyberbullying," which is hate speech or threats. And some users find that embarrassing details from their online profiles come back to haunt them years later.

Use simple strategies to stay in charge of your safety, reputation, and integrity when you are online.

Post only what you want made public and permanent. Friends, relatives, university administrators, potential employers, and police officers might be able to access your online profile. Anyone with Internet access can take your words and images and post them on a Web site or distribute them via e-mail. Don't post anything that could embarrass you later.

To avoid unwanted encounters with members of online communities, also avoid posting the following:

- Your home or school address
- Your phone number
- Your birth date
- Your screen name for instant messaging
- Your financial information
- Information about places you plan to visit in the future
- Provocative pictures or messages with sexual innuendos
- To further protect your safety, don't add strangers to your list of online friends. Also use caution and common sense when joining groups.

Be honest and polite. After you've chosen what information to post, make sure that it's accurate. False information can lead to expulsion from a community.

Politeness counts, too. Remember that the recipient on the other end is a human being. Whenever you're at a keyboard or cell phone, typing up messages, ask yourself, "Would I say this to the person's face?"

Use privacy features. Many online communities offer options for blocking messages from strangers. Several social networking sites also allow you to create both private and public profiles. (Look for a link on each site titled "Frequently Asked Questions," or "Privacy Settings.")

Be cautious about meeting community members in person. Because people can give misleading or false information about themselves online, think carefully before agreeing to meet them in person. If you do opt for a face-to-face meeting, choose a public place, and bring along a friend you trust.

Report malicious content. Report content that you consider offensive or dangerous to site administrators. In many online communities, you can do this anonymously.

You can help to prevent intolerance, prejudice, and discrimination. Set a positive counterexample by posting messages that demonstrate acceptance. *

Learn more about smart social networking.

mastering technology

MASTER STUDENTS—GET NETWORKED

Learning naturally occurs in social networks—that is, among groups of teachers and students. With technology, you can extend your network across the reach of the Internet. For example:

- Choose a topic that interests you, and search for related Web sites and podcasts.
- Use an RSS reader such as Google Reader, Bloglines, or NetNewsWire to get updated lists of articles on the Web sites you'd like to follow.
- Use e-mail, social networking, and chat rooms to contact experts on your topic.
- Use videoconferencing Web sites to converse in real time with people across the world.
- Pay special attention to well-written blogs, and join the discussion by commenting on the postings.
- Create your own blog to document your learning, and welcome comments from others.

Strategies for effective writing

Effective writing is essential to your success. Papers, presentations, essay tests, e-mail, social networking sites—and even the occasional text message—call for your ability to communicate ideas with force and clarity.

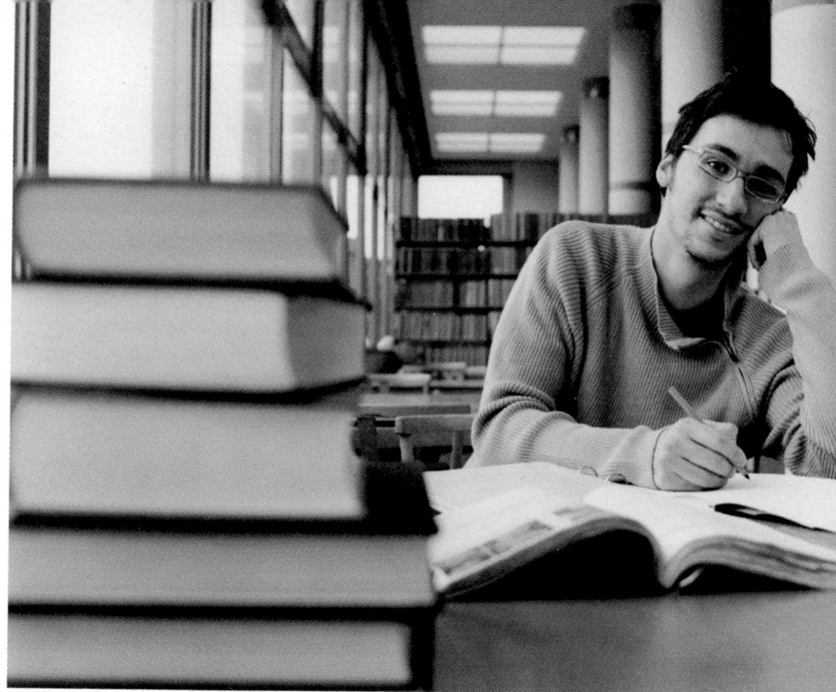
Digital Vision/Getty

Schedule and list writing tasks. You can divide the ultimate goal—such as a finished paper—into smaller steps to do right away. Estimate how long it will take to complete each step. Start with the date your paper is due and work backward to the present. Say that the due date is December 1, and you have about 3 weeks to write the paper. To give yourself a cushion, schedule November 28 as your targeted completion date. Plan what you want to get done by November 21, and then list what you want to get done by November 14.

Select a topic and working title. Using your instructor's guidelines for the paper or speech, write down a list of topics that interest you. Write as many of these ideas as you can think of in 2 minutes. Then choose one topic. A common pitfall is selecting a topic that's too broad. "Harriet Tubman" is not a useful topic for your American history paper. Instead, consider "Harriet Tubman's activities as a Union spy during the Civil War." Your topic statement can function as a working title.

Write a thesis statement. Clarify what you want to say about your topic by summarizing it in one sentence. This sentence is called a thesis statement. Unlike a topic, it is expressed in a complete sentence, including a verb. "Diversity" is a topic. "Cultural diversity is valuable" is a thesis statement.

Consider your purpose. Think about how you'd like your reader or listener to respond after considering your ideas. Do you want your audience to think differently, to feel differently, or to take a certain action? How you answer these questions greatly affects your writing strategy. If you want someone to *think* differently, make your writing clear and logical. Support your assertions with evidence. If you want someone to *feel* differently, consider crafting a story. Write about a character your audience can empathize with, and tell how that character resolves a problem that the audience can relate to. And if your purpose is to move the reader into *action*, explain exactly what steps to take and offer solid benefits for doing so.

Do initial research. At the initial stage, the objective of your research is not to uncover specific facts about your topic. That comes later. First, you want to gain an overview of the subject. Discover the structure of your topic—its major divisions and branches.

Outline. An outline is a kind of map. When you follow a map, you avoid getting lost. Likewise, an outline keeps you from wandering off the topic. To start an outline, gather a stack of 3x5 cards. Using the information gathered from your initial research, brainstorm ideas you want to include in your paper. Write one phrase or sentence per card. Then experiment with the cards. Group them into separate stacks, each stack representing one major category. After that, arrange the stacks in order. Finally, arrange the cards within each stack in a logical order. Rearrange them until you discover an organization that you like. If you write on a computer, consider using the outlining feature of your word-processing software.

Do in-depth research. You can find information about research skills in Chapter 4: "Reading" and Chapter 5: "Notes." Following are more suggestions.

One option is to take notes on 3x5 cards. Use these cards to record your own ideas and ideas from your sources, such as books, periodicals, and Web sites. Write down one idea or fact per card. This allows you to easily sort cards into different categories based on your outline.

Be sure to put quotation marks around each sentence or paragraph that you copy word for word from your sources. Write down the source of each quote as well, including author, title, publication date, and name of the publisher. (Ask your instructor for examples of what information to include about your sources.)

Instead of quoting material from your sources, you can also paraphrase or summarize them. To avoid plagiarism (see the sidebar), be sure put the author's ideas in your own words. Also record the source of paraphrased or summarized material.

Instead of taking notes on cards, you might choose to use a computer. If so, follow the same guidelines about quoting, paraphrasing, and summarizing your sources.

Write a first draft. Gather your notes and arrange them to follow your outline. Then write about the ideas in your notes. Write in paragraphs, with one main idea per paragraph. If you have organized your notes logically, related facts and ideas will appear close to one another. At this stage, don't stop to revise your writing. Your goal at this point is simply to finish a complete draft of your paper. Then let your first draft sit for a day or two before you go to the next step.

Revise, revise, revise. Schedule plenty of time to slow down and take a microscope to your work. One effective way to revise your paper is to read it out loud. Another technique is to have a friend look over your paper. This is never a substitute for your own review, but a friend can often see things you miss.

To revise efficiently, first look for pages, paragraphs, sentences, and words that you can cut. Next, rearrange what's left of your draft so that it flows logically. Finally, polish by looking for the following:

- A clear thesis statement
- Sentences that introduce your topic, guide the reader through the major sections of your paper, and summarize your conclusions
- Details—such as quotations, examples, and statistics—that support your conclusions.
- Lean sentences that are free of needless words
- Plenty of action verbs and concrete, specific nouns

Finally, proofread your writing. Correct any grammar and punctuation areas. Format your paper or presentation according to your instructor's guidelines and print out a clean copy. Then savor the feeling of finishing your paper. See every writing assignment as a chance to demonstrate mastery. *

Learn more ways to make your writing shine.

Academic integrity: Avoid plagiarism

Using another person's words, images, or other original creations without giving proper credit is called plagiarism. Plagiarism amounts to taking someone else's work and presenting it as your own—the equivalent of cheating on a test. The consequences of plagiarism can range from a failing grade to expulsion from school.

To avoid plagiarism, ask an instructor where to find your school's written policy on this issue. Read this document carefully (no kidding). Ask questions about anything you don't understand.

When writing, be sure to cite a source for each passage, sequence of ideas, or image created by another person. Although ideas cannot be copyrighted, the way that any idea is *expressed* in words and images can be.

In addition:

- If you use a direct quote from another writer or speaker, put that person's words in quotation marks. List the source of the quotation as well.
- Paraphrase and summarize with care. Paraphrasing means restating someone else's message in your own words, usually making it shorter and simpler. This does *not* mean copying a passage word for word and then just rearranging or deleting a few phrases. List a source for paraphrased or summarized material, just as you do for direct quotes.
- When you use the same sequence of ideas as one of your sources—even if you have not quoted, paraphrased, or summarized—cite that source.
- List a source for any idea that is closely identified with a particular person.
- Submit only your own work. Turning in materials that are written or revised by someone else puts your education at risk.

Learn more about avoiding plagiarism.

Speaking in class

© Masterfile Royalty Free

When you speak up in class, you step out from the sidelines and start playing full out. Polishing your presentation and discussion skills can help you think on your feet and communicate clearly. Those are skills you can use in any course—and in any career.

Analyze your audience. Developing a presentation is similar to writing a paper. Begin by choosing your topic, purpose, and thesis statement as described in "Strategies for effective writing" on page 185.

Also remember that audiences generally have one question in mind: *So what?* They want to know that your presentation relates to their desires. To convince people that you have something worthwhile to say, write down the main point of your presentation. Then see whether you can complete this sentence: *I'm telling you this because . . . .*

Organize your presentation. Consider the length of your presentation. Time yourself as you practice speaking. Aim for a lean presentation—just enough to make your point and avoid making your audience restless. Leave your listeners wanting more. When you speak, be brief and then be seated.

Communicate your message in three parts. Presentations are usually organized into three main sections: the introduction, the main body, and the conclusion.

Rambling speeches with no clear point or organization put audiences to sleep. Solve this problem with your introduction. State your main point in a way that gets attention. Then give your audience a hint of what's coming next. For example: "More people have died from hunger in the past 5 years than have been killed in all of the wars, revolutions, and murders in the past 150 years. Yet there is enough food to go around. I'm honored to be here with you today to share a solution to this problem."

In the main body of your presentation, develop your ideas in the same way that you develop a written paper. Cover each point in order. Support each point with notable facts, quotations, and interesting stories. Also be prepared to offer a source for each of these.

During this part of your presentation, transitions are especially important. Use meaningful pauses and phrases to let people know where you're at and where you're going: "On the other hand, until the public realizes what is happening to children in these countries . . . ." Or, "The second reason hunger persists is . . . ."

For the conclusion, summarize your key points and draw your conclusion in a way that no one will forget. You started with a bang; now finish with drama.

The introduction and conclusion of a speech are the most important sections. Your introduction grabs your audience's attention; your conclusion drives home the main point while making it clear that you've reached the end. Avoid endings such as "This is the end of my speech" and "Umm, I guess that's it." A simple standby is this: "In conclusion, I want to reiterate three points. . . ."

When you are finished, just stop talking.

Create speaking notes. Some professional speakers recommend writing out your speech in full and then putting key words or main points on a few 3x5 cards. Number the cards so that if you drop them, you can quickly put them in order again. As you finish the information on each card, move it to the back of the pile. Write information clearly and in letters large enough to be seen from a distance.

Other speakers prefer to use standard outlined notes instead of cards. Another option is mind mapping. Even an hour-long speech can be mapped on one sheet of paper.

Whatever method you choose, use suggestions from Chapter 3: "Memory" to remember your speech.

Create supporting visuals. Presentations often include visuals such as overhead transparencies, flip charts, or slides created with presentation software. These can reinforce your main points. Remember that effective visuals complement rather than replace your speaking. If you use too many visuals—or visuals that are too complex—your audience might focus on them and forget about you.

Overcome fear of speaking. Take steps to reduce your fear of speaking to groups of people. Start by preparing thoroughly. Do plenty of research and learn a lot about your topic. In addition, forget about "making a speech." Your job is not to perform or entertain. Your job is to give people valuable ideas and information that they can use. Focus on the content of presentation rather than on yourself. Ultimately, your classroom audience is more interested in *what* you have to say than *how* you say it.

Practice your presentation. One key to successful speaking is practice. Deliver your presentation many times in private before you give it in public. Speak loudly and clearly. If you find yourself repeating certain words—*you know, kind of, really, uh, umm, ahh*—remind yourself that you don't use those words anymore. Also avoid reading your notes word for word. When you know your material well, you can speak in a natural way.

Join class discussions. You can apply many of the above suggestions to any kind of speaking that you do in class. Get prepared for class discussions by keeping up with your reading and other assignments. In your notes, write out questions to ask in class and other ideas you want to share. Then, when it's your turn to speak, talk loudly enough to be heard and stick to the point.

In addition, accept any fear that you feel about speaking up in class. You can feel nervous and still join the discussion. Focus on your ideas rather than what other people are thinking about you. Just keep speaking—and celebrating your growing mastery. *

Making the grade in group presentations

When preparing group presentations, you can use three strategies for making a memorable impression.

Get organized. As soon as you get the assignment, select a group leader and exchange contact information. Schedule specific times and places for planning, researching, writing, and practicing your presentation.

At your first meeting, write a to-do list that includes all of the tasks involved in completing the assignment. Distribute tasks fairly, paying attention to the strengths of individuals in your group. For example, some people excel at brainstorming, whereas others prefer researching.

One powerful way to get started is to define clearly the topic and thesis, or main point, of your presentation. Then support your thesis by looking for the most powerful facts, quotations, and anecdotes you can find.

As you get organized, remember how your presentation will be evaluated. If the instructor doesn't give grading criteria, create your own.

Get coordinated. Coordinate your presentation so that you have transitions between individual speakers. Practice making those transitions smooth.

Also practice using visuals such as flip charts, posters, DVDs, videos, or slides. To give visuals their full impact, make them appropriate for the room where you will present. Make sure that text is large enough to be seen from the back of the room. For bigger rooms, consider using presentation software or making overhead transparencies.

Get cooperation. Presentations that get top scores take teamwork and planning—not egos. Communicate with group members in an open and sensitive way. Contribute your ideas, and be responsive to the viewpoints of other members. When you cooperate, your group is on the way to an effective presentation.

Employ Your Word

When you give your word, you are creating—literally. You create your life, for the most part, by the agreements you make. To learn about who you are, observe which commitments you choose to keep and which ones you choose to avoid.

Relationships are built on agreements. When we break a promise to be faithful to a spouse, to help a friend move to a new apartment, or to pay a bill on time, relationships are strained. When we keep agreements, on the other hand, relationships flourish.

The words we use to make agreements can be placed onto several different levels. Think of each level as one rung on a ladder—the ladder of powerful speaking. The farther you move up the ladder, the more effectively you commit to create the life you want. This is what it means to employ your word.

The lowest rung on the ladder is obligation. Words used at this level include *I should*, *he ought to*, *someone had better*, *they need to*, *I must*, and *I had to*. Speaking this way implies that something other than ourselves is in control of our lives. When we live at the level of obligation, we speak as if we are victims.

The next rung up is possibility. At this level, we examine new options. We play with new ideas, possible solutions, and alternative courses of action. As we do, we learn that we can make choices that dramatically affect the quality of our lives. We are not the victims of circumstance. Phrases that signal this level include *I might*, *I could*, *I'll consider*, *I hope to*, and *maybe*.

From possibility, we can move up to preference. Here we begin the process of choice. The words *I prefer* signal that we're moving toward one set of possibilities over another, perhaps setting the stage for eventual action.

Above preference is a rung called passion. Again, certain words signal this level: *I want to*, *I'm really excited to do that*, and *I can't wait*.

Action is preceded by the next rung—planning. When people use phrases such as *I intend to*, *my goal is to*, *I plan to*, and *I'll try like mad to*, they're at the level of planning. The Intention Statements you write in this book are examples of planning.

The highest rung on the ladder is promising. At this level, it's common to use phrases such as these: *I will*, *I promise to*, *I am committed*, and *you can count on it*.

Promising is where we bridge from possibility and planning to action. In making new promises, we declare our intention to change our behavior. And, in changing our behavior, we create new results in our lives.

At this level, promising becomes an act of creation. Promising brings with it all of the rewards of employing your word.

Learn more about this Power Process online.

Put it to Work

You can use strategies you learn in Becoming a Master Student to succeed at work. To discover ways in which your new communication skills can transfer to your career, reflect on the following case study.

Mark Hyland earned an associate's degree in dental hygiene and then completed a B.A. in business administration. Soon after graduating, he moved back to his hometown and went to work as an office manager for his family dentist.

Mark welcomed the chance to apply the skills he'd gained in school. He ordered supplies, managed the payroll, handled the day-to-day accounting chores, and filed tax returns for the business.

Everyone in the dental office admitted that Mark's skills in these areas were superb. His communication skills were another matter, though. Several long-term patients complained that Mark's manner was condescending—even harsh—during casual conversations at the office.

One day, the dentist who hired Mark overheard him talking to a patient.

"I just happened to glance at your records and noticed that you've got a lot of plaque on your upper teeth," said Mark. "Do you ever floss?"

The patient tried to make light of the situation. "Oh well," she said, "we all have our vices, and . . . ."

"Yeah, but it's your teeth we're talking about here," Mark said, interrupting her. "They're really stained too, from drinking too much coffee."

The dentist winced. He feared he was about to lose a valued patient. However, he'd known Mark for years and counted his parents as friends. He wanted to meet with Mark and give him feedback, yet the dentist knew that this conversation would be awkward for both of them. He found this meeting an easy thing to put off.

Review the suggestions given in this chapter for creating "I" messages. Then write an "I" message that the dentist could use to express his concerns with Mark.

____

____

____

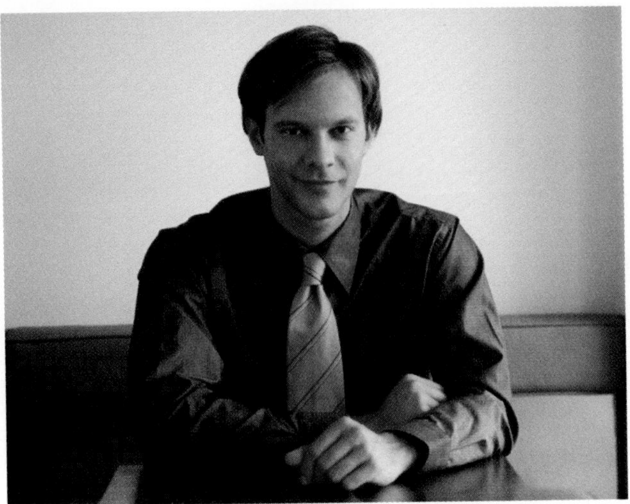

Sanna Lindberg/PhotoAlto Agency RF Collections/Getty

Also list some suggestion for Mark to keep in mind when talking to patients.

____

____

____

____

____

____

____

____

In addition, consider the following strategies for communicating effectively during your first crucial year as a new employee:

- Use memory techniques to learn coworkers' names quickly.
- Be honest when you don't understand directions—and willing to ask questions.
- Be open to feedback about your performance and willing to change your behavior on the basis of that feedback.
- Be willing to complete the mundane tasks that are part of almost every job; understand what it means to "pay your dues" in a constructive way.
- To gain credibility in your organization, get involved in a high-profile project, and then perform well.
- Each day, look for a simple way to demonstrate a positive attitude and strong work ethic.

Quiz

Name____ Date____/____/____

1. According to the text, job interviewers are more interested in technical skills than communication skills. True or false? Explain your answer.
   False. According to the National Association of Colleges and Employers (and the text), what interviewers look for most of all in job applicants is skill in communicating—the ability to write and speak clearly and persuasively. (*Communicating in a diverse world*, p. 175)
2. Explain a potential problem with asking questions while you listen.
   Asking questions while listening can take conversations in a new direction, which may not be where the speaker wants to go. Ask questions only to clarify the speaker's message. (*Choosing to listen,* p. 176)
3. Emotional intelligence involves
   (a) Naming feelings.
   (b) Accepting feelings.
   (c) Responding to feelings in skillful ways.
   (d) Expressing feelings.
   (e) All of the above.
   (e) All of the above. (*Developing emotional intelligence*, p. 179)
4. Effective "I" messages
   (a) Stick to the facts—what we can hear or see.
   (b) Offer constructive criticism of other people.
   (c) Avoid any mention of how you feel.
   (d) None of the above.
   (a) Stick to the facts—what we can hear or see. (*Choosing to speak*, p. 177)
5. Reword the following complaint as a request: "You always interrupt when I talk!"
   Possible rewordings include "Before you begin to talk, please let me finish" and "I'd like to finish making my point; please allow me to do that." (*Choosing to listen,* p. 176)
6. You can listen skillfully to a speaker even when you disagree with that person's viewpoint. True or false? Explain your answer.
   True. Effective listening does not mean that we're obligated to agree with the message. The key to effective listening is understanding before evaluating. (*Choosing to listen,* p. 176)
7. Which of the following is an effective thesis statement? Explain your answer.
   (a) Two types of thinking
   (b) Critical thinking and creative thinking go hand in hand.
   (c) The relationship between critical thinking and creative thinking
   (b) Critical thinking and creative thinking go hand in hand. This is a complete sentence (including a verb) that makes an assertion. (*Strategies for effective writing,* pp. 185–186)
8. Define plagiarism, and explain ways to avoid it.
   Plagiarism is when you use another person's words, images, or other original creations without giving proper credit. Plagiarism amounts to taking someone else's work and presenting it as your own. The basic guideline for preventing plagiarism is to cite a source for each phrase, sequence of ideas, or visual image created by another person.
   Explain one or more of the following methods for preventing plagiarism:
   - Identify direct quotes.
   - Paraphrase carefully.
   - Note details about each of your sources.
   - Submit only your own work. (*Academic integrity: Avoid plagiarism*, p. 186)
9. Describe at least three techniques for speaking in class.
   Describe three of the following:
   - Analyze your audience.
   - Organize your presentation
   - Communicate your message in three parts.
   - Create speaking notes.
   - Create supporting visuals.
   - Overcome fear of speaking.
   - Practice your presentation.
   - Join class discussions. (Answers will vary.) (*Speaking in class*, pp. 187–188)
10. Write one example of a statement on the lowest rung of the ladder of powerful speaking—and a statement on the highest rung.
    Lowest rung: I ought to study for my chemistry test this weekend. Highest rung: I am committed to studying for my chemistry test this weekend. (Answers will vary.) (*Power Process: Employ Your Word,* p. 189)

Skills Snapshot

By now you've had a chance to read this chapter and apply some of the suggestions it includes. Take a few minutes to revisit your responses to the "Communicating" section of the Discovery Wheel exercise on page 25. Then complete the following sentences.

The technique that has made the biggest difference in my skill at listening is . . .

When I hear an accomplished public speaker, the skill that I notice first and most admire is . . .

When I'm effective at managing conflict, I am remembering to . . .

I'll know that I've reached a new level of mastery with my communication skills when . . .

To reach that level of mastery, the most important thing I can do next is to . . .

Master Student PROFILE

Sampson Davis

. . . is determined.

© Michael Didyoung/Retna Ltd./Corbis

(1973–) As a teenager growing up in Newark, New Jersey, Sampson made a pact with two of his friends to "beat the street," attend college, and become a physician.

Medical school was one of the roughest periods of my life. Something unexpected was always threatening to knock me out of the game: family distractions, the results of my first state board exam, the outcome of my initial search for a residency. But through determination, discipline, and dedication, I was able to persevere.

I call them my three D's, and I believe that they are the perfect formula for survival, no matter what you are going through.

Determination is simply fixing your mind on a desired outcome, and I believe it is the first step to a successful end in practically any situation. When I made the pact with George and Rameck at the age of seventeen, I was desperate to change my life. Going to college and medical school with my friends seemed the best way to make that happen.

But, of course, I had no idea of the challenges awaiting me, and many times over the years I felt like giving up. Trust me, even if you're the most dedicated person, you can get weary when setbacks halt or interfere with your progress. But determination means nothing without the discipline to go through the steps necessary to reach your goal—whether you're trying to lose weight or finish college—and the dedication to stick with it.

When I failed the state board exam, the light in the tunnel disappeared. But I just kept crawling toward my goal. I sought counseling when I needed it, and I found at least one person with whom I could share the range of emotions I was experiencing. If you're going through a difficult time and can't see your way out alone, you should consider asking for help. I know how difficult that is for most guys. . . . But reaching out to counselors I had come to trust over the years and talking to my roommate Camille helped me unload some of the weight I was carrying. Only then was I able to focus clearly on what I needed to do to change my circumstances.

I'm grateful that I took kung fu lessons as a kid, because the discipline I learned back then really helped me to stay consistent once I started meditating, working out, and studying every single day. . . .

Another important ingredient of perseverance is surrounding yourself with friends who support your endeavor. I can't tell you how much it helped me to have George and Rameck in my life to help me reach my goal. Even though things were awkward between us for a while after I failed the state boards, just knowing they were there and that they expected me to succeed motivated me.

I found motivation wherever I could. One of my college professors once told me that I didn't have what it takes to be a doctor, and I even used that to motivate me. I love being the underdog. I love it when someone expects me to fail. That, like nothing else, can ignite my three D's.

And when success comes, I'm the one who's not surprised.

For more biographical information about Sampson Davis, visit the Master Student Hall of Fame.

9 Health

Instructor Tools & Tips

> "To be somebody you must last.
>
> —**Ruth Gordon**
>
> Emotion, which is suffering, ceases to be suffering as soon as we have a clear picture of it.
>
> —**Baruch Spinoza**

Preview

Staying healthy while pursuing higher education is an important skill all students need to master. Juggling work, college courses, and family responsibilities can be quite stressful. It is essential that first-year students start their education on the right foot with strategies for maintaining their "machine." The revised "Health" chapter in the thirteenth edition of *Becoming a Master Student Concise* provides resources for beginning conversations about such topics as eating well, exercising, personal safety, self-esteem, alcohol abuse, and addiction. Don't hesitate to seek an opinion—from your campus health center or a community outreach program—when you need an expert's voice to support the text.

Some of you may feel uncertain *how* to begin discussing serious health issues in your classroom. One way to initiate to conversation is to have students revisit the answers they filled in on their Discovery Wheel. Using the Discovery and Intention Journal Entry system, you can begin a discussion about stress by asking *what* factors are causing your students to feel stress. This discussion can lead to asking *why* these issues might be considered stressful. As a class, you can brainstorm possible *what if* scenarios to reduce students' stress. Then have your students write Intention Statements about steps they can take the next time they are experiencing high levels of stress.

Guest Speaker

Invite a guest speaker from the student wellness or health center for this portion of the class. You could even contact your county health department as a resource. Often, students will pay more attention to a visiting professional. Ask your presenter to discuss the importance of health and the relationship of health to learning. Be sure to allow time for a question-and-answer period.

Another idea is to ask whether a local chapter of Alcoholics Anonymous or Narcotics Anonymous can provide a guest speaker or, better yet, a panel of speakers. Although these programs emphasize anonymity, some participants, as part of their program of recovery, choose to share their story as a way of educating others. These individuals can have a powerful impact on your students.

Lecture

Choose to stay safe (pages 201–202). Here is a lecture idea from an instructor:

> "I've been involved in AIDS education since the 1980s. The best weapon we have to fight HIV/AIDS is education, so we spend about 30 to 45 minutes on this topic in my College Success classes. The college years are the time for many students to experiment with sexual behaviors. Many know that they need to practice abstinence to be totally safe or, if sexually active, to practice safer sex. However, many students do not know what behaviors are considered risky or what skills are involved in practicing safer sex. So I teach not only the fact that condoms may prevent the transmission of HIV but also specific skills in condom usage. My primary objectives are for students to learn effective communication skills in negotiating the use of a condom with their partners as well as the skills needed to stay safe during sexual activities. I use explicit language; I incorporate humor and frank discussion, as well as a demonstration on how to use a condom. This is one topic where you will find the entire class will "be here now."
>
> —**Deborah Warfield, Seminole Community College**

Exercises/Activities

1. Avoiding negative thinking. Here is a suggestion from an instructor:

> When change is requested of students, they often unconsciously say, "I can't . . . ." I ask my students to take a closer look at times when they say these statements and to begin to replace the "I can't" with "I won't."
>
> Have your students make a list of those "I can't" statements. From this list, have them select one and restate the sentence with "won't" instead of "can't." Then, ask your students to describe any distinction between these two statements. Generally students will say that the "I won't" statement implies some choice in the matter, and the experience changes from being one of victimization to taking some responsibility.
>
> The last step is to have students replace the "I won't" with "I don't know how." Again I ask students to describe any distinction between this statement and the "I won't" statement. Students often experience a weight off their shoulders or realize they were operating under a false expectation such as, "I should know this." Students at this point can write a Discovery and Intention Statement about their experience.
>
> Chapter 9 provides students with an opportunity to practice taking more responsibility for their thoughts (intrapersonal communications) and to use the steps in critical thinking.
>
> I have students list some of their negative thoughts. They often say things like "I'll never get as much sleep as suggested" or "I'll never reduce my anxiety before test taking."
>
> I ask students to rewrite their sentences to look like this: "I thought I would never get enough sleep" or "I thought I would never reduce my anxiety before test taking."
>
> I have students rewrite these statements over and over again, emphasizing the word *thought*. At some point, students will smile and say, "Oh I get it, I just 'thought' I would never get enough sleep," or "I see it now, I 'thought' I would never reduce my anxiety before test taking."
>
> We often turn our thoughts into reality or a belief without going through the steps in critical thinking. This is related to a self-fulfilling prophecy, or self-efficacy, described in the article "Developing self-esteem" in Chapter 9 and the Power Process: "I Create It All" in Chapter 5.
>
> **—Fred Kester, Yavapai College**

2. Master Student Profile: Randy Pausch (page 211). After students read the inspirational story about Randy Pausch, ask them to think about how their childhood dreams can be connected to their career goals.

Conversation/Sharing

Power Process: Surrender (page 207). Use the following example to open a discussion about this Power Process with your students:

Sally and Jane leave work on Friday at the same time. Both are caught in rush-hour traffic. Sally frets, honks her horn, and changes lanes as frequently as possible with the hope of saving time. She curses the light when it changes to red, gets aggravated at cars that don't start moving fast enough when the light changes to green, frantically listens to the traffic reports on the radio, agonizes about all the things she's missing at home, worries because she is getting very low on gas, and arrives home at 6:09 p.m. with a headache. Jane surrenders. Rather than fighting and resisting the traffic, she accepts it and flows with it. She listens to her favorite radio station, plans her activities for the weekend, thinks of a better way for taking purchase orders at work, sees a new Chinese restaurant she wants to try, notices the trees and plants telling her that spring is here, repeats her affirmations about self-improvement, anticipates the warm greeting she will receive from her family, and arrives home at 6:09 with a smile.

More examples like this one are available on the Instructor Companion site.

Homework

Choose to rest (page 200). College students frequently complain that they have trouble getting a good night's sleep. For a homework assignment, have your students research solutions to sleep disorders online and bring an interesting article to class. Have them share these articles in small groups and then discuss the body's need for rest and how sleep deprivation can affect their schoolwork.

Alcohol and other drugs: THE TRUTH (pages 205–206). Some college students are trying to enhance their focus, memory, and brain performance by taking controlled medications that are prescribed for other purposes. These drugs include Ritalin, Adderall, and Provigil. Assign students to research the intended medical purposes of these drugs as well as the precautions and side effects associated with them.

Evaluation

Ask students to describe strategies for finding more time to exercise. Ask students to write Discovery and Intention Statements about ways to prevent and treat eating disorders. Ask students to describe tools for dealing with emotional pain. Ask students to identify several strategies that can be used to quit smoking.

Additional Digital Resources

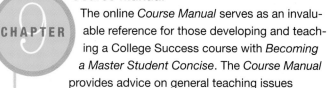

CHAPTER 9

Course Manual

The online *Course Manual* serves as an invaluable reference for those developing and teaching a College Success course with *Becoming a Master Student Concise*. The *Course Manual* provides advice on general teaching issues such as preparing for classes, classroom management, grading, and communicating with students of various backgrounds, as well as specific strategies on getting the most out of various features in *Becoming a Master Student Concise* and book-specific Web sites. Do a *Course Manual* reconnaissance to find ideas that you can use in your course right now.

Instructor Companion Site

The updated Instructor Companion Site provides resources to help you plan and customize your course. Content specific to Chapter 9 includes:

- Lecture Ideas
    - Addiction – Some Facts to Consider
    - Getting Trapped and Getting Out
    - Recognizing and Beating "Burnout"
- In-Class Exercises
    - Speeches Promote Learning
    - What I Like about Myself
    - A Nutrition Journal
- In-Text Quiz Answers
- PowerPoint Slides

The Instructor Companion Site also contains the following book specific content:

- ExamView Test Bank
- Online Course Manual
- Sample Syllabi
- Detailed Transition Guide

College Success CourseMate

To help your students gain a better understanding of the topics discussed in *Becoming a Master Student Concise*, encourage them to visit the College Success CourseMate at CengageBrain.com that provides the following resources specific to Chapter 9:

- Connect to Text content expands on specific topics marked with an icon within Chapter 9.
- Practice Tests allow students to see how well they understand the themes of *Becoming a Master Student Concise.*
- Interactive Concept Maps promote critical thinking by highlighting related ideas to show relationships among concepts.
- Video Skillbuilders bring to life techniques that will help students to excel in college and beyond. The following videos should give your students more information regarding topics covered in Chapter 9:
    - Healthy Living: Making the Right Choices
    - Keeping Your Mind and Body in Shape
- Learning Styles Application
- Discussion Topics
- Reflection Questions
- Assessment Questions
- Experiment with chapter strategies
- Remembering Cultural Differences presents readers with brief articles that touch on aspects of diversity in our rapidly changing world. For Chapter 9, the following article will prompt your students to look at contemporary issues in a new way:
    - A Holistic Approach to Health
- Master Student Profiles provide additional information on the people covered in this book feature. For Chapter 9, students will find expanded coverage and links about:
    - Randy Pausch
- Power Process Media contains video, PowerPoints, and audio files to take what your students have learned from the Power Processes in their book to the next level. For Chapter 9, students will find additional media on:
    - Surrender

Along with the chapter-specific content, a General Resources folder is available that contains Toolboxes geared toward specific student types (Community College, Adult Learner, Student Athlete), the Plagiarism Prevention Zone, and the Career Resource Center.

9 Health

Master Student Map

as you read, ask yourself

what if . . .?

I could meet the demands of daily life with energy and optimism to spare?

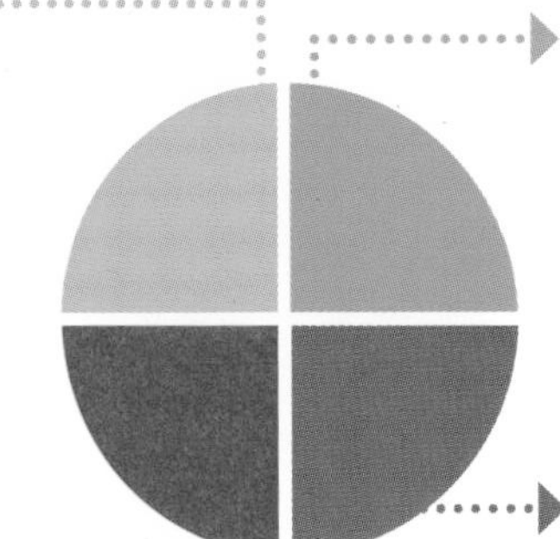

why this chapter matters . . .

Succeeding in higher education calls for a baseline of physical and emotional well-being.

how you can use this chapter . . .

- Maintain your physical and mental energy.
- Enhance your self-esteem.
- Make decisions about alcohol and other drugs in a way that supports your success.

what is included . . .

MASTER STUDENTS in *action*

I start every week with my Success Triangle: (1) Prioritize what needs to be done now and what can be done by others; (2) make a schedule, and check it daily (or more often as needed); (3) reward myself—eat right, exercise, and get more rest. When I stick to my plan there's less stress in my life.

—KAREN GRAJEDA

Courtesy of Karen Grajeda

Wake up to health

SOME PEOPLE SEE HEALTH as just a matter of common sense. These people might see little value in reading a health chapter. After all, they already know how to take care of themselves. Yet *knowing* and *doing* are two different things. Health information does not always translate into healthy habits.

Healthy people meet the demands of daily life with energy to spare. Illness or stress might slow them down for a while, but then they bounce back. They know how to relax, create loving relationships, and find satisfaction in their work.

To a large extent, your level of health is your own creation. You have two basic choices. You can remain unaware of habits that have major consequences for your health. Or you can become aware of current habits (discovery), choose new habits (intention), and take appropriate action.

Health is a choice you make every moment, with each action that you take. Wake up to this possibility by experimenting with the suggestions in this chapter. *

journal entry 21

Discovery Statement

Take a First Step about health

This structured Discovery Statement allows you to look closely at your health. If you look and feel healthy, understanding your body better can help you be aware of what you're doing well. If you are not content with your present physical or emotional health, you might discover some ways to adjust your personal habits and increase your sense of well-being. As with the Discovery Wheel exercise in Chapter 1, the usefulness of this Journal Entry will be determined by your honesty and courage.

What I would most like to change about my diet is . . .

The last time I did 20 minutes or more of heart/lung (aerobic) exercise was . . .

In the last 10 days, the number of alcoholic drinks I have had is . . .

I would describe my use of coffee, colas, and other caffeinated drinks as . . .

When it comes to drugs, what I am sometimes concerned about is . . .

Someone who knows me fairly well would say I am emotionally . . .

The best thing I could do to raise the quality of my relationships would be to . . .

I have trouble sleeping when . . .

What concerns me more than anything else about my health is . . .

The most important thing I could do right now to take charge of my health is. . .

Choose your fuel

© Iconotec/ Wonderfile

FOOD IS YOUR primary fuel for body and mind. And even though you've been eating all your life, entering higher education is bound to change the way that you fuel yourself.

There have been hundreds of books written about nutrition. Some say don't drink milk. Others say that we should buy a cow. Although such debate seems confusing, take comfort. There is actually wide agreement about how to fuel yourself for health.

Today, federal nutrition guidelines are summarized visually as a *food pyramid*. The idea is to eat more of the foods shown in the bigger sections of the pyramid and less of those in the smaller sections. To see an example and build your personal food pyramid, go online to www.mypyramid.gov.

The various food pyramids agree on several core guidelines:[1]

- Emphasize fruits, vegetables, whole grains, and fat-free or low-fat milk and milk products.
- Include lean meats, poultry, fish, beans, eggs, and nuts.
- Choose foods that are low in saturated fats, trans fats, cholesterol, salt (sodium), and added sugars.

Michael Pollan, a writer for the *New York Times Magazine*, spent several years sorting out the scientific literature on nutrition.[2] He boiled the key guidelines down to seven words in three sentences:

- *Eat food.* In other words, choose whole, fresh foods over processed products with a lot of ingredients.
- *Not too much.* If you want to manage your weight, then control how much you eat. Notice portion sizes. Pass on snacks, seconds, and desserts—or indulge just occasionally.
- *Mostly plants.* Fruits, vegetables, and grains are loaded with chemicals that help to prevent disease. Plant-based foods, on the whole, are also lower in calories than foods from animals (meat and dairy products).

Finally, forget diets. *How* you eat can matter more than *what* you eat. If you want to eat less, then eat slowly. Savor each bite. Stop when you're satisfied instead of when you feel full. Use meal times as a chance to relax, reduce stress, and connect with people. *

Discover more strategies for fueling your body.

Prevent and treat eating disorders

Eating disorders affect many students. These disorders involve serious disturbances in eating behavior. Examples are overeating or extreme reduction of food intake, as well as irrational concern about body shape or weight. Women are much more likely to develop these disorders than are men, though cases are on the rise among males.

Bulimia involves cycles of excessive eating and forced purges. A person with this disorder might gorge on a pizza, doughnuts, and ice cream and then force herself to vomit. Or she might compensate for overeating with excessive use of laxatives, enemas, or diuretics.

Anorexia nervosa is a potentially fatal illness marked by self-starvation. People with anorexia may practice extended fasting or eat only one kind of food for weeks at a time.

Binge eating disorder leads to many of the same symptoms as bulimia, without the purging behaviors.

These disorders are not due to a failure of willpower. They are real illnesses in which harmful patterns of eating take on a life of their own.

Eating disorders can lead to many complications, including life-threatening heart conditions and kidney failure. Many people with eating disorders also struggle with depression, substance abuse, and anxiety. They need immediate treatment to stabilize their health. This is usually followed by continuing medical care, counseling, and medication to promote a full recovery.

If you're worried you might have an eating disorder, visit a doctor, campus health service, or local public health clinic. If you see signs of an eating disorder in someone else, express your concern with "I" messages, as explained in Chapter 8: "Communicating."

For more information, contact the National Eating Disorders Association at 1–800–931–2237 or online at www.nationaleatingdisorders.org.

Choose to exercise

© Brand X (X Collection)/Wonderfile

OUR BODIES NEED to be exercised. The world ran on muscle power back in the era when we had to hunt down a woolly mammoth every few weeks and drag it back to the cave. Now we can grab a burger at a drive-up window. Today we need to make a special effort to exercise.

Exercise promotes weight control and reduces the symptoms of depression. It helps to prevent heart attack, diabetes, and several forms of cancer.[3] Exercise also refreshes your body and your mind. If you're stuck on a math problem or blocked on writing a paper, take an exercise break. Chances are that you'll come back with a fresh perspective and some new ideas.

If you get moving, you'll create lean muscles, a strong heart, and an alert brain. You don't have to train for the Boston Marathon, however. And if the word *exercise* turns you off, think *physical activity* instead. Here are some things you can do:

Stay active throughout the day. Park a little farther from work or school. Do your heart a favor by walking some extra blocks. Take the stairs instead of riding elevators. For an extra workout, climb two stairs at a time.

An hour of daily activity is ideal, but do whatever you can. *Some* activity is better than none.

No matter what you do, ease into it. For example, start by walking briskly for at least 15 minutes every day. Increase that time gradually, and add a little jogging.

Adapt to your campus environment. Look for exercise facilities on campus. Search for classes in aerobics, swimming, volleyball, basketball, golf, tennis, and other sports. Intramural sports are another option. School can be a great place to get in shape.

Do what you enjoy. Stay active over the long term with aerobic activities that you enjoy. You might enjoy martial arts, kickboxing, yoga, ballroom dance classes, stage combat classes, or mountain climbing. Check your school catalog for such courses.

Vary your routine. Find several activities that you enjoy, and rotate them throughout the year. Your main form of activity during winter might be ballroom dancing, riding an exercise bike, or skiing. In summer, you could switch to outdoor sports. Whenever possible, choose weight-bearing activities such as walking, running, or stair climbing.

Get active early. Work out first thing in the morning. Then it's done for the day. Make it part of your daily routine, just like brushing your teeth.

Exercise with other people. Making exercise a social affair can add a fun factor and raise your level of commitment.

Join a gym without fear. Many health clubs welcome people who are just starting to get in shape.

Look for gradual results. If your goal is to lose weight, be patient. Because 1 pound equals 3,500 calories, you might feel tempted to reduce weight loss to a simple formula: *Let's see . . . if I burn away just 100 calories each day through exercise, I should lose 1 pound every 35 days.*

Actually, the relationship between exercise and weight loss is complex. Many factors—including individual differences in metabolism and the type of exercise you do—affect the amount of weight you lose.[4]

When you step on the bathroom scale, look for small changes over time rather than sudden, dramatic losses. Gradual weight loss is more healthy, anyway—and easier to sustain over the long term.

Weight loss is just one potential benefit of exercise. Choosing to exercise can also lift your mood, increase your stamina, strengthen your bones, stabilize your joints, and help prevent heart disease. It can also reduce your risk of high blood pressure, diabetes, and several forms of cancer.[5] If you do resistance training—such as weight machines or elastic-band workouts—you'll strengthen your muscles as well. For a complete fitness program, add stretching exercises to enjoy increased flexibility.

Before beginning any vigorous exercise program, consult a health care professional. This is critical if you are overweight, over age 60, in poor condition, or a heavy smoker, or if you have a history of health problems. *

Discover more ways to follow through on your exercise goals.

Choose freedom from distress

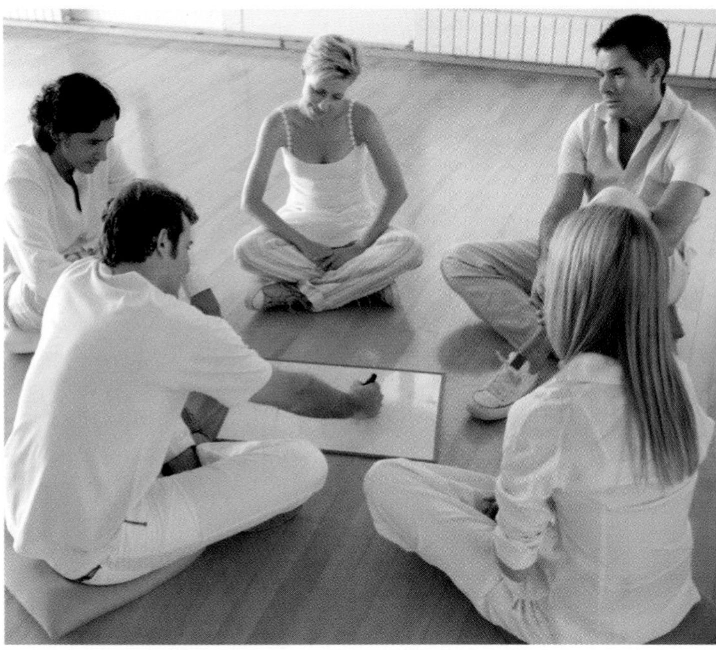
ZenShui/Alix Minde/PhotoAlto Agency RF Collections/Getty Images

IF YOU FEEL a little tension before a test, a presentation, or a date, you're normal. That feeling can keep you alert and boost your energy. The problem comes when tension is persistent and extreme. That's when average levels of stress turn into *distress*.

The number of students in higher education who cope with high levels of stress and other mental health issues is steadily increasing.[6] According to the American College Health Association, 31 percent of college students report that they have felt so depressed that it was difficult to function. Almost half of students say that they've felt overwhelming anxiety, and 60 percent report that they've felt very lonely.[7] Suicide is the second leading cause of death on college campuses.[8]

Your skill at managing stress has a profound impact on your relationships, your capacity to meet the demands of school and work, and your beliefs about your ability to succeed. If you experience thoughts, emotions, or behaviors that consistently interfere with daily life, then it's time to take a First Step about this aspect of your health.

You can take simple and immediate steps toward freedom from distress. Start with your overall health. Your thoughts and emotions can get scrambled if you go too long feeling hungry or tired. Follow the suggestions in this chapter for eating, exercise, and sleep.

Remember that the ideas in "Let go of test anxiety" on page 144 can help you manage *any* form of stress. Consider the following strategies as well.

Make contact with the present moment. If you feel anxious, see whether you can focus your attention on a specific sight, sound, or other sensation that's happening in the present moment. Examine the details of a picture. Study the branches on a tree. Observe the face of your watch right down to the tiny scratches in the glass. During an exam, take a few seconds to listen to the sounds of squeaking chairs, the scratching of pencils, the muted coughs. Touch the surface of your desk and notice the texture. Focus all of your attention on one point—anything other than the flow of thoughts through your head. Focusing in this manner is one way to use the Power Process: "Be Here Now" as a simple and quick stress buster.

Scan your body. Awareness of physical sensations can be an immediate and effective response to distress. Discover this for yourself by bringing awareness to each area of your body.

To begin, sit comfortably and close your eyes. Focus your attention on the muscles in your feet, and notice whether they are relaxed. Tell the muscles in your feet that they can relax.

Move up to your ankles, and repeat the procedure. Next, go to your calves and thighs and buttocks, telling each group of muscles to relax.

Do the same for your lower back, diaphragm, chest, upper arms, lower arms, fingers, upper back, shoulders, neck, jaw, face, and scalp.

Use guided imagery. This technique can work especially well after a body scan. Relax completely and take a quick fantasy trip. Close your eyes, free your body of tension, and imagine yourself in a beautiful, peaceful, natural setting. Create as much of the scene as you can. Be specific. Use all of your senses.

For example, you might imagine yourself at a beach. Hear the surf rolling in and the seagulls calling to each other. Feel the sun on your face and the hot sand between your toes. Smell the sea breeze. Taste the salty mist from the surf. Notice the ships on the horizon and the rolling sand dunes. Use all of your senses to create a vivid imaginary trip.

Find a place that works for you, and practice getting there. When you become proficient, you can return to it quickly for trips that might last only a few seconds.

With practice, you can use this technique even while you are taking a test.

Don't believe everything you think. According to Albert Ellis and other cognitive psychologists, stress results not from events in our lives but from the way we *think* about those events.[9] One thought that sets us up for misery is *People should always behave in exactly the way I expect.* Another one is *Events should always turn out exactly as I expect.* A more sane option is to dispute such irrational beliefs and replace them with more rational ones: *I can control my own behavior but not the behavior of others.* And *Some events are beyond my control.* Changing our beliefs can reduce our stress significantly.

Another way to deal with stressful thoughts is to release them altogether. Meditation is a way to do this. While meditating, you simply notice your thoughts as they arise and pass. Instead of reacting to them, you observe them. Eventually, your stream of thinking slows down. You might enter a state of deep relaxation that also yields life-changing insights.

Many religious organizations offer meditation classes. You can also find meditation instruction through health care providers and community education programs.

Practice detachment. Beyond questioning your thoughts is detaching from them. To *detach* means to step back from something and see it as separate from ourselves. When we detach from an emotion, we no longer identify with it. We no longer say, "*I* am afraid" or "*I* am sad." We say something like "There's fear again" or "I feel sadness right now." Using language such as this offers us a way to step back from our internal experiences and keep them in perspective.

You might find it especially useful to detach from your thoughts with ideas from acceptance and commitment therapy.[10] Take an anxiety-producing thought—such as *I always screw up on tests*—and do any of the following.

Solve the problem. Although you can't "fix" a bad feeling in the same way that you can fix a machine, you can choose to change a situation associated with that feeling. You might be able to identify a problem that needs a solution. You can use feeling bad as your motivation to take action.

Sometimes an intense feeling of sadness, anger, or fear is related to a specific situation in your life. Describe the problem. Then brainstorm solutions and choose one to implement. Reducing your course load, cutting back on hours at work, getting more financial aid, delegating a task, or taking some other concrete action might solve the problem and help you feel better.

Stay active. A related strategy is to do something—*anything* that's constructive, even if it's not a solution to a specific problem. For example, mop the kitchen floor. Clean out your dresser drawers. Iron your shirts. This sounds silly, but it works.

The basic principle is that you can separate emotions from actions. It is appropriate to feel miserable when you do. It's normal to cry and express your feelings. It is also possible to go to class, study, work, eat, and feel miserable at the same time. Unless you have a diagnosable problem with anxiety or depression, you can continue your normal activities until the misery passes.

Share what you're thinking and feeling. There are times when negative thoughts and emotions persist even when you take appropriate action. Tell a family member or friend about your feelings. This is a powerful way to gain perspective. The simple act of describing a

Men, consider your health

In a poll conducted by Louis Harris and Associates, researchers found that one in three men did not have a doctor they saw regularly for medical advice. This might be one reason why life expectancy for men averages 6 years less than that for women.[11] The U.S. Preventive Services Task Force suggests that men do the following:

- Have your body mass index (BMI) calculated to screen for obesity.
- Have your cholesterol checked regularly starting when you turn 35. If you smoke or have diabetes, or if heart disease runs in your family, start having your cholesterol checked at age 20.
- Have your blood pressure checked at least every 2 years.
- Begin regular screening for colorectal cancer starting at age 50. Ask your doctor about which test is best for you.
- Have a test to screen for diabetes if you have high blood pressure or high cholesterol.
- Talk to your doctor about a screening for depression if you've felt despondent and have had little interest or pleasure in your regular activities for 2 weeks straight.
- Talk to your doctor to see whether you should be screened for STIs, such as HIV infection.

Daily steps that you can take are to stay tobacco-free, be physically active, eat a healthy diet, stay at a healthy weight, and take preventive medicines if you need them.[12]

problem can sometimes reveal a solution or give you a fresh perspective.

Ask for help. Student health centers are not just for treating colds, allergies, and flu symptoms. Counselors expect to help students deal with adjustment to campus, changes in mood, academic problems, and drug use disorders. Your tuition helps to pay for health services. It's smart to use them now.

Students with anxiety disorders, clinical depression, bipolar disorder, and other diagnoses might get referred to a psychiatrist or psychologist who works off campus. The referral process can take time, so seek help right away.

You can find resources to promote mental health even if your campus doesn't offer counseling services. First, find a personal physician—one person who can coordinate all of your health care. A personal physician can refer you to a mental health professional if it seems appropriate.

Second, remember a basic guideline about *when* to seek help: whenever problems with your thinking, moods, or behaviors consistently interfere with your ability to sleep, eat, go to class, work, or create positive relationships.

These two suggestions can also work after you graduate. Promoting mental health is a skill to use for the rest of your life. *

Go online for more pathways to freedom from distress.

Choose to rest

You might be tempted to cut back drastically on your sleep once in a while for an all-night study session. Instead, read Chapter 2: "Time and Money" for some time management ideas. A lack of rest can decrease your immunity to illness and impair your performance in school. Depriving yourself of sleep is a choice you can avoid.

If you have trouble falling asleep, experiment with the following suggestions:

- Exercise daily. For many people, regular exercise promotes sounder sleep. However, finish exercising several hours before you want to go to sleep.
- Avoid naps during the daytime.
- Monitor your caffeine intake, especially in the afternoon and evening.
- Avoid using alcohol to induce sleep. Drinking alcohol late in the evening can disrupt your sleep during the night.
- Develop a sleep ritual—a regular sequence of calming activities that end your day. You might take a warm bath and do some light reading. Turn off the TV and computer at least 1 hour before you go to bed.
- Keep your sleeping room cool.
- Keep a regular schedule for going to sleep and waking up.
- Sleep in the same place each night. When you're there, your body gets the message: "It's time to go to sleep now."
- Practice relaxation techniques while lying in bed. A simple one is to count your breaths and release distracting thoughts as they arise.
- Make tomorrow's to-do list before you go to sleep so you won't lie there worrying that tomorrow you'll forget about something you need to do.
- Get up and study or do something else until you're tired.
- See a doctor if sleeplessness persists.

Choose to stay safe

KNOWING HOW TO stay safe can help you prevent illness, disability, and premature death. Begin with some general precautions. Then consider specific ways to avoid accidents, sexual assault, sexually transmitted infections (STIs), and unwanted pregnancy.

© George Shelley/Masterfile

Start with these three strategies

Three simple actions can significantly increase your personal safety. One is to always lock doors when you're not home. If you live in a dorm, follow the policies for keeping the front doors secure. Don't let a stranger walk in behind you. If you commute to school or have a car on campus, keep your car doors locked.

The second action is to avoid walking alone, especially at night. Many schools offer shuttle buses to central campus locations. Use them. As a backup, carry enough spare cash for a taxi ride.

Third, plan for emergencies. Look for emergency phones along campus routes that you normally walk. If you have a cell phone, you can always call 911 for help.

Prevent accidents

Accident prevention is mostly common sense, but it takes uncommon skill to practice what you know:

- Avoiding driving after drinking alcohol or using psychoactive drugs.
- Drive with the realization that other drivers may be preoccupied, intoxicated, or careless.
- Label poisons and keep them away from children.
- Keep stairs and pathways clear of clutter.
- Avoid smoking in bed; don't let candles burn unattended.
- Keep children away from hot stoves, and turn pot handles inward.
- Check electrical cords for fraying, loose connections, or breaks in insulation.
- Don't overload extension cords.
- Keep a fire extinguisher handy.
- Install smoke detectors where you live and work.

Prevent sexual assault

Sexual assault refers to any form of unwanted sexual contact, including rape and attempted rape. Both women and men can take steps to protect themselves:

- Tour your campus, looking for danger spots such as unlighted paths and unguarded buildings.
- If you take an evening class, ask whether there are security officers on duty before and after the class.
- Take a workshop on self-defense and rape prevention from your student counseling service or community education center.

If you are raped, get medical care right away. Go to the nearest rape crisis center, hospital, student health service, or police station. Also arrange for follow-up counseling. It's your decision whether to report the crime. Filing a report does not mean that you have to press charges. However, if you do choose to press charges later, having a report on file can help your case.

Date rape—the act of forcing sex on a date—is a common form of rape among college students. Date rape is rape. It is a crime.

Drugs such as Rohypnol (flunitrazepam) and GHB (gamma-hydroxybutyrate) have been used in date rape. These drugs, which can be secretly slipped into a drink, reduce resistance to sexual advances and produce an effect similar to amnesia. People who take these drugs might not remember the circumstances that led to their being raped. To protect yourself, keep an eye on your drinks, and buy your own food and beverages.

Decide what kind of sexual relationships you want. Then set firm limits, and communicate them clearly and assertively. If someone refuses to respect your limits, stay away from that person.

Prevent STIs

People with an STI can feel no symptoms for years and still be infected. Know how to protect yourself.

STIs can result from vaginal, oral, and anal sex, or any other way that people contact semen, vaginal secretions, and blood. There are at least 25 kinds of STIs, including chlamydia, gonorrhea, and syphilis. Sexual contact can also spread the human papillomavirus (HPV, the most common cause of cervical cancer) and the human immunodeficiency virus (HIV, the virus that causes acquired immune deficiency syndrome [AIDS]).

Most STIs can be cured if treated early. (Herpes and AIDS are important exceptions.) Prevention is a better course of action.

Talk to your partner. Before you have sex with someone, talk about the risk of STIs. If you are infected, tell your partner.

Use condoms. Male condoms are thin membranes stretched over the penis prior to intercourse. Condoms prevent semen from entering the vagina. For the most protection, use latex condoms—not ones made of lambskin or polyurethane. Use a condom every time you have sex, and for any type of sex. But remember that condoms can break, leak, or slip off. In addition, condoms cannot protect you from STIs that are spread by contact with herpes sores or warts.

Do not share needles. Sharing needles or other paraphernalia with other drug users can spread STIs.

Get vaccinated. Vaccines are available to prevent hepatitis B and HPV infection. See your doctor.

Get screened for STIs. The only way to find out whether you're infected is to be tested by a health care professional. If you have sex with more than one person, get screened for STIs at least once each year. Do this even if you have no symptoms. Remember that many schools offer free STI screening. Ask about it at your student health center.

Get treated right away. If you think you have an STI, see a doctor immediately. Abstain from sex until you are treated and cured.

Prevent unwanted pregnancy

There are many ways to prevent pregnancy. Choosing among them can be a challenge. Consider whether you want to have children someday, the number of sexual partners you have, your comfort using a birth control method, possible side effects, and your personal values.

Abstinence, when practiced without exception, is the only sure way to prevent pregnancy and STIs. Abstinence means choosing not to have any form of sex—vaginal, oral, or anal.

If you choose to have sex, think carefully through your options for birth control. The federal government offers up-to-date information. Go online to www.womenshealth.gov/faq/birth-control-methods.pdf. Also talk to your doctor.

To prevent pregnancy, make sure you understand your chosen method and use it correctly *every* time you have sex. Birth control methods vary in effectiveness. They may not work 100 percent of the time. *

Learn more about staying safe.

Observe thyself

You are an expert on your body. You are more likely to notice changes before anyone else does. Pay attention to these changes. They are often your first clues about the need for medical treatment or intervention.

Watch for the following signs:

- Weight loss of more than 10 pounds in 10 weeks with no apparent cause
- A sore, scab, or ulcer that does not heal in 3 weeks
- A skin blemish or mole that bleeds; itches; or changes size, shape, or color
- Persistent or severe headaches
- Sudden vomiting that is not preceded by nausea
- Fainting spells
- Double vision
- Difficulty swallowing
- Persistent hoarseness or a nagging cough
- Blood that is coughed up or vomited
- Shortness of breath for no apparent reason
- Persistent indigestion or abdominal pain
- A big change in normal bowel habits, such as alternating diarrhea and constipation
- Black and tarry bowel movements
- Rectal bleeding
- Pink, red, or unusually cloudy urine
- Discomfort or difficulty when urinating or during sexual intercourse
- Lumps or thickening in a breast
- Vaginal bleeding between menstrual periods or after menopause

If you are experiencing any of these symptoms, get help. Even if you think it might not be serious, check it out. Without timely and proper treatment, a minor illness or injury can lead to serious problems. Begin with your doctor or school health service.

23 critical thinking exercise
Addiction: How do I know?

Lectures about the reasons for avoiding alcohol and drug use can be pointless. We don't take care of our bodies because someone says we should. We might take care of ourselves when we see that the costs of using alcohol and other drugs outweigh the benefits.

People who have problems with drugs and alcohol can hide this fact from themselves and from others. It is also hard for friends and family to admit that their loved one has a problem.

The purpose of this exercise is to give you an objective way to look at your relationship with drugs or alcohol. There are signals that indicate when drug or alcohol use has become a problem that calls for getting treatment.

Answer the following questions quickly and honestly with yes, no, or n/a (not applicable). If you are concerned about someone else, rephrase each question using that person's name.

_____ Are you uncomfortable discussing drug abuse or addiction?

_____ Are you worried about your own drug or alcohol use?

_____ Are any of your friends worried about your drug or alcohol use?

_____ Have you ever hidden from a friend, spouse, employer, or coworker the fact that you were drinking? (Pretended you were sober? Covered up alcohol breath?)

_____ Do you sometimes use alcohol or drugs to escape lows rather than to produce highs?

_____ Have you ever gotten angry when confronted about your use?

_____ Do you brag about how much you consume? ("I drank her under the table.")

_____ Do you think about or do drugs when you are alone?

_____ Do you store up alcohol, drugs, cigarettes, or caffeine (in coffee or soft drinks) to be sure you won't run out?

_____ Does having a party almost always include alcohol or drugs?

_____ Do you try to control your drinking so that it won't be a problem? ("I drink only on weekends now." "I never drink before 5 p.m." "I drink only beer.")

_____ Do you often explain to other people why you are drinking? ("It's my birthday." "It's my friend's birthday." "It's Veterans Day." "It sure is a hot day.")

_____ Have you changed friends to accommodate your drinking or drug use? ("She's OK, but she isn't excited about getting high.")

_____ Has your behavior changed in the last several months? (Grades slipping? Lack of interest in a hobby? Change of values or o moral standards?)

_____ Do you drink or use drugs to relieve tension? ("What a day! I need a drink.")

_____ Do you have medical problems (stomach trouble, malnutrition, liver problems, anemia) that could be related to drinking or drugs?

_____ Have you ever decided to quit drugs or alcohol and then changed your mind?

_____ Have you had any fights, accidents, or similar incidents related to drinking or drugs in the last year?

_____ Has your drinking or drug use ever caused a problem at home?

_____ Do you envy people who go overboard with alcohol or drugs?

_____ Have you ever told yourself you can quit at any time?

_____ Have you ever been in trouble with the police after or while you were drinking?

_____ Have you ever missed school or work because you had a hangover?

_____ Have you ever had a blackout (a period you can't remember) during or after drinking?

_____ Do you wish that people would mind their own business when it comes to your use of alcohol or drugs?

_____ Is the cost of alcohol or other drugs taxing your budget or resulting in financial stress?

_____ Do you need increasing amounts of a drug to produce the desired effect?

_____ When you stop taking a drug, do you experience withdrawal?

_____ Do you spend a great deal of time obtaining and using alcohol or other drugs?

_____ Have you used alcohol or another drug when it was physically dangerous to do so (such as when driving a car or working with machines)?

_____ Have you been arrested or had other legal problems resulting from the use of a substance?

Now count the number of questions you answered *yes.* If you answered *yes* more than once, then talk with a professional. This does not necessarily mean that you are addicted. It does point out that alcohol or other drugs are adversely affecting your life. Talk to someone with training in recovery from chemical dependency. Do not rely on the opinion of anyone who lacks such training.

If you filled out this questionnaire about another person and you answered yes two or more times, then your friend might need help. You probably can't provide that help alone. Seek out a counselor and a support group such as Alcoholics Anonymous (AA) or Al-Anon.

mastering technology

SETTING LIMITS ON SCREEN TIME

Access to wireless communication offers easy ways to procrastinate. We call it "surfing," "texting," "IMing"—and sometimes "researching" or "working."

Digital devices create value. With a computer, you can stream music, watch videos, listen to podcasts, scan newspapers, read books, check e-mail, and send instant messages. With a cell phone, you can be available to key people when it counts. Any of these activities can become addicting distractions.

Discover how much time you spend online. People who update their MySpace or Facebook page every hour may be sending an unintended message—that they have no life offline.

To get an accurate picture of your involvement in social networking and other online activity, use the Time Monitor/Time Plan exercise included in Chapter 2. Then make conscious choices about how much time you want to spend online and on the phone. Don't let social networking distract you from meeting personal and academic goals.

Go offline to send the message that other people matter. It's hard to pay attention to the person who is right in front of you when you're hammering out text messages or updating your Twitter stream. You can also tell when someone else is doing these things and only half-listening to you. How engaged in your conversation do you think that person is?

An alternative is to close up your devices and "be here now." When you're eating, stop answering the phone. Notice how the food tastes. When you're with a friend, close up your laptop. Hear every word he says. Instead of using a computer or cell phone to rehash the past or plan the future, rediscover where life actually takes place—in the present moment.

Developing emotional intelligence requires being with people and away from a computer or cell phone. People who break up with a partner through text messaging are not developing that intelligence.

True friends know when to go offline and head across campus to resolve a conflict. They know when to go back home and support a family member in crisis. When it counts, your presence is your greatest present.

Alcohol and other drugs: THE TRUTH

Patrick Strattner/Getty

THE TRUTH IS that getting high can be fun. In our culture, getting high has become synonymous with having a good time.

Acknowledging that alcohol and other drugs can be fun infuriates a lot of people. Remember that this acknowledgment is *not* the same as condoning drug use. The point is this: People are most likely to abstain from alcohol and other drugs when they're convinced that using them leads to more pain than pleasure over the long run. It's your body, and you get to choose.

We are a drug-using society. Of course, some of those uses are therapeutic and lawful, including taking drugs as prescribed by a doctor.

The problem comes when we turn to drugs as *the* solution to any problem. Are you uncomfortable? Often the first response is "Take something." We live in times when reaching for instant comfort via chemicals is not only condoned but encouraged. If you're bored, tense, or anxious, you can drink a can of beer, down a glass of wine, or light up a cigarette. If you want to enhance your memory, you can take a "smart drug," which might include prescription stimulants and caffeine. And these are only the legal options.

There is a big payoff in using alcohol, tobacco, caffeine, cocaine, heroin, or other drugs—or people wouldn't do it. The payoff can be relaxation, self-confidence, comfort, excitement, or the ability to pull an all-nighter. At times, the payoff is avoiding rejection or defying authority.

In addition to the payoffs, there are costs. And sometimes these costs are much greater than the payoff. This is true for people who care about little else except finding and using drugs—friends, school, work, and family be damned.

Some people will stop using a drug when the consequences get serious enough. Other people don't stop. They continue their self-defeating behaviors, no matter the consequences for themselves, their friends, or their families. At that point, the problem goes beyond abuse. It's addiction.

With addiction, the costs can include overdose, infection, and lowered immunity to disease. These can be fatal. Long-term heavy drinking, for example, damages every organ system in the human body. And about 440,000 Americans die annually from the effects of cigarette smoking.13

Lectures about the reasons for avoiding alcohol and drug abuse and addiction can be pointless. We don't take care of our bodies because someone says we should. We might take care of ourselves when we see that the costs of using a substance outweigh the benefits.

The technical term for addiction is *alcohol use disorder* or *substance use disorder*. This disease has many signs. Examples are:

- Failing to meet major requirements for work or school
- Feeling strong cravings for drugs
- Continued use of drugs even when it leads to physical danger
- Taking drugs in larger doses over longer periods of time
- Persistent failure in reducing or quitting drug use
- Continued drug use despite other harmful consequences

Remember that behaviors such as gambling can also take on a life of their own and overtake commitments to school, work, and family.

Fortunately, help is available for these disorders. Consider the following suggestions.

Use responsibly. Show people that you can have a good time without alcohol or other drugs. If you do choose to drink, consume alcohol with food. Pace yourself. Take time between drinks.

Avoid promotions that encourage excess drinking. "Ladies Drink Free" nights are especially dangerous. Women are affected more quickly by alcohol, making them targets for rape. Also stay out of games that encourage people to guzzle. In addition, avoid people who make fun of you for choosing not to drink.

Pay attention. Whenever you use alcohol or another drug, do so with awareness. Then pay attention to the consequences. Act with deliberate decision rather than out of habit or under pressure from others.

Admit problems. People with active addictions are a varied group—rich and poor, young and old, successful and unsuccessful. Often these people do have one thing in common: They are masters of denial. They deny that they are unhappy. They deny that they have hurt anyone. They are convinced that they can quit any time they want. They sometimes become so good at hiding the problem from themselves that they die.

Take responsibility for recovery. Nobody plans to become addicted. If you have pneumonia, you seek treatment and recover without shame. Approach addiction in the same way. You can take responsibility for your recovery without blame or shame.

Get help. Two broad options exist. One is the growing self-help movement. The other is formal treatment. People who seek help often combine the two.

Many self-help groups are modeled after Alcoholics Anonymous (AA)—one of the oldest and most successful programs in this category. Groups based on AA principles exist for many other problems as well.

Some people feel uncomfortable with the AA approach. Other resources exist for them, including private therapy and group therapy. Also investigate organizations such as Women for Sobriety, the Secular Organizations for Sobriety, and Rational Recovery. Use whatever works.

Treatment programs are available in almost every community. They might be residential (you live there for weeks or months at a time) or outpatient (you visit several hours a day). Find out where these treatment centers are located by calling a doctor, a mental health professional, or a local hospital. If you don't have insurance, it is usually possible to arrange some other payment program. Cost is no reason to avoid treatment.

Get help for a friend or family member. You might know someone whose behavior meets the criteria for a drug use disorder. If so, you have every right to express your concern to that person. Wait until the person is clearheaded. Then mention specific incidents. For example: "Last night you drank five beers when we were at my apartment, and then you wanted to drive home. When I offered to call a cab for you instead, you refused." Also be prepared to offer a source of help, such as the phone number of a local treatment center. *

Learn more online about recovery from dependence.

Succeed in quitting smoking

There is no magic formula for becoming tobacco-free. However, you can take steps to succeed sooner rather than later. The American Cancer Society suggests the following.[14]

Make a firm choice to quit. All plans for quitting depend on this step. If you're not ready to quit yet, then admit it. Take another look at how smoking affects your health, finances, and relationships.

Set a date. Choose a "quit day" within the next month. That's close enough for a sense of urgency—and time to prepare. Consider a date with special meaning, such as a birthday or anniversary. Let friends and family members know about the big day.

Get personal support. Involve other people. Sign up for a quit smoking class. Attend Nicotine Anonymous or a similar group.

Consider medication. Medication can double your chances of quitting successfully.[15] Options include bupropion hydrochloride (Zyban) and varenicline (Chantix), as well as the nicotine patch, gum, nasal spray, inhaler, and lozenge.

Prepare the environment. Right before your quit day, get rid of all cigarettes and ashtrays at home and at work. Stock up on oral substitutes such as sugarless gum, candy, and low-fat snacks.

Deal with cravings for cigarettes. Distract yourself with exercise or another physical activity. Breathe deeply. Tell yourself that you can wait just a little while longer until the craving passes. Even the strongest urges to smoke will pass. Avoid alcohol use, which can increase cravings.

Learn from relapses. If you break down and light up a cigarette, don't judge yourself. Quitting often requires several attempts. Think back over your past plans for quitting and how to improve on them. Every relapse contains a lesson about how to succeed next time.

Surrender

Life can be magnificent and satisfying. It can also be devastating.

Sometimes there is too much pain or confusion. Problems can be too big and too numerous. Life can bring us to our knees in a pitiful, helpless, and hopeless state. A broken relationship with a loved one, a sudden diagnosis of cancer, total frustration with a child's behavior problem, or even the prospect of several long years of school are situations that can leave us feeling overwhelmed—powerless.

In these troubling situations, the first thing we can do is to admit that we don't have the resources to handle the problem. No matter how hard we try and no matter what skills we bring to bear, some problems remain out of our control. When this is the case, we can tell the truth: "It's too big and too mean. I can't handle it."

Desperately struggling to control a problem can easily result in the problem's controlling us. Surrender is letting go of being the master in order to avoid becoming the slave.

Many traditions make note of this idea. Western religions speak of surrendering to God. Hindus say surrender to the Self. Members of Alcoholics Anonymous talk about turning their lives over to a Higher Power. Agnostics might suggest surrendering to the ultimate source of power. Others might speak of following their intuitions, their inner guides, or their consciences.

In any case, surrender means being receptive to help. Once we admit that we're at the end of our rope, we open ourselves up to receiving help. We learn that we don't have to go it alone. We find out that other people have faced similar problems and survived.

We give up our old habits of thinking and behaving as if we have to be in control of everything. We stop acting as general manager of the universe. We surrender. And that creates a space for something new in our lives.

Surrendering is not "giving up." It is not a suggestion to quit and do nothing about your problems. Giving up is fatalistic and accomplishes nothing. You have many skills and resources. Use them. You can apply all of your energy to handling a situation and still surrender at the same time. Surrender includes doing whatever you can in a positive, trusting spirit. So let go, keep going, and recognize when the true source of control lies beyond you.

Learn more about the power of this Power Process online.

Yashuhide Fumoto/Digital Vision/Getty Images

Put it to Work

Strategies from *Becoming a Master Student* can help you succeed in your career, as well as in school. To discover how suggestions in this chapter can apply to the workplace, reflect on the following case study.[16]

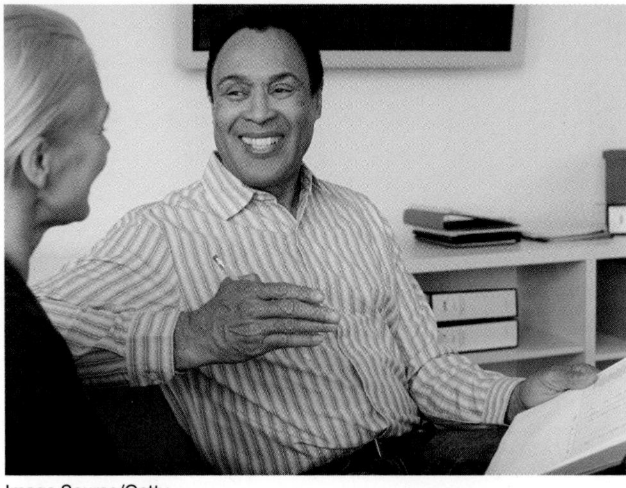
Image Source/Getty

For weeks David had been bothered by aching muscles, loss of appetite, restless sleep, and fatigue. Eventually he became so short-tempered and irritable that his wife insisted he get a checkup.

Now, sitting in the doctor's office, David barely noticed when Theresa took the seat beside him. They had been good friends when she worked in the front office at the plant. He hadn't seen her since she left 3 years ago to take a job as a customer service representative. Her gentle poke in the ribs brought him around. Within minutes they were talking freely.

"You got out just in time," he told her. "Since the reorganization, nobody feels safe. It used to be that as long as you did your work, you had a job. Now they expect the same production rates even though two guys are now doing the work of three. We're so backed up that I'm working 12-hour shifts, 6 days a week. Guys are calling in sick just to get a break."

"Well, I really miss you guys," she said. "In my new job, the computer routes the calls, and they never stop. I even have to schedule my bathroom breaks. All I hear the whole day are complaints from unhappy customers. I try to be helpful and sympathetic, but I can't promise anything until I get my boss's approval. Most of the time I'm caught between what the customer wants and company policy. The other reps are so uptight and tense they don't even talk to one another. We all go to our own little cubicles and stay there until quitting time. No wonder I'm in here with migraine headaches and high blood pressure."

David and Theresa are using a powerful strategy to promote health—talking about how they feel with a person they trust. List three other strategies that might be useful to them:

____

____

____

Imagine that you suggested those three strategies to David and Theresa. They responded, "Those are good ideas, but we can't get relief from stress until our working conditions change. And that's up to our supervisors, not us." How would you respond to them?

____

____

____

Consider these other strategies for staying healthy under pressure.

Ask for change. Use your skill with "I" messages (see Chapter 8: "Communicating") to make suggestions and ask for specific changes in working conditions. If your employer conducts a survey of workers' satisfaction with their jobs, answer honestly and completely—especially if responses are kept anonymous.

Deal with depression. Untreated depression costs the American economy as much as heart disease or AIDS.[16] However, many employees don't report symptoms of depression. They worry about confidentiality in the workplace and about paying for treatment. Yet confidential and free or low-cost help is often available through employee assistance plans. Find out whether your employer offers such a plan.

Check the full range of your health benefits. In addition to screening and treatment for depression, your employee health benefits might include screenings for other conditions, paid time off for medical appointments, and discounts for health club memberships. Set up a meeting with someone at work who can explain all the options available to you.

Quiz

Name____ Date____/____/____

1. Taking care of your overall health is not a recommended strategy for taking care of your mental health. True or false? Explain your answer.
   False. The steps toward freedom from distress begin with your overall health. Your thoughts and emotions can get scrambled if you go too long feeling hungry or tired. (*Choose freedom from distress*, pp. 198–200)
2. According to the text, the key sign that people are dependent on a drug is
   (a) They keep using the drug even though they know that this will lead to harmful consequences.
   (b) They spend a lot of time using the drug and thinking about how to get it.
   (c) They experience tolerance (a desire for greater amounts of the drug).
   (d) They experience withdrawal (physical discomfort when they use less of the drug).
   (e) All of the above.
   (e) All of the above. (*Alcohol and other drugs: THE TRUTH*, pp. 205–206)
3. How is the Power Process: "Surrender" different from giving up?
   Surrender is not a suggestion to quit and do nothing about your problems. Surrender includes doing whatever you can in a positive, trusting spirit. Surrender is the ability to let go and keep going, knowing the true source of control lies just ahead. (*Power Process: Surrender,* p. 207)
4. List three techniques for detaching from your thoughts.
   List the following three techniques: 1. Solve the problem 2. Stay active 3. Share what you are thinking and feeling (*Choose freedom from distress*, pp. 198–200)
5. Define *date rape*, and describe at least two ways to protect yourself against it.
   Date rape is the act of forcing sex on a date. It is the most common form of rape among college students. List any two of the following ways to protect yourself: • Don't leave your drinks unattended. • Buy your own food and beverages. • Set firm limits about the kind of sexual relationships you want. • Stay away from people who do not respect your limits. (Answers will vary.) (*Choose to stay safe,* pp. 201–202)
6. Ways to make contact with the present moment include
   (a) Studying the details of a picture.
   (b) Listening to sounds in your immediate environment.
   (c) Touching the surface of your desk and noticing the texture.
   (d) Taking a deep breath and noticing how far your stomach expands.
   (e) All of the above.
   (e) All of the above. (*Choose freedom from distress*, pp. 198–200)
7. One of the suggestions for dealing with addiction is "pay attention." This implies that it's okay to use any drug, as long as you do so with full awareness. True or false? Explain your answer.
   False. The suggestion to "Pay attention" refers to being aware of the consequences of behavior under the influence of drugs. Respond to that awareness with deliberate decision rather than out of habit or under pressure from others. (*Alcohol and other drugs: THE TRUTH*, pp. 205–206)
8. List five strategies for getting better sleep.
   List five of the following strategies: • Exercise daily. • Avoid naps during the daytime. • Monitor your caffeine intake, especially in the afternoon and evening. • Avoid using alcohol to induce sleep. • Develop a sleep ritual. • Keep your sleeping room cool. • See a doctor if sleeplessness persists. (Answers will vary.) (*Choose to rest*, p. 200)
9. Writer Michael Pollan reduced guidelines for healthy eating down to seven words. What are they?
   - *Eat food.* In other words, choose whole, fresh foods over processed products with a lot of ingredients.
   - *Not too much.* If you want to manage your weight, then control how much you eat. Notice portion sizes. Pass on snacks, seconds, and desserts—or indulge just occasionally.
   - *Mostly plants.* Fruits, vegetables, and grains are loaded with chemicals that help to prevent disease. Plant-based foods, on the whole, are also lower in calories than foods from animals (meat and dairy products). (*Choose your fuel*, p. 196)
10. The only option for long-term recovery from drug dependence is treatment based on the steps of Alcoholics Anonymous. True or false? Explain your answer.
    False. Many recovery groups are based on the AA system, but there are many other systems, such as private therapy and group therapy. People should explore different systems and pursue the one that works best for them.(*Alcohol and other drugs: THE TRUTH*, pp. 205–206)

Skills Snapshot

Now that you've reflected on the ideas in this chapter and experimented with some new strategies, revisit your responses to the "Health" section of the Discovery Wheel exercise on page 25. Think about the most powerful action you could take in the near future toward mastery in this area of your life. Complete the following sentences:

DISCOVERY

To monitor my current level of health, I look for specific changes in . . .

After reading and doing this chapter, my top three health concerns are . . .

INTENTION

My top three intentions for responding to these concerns are . . .

NEXT ACTION

I'll know that I've reached a new level of mastery with health when . . .

To reach that level of mastery, the most important intention for me to act on next is . . .

Master Student PROFILE

Randy Pausch

. . . was energetic

AP Photo/Daily Progress, Kaylin Bower

(1960–2008)
A professor at Carnegie Mellon University who, shortly after being diagnosed with pancreatic cancer, gave a "last lecture"—a reflection on his personal and professional journey—that became a hit on YouTube (this lecture was later adapted into a book of the same title). He devoted the remaining 9 months of his life to creating a legacy.

It's a thrill to fulfill your own childhood dreams, but as you get older, you may find that enabling the dreams of others is even more fun.

When I was teaching at the University of Virginia in 1993, a 22-year-old artist-turned-computer-graphics-wiz named Tommy Burnett wanted a job on my research team. After we talked about his life and goals, he suddenly said, "Oh, and I have always had this childhood dream."

Anyone who uses "childhood" and "dream" in the same sentence usually gets my attention.

"And what is your dream, Tommy?" I asked.

"I want to work on the next *Star Wars* film," he said.

Remember, this was in 1993. The last Star Wars movie had been made in 1983, and there were no concrete plans to make any more. I explained this. "That's a tough dream to have because it'll be hard to see it through," I told him. "Word is that they're finished making *Star Wars* films."

"No," he said, "they're going to make more, and when they do, I'm going to work on them. That's my plan."

Tommy was 6 years old when the first Star Wars film came out in 1977. "Other kids wanted to be Han Solo," he told me. "Not me. I wanted to be the guy who made the special effects—the space ships, the planets, the robots."

He told me that, as a boy, he read the most technical *Star Wars* articles he could find. He had all the books that explained how the models were built, and how the special effects were achieved. . . . I figured Tommy's big dream would never happen, but it might serve him well somehow. I could use a dreamer like that. I knew from my NFL desires that even if he didn't achieve his, they could serve him well, so I asked him to join our research team. . . .

When I moved to Carnegie Mellon, every member of my team from the University of Virginia came with me—everyone except Tommy. He couldn't make the move. Why? Because he had been hired by producer/director George Lucas' company, Industrial Light & Magic. And it's worth noting that they didn't hire him for his dream; they hired him for his skills. In his time with our research group, he had become an outstanding programmer in the Python language, which as luck would have it, was the language of choice in their shop. Luck is indeed where preparation meets opportunity.

It's not hard to guess where this story is going. Three new *Star Wars* films would be made—in 1999, 2002, and 2005—and Tommy ended up working on all of them.

On *Star Wars Episode II: Attack of the Clones*, Tommy was a lead technical director. There was an incredible 15-minute battle scene on a rocky red planet, pitting clones against 'droids, and Tommy was the guy who planned it all out. He and his team used photos of the Utah desert to create a virtual landscape for the battle. Talk about cool jobs. Tommy had one that let him spend each day on another planet.

Excerpted with permission from Randy Pausch with Jeffrey Zaslow, *The Last Lecture* (New York: Hyperion, 2008), 117–119.

Learn more about Randy Pausch online at the Master Student Hall of Fame.

10 What's Next?

Instructor Tools & Tips

Live as if you were to die tomorrow. Learn as if you were to live forever.

—Gandhi

Learning is not a task or a problem—it is a way to be in the world. Man learns as he pursues goals and projects that have meaning for him.

—Sidney Jourard

Preview

Use your class sessions at the end of the semester to help students understand that time spent in school is a stepping-stone to the future. Revisit goals set earlier in the term to help guide students from "school is something I have to do for now" to "school is the First Step toward achieving the goals I have set for my life." When students choose life missions that direct and energize their efforts both in and out of class, you and your students can celebrate this true sign of success—yours and theirs. Faculty Advisor Dean Mancina shares his thoughts on the semester's end:

I know from my own experience that as each semester draws to a close, we are rushing to get through all the material that has to be completed before final exams. For some instructors, that means skipping the last one or two chapters of a text. However, Chapter 10 of *Becoming a Master Student Concise* provides so much reflection and closure that it's essential to plan your course carefully so students will have time to read and complete the writing activities in this final chapter. You and your students will especially want to see the results of Critical Thinking Exercise 26: "The Discovery Wheel" (page 226).

Guest Speaker

A local employer who looks to your institution to find workers is an appropriate choice for a guest speaker for this chapter. Another possibility is to invite a career counselor who specializes in helping students prepare to apply for jobs, interview, and enter the workplace.

Now is also the time to ask your current students to consider coming back next term to be guest speakers on the first day of class. Your new students will be very interested in meeting your former students. These former students can be an inspiration to new students who are not fully committed to continuing in your class.

Lecture

Appropriate lecture topics for this chapter include the following:

- What students can do next term to keep the tools learned in this course fresh in their minds
- The connection between the skills learned in this course and the skills employers are looking for
- Putting together an effective résumé
- Interviewing successfully for a job
- Skills for starting a new job
- Service-learning and other types of contributing

Exercises/Activities

1. **The Discovery Wheel (page 226).** Begin this in-class assignment by having your students complete the Discovery Wheel in this final chapter. Ask them to compare the scores they have just given themselves with the scores from the Discovery Wheel they completed in Chapter 1. Then have students subtract their first Discovery Wheel scores from their second Discovery Wheel scores. Alternately, some students like to divide the first Discovery Wheel scores by the second, noting the percentage change. Either way, the difference can be very insightful. It represents the change in the students' self-confidence. Many students see dramatic improvements.
Note: Occasionally, you will have a student whose scores go down. This is an important example of the power of telling the truth and how the truth can change.

2. **Power Process: "Be It" (page 231).** As this class nears its completion, it's exciting for students to reflect on their educational and career goals one last time. Once they learn to use the tools and strategies presented in this text, many students raise their level of expectation to include

additional educational and career achievements. They now know how easy it can be to pursue goals they would never have considered before. In class, ask your students to brainstorm individually a list of their hopes, dreams, and goals. Have them answer the following questions on a sheet of paper: What do you want to be? What do you want to do? What do you want to have? For example, a student might write: I want to get a Masters from Stanford University.

Then ask your students to sit in a large circle. Ask them to change the want's to be's. In the example above, the changes might look like this: I am a Masters student at Stanford University.

Ask them to look at their revised statements and review them silently. Seeing this change on paper will make students feel as if the future is happening now! Ask your students to read their affirmation statements aloud in class. This is an opportunity to proclaim their goals. It's a First Step of the Power Process: "Be It."

3. **Create your next semester.** Here's a suggestion from an instructor:

> I try to make sure my students know what a degree plan is, how to file one, and how to follow one. Remind students that college is a long progression of acquiring knowledge and learning how to use it, but college is also a chance to explore life and take risks. Learning from the mistakes of others shows real maturity. Invite students to remember a time when they began a project, followed the appropriate steps, and completed the project successfully. Examples can be anything from baking a cake to teaching swimming lessons. This chapter might also remind students that a successful semester isn't necessarily a 4.0 GPA. In college, being successful means growing, learning, and evolving into a better person. Invite students to challenge themselves in nontraditional ways.
>
> **—Joseph Fly, South Plains College**

Conversation/Sharing

This culminating chapter focuses on the transfer of knowledge that is best displayed by Mode 4 learners, who ask *What if?* Your students will have practiced using the metacognitive map for a whole semester. Now you can challenge them to think of questions related to Chapter 10 and Mode 4. *What if* they apply the skills they learned in this course to all of their future courses? *What if* they apply these skills in the workplace? *What if* they select one major and then want to change majors because they have changed career goals? This is a great way to introduce a discussion about transferable skills.

Encourage your students to look ahead to the next semester and make a commitment to review the chapters of this textbook, one per week, to keep the concepts and strategies fresh in their mind. As part of the final week's assignments, have students reread the textbook's Introduction: "Mastering Transitions," which will make even more sense to them now that they have read the entire book. This assignment demonstrates the benefits of a second reading of the text. Ask students to engage in a group conversation about what they discovered on rereading the Introduction.

Homework

Exercise 24: Create your career plan—now (page 217). This exercise will help students focus and commit to considering a specific career and identifying in writing the steps to get there.

Creating portfolios. This course is a perfect place for students to begin collecting their work in a way that reflects their academic development and accomplishments. Encourage students to use the following portfolio exercise suggestions to personalize their portfolios and help them reflect on their growth over time. A portfolio is a work in progress. Each student's portfolio will be unique. Consider having a sharing day celebration at the end of your course so that students can review and reflect on one another's portfolios.

- **Create a personal profile.** Personal profiles help to catalog your student's background, education, employment, activities, hobbies, and college skills. The profile can also be used as a resource for learning more about your students. A sample personal profile form is available for downloading and distributing from the Instructor Companion site. Consider customizing the profile to your liking and to your campus. You can allow students to omit sensitive items if they prefer not to answer them.
- **Discover learning preferences.** Have your students include their Chapter 1 Discovery Wheel and Journal Entry in their portfolio. At the end of the course, they can use their portfolio to compare their discoveries from the first week of class with their discoveries in the second Discovery Wheel in Chapter 10.

  The Learning Style Inventory is another item that should be cataloged for future reflection. Students can pursue other inventories available on your campus (like the MBTI, Strong Interest Inventory). These tools can help students prepare for their future courses and career choices.
- **Review goal-setting exercises.** This book provides students with many opportunities for setting goals. Beginning with Exercise 8: "Get Real with Your Goals" (page 56) in Chapter 2, students can begin to plan long-term, mid-term, and short-term goals. Periodically, they are encouraged to revisit these goals and make updates. Filing this material in a portfolio enables them to easily measure their growth and note changes throughout their semester and college experience.

  The CL Assessment and Portfolio Builder provides students with another opportunity for self-reflection and future planning. You can use this online tool in your classroom to reinforce goal setting, accomplishments, attitudes, and values. Have your students assess the skills that they have brought to college, and work with your students to plan for accomplishments throughout college and in the workplace.

  As students assess their majors and career interests, they can use their portfolios to track their education plans, lists of courses they need in order to graduate, and other program requirements. Suggest that students also consider what types of materials may be relevant to share with prospective employers. For example, if a student writes for a student publication, he can add his articles to his portfolio and share them during an interview. If a student participates in campus organizations or service-learning projects, she can add photographs and materials documenting her activities to her portfolio.[1]

Use résumés and interviews to "hire" an employer (pages 221–222). The materials provided in this text that relate to résumé building should be considered preliminary guidelines. These are tools to help students get started and perhaps gain employment while they are in school. If your students are not yet ready to create their own résumés, consider having them create a résumé that answers a specific help wanted ad that they pull from the newspaper or a Web site. This mock résumé can be used as a goal-setting tool. What skills do you want to acquire? How can you successfully practice these skills in higher education, or at an internship?

Sell your résumé with an effective cover letter. Have your students follow up their work on their résumés by writing a cover letter that addresses their accomplishments and skills, aligning them to a position they are applying for (building on Critical Thinking Exercise 25: Recognize your skills, page 220). This exercise provides another opportunity for students to practice their writing skills. Have your students do peer editing in the classroom.

Evaluation

Here are some ideas for final exam questions:

1. Which Master Student Profile in the text inspired you the most? Explain your answer.

2. What were the three most valuable in-class activities in this course? Why were they valuable to you.

3. What were the three most valuable textbook articles that you read in this course? How did they change the way you behave as a student?

4. What were the three most valuable outside-of-class activities you were assigned in this course? Explain.

5. What would be your top five reasons why a student entering college should take this course?

6. Name the five most important skills you learned in this course. Explain how you will you use, and do not lose, these skills as you continue your college experience.

Additional Digital Resources

Course Manual

The online *Course Manual* serves as an invaluable reference for those developing and teaching a College Success course with *Becoming a Master Student Concise*. The *Course Manual* provides advice on general teaching issues such as preparing for classes, classroom management, grading, and communicating with students of various backgrounds, as well as specific strategies on getting the most out of various features in *Becoming a Master Student Concise* such as the Discovery Wheel and book-specific Web sites. Do a *Course Manual* reconnaissance to find ideas that you can use in your course right now.

Instructor Companion Site

The updated Instructor Companion Site provides resources to help you plan and customize your course. Content specific to Chapter 10 includes:

- ► Lecture Ideas
    - How School Fits Into the Rest of Students' Lives
    - Rehearsing Success
    - Use the SCANS Reports to Create Value for Your Students
- ► In-Class Exercises
    - From Paper to Action
    - Career Planning
    - Creating Your Diploma: A Goal-Setting
- ► In-Text Quiz Answers
- ► PowerPoint Slides

The Instructor Companion Site also contains the following book specific content:

- ► ExamView Test Bank
- ► Online Course Manual
- ► Sample Syllabi
- ► Detailed Transition Guide

College Success CourseMate

To help your students gain a better understanding of the topics discussed in *Becoming a Master Student Concise*, encourage them to visit the College Success CourseMate at CengageBrain.com that provides the following resources specific to Chapter 10:

- ► Connect to Text content expands on specific topics marked with an icon within Chapter 10.
- ► Practice Tests allow students to see how well they understand the themes of *Becoming a Master Student Concise.*
- ► Interactive Concept Maps promote critical thinking by highlighting related ideas to show relationships among concepts.
- ► Video Skillbuilders bring to life techniques that will help students to excel in college and beyond. The following videos should give your students more information regarding topics covered in Chapter 10:
    - Career Planning: In College
    - Career Planning: After College
- ► Learning Styles Application
- ► Discussion Topics
- ► Reflection Questions
- ► Assessment Questions
- ► Experiment with chapter strategies
- ► Remembering Cultural Differences presents readers with brief articles that touch on aspects of diversity in our rapidly changing world. For Chapter 10, the following article will prompt your students to look at contemporary issues in a new way:
    - Align Yourself with Tomorrow's Employment Trends
- ► Master Student Profiles provide additional information on the people covered in this book feature. For Chapter 10, students will find expanded coverage and links about:
    - Lisa Ling
- ► Power Process Media contains video, PowerPoints, and audio files to take what your students have learned from the Power Processes in their book to the next level. For Chapter 10, students will find additional media on:
    - Be It

Along with the chapter-specific content, a General Resources folder is available that contains Toolboxes geared toward specific student types (Community College, Adult Learner, Student Athlete), the Plagiarism Prevention Zone, and the Career Resource Center.

10 What's Next?

Master Student Map

as you read, ask yourself

what if . . .

I could begin creating the life of my dreams—starting today?

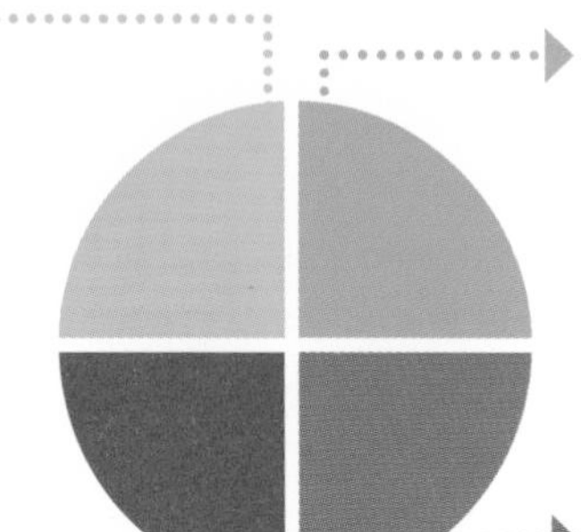

why this chapter matters . . .

You can use the techniques introduced in this book to set and achieve goals for the rest of your life.

how you can use this chapter . . .

- Choose the next steps in your education and career.
- Highlight your continuing success on résumés and in interviews.
- Experience the joys of contributing.
- Use a Power Process that enhances every technique in this book.

what is included . . .

MASTER STUDENTS in *action*

The feeling of accomplishment is a feeling like no other. To know what it is like to finish what you started and what it took to get there. . . . I believe that success is not about what you have gained, but what you have gone through.

—ALEX DENIZARD

Photo courtesy of Alex Denizard

Now that you're done—begin

IF YOU USED this book fully—if you actively read the contents, wrote Journal Entries, did exercises, practiced critical thinking, and applied the suggestions—you have had quite a journey.

Recall some high points of that journey. The first half of this book is about the nuts and bolts of education—the business of acquiring knowledge. It helps prepare you for making the transition to higher education and suggests that you take a First Step by telling the truth about your skills and setting goals to expand them. Also included are guidelines for planning your time, managing money, training your memory, improving your reading skills, taking useful notes, and succeeding at tests.

All of this activity prepares you for another aim of education—generating new knowledge and creating a unique place for yourself in the world. Meeting this aim leads you to the topics in the second half of this book: thinking for yourself, enhancing your communication skills, embracing diversity, and living with vibrant health. All are steps on the path of becoming a master student.

Now what? What's the next step?

As you answer this question, remember that the process of experimenting with your life never ends. At any moment, you can begin again.

Consider the possibility that you can create the life of your dreams. Your responses to any of the ideas, exercises, and Journal Entries in this book can lead you to think new thoughts, say new things, and do what you never believed you could do. If you're willing to master new ways to learn, the possibilities are endless. This message is more fundamental than any individual tool or technique you'll ever read about.

There are people who scoff at the suggestion that they can create the life of their dreams. These people have a perspective that is widely shared. Please set it aside.

You are on the edge of a universe so miraculous and full of wonder that your imagination, even at its most creative moment, cannot encompass it. Paths are open to lead you to worlds beyond your wildest dreams.

If this sounds like a pitch for the latest recreational drug, it might be. That drug is adrenaline, and it is automatically generated by your body when you are learning, planning, taking risks, achieving goals, and discovering new worlds inside and outside your skin.

One of the first articles in this book is about transitions. You are about to make another transition—not just to another chapter of this book, but to the next chapter of your life. Each article in this chapter is about creating your future through the skills you've gained in this course. Use the following pages to choose what's next for you. *

journal entry 22

Discovery/Intention Statement

Revisiting what you want

Review the Power Process: "Discover What You Want" on page 19. Then complete the following sentences with the first thoughts that come to mind.

I discovered that what I want most from life is . . .

____

____

____

____

____

____

____

____

____

To get what I want from my life, I intend to . . .

____

____

____

____

____

____

" . . . use the following suggestions to continue . . ."

Keep a journal. Consider buying a bound notebook in which to record your private reflections and dreams for the future. Get a notebook that will be worthy of your life. Write in this journal daily. Record what you are learning and write about your goals. Keep a record of significant events. Continue the Discovery Statements and Intention Statements that you started in this book.

Take a workshop. Schooling doesn't have to stop at graduation, and it doesn't have to take place on a campus. In most cities, a variety of organizations sponsor ongoing workshops covering topics from cosmetology to cosmology. Check them out.

Read, watch, and listen. Ask friends and instructors what they are reading. Sample a variety of books, newspapers, and magazines. None of them has all of the truth. Most of them have a piece of it.

© Photodisc/Getty Images

Take an unrelated class. Sign up for a class that is totally unrelated to your major. You can discover a lot about yourself and your intended future when you step out of old patterns. In addition to formal courses offered at your school, check into local community education courses.

Travel. See the world. Visit new neighborhoods. Travel to other countries. Explore. Find out what it looks like inside buildings that you normally have no reason to enter, museums that you never found interesting before, cities that are out of the way, forests and mountains that lie beyond your old boundaries.

Get counseling. Solving emotional problems is not the only reason to visit a counselor, therapist, or psychologist. These people are excellent resources for personal growth. You can use counseling to look at and talk about yourself in ways that might be uncomfortable for anyone except a trained professional.

Form a support group. Just as a well-organized study group can promote your success in school, an organized support group can help you reach goals in other areas of your life. Today, people in support groups help one another lose weight, stay sober, plan careers, find jobs, and achieve a host of other goals.

Find a mentor—or become one. Seek the counsel of experienced people you respect and admire. Use them as role models. If they are willing, ask them to be sounding boards for your plans and ideas. Many people are flattered to be asked. You can also become a mentor. If you want to perfect your skills as a master student, teach them to someone else.

Redo this book. Start by redoing one chapter, or maybe just one exercise, in this book. Then consider doing more, or even retaking your student success course. You'll deepen your current skills and pick up lots of new ideas as well. *

Find more suggestions online for continuing the path toward mastery.

Create your career *now*

There's an old saying: "If you enjoy what you do, you'll never work another day in your life." If you clearly define your career goals and your strategy for reaching them, you can plan your education effectively and create a seamless transition from school to the workplace. Begin now with the following ideas.

Terry Vine/Blend Images/RF/Getty

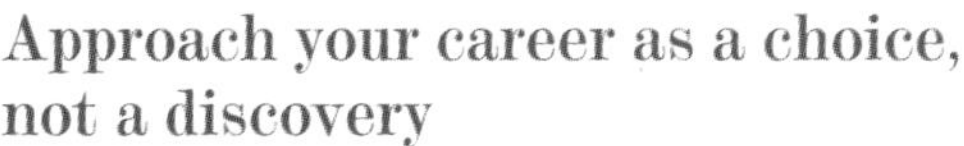

Approach your career as a choice, not a discovery

Many people approach career planning as if they were panning for gold. They keep sifting through the dirt, clearing the dust, and throwing out the rocks. They are hoping to strike it rich and discover the perfect career.

Other people believe that they'll wake up one morning, see the heavens part, and suddenly know what they're supposed to do. Many of them are still waiting for that magical day to dawn.

You can approach career planning in a different way. Instead of seeing a career as something you discover, you can see it as something you choose. You don't find the right career. You create it.

There's a big difference between these two approaches. Thinking that there's only one "correct" choice for your career can lead to a lot of anxiety: "Did I choose the right one?" "What if I made a mistake?"

Viewing your career as your creation helps you relax. Instead of anguishing over finding the right career, you can stay open to possibilities. You can choose one career today, knowing that you can choose again later.

Suppose that you've narrowed your list of possible careers to five, and you still can't decide. Then just choose one. Any one. Many people will have five careers in a lifetime anyway. You might be able to pursue all five of your careers, and you can do any one of them first. The important thing is to choose.

One caution is in order. Choosing your career is not something to do in an information vacuum. Rather, choose after you've done a lot of research. That includes research into yourself—your skills and interests—and a thorough knowledge of what careers are available.

You have a world of choices

Our society offers a limitless array of careers. You no longer have to confine yourself to a handful of traditional categories, such as business, education, government, or manufacturing. People are constantly creating new products and services to meet emerging demands. The number of job titles is expanding so rapidly that we can barely keep track of them.

The global marketplace creates even more options for you. Through Internet connections and communication satellites that bounce phone calls across the planet, you can exchange messages with almost anyone, anywhere. Your customers or clients could be located in Colorado or China, Pennsylvania or Panama. Your skills in thinking globally and communicating with a diverse world could help you create a new product or service for a new market—and perhaps a career that does not even exist today.

Describe your ideal lifestyle

In addition to choosing the content of your career, you have many options for integrating work into the context of your life. You can work full time. You can work part time. You can commute to a cubicle in a major corporation. Or you can work at home and take the 30-second commute from your bedroom to your desk.

Close your eyes. Visualize an ideal day in your life after graduation. Vividly imagine the following:

- Your work setting
- Your coworkers
- Your calendar and to-do list for that day
- Other sights and sounds in your work environment

This visualization emphasizes the importance of finding a match between your career and your lifestyle preferences—the amount of flexibility in your schedule, the number of people you see each day, the variety in your tasks, and the ways that you balance work with other activities.

Plan by naming names

One key to making your career plan real and to ensuring that you can act on it is naming. Go back over your plan to see whether you can include specific names whenever they're called for.

- *Name your job.* List the skills you enjoy using, and find out which jobs use them (the *Occupational Outlook Handbook* is a good resource for this activity). What are those jobs called? List them. Note that the same job might have different names.
- *Name your company—the agency or organization you want to work for.* If you want to be self-employed or start your own business, name the product or service you'd sell. Also list some possible names for your business. If you plan to work for others, name the organizations or agencies that are high on your list.
- *Name your contacts.* Take the list of organizations you just compiled. Find out which people in these organizations are responsible for hiring. List those people, and contact them directly. If you choose self-employment, list the names of possible customers or clients. All of these people are job contacts.
- *Name your location.* Ask whether your career choices are consistent with your preferences about where to live and work. For example, someone who wants to make a living as a studio musician might consider living in a large city such as New York or Toronto. This contrasts with the freelance graphic artist who conducts his business mainly by phone, fax, and online communication. He might be able to live anywhere and still pursue his career.

Now expand your list of contacts by brainstorming with your family and friends. Come up with a list of names—anyone who can help you with career planning and job hunting. Write each of these names on a 3x5 card or Rolodex card. You can also use a spiral-bound notebook, computer, or handheld electronic device.

Next, call the key people on your list. Ask them about their career experiences, tell them about the career path you're considering, and probe their knowledge of the industry you're interested in. After you speak with them, make brief notes about what you discussed. Also jot down any actions you agreed to take, such as a follow-up call.

Consider everyone you meet as a potential member of your job network. Be prepared to talk about what you do. Develop a "pitch"—a short statement of your career goal that you can easily share with your contacts. For example: "After I graduate, I plan to work in the travel business. I'm looking for an internship in a travel agency for next summer. Do you know of any agencies that take interns?"

Consider self-employment

Instead of joining a thriving business, you could create one of your own. If the idea of self-employment seems far-fetched, consider that as a student, you already *are* self-employed. You are setting your own goals, structuring your time, making your own financial decisions, and monitoring your performance. These are all transferable skills that you could use to become your own boss. Remember that many successful businesses—including Facebook and Yahoo!—were started by college students.

Test your choice—and be willing to change

Career-planning materials and counselors can help you test your choice and change it if you choose to do so. Read books about careers. Search for career-planning Web sites. Ask career counselors about skills assessments that can help you discover more about your skills and identify jobs that call for those skills. Take career-planning courses and workshops sponsored by your school. Visit the career-planning and job placement offices on campus.

Once you have a career choice, translate it into workplace experience. For example:

- Contact people who are actually doing the job you're researching, and ask them a lot of questions about what it's like (an *information interview*).
- Choose an internship or volunteer position in a field that interests you.
- Get a part-time or summer job in your career field.

If you find that you enjoy such experiences, you've probably made a wise career choice. The people you meet are possible sources of recommendations, referrals, and employment in the future. If you did *not* enjoy your experiences, celebrate what you learned about yourself. Now you're free to refine your initial career choice or go in a new direction.

Career planning is not a once-and-for-all proposition. Rather, career plans are made to be changed and refined as you gain new information about yourself and the world.

Career planning never ends. If your present career no longer feels right, you can choose again—no matter what stage of life you're in. The process is the same, whether you're choosing your first career or your fifth. *

Find more strategies online for career planning.

24 critical thinking exercise
Create your career plan—now

Write your career plan. Now. Start the process of career planning, even if you're not sure where to begin. Your response to this exercise can be just a rough draft of your plan, which you can revise and rewrite many times. The point is to get your ideas in writing.

The final format of your plan is up to you. You might include many details, such as the next job title you'd like to have, the courses required for your major, and other training that you want to complete. You might list companies to research and people that could hire you. You might also include target dates to complete each of these tasks.

Another option is to represent your plan visually through flowcharts, time lines, mind maps, or drawings. You can generate these by hand or use computer software.

For now, experiment with career planning by completing the following sentences. Use the space below, and continue on additional paper as needed. The goal is to begin the process of discovery. You can always change direction after some investigation.

1. The career I choose for now is . . .

2. The major steps that will guide me to this career are . . .

3. The immediate steps I will take to pursue this career are . . .

mastering technology

CONTINUE YOUR EDUCATION AT INTERNET UNIVERSITY

Access Web sites devoted to learning. Examples are eduFire (http://edufire.com), eHow (www.ehow.com), MindTools.com (www.mindtools.com), and About.com (www.about.com).

Use a newsreader to stay informed. Applications such as Google Reader, FeedDemon, and NewsGator (also called *RSS feeders*) will check your favorite Web sites for hourly or daily updates. This new content is displayed as a list of headlines with summaries.

Subscribe to audio and video podcasts. Podcasts are essentially radio and television programs delivered on demand. You can subscribe to podcasts through iTunes and sites such as Odeo (odeo.com).

Access university classes. Through iTunes U, colleges and universities across the world offer courses as podcasts for anyone to download.

Find more. For additional ways to learn online, do an Internet search using key words such as *online education*, *virtual education*, *instructional Web sites*, and *distance learning*. Make the world your classroom.

Jumpstart your education with transferable skills

FEW WORDS ARE as widely misunderstood as *skill.* Defining it carefully can have an immediate and positive impact on your career planning.

Identify two kinds of skills

One dictionary defines *skill* as "the ability to do something well, usually gained by training or experience." Some skills—such as the ability to repair fiber-optic cables or do brain surgery—are acquired through formal schooling, on-the-job training, or both. These abilities are called *technical skills.* People with such skills have mastered a specialized body of knowledge needed to do a specific kind of work.

However, there is another category of skills that we develop through experiences both inside and outside the classroom. We may never receive formal training to develop these abilities, yet they are key to success in the workplace. These are *transferable skills.* Transferable skills indicate the kind of abilities that help people thrive in any job—no matter what technical skills they have.

Perhaps you've heard someone described this way: "She's really smart and knows what she's doing, but she's got lousy people skills." People skills—such as *listening* and *negotiating*—are prime examples of transferable skills. Others include these:

- Assessing your current knowledge and skills
- Seeking out opportunities to acquire new knowledge and skills
- Choosing and applying learning strategies
- Showing flexibility by adopting new attitudes and behaviors
- Setting goals
- Scheduling time for goal-related tasks
- Monitoring progress toward goals
- Reading for key ideas and major themes
- Reading for detail
- Taking notes on material presented verbally, in print, or online
- Creating pictures, graphs, and other visuals to summarize and clarify information
- Researching by finding information online or in the library

When meeting with an academic advisor, you may be tempted to say, "I've just been taking general education and liberal arts courses. I don't have any marketable skills." Think again.

- Assessing personal performance at school or at work
- Using test results and other assessments to improve performance
- Working cooperatively in study groups and project teams
- Managing stress
- Thinking to create new ideas, products, or services
- Thinking to evaluate ideas, products, or services
- Choosing appropriate strategies for making decisions
- Choosing ethical behaviors
- Generating possible solutions to problems
- Choosing and implementing solutions
- Giving people feedback about the quality of their performance
- Resolving conflicts
- Speaking to diverse audiences
- Writing
- Monitoring income and expenses
- Decreasing expenses

This book includes articles, exercises, and Journal Entries that can assist you in developing all of the above skills.

Define your transferable skills

Transferable skills are often invisible to us. The problem begins when we assume that a given skill can be used in only one context, such as being in school or working at a particular job. Thinking in this way places an artificial limit on our possibilities.

As an alternative, think about the things you routinely do to succeed in school. Analyze your activities to isolate specific skills. Then brainstorm a list of jobs where you could use the same skills.

As an example, consider the task of writing a research paper. This calls for the following skills:

- *Planning*, including setting goals for completing your outline, first draft, second draft, and final draft.
- *Managing time* to meet your writing goals.
- *Interviewing* people who know a lot about the topic of your paper.
- *Researching*, using the Internet and campus library to discover key facts and ideas to include in your paper.
- *Writing* to present those facts and ideas in an original way.
- *Editing* your drafts for clarity and correctness.

Now consider the kinds of jobs that draw on these skills.

For example, you could transfer your skill at writing papers to a possible career in journalism, technical writing, or advertising copywriting.

You could use your editing skills to work in the field of publishing as a magazine or book editor.

Interviewing and research skills could help you enter the field of market research. And the abilities to plan, manage time, and meet deadlines will help you succeed in all the jobs mentioned so far.

Use the same kind of analysis to think about transferring skills from one job to another. Say that you work part-time as an administrative assistant at a computer dealer that sells a variety of hardware and software. You take phone calls from potential customers, help current customers solve problems using their computers, and attend meetings where your coworkers plan ways to market new products. You are developing skills at *selling*, *serving customers*, and *working on teams*. These skills could help you land a job as a sales representative for a computer manufacturer or software developer.

The basic idea is to take a cue from the word *transferable*. Almost any skill you use to succeed in one situation can *transfer* to success in another situation.

The concept of transferable skills creates a powerful link between higher education and the work world. Skills are the core elements of any job. While taking any course, list the specific skills you are developing and how you can transfer them to the work world. Almost everything you do in school can be applied to your career—if you consistently pursue this line of thought.

Ask four questions

To experiment further with this concept of transferable skills, ask and answer four questions derived from the Master Student Map.

Why identify my transferable skills?

Getting past the "I-don't-have-any-skills" syndrome means that you can approach job hunting with more confidence. As you uncover transferable skills, your list of qualifications will grow as if by magic. You won't be padding your résumé. You'll simply be using action words to tell the full truth about what you can do.

Identifying your transferable skills takes a little time. And the payoffs are numerous. A complete and accurate list of transferable skills can help you land jobs that involve more responsibility, more variety, more freedom to structure your time, and more money. Careers can be made—or broken—by transferable skills at defining your job, managing your workload, and getting along with people.

Transferable skills can also help you thrive in the midst of constant change. Technology will continue to develop. Ongoing discoveries in many fields could render current knowledge obsolete. Jobs that exist today may disappear in a few years, only to be replaced by entirely new ones.

In the economy of the twenty-first century, you might not be able to count on job security. What you *can* count on is "skills security"—abilities that you can carry from one career to another or acquire as needed. Even though he only completed 8 years of formal schooling,[1] Henry Ford said, "The only real security that a person can have in this world is a reserve of knowledge, experience, and ability. Without these qualities, money is practically useless."[2]

What are my transferable skills?

Discover your transferable skills by reflecting on key experiences. Recall a time when you performed at the peak of your ability, overcame obstacles, won an award, gained a high grade, or met a significant goal. List the skills you used to create those successes.

For a more complete picture of your transferable skills, describe the object of your action. Say that one of the skills on your list is *organizing*. This could refer to organizing ideas, organizing people, or organizing objects in a room. Specify the kind of organizing that you like to do.

How do I perform these skills?

You can bring your transferable skills into even sharper focus by adding adverbs—words that describe *how* you take action. You might say that you edit *accurately* or learn *quickly*.

In summary, you can use a three-column chart to list your transferable skills. For example:

Verb	Object	Adverb
Organizing	Records	Effectively
Serving	Customers	Courteously
Coordinating	Special events	Efficiently

Add a specific example of each transferable skill to your skills list, and you're well on the way to an engaging résumé and a winning job interview.

What if I could expand my transferable skills?

In addition to thinking about the skills you already have, consider the skills you'd like to acquire. Describe them in detail. List experiences that can help you develop them. Let your list of transferable skills grow and develop as you do. *

Learn more about transferable skills online.

25 critical thinking exercise Recognize your skills

This exercise about discovering your skills includes three steps. Before you begin, gather at least a hundred 3 x5 cards and a pen or pencil. Allow about 1 hour to complete the exercise.

Step 1

Recall your activities during the past week or month. To refresh your memory, review your responses to Critical Thining Exercise 7: "The Time Monitor/Time Plan Process" in Chapter 2 . (You might even benefit from doing that exercise again.)

Write down as many activities as you can, listing each one on a separate 3x5 card. Include work-related activities, school activities, and hobbies.

In addition to daily activities, recall and write down any rewards you've received or recognition of your achievements during the past year. Examples include scholarship awards, athletic awards, or recognitions for volunteer work.

Spend 20 minutes on this step, listing all of the activities, rewards, and recognitions you can recall.

Step 2

Next, look over your activity cards. Then take another 20 minutes to list any specialized knowledge or procedures needed to complete those activities or merit those awards and recognitions. These are your *technical skills*. For example, tutoring a French class requires a working knowledge of that language. Write each skill on a separate card, and label it "technical skill."

Step 3

Go over your activity cards one more time. Look for examples of *transferable skills*—those that can be applied to a variety of careers. For instance, giving a speech or working as a salesperson in a computer store requires the ability to persuade people. Tuning a car means that you can attend to details and troubleshoot. These are all transferable skills.

Write each of these on a separate card labeled "transferable skill."

Congratulations—you now have a detailed picture of your skills. Keep your lists of technical skills and transferable skills on hand when writing your résumé, preparing for job interviews, and doing other career-planning tasks. As you think of new skills, add them to the lists.

Use résumés and interviews to "hire" an employer

The logical outcome of your career plan is a focused job hunt.

© Thinkstock/Alamy

MENTION THE PHRASE *job hunting*, and many people see themselves poring through the help-wanted sections in newspapers or on Web sites, sending out hundreds of résumés, or enlisting the services of employment agencies to find job openings and set up interviews.

There's a big problem with these job-hunting strategies: *Most job openings are not advertised.* Many employers turn to help-wanted listings, résumés, and employment agencies only as a last resort. When they have positions to fill, they prefer instead to hire people they know—friends and colleagues—or people who walk through the door and prove that they're excellent candidates for available jobs.

Remembering this can help you overcome frustration, tap the hidden job market, and succeed more often at getting the position you want.

One powerful source of information about new jobs is people. Ask around. Tell everyone—friends, relatives, coworkers, and fellow students—that you want a job. In particular, tell people who have the power to hire you. Some jobs are created on the spot when a person with potential simply shows up and asks.

Richard Bolles, author of *What Color Is Your Parachute? A Practical Manual for Job-Hunters and Career-Changers*, recommends the following steps in job hunting:

- Discover what skills you want to use in your career.
- Discover what jobs draw on the skills you want to use.
- Interview people who are doing the kind of jobs you'd want to do.
- Research companies you'd like to work for, and find out what kinds of problems they face on a daily basis.
- Identify your contacts—a person at each one of these companies who has the power to hire you.
- Arrange an interview with that person, even if the company has no job openings at the moment.
- Stay in contact with the people who interviewed you, knowing that a job opening can occur at any time.[3]

Use résumés to get interviews. A résumé is a piece of persuasive writing, not a dry recitation of facts or a laundry list of previous jobs. It has a basic purpose—to get you to the next step in the hiring process, usually an interview.

Begin your résumé with your name, address, phone number, and e-mail address. Then name your desired job, often called an "objective" or "goal." Follow with the body of your résumé—your skills, work experience, and education.

Many résumés follow the contact information with an *objective*. This is a description of the job that you want. Keep this to one sentence, and tailor it to the specific position for which you're applying.

Craft your objective to get attention. Ask yourself: *From an employer's perspective, what kind of person would make an ideal candidate for this job?* Then write your objective to directly answer this question with two or three specific qualities that you can demonstrate.

Focus the objective on what you can do for the employer. Here is the first place to state the benefits you can deliver. Avoid self-centered phrases like "a job in the software industry where I can develop my sales skills." Instead, state your objective as "a sales position for a software company that wants to continually generate new customers and exceed its revenue goals."

Write your résumé so that the facts leap off the page. Describe your work experiences in short phrases that start with active verbs: "*Supervised* three people." "*Wrote* two annual reports." "*Set up* sales calls." Also leave reasonable margins and space between paragraphs.

As you draft your résumé, remember that every organization has problems to solve. Show in your résumé that you know about those problems and can offer your skills as solutions. Give evidence that you've used those skills to get measurable results. Show a potential employer how you can contribute value and help create profits.

Use interviews to screen employers. You might think of job interviews as times when potential employers size you up and possibly screen you out. Consider another viewpoint—that interviews offer you a chance to size up potential employers and possibly screen *them* out.

To get the most from your interviews, learn everything you can about each organization that interests you. Get a feel for its strong points. Learn about its successes in the marketplace. Also find out what challenges the organization faces. As in a résumé, use interviews to present your skills as unique solutions for those challenges.

Job interviewers have many standard questions. Most of them boil down to a few major concerns:

- How did you find out about us?
- Would we be comfortable working with you?
- How can you help us?
- Will you learn this job quickly?
- What makes you different from other applicants?
- Can we afford you?

Before your interview, prepare some answers to these questions.

If you get turned down for the job after your interview, don't take it personally. Every interview is a source of feedback about what works—and what doesn't work—in contacting employers. Use that feedback to interview more effectively next time.

Counter bias and discrimination. During your job hunt, you might worry about discrimination based on your race, ethnic background, gender, or sexual orientation. Protect yourself by keeping records, including copies of all correspondence from prospective employers. Remember that Title VII of the Civil Rights Act bans discrimination in almost all aspects of the workplace, from hiring to firing. Congress set up the Equal Employment Opportunity Commission (EEOC) to enforce this act. You can contact this agency at 1-800-669-4000 and get more information through its Web site at www.eeoc.gov.

Give yourself a raise before you start work. Preparing for salary negotiation can immediately increase your income by hundreds or thousands of dollars. To get the money you deserve:

- Use Critical Thinking Exercise 28: "The Money Monitor/Money Plan" in Chapter 9 to determine how much you'll need each month to meet your expenses—and still have some money left over to save.
- Maintain flexibility by settling on a salary *range* that you want rather than a specific figure.
- Through information interviews, library research, and Internet searches, discover typical salary ranges for jobs in your field.
- Remember that where you live has an effect on your salary, too. The national average for a job in your field may be different than what you can expect to make in your region, depending on living and housing costs.
- Based on your research, estimate how much the employer is likely to offer you.
- Postpone salary discussions until the end of the interview process—when you're confident an employer wants to hire you.
- Let the employer be the first to mention a salary range.
- Ask for a figure near the top of that range.
- Ask whether there's room to negotiate benefit packages as well.

Be prepared to act like a free agent. International competition, corporate downsizing, and new technology could make the typical job as we know it a thing of the past. The workplace of the future might be organized around projects done by flexible teams of free agents instead of employees who spend years with a single company.

If this happens, you can prosper by seeing yourself as self-employed—even if you have a "regular" job. Think like a freelance or contract employee who's hired to complete a specific project. Demonstrate your value in each project, continually revise your job goals, and expand your contacts. Use what you have learned in this course to constantly update your skills, manage job transitions, and stay in charge of your career path. *

Go online to discover more job-hunting strategies.

Choosing schools . . . *again*

THE WAY THAT you choose a new school will have a major impact on your education. This is true if you're transferring from a community or technical college to a 4-year school or if you're choosing a graduate school. Even if you don't plan to transfer, you can use the following ideas to evaluate your current school.

Know key terms

As you begin researching schools, take a few minutes to review some key terms.

Articulation agreements are official documents that spell out the course equivalents that a school accepts.

An *associate of arts (A.A.)* or *associate of science (A.S.)* is the degree title conferred by many 2-year colleges. Having a degree from a 2-year college can make it easier to change schools than transferring without a degree.

Course equivalents are courses you've already taken that another school will accept as meeting its requirements for graduation.

Prerequisites are courses or skills that a school requires students to complete or have before they enter or graduate.

Gather information

To research schools, start with publications. These include print sources, such as school catalogs, and school Web sites. Next, contact people—academic advisors, counselors, other school staff members, and current or former students from the schools you're considering. Contact the advisor at the new school to find out what the acceptance and graduation requirements will be. Finally, take trips to the two or three schools that interest you most.

Use your research to dig up key facts about each school you're considering, such as the following:

- Location
- Number of students
- Class sizes
- Possibilities for contact with instructors outside class
- Percentage of full-time faculty members
- Admissions criteria
- Availability of degrees that interest you
- Tuition and fees
- Housing plans
- Financial aid programs
- Religious affiliation
- Diversity of students and staff
- Course requirements
- Retention rates (how many students come back to school after their freshman year

To learn the most about a school, go beyond the first statistics you see. For example, a statement that "30 percent of our students are persons of color" doesn't tell you much about the numbers of people from specific ethnic or racial groups. Also remember that any statement about average class size is just that—an average. To gain more details, ask how often you can expect to enroll in smaller classes, especially during your final terms.

In addition, gather facts about your current academic profile. Include your grades, courses completed, any degrees attained, grade point average (GPA), and standardized test scores.

Choose your new school

If you follow the above suggestions, you'll end up with stacks of publications and pages of notes. As you sort through all this information, remember that your impressions of a school will go beyond a dry list of facts. Also pay attention to your instincts and intuitions—your "gut feelings" of attraction to one school or hesitation about another. These impressions can be important to your choice. Allow time for such feelings to emerge.

You can also benefit from putting your choice of schools in a bigger context. Consider the purposes, values, and long-term goals you've generated by doing the exercises and Journal Entries in this book. Consider which school is most likely to support the body of discoveries and intentions that you've created.

As you choose your new school, consider the needs and wishes of your family members and friends. Ask for their guidance and support. If you involve them in the decision, they'll have more of a stake in your success.

At some point, you'll just choose a school. Remember that there is no one "right" choice. You could probably thrive at many schools—perhaps even at your current one. Use the suggestions in this book to practice self-responsibility. Take charge of your education no matter which school you attend. *

Service-learning: The art of learning by contributing

AS PART OF a service-learning project for a sociology course, students volunteer at a community center for older adults. For another service-learning project, history students interview people in veterans' hospitals about their war experiences. These students plan to share their interview results with a psychiatrist on the hospital staff.

Meanwhile, business students provide free tax-preparation help at a center for low-income people. Students in graphic arts classes create free promotional materials for charities. Other students staff a food cooperative and a community credit union.

These examples of actual projects from the National Service-Learning Clearinghouse demonstrate the working premise of service-learning—that volunteer work and other forms of contributing can become a vehicle for higher education.

Service-learning generally includes three elements: meaningful community service, a formal academic curriculum, and time for students to reflect on what they learn from service. That reflection can include speeches, journal writing, and research papers.

Service-learning creates a win–win scenario. For one thing, students gain the satisfaction of contributing. They also gain experiences that can guide their career choices and help them develop job skills.

At the same time, service-learning adds to the community a resource with a handsome return on investment. For example, participants in the Learn and Serve America program (administered by the Corporation for National and Community Service) provided community services valued at four times the program cost.[4]

When you design or participate in a service-learning project, consider these suggestions:

- **Choose partners carefully.** Work with a community agency that has experience with students. Make sure that the agency has liability insurance to cover volunteers.
- **Handle logistics**. Integrating service-learning into your schedule can call for detailed planning. If your volunteer work takes place off campus, arrange for transportation, and allow for travel time.
- **Reflect on your service-learning project.** Turn to a tool you've used throughout this book—the Discovery and Intention Journal Entry system. Write Discovery Statements about what you want to gain from service-learning and how you feel about what you're doing. Follow up with Intention Statements about what you'll do differently for your next volunteer experience.
- **Include ways to evaluate your project.** From your Intention Statements, create action goals and outcome goals. *Action goals* state what you plan to do and how many people you intend to serve; for instance, "We plan to provide 100 hours of literacy tutoring to 10 people in the community." *Outcome goals* describe the actual impact that your project will have: "At the end of our project, 60 percent of the people we tutor will be able to write a résumé and fill out a job application." Build numbers into your goals whenever possible. That makes it easier to evaluate the success of your project.
- **Build long-term impact into your project.** One potential pitfall of service-learning is that the programs are often short lived. After students pack up and return to campus, programs can die. To avoid this outcome, make sure that other students or community members are willing to step in and take over for you when the semester ends.
- **Build transferable skills.** Review the list of transferable skills on page 218. Use this list as way to stimulate your thinking. List the specific skills that you're developing through service-learning. Keep this list. It will come in handy when you write a résumé and fill out job applications. And before you plan to do another service-learning project, think about the skills you'd like to develop from that experience.
- **Celebrate mistakes.** If your project fails to meet its goals, have a party. State—in writing—the obstacles you encountered and ways to overcome them. The solutions you offer will be worth gold to the people who follow in your footsteps. Sharing the lessons learned from your mistakes is an act of service in itself. *

Join a diverse workplace

As companies look for ways to gain overseas market share, they will look for people who enter this global environment with ease. Diversity in the workplace will be seen as good for people—and good for business. People of all races and cultures can use several strategies to reach common ground at work.

Expect differences

Most of us unconsciously judge others by a single set of standards—our own. That can lead to communication breakdown. For example:

- A man in Costa Rica works for a multinational company. He turns down a promotion that would take his family to California. This choice mystifies the company's executives. Yet the man has grandparents who are in ill health, and leaving them behind would be taboo in his country.
- A Native American woman avoids eye contact with her superiors. Her coworkers see her as aloof. However, she comes from a culture where people seldom make eye contact with their superiors.
- A woman from Ohio travels to Mexico City on business. She shows up promptly for a 9 a.m. meeting and finds that it starts 30 minutes late and goes an hour beyond its scheduled ending time. She's entered a culture with a flexible sense of time.

To prevent misunderstandings, remember that culture touches every aspect of human behavior, ranging from the ways people greet one another to the ways they resolve conflict. Differences in culture could affect any encounter you have with another person. Expecting differences up front helps you keep an open mind.

Mind the details

Pay attention to details that people from any culture will use to form first impressions of you. Lydia Ramsey, author of *Manners That Sell: Adding the Polish That Builds Profits*, suggests the following practices. You might find them especially useful if you travel overseas for your job:

- Shake hands appropriately. While the handshake is a near-universal form of greeting, people do it differently across the world. You might have been coached to take a firm grip, make eye contact, pump twice, and then let go. In other countries, however, people might prefer a lighter grip or longer contact. When traveling to the Middle East, you might even be greeted with a kiss or hug. Observe closely to discover the norm.
- When in doubt, dress up. Americans are relatively informal about workplace fashion. In many cultures, there are no "casual days." Formal business wear is expected every day. Dress up unless it's clearly OK to do otherwise.
- Treat business cards carefully. In many cultures, the way that you exchange cards conveys your respect for others. When someone gives you a card, take a second to look at it. Then offer your thanks and place the card in a folder or briefcase with other work-related documents. Don't stash it quickly in a pocket or purse.
- Respect titles and names. Though Americans like to do business on a first-name basis, this is acceptable in some cultures only among family members. Avoid misunderstandings by using last names and job titles when you greet people in work settings.[5]

Use language with care

Even people who speak the same language sometimes use simple words that can be confused with each other. For instance, giving someone a "mickey" can mean pulling a practical joke—or slipping a drug into someone's drink. We can find it tough to communicate simple observations, let alone abstract concepts.

You can help by communicating simply and directly. When meeting with people who speak English as a second language, think twice before using figures of speech or slang expressions. Stick to standard English and enunciate clearly.

Be willing to bridge gaps

Simply being *willing* to bridge culture gaps can be just as crucial as knowing about another group's customs or learning their language. People from other cultures might sense your attitude and be willing to reach out to you. *

26 critical thinking exercise
The Discovery Wheel

This book doesn't work. It is worthless. Only you can work. Only you can make a difference and use this book to become a more effective student.

The purpose of this book is to give you the opportunity to change your behavior. The fact that something seems like a good idea doesn't necessarily mean that you will put it into practice. This exercise gives you a chance to see what behaviors you have changed on your journey toward becoming a master student.

Answer each question quickly and honestly. Record your results on the Discovery Wheel on page 229. Then compare your new wheel with the one you completed in Chapter 1.

The scores on this Discovery Wheel indicate your current strengths and weaknesses on your path toward becoming a master student. The last Journal Entry in this chapter provides an opportunity to write about how you intend to change. As you complete this self-evaluation, keep in mind that your commitment to change allows you to become a master student. *Your scores might be lower here than on your earlier Discovery Wheel.* That's OK. Lower scores might result from increased self-awareness and honesty, as well as other valuable assets.

Note: The online version of this exercise does not include number ratings, so the results will be formatted differently than described here. If you did your previous Discovery Wheel online, do it online again. This will help you compare your two sets of responses more accurately.

5 points: This statement is always or almost always true of me.
4 points: This statement is often true of me.
3 points: This statement is true of me about half the time.
2 points: This statement is seldom true of me.
1 point: This statement is never or almost never true of me.

1. ______ I enjoy learning.
2. ______ I understand and apply the concept of multiple intelligences.
3. ______ I connect my courses to my purpose for being in school.
4. ______ I make a habit of assessing my personal strengths and areas for improvement.
5. ______ I am satisfied with how I am progressing toward achieving my goals.
6. ______ I use my knowledge of learning styles to support my success in school.
7. ______ I am willing to consider any idea that can help me succeed in school—even if I initially disagree with that idea.
8. ______ I regularly remind myself of the benefits I intend to get from my education.

______ **Total score (1) Attitude**

1. ______ I set long-term goals and periodically review them.
2. ______ I set short-term goals to support my long-term goals.
3. ______ I write a plan for each day and each week.
4. ______ I assign priorities to what I choose to do each day.
5. ______ I am in control of my personal finances.
6. ______ I can access a variety of resources to finance my education.
7. ______ I am confident that I will have enough money to complete my education.
8. ______ I take on debts carefully and repay them on time.

______ **Total score (2) Time and Money**

1. ______ I am confident of my ability to remember.

2. ______ I can remember people's names.

3. ______ At the end of a lecture, I can summarize what was presented.

4. ______ I apply techniques that enhance my memory skills.

5. ______ I can recall information when I'm under pressure.

6. ______ I remember important information clearly and easily.

7. ______ I can jog my memory when I have difficulty recalling.

8. ______ I can relate new information to what I've already learned.

______ **Total score (3) Memory**

1. ______ I preview and review reading assignments.

2. ______ When reading, I ask myself questions about the material.

3. ______ I underline or highlight important passages when reading.

4. ______ When I read textbooks, I am alert and awake.

5. ______ I relate what I read to my life.

6. ______ I select a reading strategy to fit the type of material I'm reading.

7. ______ I take effective notes when I read.

8. ______ When I don't understand what I'm reading, I note my questions and find answers.

______ **Total score (4) Reading**

1. ______ When I am in class, I focus my attention.

2. ______ I take notes in class.

3. ______ I am aware of various methods for taking notes and choose those that work best for me.

4. ______ I distinguish important material and note key phrases in a lecture.

5. ______ I copy down material that the instructor writes on the chalkboard or overhead display.

6. ______ I can put important concepts into my own words.

7. ______ My notes are valuable for review.

8. ______ I review class notes within 24 hours.

______ **Total score (5) Notes**

1. ______ I use techniques to manage stress related to exams.

2. ______ I manage my time during exams and am able to complete them.

3. ______ I am able to predict test questions.

4. ______ I adapt my test-taking strategy to the kind of test I'm taking.

5. ______ I understand what essay questions ask and can answer them completely and accurately.

6. ______ I start reviewing for tests at the beginning of the term.

7. ______ I continue reviewing for tests throughout the term.

8. ______ My sense of personal worth is independent of my test scores.

______ **Total score (6) Tests**

1. ______ I have flashes of insight and think of solutions to problems at unusual times.

2. ______ I use brainstorming to generate solutions to a variety of problems.

3. ______ When I get stuck on a creative project, I use specific methods to get unstuck.

4. ______ I see problems and tough choices as opportunities for learning and personal growth.

5. ______ I am willing to consider different points of view and alternate solutions.

6. ______ I can detect common errors in logic.

7. ______ I construct viewpoints by drawing on information and ideas from many sources.

8. ______ As I share my viewpoints with others, I am open to their feedback.

______ Total score (7) Thinking

1. ______ I am candid with others about who I am, what I feel, and what I want.

2. ______ Other people tell me that I am a good listener.

3. ______ I can communicate my upset and anger without blaming others.

4. ______ I can make friends and create valuable relationships in a new setting.

5. ______ I am open to being with people I don't especially like in order to learn from them.

6. ______ I can effectively plan, research, and complete a large writing assignment.

7. ______ I approach conflict with other people as a problem to solve, not a contest to win.

8. ______ I speak confidently in class and make effective presentations.

______ Total score (8) Communicating

1. ______ I have enough energy to study and work—and still enjoy other areas of my life.

2. ______ If the situation calls for it, I have enough reserve energy to put in a long day.

3. ______ The way I eat supports my long-term health.

4. ______ The way I eat is independent of my feelings of self-worth.

5. ______ I exercise regularly to maintain a healthful weight.

6. ______ My emotional health supports my ability to learn.

7. ______ I notice changes in my physical condition and respond effectively.

8. ______ I am in control of any alcohol or other drugs I put into my body.

______ Total score (9) Health

1. ______ I see learning as a lifelong process.

2. ______ I relate school to what I plan to do for the rest of my life.

3. ______ I learn by making a contribution to the lives of other people.

4. ______ I have a written career plan and update it regularly.

5. ______ I am gaining skills to succeed in a diverse workplace.

6. ______ I take responsibility for the quality of my education—and my life.

7. ______ I live by a set of values that translates into daily actions.

8. ______ I am willing to accept challenges even when I'm not sure how to meet them.

______ Total score (10) Purpose

Filling in your Discovery Wheel

Using the total score from each category, shade in each section of the Discovery Wheel. Use different colors, if you want. For example, you could use green to denote areas you want to work on. When you have finished, complete the Journal Entry on the next page.

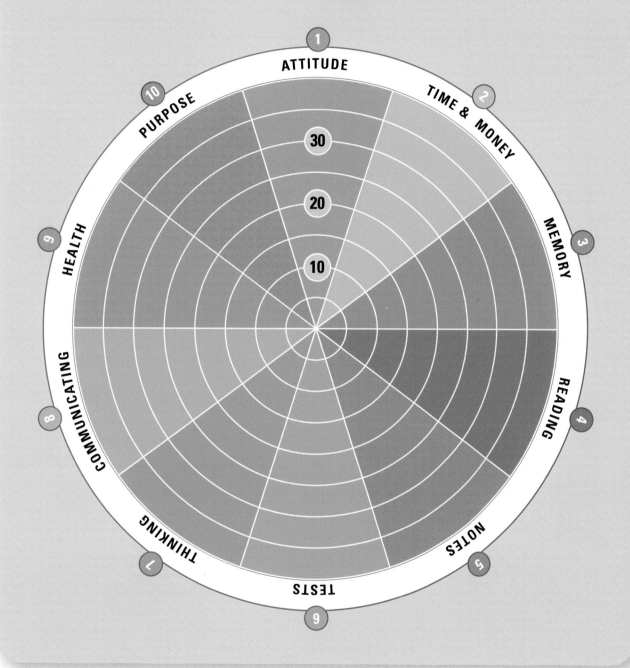

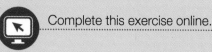

1 ATTITUDE
2 TIME & MONEY
3 MEMORY
4 READING
5 NOTES
6 TESTS
7 THINKING
8 COMMUNICATING
9 HEALTH
10 PURPOSE

30
20
10

journal entry 23

Discovery/Intention Statement

Revisiting your Discovery Wheels

The purpose of this Journal Entry is to (1) review both of the Discovery Wheels you completed in this book, (2) summarize your insights from doing them, and (3) declare how you will use these insights to promote your continued success in school.

Again, a lower score on the second Discovery Wheel does not necessarily indicate decreased personal effectiveness. Instead, the lower score could result from increased honesty and greater self-awareness.

Enter your Discovery Wheel scores from both chapters in the space below.

	Chapter 1	Chapter 10
Attitude	________	________
Time and Money	________	________
Memory	________	________
Reading	________	________
Notes	________	________
Tests	________	________
Thinking	________	________
Communicating	________	________
Health	________	________
Purpose	________	________

Comparing the Discovery Wheel in this chapter with the Discovery Wheel in Chapter 1, I discovered that I . . .

In the next 6 months, I intend to review the following articles from this book for additional suggestions I could use:

27 critical thinking exercise

This book shouts, "Use me!"

Becoming a Master Student is designed to be used for years. The success strategies presented here are not likely to become habits overnight. There are more suggestions than can be put into action immediately. Some of what is discussed might not apply to your life right now, but it might be just what you could use in a few months.

Plan to keep this book and use it again. Imagine that your book has a mouth. (Visualize the mouth.) Also imagine that it has arms and legs. (Visualize them.)

Now picture your book sitting on a shelf or table that you see every day. Imagine a time when you are having trouble in school and struggling to be successful as a student. Visualize your book jumping up and down, shouting, "Use me! Read me! I might have the solution to your problem, and I know I can help you solve it."

This is a memory technique to remind you to use a resource. Sometimes when you are stuck, all you need is a small push or a list of possible actions. At those times, hear your book shout, "Use me!"

Be It

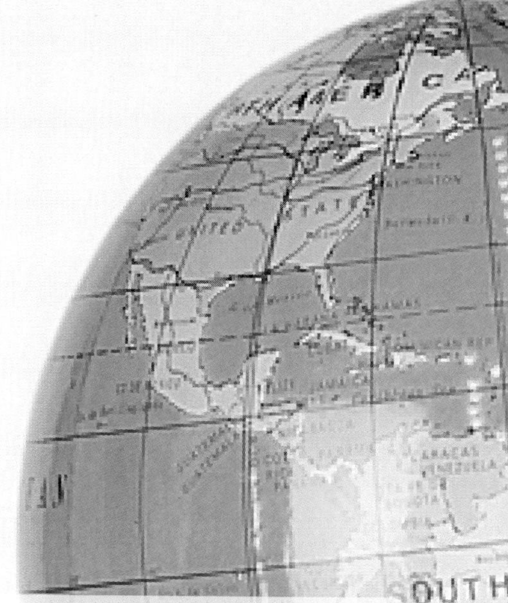

Use this Power Process to enhance all of the techniques in this book.

Consider that most of our choices in life fall into three categories. We can do the following:

- Increase our material wealth (what we have).
- Improve our skills (what we do).
- Develop our "being" (who we are).

Many people devote their entire lifetimes to the first two categories. They act as if they are "human havings" instead of human beings. For them, the quality of life hinges on what they have. They devote most of their waking hours to getting more—more clothes, more cars, more relationships, more degrees, more trophies. "Human havings" define themselves by looking at the circumstances in their lives—what they have.

Some people escape this materialist trap by adding another dimension to their identities. In addition to living as "human havings," they also live as "human doings." They thrive on working hard and doing everything well. They define themselves by how efficiently they do their jobs, how effectively they raise their children, and how actively they participate in clubs and organizations. Their thoughts are constantly about methods, techniques, and skills.

In addition to focusing on what we have and what we do, we can also focus on our being. That last word describes how we *see* ourselves.

All of the techniques in this book can be worthless if you operate with the idea that you are an ineffective student. You might do almost everything this book suggests and still never achieve the success in school that you desire.

Instead, picture yourself as a master student right now. Through higher education, you are simply gaining knowledge and skills that reflect and reinforce this view of yourself. Change the way you see yourself. Then watch your actions and results shift as if by magic.

Remember that "Be It" is not positive thinking or mental cheerleading. This Power Process works well when you take a First Step—when you tell the truth about your current abilities. The very act of accepting who you are and what you can do right now unleashes a powerful force for personal change.

If you can first visualize where you want to be, if you can go there in your imagination, if you can *be* it today, then you set yourself up to succeed.

If you want it, be it.

Learn more about this Power Process online.

Put it to Work

Strategies from *Becoming a Master Student* can help you succeed in your career, as well as in school. To discover how suggestions in this chapter can apply to the workplace, reflect on the following case study.

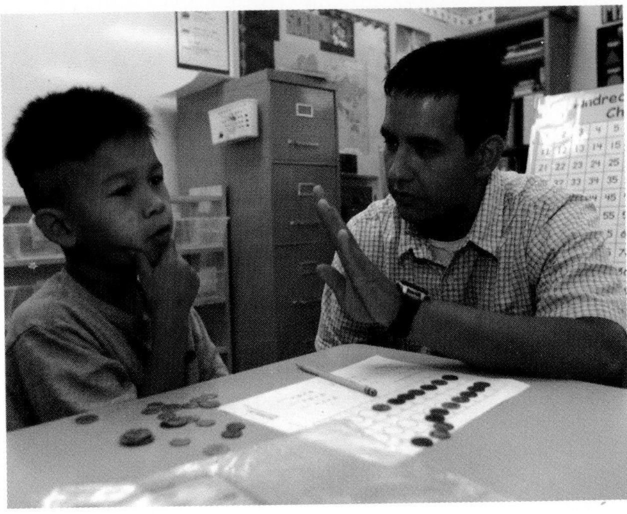

© Ed Kashi/CORBIS

Duane Bigeagle earned his B.A. in elementary education and found a job teaching kindergarten in an urban public school.

To his surprise, the hardest thing about the job was not interacting with students—whom he enjoyed greatly—but interacting with his coworkers. Although Duane had heard of office politics, he did not expect to encounter them much in an educational setting.

Duane's greatest concern was a colleague named Reneé, a teacher with 25 years of experience. During weekly staff meetings, the school's principal asked teachers to share any problems they were experiencing with students and to collectively brainstorm solutions. Reneé smiled a lot, offered suggestions, and freely offered praise for anyone who was willing to share a problem. During informal conversations with Duane before or after school, however, Reneé complained bitterly about other teachers on staff—including those she'd just praised during staff meetings.

Being new to the school and a first-year teacher, Duane decided that he wanted to avoid making enemies. His goal in relating to staff members was simply to learn everything he could from them. With that goal in mind, Duane adopted the habits of carefully observing the classroom strategies used by other teachers and listening without judgment to any coaching they offered him.

Reneé talked with Duane every day and, after gossiping about other teachers, freely offered advice for managing his classroom. By the end of the school year, Duane had had enough of this. He worried that Reneé was taking on the role of a self-appointed mentor to him, and he disagreed with many of her ideas about teaching. He also worried that other teachers would perceive he and Reneé as a "team," and that her mixed reputation in the workplace would reflect negatively on him as well.

During his first year on a new job, Duane is using several transferable skills, including listening without judgment. Describe some other transferable skills that he demonstrates:

____

____

____

____

Also describe some strategies that Duane could use to resolve his conflict with Reneé:

____

____

____

To get continuing benefits from this course, continue the conversation about creating success in the workplace and every other area of your life. For example, put your vision in front of you. Write your goals on 3x5 cards or sticky notes. Place these reminders of your vision in places where you can't miss them—your desk, your bathroom mirror, your car.

Also consider starting a book group focused on success. There are plenty of books about success that complement this one. (See Additional Reading on page 239.) Gather with friends to digest and discuss some of them.

Quiz

Name______________________________ Date___/___/___

1. According to the text, you can create a career plan through the process of "naming names." True or false? Explain your answer.
   True. Naming names means being very specific: *Name* your specific job, *name* the company you want to work for, *name* your contacts in securing that job, and *name* where you want to live and work. (*Create your career* now, pp. 215–217)
2. Explain how *technical skills* and *transferable skills* differ. Give one example of each kind of skill.
   A technical skill is an ability gained by training or experience. It involves a specialized body of knowledge needed to do a specific kind of work. An example is the ability to repair fiber-optic cable. A transferable skill is an ability developed without formal training that helps people thrive in any job. Examples include listening and negotiating.
   (Answers will vary.) (*Jumpstart your education with transferable skills,* pp. 218–220)
3. Explain how career planning can become a process of choosing instead of a process of discovery.
   While we may discover skills through career planning, we don't find the right career. We create it. We choose our careers because we are the only ones who can do research into ourselves and truly know our own skills and interests. Knowing that we make the choice can be relaxing. There is not just one "correct" choice for a career.
   (*Create your career* now, pp. 215–217)
4. List three suggestions for designing an effective service-learning project.
   List at least three of the following:
   - Choose partners carefully.
   - Handle logistics.
   - Reflect on your project using the Discovery and Intention Journal Entry system.
   - Include ways to evaluate your project.
   - Build long-term impact into your project.
   - Celebrate mistakes.

   (Answers will vary.) (*Service-learning: The art of learning by contributing,* p. 224)
5. Describe the three main types of life choices explained in the Power Process: "Be It."
   List and describe the following:
   (a) What we have (b) What we do (c) Who we are (*Power Process: Be It*, p. 231)
6. List three strategies for negotiating a starting salary during the interview process.
   List any three of the following:
   - Use the Money Monitor/Money Plan to determine how much money you'll need.
   - Maintain flexibility by settling on a salary range rather than a specific figure.
   - Discover typical salary ranges for jobs in your field.
   - Estimate how much the employer is likely to offer you.
   - Postpone salary discussions until the end of the interview process (when you're confident the employer wants to hire you).
   - Let the employer be the first to mention a salary range.
   - Ask for a figure near the top of the employer-proposed salary range.
   - Ask if there's room to negotiate benefit packages and vacation time. (Answers will vary.) (*Use résumés and interviews to "hire" an employer,* pp. 221–222)
7. If your scores are lower on the Discovery Wheel the second time you complete it, this means you are less effective as a student. True or false? Explain your answer.
   False. Lower scores the second time you complete the Discovery Wheel might result from increased self-awareness and honesty, among other valuable assets. (*Exercise 26: The Discovery Wheel—Coming full circle,* pp. 226–229)
8. Give three examples of ways to test your career choice.
   Three ways to test a career choice are to interview people who are actually doing the job, obtain an internship or volunteer position in that field, and get a part-time or summer job in that field. For example, a person considering a career as a veterinarian might interview and ask questions of a working veterinarian, seek out a volunteer or internship position at a local animal care shelter, and get a part-time job at a veterinarian's office for the summer.
   (Answers will vary.) (*Create your career* now, pp. 215–217)
9. Describe a flaw associated with the typical job-hunting strategy of looking through help-wanted advertisements. Then briefly describe an alternative approach to job hunting.
   A major flaw is that most job openings are never advertised. Many employers use help-wanted listings, along with résumés and employment agencies, only as a last resort. An example of a strategy that might be used instead is to research a company you would like to work for, identify a contact there, and arrange an interview with that person. Employers often prefer to hire people they know. (*Use résumés and interviews to "hire" an employer,* pp. 221–222)
10. List at least four ways to continue on your path of becoming a master student after completing this book.
    List at least four:
    - Keep a journal.
    - Take a workshop.
    - Read, watch, and listen.
    - Take an unrelated class.
    - Travel.
    - Get counseling.
    - Form a support group.
    - Find a mentor—or become one.
    - Redo this book.

    (Answers will vary.) ("*. . . use the following suggestions to continue . . . ,*" p. 214)

Skills Snapshot

Jerry Seinfeld told one aspiring comedian that "the way to be a better comic was to create better jokes and the way to create better jokes was to write every day."[6] Seinfeld also revealed his own system for creating a writing habit: He bought a big wall calendar that displayed the whole year on one page. On each day that he wrote jokes, Seinfeld marked a big red "X" on the appropriate day on the wall calendar. He knew that he'd established a new habit when he looked at the calendar and saw an unbroken chain of "X's."

So much of success boils down to changing habits. Take a snapshot of your habits as they exist today, after reading and doing this book. Then take the next step toward mastery by committing to a specific action in the near future.

DISCOVERY

During this course, it has been my intention to change the following habits . . .

I would describe my skill at changing those habits as . . .

INTENTION

Three habits that I am committed to changing in the future are . . .

NEXT ACTION

Of the three habits listed above, the one I would like to focus on next is . . .

To experience a new level of mastery at making this habit change, i will . . .

Master Student PROFILE

Lisa Ling

. . . is inquisitive

Excerpted from "Journalist and Correspondent Lisa Ling," broadcast on Profiles, a radio program from WFIU, Indiana University, and hosted by Owen Johnson, November 11, 2007, http://wfiu.org/profiles/lisa-ling.

I had heard about auditions for a teen magazine show called *Scratch*. They were holding auditions in a mall, and one Saturday in Sacramento I showed up along with hundreds of other students. They chose four of us to host this show—a fun teen magazine where I interviewed celebrities and did makeovers and silly things like that. But what was cool was that it was produced by a local news affiliate, and I used that entré into the station to get an internship in the newsroom. I hung out with the writers and learned to run the teleprompter. I was sort of an eager and aggressive young kid who wanted to learn about the business, and I would show up at the TV station at 4:30 or 5:00 in the morning before classes.

After doing 3 years on a teen magazine show, I was ready to go to college. Then the director of Channel One called me and said, "We'd like you to come audition." I did and got the job. It was based in Los Angeles, so I ended up going to the University of Southern California while doing Channel One at the same time.

Channel One has been plagued by . . . controversy because it airs commercials within the broadcast. But for me as a reporter it was the most incredible opportunity, and the editorial content of Channel One I would put up against any network news show. I was a 19- and 20-year old kid covering the civil war in Afghanistan, the Russian referendum elections, the civil war in Algeria, the drug war in Colombia, overpopulation in China, globalization in India. I would work on a series about the democracy movement in Iran in 1995 that would run about 25 minutes throughout the course of a week. And at that time what news outlet would cover Iran for 25 minutes?

I actually think that was some of my best journalism. While I did do research on the various stories and countries, I kind of went into them not knowing so much—just being open and not having a lot of preconceived ideas or notions. You know, these days we are almost brainwashed. When our leadership characterizes entire countries as evil, how do you *not* go into stories with preconceived ideas? What we did as young people was pick these places in the world that no one was covering and went there. We didn't tell our viewers what to think. We just gave them an opportunity to experience what *we* were experiencing.

I majored in history because I wanted to have as broad-based an education as I could possibly get. My history background and my political science background and my travels have been my biggest assets as a journalist.

People are always asking me: How did you get your job? And my answer is, I just got it. I just kind of willed it into existence. I just kind of created this situation.

My advice to young people is: Before you get hampered by a job and family and financial obligations, try to get out of your comfort zone. If you can, live in another country for a year or so. You won't regret it.

Excerpted from "Journalist and Correspondent Lisa Ling," broadcast on *Profiles*, a radio program from WFIU, Indiana University, and hosted by Owen Johnson, November 11, 2007, http://wfiu.org/profiles/lisa-ling.

(1973–) Host of National Geographic Channel's *Explorer*, special correspondent for *The Oprah Winfrey Show*, and a former cohost of ABC's *The View*, Ling was one of the youngest reporters for Channel One News, whose programming is aimed at middle and high schools.

Learn more about Lisa Ling at the Master Student Hall of Fame.

Endnotes

Introduction

1. U.S. Department of Labor, Bureau of Labor Statistics, "Education Pays . . .," December 22, 2009, www.bls.gov/emp/emptab7.htm (accessed January 29, 2010).
2. Robert Mager, *Preparing Instructional Objectives* (Belmont, CA: Fearon, 1975).
3. Randy Moore, "The Importance of Admissions Scores and Attendance to First-Year Performance," *Journal of The First-Year Experience & Students in Transition*, 2006, vol. 18, no. 1 (2006): 105–125.
4. Albert Bandura, *Self-Efficacy: The Exercise of Control* (New York: F. H. Freeman, 1997), 131–136.
5. U.S. Census Bureau, "Facts for Feature: Back to School 2007–2008," June 14, 2008, www.prnewswire.com/cgi-bin/stories.pl?ACCT=104&STORY=/www/story/06-14-2007/0004608454&EDATE= (accessed January 29, 2010).
6. Excerpts from *Creating Your Future*. Copyright © 1998 by David B. Ellis. Adapted by permission of Houghton Mifflin Company. All rights reserved.

Chapter 1

1. Douglas A. Bernstein, Louis A. Penner, Alison Clarke-Stewart, and Edward J. Roy, *Psychology* (Boston: Houghton Mifflin, 2006), pp. 368–369.
2. Howard Gardner, *Frames of Mind: The Theory of Multiple Intelligences* (New York: Basic Books, 1993).
3. David A. Kolb, *Experiential Learning: Experience as the Source of Learning and Development* (Englewood Cliffs, NJ: Prentice-Hall, 1984).

Chapter 2

1. Alan Lakein, *How to Get Control of Your Time and Your Life* (New York: New American Library, 1973; reissue 1996).
2. Stephen R. Covey, *The Seven Habits of Highly Effective People: Restoring the Character Ethic* (New York: Simon & Schuster, 1990).

Chapter 3

1. Donald Hebb, quoted in D. J. Siegel, "Memory: An Overview," *Journal of the American Academy of Child and Adolescent Psychiatry*, vol. 40, no. 9 (2001): 997–1011.
2. From *Information Anxiety* by Richard Saul Wurman. Copyright © 1989 by Richard Saul Wurman. Used by permission of Doubleday, a division of Bantam Doubleday Dell Publishing Group, Inc.
3. Daniel L. Schacter, *The Seven Sins of Memory: How the Mind Forgets and Remembers* (Boston: Houghton Mifflin, 2001), 14.
4. Alzheimer's Association, "Brain Health," 2009, www.alz.org/brainhealth/overview.asp (accessed January 27, 2010).

Chapter 4

1. From *Master Student Guide to Academic Success*, 115.
2. Joseph Novak and D. Bob Gowin, *Learning How to Learn* (New York: Cambridge University Press, 1984).
3. Adapted from Ann Raimes, *Universal Keys for Writers* (Boston: Houghton Mifflin, 2002), 709–712.

Chapter 5

1. Walter Pauk and Ross J. Q. Owens, *How to Study in College*, 10th ed. (Florence, KY: Cengage, 2011).
2. Tony Buzan, *Use Both Sides of Your Brain* (New York: Dutton, 1991).

Chapter 6

1. Joe Cuseo, "Academic-Support Strategies for Promoting Student Retention and Achievement during the First Year of College," University of Ulster Office of Student Transition and Retention, www.ulster.ac.uk/star/resources/acdemic_support_strat_first_years.pdf (accessed September 4, 2003).
2. Ibid.
3. Jonathan D. Glater, "Colleges Chase as Cheats Shift to Higher Tech," *New York Times*, May 18, 2006, www.nytimes.com/2006/05/18/education/18cheating.html (accessed March 1, 2009).
4. This article incorporates detailed suggestions from reviewer Frank Baker.

Chapter 7

1. Robert Manning, "Hemingway in Cuba," *Atlantic Monthly*, August 1965, www.theatlantic.com/issues/65aug/6508manning.htm (accessed January 30, 2010).

Chapter 8

1. "How You Fit Into the Tight Job Market," National Association of Colleges and Employers, 2009, www.jobweb.org/studentarticles.aspx?id=2121 (accessed January 30, 2010).
2. "Working in the 21st Century," U. S. Bureau of Labor Statistics, www.bls.gov/opub/working/page4a.htm (accessed January 30, 2010).
3. Thomas Gordon, *Parent Effectiveness Training: The Tested New Way to Raise Responsible Children* (New York: New American Library, 1975).
4. Sidney Jourard, *The Transparent Self* (New York: Van Nostrand, 1971).
5. Daniel Goleman, *Emotional Intelligence: Why It Can Matter More Than IQ* (New York: Bantam, 1995), pp. xiv–xv.
6. Maia Szalavitz, "Race and the Genome," Howard University Human Genome Center, March 2, 2001, www.genomecenter.howard.edu/article.htm (accessed January 30, 2010).

Chapter 9

1. U.S. Department of Agriculture, "MyPyramid.gov," mypyramid.gov/guidelines/index.html, September 10, 2009 (accessed January 30, 2010).
2. Michael Pollan, "Unhappy Meals," *New York Times*, January 28, 2007, www.nytimes.com/2007/01/28/magazine/28nutritionism.t.html (accessed January 30, 2010).
3. Harvard Medical School, *HEALTHbeat: 20 No-Sweat Ways to Get More Exercise* (Boston: Harvard Health Publications, October 14, 2008).
4. Jane Brody, "Exercise = Weight Loss, Except When It Doesn't," *New York Times*, September 12, 2006, www.nytimes.com/2006/09/12/health/nutrition/12brody.html (accessed January 30, 2010).
5. Harvard Medical School, *HEALTHbeat Extra: The Secret to Better Health—Exercise* (Boston: Harvard Health Publications, January 27, 2009).
6. Mary Duenwald, "The Dorms May Be Great, but How's the Counseling?" *New York Times*, October 26, 2004, www.nytimes.com/2004/10/26/health/psychology/26cons.html (accessed January 30, 2010).
7. American College Health Association, *American College Health Association–National College Health Assessment II: Reference Group, Executive Summary Fall 2008*, www.acha-ncha.org/docs/ACHA-NCHA_Reference_Group_ExecutiveSummary_Fall2008.pdf, 2009 (accessed January 30, 2010).
8. M. Schaffer, E. L. Jeglic, and B. Stanley, "The Relationship between Suicidal Behavior, Ideation, and Binge Drinking among College Students," *Archives of Suicide Research* 12, no. 2 (2008): 124–132.
9. Albert Ellis, *Overcoming Destructive Beliefs, Feelings, and Behaviors: New Directions for Rational Emotive Behavior Therapy* (Amherst, NY: Prometheus, 2001).
10. Steven C. Hayes, *Get Out of Your Mind and Into Your Life: The New Acceptance and Commitment Therapy* (Oakland, CA: New Harbinger, 2004).
11. David Sandman, Elisabeth Simantov,a nd Christina An, "Out of Touch: American Men and the Health Care System," www.commonwealthfund.org/Content/Publications/Fund-Reports/2000/Mar/Out-of-Touch--American-Men-and-the-Health-Care-System.aspx, The Commonwealth Fund, 2000 (accessed April 10, 2009)
12. Agency for Healthcare Research and Quality, "Men: Stay Healthy at Any Age," February 2007, www.ahrq.gov/ppip/healthymen.htm (accessed April 10, 2009)
13. American Cancer Society, "Guide to Quitting Smoking," www.cancer.org/docroot/PED/content/PED_10_13X_Guide_for_Quitting_Smoking.asp, November 23, 2009 (accessed January 30, 2010).
14. American Cancer Society, "Double Your Chances of Quitting Smoking," www.cancer.org/docroot/PED/content/PED_10_3x_Double_Your_Chances.asp, October 10, 2009 (accessed January 30, 2010).
15. *Stress . . . at Work*, Adapted from National Institute of Occupational Safety and Health, www.cdc.gov/niosh/docs/99-101/ (accessed January 30, 2010).
16. Mental Health America, "Depression in the Workplace," www.mentalhealthamerica.net/go/information/get-info/depression/depression-in-the-workplace, 2010 (accessed January 30, 2010).

Chapter 10

1. Encyclopaedia Britannica Online Reference Center, "Ford, Henry," www.library.eb.com/eb/article-22461 (accessed January 30, 2010).
2. FordCarz, "Henry Ford Quotations," 2003, www.fordcarz.com/henry_ford_quotes.htm (accessed January 30, 2010).
3. Richard N. Bolles, *What Color Is Your Parachute? A Practical Manual for Job-Hunters and Career-Changers* (Berkeley, CA: 2005), 38.
4. Center for Human Resources, *National Evaluation of Learn and Serve America*, www.cpn.org/topics/youth/k12/pdfs/Learn_and_Serve1999.pdf, July 1999 (accessed January 30, 2010).
5. Lydia Ramsey, "Minding Your Global Manners," 2008, http://www.mannersthatsell.com/articles/globalmanners.html (accessed November 27, 2009).
6. Brad Isaac, "Jerry Seinfeld's Productivity Secret," *Lifehacker*, July 24, 2007, lifehacker.com/software/motivation/jerry-seinfelds-productivity-secret-281626.php (accessed January 30, 2010).

Additional Reading

Adler, Mortimer, and Charles Van Doren. *How to Read a Book: The Classic Guide to Intelligent Reading.* New York: Touchstone, 1972.

Allen, David. *Getting Things Done: The Art of Stress-Free Productivity.* New York: Penguin, 2001.

Allen, David. *Ready for Anything: 52 Productivity Principles for Work and Life.* New York: Viking, 2003.

Bandler, Richard, and John Grinder. *Frogs into Princes: Neuro-Linguistic Programming.* Moab, UT: Real People, 1979.

Becoming a Master Student Athlete. Florence, KY: Cengage, 2006.

Bolles, Richard N. *What Color Is Your Parachute? A Practical Manual for Job-Hunters and Career-Changers.* Berkeley, CA: Ten Speed, updated annually.

Boston Women's Health Book Collective. *The New Our Bodies, Ourselves.* New York: Simon & Schuster, 1996.

Brown, Alan C. *Maximizing Memory Power.* New York: Wiley, 1986.

Buzan, Tony. *Make the Most of Your Mind.* New York: Simon & Schuster, 1977.

Chaffee, John. *Thinking Critically.* Florence, KY: Cengage, 2009.

Coplin, Bill. *10 Things Employers Want You to Learn in College.* Berkeley, CA: Ten Speed, 2003.

Covey, Stephen R. *The Seven Habits of Highly Effective People: Powerful Lessons in Personal Change.* New York: Simon & Schuster, 1989.

Davis, Deborah. *The Adult Learner's Companion.* Florence, KY: Cengage, 2007.

Downing, Skip. *On Course: Strategies for Creating Success in College and in Life,* 4th ed. Florence, KY: Cengage, 2008.

Dumond, Val. *The Elements of Nonsexist Usage.* New York: Prentice-Hall, 1990.

Elgin, Duane. *Voluntary Simplicity.* New York: Morrow, 1993.

Ellis, Dave. *Falling Awake: Creating the Life of Your Dreams.* Rapid City, SD: Breakthrough Enterprises, 2000.

Facione, Peter. *Critical Thinking: What It Is and Why It Counts.* Millbrae, CA: California Academic Press, 1996.

Fletcher, Anne. *Sober for Good.* Boston: Houghton Mifflin, 2001.

From *Master Student to Master Employee.* Florence, KY: Cengage, 2009.

Gawain, Shakti. *Creative Visualization.* New York: New World Library, 1998.

Gibaldi, Joseph. *MLA Handbook for Writers of Research Papers.* New York: Modern Language Association, 1999.

Glasser, William. *Take Effective Control of Your Life.* New York: HarperCollins, 1984.

Golas, Thaddeus. *The Lazy Man's Guide to Enlightenment.* New York: Bantam, 1993.

Greene, Susan D., and Melanie C. L.Martel. *The Ultimate Job Hunter's Guidebook.* Florence, KY, 2008.

Hallowell, Edward M. *CrazyBusy: Overstretched, Overbooked, and About to Snap!* New York: Ballantine, 2006.

Higbee, Kenneth L. *Your Memory: How It Works and How to Improve It.* Englewood Cliffs, NJ: Prentice-Hall, 1996.

Hill, Napolean. *Think and Grow Rich.* New York: Fawcett, 1996.

Keyes, Ken, Jr. *Handbook to Higher Consciousness.* Berkeley, CA: Living Love, 1974.

Kolb, David A. *Experiential Learning: Experience as the Source of Learning and Development.* Englewood Cliffs: Prentice-Hall, 1984.

Levy, Frank, and Richard J. Murname. *The New Division of Labor: How Computers Are Creating the Next Job Market.* Princeton, NJ: Princeton University Press, 2004.

Lucas, Jerry, and Harry Lorayne. *The Memory Book.* New York: Ballantine Books, 1975.

Mallow, Jeffry V. *Science Anxiety: Fear of Science and How to Overcome It.* New York: Thomond, 1986.

Newport, Cal. *How to Win at College.* New York: Random House, 2005.

Nolting, Paul D. *Math Study Skills Workbook,* 3rd ed. Florence, KY: Cengage, 2008.

Pauk, Walter, and Ross J. Q. Owens. *How to Study in College.* Florence, KY: Cengage, 2008.

Pirsig, Robert. *Zen and the Art of Motorcycle Maintenance.* New York: Perennial Classics, 2000.

Raimes, Anne and Maria Jerskey. *Universal Keys for Writers.* Florence, KY: Cengage, 2008.

Robinson, Adam. *What Smart Students Know: Maximum Grades, Optimum Learning, Minimum Time.* New York: Crown, 1993.

Ruggiero, Vincent Ryan. *Becoming a Critical Thinker.* Florence, KY: Cengage, 2009.

Schacter, Daniel L. *Searching for Memory: The Brain, the Mind, and the Past.* New York: HarperCollins, 1997.

Strunk, William, Jr., and E. B.White. *The Elements of Style.* New York: Macmillan, 1979.

Tobias, Sheila. *Succeed with Math: Every Student's Guide to Conquering Math Anxiety.* New York: College Board, 1995.

Toft, Doug, ed. *Master Student Guide to Academic Success.* Florence, KY: Cengage, 2005.

Ueland, Brenda. *If You Want to Write: A Book About Art, Independence and Spirit.* St. Paul, MN: Graywolf, 1987.

U.S. Department of Education. *Funding Education Beyond High School: The Guide to Federal Student Aid.* Published yearly. http://studentaid.ed.gov/students/publications/student_guide/index.html

Watkins, Ryan, and Michael Corry. *E-learning Companion: A Student's Guide to Online Success.* Florence, KY: Cengage, 2008.

Weil, Andrew. *Health and Healing.* Boston: Houghton Mifflin, 1998.

Wurman, Saul Richard. *Information Anxiety 2.* Indianapolis: QUE, 2001.

Index

Master Instructor Notes

Master Instructor Notes

Master Instructor Notes

Master Instructor Notes